STUDIES IN PURĀṆIC RECORDS ON HINDU RITES AND CUSTOMS

STUDIES IN THE
PURĀṆIC RECORDS
ON
HINDU RITES AND CUSTOMS

R.C. HAZRA

MOTILAL BANARSIDASS PUBLISHERS
PRIVATE LIMITED • DELHI

2nd Reprint : Delhi, **2017**
Second Revised Edition: Delhi, 1975
First Edition: Delhi, 1987

ISBN: 978-81-208-0422-7

Also Available at

MOTILAL BANARSIDASS

41 U.A. Bungalow Road, Jawahar Nagar, Delhi 110 007
1 B, Jyoti Studio Compound, Kennedy Bridge, Nana Chowk, Mumbai 400 007
203 Royapettah High Road, Mylapore, Chennai 600 004
236, 9th Main III Block, Jayanagar, Bengaluru 560 011
8 Camac Street, Kolkata 700 017
Ashok Rajpath, Patna 800 004
Chowk, Varanasi 221 001

MLBD Cataloging-in-Publication Data
Studies in the Purāṇic Recrods on Hindu Rites and Customs
by R.C. Hazra
Includes Appendix, Bibliography and Index
ISBN : 978-81-208-0422-7
I. Hinduism II. Puranic Records
III. Hindu Rites IV. Hindu Custom

Printed in India

by RP Jain at NAB Printing Unit,
A-44, Naraina Industrial Area, Phase I, New Delhi-110028
and published by JP Jain for Motilal Banarsidass Publishers (P) Ltd,
41 U.A. Bungalow Road, Jawahar Nagar, Delhi-110007

yo vidyāc caturo vedān sāṅgopaniṣado dvijaḥ|
na cet purāṇaṃ saṃvidyān naiva sa syād vicakṣaṇaḥ||
itihāsa-purāṇābhyāṃ vedaṃ samupabṛṃhayet|
vibhety alpa-śrutād vedo mām ayaṃ prahariṣyati||

To Professor S. K. De, M.A., D.LIT., this humble work is dedicated as a token of deep reverence and sincere gratitude by his pupil, the author.

APOLOGY FOR REPRINT

The present work (*Studies in the Purāṇic Records on Hindu Rites and Customs*) was written in 1933-35, when I was a Research Student at the University of Dacca (now in Bangla Desh); and it was published by the said University a few years later, in 1940. At that time no critical edition of the Mahābhārata, Rāmāyaṇa, or any of the Purāṇas or Upapurāṇas had been published, nor was there in printed form any of the parts of Lakṣmīdhara's voluminous Smṛti work Kṛtya-kalpataru, which abounds in references to and quotations from the Epics and the Purāṇas and Upapurāṇas and is thus extremely helpful in checking their contents and determining their chronology. I could not even find within my reach any complete or incomplete Ms. of Lakṣmīdhara's work. Of Ballālasena's Dānasāgara, which is equally valuable for its quotations from the Purāṇic works and records highly interesting information about some of these works, I could use only the India Office (London) Ms., the Bibliotheca Indica edition of this work being published much later.

On the other hand, the publication of my work, as the late Professor P. K. Gode predicted in New Indian Antiquary, Vol. IV, 1941, pp. 250-251, opened up new avenues of research and gave an impetus to the study of the Purāṇas, particularly on their social and religious sides, and added very much to their popularity.

So, there is no denying the fact that my work ought to have been revised and improved thoroughly by this time. But, unfortunately, having little freedom of work and being compelled under unavoidable circumstances to divert my attention very often to subjects other than Purāṇic from about 1956 after I had joined service at the Sanskrit College, Calcutta, in 1951, I found little time to take up the work of revision in right earnest. In the meantime my work went out of print, and interested scholars from different parts of India and outside pressed me hard from time to time for a revised edition or at least for a reprint of the book.

Under these circumstances I was naturally feeling helpless, but fortunately, to my great relief, the generous and widely reputed publishers of Delhi, Messrs Motilal Banarsidass, came forward to remove this long felt want of scholars by bringing out immediately at their own risk a reprint of this book, with a short list of most unavoidable *Additions and Corrections*. But I hope to be able to revise this work thoroughly very soon after getting relieved of my present encumbrances.

Calcutta,
April, 1975.

R. C. Hazra

ADDITIONS AND CORRECTIONS

At p. 6. (in lines 9-15) *omit* "Vijñāneśvara tells us .. .. are perhaps sufficient to show that" and *read instead* "Varied Smṛti topics are dealt with in the fairly early Upapurāṇas such as the Narasiṃha-p., which come down from about the fifth or sixth century A.D. and claim to be parts of the Matsya and other Purāṇas. From these it is evident that."

At p. 6 *omit* foot-notes 36-37.

At p. 43 (in lines 37-38) *omit* "which borrows, among others, chaps. 207 (24b to the end) and 115-120 from the Matsyap." and *read instead* "from which the Matsya-p. has borrowed a large number of chapters."

At p. 44 *omit* the first 8 lines of the foot-notes.

At p.101 (in lines 23-25) *omit* "and 112,......, it is probable" and *read instead* "and 112, 52-59 tally respectively with Padma-p. (Sṛṣṭi-kh.) 31, verses 105-145 and 150-157, it is probable".

At p.128 (in line 12), immediately after "(I, 25, 23)" *add* "and the Ekāmra-p."

At p.129 (in line 18), *transpose* "Sattva" and "Rajas".

At p.198 (in line 20), *for* "(sammita)" *read* "(samita)".

At p.201 (in line 20), immediately after "(II, 311)" *add* "and ascribed to the Brahmāṇḍa-p."

At p.201 (at the end of the foot-note) *add* "So, their early origin cannot be denied."

At p.204 (in line 11), *for* "devotion" *read* "faith".

At p.262 (in line 36), *for* "sections" *read* "groups".

At p.282 *for* line 12 of the first column *read* "p. 490 = 241, 2".

TABLE OF CONTENTS

PREFACE

The extant Purāṇas present a very rich collection of materials for the study of the development of Hindu rites and customs during the centuries intervening between Yājñavalkya and the Smṛti-Nibandhas. During this long period, the Hindu society passed through numerous vicissitudes, so much so that in many respects the Hindu rites and customs, as found in the Nibandhas, differ from those in the Codes of Manu and Yājñavalkya. Hence the study of the Purāṇas is of immense importance for a clear understanding of the whole course of the development. But none of the extant Purāṇas being assignable to any positive date, the greatest difficulty which makes their study impracticable and unscientific is the want of a proper chronology of the chapters constituting the individual Purāṇas. Unfortunately no systematic attempt was made to remove this long felt want, probably because, as Mr. P. V. Kane says, 'the chronology of the Purāṇas is, like that of the epics, a subject full of perplexing problems'. The work, done by such eminent scholars as H. H. Wilson, F. E. Pargiter and Haraprasad Shastri even in regard to the approximate dates of only a few of the Purāṇic works, is not at all considerable, nor are their conclusions always acceptable. Hence the first thing, on which attention has been directed in this work, has been to determine as approximately as possible the chronology of the Purāṇic chapters, or parts thereof, on Hindu rites and customs. I should mention here that in this chronology, which is based only on such evidences as are contained in the majority of the editions of the individual Purāṇas, attention has been given especially to those chapters which are devoted mainly to the treatment of the above mentioned topics; and, the scope of this work being limited to the study of these matters during the period ranging approximately from 200 to 1000 A.D., those Purāṇas, which have been found to be hardly earlier than the tenth century, have been dealt with very briefly. However, on the basis of this chronology, which forms Part I of this work, I have attempted to describe in Part II the different stages in the development of the Purāṇic rites and customs. I have tried to show that these rites and customs are not the productions of a single social dictator or of a particular period of time, but were revised from generation to generation and reshaped gradually to their present character with such additions as the changes in society demanded. With an eye to the notable changes in the religious and political history of ancient India, I have tried, further, to ascertain the factors which determined the stages in the development of the Purāṇic Dharma (i.e. law and custom) and moulded its character. This enquiry, which has been found absolutely necessary for a clear understanding of the nature and growth of the Purāṇic rites and customs, and which has in many cases led to interesting results, has involved an investigation into the origin of Purāṇic Hinduism, because in India, as in all other eastern countries, religion is inseparably connected with customs.

Besides the two parts, of which the present work mainly consists, there is an Appendix containing a long list of quotations which I have traced in the extant Purāṇas. This list has been extremely necessary not only for understanding the nature of the Purāṇas during the ages they were used by the commentators and Nibandha-writers but also for determining the dates of those Purāṇic chapters from which the quotations were made. This list may also be of some use to those scholars who will, in future, set themselves to the solution of textual problems relating to the Purāṇas.

Being concerned with a field of research hitherto almost unexplored, this work may interest those who want to study the Purāṇic literature and the Hindu social institutions. Attempts have been made to solve many problems relating to the Purāṇas and the Purāṇic Dharma; but no conclusion has been drawn which has not been sufficiently evidenced by the facts of the case. The chronological scheme in Part I is necessarily tentative, but all available materials have been fully considered and taken into account.

As this work is the result of a general study of the Purāṇic chapters on Hindu rites and customs, no attention has been given to the divergent opinions held by the different Purāṇas on the niceties of any particular rite or custom. Such detailed study would require a separate volume and has consequently been avoided.

Though this work is based on a first-hand study of the original sources, the accounts given in it of the rise and spread of Jainism, Buddhism and Ājīvakism (i.e. the religion preached by Gosāla Maṅkhaliputta) are mainly based on those given in such authoritative works as the Cambridge History of India (Vol. I), V. A. Smith's Early History of India, and the like. In translating some of the passages of the Purāṇas and Smṛti works, H. H. Wilson's Viṣṇu Purāṇa, F. E. Pargiter's Mārkaṇḍeya Purāṇa, Taluqdar's Matsya Purāṇa (S.B.H., Vol. XVII), Mahendra Nath Chatterjee's Śrīmadbhāgavata, and Bühler's Laws of Manu (S.B.E., Vol. XXV), Institutes of Gautama (S.B.E., Vol. II) and Institutes of Baudhāyana (S.B.E., Vol. XIV) have been extremely helpful to me. In studying the Purāṇas I have, in addition to the different printed editions, utilised the large collection of Purāṇa and Smṛti manuscripts existing in the Dacca University Library. Of the Dānasāgara of Ballālasena I consulted the India Office manuscript, which was secured for me on loan by the Dacca University Library. As to the dates of the Smṛti-Saṃhitās and the Nibandhas, I have been generally guided by the indications of the veteran scholar Mr. P. V. Kane, M.A., LL.M., whose History of Dharmaśāstra (Vol. I) is undoubtedly the most valuable work on the subject.

By way of explaining why in a few cases I have used the Vaṅgavāsī editions of the Purāṇas, printed in Bengali characters, in preference to the more widely used Devanāgarī editions, I should only say that these editions, though not critically accomplished from sufficient Manuscript material, are not always so negligible as scholars may take them to be. They are often, if not in all cases, based on Bengal Mss and have consequently different texts with less number of additional passages than the South Indian editions. However, the comparative notes on the different editions, which have been added to the analyses of the Purāṇas, will enable scholars to trace the references in the South Indian and other Devanāgarī editions.

My thankful obligations are due to my professor Dr. S. K. De, M.A., D.LIT., for his valuable suggestions and guidance. It was at his instance that I took up the Purāṇas as a subject of study. During the three years I worked with him on this subject he took very keen personal interest in the progress of my work and accorded to me such facilities as very few students of his department have ever enjoyed. In spite of his heavy duties and responsibilities he ungrudgingly took the trouble of going through the whole thesis step by step, as well as when it was finally completed. I am particularly grateful to our Vice-Chancellor, Dr. R. C. Majumder, M.A., PH.D., for kindly securing books and manuscripts for my use from different libraries as well as for enabling me to publish my work as a Bulletin of the University. But for his help and sympathy the book would never have seen light so soon. I am also much obliged to Mr. Subodh Chandra Banerjee, M.A., of the Dacca University Mss Library, for giving me all possible help in consulting the valuable collections of Sanskrit manuscripts in his charge, as well as for pointing out to me the reference to the Padma-purāṇa in a marginal note contained in a manuscript of the Yathārtha-mañjarī.

All necessary information regarding the editions of the Purāṇas and other works, which have been utilised, has been given in the Bibliography. Words, admitting of alternative spellings, have sometimes been used in both forms, viz., Vaśiṣṭha and Vasiṣṭha, Lomaharṣaṇa and Romaharṣaṇa, Kalkin and Kalki, Śaṃbhala and Saṃbhala, Pāṃśula, and Pāṃsula, Sātvata and Sāttvata, etc.; and, except in only one place (in Part I, Chapter I), the word 'Smṛti' has been used in its restricted sense to mean 'Dharma' i.e. 'law and custom'.

Though a portion of this work was published as isolated articles in different oriental journals, I have considerably improved the whole work, including the published portion, by adding much new material and, in a few cases, by modifying my views already expressed in those articles.

DACCA
February, 1940. RAJENDRA CHANDRA HAZRA

ABBREVIATIONS.

ABORI	=	Annals of the Bhandarkar Oriental Research Institute, Poona.
Adbhs.	=	Adbhuta-sāgara (of Ballālasena).
Ag	=	Agni-purāṇa.
AnSS	=	Ānandāśrama Sanskrit Series (Poona).
Āpas.	=	Āpastamba-dharmasūtra.
App.	=	Appendix or Appendices, as the case may be.
ASB	=	Asiatic Society of Bengal (Calcutta).
ASI	=	Archæological Survey of India.
Bḍ	=	Brahmāṇḍa-purāṇa.
Bhāg	=	Bhāgavata-purāṇa.
Bhandarkar, Vaiṣṇavism etc.	=	R. G. Bhandarkar, Vaiṣṇavism, Śaivism and Minor Religious Systems.
Bhav	=	Bhaviṣya-purāṇa.
Bibl. Ind. Ser.	=	Bibliotheca Indica Series.
Bnār	=	Bṛhannāradīya-purāṇa.
Bod. Cat., or Bodleian Catalogue	=	Catalogus Codicum Manuscriptorum Sanscriticorum Bibliothecae Bodleianae.
Br	=	Brahma-purāṇa.
BSOS	=	Bulletin of the School of Oriental Studies, London.
Bv	=	Brahmavaivarta-purāṇa.
Chap. or chaps.	=	Chapter or chapters.
CHI	=	The Cambridge History of India.
Com.	=	Commentary.
Corp. Inscr. Ind.	=	Corpus Inscriptionum Indicarum.
Dbh	=	Devībhāgavata-purāṇa.
D. U. Mss Lib.	=	Dacca University Manuscripts Library.
Ed.	=	Edition.
Ep. Ind.	=	Epigraphia Indica.
ERE	=	Hastings' Encyclopædia of Religion and Ethics.
Farquhar, Outline	=	J. N. Farquhar, An Outline of the Religious Literature of India.
Faus.	=	Fausbôll's Jātaka.
Fick, Social Organisation	=	Richard Fick, Social Organisation in North-east India in Buddha's time.
Fol.	=	Folio or folios.
Gaut.	=	Gautama-dharmasūtra.
Gḍ	=	Garuḍa-purāṇa.

Hv	=	Harivaṃśa.
IHQ	=	Indian Historical Quarterly (Calcutta).
Ind. Ant.	=	Indian Antiquary.
Ind. Off. Cat., or India Office Catalogue	=	A Descriptive Catalogue of the Sanskrit Manuscripts in the the Library of the India Office, London.
JASB	=	Journal of the Asiatic Society of Bengal.
JBBRAS	=	Journal of the Bombay Branch of the Royal Asiatic Society.
JBORS	=	Journal of the Behar and Orissa Research Society.
JAOS	=	Journal of the American Oriental Society.
JRAS	=	Journal of the Royal Asiatic Society.
Kane, Hist. of Dhs.	=	P. V. Kane, History of Dharmaśāstra.
Kh.	=	Khaṇḍa.
Kūr	=	Kūrma-purāṇa.
Lg	=	Liṅga-purāṇa.
Macdonell, Skt. Lit.	=	A. A. Macdonell, A History of Sanskrit Literature.
Mārk	=	Mārkaṇḍeya-purāṇa.
Mat	=	Matsya-purāṇa.
Mbh	=	Mahābhārata.
McCrindle, Ancient India	=	J. W. McCrindle, Ancient India as described by Megasthenes and Arrian.
Ms, Mss	=	Manuscript, Manuscripts.
Nār	=	Nāradīya-purāṇa.
P.; -p.	=	Purāṇa; -purāṇa.
Pargiter, AIHT	=	F. E. Pargiter, Ancient Indian Historical Tradition.
Pd	=	Padma-purāṇa.
Rapson, Cat. of Ind. Coins in the Brit. Mus.	=	E. J. Rapson, A Catalogue of Indian Coins in the British Museum.
S.B.E.	=	Sacred Books of the East.
Shastri, Cat. of Sans. Mss, ASB	=	Haraprasad Shastri, A Descriptive Catalogue of Sanskrit Manuscripts in the collection of the Asiatic Society of Bengal, Calcutta.
Shastri and Gui, Cat. of Sans. Mss, Cal. Sans. Coll.	=	Hrishikesh Shastri and Siva Chandra Gui, A Descriptive Catalogue of Sanskrit Manuscripts in the Library of Calcutta Sanskrit College.
Śiv	=	Śiva-purāṇa.
Sk	=	Skanda-purāṇa.
Smith, EHI	=	V. A. Smith, The Early History of India including Alexander's Campaigns. Fourth edition.

Tīrtha-c.	=	Tīrtha-cintāmaṇi (of Vācaspatimiśra).
Uś.-saṃ.	=	Uśanas-saṃhitā.
Vā	=	Vāyu-purāṇa.
Vām	=	Vāmana-purāṇa.
Vaṅga.	=	Vaṅgavāsī Press (Calcutta).
Var	=	Varāha-purāṇa.
Veṅk.	=	Veṅkaṭeśvara Press (Bombay).
Viṣ	=	Viṣṇu-purāṇa.
Viṣṇudh.	=	Viṣṇudharmottara.
Wilson, Essays	=	H. H. Wilson, Essays Analytical, Critical and Philological.
Winternitz, Ind. Lit.	=	M. Winternitz, A History of Indian Literature.
Yāj.	=	Yājñavalkya or Yājñavalkya-smṛti (as the case may be).

PART I

CHAPTER I

THE MAHĀPURĀṆAS

The only species of Indian literature, which can claim, next to the Vedas, to reach back to great antiquity, is the 'Purāṇa'[1]. It is mentioned, mostly in connection with Itihāsa, in such early works as the Atharva-veda[2], Śatapatha-brāhmaṇa[3], Gopatha-brāhmaṇa[4], Jaiminīya-upaniṣad-brāhmaṇa[5], Bṛhadāraṇyaka-upaniṣad[6], Chāndogya-upaniṣad[7], Taittirīya-āraṇyaka[8], Sāṅkhyāyana-śrautasūtra[9] and Gautama-dharmasūtra[10].

According to the Brahmanical traditions as recorded in the Atharva-veda and the Bṛhadāraṇyaka-upaniṣad, the 'Purāṇa' has as much a sacred origin as the Vedas. The former says that the Ṛcs, the Samans, the Metres and the Purāṇa originated from the residue of the sacrifice together with the Yajus[11]. The latter, on the other hand, ascribes the origin of the four Vedas, Itihāsa, Purāṇa etc. to the breath of Mahābhūta[12]. These traditions, though fundamentally different, are unanimous in their recognition of the sacredness of the 'Purāṇa'. In many of the works of the Vedic literature, the 'Purāṇa' is even called the fifth Veda[13] This traditionally sacred character has been retained by the literature even to the present day; but it

[1] For the antiquity of the 'Purāṇa', see Sir Ashutosh Mukherjee Silver Jubilee Volumes (Calcutta), III, Part 2, pp. 7 f.

[2] XI, 7, 24 and XV, 6, 4.

[3] XIII, 4, 3, 13; XI, 5, 6, 8 and 7, 9.

[4] I, 10.

[5] I, 53.

[6] II, 4, 10; IV, 1, 2 and 5, 11.

[7] III, 4, 1 and 2; VII, 1, 2 and 4; VII, 2, 1 and 7, 1.

[8] II, 9.

[9] XVI, 2, 27.

[10] VIII, 6 and XI, 19.

[11] *ṛcaḥ sāmāni chandāṃsi purāṇaṃ yajuṣā saha| ucchiṣṭāj jajñire.....||* Atharva-veda, XI, 7, 24.

[12] *.....mahato bhūtasya niśvasitam etad yad ṛgvedo yajur-vedaḥ sāmavedo 'tharvāṅgirasa itihāsaḥ purāṇam..........|* Bṛhadāraṇyaka, II, 4, 10.

[13] Cf. Śatapatha-brāhmaṇa, Chāndogya-upaniṣad, Sāṅkhyāyana-śrautasūtra, etc.

never attained the position of 'Śruti', being always recognised as 'Smṛti'.

Though the theory of the existence of a single original Purāṇa is open to serious doubts, it can hardly be denied that more Purāṇas than one had come into existence long before the beginning of the Christian era. In the Saṃhitās of Manu and Yājñavalkya[14] and in the Taittirīya-āraṇyaka[15], the word 'Purāṇa' has been used in the plural number; the Mahābhārata speaks of a 'Purāṇa proclaimed by Vāyu'[16]; and the Āpastamba-dharmasūtra has a passage quoted from a 'Bhaviṣyat-purāṇa'[17]. The self-contradicting title 'Bhaviṣyat-purāṇa' given to a distinct work of the Purāṇa literature indicates that in Āpastamba's time 'the term Purāṇa had become so thoroughly specialised as to have lost its proper meaning, and had become merely the designation of a particular class of books. It would have required the existence of a number of books called Purāṇas to produce that change, and manifestly they must have had their own special names to distinguish from one another, and so convert their common title Purāṇa into a class designation'[18]. Hence it can be held that the number of the Purāṇas had begun to be multiplied even before the time of Āpastamba.

The existence of more Purāṇas than one in Āpastamba's time or earlier does not, however, mean that the canon of 'eighteen Mahāpurāṇas'[19] came into vogue at such an early period. As a matter of fact this canon can scarcely be dated earlier than the third century A.D.[20]. There is, of course, mention of 'eighteen Purāṇas' in the Svargārohaṇa-parvan(5,45 & 46 & 6, 97) of the Mahābhārata,

[14] Manu III, 232—*svādhyāyaṃ śrāvayet pitrye*.......................... *purāṇāni khilāni ca||* Yāj. III, 189—*yato vedāḥ purāṇāni vidyopaniṣadas tathā* etc.

[15] II, 9— * * * * *itihāsa-purāṇāni.*

[16] Mbh III, 191, 16.

[17] Āpas II, 24, 5-6.

[18] Pargiter, AIHT, pp. 50-51.

[19] The name 'Mahāpurāṇa' is of late origin. It is found only in Bhāg XII, 7 and Bv IV, 131. What are now known as Mahāpurāṇas, are called simply Purāṇas in the earlier works.

[20] Of the *earliest* of the extant Purāṇas, the Viṣṇu (III, 6) and the Mārkaṇḍeya (chap. 137) contain lists of eighteen Mahāpurāṇas. Though the former Purāṇa is to be dated between 100 and 350 A.D., and most probably in the last quarter of the third or the first quarter of the fourth century (see under Viṣṇu-purāṇa below), there is sufficient reason to hold that the list of the Mahāpurāṇas in Viṣ III, 6 was revised to its present form in later days, or that verses 21-26 (on the names of the eighteen Purāṇas and their five characteristics) were interpolated, especially when we take into consideration Viṣ III, 6, 20 which says that the Viṣṇu-purāṇa was based on the four Purāṇa-saṃhitās compiled by Romaharṣaṇa, Akṛtabraṇa, Sāvarṇi and Śāṃśapāyana. The list, however, must be dated earlier than Alberūnī who gives it in his account of India.

and on the strength of this mention scholars have sometimes tried to assign the canon to a very early date[21]. But an examination of the text of the Svargārohaṇa-parvan as occurring in the Bengal Mss as well as in the printed editions of the Mahābhārata, shows that the portions in which 'eighteen Purāṇas' have been mentioned are in all probability later additions. Svargārohaṇa-parvan 5, 46 (Vaṅga. ed.), which corresponds to the same verse in the Bombay ed., is found neither in the ASB ed. nor in any one of about a dozen Bengal Mss which we have consulted in this connection in the Dacca University Library. Svargārohaṇa-parvan, chap. 6 also, though found both in the ASB and Bombay editions, does not occur in the Bengal Mss. At the close of the Vaṅgavāsī ed. of the Mahābhārata the commentator Nīlakaṇṭha says that this chapter, which begins with the verse '*bhagavan kena vidhinā*' and in which the merits of listening to the Mahābhārata and the gifts to be made to the reader of its Parvans have been described, was transferred from the Harivaṃśa to the Mahābhārata for the encouragement of the audience of the latter[22]. The validity of this information supplied by Nīlakaṇṭha is fully realised when we see that Svargārohaṇa-parvan, chap. 6 is the same as Hv III, 132, 1-97 and 135, 2b to the end, and that in this chapter of the Svargārohaṇa-parvan the gifts to be made to the reader of the Harivaṃśa also are described along with those of the other Parvans of the Mahābhārata. This is certainly against the proper order of things, for if, as the enumeration of the Parvans in this chapter shows, the Harivaṃśa constitutes the eighteenth book of the Mahābhārata, then the results of listening to the whole epic cannot be described in the book previous to the eighteenth. Hence there can scarcely be any doubt regarding the spuriousness of Svargārohaṇa-parvan, chap. 6.

The second mention of 'eighteen Purāṇas' is found in verse 3 of Hv III, 135. Though this chapter is found to be one of the two sources of chap. 6 of the Svargārohaṇa-parvan, it is very doubtful whether it can be placed as early as about 400 A.D., the probable date of the Harivaṃśa. This chapter is not found in many of the Bengal Mss of the Harivaṃśa[23].

Mārk 137 (on Purāṇa-māhātmya) does not occur in all the editions. Hence its authenticity is extremely doubtful.

Vā 104 also contains a list of the Purāṇas, but we shall see later (under Vāmana-purāṇa) that this chapter was added very late to the Vāyu.

For the date of Mat 53 which also contains a list, see under Matsya-purāṇa.

21 Macdonell, Skt. Lit., p. 299. Pargiter, *op. cit.*, p. 22. IHQ, Vol. VIII, p. 761.

22 *bhagavannityādiḥ phalādhyayo vyāsena harivaṃśānte uktaḥ, atra śrotṛ-prarocanārtham ukta iti jñeyam*

23 For instance, cf. Mss No. 508 (dated 1549 Śaka), No. 514A (dated 1765 Śaka), No. 1041 and No. 1718 in the Dacca University Mss Library.

Inspite of the little value which can be attached to the mention of 'eighteen Purāṇas' in the Mahābhārata and the Harivaṃśa, it can hardly be doubted that the canon originated not later than the first quarter of the seventh century A.D. In Mat 53 the eighteen Purāṇas have been named, and it will be seen afterwards that the date of this chapter (especially except verses 59-63) is to be placed between 550 and 650 A.D. Gauḍapāda, in his Sāṃkhyakārikā-bhāṣya, uses the word '*purāṇa*' in the plural number to mean distinct Purāṇic works[24], and, in his Uttaragītā-bhāṣya, explains the word (*purāṇa*) occurring in chap. 2 of the Gītā, as '*purāṇāni brahmāṇḍādīni*'[25]. This word '*brahmāṇḍādīni*' betrays Gauḍapāda's acquaintance with the eighteen Purāṇas. That the word *brahmāṇḍādīni* was used, as much as *brāhmādīni*, to mean the group of the eighteen Purāṇas, is evidenced by Sāyaṇācārya who explains the word *purāṇa*, occurring in the Taittirīya-āraṇyaka (II, 9), as '*purāṇāni brahmāṇḍādīni*' in his Bhāṣya on the same. Sāyaṇa's knowledge of the group of the eighteen Purāṇas can by no means be denied.

It is not known definitely of what the Purāṇas in their earliest form treated. A very old definition, contained in the famous lexicon Amarakoṣa and in most of the extant Purāṇas, says that a Purāṇa is to have five characteristics: (1) creation (Sarga), (2) re-creation (Pratisarga), (3) genealogy (Vaṃśa, of gods and sages), (4) cosmic cycles (Manvantara), and (5) accounts of royal dynasties (Vaṃśānucarita). All these characteristics have their roots in the materials, viz., Ākhyānas (tales), Upākhyānas (anecdotes), Gāthās (songs) and Kalpajoktis (lore that had come down through ages), which, as the Brahmāṇḍa, Vāyu and Viṣṇu say, were used by Vyāsa in compiling

[24] *tatra bāhyaṃ nāma vedāḥ śikṣā-kalpa-vyākaraṇa-nirukta-cchando-jyotiṣākhya-ṣaḍaṅga-sahitāḥ purāṇāni nyāya-mīmāṃsā- dharmaśāstrāṇi. ceti.* —Sāṃkhya-kārikā with Gauḍapāda-bhāṣya (ed. Pandit Bechanarāma Tripāṭhī, Benares Sanskrit Series, No. 9, Benares 1905), p. 16.

[25] Uttaragītā, p. 52.

In the Bombay edition of the Uttaragītā with Gauḍapāda-bhāṣya (ed. Mahādeva Śarman and published by the Gujarati Printing Press, Bombay 1912) the reading is '*purāṇāni bra(ā?)hmādīni*'.

In the D. U. Mss Lib. there are two Mss, Nos. 4504 and K558E, of the Uttaragītā-bhāṣya. Of these, the former, which is concise and is written in a terse style smacking of an early date, reads '*purāṇāni brāhmādīni*'. The latter Ms, on the other hand, says in its post-colophon statement that it was copied at Benares and brought from there by post. It is comparatively elaborate, agrees more with the printed editions than with the other Ms, and reads '*purāṇāni brahmāṇḍādīni*'.

Regarding Gauḍapāda's authorship of the Bhāṣya, S. K. Belvalkar says: "We can, for the present, only assert that there is nothing, so far discovered, in these two commentaries (*i.e.*, the Sāṃkhyakārikā-vṛtti and the Uttaragītā-vṛtti) that necessarily militates against the traditional identification of their author with the author of the Māṇḍukya Kārikās". See, Belvalkar, Basu Mallik Lectures on Vedānta, 1925, p. 189.

the original Purāṇa[26]. These characteristics, therefore, indicate the real nature of the Purāṇas in their early, if not the earliest, form. In most of the present Purāṇas, on the other hand, the five characteristics have been neglected partially or totally and great importance has been given to matters religious and social. In those few Purāṇas also, in which the five topics have been dealt with, there are to be found chapters on social customs and glories of gods. Thus, the present Purāṇas have practically turned into Smṛti-codes. This new form the Purāṇas do not seem to have attained before the beginning of the Christian era. The few passages quoted in the Āpastamba-dharmasūtra from a Purāṇa and a Bhaviṣyat-purāṇa cannot be made the basis of the statement that Smṛti-matter began to be imported into the Purāṇas in Āpastamba's time. These passages are most probably Gāthās, or summaries thereof, which were current among the people in ancient times and received admission into the Purāṇas especially in connection with the patriarchs. That at least some of the ancient Gāthās were concerned with Smṛti-matter is evidenced not only by the Purāṇas[27] and the Mahābhārata but also by the Manu-smṛti which refers to one sung by Vāyu[28]. The fact that Manu incorporates the verses found in Āpas I, 19, 13 without calling them Gāthās is not very important, because in several other cases also Manu is found to insert verses, not of his own composition, without naming the sources. For instance, Manu II, 94 *(na jātu kāmaḥ kāmānām)* occurs in the Purāṇas as spoken by Yayāti who became tired of worldly enjoyment[29], and Manu III, 274a *(api naḥ sa kule jāyāt)* is found in some Purāṇas as a part of a Gāthā sung by the patriarchs[30]. There are also numerous other references to the Purāṇa literature in the works of the pre-Christian era, but nowhere there is any reference to its Smṛti-contents.

On the other hand, there are evidences to show that the Purāṇas began to incorporate matters on Hindu rites and customs from a period earlier than the sixth century A.D. Medhātithi quotes in his Bhāṣya on the Manu-smṛti a number of verses from the Purāṇas. Though the majority of these verses are concerned with creation, philosophy etc., a few of them relate definitely to Smṛti. These

[26] *ākhyānaiś cāpyupākhyānair gāthābhiḥ kalpajoktibhiḥ purāṇa-saṃhitāṃ cakre purāṇārtha-viśāradaḥ* Bḍ II, 34, 21 ; Vā 60, 21 ; and Viṣ III, 6, 16.

The last two Purāṇas differ slightly in readings from the first. Also cf. Vā 103, 51 ; 104, 20

[27] See, for example, Mārk 29, 43-46.

[28] Manu IX, 42—*atra gāthā vāyu-gītāḥ* etc.

[29] Viz., Mat 34, 10 ; Viṣ IV, 10, 9 ; Hv I, 30, 38 ; and so on.

[30] Cf. Bḍ III 19, 9 f.

latter verses testify to the fact that the Purāṇas in Medhātithi's time contained chapters on holy places, funeral sacrifices, etc[31]. Kumārilabhaṭṭa, in his Tantravārttika, looks upon the Purāṇas as authoritative works on Dharma and names them along with the Dharmaśāstras[32]. The Hārīta-saṃhitā[33] says that the Anadhyāya days should be known from the Smṛti works as well as the Purāṇas[34]. An old Ms of the Skanda-purāṇa, discovered in Nepal by Haraprasad Shastri, contains several sections on hells and one on the method of worshipping the god (Śiva)[35]. Vijñāneśvara tells us of Hārīta's reference to the opinion of the Purāṇas in prescribing penance, in normal circumstances, to those who eat up the food dedicated to the patriarchs[36]. The date of the Hārīta-smṛti used by Vijñāneśvara cannot be later than the sixth century A.D.[37]. The above evidences are perhaps sufficient to show that topics on Hindu rites and customs began to be dealt with in the Purāṇas from a period not later than the middle of the fourth century A.D. As a result, the Purāṇas came gradually to lose their original character and turn into important codes of Hindu rites and customs by including chapters on Varṇāśramadharma, Ācāra, Śrāddha, Prāyaścitta, Dāna, Pūjā, Vrata, Tīrtha, Pratiṣṭhā, Dīkṣā, Utsarga, etc.

But in the great majority of cases the Purāṇas have not come down to us with their early incorporations, because tradition demanded that they should be re-edited with the changes in society so that their importance as works of authority might not decrease[38]. Now, the work of re-editing could be done in three ways : viz., (i) by

[31] Cf. Medhātithi on Manu II, 24; III, 124 & 232; etc.

As Medhātithi does not expressly name any Purāṇa, the Purāṇic verses quoted by him should not be used in determining the dates of the extant Purāṇas even in those cases where they are traceable. Cf. footnote 31 (under Viṣṇu-p.).

[32] Kane, JBBRAS, Vol. I, 1925, p. 102.

Tantravārttika, p. 179—*purāṇa-mānavetihāsa-vyatirikta-gautama-vasiṣṭha*..... ....*baudhāyanādi-praṇīta-dharmaśāstrāṇām*.........etc.

[33] Ūnaviṃśati Saṃhitā, pp. 127-139. It is called Laghuhārīta-smṛti in Jīvānanda Vidyāsāgara's collection of Dharmaśātras, Vol. I, pp. 177-193.

[34] Hārīta-saṃhitā IV, 70

[35] H. P. Shastri, Catalogue of Palm Leaf and Selected Paper Mss belonging to the Durbar Library, Nepal, Calcutta, 1905, pp. lii, 141 f. The Ms, which is written in old Gupta script, has been assigned to the seventh century A. D. by Shastri and C. Bendall.

[36] Vijñāneśvara on Yāj. III, 289.

[37] Kane, Hist. of Dhs., Vol. I, pp. 75 and 246.

[38] Cf. Mat 53, 8-9 wherein the Fish says to Manu:

kālenāgrahaṇaṃ dṛṣṭvā purāṇasya tato nṛpa|
vyāsa-rūpam ahaṃ kṛtvā saṃharāmi yuge yuge||

Cf. also Pd (Sṛṣṭi-khaṇḍa) 1, 49-50; Dbh I, 3, 20; Sk V, iii, 1, 26-28; and so on.

adding fresh chapters to the already existing ones, (ii) by substituting the latter by the former, and (iii) by writing new works bearing old titles. All these processes being equally practised with respect to the Purāṇas, some retained their earlier materials, some lost many of the earlier chapters which were replaced by others of later dates, and some became totally new works. But they had a common feature in that all of them came to have units belonging to different ages. It should be mentioned here that the fresh additions to the Purāṇas were not always fresh compositions, but chapters and verses were often transferred from one Purāṇa to another or from the Smṛti and other works to the Purāṇas, obviously to enrich the latter. That this practice of transference began much earlier than 1100 A.D. is evidenced by Ballālasena who says that the Liṅga-p. took its chapters on the big donations (Mahādāna) from the Matsya, and that the Viṣṇu-rahasya and Śiva-rahasya were mere compilations[39].

The great importance given to the Purāṇas as authoritative works on Hindu rites and customs perverted the idea of the people of later ages as to the real contents of these works. It was thought that the five characteristics—creation, re-creation etc.—were meant for the Upapurāṇas, whereas the Mahāpuraṇas were to have not less than ten characteristics relating to cosmogony, religion and society[40]. Consequently, the accounts of the genealogies of kings and sages were little cared for, and often fabricated[41]; and sections on holy places etc. were composed by different people at different times and freely attached to the Purāṇas as their integral parts, so that the extents of these works varied[42]. People also took absolute liberty in making changes in the texts of the Purāṇas. Consequently, textual corruptions increased hopelessly. Of such corruptions, the Vāyu is the best example.

[39] *'bṛhad api liṅga-purāṇaṃ matsya-purāṇoditair mahādānaiḥ'* and *'loke prasiddham etad viṣṇu-rahasyaṃ ca śiva-rahasyaṃ ca| dvayam iha na parigṛhītaṃ saṃgraha-rūpatvam avadhārya||'* Dānasāgara, fol. 3b.

[40] Cf. Bv IV, 131, 6-10. Also, Bhāg II, 9, 43; II, 10, 1; and XII, 7, 8 f.

[41] Cf. *'mṛṣāvaṃśānucaritaiḥ* * * * '—Dānasāgara, fol. 4a.

[42] For instance, according to the Matsya, the Kūrma-p. consisted of 18,000 verses; according to the Agni, of 8,000 verses; and according to the Nāradīya, of 17,000 verses. According to the Matsya and Skanda, the Varāha-p. contained 24,000 verses, whereas the Agni gives its extent as consisting of 14,000 verses only.

An examination of the quotations made by the commentators and Nibandhakāras from the Purāṇas shows that even at a particular period of time the extent and contents of a particular Purāṇa were more or less different in different parts of India.

CHAPTER II

THE CHRONOLOGY OF THE PURĀṆIC CHAPTERS ON HINDU RITES AND CUSTOMS

THE MAJOR PURĀṆAS

It has been said in the previous chapter that from an early date the Purāṇas grew up into important codes of Hindu rites and customs, and that they came to contain chapters or groups of chapters which often belonged to different dates. Hence the chronology of these chapters is of immense importance for tracing the course of the changes that took place in Hindu society earlier than the time of the Smṛti-Nibandhas.

Any attempt at determining the chronology of the Smṛti-chapters means a detailed study of all the eighteen Purāṇas, and this has been done as far as possible in this and the following two chapters. Of these, the present chapter includes the major Purāṇas, viz., Mārkaṇḍeya, Vāyu, Brahmāṇḍa, Viṣṇu, Matsya, Bhāgavata and Kūrma, which are of earlier dates and have preserved much of their older materials; chapter III comprises the minor Purāṇas, *i.e.*, those which, being subjected to the interfering hands of the later redactors, have lost their earlier forms and contents; and chapter IV embodies the results arrived at in chapters II and III.

We shall now proceed to analyse the Purāṇas.

1 THE MĀRKAṆḌEYA-PURĀṆA :

This is one of the oldest and most important of the extant Purāṇas. It commences with Jaimini, a pupil of Vyāsa, who approaches the sage Mārkaṇḍeya for the solution of some doubts raised in his mind by the study of the Mahābhārata. For want of sufficient time Mārkaṇḍeya does not answer the questions put to him by Jaimini but refers the latter to the four wise birds living on the Vindhyas. This beginning of the Mārkaṇḍeya-purāna agrees with its description given in the Matsya, which says: "That Purāṇa in which, in reply to the Muni, the duties and non-duties have been explained by the holy sages in connection with the birds and which, again, is narrated fully by Mārkaṇḍeya is called the Mārkaṇḍeya (-purāṇa), containing 9,000 verses"[1].

Though this Purāṇa is generally true to the old definition of the Purāṇa of five characteristics, it contains a few chapters on topics which come within the description of Dharma; viz., chaps. 12 and 14 dealing with hells (Naraka), chap. 15 with the results of actions done (Karma-vipāka), chaps. 28-29 with the duties of the castes and Āśramas, chaps. 30-33 with funeral sacrifices, chap. 34 with customs in general (Ācāra), and chap. 35 with eatables and non-eatables[2].

Mārk 28-35 form parts of the story of Alarka and Madālasā which is interwoven in the story of Sumati (also called Jaḍa) and his father Mahāmati (in Mārk 10-44). This story of Sumati and his father is a lengthy amplification of the dialogue between Medhāvin and his father found in one of the latest books of the Mahābhārata (viz., XII, 175 and 276). Hence it can be supposed that the story of Sumati (or Jaḍa) was put into the Mārkaṇḍeya-p. after the Mahābhārata had attained its final form. This supposition is strengthened by the information, regarding the nature of the contents of the Mahābhārata, that is supplied by the Mārkaṇḍeya-p. in chap. 1, wherein Jaimini approaches the sage Mārkaṇḍeya for the solution of the doubts. Before giving expression to these, Jaimini praises the Mahābhārata as:

> *....sarva-śāstrāṇāṃ mahābhāratam uttamam||*
> *atrārthaś caiva dharmaś ca kāmo mokṣaś ca varṇyate|*
> *parasparānubandhaś ca sānubandhaś ca te pṛthak||*
> *dharmaśāstram idaṃ śreṣṭham arthaśāstram idaṃ param|*
> *kāmaśāstram idaṃ cāgryaṃ mokṣaśāstraṃ tathottamam||*
> *caturāśrama-dharmāṇām ācāra-sthiti-sādhanam|*
>
> (Mārk 1, 5b-8a).

From this it is clear that at the time of composition of at least Mārk 1, 1-22 the Mahābhārata came to be regarded as the best Dharmaśāstra, the greatest Arthaśāstra, the foremost Kāmaśāstra and the highest Mokṣaśāstra. A comparison between Mārk 34 (dealing with customs in general) and Mbh XIII, 104 also shows

[1] *yatrādhikṛtya śakunīn dharmādharma-vicāraṇā|*
vyākhyātā vai muni-praśne munibhir dharmacāribhiḥ||
mārkaṇḍeyena kathitaṃ tat sarvaṃ vistareṇa tu|
purāṇaṃ nava-sāhasraṃ mārkaṇḍeyam ihocyate|| Mat 53, 25-26.

[2] These chapters correspond to chaps. 12, 14, 15 and 28-35 in the editions of Jīvānanda Vidyāsāgara and the Bibl. Ind. Ser., and to chaps. 12, 14, 15 and 25-32 in the Veṅk. ed. Though there are variations in readings and numbers of verses in the corresponding chapters of the different editions, they are not many and important for our purpose.

that the former has the latter as its prototype[3]. Mbh XIII, 104 has many lines borrowed from the Code of Manu; the style is often defective and elaborate; and the contents are not arranged properly. In Mārk 34, on the other hand, plagiarism has been avoided as far as practicable, and the subject-matter, though changed at places, has been dealt with in an improved and terse style. The few lines of Manu, which have been retained, have not escaped changes more or less. The readings of these lines, when compared with those occurring in Mbh XIII, 104 and the Code of Manu, show that the Mahābhārata approaches more the Code of Manu than the Mārkaṇḍeya-p. does.

From what has been said above it seems highly probable that the story of Sumati was inserted into the Mārkaṇḍeya-p. after the great epic had attained its present extent, content and character. Regarding the approximate dates of the different strata in the Mahābhārata Hopkins says: "We may tentatively assume as approximate dates of the whole work in its different stages. Bhārata (Kuru) lays, perhaps combined into one, but with no evidence of an epic before 400 B.C. A Mahābhārata tale with Pāṇḍu heroes, lays and legends combined by the Purāṇic diaskeuasts, Kṛṣṇa as a demi-god (no evidence of didactic form or of Kṛṣṇa's divine supremacy), 400-200 B.C. Remaking of the epic with Kṛṣṇa as all-god, intrusion of masses of didactic matter, addition of Purāṇic material old and new, multiplication of exploits, 200 B.C. to 100-200 A.D. The later books added with the introduction to the first book, the swollen Anuśāsana separated from Śānti and recognised as a separate book, 200 to 400 A.D.; and finally 400 A.D. + occasional amplifications"[4]. On the strength of this tentative chronological scheme, which is the most acceptable of all that have been put forth, we may hold in the present state of our knowledge that the story of Sumati as found in the Mārkaṇḍeya-p. cannot possibly be earlier than 200 A.D.

The story of Sumati, including that of Alarka, extends over Mārk 10-44, and at the beginning of chapter 45 Jaimini praises the birds saying:

samyag etan mamākhyātaṃ bhavadbhir dvija-sattamāḥ|
pravṛttiś ca nivṛttiś ca dvividhaṃ karma vaidikum||

* * * * *

pravṛtte ca nivṛtte ca bhavatāṃ jñāna-karmaṇi|
matim asta-malāṃ manye yathā nānyasya kasyacit||

* * * * *

[3] Cf. Mbh XIII, 104, verses 16, 20b-21, 23, 37, 41, 48a, 51b-52a, 59a etc with Mārk 34, verses 17, 61b, 62b-63a, 21, 47b, 48b, 50b, 52b-53a, 24b etc.

[4] Hopkins, The Great Epic of India, pp. 397-398 and 398-402.

These references to Pravṛtti- and Nivṛtti-dharma certainly point to chapters 27-35 dealing with Pravṛtti-dharma and to chapters 39-43 dealing with Nivṛtti-dharma or Yoga. Now, chap. 45, which glorifies Brahmā as unborn, imperishable, changeless, incomparable *(anaupamya)* etc. and thus identifies him with the supreme Brahma of the Upaniṣads, certainly belongs to the Brahmā-sect. The opinion of scholars that the sect of Brahmā became prominent during the period ranging from 200 to 600 A.D. and that the five-gods of the Smārtas threw Brahmā into the back-ground towards the beginning of the seventh century[5], tends to show that the chapters dealing with Pravṛtti- and Nivṛtti-dharma cannot possibly be later than the seventh century A.D.

In relation to the effect of performing funeral sacrifices under different Tithis and Nakṣatras, the latter are mentioned in the order from Kṛttikā to Bharaṇī in Mārk 33, 8 ff. This order of the Nakṣatras is important. We know from the evidence of the Yājñavalkya-smṛti[6] and the latest books of the Mahābhārata[7] that the old arrangement of the Nakṣatras from Kṛttikā to Bharaṇī was in vogue at least some time after the beginning of the third century A.D. When this order of the Nakṣatras was changed we do not know definitely. It is only as late as about 550 A.D. that we find in the Bṛhat-saṃhitā of Varāhamihira the order of the Nakṣatras from Aśvinī to Revatī to be an established fact in all parts of India. So it can be held, and not quite unreasonably, that the old order of the Nakṣatras held ground at best down to the latter half of the fifth century A.D. Hence those chapters of the Mārkaṇḍeya-p., which treat of Hindu customs and Yoga, cannot possibly be later than the latter half of the fifth century A.D.

Mārk 33, 8 ff., which describe the results of performing funeral sacrifices under different Nakṣatras, *seem to have been added later than the other chapters on Hindu customs*, because in Mārk 32, 38 *(kāmyānāṃ śrūyatāṃ vatsa Śrāddhānāṃ tithi-kīrtanam)*, which points to the subject-matter of the chapter to follow, there is no mention of the Nakṣatras. If a gap of at least fifty years be allowed

[5] Farquhar, Outline, pp. 148 and 179-180.

Cf. also Bṛhat-saṃhitā, chapters 58 *(pratimā-lakṣaṇaṃ nāma)* and 60 *(pratimā-sthāpanaṃ nāma)*, wherein there are rules for the construction and erection of the image of Brahmā, thus proving the wide spread of the worship of the god in Varāhamihira's time.

[6] I, 268—*kṛttikādi-bharaṇyantaṃ*. In Kane's opinion the Yājñavalkya-smṛti was composed between the first century B.C. and the third century A.D. See Kane, Hist. of Dhs., Vol. I, p. 184.

[7] Viz., XIII, 64 wherein the Nakṣatras are mentioned in connection with the effect of making gifts under these; XIII, 89 which describes the results of performing the Kāmya-śrāddha under different Nakṣatras; and XIII, 110.

between this portion of Mārk 33 and the other chapters, then the lower limit of the date of composition of these chapters (28-35, except 33, 8 ff.) should be pushed up to the beginning of the fifth century A.D.

Here a question may arise as to whether all the Smṛti-chapters (except 33, 8 ff.) of the Mārkaṇḍeya-p. were inserted simultaneously. Such a doubt is removed by the fact that when, in Mārk 26, Madālasā is about to give instructions on self-knowledge (Ātma-jñāna) to the new-born Alarka, king Ṛtadhvaja forbids her saying, "Why dost thou deal thus, O foolish one, with the temperament of my child, by giving him a mischievous education as thou didst before to my other sons. If thou shouldest do what pleases me, if my word should be accepted, then restrain this son within the path of activity *(mārge pravṛttch).* So the path of action will not lead to utter destruction, O lady ; and so the Piṇḍa offering to the Pitṛs will not cease, O virtuous one. The Pitṛs dwell in the Deva-loka, they are also born as brutes, they become men likewise, and they reside within the class of elements. By offering the Piṇḍa and water a man, busied in the ceremonies, ever nourishes them, O fine-browed one, both the righteous and the unrighteous, those worn out with hunger, those harassed by thirst ; he nourishes the gods likewise and guests. The gods, mankind, the Pitṛs, departed spirits, goblins, and Guhyakas, birds, worms and insects live upon man indeed. Therefore, O slender-limbed, cause my son to acquire thoroughly the whole duty of Kṣatriyas, as regards this life and life in the next world". This request of the king to his wife Madālasā to give instructions to Alarka about the duties of Kṣatriyas and to train him in the Pravṛtti-mārga so that the Pitṛs may not be deprived of the offerings of water and rice-balls and the gods, men and lower animals may get their respective shares, presupposes the instructions on the duties of kings, on the duties of the castes and Āśramas, and on funeral sacrifices given by Madālasā to Alarka in chaps. 27-35.

From the above discussion it appears that *Mārk 28-35 (except 33, 8 to the end) were inserted some time about the third and fourth centuries A.D. It is highly probable that these chapters were added in the third century.*

Chapters 12, 14 and 15 also, forming parts of the story of Sumati, should be assigned to the above date.

The above conclusion about the date of the chapters under discussion agrees remarkably with the view of Pargiter, who says : "The Devī-māhātmya, the latest part, was certainly complete in the 9th century and very probably in the 5th or 6th century A.D. The third and fifth parts (i.e., chaps. 45-81 and 93-136 respectively), which constituted the original Purāṇa, were very probably in existence in the third century, and perhaps even earlier; and the first and second parts (i.e., chaps. 1-9 and 10-44 respectively) were composed between those two periods"[8].

The Smṛti-chapters of the Mārkaṇḍeya-p. have been frequently drawn upon by the commentators and the Nibandhakāras. For instance, Aparārka quotes numerous verses from chaps. 11, 29, 30, 32, 34, 35, 39 and 40 in his commentary on Yāj.; Ballālasena from chaps. 43 and 58 in his Adbhutasāgara and from chaps. 10 and 16 in his Dānasāgara; Devaṇabhaṭṭa from chaps. 29-35 in his Smṛti-candrikā; Hemādri from chaps. 15-16, 29-35, 46, 49, 57, 88 and 95-97 in his Caturvarga-cintāmaṇi; and so forth (see App.).

There are lines in the Smṛti-chapters of the Mārkaṇḍeya-p. which have their parallels in the Code of Manu. For example, Mārk 29, 29a; 29, 33a; 34, 8; and 34, 17 and 24 may be compared to Manu III, 102b and 82a; and IV, 156b-157a, 92, 56a and 78a.

2. THE VĀYU-PURĀṆA :

The Vāyu is perhaps the oldest of the extant Purāṇas[9]. The Mahābhārata (III, 191, 16) speaks of a 'Purāṇa proclaimed by Vāyu;' the Harivaṃśa (I, 7, 13 and 25) refers to 'Vāyu' as an authority; Bāṇabhaṭṭa says in his Harṣa-carita that he attended the reading of the Vāyu-p. in his native village[10]; and Alberūnī repeatedly quotes and names a Vāyu-p. in his account of India[11].

The character of the Vāyu as a Mahāpurāṇa has sometimes been called in question[12]. The cause of this doubt is the use of the title 'Śiva' or 'Śaiva' for 'Vāyavīya' in the majority of the lists of the 'eighteen Mahāpurāṇas'[13]. But this substitution, which has

[8] Pargiter, Mārkaṇḍeya-Purāṇa (English translation), Introduction, p. XX.

[9] The word 'oldest' is applicable only to the main skeleton of the work, because this Purāṇa also, like the others, was subjected to later additions and alterations. As an example, chap. 104 may be cited. This chapter mentions Rādhā, the Tantras, and the Śākta philosophy. Mr. Dikshitar rightly says that 'the Purāṇa compilation extended over a number of centuries'.

[10] Harṣa-carita, chap. III, *(pavamāna-proktaṃ purāṇaṃ papāṭha)*.

[11] Sachau, Alberūnī's India, I, pp. 41-42, 130, 168, 194 247, 287 etc.

[12] Narasiṃha Vājapeyin includes the 'Vāyu-p.' among the Upapurāṇas.—See Nityācārapradīpa, p. 19. In his com. on the Bhāgavata-purāṇa Śrīdhara Svāmin explains the word *śaivaka* as 'Śiva-purāṇa'.—See his com. on Bhāg XII, 13, 4. Mitra Miśra recognises the Śaiva as a Mahāpurāṇa and says: *'yā'pi viṣṇupurāṇe brahmāṇḍam ādāya vāyavīya-tyāgena, yā ca brahmavaivarte vāyavīyam upādāya brahmāṇḍapurāṇa-parityāgena aṣṭādaśa-saṃkhyā uktā sā kalpa-bhedena vyavasthāpanīyā'*.—See Vīramitrodaya, Paribhāṣā-prakāśa (ed. Parvatīya Nityānanda Śarma, Chowkhamba Sanskrit Series, Benares 1906), p. 13.

[13] See Viṣ III, 6, 21 ff.; Bhāg XII, 7, 23 ff. and XII, 13, 4 ff.; Kūr I, 1, 13 ff.; Pd I, 62, 2 ff., IV, 111, 90 ff., VI, 219, 25 ff., and VI, 263, 77 ff.: Var 112, 69 ff.; Mārk 137, 8 ff.; Lg I, 39, 61 ff.; Śiv V (Vāyavīya-saṃhitā), i, 1, 38 ff.; Śiva-

been taken wrongly in favour of the comparatively late sectarian Upapurāṇa called 'Śiva-purāṇa', is based on the Śaiva character of the Vāyu. The Skanda says: "The fourth (Purāṇa), declared by Vāyu, is known as Vāyavīya. It is also called Śaiva on account of its connection with (i.e., treatment of) Śiva-bhakti...........It contains 24,000 Ślokas"[14]. The description of the fourth Mahā-purāṇa, as given in the Matsya, Nāradīya and Agni, also agrees with the contents of the present Vāyu-p[15]. None of the Nibandha-writers, who have drawn upon the Vāyu and the Śiva-purāṇa, has been found to make any confusion between the two; because the verses quoted from the 'Vāyavīya' or 'Vāyu-purāṇa' are, in the majority of cases, found only in the present Vāyu but not in the Śiva, and those quoted from the 'Śaiva' or 'Śiva-purāṇa' are sometimes traceable in the present Śiva but never in the Vāyu. That the Vāyu was more important in the eyes of at least the Nibandha-kāras is shown by the fact that almost all of them quote verses from it, whereas the Śiva-p. is drawn upon by a very few of them. Hence it seems that the attempt to raise the Śiva-p. to the status

māhātmya-khaṇḍa of the Sūta-saṃhitā commented on by Mādhavācārya (Eggeling, Ind. off. Cat., Part VI, p. 1377); Saura-saṃhitā of the Skanda-p. (Eggeling, *op. cit.*, Part VI, p. 1382); Saṃbhava-kāṇḍa of the Śivarahasya-khaṇḍa of the Śaṃkara-saṃhitā of the Skanda-p. (Eggeling, *op. cit.*, Part VI, p. 1363); and so forth.

[14] *caturthaṃ vāyunā proktaṃ vāyavīyam iti smṛtam|*
śiva-bhakti-samāyogāc chaivaṃ tac cāparākhyayā||
caturviṃśati-saṃkhyātaṃ sahasrāṇi tu śaunaka|

Sk V, iii (Revā-kh.), 1, 33-34a.

These verses are also found in the Revā-māhātmya which claims to be a part of the Vāyu-purāṇa.—See, Aufrecht, Bodleian Catalogue, p. 65.

[15] See Mat 53, 18, Nār I, 95, and Ag 272, 4b-5.

The mention of the Śveta-kalpa as connected with the declaration of the 'Vāyavīya' Purāṇa should not create any difficulty, for the Vāyu-p. seems to connect itself with the Varāha-kalpa (Vā 6, 11 and 13; 7, 5; 21, 12 and 23) and to identify this Kalpa with the Śveta-kalpa (Vā 6, 13; 23, 63 ff. and 114 ff.). Moreover, the Nāradīya-p., whose list of contents of the 'Vāyavīya' Purāṇa agrees much with those of our Vāyu but not even partially with those of the Śiva, also speaks of the connection of the 'Vāyavīya' with the Śveta-kalpa. The word *bhāgadvaya-samanvita* used by the Nāradīya-p. with respect to the 'Vāyavīya' should not be taken to point to the Vāyavīya-saṃhitā (of the Śiva-p.) which also consists of two Bhāgas (parts). Eggeling, in his Ind. Off. Cat., Part VI, pp. 1299-1301, describes a few Mss of a Purāṇa which is called *vāyuprokta-purāṇa or vāyu-purāṇa* in the colophons of chapters, is generally the same as our present Vāyu, and is divided into two Khaṇḍas (or Kāṇḍas) or four Pādas. The ASB edition of the Vāyu also is divided into two Bhāgas.

Of the twelve Saṃhitās of the Śiva-p. the Vāyavīya-saṃhitā only is declared by Vāyu. So, how could the words *vāyavīya, vāyu-prokta* etc. be applicable to the entire Śiva-p. which begins with a Saṃhitā other than the Vāyavīya?

of a Mahāpurāṇa[16] was due to a comparatively late sectarian zeal[17]. The Devībhāgavata (I, 3, 14) and the 'Padma-p.' referred to by Gaṅgādhara in his com. on the Dharma-saṃhitā of the Śiva-p.[18], include the Śiva among the Upapurāṇas.

The Vāyu consists of four Pādas—(1) Prakriyā, comprising chaps. 1-6, (2) Anuṣaṅga, chaps. 7-64, (3) Upodghāta, chaps. 65-99, and (4) Upasaṃhāra, chaps. 100 to the end. It deals with all the five topics characteristic of the old Purāṇas. Over and above these, there are a few chapters on Smṛti-matter; viz.,

chaps. 16-17 .. on the duties of the castes and Āśramas,
chap. 18 .. on the penances for Yatis,
chaps. 57-59 .. on Yuga-dharma,
„ 73-83 .. on funeral sacrifices (including impurity due to births and deaths, and purification of things),
chap. 101 .. on hells and the results of actions done,
and chaps. 105-112 .. on the glories of Gayā.

These chapters do not seem to have belonged to the present Vāyu in its earliest form. They are in all likelihood later additions. Of these, chaps. 16-18 are comprised in the section on Pāśupata Yoga which betrays the influence of chaps. 39-43 of the Mārkaṇḍeya-p. In this section, which extends from chap. 10 (verses 68 ff.) to 20, the Vāyu has not only a good number of verses in common with the Mārkaṇḍeya[19] but has also improved upon the latter with fresh additions of chapters and verses. Now, we have seen that Mārk 39-43 cannot possibly be dated earlier than 200 A.D. Therefore chaps. 16-18 of the Vāyu-p. should be dated later still. The fact that the section on Pāśupata Yoga is not found in the Brahmāṇḍa-p. tends to show that it was interpolated after 400 A.D., because, we shall see presently, the Vāyu and Brahmāṇḍa could not have been separated earlier than 400 A.D. Consequently, Vā 16-18 also are to be dated later than that period. As Śūlapāṇi quotes a

[16] In its Vāyavīya-saṃhitā, the Śiva-p. lays claim to the position of a Mahāpurāṇa saying that the fourth Mahāpurāṇa is the Śaiva which consists of twelve Saṃhitās. See Śiv V, 1, 41.

[17] The verse '........*vāyavīyam anuttamam| aṣṭādaśaṃ samuddiṣṭaṃ brahmāṇḍam iti saṃjñitam||*' in Kūr I, 1, which includes the 'Śaiva' among the Mahāpurāṇas, should not be taken strongly in support of the early date of the Śiva-p. and its character as a Mahāpurāṇa. This verse most probably means, "That excellent (Purāṇa) *proclaimed by Vāyu* is enumerated as the eighteenth and is known as Brahmāṇḍa", because the Brahmāṇḍa-p. also is proclaimed by Vāyu and is called '*vāyu-prokta brahmāṇḍa*' in the colophons of its chapters.

[18] Shastri, Cat. of Sans. Mss, ASB, Vol. V, p. 289.

[19] Cf. Vā 16 with Mārk 41, 3 ff.; Vā 17 with Mārk 41, 18 ff.; Vā 19 with Mārk 43; and Vā 20 with Mārk 42, 5 ff.

verse from chap. 18 in his Prāyaścitta-viveka, they are certainly earlier than 1300 A.D. None of the earlier Nibandhakāras being found to draw upon them, it is difficult to place the lower limit of the date at a still earlier period.

Chaps. 57-59, dealing with Yuga-dharma, give an account of the period ranging from the reign of the Nandas to the end of the Āndhra rule in western India (see Part II, chap. I). Therefore these chapters should not be dated earlier than 200 A.D. They were, however, written earlier than 275 A.D., because the Matsya-p. borrowed from the Vāyu a good number of chapters, including the three mentioned above, in the last quarter of the third or the first quarter of the fourth century A.D. (see below, under Matsya-p.). Of these three chapters, chap. 59 has been drawn upon by Devaṇabhaṭṭa in his Smṛti-candrikā (see App.).

Chaps. 73-83, on Śrāddha, are included in the section Śrāddhakalpa (covering chaps. 71-85), the greater part of which is given as an interlocution between Bṛhaspati and his son Śaṃyu. In these chapters Yogins have been given remarkable prominence as invited guests[20]. It is said: "Śrāddhas should be carefully offered to Yogins......What is eaten by an adept in Yoga saves one from great fear. A Yogin is superior to a thousand house-holders, a hundred forest-hermits and a thousand students". Such prominence given to Yogins is not traceable in the Codes of Manu and Yāj., who do not seem to have held Yogins in high esteem. On the other hand, Yogins are given great prominence in the existing Pāñcarātra Saṃhitās which are certainly later in date than the above mentioned Codes. It is, therefore, highly probable that the chapters on Śrāddha in the Vāyu-p. come from a date not earlier than 200 A.D. This date seems also to be supported by the hatred with which the Nagnas (the naked) have been mentioned in chaps. 78 and 79[21]. The word *nagna* is said to mean those people who are stripped of the garments consisting metaphorically of the Vedas. Such people are clearly the Jains and the Buddhists, because the terms 'Nirgrantha' and 'Pāṣaṇḍa' also have been used in these chapters of the Vāyu. The contempt shown to these religious sects could be possible only when their religions were in a decadent state. Buddhism, which found its strongest upholders in Aśoka Maurya and Kaniṣka, was probably in a flourishing condition to the end of the second century A.D. So the chapters of the Vāyu cannot possibly be earlier than that time. The mention of the Nakṣatras from Kṛttikā to Bharaṇī in Vā 82 points to a date earlier than 500 A.D. It is probable that the chapters under discussion were added to the Vāyu about the middle of the third century A.D.

[20] Vā 71, 50 ff.   [21] Vā 78, 24, and 79, 25.

Most of the above mentioned chapters on Śrāddha have been drawn upon by the commentators and Nibandha-writers early and late; viz., Śūlapāṇi has quoted verses from chaps. 78 and 79 in his Prāyaścitta-viveka; Vācaspatimiśra from chaps. 77 and 82 in his Tīrtha-cintāmaṇi; Kullūkabhaṭṭa from chap. 78 in his com. on the Manu-smṛti; Mādhavācārya from chaps. 75 and 76 in his Bhāṣya on the Parāśara-smṛti; Madanapāla from chaps. 75 and 79-81 in his Madana-pārijāta; Srīdatta Upādhyāya from chaps. 78 and 79 in his Kṛtyācāra; Caṇḍeśvara from chap. 81 in his Kṛtya-ratnākara; Hemādri from chaps. 73-76, 78-81 and 83 (as also from chaps. 30-31 and 71) in his Caturvarga-cintāmaṇi; Devaṇabhaṭṭa from chaps. 75 and 78-80 in his Smṛti-candrikā; Ballālasena from chap. 80 in his Dānasāgara, and from chap. 19 in his Adbhutasāgara; and Aparārka from chaps. 74-82 in his com. on Yāj. (see App.).

All of the verses in Vā 73-83 do not seem to have come from the same date. Verses 14-42 of Vā 82 are most probably spurious. They do not occur in the great majority of Mss, nor are they to be found in the corresponding chapter of the Brahmāṇḍa-p. Besides these verses, there are certainly others which were interpolated later. But it is very difficult to separate them. The fact that many of the quoted verses, especially on Śrāddha, are not found in the present Vāyu, proves that the Purāṇa has undergone serious losses also. A perusal of the Caturvarga-cintāmaṇi shows that the 'Vāyu-p.,' used by Hemādri, contained a good number of chapters on big donations such as those of golden cows, silver bulls, gold, lotuses made of gold or sesamum, the image of Sarasvatī made of gold or silver, and the like, all these being meant for removing sins or curing diseases. This 'Vāyu-p.' dealt with Ekādaśī also.

Chap. 101, on hells and results of actions, probably comes from the same date as chaps. 57-59. As there is no evidence sufficient for the determination of its date, it is impossible to say anything definitely.

Chaps. 105-112, on Gayā-māhātmya, did not really belong to the Vāyu. In many Mss of the Purāṇa this Māhātmya has been omitted[22]. On the other hand, it is often found to appear as an independent text in Mss as well as in printed editions. That this appendage was attached to the Vāyu earlier than 1,400 A.D., is certain, for Vācaspatimiśra quotes numerous verses from chaps. 105 and 111-112 (see App.).

3. THE BRAHMĀṆḌA-PURĀṆA:

The Brahmāṇḍa[23], though one of the oldest of the extant Purāṇas, is assigned the eighteenth place in almost all the lists of

[22] See Vāyu-p., p. 426, footnote.

[23] The text of the Vaṅga. ed. of the Brahmāṇḍa is almost the same as the

Mahāpurāṇas. From the facts that it has sometimes been called 'Vāyavīya Brahmāṇḍa', that it also, like the Vāyu-p., is said to have been proclaimed by Vāyu, and that its chapters often agree almost literally with those of the Vāyu, F. E. Pargiter has rightly said that originally these two Purāṇas were not separate[24]. This view of Pargiter seems to be supported by some of the verses quoted in the Nibandhas from the 'Vāyu-p.' or 'Vāyavīya' but found only in the present Brahmāṇḍa. In a few cases, verses quoted by Ballālasena, Devaṇabhaṭṭa and Hemādri from the 'Brahmāṇḍa-p'. are found not in the present Brahmāṇḍa but in the Vāyu (see App.). This proves the original unity of the texts of the two Purāṇas.

It is not known definitely when and why the same original Purāṇa, which was named most probably after Vāyu[25], came to have a second version with a different title. A comparison between the dynastic accounts given in the Vāyu and Brahmāṇḍa, shows that the separation took place after 325 A.D., and most probably not earlier than 400 A.D., for the Brahmāṇḍa has not only the extended portion of the Vāyu's account of the dynasties of the Kali age but agrees very closely with the text of the present Vāyu (also see under Matsya-p.). The cause of separation may be sectarian, because in the Brahmāṇḍa there are a few chapters (viz., III, 21 ff.) which smack of Vaiṣṇavism. Or, it may be that some people gave the title 'Brahmāṇḍa' to a version of 'the great Purāṇa proclaimed by Vāyu'[26], on account of the latter's giving information about the cosmic egg.

The Brahmāṇḍa-p. contains a few chapters on Smṛti-topics. All these chapters have their parallels in the Vāyu-p.; viz.,

Bḍ II, 29-32 (on Yuga-dharma) = Vā 57-59;
„ III, 10, 52 to III, 23 (on Śrāddha) = „ 73-83 (except 82, 14-42);
and „ IV, 2 (on Naraka and Karma-vipāka) .. .. = „ 101.

So their dates are not different from those of the corresponding chapters of the Vāyu.

Prąkriyā and Anuṣaṅga Pādas of the Vāyu of the AnSS ed., the main differences being that Bḍ 35 (verses 78-87), 36 (verses 1-16a), and 70 are not found in the Vāyu, and Vā 25 is not found in the Brahmāṇḍa. Besides these, there are variations in readings and numbers of verses in the corresponding chapters, as one may expect in any two Mss of the same Purāṇa.

24 Pargiter, AIHT, pp. 23 and 77.

25 Cf. Mbh III, 191, 16; Hv I, 7, 13 and 25; and Harṣacarita, chap. III. No early non-Purāṇic work, except the Uttaragītā-bhāṣya of Gauḍapāda, has been found to name the Brahmāṇḍa-p. In the Bhāṣya even, the reading *brahmāṇḍādīni* is dubious.

26 This is the title given to the Vāyu in the colophons of its chapters.

Some of the above mentioned chapters of the Brahmāṇḍa have been drawn upon by the commentators and Nibandhakāras. For instance, Jīmūtavāhana quotes verses from Bḍ II, 21, 24 and 28 and III, 19 in his Kālaviveka; Aparārka from Bḍ III, 9, 11-12, 14-16 and 19 in his com. on Yāj.; Devaṇabhaṭṭa from Bḍ III, 9, 11, 14 and 15 in his Smṛti-candrikā; Hemādri from Bḍ III, 9-12, 14-17 and 19 in his Caturvarga-cintāmaṇi; and so forth (see App.).

The numerous large extracts and isolated verses, quoted from the 'Brahmāṇḍa-p.' in the Caturvarga-cintāmaṇi on various big donations (such as those of Jambu-dvīpa, Sapta-dvīpa, Pṛthivī-padma, Dhānya-parvata, Trimūrti, Caturmūrti, Panca-mūrti, and the like) and vows (Vrata, viz., Ṛṣi-pañcamī, Daśāditya, Karaṇa, Ardha-śrāvaṇikā, etc.) but not found in the present Brahmāṇḍa, show that the text of the 'Brahmāṇḍa', used by Hemādri, was in many respects different from that of our present edition as well as from that of the Brahmāṇḍa known to Ballālasena (cf. '. . . . *purāṇaṃ brahmāṇḍaṃ. . . . dāna-vidhi-śūnyaṃ. . . .*' —Dānasāgara, fol. 3b).

4. THE VIṢṆU-PURĀṆA:

This is one of the most important of the extant Purāṇas. It belongs to the Pāñcarātra sect and 'is the best representative of the whole class of sectarian Purāṇas, since it is purely Vaiṣṇava in its teaching from beginning to end and yet retains with considerable faithfulness the character of the old unsectarian Purāṇas'. Inspite of this distinctive character, it contains, like the other Purāṇas, several chapters on Smṛti-matter; viz., II, 6 (on hells), III, 8-16 (on the duties of the castes and Āśramas, general customs, impurity and funeral sacrifices), and VI, 1-2 (on Yuga-dharma and Karma-vipāka) and 5 (on hells).

The problem of the date of this Purāṇa is a very difficult one, and scholars hold different opinions about it. Pargiter says: "It is a late Purāṇa composed as a single whole upon a consistent plan, and not a collection of materials of various times, as we find in the Vāyu, Brahma and Matsya. From its account of Buddhism and Jainism it appears to have been composed after Brahmanism had recovered its supremacy, so that it cannot be earlier than about the fifth century A.D., and it is Brahmanical"[27]. Farquhar opines: "The Harivaṃśa clearly cannot be dated later than A.D. 400, and the Viṣṇu-purāṇa is so like it in most of its features that it is probable that it belongs to the same general date"[28]. Winternitz says: "Pargiter may be right in thinking that it cannot be earlier than the fifth century A.D. However, I do not think that it is much later"[29].

[27] Pargiter, AIHT, p. 80. [28] Farquhar, Outline, p. 143.
[29] Winternitz, Ind. Lit., Vol. I, p. 545, footnote 2.

C. V. Vaidya tries to prove that the Viṣṇu-purāṇa is not earlier than the ninth century A.D. on the hypothetical assumption that the Kailakila or Kaiṅkila Yavanas, mentioned in Viṣ IV, 24, 16, reigned in Andhra between 575 and 900 A.D. and were at the height of their power about 782 A.D[30]. All these views, except that of Winternitz, are not beyond objection. It is necessary, therefore, to determine afresh the date of the Viṣṇu-p., which has been referred to by Alberūnī and drawn upon by the Nibandha-writers and the religious teachers like Rāmānuja from the eleventh century[31].

[30] Vaidya, History of Mediæval Hindu India, I, Poona, 1921, pp. 350 ff; and JBBRAS, 1925, pp. 155 ff.

[31] In his Bhāṣyas on the Brahmasūtra and the Upaniṣads Śaṃkarācārya gives from 'Smṛti' and 'Purāṇa' a number of verses without expressly naming the sources, and some of these verses are traceable not only in the extant Viṣṇu-purāṇa but in other Purāṇas also; viz., the verses quoted on:

(i) Brahmasūtra I, 2, 19 (p. 196—*apratarkyam avijñeyam*)	= Manu I, 5b; = Devī-p. 127, 42b; and so forth.
(ii) Brahmasūtra I, 3, 28 (p. 288—*anādinidhanā*)	= Kūr I, 2, 28.
(iii) Brahmasūtra I, 3, 28 (p. 288—*nāmarūpe ca bhūtānām*)	= Viṣ I, 5, 62; = Kūr I, 7, 66; = Vā 9, 63; = Bd I, 8, 65; = Mārk 48, 42; and so on.
(iv) Brahmasūtra I, 3, 30 (p. 302—*teṣāṃ ye yāni*)	= Viṣ I, 5, 59b-60; = Kūr I, 7, 63-64; = Mārk 48, 39-40; and so forth.
(v) Brahmasūtra I, 3, 30 (pp. 304-5—*ṛṣīṇāṃ nāma-dheyāni*)	= Viṣ I, 5, 63-64 (readings differ in verse 63); = Kūr I, 7, 67-68; = Śiv V (Vāyavīya-saṃhitā), i, 10, 70-71; = Vā 9, 64-65; = Bd I, 8, 66; = Mārk 48, 43-44; and so forth. In none of the above Purāṇas the verse *'yathābhimāninaḥ'* is found.
(vi) Brahmasūtra III, 2, 24 (p. 828—*yaṃ vinidrāḥ*)	= Kūr I, 10, 67. (The line *'yoginas taṃ'* is not found).

It will be shown below that the extant Kūrma-p. has come down to us through two main stages; that in its earlier form it was a Pāñcarātra document composed between 550 and 650 A.D. but was later recast by the Pāśupatas between 700 and 800 A.D.; and that the theology of those chapters, which have been retained in it, has considerable Śākta element like that of the Ahirbudhnya-saṃhitā (see under Kūrma-p.). Now, a comparison, so far as theology is concerned, between the Viṣṇu and the Viṣṇuite Kūrma-p., shows that the former is older than the latter. In the Viṣṇu-p. Lakṣmī plays no part in creation as Viṣṇu's Śakti. Even, except in only one place (viz., Viṣ I, 8, 27—*aviṣṭambho gadā-pāṇiḥ śaktir lakṣmīr dvijottama*), there is no second mention of Lakṣmī as Viṣṇu's Śakti. The portion, viz., verses 15-32 of Viṣ I, 8, in which this mention occurs and in which the inseparable connection of Viṣṇu and Lakṣmī has been put forth, seems to have been interpolated on account of the fact that the Padma-purāṇa (Sṛṣṭi-khaṇḍa), which has borrowed Viṣ I, 8 along with many other chapters, does not contain it. The Viṣṇu-p. itself also seems to prove the spuriousness of these verses. In Viṣ I, 8, 14 Maitreya asks: "It is heard that Śrī came out of the ocean of milk during the churning. Then how do you say that she

(*vii*) Brahmasūtra III, 3, 16 (p. 872—*sa vai śarīraḥ*) = Kūr I, 4, 33.

(*viii*) Bṛhadāraṇyaka-upaniṣad I, 4, 6 (p. 113—*brahmavṛkṣaḥ sanātanaḥ*) = Śiv V (Vāyavīya-saṃhitā), i, 10, 76c; = Vā 9, 116a (in Mss *kh*, *gh* and *ṅ* used in the AnSS ed.); = Narasiṃha-p. 16, 7a; and so on.

It is quite evident that the above coincidences cannot carry us far in determining the date of the Viṣṇu-purāṇa.

In numerous cases the individual Purāṇas are found to contain chapters or verses common to two or more of them, or to have retained extracts or isolated verses from their older prototypes or other Sanskrit works. In the Nibandhas also there are numerous extracts or verses which have been quoted with the mention of the names of two or more Purāṇic or non-Purāṇic works as common sources. For instance, see Caturvarga-cintāmaṇi, Vol. III (Pariśeṣa-khaṇḍa), Part i, pp. 10 (*brahmavaivarta-vāyupurāṇayoḥ*), 12 (*mārkaṇḍeya-skānda-brahmapurāṇeṣu*), 14 (*pādma-mātsyayoḥ*), 15 (*pādma-mātsyayoḥ*), 1079 (*viṣṇudharmottara-bhaviṣyat-purāṇa-brahmavaivarta - brahmapurāṇa -vāyupurāṇa-prabhāsakhaṇḍa-bhaviṣyottareṣu*), 1095 (*yama - yājñavalkya - viṣṇudharmottara - brahmavaivarta - bhaviṣyottara - kūrma-purāṇeṣu*), 1139 (*śātātapasmṛti-prabhāsakhaṇḍeṣu*), 1146 (*vasiṣṭhasmṛti-kūrma-purāṇayoḥ*), etc. etc. So, it is not at all safe to use in determining the date of any particular work any verses which have been quoted without any express mention of the sources, even if those quoted verses are traceable in that particular work.

was born of Khyāti by Bhṛgu?" To this Parāśara's reply comes in a much later passage in Viṣ I, 9, 1: "Hear, O Maitreya, what you have asked me about. This (story) about Śrī I heard from Marīci". He then narrates the story. The nature of the answer mentioned above shows that it should follow the query immediately and should have nothing intervening. Therefore, *the irrelevant verses, which separate the answer from the query, appear to be spurious.* Now, if the Viṣṇuite Kūrma-p. was composed between 550 and 650 A.D., then the Viṣṇu-p. cannot be dated later than the beginning of the seventh century A.D.

Let the Bhāgavata and the Viṣṇu-p. be now compared. As regards contents the Bhāgavata is 'closely connected with the Viṣṇu-p. with which it often agrees literally, and it is undoubtedly dependent upon the latter'[32]. By comparing the genealogies in both the Purāṇas, Pargiter has come to the conclusion that 'the Bhāgavata has used the Viṣṇu in its composition'[33]. Many myths and legends, which are found in a concise and older form in the Viṣṇu-p., appear in the Bhāgavata in a much enlarged and elaborate version. For instances, the stories of Dhruva, Veṇa, Pṛthu, Prahlāda, Jaḍa Bharata and others, occurring in both the Purāṇas, may be compared. The Bhāgavata (book X) 'contains the biography of Kṛṣṇa which is here given in much greater detail than in the Viṣṇu-p. and in the Harivaṃśa. In particular the love scenes with the cowherdesses (Gopīs) occupy a much larger space'[34]. In the Viṣṇu-p. a hair of Viṣṇu is said to be incarnated as Kṛṣṇa[35], i.e., Kṛṣṇa is an incarnation of an exceedingly small portion of Viṣṇu; but in the Bhāgavata he is called an Aṃśāvatāra[36] or the Bhagavat himself *(kṛṣṇas tu bhagavān svayam).* In the Bhāgavata there are stories which are not found in the Viṣṇu. The story of Kapila (in Bhāg III, 24-33) may be cited as an example. From all this it appears that the Viṣṇu-p. is older than the Bhāgavata. If the latter Purāṇa is assigned to the sixth century A.D. (see under Bhāgavata-p. below), then the date of the former should be placed earlier.

In Viṣ II, 9, 16 the Nakṣatras are mentioned as beginning with Kṛttikā *(kṛttikādiṣu ṛkṣeṣu).* The evidence of Varāhamihira (about 550 A.D.) that the old order of the Nakṣatras from Kṛttikā to Bharaṇī was changed for that from Aśvinī to Revatī in his time, shows that the old order held ground up to a time not posterior to the end of the fifth century A.D. Therefore the Viṣṇu-p., which

[32] Winternitz, Ind. Lit., Vol. I, p. 555.

[33] Pargiter, AIHT, p. 80.

[34] Winternitz, Ind. Lit., Vol. I, p. 557.

[35] Viṣ V, 1, 59-60. [36] Bhāg X, 2, 9 and 16.

speaks of the old order, should be dated not later than the end of that century.

We may now compare the Viṣṇu-p. with the Harivaṃśa to see if the date of the former can be pushed further up. In the Harivaṃśa the biography of Kṛṣṇa is given at greater length and in greater detail, and Kṛṣṇa is called an Aṃśāvatāra[37] in the sense that Viṣṇu divided himself into Kṛṣṇa and Saṃkarṣaṇa for the good of the world[38]. In the Viṣṇu-p. the Hallīśa sport has got various erotic touches, but 'in the Harivaṃśa the whole story of his (*i.e.*, Kṛṣṇa's) youth is told at much greater length and the Hallīśa is treated as involving sexual intercourse'[39]. The stories have been developed and expanded in the Harivaṃśa. The story of Jarāsandha and that of the carrying away of the Pārijāta tree by Kṛṣṇa may be cited as examples. Besides these, there are many new additions found in the Harivaṃśa. For instance, there are the Āryāstava (Hv II, 3) and the Puṇyaka-vrata observed by Satyabhāmā (Hv II, 77-81). From all this it can be concluded that the Viṣṇu-p. is of earlier origin than at least this portion of the Harivaṃśa. If the lower limit of the date of the Harivaṃśa, which is named and quoted by Gauḍapāda in his Uttaragītā-bhāṣya[40] and cannot possibly, therefore, be later than the sixth century A.D., be placed about 400 A.D[41]., then the Viṣṇu must be dated not later than the middle of the fourth century A.D. This will give us the lower limit of the date of the Viṣṇu-p.

The mention of the zodiacal signs (Rāśi) at various places in the Viṣṇu-p.[42] shows that at the time of composition of the Purāṇa these signs became quite familiar and were widely used. The familiarity of the ancient people with the Tithis, Nakṣatras and planets but the total absence of the term *rāśi* in all early works down to the time of the Yājñavalkya-smṛti, tends to show that the Indians were not familiar with the Rāśis earlier than the second century A.D. The mention of the word *horā* in Viṣ IV, 12, 13 is also significant. Though the occurrence of the term *horā* in two verses quoted by

[37] Hv II, 49, 32. [38] Ibid., II, 14, 46.

[39] Farquhar, Outline, p. 144.

[40] Uttaragītā, p. 68—*uktaṃ ca harivaṃśe—*
asatkīrtana-kāntāra-parivartana-pāṃsubhiḥ (°pāṃsulāṃ?)
vācaṃ hari-kathālāpa-gaṅgayaiva punīmahe||
Also see chap. 3 in Mss Nos. 4504 and K558E of the Uttargītā in the D. U. Mss Lib. In the Mss the readings of the verse slightly differ.

[41] Farquhar, Outline, p. 143.
Winternitz, Ind. Lit., I, p. 464, footnote 2.

[42] Viz., Viṣ II, 8, 28 and 30; II, 8, 41-42; II, 8, 62-63; II, 8, 70; II, 12, 19; III, 14, 5; and IV, 24, 30.

Varāhamihira from Garga[43] shows that it came to be used by the Indians much earlier than the sixth century A.D., there is nothing to prove that it was used by them earlier than the end of the first century A.D. Hence it can be held, and not quite unreasonably, that the Viṣṇu-p., which is familiar with the Rāśis and the Horā, was written not earlier than the end of the first century A.D.

Thus, the date of composition of the Viṣṇu-p. falls between the end of the first and the middle of the fourth century A.D., i.e., between 100 and 350 A.D. The nature of the Smṛti-contents of the Viṣṇu-p., as compared with those of the Mārkaṇḍeya, tends to show that the former is later than the latter. So *it is highly probable that the Viṣṇu-p. was written in the last quarter of the third or the first quarter of the fourth century A.D.*

The view of Pargiter that the Viṣṇu-p. 'cannot be earlier than about the 5th century A.D.' is based on *Viṣ III, 17 and 18 describing the story of Māyāmoha.* It will be seen below that these chapters *were most probably interpolated at a later date.*

The summary of contents of Viṣ III, 17 and 18 is as follows :

Maitreya asks Parāśara to explain the word *nagna* used by the latter in connection with those who are to be shunned in a Śrāddha ceremony. Accordingly, Parāśara begins a story, which he says, was narrated to Bhīṣma by Parāśara's grandfather Vaśiṣṭha. This story says that in ancient times the gods, being defeated by the demons (Asuras) in a war which was continued for a divine year, went to the northern side of the ocean of milk and eulogised Viṣṇu who, consequently, produced Māyāmoha from his own body and gave him to the gods. This Māyāmoha, with his body stripped of all garments, his head shaved and a peacock feather in hand, went to the banks of the Narmadā where the demons were living, preached to them the religion of 'the naked' (i.e., Jainism) and turned them 'Ārhatas'. Next, Māyāmoha put on red clothes, painted his eyes with collyrium and preached Ahiṃsā (i.e., Buddhism) to the remaining demons. As a result of this preaching the demons soon gave up the Vedic religion and got weakened. Consequently, they were attacked by the gods, defeated and massacred.

The above story of delusion, in which Viṣṇu creates Māyāmoha from his own body with a view to deluding the demons, is certainly later than that found in Mat 24, 43-49. This Purāṇa says that once the sons of Raji became very powerful by virtue of their penance, took possession of the heavenly kingdom of Indra, and deprived him of his share in the sacrifices. Consequently, Indra sought the help of Bṛhaspati, who first increased the power of the god through

[43] Bṛhat-saṃhitā, pp. 7 and 9.

various mystic rites and then deluded *(mohayāmāsa)* the sons of Raji by preaching to them the non-Vedic religion of the Jina[44]. The sons of Raji thus got out of the pale of the Vedic religion and were killed by Indra. In this story it is Bṛhaspati who preaches the religion of the Jina. That this connection of Bṛhaspati with delusion through the Jina-dharma was well-known in ancient India is shown by the Devībhāgavata (IV, 13), in which Bṛhaspati appears in the guise of Śukra during the latter's absence and deludes the demons by preaching the 'Jaina dharma'. In the Harivaṃśa also, Bṛhaspati is said to have 'deluded' the sons of Raji by writing some heretical works for them[45]. Now, the date of Mat 24, in which the above mentioned story of Bṛhaspati occurs, is to be placed either in the last quarter of the third or the first quarter of the fourth century A.D. (See under Matsya-p. below). Therefore the story of Māyāmoha in the Viṣṇu-p. is to be dated later than the middle of the fourth century A.D. It is probable that the story did not originate earlier than 500 A.D. (see also under Matsya-p.).

That the story of Māyāmoha is spurious seems further to be shown by the fact that though the Viṣṇu-p. knows many incarnations of Viṣṇu including the Kalki, it is remarkably silent about the Buddha incarnation. So it seems that the Buddha did not come to be regarded as an incarnation of Viṣṇu at the time of composition of the Viṣṇu-p.

The story of Māyāmoha is also found in a much elaborate form in the Padma-p., Sṛṣṭi-khaṇḍa, chap. 13. The story here is clearly an amalgamation of those in the Matsya (24, 43-49) and the Devībhāgavata (IV, 13) on the one hand, and that in the Viṣṇu (III, 17-18) on the other. The date of the Padma-p. (Sṛṣṭi-kh.) being not earlier than about 650 A.D. (see below, under Padma-p.), this story does not affect the above date of Viṣ III, 17-18.

In Padma-p., Bhūmi-kh., 36-39 also, Viṣṇu is said to have deluded Veṇa by preaching the 'Jaina dharma'. As this Khaṇḍa cannot be placed earlier than 900 A.D., the story in it can be ignored.

As to the Smṛti-chapters of the Viṣṇu-p., there is nothing to show that they were added later. Hence it should be admitted that they come from the same general date as that of the Purāṇa itself. They have been profusely drawn upon by the commentators and Nibandhakāras like Jīmūtavāhana, Aparārka, Vijñāneśvara, Aniruddhabhaṭṭa, Ballālasena, Devaṇabhaṭṭa, Hemādri, Kullūkabhaṭṭa and others (see App.).

Of all the extant Purāṇas, the Viṣṇu has preserved the best text. Additions and alterations have been made in it much less freely than

[44] Mat 24, 47.

[45] Hv I, 28, 29 ff.

in the other Purāṇas. Consequently, the great majority of the verses quoted in the commentaries and Nibandhas from the 'Viṣṇu-p.' or 'Vaiṣṇava' occur in the present Viṣṇu and agree very closely in readings with those of the Purāṇa. From the verses quoted in the Adbhutasāgara (pp. 383, 499-500 and 564) but not traceable in the extant Viṣṇu it is evident that the Purāṇa, in its earlier form or in a different recension, contained chapters (on the different Adbhutas) which are now lost. The verses on Nārāyaṇa-bali (offering to Nārāyaṇa), quoted in the Mitākṣarā (on Yāj. III, 6) from the 'Vaiṣṇava', does not seem to have been taken from the Viṣṇu-p., because these verses, which are not found in the present Viṣṇu-p., are quoted in the Madana-pārijāta (pp. 410-411) with the words '*nārāyaṇa-bali-svarūpaṃ ca viṣṇunābhihitam*', wherein the word '*viṣṇu*' seems to mean a person (most probably a Saṃhitākāra) and not a book.

It was perhaps the great fame and popularity of the Viṣṇu-p. that encouraged the composition of a spurious work of the same title and extent as those of the Viṣṇu at a time earlier than the beginning of the twelfth century A.D[46]. As no Ms of this spurious work has been found as yet, it seems to have been lost.

5. THE MATSYA-PURĀṆA[47].

The determination of the date of composition of the Matsya-purāṇa, as we have it now, is rather difficult. No one date is sufficient for it, because it has suffered through repeated additions and losses. Hence, for the date of this Purāṇa in its earlier form, we shall have to look to the chapters dealing with the genealogies of the kings of the Solar and Lunar dynasties, for these chapters are undoubtedly the oldest parts in the present Matsya. These chapters, again, should be divided into two groups; viz.,

(1) chaps. 11-12, 23-24, and 43-46—which have not yet been traced anywhere else, and (2) chaps. 47-50 and 271-273—which greatly resemble chaps. 96 (verses 192 ff.), 97-98 and 99 (especially except verses 367-391) of the Vāyu-p. Besides these, there are also other chapters which are common to the Matsya and Vāyu; viz., Matsya-p., chaps. 51, 114, 124-128 and 141-145, and Vāyu-p., chaps. 29, 45 (verses 69 to the end), 46 (verses 1 to the end, except a few verses), 50 (verses 56 to the end), 51, 52 (verses 1-71a), 52 (71b to the end), and 53. We shall first turn our attention to the chapters

[46] See Dānasāgara, fol. 4a; also footnote 131 under Agni-purāṇa in chap. III.

[47] The Vaṅga. ed. is chapter by chapter the same as the AnSS ed., the main difference being that the section on the merits of listening to the Purāṇa, which is found at the end of the AnSS ed., does not occur in the Vaṅga. ed. There are also occasional differences in readings, but those are not many.

of the second group, and especially to chaps. 50 (verses 72 ff.) and 271-273 dealing with the future dynasties, because their date will help us to ascertain the date of the present Matsya-p.

The striking agreement between the chapters common to the Matsya and the Vāyu-p. naturally raises the question as to whether these two Purāṇas borrowed their accounts from the same original source or one of them copied these from the other. As a solution F. E. Pargiter has put forth the theory that about the last quarter of the third century A.D. the Matsya borrowed from the Bhaviṣya the shorter account (of the future dynasties) which ended with the downfall of the Āndhras and the local kingdoms that survived them a while. 'The Bhaviṣya account was then extended down to the time when the Gupta kingdom had acquired the territories assigned to it, and its language was revised; that would be (say) about 320-325 A.D. The Vāyu copied that extended and revised account from the Bhaviṣya almost immediately, and that is the version found in eVāyu (i.e., a Ms of the Vāyu-p., preserved in the India Office Library and called eVāyu by Pargiter for differentiation). Afterwards, the language of the Bhaviṣya version was revised again..... ......about 330-335.........This second revision was soon adopted by the Vāyu and is the version found now in Vāyu Mss generally'[48]. This theory, with all its attractiveness and reasonings, is not free from defects. The way in which the Matsya and the Vāyu refer to the 'Bhaviṣya'[49], shows clearly that their versions were not copied *verbatim* from this original source, viz., 'Bhavisya-p.'; for in the 'Bhaviṣya' itself such references would be absurd and meaningless. If so, why then do the two versions agree almost literally not only in the genealogies but also in the stories of kings, sages and demons; viz., Mat 47 = Vā 96 (verses 192 ff.)—98 (on Viṣṇu's different incarnations and the war between the gods and demons); Mat 48, 30-89 = Vā 99, 35-98 (containing the story of the birth of Dīrghatamas, his practice of Go-dharma, and his begetting of five sons on the maid servant and the wife of king Bali); Mat 49, 15-34 = Vā 99, 139-158 (on the story of the birth of Bharadvāja); and so forth? The genealogies of kings are given in some other Purāṇas also; and there are, of course, certain verses which are found common to two or more of them, but the striking agreement which is found between the Matsya and the Vāyu is to be met with nowhere else. So, the

[48] Pargiter, Dynasties of the Kali age, Introduction, p. xiii.

[49] Viz., in '*tān sarvān kīrtayiṣyāmi bhaviṣye Kathitān nṛpān*'—Mat 50, 75 = Vā 99, 267 (the Vāyu reads '*paṭhitān*' for '*kathitān*'); '*tasyānvavāye vakṣyāmi bhaviṣye kathitān nṛpān*'—Mat 50, 77 = Vā 99, 270 (the Vāyu reads '*tāvato*' for '*kathitān*'); and '*bhaviṣye te prasaṃkhyātāḥ purāṇajñaiḥ śrutarṣibhiḥ*'—Mat 273, 37 = Vā 99, 417 (the latter reads '*bhaviṣyais tatra saṃkhyātāḥ*' for '*bhaviṣye* etc'.).

mutually agreeing Matsya and Vāyu versions, which are not copies made from the 'Bhaviṣya', could not be based independently upon this source, because in that case they would never agree so literally. It seems therefore that one of them must have drawn upon the other.

The expressions '....*bhaviṣye kathitān nṛpān*', '*bhaviṣye te prasaṃkhyātāḥ*....' etc., occurring both in the Vāyu and the Matsya, should not be taken to be due to the independent use of the same original source (viz., the 'Bhaviṣya-p'.) by these two Purāṇas. But the reason is that, as we shall see below, the version of the Vāyu was based on the 'Bhaviṣya' to which it refers by name, and the Matsya version is only a copy of the Vāyu version. So the references also have been retained in the Matsya.

It may be questioned, 'If one of the Purāṇas, viz., the Matsya and the Vāyu, used the other as the source, then how are we to explain the differences between the two Purāṇas in readings and additional verses?' The answer is that such differences are to be ascribed to the later additions, alterations, losses, and mistakes made by the scribes. Even the different Mss of a particular Purāṇa are always found to differ considerably in readings and numbers of verses; but inspite of such differences the work is substantially the same. So, the Matsya and Vāyu versions should not be taken as distinct from, and independent of, each other merely on account of such differences. On the other hand, a comparison of readings and verses given from different Mss in the AnSS editions of the Vāyu and Matsya reduces the number of such variations to a very great extent. It should be remembered that no one Ms of a Purāṇa is reliable for such comparison, for it is sometimes found that while one Ms preserves a correct reading in a particular place another makes a mistake, and the verses omitted by one Ms in one place are found in another. For example, Vā 99, 14 (= Bḍ III, 74, 14 = Mat 48, 11b-12a ; the Matsya reads '*kolāhalasya*' for '*kālānalasya*' of the Vāyu and Brahmāṇḍa) is not found in Ms *g* of the Vāyu[50]; Vā 99, 17a (= Bḍ III, 74, 16a = Mat 48, 14b; reading differs) is not found in Ms *kh* of the same Purāṇa ; and so on. Similarly, Mat 49, 52b-59 (= Vā 99, 175-182; readings differ) are not found in Ms *g* of the Matsya[51]; and so on. On the other hand, Mat 49, 61-69, which are not found in the Vāyu-p., are also not found in Mss *gh* and *ṅ* of the Matsya[52]; Mat 50, 41b, not occurring in the Vāyu, does not also occur in Mss *k* and *kh*[53]; and so on. As regards readings also a good number of such examples may be given.

[50] See Vāyu-p., p. 370, footnote.

[51] See Matsya-p., AnSS ed., p. 102, footnote.

[52] Ibid., p. 102, footnote. [53] Ibid., p. 105, footnote.

As to the interrelation among the Vāyu, Brahmāṇḍa and Matsya, it may be said that the Vāyu and Brahmāṇḍa, though originally one, were separated at some early time. Since separation they have been subjected independently to additions, alterations, losses, and mistakes made by the scribes. As the same additions, alterations etc. were not, and could not possibly be, made in these two separate works by different hands belonging to different climes and ages, it is found that where one is found to preserve the original text, the other makes a mistake. It is only for this reason that "where the Vāyu and Brahmāṇḍa differ, one of them not seldom agrees with the Matsya" which also has not escaped additions, alterations etc.; that "single Mss of them sometimes vary so as to agree with the reading of the Matsya", and that "one Purāṇa occasionally omits a verse which appears in one or both of the two others, yet a single Ms (or a very few Mss) of it has at times preserved that verse"[54].

From the above discussion it follows that the Matsya and Vāyu versions were not based independently on the original source 'Bhaviṣya' nor were they copied *Verbatim* from it, but that either the Matsya version was copied from that of the Vāyu or *vice versa*. We shall now try to see which one is the borrower.

In Mat 142 (= Vā 57, 1-85) the genealogies of sages are referred to as narrated before[55], but there is no chapter in the Matsya dealing with these and preceding chap. 142, whereas in the Vāyu there is a chapter (viz., 28) which deals with Ṛṣi-vaṃśa. In the Matsya the genealogies of sages are given as late as in chapters 195-202, which, on account of their position and elaborate character, seem to be later additions. Moreover, the opening verses contain Manu's mention of Śiva's curse on the sage—a curse which has really not been referred to by the Fish anywhere in the Matsya-p. These chapters (195-202), which practically treat of the Gotras and Pravaras, may have been based on the works on Pravaras ascribed to Baudhāyana, Kātyāyana, Viśvāmitra, Garga and others[56]. Again, in Mat 50, 68-71 (= Vā 99, 260-263; the Vāyu differs in readings in several places) the sages, wishing to hear of the future, put to Sūta several questions about (1) the future kings—their names and the periods of their reigns, and (2) the future ages—their characteristic

[54] Pargiter, Dynasties of the Kali age, Introduction, p. vi.

[55] Cf. *kramāgataṃ mayāpy etat tubhyaṃ noktaṃ yuga-dvayam|*
ṛṣi-vaṃśa-prasaṅgena vyākulatvāt tathātmanaḥ||

Mat 142, 39 = Vā 57, 38. The latter reads '*hi*' for '*api*', '*proktam*' for '*noktaṃ*', and '*tathaiva ca*' for '*tathātmanaḥ*'.

[56] Cf. '*pravara-gotrayoḥ samānatvāsamānatve baudhāyana-kātyāyana-viśvāmitra-gargādi-praṇīteṣu pravara-grantheṣu prasiddhe*'—Mādhava-bhāṣya on the Parāśara-smṛti, Vol. I, part ii, p. 72.

signs, their merits and defects, and the happiness and miseries of the people during these ages. Consequently, Sūta, promising to narrate to them the future Kali age, the future Manvantaras and the future kingships[57], begins with the future kings and answers all the questions in Mat 50 (verses 77 to the end = Vā 99, 270-280a) and 271-273 (= Vā 99, 281 to the end). About the future Manvantaras, which Sūta himself wants to narrate, nothing is said in the Matsya-p., whereas in the Vāyu these are dealt with in the following chapter (i.e., chap. 100). From these disagreements between the two Purāṇas it follows that the Matsya-p. borrowed only those chapters from the Vāyu which it found necessary, without caring for the lines containing references to other chapters of the Vāyu. So it may be concluded that the Matsya borrowed the chapters, common to itself and the Vāyu, from the latter, and not from the 'Bhaviṣya'. And this priority of the Vāyu account explains why "the Vāyu has Prakritisms sometimes where the Matsya has correct Sanskrit"[58].

The above view is supported by the Vāyu Mss themselves. One Vāyu Ms (referred to as eVāyu by Pargiter and belonging to the India Office Library) is described as follows: "Very valuable, because it has readings different from the printed editions, and some verses not contained therein; and where it differs therefrom it often agrees with the Matsya"[59]. Moreover, in that portion of the account, which deals with the evils of the Kali age and a chronological-astronomical summary of the age, "the Vāyu and Brahmāṇḍa version contains 32 more lines and is nearly twice as long as the Matsya", whereas "the account in eVāyu has the full description with the exception of a few verses". From these it follows that the agreement between the Vāyu and Matsya versions was once much greater than it is now, and that the text of the Vāyu has been much tampered with, with the result that it has suffered through additions, losses and mistakes. It should be noted here that the Vāyu Ms referred to cannot be proved to have preserved the original readings of the Vāyu, and that there might have been other Mss containing better readings.

Before we proceed further we are confronted with another problem, viz., why Vā 99, 365-391, which carry the narrative down to the rise of the Guptas, do not occur in the Matsya-p., though the latter drew upon the former. The explanation is that the Vāyu version of the dynasties of the Kali age must have had two stages of termination. In its earlier stage it ended with the downfall of the Āndhras and the local kingdoms that survived them a while,

[57] Cf. Mat 50, 72-76 = Vā 99, 264-269; readings differ in a few cases.

[58] Pargiter, Dynasties of the Kali age, Introduction, p. xiv.

[59] Ibid., Introduction, p. xxiii.

and it was in this stage that the Matsya copied the Vāyu version. In the second stage the Vāyu account was extended to the rise of the Guptas by the addition of verses 365-391 of Vā 99. There being no mention of Samudragupta's conquests in this later addition, Pargiter thinks, and not unreasonably, that this addition was made not later than 335 A.D.[60] Hence the date of the Vāyu version in its earlier stage should be placed not earlier than the middle of the third century A.D. when the Āndhra kingdom fell and not later than 335 A.D., and most probably about the last quarter of the third century A.D.[61] So, the date of the Matsya version also falls either in the last quarter of the third or the first quarter of the fourth century A.D. The occasionally crude style of the Matsya version and the agreement between the Vāyu and Brahmāṇḍa as regards the extended portion of the dynastic account need not go against the priority of the shorter account of the Vāyu. It has already been said that the text of the Vāyu was revised and emended more than once. Hence it is not at all improbable that the crude portions also should have been rewritten. Further, the Vāyu and Brahmāṇḍa were separated undoubtedly after the Vāyu account had been extended to the rise of the Guptas and also even after the text of the Vāyu had begun to be worked upon, for the Brahmāṇḍa not only contains the extended portion of the dynastic account of the Vāyu but agrees more closely with the printed text of the Vāyu than with the Ms (eVāyu) referred to above.

The view of Pargiter that the Bhaviṣya was subjected to two revisions in the early centuries of the Christian era[62] is purely an assumption without any evidence in its support. The accounts in the three Purāṇas—Matsya, Vāyu and Brahmāṇḍa—do not also seem to have been compared at times, because in that case the readings of the Matsya, while agreeing more with those of the Ms eVāyu, would not have differed so much from those of the printed editions of the Vāyu and Brahmāṇḍa, and there would have been every possibility of extending the Matsya account to the rise of the Guptas.

We have seen above that the chapters of the second group in the Matsya-p. (i.e., those chapters on the genealogies of kings in the Matsya which are common to itself and the Vāyu) were borrowed from the Vāyu about the last quarter of the third century A.D. Now, the chapters of the first group (i.e., chaps. 11-12, 23-24 and 43-46) may either be contemporaneous with those of the second or may belong to different ages. The close interrelation of the contents of the chapters of the two groups, however, tends to

[60] Ibid., Introduction, p. xiii. [61] Ibid., Introduction, p. xiii.
[62] Ibid., Introduction, p. xiii.

point to the former alternative. In the first group chap. 11 opens with a request to Sūta to describe the Solar and Lunar dynasties, and chap. 12 accordingly names the descendants of Ikṣvāku of the Solar dynasty. Next, the Lunar dynasty is taken up. Accordingly, in chaps. 23-24 the story of the birth of Budha is narrated and his descendants down to Yadu, Turvasu, Druhyu, Anu and Puru are named; and chaps. 43-46 name the descendants of Yadu and give accounts of some of them. In the second group, chap. 47 narrates the stories of the Yādavas, of Kṛṣṇa, of the wars between the gods and demons, etc.; chap. 48 names and describes the descendants of Turvasu, Druhyu and Anu; chaps. 49-50 (verses 1-67) name the descendants of Puru down to Adhisomakṛṣṇa; chap. 50 (verses 68 to the end) names the future kings from Adhisomakṛṣṇa to Kṣemaka; and chaps. 271-273 further continue the names and accounts of the future kings and races.

The contents enumerated above will show how closely the chapters of the two groups are interrelated. Without the chapters of the second group, the accounts given by those of the first are incomplete; for the descendants of Turvasu, Druhyu, Anu and Puru are no less important than those of Yadu, but are equally required for the completion of the account. It is therefore highly probable that the original author, or rather compiler, of the present Matsya wrote, or borrowed from some unknown source, the chapters of the first group and supplemented them with those of the second. Consequently, *the date of the earlier form of the present Matsya seems to be the same as that of the Matsya's borrowing the chapters of the second group from the Vāyu, i.e., about the last quarter of the third or the first quarter of the fourth century A.D.*

Let us now pass on to the Smṛti-chapters, which form the major portion of the present Matsya-p. In this Purāṇa funeral sacrifices are dealt with in chaps. 16-22; Vratas in chaps. 7, 54-57, 60-66, 69-81 and 95-101; gifts in chaps. 53, 82-92, 205-206 and 274-289; holy places in chaps. 13 (verses 10 to the end), 22, 103-112 (on the glories of Prayāga), 180-185 (on the glories of Benares), and 186-194 (on the glories of the river Narmadā); duties of the Āśramas in chap. 40; bath in chaps. 67, 68 and 102; Pratiṣṭhā (consecration) in chaps. 58-59 and 264-270; duties of women in chap. 7 (verses 37-49); hells in chap. 39; sacrifices to the planets (Graha-yajña) and their pacification (Śānti) in chaps. 93, 94 and 228-239; duties of kings in chaps. 215-243; law (Vyavahāra) in chap. 227; dedication (Utsarga) in chap. 207; Yuga-dharma in chaps. 142, 144, 145 and 165; penances in chap. 227 (verses 34 ff.); and Vāstu in chaps. 252-257 and 268-270

Before proceeding to discuss the dates of these chapters it is necessary to examine the chapters common to the Matsya and the

Padma-p. (Sṛṣṭi-kh.) in order to see whether the former borrowed these chapters from the latter or *vice versa*. The chapters common to the two Purāṇas are the following :

Matsya-p.		Padma-p. (Sṛṣṭi-kh.)
Chaps. 5-6	=	Chap. 6.
„ 7-9	=	„ 7.
„ 10-12	=	„ 8.
Chap. 13 (verses 1-10a) Chaps. 14-17	=	„ 9.
„ 18-21	=	„ 10.
Chap. 22	=	„ 11 (especially except verses 69-81).
„ 23, „ 24 (verses 1-54)	=	„ 12 (verses 1-108a).
„ 43	=	„ 12 (verses 110 to the end).
„ 44 (especially except verses 1-14a), Chaps. 45-46, Chap. 47 (verses 1-181)	=	„ 13 (verses 1-284a).
Chaps. 100-102	=	„ 20 (verses 4-176).
„ 81-92, „ 74-80	=	„ 21.
„ 61-64 Chap. 66	=	„ 22 (especially except verses 165-175)
Chaps. 60-70	=	„ 23.
„ 71-72	=	„ 24 (verses 1-63).
Chap. 55	=	„ 24 (verses 64-96).
Chaps. 57-58	=	„ 24 (verses 101-190).
„ 59-60	=	„ 24 (verses 191-end)
„ 164-168	=	„ 36.
„ 169-173	=	„ 37.
„ 174-178	=	„ 38.
Chap. 146 (verses 41-end) Chaps. 147-148	=	„ 39 (verses 5-102).
Chap. 153 (verses 222-228a)	=	„ 39 (verses 103-end)
„ 154 (especially except verses 447-485)	=	„ 40.
Chaps. 155-160	=	„ 41.
Chap. 161, „ 162 (verses 1-34) „ 163 (verses 25b-end)	=	„ 42

Matsya-p.		Padma-p. (Sṛṣṭi-kh.)
Chap. 179 (verses 1-13a)	=	Chap. 43 (verses 6b-9a and 77-85a)[63].

The close agreement of multifarious subjects and stories dealt with in these chapters proves that they could not be based independently on tradition, but one of them must have drawn upon the other. A comparison between the two Purāṇas, however, shows that the Padma (Sṛṣṭi-kh.) is the borrower. In those chapters which are common to the Vāyu, Matsya and Padma (Sṛṣṭi-kh.)[64], the Padma follows more the Matsya than the Vāyu. It has been said above that the Matsya drew upon the Vāyu. So it seems that the Matsya first borrowed these common chapters from the Vāyu, and the Padma (Sṛṣṭi-kh.) next took them from the Matsya. A comparison of the chapters common to the Harivaṃśa, Matsya and Padma (Sṛṣṭi-kh.)[65] also shows that the Padma (Sṛṣṭi-kh.) resembles more the Matsya than the Harivaṃsa. The reading '*purāṇaṃ pauṣkare caiva mayā dvaipāyanācchrutam*' of Hv III, 14, 66a need not mislead one to hold that the Harivaṃśa was based on the Padma (Sṛṣṭi-kh. which is also known as Pauṣkara), for both the Matsya and the Vaṅga. ed. of the Padma (Sṛṣṭi-kh.) read '*purāṇaṃ puruṣaś caiva mayā* (Padma reads '*māyāṃ*') *viṣṇur hariḥ prabhuḥ*' in the corresponding passages[66]. There are also other evidences to show that the Padma (Sṛṣṭi-kh.) is the borrower. Both in Vā 98 (verses 9, 12, 15, 19 and 31) and Mat 47 (verses 176, 179, 182, 186 and 197) Śukra, the preceptor of the demons, is said to have lived invisibly with Jayantī for ten years, whereas in Pd (Sṛṣṭi-kh.) 13 (verses 278, 281 and 287) the period is lengthened to one hundred years. The occurrence of the words *śata-varṣāṇi* and *varṣa-śataṃ* in three places in the Padma (Sṛṣṭi-kh.) shows that it is not due to the mistake of the scribes but is to be ascribed to the spirit of exaggeration of the people of later ages. Further, in some of the chapters of the Padma (Sṛṣṭi-kh.), which are traceable in the Matsya and Viṣṇu, the names of Viṣṇu have been changed for those of Brahmā, while in others

[63] The corresponding chapters in the two Purāṇas have often different readings or numbers of verses. Even besides the additional verses mentioned above, there are others which are too numerous to be given in the above list. Of the chapters containing such extra verses, Mat 147-148 and 154 and Pd (Sṛṣṭi-kh.) 40 deserve special mention.

[64] Vā 73, 96 (verses 192 ff.) and 97-98; Mat 14-15 and 47; and Pd (Sṛṣṭi-kh.) 9 (verses 11-72) and 13 (verses 139-284a).

[65] Hv III, 41-47 and 7-14; Mat 161-171; Pd (Sṛṣṭi-kh.) chapters 42, 36 and 37.

[66] The AnSS ed. of the Pd (Sṛṣṭi-kh.) reads '*suparṇaṃ pakṣiṇaś caiva māyāṃ* etc'.

the names or glorifications of Viṣṇu have been left unchanged. Even in those chapters wherein such changes have been made, there are marks left to testify to their originally Vaiṣṇava character[67]. Such Vaiṣṇava character of these chapters shows that they did not belong to the Padma (Sṛṣṭi-kh.), which, it will be shown afterwards, was originally meant for the revival of Brahmā-worship. That the Padma-p. (Sṛṣṭi-kh.) borrowed the common chapters from the Matsya does not seem to have been unknown to the early Smṛti-writers. For instance, Aniruddhabhaṭṭa, who lived about 1150 A.D., quotes Pd (Sṛṣṭi-kh.) 10, 13b and refers to Pd (Sṛṣṭi-kh.) 10, 15-20a saying :

> *"yat tu padmapurāṇe—saṃpūjya dvija-dāṃpatyaṃ nānābharaṇa-bhūṣitam|| ityevamantaṃ matsya-purāṇa-tulyam abhidhāyādhikaṃ śayyā-dāna-vidhānam uktaṃ tat pārvatīyānām eva kāmarūpādi-vāsināṃ brāhmaṇādīnām avaśyānuṣṭheyam iti tatraivoktam"*[68].

The evidences adduced above are perhaps sufficient to prove that the Padma (Sṛṣṭi-kh.) is the borrower. It is probably due to this plagiarism that the Padma-p. has been rarely drawn upon by the early Nibandha-writers.

Let us now proceed to discuss the dates of the Smṛti-chapters. We shall first take up the chapters (16-22) on funeral sacrifices (Śrāddha). These chapters were written by a Vaiṣṇava[69] and introduced into the Matsya-p. in connection with the Pitṛvaṃśa (i.e., the genealogy of the patriarchs) given in chaps. 13-15. The spurious character of all these chapters from 13 to 22 seems to be proved by their very position. At the outset of chap. 11 Sūta is requested to narrate the Solar and Lunar dynasties. Chap. 12, accordingly dealing with the Solar race, ends thus : "*iti.......surya-vaṃśanukīrtanaṃ nāma dvādaśo 'dhyāyaḥ*". But the Lunar race is taken up as late as in chap. 23. Hence the intervening chaps. 13-22 seem to have been interpolated later. The spuriousness of the chapters is further proved by the fact that they are wholly unconnected and are introduced all on a sudden without any hint being given beforehand. So, they are to be dated later than the first quarter of the fourth century A.D. Again, chaps. 16-22 (on funeral sacrifices) and chaps. 13-15 (on the genealogy of the patriarchs) do not appear to have belonged to the same date. At the beginning of chap. 13 Manu

[67] Cf. Pd (Sṛṣṭi-kh.) 7, 115—'*brahmādyā viṣṇu-sāyujyaṃ tato yāsyanti vai nṛpa;*' 9, 113; etc.

[68] Hāralatā, p. 199. Cf. also Smṛti-tattva, II, p. 531.

[69] Cf. Mat 16, 45b; 17, 1a; 17, 30b; and so on.

requests the Fish to tell him about the Pitṛ-vaṃśa and the Śrāddha-devatva of the Sun and the Moon. The Fish accordingly narrates the Pitṛ-vaṃśa in chaps. 13-15, refers to the Sun and the Moon in the course of chap. 15, and finishes saying:

> "*haviṣmatām ādhipatye śrāddha-devaḥ smṛto raviḥ|*
> *etad vaḥ sarvam ākhyātaṃ pitṛ-vaṃśānukīrtanam|*
> *puṇyaṃ pavitram āyuṣyaṃ kīrtanīyaṃ sadā nṛbhiḥ||*
>
> (Mat 15, 43).

As in chaps. 13-15 there is no reference to the chapters on funeral sacrifices, as the genealogy of the patriarchs is complete in chaps. 13-15, and as there is no second reference to the Śrāddha-devatva of the Sun and the Moon anywhere in chaps. 16-22, we may hold that chaps. 13-15 formed a distinct unit by themselves and were originally not followed by any chapter or chapters on funeral sacrifices. It is, therefore, probable that chaps. 16-22 on funeral sacrifices were interpolated at a date later than that of chaps. 13-15. If a period of at least 50 years be allowed between the latter and chaps. 16-22, then these chapters on funeral sacrifices cannot possibly be earlier than the beginning of the fifth century A.D. Now, Devaṇa-bhaṭṭa quotes numerous verses from chaps. 15-19 and 22 in his Smṛti-candrikā, Hemādri from chaps. 16-22 in his Caturvarga-cintāmaṇi, Jīmūtavāhana from chaps. 17 and 22 in his Kālaviveka, Aniruddhabhaṭṭa from chap. 18 in his Hāralatā, Ballālasena from chap. 22 in his Dānasāgara, Aparārka from chaps. 15-18 and 22 in his com. on Yāj., Haradatta from chap. 18 in his com. on the Gautama-dharmasūtra, Kullūkabhaṭṭa from chaps. 17 and 18 in his com. on the Manu-smṛti, Mādhavācārya from chaps. 16-18 in his Bhāṣya on the Parāśara-smṛti, Madanapāla from chaps. 16 and 17 in his Madana-pārijāta, Śrīdatta Upādhyāya from chap. 16 in his Kṛtyācāra, Caṇḍeśvara from chap. 17 in his Kṛtya-ratnākara, Narasiṃha Vājapeyin from chap. 18 in his Nityācārapradīpa, and Govindānanda from chaps. 15-18 and 22 in his Dānakriyā-kaumudī, Śuddhikriyā-kaumudī and Śrāddhakriyā-kaumudī (see App.). These quotations made by the Nibandha-writers from different parts of India show that chaps. 16-22 must be dated not later than 1000 A.D. Again, chaps. 16-22 are among those which are found common to the Matsya and the Padma (Sṛṣṭi-kh.). The quotations made by the early Nibandha-writers like Aniruddhabhaṭṭa, Aparārka, Ballālasena, Devaṇabhaṭṭa, Hemādri and Śrīdatta Upādhyāya from the chapters of the Padma (Sṛṣṭi-kh.), common also to the Matsya, show that the Padma (Sṛṣṭi-kh.) borrowed these chapters so early that this Purāṇa, with its new additions, had sufficient time not only for circulation in all parts of India but also for replacing the earlier form of the Purāṇa. If at least a century and a half be allowed for such effective circulation, then the lower limit of the date of borrowing is to be placed not later than about 950 A.D. Consequently, the common chapters of the Matsya are to be dated earlier still, and most probably not later than 850 A.D. As chaps. 16-22 betray Vaiṣṇava authorship, it is probable that they come from the same date as the chapters on vows and gifts[70].

We shall now take up the chapters on vows, gifts, bath etc. The position of chaps. 51-270 between chaps. 43-50 on the one hand and chaps. 271-273 on the other appears to prove their spurious character, for the latter two groups of chapters are intimately connected with each other. The Lunar dynasty is taken up in chap. 23 and is described in chaps. 23-24 and 43-50. In Mat 50, 68-71 the sages request Sūta to tell them about the future kings and ages. In compliance with this request Sūta undertakes, in Mat 50, 72-76, to speak on the future Kali age and the Manvantaras and also to give accounts not only of the future kings in the families of Ila, Ikṣvāku and Puru but also of the Āndhras, Śakas, Yavanas, Pulindas, Kaivartas, Ābhīras and others who attained regal power. He then gives the list of the future kings only of the line of Puru in Mat 50, 77 to the end, the chapter ending thus:

> *ityeṣa pauravo vaṃśo yathāvad iha kīrtitaḥ|*
> *dhīmataḥ pāṇḍu-putrasya arjunasya mahātmanaḥ||*

At the beginning of chap. 271 the sages say to Sūta,

> *'puror vaṃśas tvayā sūta sabhaviṣyo niveditaḥ|*
> *sūrya-vaṃśe nṛpā ye tu bhaviṣyanti hi tān vada||'*

Consequently, the latter continues to give lists and accounts of the other future kings and the future ages in accordance with the promise he makes in Mat 50, 72-76. From all this it is quite evident that chaps. 271-273 have been separated from chap. 50. Of course, this separation might be due to the misplacement of chaps. 271-273

[70] If the word *brahmaṇya*, used along with the words *śiva-bhakta*, *sūrya-bhakta* and *vaiṣṇava* in Mat 16, 9-10, is taken to mean 'a worshipper of Brahmā', then it must be admitted that Brahmā-worship was still prevalent, otherwise his worshippers would not have been classed with the Paṅkti-pāvanas. Hence Mat 16-22 could not be later than 650 A.D. Though the Padma (Sṛṣṭi-kh.) reads '*brāhmaṇa*' in the corresponding line (cf. Pd, Sṛṣṭi-kh., 9, 82b), the reading '*brahmaṇya*' of the Matsya is the correct one, for this latter reading is supported by Devaṇabhaṭṭa (Smṛti-candrikā, IV, p. 156), Aparārka (com., p. 443), Hemādri (Caturvarga-cintāmaṇi, III, i, p. 386) and Govindānanda (Śrāddhakriyā-kaumudī, p. 35). The change from '*brahmaṇya*' to '*brāhmaṇa*' made by the Padma (Sṛṣṭi-kh.) is most probably due to the fact that in the just preceding line it changes '*śiva-bhakta*' to '*brahma-bhakta*'.

or chaps. 51-270, which is not quite unlikely. We should, therefore, turn our attention to other things.

The internal evidences show that at least a good number of the chapters on gifts, vows, bath etc. was inserted into the Matsya-p. at the same time. In Mat 53, 1 the sages ask Sūta not only to enumerate the Purāṇas but also to 'deal exhaustively with the piety of making gifts' (*dāna-dharmān aśeṣaṃ tu*). Consequently, in chap. 53, (verses 3 ff.) Sūta speaks of the Purāṇas and Upapurāṇas and the gifts of the former on particular occasions. Next, proceeding to speak on the gifts connected with vows and fasts in chapters 54 ff., he begins saying :

> '*ataḥ paraṃ pravakṣyāmi dāna-dharmān aśeṣataḥ|*
> *vratopavāsa-saṃyuktān yathā matsyoditān iha|*
> *mahādevasya saṃvāde nāradasya ca dhīmataḥ||*'

The expression '*pravakṣyāmi dāna-dharmān aśeṣataḥ*' is certainly used by Sūta in compliance with the request made by the sages in Mat 53, 1. It, therefore, shows that chap. 53 and those chapters (viz., 54-57, 61, 68 and 83-92) on vows and gifts (because the making of ceremonial gifts also is to be accompanied with fasting) in which Mahādeva and Nārada are the interlocutors are contemporaneous[71]. The genuineness of these latter chapters need not be doubted, for the request made by Nārada to Śiva in Mat 54, 4 to tell him how the Śiva- and Viṣṇu-worshippers could attain health, wealth, beauty etc., shows that the chapters in which Mahādeva and Nārada are to be

[71] Verses 59-63 of chap. 53, which give the titles and contents of the Upapurāṇas, must be taken as spurious for the following reasons :—

(i) Nothing is said about the gift of any of the Upapurāṇas though the chapter is on *dāna-dharma* ;

(ii) there is no mention of the Upapurāṇas in verses other than those mentioned above ;

(iii) though in verses following verse 63 the classification and contents of the Purāṇas and the titles and extents of the epics are given, there is not even a single word on the Upapurāṇas.

These verses are, however, not very late additions ; for Narasiṃha Vājapeyin, who quotes all these verses except 59a in his Nityācārapradīpa, refers to Lakṣmīdhara's explanation of verse 63 (*aṣṭādaśabhyas tu pṛthak purāṇaṃ*) as meaning the Kālikā-purāṇa etc. (see Nityācārapradīpa, p. 18), and Hemādri quotes verses 59b-61 and 62c-63 in his Caturvarga-cintāmaṇi, vol. II, part i, pp. 21-22.

The omission of these verses by Aparārka who quotes verses 3-4, 11-20, 22-25a and 26b-56a in his com. on Yāj, by Ballālasena who quotes verses 3-4 and 11-56 in his Dānasāgara, by Caṇḍeśvara who has a few verses in his Kṛtya-ratnākara, and by Govindānanda who has a few lines in his Dānakriyā-Kaumudī, should not be taken in favour of a very late date. These authors, who drew upon Mat 53 in connection with gifts, had nothing to do with verses 59-63 in which there is no mention of gift.

the interlocutors should be Śaiva and Vaiṣṇava; and in fact they are so with the only exception of chap. 61 (dealing with Agastya-pūjā). Chapters 83-92 were all inserted at the same time in a group, for they are all enumerated by Śiva at the very beginning of these chapters (viz., in Mat 83, 4-6). All these contemporaneous chapters (viz., 54-57, 61, 68 and 83-92) are interspersed by many others (viz., chaps. 58-60, 62-65, 66-67, 69-80 and 81-82) on vows, consecration, bath and gifts, in which the interlocutors differ[72]. The unconnected position of these chapters, and the breaches they create in the dialogue between Mahādeva and Nārada, prove their comparatively late dates. In these comparatively late chapters, again, there are some which seem to date still later. These are chapters 65, 73 and 76. The list of contents of the Matsya given in chap. 291 does not mention the Akṣaya-tṛtīyā-vrata (chap. 65), Guru-śukra-pūjā-vidhi (chap. 73) and Viṣṇu-vrata (chap. 99). Therefore, these seem to be later additions. This doubt is further strengthened by their absence from the Padma-p. (Sṛṣṭi-kh.). The late age of chap. 76 (dealing with the Phalasaptamī-vrata) is evidenced by the non-mention of this Vrata in Mat 74, 2-3 wherein Śiva names the Saura Vratas he afterwards speaks of in chaps. 74-75 and 77-80.

Thus we get three groups of chapters which are arranged in order of priority:

(1) chaps. 53 (especially verses 1-58 and 64 to the end), 54-57, 61, 68 and 83-92,

(2) chaps. 58-60, 62-64, 66-67, 69-72, 74-75, 77-80 and 81-82,

and (3) chaps. 65, 73 and 76.

Now, Narasiṃha Vājapeyin of Orissa quotes one verse from chap. 53 in his Nityācārapradīpa; Govindānanda quotes a number of verses from chaps. 53 and 58 in his Dānakriyā-kaumudī; Caṇḍeśvara quotes the entire chapters 56 and 63 and also some verses from chaps. 53, 61 and 70 in his Kṛtya-ratnākara; Madanapāla quotes verses from chap. 53 in his Madana-pārijāta; Hemādri draws profusely upon chaps. 53-54, 58-60, 62, 67, 71-72 and 82 in his Caturvarga-cintāmaṇi;

[72]

Chaps.	54-57	are	told by	Mahādeva to Nārada.
„	58-60	„	„ „	Matsya to Manu.
Chap.	61	is	„ „	Mahādeva to Nārada.
Chaps.	62-65	are	„ „	Mahādeva to Umā.
„	66-67	„	„ „	Matsya to Manu.
Chap.	68	is	„ „	Mahādeva to Nārada.
Chaps.	69-80	are	„ „	Śiva to Brahmā.
„	81-82	„	„ „	Matsya to Manu.
„	83-92	„	„ „	Mahādeva to Nārada.
Chap.	93	is	„ „	Vaiśampāyana to Śaunaka.
„	94	„	„ „	Śiva to (?).
Chaps.	95-112	are	„ „	Nandikeśvara to Nārada

Ballālasena quotes the entire chapters 82-92 and also verses from chap. 53 in his Dānasāgara; he also quotes five verses from chap. 67 in his Adbhutasāgara; Aparārka quotes almost the entire chapters 53, 58-59 and 82-92 in his com. on Yāj.; and Jīmūtavāhana quotes a verse from chap. 53 in his Kālaviveka (see App.). These quotations made by the Nibandha-writers hailing from different parts of India show that the chapters of at least the first two groups were inserted into the Matsya-p. much earlier than the age in which they flourished. Otherwise, such widespread circulation would have been impossible. So these chapters must be dated not later than 950 A.D. Again, many of the chapters of the first and second groups and chap. 76 of the third group have been borrowed by the Padma-p. (Sṛṣṭi-kh.) from the Matsya. It has already been said that this borrowing took place not later than about 950 A.D. Hence the date of the above mentioned Smṛti-chapters of the Matsya, including chap. 76, are to be placed earlier still and most probably not later than at least 900 A.D. We have said above that chap. 76 (on Phalasaptamī-vrata) was added later than chaps. 74-75 and 77-80 which belong to the second group. Hence at least these chapters of the second group, and consequently also those of the first, are to be dated earlier still.

The gifts of hillocks (Acala-dāna, chaps. 83-92) require the image of Brahmā, Viṣṇu and Śiva, which are to be placed on the artificial hillocks to be given away (cf. Mat 83, 15 and 91, 5), and in Mat 58, 24 Brahmā is found to be worshipped equally with the other two gods of the triad. These evidences show that the worship of Brahmā did not die out at the time of insertion of these chapters. Varāhamihira's mention of the most prominent sects of his time[73] shows that Brahmā-worship was still popular. If, as scholars hold, this god was thrown into the background about the beginning of the 7th century A.D., then the date of chap. 58 and of the chapters on Acala-dāna cannot be placed later than 650 A.D. Thus we get the lower limit.

The mention of the names of the weekdays in connection with vows etc.,[74] shows that these were well-known when these chapters were added. The earliest dated mention of a weekday being traced

[73] *viṣṇor bhāgavatān magāṃś ca savituḥ śambhoḥ sabhasma-dvijān*
mātṝṇām api mātṛ-maṇḍala-vido viprān vidur brahmaṇaḥ|
śākyān sarva-hitasya śānta-manaso nagnān jinānāṃ vidur
ye yaṃ devam upāśritāḥ sva-vidhinā tais tasya kāryā kriyā||

Bṛhat-saṃhitā 60, 19.

The mention of only the Bhāgavatas, and not the Pāñcarātras, among the worshippers of Viṣṇu shows that Varāhamihira mentions only the most powerful sects of his time. We know that the Bhāgavatas grew in power under the Gupta emperors who called themselves 'parama-bhāgavata'.

[74] Cf. Mat 55, 4; 57, 4; 66, 5; 70, 83; etc.

in the Eran inscription of 484 A.D.,[75] these chapters should not be placed very much earlier than this date. Mat 53, 46-7 describe the Kūrma-p. in its Vaiṣṇava form. As it will be seen that the Viṣṇuite Kūrma-p. was written between 550 and 650 A.D., this chapter cannot be earlier than 550 A.D. The mention of the ten incarnations of Viṣṇu during the worship of the Nakṣatra-puruṣa in Mat 54 (dealing with the Nakṣatrapuruṣa-vrata) and their total absence in Bṛhat-saṃhitā, chap. 105 (dealing with the same Vrata) prove the later date of the former. The Bṛhat-saṃhitā was written about 550 A.D. Therefore the date of Mat 54 is later than 550 A.D. The inclusion of the Buddha, in Mat 54, among the ten incarnations of Viṣṇu also shows that this chapter could not have been written earlier than 550 A.D. The Mahābhārata does not mention the Buddha incarnation, though it mentions Kalki in one of the spurious verses in XII, 339. Mārk 4 names a few incarnations beginning with the Varāha and ending with Māthura (i.e., Kṛṣṇa), there being no mention of the Buddha. The Viṣṇu-p. mentions Kalki but not the Buddha. The Harivaṃśa also does not mention the Buddha, though it mentions Kalki. The Kūrma-p. is silent about the Buddha and Kalki. The lists of incarnations, or rather manifestations, in the Brahma-p. are the same as those in the Mārkaṇḍeya-p. and the Harivaṃśa. The Jayākhya-saṃhitā (about 450 A.D.) of the Pāñcarātras does not mention the Buddha, though it mentions some of the other incarnations. The Ahirbudhnya-saṃhitā, which is certainly later than the Jayākhya, mentions 39 Vibhavas in which Kalki is one, but the name of the Buddha is wanting. Thus the Buddha incarnation seems to have been unknown in the beginning of the sixth century A.D. Mat 47, 247, which mentions the Buddha, is undoubtedly a later interpolation, for this verse is not found in the corresponding chapters of the Vāyu and Brahmāṇḍa. Now, the mention of the Buddha incarnation in the Gītagovinda of Jayadeva (about the end of the 12th century), the Daśāvatāra-carita of Kṣemendra (11th century A.D.), a hymn by Nammalvar (alias saint Śaṭagopa, 9th century)[76], the Viṣṇupura cards (end of the 7th and beginning of the 8th century), and a Pallava inscription of about the latter half of the 7th century A.D.,[77] shows that this incarnation attained popularity by the beginning of the 7th century A.D. It is highly probable, therefore, that the Buddha began to be regarded as an incarnation of Viṣṇu from about 550 A.D. That during this time the founders of the heretical religions came to be identified

[75] Fleet, Gupta Inscriptions, pp. 88-89.

[76] ABORI, Vol. XIV, 1932-33, pp. 200-201.

[77] H. Krishna Shastri, The Memoirs of the Archæological Survey of India, Vol. 26, p. 5.

with Viṣṇu is shown by the Bṛhat-saṃhitā (58, 45), according to which the image of the god of the Arhats (*arhatāṃ devaḥ*) is to be marked with the Śrī-vatsa.

From the above discussion it appears that the chapters of the first two groups were written not earlier than 550 and not later than 650 A.D.

Of the chapters of the third group, chap. 76 is, as we have seen, later than the chapters (74-75 and 77-80) of the second group. As it is found in the Padma (Sṛṣṭi-kh.), it is earlier than 950 A.D. The other two chapters (65 and 73) are neither mentioned in the list of contents of the Matsya given in chap. 291 nor found in the Padma (Sṛṣṭi-kh.). They are also not drawn upon by any Nibandha-writer. Therefore they may be taken to be very late additions.

Mat 7, 6-30 deal with the Madanadvādaśī-vrata observed by Diti for a son capable of killing the enemies of the Daityas. As in no other Purāṇa (except the Padma) Diti is found to observe this vow, this portion of Mat 7 seems to have been interpolated later. This interpolation was, however, made earlier than Hemādri (see App.) and most probably than 900 A.D., for these verses occur in the Padma-p. (Sṛṣṭi-kh.).

Mat 95-101 deal with vows (Vratas)—Śaiva, Saura and Vaiṣṇava. All of these chapters do not seem to belong to the same date. In Mat 95 Śiva, the speaker in the earlier chapters on vows and gifts, refers Nārada to Nandikeśvara, who is to speak on 'Māheśvara Dharma'. Consequently, Nārada asks Nandikeśvara to tell him about 'Māheśvara Vrata', and the latter describes the Śiva-caturdaśī-vrata (chap. 95) and the Sarvaphalatyāga-vrata (chap. 96), both of which are Śaiva. But in chaps. 97-112, which also are ascribed to Nandikeśvara, the Saura and Vaiṣṇava Vratas and Prayāga-māhātmya are treated of. Hence these chapters (97-112) must have been added by the non-Śaivas later than chaps. 95-96. The strictly Śaiva character of chaps. 95-96, as contrasted with those chapters on vows and gifts in which Śiva and Nārada are the interlocutors, and the fact that Nandikeśvara, the narrator in chaps. 95-96, is introduced to Nārada by Śiva, show that chaps. 95-96 were added by a Śaiva later than those chapters in which Śiva and Nārada are the interlocutors. Therefore, these two chapters (95-96) cannot be dated earlier t ın 600 A.D. Now, Caṇḍeśvara quotes verses from chaps. 95 ano 101 in his Kṛtya-ratnākara, Madanapāla from chap. 101 in his Maaana-pārijāta, Hemādri from chaps. 95-97, 99 and 101 in his Caturvarga-cintāmaṇi, and Devaṇabhaṭṭa from chap. 101 in his Smṛti-candrikā (see App.). These quotations show that chaps. 95-97, 99 and 101 are to be dated earlier than 1100 A.D. Chaps. 100 and 101 have been borrowed by the Padma-p. (Sṛṣti-kh.). Therefore, these two chapters should not be placed later than about 900 A.D. The Bhaviṣya-p. also has borrowed chaps. 95-100. Hence the dates of Mat 95-101 fall between 600 and 900 A.D. Chaps. 95-96 being earlier than chaps. 97-101, the former should be dated in the former part and the latter in the latter part of this period.

Mat 205-206, on gifts, and chap. 207, on the dedication of bulls, seem to have been misplaced. Chap. 115 opens thus:

manur uvāca
caritaṃ budha-putrasya janārdana mayā śrutam|
śrutaḥ śrāddha-vidhiḥ puṇyaḥ sarva-pāpa-praṇāśanaḥ||
dhenvāḥ prasūyamānāyāḥ phalaṃ dānasya me śrutam|
kṛṣṇājina-pradānaṃ ca vṛṣotsargas tathaiva ca||
śrutvā rūpaṃ narendrasya budha-putrasya keśava|
kautūhalaṃ samutpannaṃ tan mamācakṣva pṛcchataḥ||
&c. &c.

This opening shows that this chapter was immediately preceded by the story of Purūravas (son of Budha) in which he was praised for his physical beauty, and also by chapters on Śrāddha, Prasūyamānadhenu-dāna, Kṛṣṇājina-dāna and Vṛṣotsarga. Now, the story of Purūravas is found in chap. 24 (verses 11-32), Śrāddha in chaps. 16-22, Prasūyamānadhenu-dāna in chap. 205, Kṛṣṇājina-dāna in chap. 206, and Vṛṣa-lakṣaṇa in chap. 207. That Mat 24 (11-32), dealing with the story of Purūravas, is meant by the expression '*caritaṃ budha-putrasya*.... etc.' is shown by the fact that it is in this portion (viz., Mat 24, 12) that Purūravas is called very beautiful so much so that Urvaśī, the divine nymph, falls in love with him. There are also other evidences to show that chaps. 205-207 immediately followed the chapters (16-22) on Śrāddha. Mat 204, in which the Pitṛ-gāthās only are laid down but which ends with the verse '*etāvad uktaṃ tava bhūmipāla śrāddhasya kalpaṃ muni-saṃpradiṣṭam|* etc.', points to chaps. 16-22 termed 'Śrāddha-kalpa' and is, therefore, a continuation of these chapters. The mention of Prasūyamānadhenu-dāna, Kṛṣṇājina-dāna and Vṛṣotsarga in this chapter (i.e., chap. 204) shows that it preceded chaps. 205-207 dealing with these topics. Hence the real order of these misplaced chapters seems to have been as follows:

Chaps. 16-22, chaps. 204-207, chap. 24 and chaps. 115-120. This order is supported by the Viṣṇudharmottara which borrows, among others, chaps. 207 (24b to the end) and 115-120 from the Matsya and in which the story of Purūravas is immediately preceded by Vṛṣotsarga[78]. We have seen above that chaps. 205-207 stand in close

[78] See Viṣṇudharmottara I, 146, 41b to the end and I, 148-154 (verses 1-7) which are the same as Mat 207 (verses 24b to the end) and 115-120 respectively.

connection with the chapters (16-22) on Śrāddha. This connection shows that the former could by no means be earlier than the latter, and it is highly probable that these two groups of chapters belong to the same date. That chaps. 205-207 were inserted into the Matsya earlier than 1100 A.D. is doubtless, because Govindānanda quotes verses from chaps. 205-207 in his Dānakriyā-kaumudī and Śuddhi-kriyā-kaumudī, Hemādri quotes almost the entire chaps. 205-207 in his Caturvarga-cintāmaṇi, Ballālasena quotes the entire chapters 205 (except verse 1) and 206 (except the last verse) and three verses from chap. 207 in his Dānasāgara, and Aparārka quotes chaps. 205 (except verse 1) and 206 (except the first and the last verse) in his com. on Yāj. (see App.).

Mat 274-289 deal with the sixteen Mahādānas (big donations), which, requiring the worship of Viṣṇu, are certainly Vaiṣṇava in character. The mention of these sixteen Mahādānas in chap. 274 (4-10) shows that all the chapters 274-289 belong to the same date. These chapters are frequently drawn upon by the commentators and Nibandha-writers, early and late. Govindānanda quotes verses from Mat 274 in his Śuddhikriyā-kaumudī; Hemādri quotes almost the entire chaps. 274-289 in his Caturvarga-cintāmaṇi; Ballālasena gives the entire chaps. 274-289 in his Dānasāgara; and Aparārka quotes chapters 274 (except verses 3a, 13b and 28b), 275 (except the last verse), 277 (except the last verse), 278 (except the last verse), 279, 280 (except the last verse) and 281-289 in his com. (see App.). These quotations show that these chapters must be dated not later than 1050 A.D. The Liṅga-purāṇa deals with the Mahādānas in II, 28 ff. Ballālasena says that the Mahādānas, dealt with in the Liṅga, were based on those in the Matsya[79]. As in the Liṅga the chapters on the Mahādānas were inserted before the time of Ballālasena, the chapters (274-289) of the Matsya should be dated earlier still, and reasonably not later than 1000 A.D. The references to the worship of the images of Brahmā during the different Mahādānas[80] prove

The Viṣṇudharmottara is suspected to be the borrower for the following reasons:

(1) In the Viṣṇudh. the story of Purūravas is further continued to chap. 156.

(2) Though the opening verses of Viṣṇudh. I, 148 are the same as those of Mat 115, in the former there is no chapter on Prasūyamānadhenu-dāna or Kṛṣṇājina-dāna preceding chap. 148.

(3) In the Viṣṇudh. the chapters on Vṛṣotsarga and the story of Purūravas are introduced almost abruptly.

[79] Dānasāgara, fol. 3b—*bṛhad api liṅga-purāṇaṃ matsya-purāṇoditair mahādānaiḥ.*

[80] Brahmā, Śiva and Viṣṇu are to be worshipped on the altar constructed during the Tulāpuruṣa-mahādāna etc. (Mat 274, 30); in the Kalpapādapa-mahādāna, the Kalpapādapa is to be placed on a heap of coarse sugar *(guḍa)* with Brahmā, Viṣṇu,

that the worship of the god was still popular. So these chapters (274-289) cannot possibly be dated later than 650 A.D. The ten incarnations of Viṣṇu including the Buddha and Kalki being mentioned in Mat 285, 7, these chapters should not be dated earlier than 550 A.D. Therefore, their date falls between 550 and 650 A.D.

Let us now take up the chapters on Tīrtha. Mat 13, verses 10 to the end describe, quite incoherently, the story of the self-immolation of Satī, daughter of Dakṣa, in which she is appeased and requested to name the numerous holy places sacred to herself. The position of these verses in chap. 13 (dealing with the Pitṛs) and their obvious Śākta character testify to their late date which is further proved by their mention of Rādhā (in Mat 13, 38—*rādhā vṛndāvane vane*) as well as by their position in the Padma-p. (Sṛṣṭi-kh.). Though chap. 9 of this Purāṇa is the same as Mat 13 (verses 1-9) and 14-17, these verses, which are included in Mat 13, are found in the Padma (Sṛṣṭi-kh.) as late as in chap. 17, verses 182-216a. Hence we may be sure that these verses were taken by the Śāktas from a common source and interpolated independently in those parts of these two Purāṇas which the interpolators thought suited for them.

Chaps. 103-112 (on Prayāga-māhātmya) of the Matsya are later than Kūr I, 35-38 which, again, cannot be dated earlier than 750 or rather 800 A.D. (see under Kūrma-p.). Hence the chapters of the Matsya should be dated not earlier than 850 A.D. As most of these chapters are profusely drawn upon by Vācaspatimiśra and Caṇḍeśvara, they are certainly not later than 1250 A.D.

The chapters on Prayāga-māhātmya, told by Mārkaṇḍeya to Yudhiṣṭhira, are not free from interpolation, for there are evidences which go against the authenticity of at least verses 1-17 of chap. 112. Though up to Mat 112, 17 the sage Mārkaṇḍeya is nowhere said to have parted with Yudhiṣṭhira, in Mat 112, 4 the former is said to have come to the latter, blessed him and then repaired to his hermitage. This is quite contradictory. Again, in Mat 112, 18 Nandikeśvara says:

> *'ityuktvā sa mahābhāgo mārkaṇḍeyo mahātapāḥ* |
> *yudhiṣṭhirasya nṛpates tatraivāntaradhīyata* ||'

The word *ityuktvā* would have been meaningless if the preceding verses were not spurious, for these verses are spoken by Vāsudeva. Hence it seems that Mat 112, 1-17 are interpolated.

Mat 180-185 (on Avimukta-kṣetra or Benares) come from a fairly early date. A comparison between these chapters and Kūr I,

Śiva and Sūrya (Mat 277, 6); the images of Brāhmī and Ananta-śakti are to be placed on a heap of salt in the Hema-kalpalatā-dāna (Mat 286, 6); and the golden image of Brahmā is to be placed on salt during the Saptasāgara-dāna (Mat 287, 7).

30-34 (on Benares) shows that the former are earlier than the latter. Though in both the Purāṇas (Mat 181, 6-7 and Kūr I, 30, 16) the glories of Benares are said to have been told by Śiva to Umā on the mount Meru, the chapters of the latter consist of the glorification of some Śiva-liṅgas, viz., Oṃkāra, Kṛttivāseśvara, Madhyameśvara etc., at Benares. They also contain some fanciful stories about the origin or power of these Liṅgas. Besides these, there is a story glorifying the Piśācamocana-kuṇḍa lying near the Kapardīśvara Liṅga. These names and stories, which are undoubtedly of later origin, are not found in the Matsya. Now, Kūr I, 30-34 are to be dated not later than the middle of the 13th century A.D. (see under Kūrma-p.). Therefore, chaps. 180-185 of the Matsya should not be placed later than 1200 A.D. As Govindānanda quotes verses from chap. 184 in his Śrāddhakriyā-kaumudī, Vācaspatimiśra from chaps. 180-184 in his Tīrtha-cintāmaṇi, Madanapāla from chap. 184 in his Madana-pārijāta, Mādhavācārya from the same chapter in his Bhāṣya on the Parāśara-smṛti, and Aparārka from chap. 184 in his com. on Yāj., it is certain that chaps. 180-185 were inserted into the Matsya not later than at least 1075 A.D. The strictly Śaiva character of these chapters tends to show that they were added later than 700 A. D.

Mat 186-194, on Narmadā-māhātmya, must have been composed by a Śaiva living somewhere about the northern bank of the river Narmadā[81]. These chapters must have been interpolated at a very late date. They seem to be later than Kūr II, 38-39 which, again, are later than 800 A. D. (see under Kūrma-p.). Their late date seems further to be proved by the fact that no Nibandha-writer has been found to draw upon them.

Mat 39 and 40, treating respectively of Naraka and Āśrama-dharma, are included in the story of Yayāti extending over chaps. 25-43. This story seems to have been interpolated later, because the Padma-p. (Sṛṣṭi-kh.), in which Mat 5-24 and 44 ff. are found borrowed in the same order, omits this story. As no Nibandha-writer has been found to quote from these chapters, we are not sure about the lower limit of their date.

Bath (Snāna) is dealt with in Mat 67-68 and 102. Of these, chaps. 67 and 68 have already been dated between 550 and 650 A. D. Chap. 102, being drawn upon by Govindānanda in his Śuddhikriyā-kaumudī, by Hemādri in his Caturvarga-cintāmaṇi and by Devaṇa-bhaṭṭa in his Smṛti-candrikā, cannot be later than 1100 A. D. As this chapter has been borrowed by the Padma-p. (Sṛṣṭi-kh.), it

[81] Cf. chap. 186, verses 8a, 10 and 11 in which the Narmadā is glorified even over the Gaṅgā, Yamunā and Sarasvati. Also cf. Mat 186, 52a; 190, 1 ff; etc.; wherein the northern bank of the Narmadā is said to be equal to the Rudra-loka. The Śaiva character of these chapters is quite obvious.

should not be placed later than 950 A.D. It has been shown that chaps. 97-112 are later than chaps. 95-96 which, again, are later than 600 A.D. Therefore, chap. 102 cannot possibly be earlier than 650 A. D. Thus the date of this chapter falls between 650 and 950 A. D.

Pratiṣṭhā (consecration) is the subject-matter of Mat 58-59 and 264-270. Of these, the former two have been dated between 550 and 650 A. D. The latter seven chapters, dealing with the consecration of the images of gods, are certainly contemporaneous with chaps. 258-263 in which the characteristics of the different images of gods have been laid down. A comparison between Bṛhat-saṃhitā, chap. 58 (dealing with Pratimā-lakṣaṇa) and Mat 258-270 shows that the former must have been earlier than the latter. The Bṛhat-saṃhitā names the following gods with their respective characteristics :

(1) Rāma, son of Daśaratha, (2) Bali, son of Virocana, (3) Baladeva, the carrier of the plough, (4) Devī (i.e., Lakṣmī), (5) Śāmba, (6) Pradyumna, (7) the two wives of Śāmba and Pradyumna, (8) Brahmā, (9) Skanda, (10) Mahendra, (11) Śambhu, (12) the Buddha (for the Buddhists), and (13) the god of the Arhats (for the Jains).

The Matsya omits (3), (6), (7), (12) and (13) but adds the following: Matsya, Kūrma, Varāha, Nṛsiṃha, Vāmana, Rudra, Ardha-nārīśvara, Umā-Maheśvara, Śiva-Nārāyaṇa, Vināyaka, Kātyāyanī, Agni, Yama, Nairta, Varuṇa, Vāyu, Kuvera, Gadādhara, the Mātṛs (viz., Brahmāṇī, Māheśvarī, Kaumārī, Vaiṣṇavī, Vārāhī, Indrāṇī, Yogeśvarī, Cāmuṇḍā and Kālikā) and Kusumāyudha. The innovations made in the chapters of the Matsya prove that they cannot be earlier than 550 A. D. As Aparārka quotes verses from chaps. 265 and 267 and Hemādri from chaps. 260 and 268, they cannot be later than 1100 A. D. The retention of Brahmā by the Matsya, inspite of its additions and alterations in the list of gods given by the Bṛhat-saṃhitā, shows that Brahmā-worship did not die out. Moreover, according to the Matsya, the priest is required to be 'brahmopendra-hara-priya' (Mat 265, 4); Brāhma Mantras are to be used in consecrating the image of Brahmā (Mat 266, 39); and the gods, who are to be summoned at the time of consecrating the image of any god, include Brahmā (Mat 266, 42). All these references prove the popularity of Brahmā-worship at the time when Mat 258-270 were written. Hence these chapters are to be dated earlier than about 650 A. D.; and thus their date falls between 550 and 650 A. D.

Mat 7, 37-49 lay down the duties of pregnant women. These verses, being closely connected with the story of the birth of the Maruts, appear to come from the date when the extant Matsya was first written, or rather compiled. That they are not later than 1100 A. D., and most probably also than 950 A. D., is shown by the quotations made from them by Devaṇabhaṭṭa in his Smṛti-candrikā and by the occurrence of these verses in the Padma-p. (Sṛṣṭi-kh.).

Mat 215-243 and 252-257, treating of Rāja-dharma, Graha-yajña, Adbhuta-śānti[82], Yātrākāla-vidhāna, Śubhāśubha-nirūpaṇa, Vāstu and Vyavahāra, should belong to the same date, because all these are meant for the king. The determination of even their approximate date is rather difficult. That they are not later than 1000 A. D. is sure, for Bhavadeva quotes verses from chap. 227 in his Prāyaścitta-prakaraṇa, Aparārka from chap. 253 in his com. on Yāj., Devaṇabhaṭṭa from chap. 227 in his Smṛti-candrikā, Hemādri from chaps. 228-238 and 252-253 in his Caturvarga-cintāmaṇi, and Ballālasena from chaps. 228-238 and 240-243 in his Adbhuta-sāgara (see App.). The reference to the unpopularity of the worship of Brahmā in Mat 225, 12-14, wherein it is said that the people worshipped the fierce (*daṇḍinaḥ*—punishing) gods,—Rudra, Agni, Sūrya, Viṣṇu and others,—instead of the mild (*praśānta*—serene) Brahmā, Pūṣan and Aryaman, shows that Mat 215-243 and 252-257 cannot possibly be dated earlier than 600 or rather 650 A.D.

Mat 93 and 94 deal with Graha-śānti and Graharūpākhyāna respectively. These chapters are certainly not later than 1000 A. D., because Śūlapāṇi quotes two lines from chap. 93 in his Vratakālaviveka, Hemādri quotes a good number of lines from chaps. 93 and 94 in his Caturvarga-cintāmaṇi, Devaṇabhaṭṭa quotes a verse from chap. 93 in his Smṛti-candrikā, Aparārka quotes the entire chap. 94 and a good number of verses from chap. 93 in his com. on Yāj., an anonymous commentary on the Trikāṇḍamaṇḍana of Trikāṇḍamaṇḍana Bhāskaramiśra has one verse from chap. 93, and Vijñāneśvara quotes the entire chap. 94 in his Mitākṣarā (see App.). The interlocutors (viz., Vaiśampāyana and Śaunaka in chap. 93, and Śiva alone in chap. 94), who appear abruptly without any introduction but who are not found in the chapters preceding or following chaps. 93 and 94, prove that these two chapters are later than at least those chapters on Vrata and Dāna in which Śiva and Nārada are the interlocutors. These latter chapters are assigned to 550-650 A. D. Therefore, chaps. 93-94 cannot be earlier than about 650 A. D. Thus their date falls between 650 and 1000 A. D.

Yuga-dharma is dealt with in chaps. 142, 144, 145 and 165. Of these, the first three are the same as Vā 57 (verses 1-85), 58 and 59

[82] Mat 229-238, on Adbhuta-śānti, were not written by Vṛddha-garga himself as the Matsya claims but are based on the Utpāta-śānti sections of a work (viz., Vṛddhagarga-saṃhitā ?) of the renowned astrologer. See my article in Indian Culture, Vol. I, 1935, pp. 587 ff.

respectively. They most probably belong to the time when the extant Matsya-p. borrowed some of its chapters from the Vāyu. Their position between Mat 50 and 271-273 (on the future dynasties and ages) must be due to misplacement. Mat 165, which has been borrowed by the Padma (Sṛṣṭi-kh.), should be dated not later than about 950 A.D.

In connection with the Smṛti-chapters a few words may be said here on the date and authenticity of some of the remaining chapters.

Mat 52, dealing with Karma-yoga, recommends the worship of Brahmā, Viṣṇu, Śiva and Sūrya who are to be considered as 'abheda' (not different from one another—Mat 52, 23 ff.). The author of this chapter seems to be a Viṣṇu-worshipper, for he defines Vāsudeva as 'atīndriya', 'śānta', 'sūkṣma', 'avyakta', 'sanātana' and 'jaganmūrti', and calls Brahmā, Śiva, Sūrya and others his 'vibhūti'. Therefore, the date of this chapter cannot possibly be later than 650 A.D.

The story of Purūravas in chaps. 115-120 is of comparatively late origin. It says how Purūravas, son of Budha, attained extraordinary physical beauty by fasting on every Dvādaśī Tithi and by worshipping Viṣṇu in the Himalayas respectively in two of his previous births. Hemādri and Ballālasena's quotations from Mat 115 in their Caturvarga-cintāmaṇi and Dānasāgara respectively show that chaps. 115-120 are at least not later than 1100 A.D.

The story of the origin and destruction of Tripura, a city built by the demon architect Maya, is dealt with in chaps. 129-140. These chapters, except the interpolated portions if any, are earlier than the beginning of twelfth century A.D., because Ballālasena quotes a line from chap. 134 in connection with 'the burning of Tripura'.

Chaps. 146-160 deal with the birth of the demon Tāraka and his death at the hand of Kārttikeya. Of these, only chaps. 146-148 (especially except verses 1-40 of chap. 146) and chaps. 153-160 (especially except verses 1-221 and 228b to the end of chap. 153, and verses 447-485 of chap. 154) have been borrowed by the Padma-p. (Sṛṣṭi-kh.). So, the intervening chaps. 149-152, on the description of a war between the gods and demons, seem to be interpolations. As Ballālasena quotes in his Adbhutasāgara a line from chap. 153 by mentioning that it is taken from the story of the war between the gods and demons[83], we can be sure that chaps. 146-148 and 153-160, especially except the verses noted above, are earlier than 1100 A.D. Again, chaps. 39-41 of the Padma-p. (Sṛṣṭi-kh.), which tally considerably with chaps. 146-148 and 153-160, are to be dated between 800 and 950 A.D., and most probably in the latter half of the eighth

[83] Cf. Adbhs., p. 478—*matsya-purāṇe devāsura-yuddha-nimittam.*

century A.D. (see under Padma-p.). So, Mat 146-148 and 153-160 (especially except the verses noted above) are to be dated earlier than 800 A.D.

Chaps. 161-163 deal with the killing of Hiraṇyakaśipu by the Man-lion, and chap. 172, which belongs to the group consisting of the closely interrelated chaps. 169-179, with the Tārakāmaya-yuddha between the gods on the one side and the demons, Yakṣas, serpents, Rākṣasas etc. on the other. As Ballālasena quotes in his Adbhuta-sāgara a good number of verses from chaps. 163 and 172 by expressly mentioning the stories[84] and as Padma-p. (Sṛṣṭi-kh.), chaps. 42, 37-38 and 43 (verses 6b-9a and 77-85a), which are borrowed from Mat 161-163, 169-178 and 179 (verses 1-13a) respectively, are to be dated between 800 and 950 A.D. and most probably in the former half of the eighth century A.D.[85], the above-mentioned chapters (161-163, 169-178, and verses 1-13a of chap. 179) of the Matsya-p. must be placed earlier than 750 A.D., if not 700.

The story of Sāvitrī in chaps. 208-214, on account of its innovations befitting later taste, can be taken to be a late interpolation. It says that Aśvapati, king of Madra, worshipped the goddess Sāvitrī and was gifted with a daughter who was consequently named after the goddess, and that four days before the death of Satyavat, Sāvitrī fasted for three days and observed the Sāvitrī-vrata. Besides these, there are also other innovations.

Pitṛ-vaṃśa has been dealt with in chaps. 13-15, Pitṛ-gāthā in chap. 204 and Kalpa-kīrtana in chap. 290. Of these, chap. 15 has been drawn upon by Hemādri and Aparārka, and chaps. 13-14, 204 and 290 by the former. So, all these chapters should be dated earlier than 1100 A.D.

The results of the above analysis are as follows:

<table>
<tr><td>Chaps.</td><td>1-10 (especially except verses 6-30 of chap. 7);</td><td rowspan="4">—Either in the last quarter of the third or the first quarter of the fourth century A.D.</td></tr>
<tr><td>„</td><td>11-12, 23-24 and 43-46;</td></tr>
<tr><td>„</td><td>47-50 and 271-273; and</td></tr>
<tr><td>„</td><td>51, 114, 124-8, 141-5.</td></tr>
<tr><td>„</td><td>13-15 .. .. ..</td><td>Earlier than 1100 A.D.</td></tr>
<tr><td>Chap.</td><td>52 .. ..</td><td>Not later than 650 A.D.</td></tr>
<tr><td>Chaps.</td><td>115-120 .. .. ..</td><td>Comparatively late, but not later than 1100 A.D.</td></tr>
</table>

[84] See Adbhs., pp. 20, 23, 50, etc., and pp. 319, 358 and 701.

[85] See under Padma-p.

Chaps.	129-140	Earlier than 1100 A.D.
Chap.	146 (except verses 1-40);	—Earlier than 1100 A.D. and most probably than 800 A.D.
Chaps.	147-148;	
Chap.	153 (except verses 1-221 and 228b to the end);	
„	154 (except verses 447-485);	
Chaps.	155-160.	
Chaps.	149-152	Interpolated most probably later than the chapters of the immediately preceding group.
Chaps.	161-163;	—Earlier than 750 A.D., if not 700.
„	169-178; and	
Chap.	179 (verses 1-13a).	
Chap.	204	Earlier than 1100 A.D.
Chaps.	208-214	Late interpolations.
Chap.	290	Earlier than 1100 A.D.

For the dates of the Smṛti-chapters see the chronological table under Matsya-purāṇa in Chap. IV.

From what has been said above about the dates of the different chapters of the Matsya-p. it appears that this Purāṇa was subjected to additions, and also perhaps to alterations, more than once. That some of its chapters have been lost is shown by those quotations (made by Hemādri, Devaṇabhaṭṭa and Aparārka on Vrata, Dāna, Ekādaśī-upavāsa, Prāyaścitta etc.) which are not found in the extant Matsya.

The extant Matsya-p. seems to have been written, or rather compiled, originally by the Vaiṣṇavas. At least this impression is created by the earlier portions that have been retained. In Mat 1, 23-25 the supernatural power, which the Fish displays in rapid growth and huge size, is said to be possible only with Vāsudeva, for, Manu says, 'none other than he can be such'; Mat 9, 39 says that at the end of each thousand years Manus perish and 'Brahmā and other gods' attain the proximity of Viṣṇu; in Mat 23, 17 Nārāyaṇa is called *paramātman;* in Mat 24 (verses 11, 36 etc.) many ancient kings, viz., Purūravas, Raji and others, are said to have practised austerity for the favour of Viṣṇu; and so on. In the verses referred to above Viṣṇu has been assigned the highest position, and these seem to be the traces of the originally Vaiṣṇava character of the Matsya.

On the strength of the great prominence given to the region about the river Godāvarī in Mat 114, 37-39 (on geography) it has been suggested that the place of composition of the Matsya-p. was Nasi [86]. This suggestion seems to have a very weak basis, for these verses of the Matsya tally with Vā 45, 112-114, and it has been shown that the Matsya borrowed some chapters from the Vāyu. The close agreement of the majority of the geographical chapters in the two Purāṇas seems to confirm the indebtedness of the Matsya to the Vāyu. Hence to find out the place of origin of the present Matsya we shall have to look to those of its original chapters which have not been found borrowed from any other work. Such an one is chap. 2. In it the river Narmadā, and not the famous Ganges, is said to remain even after the destruction of the world (cf. Mat 2, 13-14). Elsewhere, in chap. 15 (which most probably belongs to a little later date and which has a few verses in common with Vā 73), this river, "which flows through the Deccan", is called the 'mind-born daughter' of the Somapa Pitṛs living in the Mānasa-loka (cf. Mat 15, 25-28). These passages tend to show that the Matsya-p. was composed and circulated by Vaiṣṇavite people living somewhere about the river Narmadā.

6. THE BHĀGAVATA-PURĀṆA.

The Bhāgavata is the most popular of the extant Purāṇas. It belongs to the Bhāgavatas and is divided into 12 Skandhas or books dealing with cosmogony, genealogies, myths, legends etc. It also contains a few chapters on Smṛti-matter, viz., III, 30 on the results of actions (Karma-vipāka), VII, 11-13 and XI, 17-18 on the duties of the castes and Āśramas, and VII, 14-15 on funeral sacrifices and holy places.

It has been held by the Śāktas that the Bhāgavata is not a Mahāpurāṇa as the Vaiṣṇavas claim. But these Śāktas themselves are not unanimous about the indentity of the 'Bhāgavata' named in the lists of the eighteen Mahāpurāṇas. Some of them say that it is the Kālikā-purāṇa which, on account of its treatment of the birth and exploits of Bhagavatī, is called 'Bhāgavata'. Some, again, claim that it is the Devībhāgavata. It is, therefore, necessary to see which one is the real Mahāpurāṇa.

An examination of the Nibandhas shows that the authors of these works are all in favour of the Bhāgavata (i.e., Vaiṣṇava Bhāgavata). Narasiṃha Vājapeyin, a noted Nibandha-writer of Orissa, disapproves the claim of the Kālikā-purāṇa to be the 'Bhāga-

[86] Haraprasad Shastri, Cat. of Sans. Mss, ASB, Vol. V, Purāṇa, Preface, p. cxc.

vata Mahāpurāṇa' by referring to the opinion of Lakṣmīdhara[87]. The verses quoted from the 'Bhāgavata' by Ballālasena, Madhvācārya, Hemādri, Govindānanda, Raghunandana, Gapālabhaṭṭa and others, are very often found in the present Bhāgavata but not in the Kālikā-p. or the Devībhāgavata. Of these two latter Purāṇas, or rather Upapurāṇas, the Kālikā has been quoted by Aparārka, Ballālasena, Hemādri, Mādhavācārya, Madanapāla, Śūlapāṇi, Govindānanda, Raghunandana and others with the express mention of its well-known title; whereas the name of the Devībhāgavata has not been mentioned in any of the numerous Nibandhas we have examined. The superior position of the Bhāgavata over the Devībhāgavata is further established by a comparison of their contents. In the Bhāgavata there is no mention of the Devībhāgavata nor is there any attempt to prove its own superior position, but in the Devībhāgavata (I, 3, 16) the Bhāgavata has been included among the Upapurāṇas obviously with a view to establishing the former's claim to the position of a Mahāpurāṇa. Further, in the Bhāgavata, Śuka, son of Vyāsa, is presented as given to complete renunciation of the world from his childhood. But the author of the Devībhāgavata probably saw that an ideal character like Śuka might instigate others, having much less indifference, to renounce the world and thus disturb the discipline in society. Hence he painted Śuka in a quite different colour in the Devībhāgavata. Here Śuka, who is about to give up the world, goes to Janaka at the request of Vyāsa. Janaka convinces him that it is highly necessary to pass through all the stages of life before taking up Saṃnyāsa; otherwise the real taste of worldly enjoyments remains unknown and the mind is not strengthened. Consequently, Śuka gives up the idea of renunciation and repairs to his father's hermitage to live with him. All the above evidences taken together make it likely that the Bhāgavata is the real Mahāpurāṇa.

As to the date of the Bhāgavata, scholars are generally of opinion that it is a very late work not earlier than the 9th century A.D.[88] But such a late date cannot reasonably be given to the Purāṇa. It has been said above that the verses quoted by Ballālasena (in his

[87] *aṣṭādaśabhyas tu pṛthak purāṇaṃ yat tu dṛśyate|*
vijānīdhvaṃ muni-śreṣṭhās tad etebhyo vinirgatam||
vinirgataṃ samudbhūtam|yathā kālikā-purāṇādīnīti lakṣmīdharaḥ|evaṃ ca sati bhagavatyā idaṃ bhāgavatam iti kālikā-purāṇaṃ bhāgavata-padenoktam iti ye vadanti te nirastāḥ|—**Nityācārapradīpa, pp. 18-19.**

[88] C. V. Vaidya, JBBRAS, 1925, pp. 144 ff.; Bhandarkar, Vaiṣṇavism etc., p. 49; Pargiter, AIHT, p. 80; Farquhar, outline, pp. 229 ff.; Winternitz, Ind. Lit., Vol. I, p. 556; and so on.

Wilson, Macdonell, Colebrooke and Burnouf placed the Bhāgavata in the 13th century A.D.

Adbhs.), Hemādri, Madhvācārya, Raghunandana, Gopālabhaṭṭa and others from the 'Bhāgavata', are very often found in the present Bhāgavata. In his Smṛti-candrikā (Vol. I, p. 3) Devaṇabhaṭṭa quotes a few verses containing the names of the eighteen Mahāpurāṇas including the 'Bhāgavata'. Ballālasena names a Bhāgavata-purāṇa in his Dānasāgara (fol. 3b). That the Bhāgavata-purāṇa mentioned in the Dānasāgara is the same as the present Bhāgavata is proved by the following evidences. On fol. 3b of the Dānasāgara Ballālasena says that he did not draw upon the 'Bhāgavata' because it did not contain any chapter on gifts[89]. As a matter of fact the present Bhāgavata contains no chapter on this topic, whereas in the Devībhāgavata there is one, viz., IX, 29. Hence the Devībhāgavata is not the 'Bhāgavata' which Ballālasena means. As Ballālasena quotes in his Dānasāgara a number of verses from the Kālikā-p. by expressly mentioning its title, this Purāṇa also cannot be meant by the name 'Bhāgavata'. Further, Ballālasena names with derision those Purāṇas which were influenced by Tantricism. But he expresses no such feeling about the 'Bhāgavata'. Hence it is sure that Ballālasena means the present Bhāgavata, which is, therefore, to be dated not later than 1050 A.D. Ānandatīrtha Madhva wrote a well-known com. on the Bhāgavata. He also draws upon the Purāṇa in his Bhāṣyas on the Brahmasūtra (? see App. II) and the Bhagavadgītā. In the Gītā-bhāṣya (p. 7) he quotes from the Nārāyaṇāṣṭākṣarakalpa a verse which mentions the Bhāgavata as a work of Vyāsa, and in another quotation from the 'Nāradīya' the Purāṇa is called 'Viṣṇu-veda' (see Gītā-bhāṣya, p. 152). In his Madhva-vijaya (IV, 49-52), Nārāyaṇa Paṇḍitācārya, son of a direct disciple of Madhva, informs us that textual problems relating to the Bhāgavata had already begun in Madhva's time. The great teacher Rāmānuja also was not unacquainted with the Bhāgavata[90]. Alberūnī, in his account of India, gives two lists of Purāṇas. About one of these lists he says: "Another somewhat different list of Purāṇas has been read to me from the Viṣṇu-purāṇa. I give it here in extenso ....Brāhma, Pādma, Viṣṇu, Śiva, Bhāgavata, i.e., Vāsudeva ...."[91]. The use of the term 'Vāsudeva' with reference to the Bhāgavata shows that Alberūnī means the (Vaiṣṇava) Bhāgavata, and that claims had already begun to be made by other works to be known as Bhāgavata. Hence the date of the Bhāgavata preceded that of Alberūnī by such a long period of time that the position of the Bhāgavata had already become enviable. Hence the date of the Bhāgavata cannot possibly be later than 800 A.D.

89 *bhāgavataṃ ca purāṇaṃ brahmāṇḍaṃ caiva nāradīyaṃ ca|*
dāna-vidhi-śūnyam etat trayam iha na niban(d ?)dham avadhārya||.

90 ABORI, XIV, 1932-33, pp. 186 ff. 91 Sachau, Alberūnī's India, I, p. 131.

A few verses are found quoted from the 'Śrīmad-bhāgavata' in Abhinavagupta's Gītārtha-saṃgraha, a com. on the Bhagavad-gītā. But these verses, which tally with Bhāg II, 1, 3-4 and 12 and XI, 20, 17, are not reliable; because in an old Ms written in Sāradā characters they are found not in the running text of the commentary but on the margin. Hence it may be that these verses were written by some one on the margin of his Ms but were later incorporated into the text by the scribes who copied from this Ms.[92] Abhinavagupta's mention of 'gajendra-mokṣaṇa' also need not be taken to point to the Bhāgavata, because chapters on 'gajendra-mokṣaṇa' are found in other Purāṇas also. For instance, Vām 85 and Viṣṇudharmottara I, 194 deal with 'gajendra-mokṣaṇa'. The verse quoted from the 'Bhāgavata' in Gauḍapāda's Uttaragītā-bhāṣya (p. 66; Bombay ed., p. 27) is also equally doubtful. In a Ms[93], which appears to preserve an older version of the Bhāṣya, this verse is not found. How the text of the Bhāṣya was corrupted with later additions and alterations is shown best by a quotation from a Tantra occurring in another Ms[94] of the same work. It is to be noted that no quotation from any Tantra is found in the printed editions or the other Ms referred to above. Hence it seems that the verse under consideration is spurious.

Inspite of the little help rendered by the doubtful verses mentioned above, the Bhāgavata does not seem to be a late work. A comparison, so far as theology is concerned, between this and the Kūrma-p. shows that the Bhāgavata is earlier than the Viṣṇuite Kūrma-p., which was, unlike the Bhāgavata, much influenced by Śākta ideas (see under Kūrma-p.). The date of the Viṣṇuite Kūrma-p. is to be placed between 550 and 650 A.D. So the Bhāgavata cannot possibly be dated later than 600 A.D. Thus we get the lower limit of its date.

It has been said[95] that the Viṣṇu-p. is earlier than the Bhāgavata. The latter 'contains the biography of Kṛṣṇa which is here given in much greater detail than in the Viṣṇu-p. and in the Harivaṃśa[96]'. Hence it seems to be later than the Harivaṃśa also. The latter being dated about 400 A.D., the Bhāgavata cannot possibly be earlier than about 500 A.D. Thus *the date of composition of the Bhāgavata falls in the sixth century A.D. It is highly probable that the Purāṇa was composed in the former half of this century*[97].

92 ABORI, XV, 1933-34, p. 248. 93 No. 4504, D. U. Mss Lib.

94 No. K558E, D. U. Mss Lib., fol. 10a. 95 See under Viṣṇu-purāṇa.

96 Winternitz, Ind. Lit., I, p. 557.

97 There are also other evidences which confirm the above date of the Purāṇa. Viz., I. (i) The two verses of the Māṭhara-vṛtti (on Īśvarakṛṣṇa's Sāṃkhya-kārikās 2 and 51), which, as B. N. Krishnamurti Sharma has pointed

The date of the Smṛti-chapters of the Bhāgavata is most probably the same as that of the Purāṇa itself. It is not, however, possible to say anything definitely. If they are interpolated, they

out in ABORI, XIV, pp. 216-7, have their parallels in the Bhāgavata-p. (I, 8, 52 and I, 6, 35), do not appear in Paramārtha's Chinese translation of the Vṛtti. So, the text of the Māṭhara-vṛtti is doubtful and cannot, therefore, be used to assign the Bhāgavata to a date earlier than that of the Vṛtti.

(ii) The mention of the Tamil Vaiṣṇava saints in Bhāg XI, 5, 38-40, and of the Hūṇas as accepting Vaiṣṇavism in Bhāg II, 4, 18 and II, 7, 46 shows that the Bhāgavata cannot be earlier than the last quarter of the fifth century A.D.

II. (i) Nār I, 96 gives the contents of a 'Bhāgavata' which agree with those of our present Bhāgavata.

(ii) In its incomplete list of the Mahāpurāṇas the Bṛhaddharma-purāṇa (25, 20 f.) names, in place of the 'Bhāgavata', the Mahābhāgavata which is a clear protest against the supremacy of Kṛṣṇa in the Bhāgavata.

(iii) 'If the Govindāṣṭaka be a genuine work of Śaṃkara, as the sixteenth-century Bengal Vaiṣṇava writer, Jīva Gosvāmin, thought and as Belvalkar and others of this day think, Saṃkara must have known the Bhāgavata'.

(iv) 'While the author of the Purāṇa appears to be familiar with the "Ajātavāda" doctrine, he does not know the "Anirvacanīyatā" doctrine posited by Śaṃkara'.

(v) In the chapter on Balarāma's pilgrimage in Bhāg X., there is no mention of Puri which is said to have been known to Śaṃkara and Rāmānuja.

The view put forth by Amarnath Roy in BSOS, Vol. VIII, 1935-7, pp. 107 ff. that the Bhāgavata has been influenced by the Kārikās of Gauḍapāda seems to have a very weak basis, because the philosophical ideas, words and similes found common to the Bhāgavata and the Kārikās are of a general character and might have been derived by the former from works used by Gauḍapāda as his sources. The use of old terms and ideas is not at all exceptional with the Bhāgavata. Other purāṇas also are often found to have derived words, ideas and similes from very ancient sources.

Even if the influence of the Gauḍapāda-kārikās on the Bhāgavata could be proved finally, it would hardly affect the date to which we have assigned the Purāṇa, the date of Gauḍapāda himself being more or less debatable. Barnett (JRAS, 1910, pp. 1361 f.) and Jacobi (JAOS, 1913, pp. 51 f.) place Gauḍapāda not later than 500 A.D.

Mat 53, 20-21 describe the 'Bhāgavata as follows:

yatrādhikṛtya gāyatrīṃ varṇyate dharma-vistaraḥ|
vṛtrāsura-vadhopetaṃ tad bhāgavatam ucyate||
sārasvatasya kalpasya madhye ye syur narottamāḥ|
tad-vṛttāntodbhavaṃ loke tad bhāgavatam ucyate||

This description does not agree fully with the contents of the present Bhāgavata which begins with the Gāyatrī and contains the story of the killing of Vṛtra but does not refer to the Sārasvata Kalpa. On the other hand, it is said in Bhāg II, 8, 28 that the Bhagavat declared the Bhāgavata to Brahmā in the Brahma-kalpa. So, it seems that there was an earlier Bhāgavata which was the prototype of the present Bhāgavata and from which chapters have been retained in the latter. It is most probably this earlier work which is mentioned in Viṣ III, 6, 22, Kūr I, 1, 13, etc.

have been connected with the original parts in such a way that it is very difficult to separate them.

The inclusion of the Buddha in the three lists of the incarnations of Viṣṇu[98] need not disprove the above date. These lists differ from one another in length as well as order. So they can never be the works of a single hand. Of these three, those given in Bhāg I, 3 and VI, 8 are undoubtedly spurious[99]. The remaining one also does not seem to have belonged originally to the Bhāgavata.

It can hardly be denied that the Bhāgavata has been revised and emended at times. But the emendations have been made so carefully that it is very difficult to find them out. The mention of Tulasī, Tantra, the ten characteristics of a 'Mahāpurāṇa', etc. may be due to these revisions and emendations.

7. THE KŪRMA-PURĀṆA[100].

The extant Kūrma-p., which is divided into two books Pūrva and Uttara, contains a good number of chapters on Hindu customs; viz., Kūr I, 2-3 and II, 12-15, 19, 24-25 and 27-29 deal with the duties of the four castes and Āśramas, II, 16 with customs in general, II, 18-19 with the daily duties, II, 17 with eatables and non-eatables, II, 20-22 with funeral ceremony, II, 23 with impurity due to births and deaths, II, 26 with gifts, II, 30 and 32-33 with expiation, I, 30-38 and II, 34-42 with holy places, I, 28 with Yuga-dharma, and I, 29 with the nature of the Kali age (Kali-svarūpa).

The Kūrma-p. informs us that the entire Purāṇa of this title consisted of four Saṃhitās, viz., Brāhmī, Bhāgavatī, Saurī and Vaiṣṇavī, and that the copy of the Purāṇa which is now available is only a part named Brāhmī Saṃhitā[101]. Of the other three Saṃhitās

[98] See Bhāg I, 3, II, 7 and VI, 8.

[99] See IHQ, Vol. VIII, 1932, pp. 253-250.

[100] The ASB ed. is generally the same as the Vaṅga. ed. The corresponding chapters in the two editions are the following:

	ASB ed.			Vaṅga. ed.	
I,	1-27	=	I,	1-27	respectively.
	28-29	=		28.	
	30-53	=		29-52	respectively.
II,	1-31	=	II,	1-31	respectively.
	32-33	=		32.	
	34-45	=		33-44	respectively.

There are, of course, occasional variations in readings and numbers of verses in the corresponding chapters.

[101] Cf. Kūr I, 1, 21-23.

By their mention of the Kūrma-p. as consisting of two Bhāgas, the Saura-p. (9, 11), Skanda-p. (V, iii, 1, 42), etc. refer definitely to the extant Kūrma.

which seem to be lost, the extant Kūrma-p. gives us no information. The Nāradīya-purāṇa, however, contains a list of contents of all the four Saṃhitās, the contents of the Brāhmī Saṃhitā tallying fully with those of the extant Kūrma. According to the Nāradīya, the Bhāgavatī Saṃhitā, which consisted of five Pādas (parts) and was termed 'Pañca-padī', dealt separately with the means of livelihood of the different castes,—the first Pāda being given to the means of livelihood of the Brāhmans, the second to those of the Kṣatriyas, the third to those of the Vaiśyas, the fourth to those of the Śūdras, and the fifth to those of the mixed castes; the Saurī Saṃhitā was divided into six parts dealing with the methods of performing the 'six acts' (Ṣaṭkarma, viz., Vaśīkaraṇa, Māraṇa, Uccāṭana etc.); and the Vaiṣṇavī Saṃhitā was divided into four Pādas dealing with Mokṣa-dharma for the twice-born. As regards the lengths of these four Saṃhitās the Nāradīya-p. says that they contained 6000, 4000, 2000 and 5000 verses respectively[102].

The present Kūrma-p. betrays the two main stages[103] through which it has passed to attain its present form. The earlier portions —especially the first two chapters of book I—which have escaped, of course not totally, the interfering hands of the rival sectaries, show that the Kūrma originally belonged most probably to the Pāñcarātras and that afterwards it was appropriated by the Pāśupatas who added to it many new myths, legends, accounts of holy places and the like in order to attain their sectarian end.

The first two chapters of the Kūrma-p. strike the keynote of the whole work. The summary of contents of these two introductory chapters is given with a view to showing not only the originality of these two chapters but also their vital connection with the contents of those other chapters which seem to have belonged to the Kūrma-p. in its Viṣṇuite form. In Kūr I, 1 the sages of the Naimiṣa forest ask Lomaharṣaṇa to narrate the Purāṇa. Consequently, Lomaharṣaṇa refers to the five characteristics of the Purāṇas, names the eighteen Mahāpurāṇas and Upapurāṇas, mentions the four Saṃhitās of the Kūrma, and proceeds to report what Viṣṇu in the form of the Tortoise said to the gods and sages who attended the churning of the ocean of milk. During the churning, Lomaharṣaṇa says, Śrī arose and was taken by Viṣṇu who introduced her as his own Śakti to the inquisitive gods and sages. The latter then asked the Tortoise to narrate what would happen at 'kāla-kṣaya'. Consequently, the Tortoise began with the story of Indradyumna to whom, he said, he had formerly narrated the Purāṇa-saṃhitā and given instructions

[102] Nār I (Pūrva-khaṇḍa), 106, 1-22.

[103] Though there are traces of Śākta and Nakulīśa influence in Kūr I, 12 and I, 52 respectively, they are negligible.

on Karman (meaning the duties of the castes and Āśramas) and Jñāna. Though the Tortoise narrated briefly the story of Indradyumna referring to the latter's desire to gain knowledge of the supreme God (i.e., Viṣṇu-Brahma), the appearance of Śrī who had referred him to Viṣṇu, and the appearance of Viṣṇu who had told Indradyumna how the supreme God could be experienced through Jñāna and Bhakti by those obeying the rules of castes and stages, the gods and the sages were not satisfied with it. They asked the Tortoise to repeat what he had said to Indradyumna. Here ends Kūr I, 1. The next chapter narrates what the Tortoise said to his audience; viz., the origin of Brahmā, Rudra and Śrī from Viṣṇu himself; the appointment of Śrī to delude the people with a view to compelling them to undergo rebirths; the creation of the nine sages, the four Vedas and the four castes by Brahmā; and the establishment of the rules of Dharma for the different castes and stages of life.

The originality of these two introductory chapters is shown by the vital connection which the story of Indradyumna has with the narration of the Purāṇa. As regards the contents of the Kūrma-p. the Matsya says: "That in which Janārdana, in the form of a Tortoise, in the region under the earth, explained the glories of duty, wealth, pleasure and liberation through the story of Indradyumna to the sages in the proximity of Śakra, which refers to the Lakṣmī-kalpa, and contains eighteen thousand verses, is the Kūrma-purāṇa"[104]. The Agni[105] and the Nāradīya-p.[106] also say that the Kūrma-p. was narrated by the Tortoise through the story of Indradyumna. Thus these Purāṇas testify to the traditional connection of the story of Indradyumna with the narration of the Purāṇa. The originality of these two chapters is further established by the interpolations, some of which were made by the worshippers of Śiva and Brahmā, even in these chapters. For examples we may refer to Kūr I, 1, 107-121 in which Indradyumna is made quite irrelevantly to go to see Brahmā, obviously with a view to adding to the glory of the latter; to Kūr I, 2, 91 ff. wherein the position of Śiva seems

[104] *yatra dharmārtha-kāmānāṃ mokṣasya ca rasātale|*
māhātmyaṃ kathayāmāsa kūrmarūpī janārdanaḥ||
indradyumna-prasaṅgena ṛṣibhyaḥ śakra-saṃnidhau|
aṣṭādaśa sahasrāṇi lakṣmī-kalpānuṣaṅgikam|| Mat 53, 46-47.

[105] *kūrmaṃ cāṣṭa-sahasraṃ ca kūrmoktāṃ ca rasātale|*
indradyumna-prasaṅgena * * * * || Ag 272, 19.

[106] *lakṣmī-kalpānucaritaṃ yatra kūrma-vapur hariḥ||*
dharmārtha-kāma-mokṣāṇāṃ māhātmyaṃ ca pṛthak pṛthak|
indradyumna-prasaṅgena prāharṣibhyo dayānvitaḥ||
tat saptadaśa-sāhasraṃ sa-catuḥsaṃhitaṃ śubham|

to be raised higher than that of Viṣṇu by directing the application of the three kinds of meditation (bhāvanā) to him and by attaching more importance to the Śaiva sect-mark 'tripuṇḍra', wherein Pradhāna comprising Brahmā, Viṣṇu and Śiva is said to dwell; and most probably also to Kūr I, 1, 16-20 in which the eighteen Upapurāṇas have been named.

We now turn to examine the theology of these two chapters, because this examination will reveal the earlier character of the Purāṇa. In these two chapters Viṣṇu (also called Nārāyaṇa Hṛṣīkeśa, Vāsudeva etc.) is identified with the supreme Brahma. He is described as imperishable, eternal, indivisible and higher than the highest[107]. In Kūr I, 1, 69-79 Indradyumna eulogises Viṣṇu by attaching to him all the attributes which are expressive of the supreme Brahma. Here Viṣṇu is described as 'viśvātman', 'paramātman', 'nirguṇa', 'niṣkala', 'viśvarūpa', 'nirvikāra', 'niṣprapañca', 'ādimadhyānta-hīna', 'jñāna-gamya', 'bhedābheda-vihīna', 'ānandarūpin', 'ananta-mūrti', 'cinmātra' and the like and is called Brahma capable of being experienced only through knowledge. In several other places Viṣṇu identifies his own self with the only Reality—the supreme Brahma[108]. There seems to be a distinction made between Viṣṇu-Brahma and the inferior Viṣṇu of the Trinity. The former is 'akṣara' and 'gūḍha-rūpa', but the latter is under the influence of Kāla and manifests himself before worshippers.

Śrī, the wife of Viṣṇu, is his Śakti. She is said to have been born of Viṣṇu himself in the Śrī-kalpa[109] and is characterised by the same signs as those of her consort[110], viz., she has four arms, carries the conch, the disc and the lotus, and is adorned with a garland[111]. She is the main source from which Brahmā, Śiva and other gods derive their own Śaktis and become known as 'śaktimat'[112]. In the supreme state Viṣṇu and his Śakti are indistinguishable and constitute the supreme Brahma[113], but in creation the latter manifests herself as Māyā Śakti and is vested with the three Guṇas[114]. It is this Mahāmāyā who deludes the people and compels them to undergo rebirths[115].

The position, which Śiva and Brahmā occupy in the earlier portions of the extant Kūrma-p., is certainly inferior to that of Viṣṇu.

[107] See Kūr I, 1, 63, 68 and 71.

[108] Kūr I, 1, 51-52; 1, 95; and 2, 3.

[109] Kūr I, 1, 38; and I, 2, 7.

[110] Kūr I, 1, 56.

[111] Kūr I, 1, 39.

[112] Kūr I, 1, 37. Cf. also Kūr I, 1, 44-45, wherein Viṣṇu says: "(Indradyumna) resorted to me after knowing that Brahmā, Mahādeva and other gods with their own Śaktis are situated in my Śakti".

[113] Cf. Kūr I, 1, 59.

[114] Kūr I, 1, 34-38.

[115] Cf. Kūr I, 2, 12.

They are ranked as common gods, so much so that even Indradyumna, as Viṣṇu says, was invincible to Śaṃkara and others[116] in his previous birth. Regarding the origin of these two gods Viṣṇu himself says that before creation he was sleeping alone on the serpent-bed; at the end of the night he awoke and thought of creation, and the four-faced Brahmā was born of his grace and the three-eyed Rudra of his anger[117]. Viṣṇu further says that Brahmā created beings at his command[118]. As Viṣṇu himself is the creator, preserver and destroyer and as Śiva and Brahmā are said to have been born of Viṣṇu, he is sometimes addressed with the names of these two gods. When, in Kūr I, 1, 67 ff., Viṣṇu appears before Indradyumna, the latter addresses him with various names including 'mahādeva', 'śiva' and 'parameṣṭhin'. The epithets 'maheśvara', 'parameśvara' and 'īśa' also are applied to mean Viṣṇu, but these are probably to be taken in their literal sense and not as names. For instance, Viṣṇu calls himself 'īśvara' which is synonymous with 'īśa'. Hence we shall be in the wrong if we think that Indradyumna 'desired to gain knowledge of the glory of Śiva'. But it seems highly probable that Indradyumna wanted to realise Viṣṇu-Brahma[119] who remains screened by his Māyā, namely Lakṣmī. But none can realise Viṣṇu-Brahma until one knows the true self of this Māyā, and thus surpasses her, by worshipping Viṣṇu[120]. Hence Indradyumna is found to worship the great god Viṣṇu, and as a result Lakṣmī, the Māyā of Viṣṇu, reveals her true self, explains her identity and refers him to Viṣṇu—of course, the inferior Viṣṇu of the Trinity—for true knowledge. Indradyumna is, however, found afterwards to gain it from Viṣṇu and realise the One, viz., supreme Brahma. It should be noted that if Indradyumna desired to gain knowledge of Śiva, he would not have to surpass the Māyā of Viṣṇu, as, we know, Śiva has his own Māyā Śakti.

The theology of these two introductory chapters of the Kūrma-p., in which there is a considerable amount of Śākta element, approaches very closely to that of the Pāñcarātra Saṃhitās like the Ahirbudhnya[121]. The philosophy is in both based on the theistic Yoga.

The very name 'Brāhmī Saṃhitā' which is given to our extant Kūrma-p. and the numerous references to Jñāna in the first two

[116] Kūr I, 1, 43.

[117] Kūr I, 2, 3-6.

[118] Kūr I, 2, 22.

[119] Kūr I, 1, 63. In this verse the word *acyuta*, one of the names of Viṣṇu, occurs.

[120] Cf. Kūr I, 1, 60 wherein Lakṣmī says to Indradyumna: "I fail to overpower those who worship Puruṣottama, the prop of all beings, with Jñāna- and Karma-yoga". Also cf. Kūr I, 1, 122.

[121] See, Dr. Schrader, Introduction to the Pāñcarātra and the Ahirbudhnya-saṃhitā.

chapters[122] naturally raise the doubt that the Kūrma-p. in its Viṣṇuite form must have contained some chapters on the knowledge of Viṣṇu-Brahma. There are, of course, some chapters (viz., II, 1-11) in the extant Kūrma which deal with Jñāna-yoga and constitute the Īśvara-gītā, but these are Pāśupata documents pure and simple. Then the question arises as to the presence of the original chapters on knowledge. In the extant Kūrma-p. itself there are evidences to show that the chapters, which now go by the name 'Īśvara-gītā', once belonged to the Viṣṇuite Kūrma-purāṇa in some other form, and that these were first spoken by Viṣṇu in the form of the Tortoise but reported perhaps by Vyāsa to the sages of the Naimiṣa forest at the request of Sūta Lomaharṣaṇa. At the very outset of the extant Kūrma-p. there are lines which tend to ascribe the authorship of these chapters to Viṣṇu himself. For instance, in Kūr I, 1, 47 it is said that in a previous birth of Indradyumna Viṣṇu promised to impart to him the most secret knowledge so that Indradyumna might merge into himself in the end; and in Kūr I, 1, 64 Lakṣmī, the Māyā of Viṣṇu, reveals herself to Indradyumna and, being asked to tell him how Viṣṇu-Brahma could be realised, says: "Nārāyaṇa himself will impart the knowledge to you". Towards the end of the Kūrma-p. also the knowledge (of Brahma) is said to have been declared by Nārāyaṇa[123]. These evidences are corroborated by the Īśvara-gītā itself. At the very beginning of this Gītā the sages refer to the topics, viz., creation in the Svāyambhuva Manvantara, the expansion of the universe, and the description of the Manavantaras, as matters already explained by Lomaharṣaṇa, and want to hear from him that knowledge which will enable them to experience the supreme Brahma (which is, as we have seen above, no other than Viṣṇu himself in his supreme state). Accordingly Lomaharṣaṇa first remembers his teacher Vyāsa and is about to begin when the latter arrives there all on a sudden. Lomaharṣaṇa receives him with due honour and requests him to narrate the knowledge of Brahma saying:

"*ime hi munayaḥ śāntās tāpasā dharma-tatparāḥ*|
śuśrūṣā jāyate caiṣāṃ vaktum arhasi tattvataḥ||
jñānaṃ vimuktidaṃ divyaṃ yan me sākṣāt tvayoditam|
munīnāṃ vyāhṛtaṃ pūrvaṃ viṣṇunā kūrmarūpiṇā||"
(Kūr II, 1, 12-13).

But Vyāsa replies: "I shall tell you what Śiva himself, being asked by the sages Sanatkumāra and others, spoke out to them in ancient times", making no mention of the Tortoise, and begins with the story in which Śiva is brought in to declare the knowledge of Śiva-

[122] Kūr I, 1, verses 47, 64, 86, 124-5 and so on.
[123] Kūr II, 43, 1.

Brahma to the sages Sanatkumāra, Sanaka and others. Vyāsa's reply to Lomaharṣaṇa's request is so irrelevant that the touches of later hands are easily detectable in these chapters.

We have now sufficient reason to hold that the extant Kūrma-p. was originally a Pāñcarātra document[124]. It was afterwards recast so successfully by the Pāśupatas that its Viṣṇuite character was obscured almost totally. The Pāśupatas not only rewrote some of the original sections, giving up others that went against their own interest, but introduced much new material in the form of myths and legends for the glorification of Śiva and the Pāśupata Vrata and Yoga. They were not satisfied with these changes even. In Kūr I, 25 Viṣṇu is presented as worshipping the Śiva-liṅgas and accepting the Pāśupata Vrata and Yoga for obtaining a son through Śiva's favour.

It is necessary to give here a brief account of the Pāśupatas as they are described in the Kūrma-p. in order to understand their true character and to distinguish them from the other sects of Śiva-worshippers. In Kūr I, 14, 22 ff. there is a story about Suśīla, one of the grandsons of king Pṛthu, wherein an ascetic named Śvetāśvatara is said to have founded the Pāśupata order. The story narrates that Suśīla went to the Himalayas with a view to practising asceticism and worshipped Śiva. All on a sudden there came a Pāśupata ascetic named Śvetāśvatara and gave him instructions on divine knowledge as well as on the vow of his own order. He also addressed his disciples present there and referred to the holiness of the place adding, "Yogins, who have studied the order founded by me, sit absorbed in meditation on the impartible and blissful Mahādeva"[125]. This Śvetāśvatara seems to be identical with the first incarnation of Mahādeva, namely Śveta, according to the Nakulīśa Pāśupatas. This Śveta also is said to have been incarnated on the Himalayas and to have had a large following[126]. Or the legend may connect the Sampradāya with the inchoate Pāśupata-Brahma doctrine of the Śvetāśvatara Upaniṣad. The scriptures of this Pāśupata order are the Atharvaśiras-upaniṣad and the Śatarudrīya section of the Yajurveda[127]. These Pāśupatas hold the Vedas

[124] A careful analysis of the contents of the present Kūrma shows that the Purāṇa in its Viṣṇuite character approached much, like the Viṣṇu-purāṇa, to the old definition of the Purāṇa of 'five characteristics' and that it lacked the chapters on Tīrtha-māhātmya. Cf. Kūr II, 1, 1-2 and II, 43, 1-2, both of which certainly belonged to the earlier Kūrma as they do not mention the contents of those preceding chapters which were interpolated by the Pāśupatas.

[125] Kūr I, 14, 40.

[126] Kūr I, 52, 2 ff.

[127] Kūr I, 20, 69 and I, 14, 30.

in high esteem and look down upon those who decry these holy scriptures. The regular study of the Vedas is one of their main duties[128]. They cite only the Vedic hymns, perform the Agnihotra, use the Vedic Mantras, follow Vedic rules and meditate on the syllable 'Oṃ'[129]. Once Śiva is even made to say: "Oh Brāhmans, my form is the Vedas; none versed in other Śāstras realises my true self * * * "[130]. The Pāśupata vow consists in besmearing the body with ashes, wearing a piece of rag or remaining naked, putting on the sacred thread, living on roots and fruits, bathing thrice daily, bearing strange signs, holding a torch in the hand, laughing, singing, dancing, making amorous jestures, and so forth. The Pāśupatas also worship Śiva with flowers and meditate on the god as seated in the sun. Those who enter heart and soul into the Pāśupata order are required to do 'saṃnyāsa' and practise the Pāśupata Yoga which is described in the Īśvara-gītā. The Pāśupatas hate those sects which are guided by the Tantras. These scirptures, they say, were originally promulgated by Śiva with a view to deluding the sages cursed by Gautama[131].

It has been shown above that the extant Kūrma-p. belonged originally to the Pāñcarātras but was later appropriated by the Pāśupatas who should be distinguished from the Āgamic Śaivas and other Śivaite sects. An attempt will now be made to determine the date of composition of the Viṣṇuite Kūrma-p. and also of that of its appropriation by the Pāśupatas, because that will help us to ascertain the periods during which the chapters on Hindu customs were interpolated[132].

A comparison between these two chapters on the one hand and the Viṣṇu-p., Harivaṃśa and Bhāgavata-p. on the other shows the advance, so far as theology is concerned, made by the Kūrma-p. over these Vaiṣṇavite documents, in none of which there is traceable any Śākta influence. In the Viṣṇu-p. there is, of course, a solitary

[128] Kūr I, 25, 8; I, 14, 48; etc.

[129] Kūr I, 14, 30; II, 37, 89; 37, 88; and I, 33, 7.

[130] Kūr II, 37, 148.

[131] Kūr I, 16, 96-122.

[132] I have shown in Indian Culture, Vol. I, pp. 587-614, that the Smṛti-chapters (12-33) of Kūr II, which constitute the Vyāsa-gītā, are nothing but the Uśanas-saṃhitā with a few additional chapters. That in the Viṣṇuite Kūrma-p. nothing intervened between the section on Mokṣa-jñāna (which now appears in a changed form under the name of Īśvara-gītā constituting Kūr II, 1-11) and Kūr II, 43 dealing with Pralaya, is shown by the opening verses of the latter. These verses are:

sūta uvāca—

etad ākarṇya vijñānaṃ nārāyaṇa-mukheritam|
kūrma-rūpadharaṃ devaṃ papracchur munayaḥ prabhum||

line in which Lakṣmī has been called Viṣṇu's Śakti[133], but it has already been shown that the verses 15 to the end of Viṣ I, 8, including the line referred to above, were interpolated. Now, if the Harivaṃśa was added to the Mahābhārata after the latter had attained its present form, if the date of the Viṣṇu-p. is pushed up as early as the fourth century A.D. and if the Bhāgavata is placed somewhere about the sixth century A.D., then the date of the Viṣṇuite Kūrma-p. cannot possibly be earlier than the middle of the sixth century. This upper limit of the date of the Kūrma-p. is supported by a Pāñcarātra Saṃhitā named Jayākhya, which, though replete with Tantric rites, remarkably lacks the Śakti theory unlike the Ahirbudhnya-saṃhitā. The Jayākhya mentions Lakṣmī and three others, viz., Jayā, Kīrti and Māyā, as Viṣṇu's wives and Śaktis[134], but they play no part at all in creation. Hence the very nature of the theology of the Jayākhya shows that it is earlier than the Ahirbudhnya. B. Bhattacarya, in his Foreword (pp. 26-34) to the Jayākhya-saṃhitā, assigns it to about 450 A.D. on the strength of doctrinal and palæographical viewpoints. If a period of at least 100 years be allowed for the Pāñcarātras' acceptance of the Śakti theory and their writing or re-writing of the Kūrma-p.,—for it is more probable that the Śakti

ṛṣaya ūcuḥ—

kathito bhavatā dharmo mokṣa-jñānaṃ savistaram|
lokānāṃ sarga-vistāro vaṃśo manvantarāṇi ca||
idānīṃ deva-deveśa pralayaṃ vaktum arhasi|

* * * * *

The word *vijñāna* in the first verse certainly points to the so-called Īśvara-gītā, at the beginning of which the sages request Sūta to narrate to them that 'vijñāna' (knowledge) which he has received from Kṛṣṇa Dvaipāyana (cf. Kūr II, 1, 4). Moreover, the knowledge that is dealt with in the Īśvara-gītā is often called 'vijñāna' (Cf. Kūr II, 2, verses 1, 36, 38, 39, 55 and so on). Therefore the fact that in the Viṣṇuite Kūrma-p. the chapter on Pralaya was immediately preceded by the so-called Īśvara-gītā seems to be undeniable. The word *dharma* in the second verse quoted above points not to the Vyāsa-gītā but to the Smṛti-sections (viz., Kūr I, 2-3) which occur at the very beginning and which belonged, as we shall see below, to the Viṣṇuite Kūrma-p. These original Smṛti-sections are also referred to by the opening verses of the Īśvara-gītā.

From all this it appears that the Vyāsa-gītā was interpolated by the Pāśupatas most probably at the time of recasting the Viṣṇuite Kūrma-p., there being nothing to show that it was interpolated afterwards. On the other hand, in the Vyāsa-gītā the Āgamic Śaivas are called Pāśupatas but are classed with the Pāṣaṇḍas (i.e., the non-Vedic sects). Of the Śāktas, only the Vāmas are mentioned. That such a state of things cannot but point to a date earlier than 800 A.D. we shall see below. The Pāśupata tinge of the Vyāsa-gītā seems to strengthen the above supposition. It speaks so often of the Pāśupata Vrata and Yoga that it could have been interpolated by none but the Pāśupatas.

133 Viṣ I, 8, 27a—*aviṣṭambho gadāpāṇiḥ śaktir lakṣmīr dvijottama.*

theory was first imbibed by the Pāñcarātra Saṃhitās which are the main literature of the sect and then by other works,—then the date of the Viṣṇuite Kūrma-p. cannot be earlier than about 550 A.D. Thus we get the upper limit of the date of composition of the extant Kūrma. It may be questioned whether the upper limit can be placed so late. As an answer we may refer to the opinion of Pargiter who says: "The Kūrma account (of the dynasties) is a composite production. Now and again it has a few lines like the Vāyu text, and like the Matsya text, in the Aikṣvāku genealogy, but it follows the Matsya rather, where they differ. It is a late composition and shows Brahmanical features; thus it omits most of the Vāyu's tales and introduces Brahmanical fabrications instead: for instance, it makes Gautama (who was far later) a contemporary of Yuvanāśva I, and tells long fables about king Vasumanas and the Haihaya kings Jayadhvaja and Durjaya"[135]. It should be remembered that the age of a Purāṇa depends more upon the genuineness of its most vital constituents, viz., account of creation and the dynastic lists, than upon anything else.

Let us now try to determine the period when the Viṣṇuite Kūrma-p. was recast by the Pāśupatas, because that will help us to determine the lower limit. Vidyākara Vājapeyin quotes verses from Kūr I, 22 and II, 37 in his Nityācārapaddhati; Narasiṃha Vājapeyin from Kūr I, 1 and II, 18, 23 and 37 in his Nityācārapradīpa; Vācaspatimiśra from Kūr I, 36 and 37 in his Tīrthacintāmaṇi; Śūlapāṇi from Kūr II, 30 and 33 in his Prāyaścittaviveka; Madanapāla from Kūr II, 18 in his Madana-pārijāta; Mādhavācārya from Kūr II, 12-16, 18-20, 22-25, 27-29, 33, 36, 39 and 43 in his Bhāṣya on the Parāśara-smṛti; Hemādri from Kūr I, 1-3, 5 and 36 and II, 12, 13, 15, 18, 20-23, 26 and 44 in his Caturvarga-cintāmaṇi; Devaṇabhaṭṭa from Kūr I, 3 and II, 12, 13, 15, 16, 18-20, 24 and 25 in his Smṛti-candrikā; Aniruddhabhaṭṭa from Kūr II, 23 in his Hāralatā; and Ballālasena from Kūr II, 18, 26 and 44 in his Dānasāgara (see App.). These quotations show that the Kūrma became a Pāśupata document not later than at least 1100 A.D. Bhāskarācārya, in his Brahmasūtra-bhāṣya, p. 62, quotes three verses (*anādinidhanā* etc.) as declared by the Paurāṇikas. Two of these verses tally with Kūr I, 2, 28 and I, 7, 66. On pp. 64-65 Bhāskarācārya quotes from 'Smṛti'[136] three more verses, two of which are traceable in the Kūrma-p. (viz., I, 7, 67 and 68). One of

[134] Jayākhya-saṃhitā, VI, 77 and 84; and XII, 30 and 31.

[135] Pargiter, AIHT, p. 81.

[136] The term 'Smṛti' as distinct from 'Śruti' is used by Śaṃkarācārya, Bhāskara and others to mean all works except Vedic.

these four verses, which are common to the Bhāskara-bhāṣya and the Kūrma-p., contains the word *maheśvara.* But these do not carry us further, as the word *maheśvara* has been used in its literal sense to mean Viṣṇu in the introductory chapters of the Kūrma-p. and as it is not sure that the verses were quoted by Bhāskara from the Kūrma-p. So we are in need of other evidences. A perusal of the extant Kūrma-p. convinces one of the fact that the object of appropriating the Purāṇa was not only to ventilate the antagonistic attitude which the Pāśupatas bore against their Pāñcarātra rivals but also to make an attempt to popularise their faith which was in a decadent condition[137]. In several places of the Kūrma-p. the sects, which are originally Tantric or which have imbibed Tantric rites and practices, are mentioned with hatred. The non-Vedic Pāṣaṇḍa Śāstras, viz., Kāpāla[138], Bhairava, Yāmala, Vāma, Ārhata, Kāpila, Pāñcarātra, Ḍāmara, Nākula, Pūrva-paścima, Pāśupata, Soma, Lāṅgala, Sāttvata[139], and many others *(anyāni sahasraśaḥ)*, are said to have been declared by Śiva with a view to deluding the sages who were cursed by Gautama[140]. The Vedic Pāśupatas hate even to speak with the followers of these Pāṣaṇḍa Śāstras[141] and consider the latter's presence in funeral ceremonies as sinful[142]. It is to be noted that in the Kūrma-p. those Pāśupatas who accept Tantric practices and attach more importance to the Tantras are also called Pāśupatas but are characterised by the epithet 'Pāṣaṇḍa'. The

137 Cf. Kūr I, 29, 9 and 25.

138 This is the literature of the Kāpāla or Kāpālika sect which is very old. In an inscription dating from the first half of the 7th century A.D. Kapāleśvara and his ascetics are mentioned (cf. Bhandarkar, Vaiṣṇavism etc., p. 118). Varāhamihira knew the Kāpālas (cf. *keśāsthi-śakala-śavalā kāpālam iva vratam dhatte*—Bṛhat-saṃhitā, p. 61. This line has been quoted by Ballālasena in his Adbhutasāgara, p. 237). According to Aparārka the Śivaite sects (the Kāpālikas?) are intended by a Sūtra of Āpastamba which includes the word *kapāla* (see Aparārka's com. on Yāj., pp. 12-13).

139 According to Kūr I, 24, 31-33 Sāttvata, son of Aṃśu of the Yadu family, is said to have worshipped Vāsudeva and promulgated the Sāttvata Śāstra which was heard by the bastards *(kuṇḍa-golādibhiḥ śrutam)*. This Sāttvata Śāstra is most probably a branch of the literature of the Pāñcarātras. 'In the Īśvara-saṃhitā * * * * * the Pāñcarātra literature is divided into two broad classes— Divya and Munibhāṣita, or as Revealed and Traditional. The prominent among the Divya class are considered to be three, namely, the Sāttvata, Pauṣkara and the Jayākhya called as the three jewels of the Pāñcarātra literature'. (Foreword to the Jayākhya-saṃhitā, p. 12).

140 Cf. Kūr I, 12, 256-258; I, 16, 115-117; I, 24, 31-33; I, 29, 25; II, 16, 15-16; II, 21, 32-33; and II, 37, 146-147.

141 Kūr II, 16, 15.

142 Kūr II, 21, 32-33.

literature of the Pāṣaṇḍa Pāśupatas is called Pāśupata Śāstra. It is clear that the distinctive names 'Śaiva' for these Pāṣaṇḍa Pāśupatas and 'Āgama' for their literature did not come into use at the time the Kūrma-p. was recast by the Pāśupatas who acknowledged Vedic sanction. If these terms were known at that time, these Vedic Pāśupatas would never have called their 'unworthy' rivals 'Pāśupatas'; nor would they have liked to connect the name of their deity with the literature which they hated so much. Now, the evidences of Aparārka, Bhāskarācārya and others show that the distinctive epithets 'Śaiva' and 'Āgama' to mean the Pāṣaṇḍa Pāśupatas and their literature respectively had been widely recognised before the 10th century A.D. The Skandapurāṇa mentions the 'Śaivas' and the 'Āgamas' at every step. The Śravaṇa-Belgola inscription of Mallisena (1129 A.D.) mentions the Śaivas, Pāśupatas, Bauddhas, Kāpālikas and Kāpilas[143]. The repeated mention of the Śaivas and Pāśupatas together by Aparārka shows that he was familiar with the distinction between these two sects. In his time the literature of the Śaivas was called Śaivāgama or Śaiva Śāstra. He also refers to the philosophical doctrines of the Śaivas, Pāśupatas, Pāñcarātras, Sāṃkhyas and Pātañjalas[144]. On pp. 10-11 and 18 of his com. Aparārka quotes two verses common to the Devīpurāṇa and Yoga-yājñavalkya, and a third from a 'Smṛti'. In these verses the Śaivas and Pāśupatas have been clearly differentiated. These quotations show that the names 'Śaiva' and 'Āgama' began to be used before the time of composition of at least those portions of the Devī-purāṇa, Yoga-yājñavalkya and 'Smṛti' from which the quotations have been made. Aparārka flourished about 1125 A.D. Therefore these distinctive epithets could not have possibly come into vogue later than the beginning of the eleventh century. The evidence of the Varāha-purāṇa also points to the same lower limit. In Var 70 and 71, which are included in the Rudra-gītā, Rudra is brought in to declare the supremacy of Viṣṇu over all other gods including himself and to denounce the non-Vedic *(veda-bāhya)* Śaiva scriptures, namely the Niḥśvāsa-saṃhitā and the Śivasiddhāntas, of the Pāśupatas meaning undoubtedly the Āgamic Śaivas. These non-Vedic scriptures, Rudra adds, were first declared by himself at the request of Viṣṇu in order to delude the people who were crowding the heaven as a result of Viṣṇu-worship. To explain why Rudra declared such 'filthy' scriptures the story of Gautama's curse on the sages, who sought his shelter on account of famine, is introduced. This story runs as follows :

[143] Ep. Ind., III, 1894-95, p. 192.

[144] Aparārka's com. on Yāj., p. 11.

Gautama practised austerities in the Daṇḍaka forest and received a boon from Brahmā to have plenty of crops. Now, in course of time there broke out a severe famine which lasted for twelve years and compelled the sages, who lived in the forests, to have recourse to Gautama for maintenance. Gautama supported the sages throughout the whole period and requested them to stay with him even when the famine was over. So, for a pretext to leave the place the sages thought out a plan. They created a cow by virtue of their magic power and put her in the hermitage. Gautama understood that it was a magic cow and sprinkled water on her citing '*jahi*' (kill). The cow fell down, and the sages also left the hermitage. Gautama then began austerities anew. As a result Rudra was pleased to come and give him a piece of his matted hair which Gautama brought to his hermitage. This hair caused the Ganges to flow through the place where the magic cow lay senseless. The touch of the water revived the cow, and consequently the river was named Godāvarī. At the sight of this strange event the 'seven sages' came and thanked Gautama for causing the Ganges to flow through the Daṇḍaka forest. Gautama then realised the whole plan and cursed the sages to be outside the pale of Veda-dharma. As a result of this curse Rudra was compelled to declare the Niḥśvāsa-saṃhitā.

A comparison between this story and that found in Kūr I, 16, 95 ff. at once suggests that the Rudra-gītā was written later than Kūr I, 16, 95-123. In the Kūrma-p. the story is shorter as well as simpler. It does not refer to Gautama's austerities for plenty of crops or to the origin of the river Godāvarī. The story of Gautama's killing the magic cow is not so clumsy as in the Varāha-p. As there are verses common to the Varāha and the Kūrma-p.[145] it is highly probable that the story in the former had its prototype in that of the latter. As Aparārka quotes verses from Var 70 and 71 in his com., Kūr I, 16, 95-123, which seem to be earlier than Var 70 and 71, cannot be dated later than 1000 A.D. The repeated mention of only the Vāmas[146] among the Śākta sects tends to suggest that the Right-hand school, even if it did originate, was not so prominent at the time of recasting the Viṣṇuite Kūrma-p. As the Kūrma names a good number of sects which were influenced by the Śāktas, it is not probable that it would have left out the name of one of the two most important divisions of the Śāktas themselves, if it were aware of the importance of those two divisions. Now, Aparārka is quite familiar with the Left- and Right-hand Śāktas. He not only mentions

[145] For instance, Var 70, 43 (*veda-mūrtir ahaṃ* etc.) = Kūr II, 37, 148.

[146] Cf. Kūr I, 12, 258; I, 16, 117; I, 29, 25; II, 16, 15; and II, 37, 147.

these two schools himself in his com.[147] but quotes from the 'Devī-purāṇa' a few verses in one of which these two Śākta schools are mentioned[148]. The nature of the quoted verses shows that the two Śākta schools were well-known to the people at the time this part of the Devī-purāṇa was written. So the Right-hand school must have begun not later than the beginning of the eleventh century.

The evidences adduced above show that the Kūrma-p. must have been recast not later than 1000 A.D. Let us see if the date can be placed earlier still. Bhāskarācārya in his Brahmasūtra-bhāṣya speaks of the four sects of the Māheśvaras—Pāśupatas, Śaivas, Kāpālikas and Kāṭhaka-siddhāntins[149]. As Bhāskara is placed between 850 and 980 A.D. and 'probably at some point near the beginning of the period' (ranging from 900 to 1350 A.D.)[150], the epithet 'Śaiva' as distinct from 'Pāśupata' must be dated not later than 900 A.D. 'The Tamil poets Tirumūlar who lived somewhere about A.D. 800, Sundarar, who was either a contemporary of Tirumūlar or came a little later, and Māṇikka Vāchakar, whose date is not far removed from A.D. 900, all refer to the Āgamas, and both Tirumūlar and Māṇikka use much of their phraseology'[151]. J. C. Chatterji informs us that the teaching of the Āgamas was popular in Kashmir before Vasugupta who flourished about 850 A.D. and supports this statement by references to the Āgamas[152]. These evidences show that the 'Āgamas' became current not later than about 800 A.D. Therefore the Kūrma-p., which, as we have seen above, does not seem to be familiar with the 'Āgamas', cannot possibly be later than 800 A.D. References to the worship of Brahmā[153] in

[147] Com., pp. 16 and 17.

[148] Aparārka's com., p. 16.—*yad api devīpurāṇe—' vāma-dakṣiṇa-vettā yo mūtr-vedārtha-pāragaḥ*| etc.'

[149] Bhāskara-bhāṣya, p. 127. In some places the reading 'kāruka-siddhāntin' for 'kāṭhaka-siddhāntin' is found. Cf. Brahmasūtra with the com. of Govindānanda, published by the ASB, p. 592.

[150] Farquhar, Outline, pp. 221-222. Cf. also the Bhūmikā to Vindhyeśvarī. Prasāda's edition of the Brahmasūtra with Bhāskara-bhāṣya.

[152] Farquhar, Outline, p. 193.

[152] Kashmir Śaivism, pp. 7-10 and 36a.

[153] In Kūr I, 2, 100b each of the four Āśramas is further divided into three kinds, viz., the Vaiṣṇava, the Brāhma and the Hara-āśrama. (Note that Kūr I, 2, 99 to the end deal with the different sect-marks, of which the Śaiva sect-mark is said to be the most effective. Therefore this part of the chapter was certainly added by the Pāśupatas). In Kūr I, 2, 104 it is said that those who take recourse to Brahmā should always bear the sect-mark *(tilaka)* on the forehead; and in Kūr I, 28, 19 Brahmā, Viṣṇu and Sūrya are said to be worshipped in the Kali age. Also cf. Kūr II, 18, 90-91 and II, 26, 39 in which there are directions for the worship of Brahmā.

those parts of the Kūrma-p. which did not certainly belong to the Viṣṇuite Kūrma tend to indicate that at the time of the recast the worship of the god did not die out totally. Hence from the consideration of Brahmā-worship also the date of the recast cannot be placed later than 800 A.D. Thus we get the lower limit of the date of recasting.

It has been shown above that the upper limit of the date of composition of the Viṣṇuite Kūrma-p. cannot possibly be earlier than 500 A.D., and now we get the lower limit of the date of recasting. If a period of at least fifty years be allowed to intervene between the date of composition of the Viṣṇuite Kūrma-p. and that of its recasting, then *the date of composition of the Viṣṇuite Kūrma-p. falls between 550 and 650 A.D. and that of its recasting between 700 and 800 A.D.* As in the Rudra-gītā of the Varāha-p. the words *raudra* and *pāśupata* are used to mean the Āgamic Śaivas as well as their literature, the Rudra-gītā should not be placed later than about the beginning of the ninth century A.D. Now, *the Kūrma-p. being earlier than the Rudra-gītā, the date of recasting the former should be placed towards the beginning of the 8th century A.D.*

We shall now pass on to the Smṛti-chapters with which we are really concerned. In the introductory chapters of the Kūrma-p., Jñāna and Karman (meaning the duties of the castes and Āśramas) are mentioned more than once as the two main factors in the attainment of final beatitude. The Indradyumna story being inseparably connected with the description of these two factors, it is highly probable that the Viṣṇuite Kūrma-p. contained chapters on Varṇāśramadharma. Kūr I, 2, 36-75 and I, 3 seem to be parts, if not the whole, of these earlier chapters. The topics of Varṇāśramadharma in these chapters have been interwoven with the accounts of creation in such a manner that they cannot be considered as interpolations. Hence it is highly probable that these chapters also come from the same date as that of the Viṣṇuite Kūrma-p.

The whole of Kūr I, 2 is certainly not the work of a single hand. Verses 76-87 seem to have been added later. In Kūr I, 2, 73-75 Yogins are mentioned separately and said to constitute a fifth Āśrama. But in Kūr I, 2, 76-87, wherein the four Āśramas are further subdivided, the existence of a fifth Āśrama is denied. This contradiction cannot be ascribed to one and the same hand.

It has already been said that in the Viṣṇuite Kūrma-p. nothing intervened between the so-called Īśvara-gītā (i.e., Kūr II, 1-11) and Kūr II, 43, and that the Vyāsa-gītā (comprising Kūr II, 12-33) was added by the Pāśupatas at the time of recasting the Viṣṇuite Kūrma-p. Therefore the date of this Vyāsa-gītā is the same as that of the recast.

The whole of the Vyāsa-gītā, however, should not be assigned to the above date. Kūr II, 14, 57b-61a, dealing with Gāyatrī-uddhāra after the manner of the Tantriks, are most probably spurious. They are not found in the Veṅk. ed. of the Kūrma or in the corresponding chapter of the Padma-p. (Ādi-kh.). Kūr II, 31 also, treating of the glories of the holy place named Kapālamocana, seems to be a later interpolation on account of its irrelevant character and the breach it creates in the treatment of the subject-matter of the Vyāsa-gītā.

Here a question may be raised as to whether the Uśanas-saṃhitā was incorporated into the Kūrma-p. to form the Vyāsa-gītā or it was some chapters of the Vyāsa-gītā which were taken off from their source and given the name 'Uśanas-saṃhitā'. The Pāśupata character of the Saṃhitā, of course, appears to indicate that the Kūrma-p. was the source of the Saṃhitā. But a comparison of readings of the Uśanas-saṃhitā, the Vyāsa-gītā and the chapters (51-60) of the Padma-p. (Ādi-kh.) shows that the Uśanas-saṃhitā is the original. That the sectarian character of the Saṃhitā is no argument against its originality is further proved by a verse quoted by Vijñāneśvara under Yāj. I, 253-254. The verse is ascribed to Uśanas, and it pretends to report the speech of Bhagavat Śiva himself[154]. As this verse and many others, also ascribed to Uśanas, are not traceable in our Uśanas-saṃhitā, it is highly probable that there existed another Smṛti of Uśanas and that it was influenced by the Śiva-worshippers.

Kūr I, 28-38, treating of Yuga-dharma and glorification of Benares and Prayāga, did not certainly belong to the Kūrma-p. in its Viṣṇuite character. In Kūr I, 1 the contents of the Purāṇa are enumerated as follows :

> *yatra dharmārtha-kāmānāṃ mokṣasya ca munīśvarāḥ|*
> *māhātmyam akhilaṃ brahma jñāyate parameśvaraḥ||*
> *sargaś ca pratisargaś ca vaṃśo manvantarāṇi ca|*
> *vaṃśānucaritaṃ puṇyā divyā prāsaṅgikī kathā||*

It is to be noted that in this enumeration there is no mention of the glorification of holy places. Moreover, at the beginning of Kūr I, 39 the sages, before they ask Sūta to speak on the geography of the world, refer to the topic of creation by Svayaṃbhū as just finished by him[155]. This reference points to Kūr I, 27 and the other chapters preceding it, in which the creation has been described. So the spurious

154 *uśanasā tu. . . . .| tathā—'pitā pitāmahe yojyaḥ pūrṇe saṃvatsare sutaiḥ| mātā mātāmahe tāvad ityāha bhagavāñ śivaḥ||*

155 *kathito bhavatā sūta sargaḥ svāyaṃbhuvaḥ śubhaḥ|*
idānīṃ śrotum icchāmas trilokasyāsya maṇḍalam|| Kūr I, 39, 2.

character of Kūr I, 28-38, which intervene between Kūr I, 27 and I, 39, is obvious.

Of these eleven spurious chapters, the first two (i.e., Kūr I, 28 and 29) seem to have been added by the Pāśupatas. These two chapters narrate the story of the meeting of, and conversation between, the bereaved Arjuna and the sage Vyāsa, who was going to Benares on account of the advent of the vicious Kali age. The former asked the latter what his duty was, and the latter preached the glory of Benares and the worship of Śiva. As a result of this preaching, Arjuna turned a staunch Śivaite. The way in which Śiva and Benares are praised in the story, shows that these two chapters could have been written by none but a Śiva-worshipper. Hence they are to be dated not earlier than 700 A.D. They are probably to be dated between 700 and 800 A.D., the time when the Pāśupatas recast the Viṣṇuite Kūrma-p. It is, however, sure that as Vyāsa, who narrates the Vārāṇasī-māhātmya in Kūr I, 30-34, is introduced first in I, 28 as proceeding to Benares, Kūr I, 28-29 cannot be later than I, 30-34, which are drawn upon by Vācaspatimiśra and cannot, therefore, be placed later than the 14th century A.D.

In Kūr I, 30-34, the greatness of Benares and the results of living, performing various pious acts, and meeting death there, are described. The different Śiva-lingas (viz., Oṃkāra, Kṛttivāseśvara, Madhyameśvara etc.) of the place are named and glorified, and stories are narrated for the purpose. A pool (kuṇḍa) named Piśāca-mocana is glorified with a story, according to which a fiend (piśāca) is said to have bathed in it to get rid of his fiendhood. There are also names of various other holy places which Vyāsa visited.

The above contents of Kūr I, 30-34 are sufficient to prove their Śivaite character and origin. That these chapters are to be ascribed to the Pāśupatas is further proved by references to the Pāśupatas and their systems and vows[156]. So these chapters should not be dated earlier than 700 A.D. The opening verse

māhātmyam avimuktasya yathāvat samudīritam|
idānīṃ ca prayāgasya māhātmyaṃ brūhi suvrata||

of Kūr I, 35 seems to presuppose Kūr I, 30-34 (on Benares). Kur I, 35-38 (treating of Prayāga-māhātmya), which are drawn upon by Hemādri in his Canturvarga-cintāmaṇi and by Vācaspatimiśra in his Tīrtha-cintāmaṇi and are earlier than Mat 103-112, also drawn upon by him and Caṇḍeśvara, cannot be dated later than the end of the 12th century A.D. (see next para.). So Kūr I, 30-34 cannot possibly be later than the middle of that century, and are probably

[156] Kūr I, 31, 6; 33, 6 ff.; 33, 21-22; and so on.

to be dated between 700 and 800 A.D., there being nothing to prove a later date.

Kūr I, 35-38, which deal with the glorification of Prayāga, are quite unconnected with the chapters preceding or following them, and form a separate unit by themselves. They exhibit very little Śivaite colour unlike the chapters interpolated by the Pāśupatas. So it is highly probable that they were inserted into the Kūrma-p. by a non-Pāśupata who wanted to glorify only the place and the river Ganges but not any particular deity, and that this insertion was made after the appropriation of the Kūrma-p. by the Pāśupatas. Hence these chapters are to be dated later than 750 A.D., if not 800. As verses have been quoted from chap. 36 in the Caturvarga-cintāmaṇi of Hemādri and from chaps. 36 and 37 in the Tīrtha-cintāmaṇi of Vācaspatimiśra[157], their date cannot be placed later than the beginning of the thirteenth century A.D. In Kūr II, 38, 3 there is a clear reference to the chapters (I, 35-38) on Prayāga-māhātmya. So, these chapters cannot be later than Kūr II, 38. Now, Kūr II, 34-42, being drawn upon by Vidyākara Vājapeyin, Narasiṃha Vājapeyin and Mādhavācārya[158], cannot be later than 1250 A.D. Hence Kūr I, 35-38 also must be earlier than 1250 A.D. A comparison between the glorification of Prayāga in Kūr I, 35-38 and Mat 103-112 shows the earlier date of the former. In the Matsya the number of chapters dealing with the Māhātmya is greater; and in those of its chapters which are common to the two Purāṇas there are many additional verses not found in the Kūrma. That these additional chapters and verses of the Matsya are not very late interpolations but are to be dated earlier than 1300 A.D. is shown by the numerous quotations made from them and the common chapters by Vācaspatimiśra and Caṇḍeśvara (see App.). If gaps of at least 50 years each be allowed between Caṇḍeśvara and Mat 103-112 and between the latter and Kūr I, 35-38, then the lower limit of the date of the chapters of the Kūrma cannot be placed after the end of the 12th century A.D.

Kūr II, 34-42 name a good number of holy places sacred to Śiva, and stories are often told for their glorification. References to the 'Purāṇas'[159] in these chapters show that their contents are derived from other Purāṇas. It is not known when these chapters were inserted into the Kūrma-p. The Pāśupata character of these chapters, and the expression that 'the glory of the holy places is told in connection with penances[160]' show that these chapters cannot

157 See App. 158 See App.

159 Kūr II, 34, 2; II, 37, 264; II, 38, 6.

160 Kūr II, 42, 24.

be earlier than the Vyāsa-gītā in which the penances are dealt with. In Kūr II, 38, 3 there is a clear reference to the chapters (viz., I, 35-38) on Prayāga-māhātmya which are to be dated not earlier than 750 A.D., or rather 800. So Kūr II, 34-42 also cannot be assigned to an earlier date. As Vidyākara Vājapeyin and Narasiṃha Vājapeyin have drawn upon Kūr II, 37, and as Mādhavācārya has also drawn upon Kūr II, 36 and 39[161], the date of Kūr II, 34-42 can by no means be placed later than 1250 A.D.

[161] See App.

CHAPTER III

THE CHRONOLOGY OF THE PURĀṆIC CHAPTERS ON HINDU RITES AND CUSTOMS

THE MINOR PURĀṆAS

1. THE VĀMANA-PURĀṆA [1]

The extant Vāmana deals in chap. 11 with hells, in chap. 12 with Karma-vipāka, in chap. 14 with the duties of the castes and Āśramas, general customs, eatables and noneatables, purification and impurity, in chaps. 16 and 80 with Vratas, and in chap. 95 with Viṣṇu-worship. It lacks, however, almost all the five themes characteristic of the older Mahāpurāṇas. It is mainly given to the glorification of Kurukṣetra and the adjoining holy places, and in connection with this glorification, legends of gods and demons have been narrated. The contents of this Purāṇa do not agree with the information regarding the 'Vāmana-purāṇa' contained in the Matsya and the Skanda. These two Purāṇas describe the 'Vāmana' as follows:

"That in which the four-faced god (Brahmā) taught the three objects of existence in connection with the greatness of Trivikrama, which treats, also, of the Kūrma-kalpa, and which consists of ten thousand verses, is called the Vāmana-purāṇa"[2].

[1] The Vaṅga. ed. is the same as the Veṅk. ed. Both consist of 95 chapters. The variations in readings in these two editions are so small in number that one seems to be a reprint of the other.
The Ms of the Vāmana-purāṇa described by H. P. Shastri in his Cat. of Sans. Mss, ASB, Vol. V, pp. 645 ff. seems to differ much our printed editions.

[2] *trivikramasya māhātmyam adhikṛtya caturmukhaḥ|*
trivargam abhyadhāt tac ca vāmanaṃ parikīrtitam||
purāṇaṃ daśa-sāhasraṃ kūrma-kalpānugaṃ śivam|
* * * * * *

Mat 53, 44-45 and Sk VII, i, 2, 63-64.

In the extant Vāmana-p., however, there is no mention of the Kūrma-kalpa, nor is the Purāṇa said to have been narrated by Brahmā. On the other hand, it is narrated by Pulastya to Nārada, and not even by Lomaharṣaṇa to the sages of the Naimiṣa forest, as is generally the case with the other Purāṇas. These facts prove that the extant Vāmana is not the same as noticed by the Matsya and the Skanda-p. It can safely be called an Upapurāṇa rather than a Mahāpurāṇa. The Kūrma (I, 1, 19) and the Garuḍa-p. (I, 227, 19) mention a Vāmana among the Upapurāṇas. It is not, however, possible to say definitely whether the extant Vāmana is the same as the Vāmana-upapurāṇa mentioned in these two Purāṇas.

The Śaiva materials in the present Vāmana as contrasted with the title and contents given in the Matsya and Skanda, show that the Purāṇa in its earlier form was a Vaiṣṇava work, and that it was later recast by the Śiva-worshippers who changed the work with additions and alterations in such a way that very little of its earlier contents was retained. The appearance of Lomaharṣaṇa as an interlocutor in a few chapters from Vām 22, 47 seems to indicate that the Vāmana-p. in its earlier form probably began with the verses in chap. 23, the opening verse being Vām 22, 47 (of course, with some change in the third line). If we connect this supposed opening verse with chap. 23, we have

sarasvatī-dṛṣadvatyor antare kurujāṅgale|
munipravaram āsīnaṃ purāṇaṃ lomaharṣaṇam|
apṛcchanta dvijavarāḥ prabhavaṃ surasattamāḥ||

ṛṣaya ūcuḥ—

brūhi vāmana-māhātmyam utpattiṃ ca viśeṣataḥ|
yathā balir niyamito dattaṃ rājyaṃ śatakratoḥ||

lomaharṣaṇa uvāca—

śṛṇvantu munayaḥ prītā vāmanasya mahātmanaḥ|
utpattiṃ ca prabhāvaṃ ca nivāsaṃ kurujāṅgale||

&c &c &c

Such a beginning agrees considerably with the accounts contained in the Matsya, Skanda and Agni-purāṇa referred to above, and in this case Lomaharṣaṇa becomes the narrator of the Purāṇa. All the chapters ascribed to Lomaharṣaṇa in our present Vāmana cannot, however, be taken to have belonged to the Purāṇa in its

Sk reads '*tu*' for '*ca*' in the second line. The Agni-p. (272, 18), on the other hand, says that the Vāmana-p. was declared in the Dhaumya-kalpa (*vāmanaṃ daśa-sāhasraṃ dhaumya-kalpe hareḥ kathām*).

earlier form. Most of these are undoubtedly of comparatively late origin. Even chap. 23, which seems to contain verses from the earlier Vāmana, have others which were added at the time of recasting, because these latter verses presuppose the preceding chapters which are Śaiva in character. These facts show that inspite of the probable retention of verses from the earlier Vāmana, our present Purāṇa is practically a new work.

As to the date of composition of the present Vāmana there are two divergent opinions, viz., those of Haraprasad Shastri and H. H. Wilson. Of these two scholars, the former says: "The Vāmana-purāṇa, so far as we find it, seems to be very old.

(1) The incarnations of Viṣṇu are not limited to the number of ten. Hayaśīrṣa is prominently mentioned as the third incarnation. No Avatāra after Vāmana is mentioned. The word 'avatāra' is rarely used in connection with Viṣṇu, but the word 'prādurbhāva' in its stead has been used.

(2) There is no sectarian spirit in this work,—Brahmā, Viṣṇu and Śiva are equally respected.

(3) Some of the islands of the Indian Ocean seem to be mentioned, viz., Indradvīpa, Nāgadvīpa, Kaṭāha, Siṃhala and Varuṇa.

(4) The boundary of India as given in chap. 13, verses 11-12, cannot be later than the 2nd century A.D. The boundaries are: Kirātas to the east, Yavanas to the west, Āndhras to the south and Turks to the north. The geography as given in the Vāmana-purāṇa is older than that of Rājaśekhara's Kāvya-mīmāṃsā (chap. 17) and that of the Bṛhat-saṃhitā of Varāhamihira. It can be placed in the 2nd century A.D. with great probability.

(5) One of the reasons to consider this work old, is that Tulasī is never mentioned to be a sacred leaf in the worship of Viṣṇu. Tulasī has now come to universal use, and its origin from Vruḍā, the wife of Jālandhara, is given in the Padma-purāṇa"[3].

None of the above arguments adduced by H. P. Shastri in support of his view seems to be very convincing for the following reasons. Firstly, in the Purāṇa there is no exhaustive and systematic list of incarnations of Viṣṇu. So the disordered, and often stray, mention of the names of incarnations cannot be relied upon to form an idea of the list of incarnations which was known to the author of the present Vāmana or to assign any particular name to any particular position in this list. Secondly, any list of Viṣṇu's incarnations which contains more names than the famous ten, cannot be taken to point unmistakably to an early date, because long lists of incar-

[3] Shastri, Cat. of Sans. Mss, ASB, Vol. V, Preface, pp. clxxxii-clxxxiii.

nations are found to occur in the later works also[4]. Thirdly, in total contradiction to Shastri's statement, the word 'avatīrṇa' has been used as often as five times in connection with Viṣṇu[5] and once in connection with Devī[6], whereas the word 'prādurbhāva' has been used only once[7]. Fourthly, the absence of sectarian spirit is not characteristic of the early works only. The 'Pañcāyatana-pūjā' or Pañcopāsanā, i.e., the worship of the five deities—Viṣṇu, Śiva, Gaṇeśa, Sūrya and Durgā, which is certainly not of very early origin, testifies to the compromising spirit of the people of later ages. Further, we learn from Vidyākara Vājapeyin (1370-1500 A.D.), one of the noted Smṛti-writers of Orissa, that in his time there were people who equally revered Viṣṇu and Śiva[8]. Fifthly, the geographical portion of the Vāmana-p., in which Indradvīpa, Nāgadvīpa etc. are mentioned and the boundaries of India are given, is undoubtedly based on that of the Mārkaṇḍeya-p., for the greater part of this portion of the Vāmana agrees remarkably with the Mārkaṇḍeya-p. (chap. 57). Sixthly, in a verse *(bilva-patraṃ śamī-patraṃ* etc.*)* quoted in Raghunandana's Smṛti-tattva (vol. I, p. 411) from the 'Vāmana-p'., there is mention of 'Tulasī' and 'Kṛṣṇa-tulasī'. This verse, which is not found in our edition, has most probably been lost, for in several other cases also our edition contains traces of losses and corruptions. For instance, in Vām 95, 23-43, which enumerate the articles to be given away for the pleasure of Viṣṇu in the different months from Māgha, there is no mention of the month of Śrāvaṇa. That a verse on the gifts in Śrāvaṇa occurred between the verses 38 and 39 (on the gifts in Āṣāḍha and Bhādra) of Vām 95, is evidenced not only by its remarkable absence but also by the verses quoted in Aparārka's com. on Yāj. (pp. 364-365), Ballālasena's Dānasāgara (fol. 237a) and Hemādri's Caturvarga-cintāmaṇi, (I, pp. 885-886).

All the above facts go seriously against the arguments put forth by H. P. Shastri in favour of an early date of the present Vāmana.

Professor Wilson's view that the Vāmana-p. was probably compiled three or four centuries ago[9] is equally untenable. Had the Purāṇa been so late, the verses quoted by the early commentators and Nibandha-writers from the 'Vāmana-purāṇa' would not have been found in our present text.

[4] See, Grierson, JRAS, 1909, pp. 607 f; and 1910, pp. 87 f.

[5] Cf. Vām 29, verses 19, 20 and 26; 30, 14; and 31, 4.

[6] Ibid., 56, 67.

[7] Ibid., 92, 65.

[8] Nityācārapaddhati, p. 155.

[9] Wilson, Viṣṇu-Purāṇa, Preface, p. lxxvi.

The above two views being thus found untenable, we shall have to try in our own way to determine the date of the Purāṇa. The repeated mention of the Rāśis and the Nakṣatras from Aśvinī to Revatī shows that the Purāṇa cannot possibly be earlier than 200 A.D. The repeated mention of the 'Śaivas' and 'Pāśupatas' as two distinct sections of the Śiva-worshippers[10] points to a still later date of the Purāṇa. From the Kūrma-p. we understand that these two distinctive epithets were unknown to the beginning of the 8th century A.D.[11] Therefore, the Vāmana-p. cannot be earlier than 700 A.D. Vidyākara Vājapeyin refers to chap. 85 (on 'gajendramokṣaṇa') of this Purāṇa in his Nityācārapaddhati, Gadādhara quotes verses from chap. 94 in his Kālasāra, Gopālabhaṭṭa from chaps. 94 and 95 in his Haribhaktivilāsa, Narasiṃha Vājapeyin from chaps. 14 and 95 in his Nityācārapradīpa, Govindānanda from chaps. 14, 16 and 95 in his Varṣakriyā-kaumudī, Śuddhikriyā-kaumudī and Śrāddhakriyā-kaumudī, Raghunandana from chaps. 14, 16, 94 and 95 in his Smṛti-tattva, Vācaspatimiśra from chaps. 79 and 83 in his Tīrtha-cintāmaṇi, Śūlapāṇi from chap. 95 in his Śrāddha-viveka, Śrīdatta Upādhyāya from chaps. 14 and 95 in his Kṛtyācāra, Caṇḍeśvara from chaps. 14 and 95 in his Kṛtya-ratnākara, Mādhavācārya from chap. 14 in his Bhāṣya on the Parāśarasmṛti, Hemādri from chaps. 14, 16, 17, 34, 92 and 95 in his Caturvarga-cintāmaṇi, Devaṇabhaṭṭa from chaps. 14 and 34 in his Smṛti-candrikā, Ballālasena from chap. 95 in his Dānasāgara, and Aparārka from chap. 95 in his com. on Yāj. (see App.). So, the date of the present Vāmana-p. can never be placed later than 1000 A.D., because the commentators and Nibandha-writers, who draw upon this Purāṇa, hail from different parts of India. Thus the date of the Purāṇa falls between 700 and 1000 A.D. Let us see if it is possible to place the date within narrower limits. For this purpose we shall have to determine the date of composition of chap. 14 dealing with Smṛti-matter. This chapter is included in the story of Sukeśin which constitutes Vām 11-15 and which is put into the Purāṇa on a chance allusion that serves as a clue to its narration. The outline of this story is as follows:

Sukeśin, the king of the Rākṣasas, worships Śiva and receives an aerial city of voluntary movement. Once he goes to the land of Magadha and meets many sages who, at his request, narrate to him the twelve kinds of Dharma meant for Devas, Daityas, Rākṣasas, Mānavas and others. Going to describe the Dharma of the Mānavas at the request of Sukeśin, the sages tell him of the division of the

[10] Vām 6, 87; 53, 3; and 67, 10-11. [11] See under Kūrma-p. above.

earth into islands (dvīpa), the areas, locations and inhabitants of these islands, and the hells to be found in the Puṣkara-dvīpa. The mention of hells rouses curiosity in Sukeśin to hear something of Karma-vipāka, and the sages satisfy him accordingly. Next, the sages name the divisions and sub-divisions of the Jambu-dvīpa, enumerate the rivers, mountains and races of the Kumāra-dvīpa, one of the sub-divisions of the Jambu-dvīpa, and describe the duties of the castes and Āśramas to be found there. Sukeśin then repairs to his city and orders the practice of the Dharma proclaimed by the sages. By virtue of its practice, the Rākṣasas attain heavenly effulgence, and as a result the Sun-god is enraged and causes the city to fall down on the pretext of the crime which the Rākṣasas have committed by forsaking their Svadharma and accepting Para-dharma. At this conduct of the Sun Śiva becomes angry and casts the Sun-god down to the earth. At last, being propitiated, he places the Sun-god and the city in their respective places.

The above outline shows that the story consists of quite different parts put carelessly together. Here we shall not trouble ourselves so much with the question as to whether these parts were added to the main story at the time the latter was inserted into the Purāṇa or at a later age, as with that of the contemporaneity of composition of chaps. 12-14; for in the latter case we shall be in a position to make a nearer approach to the date of composition of chap. 14.

At the beginning of chap. 15 Sukeśin orders his people to practise the thirteen characteristic branches of Dharma which he enumerates as follows:

ahiṃsā satyam asteyaṃ śaucam indriya-saṃyamaḥ|
dānaṃ dayā ca kṣāntiś ca brahmacaryam amānitā||
śubhā satyā ca madhurā vāṅ nityaṃ satkriyā-ratiḥ|
sadācāra-niṣevitvaṃ paraloka-pradāyakāḥ||[12]

As on the one hand this enumeration is necessary for giving the Rākṣasas an idea of the Dharma they are to practise and is, therefore, vitally connected with the chapter, on the other hand it presupposes the existence of chap. 14, for it is in this chapter that we can trace these characteristics. At the beginning of chap. 14 the sages enumerate the ten limbs of Dharma thus:

ahiṃsā satyam asteyaṃ dānaṃ kṣāntir damaḥ śamaḥ|
akārpaṇyaṃ ca śaucaṃ ca tapaś ca rajanīcara||
daśāṅgo rākṣasa-śreṣṭha dharmo 'sau sārvavarṇikaḥ||[13]

Some of the thirteen characteristics in Sukeśin's enumeration are found in that of the sages given here. Not only so, the beginnings

[12] Vām 15, 2-3.

[13] Vām 14, 1-2a.

in both the enumerations are similar. For those characteristics mentioned by Sukeśin which are not found in the enumeration of the sages, we can refer to the body of chap. 14. For example, the characteristics 'brahmacarya' and 'amānitā' mentioned by Sukeśin are found in verse 114 of chap. 14 *(sarva-saṅga-parityāgo brahmacaryam amānitā)*; for 'sadācāra-niṣevitva' we may refer to verses 14-17 wherein the sages glorify the practice of Sadācāra; *'satyā madhurā ca vāk'* has its parallel in verse 39 *(na niṣṭhuraṃ nāgamaśāstrahīnaṃ vākyaṃ vadet)*; and so on. The characteristics of Mānava-dharma, mentioned by the sages while describing the twelve kinds of Dharma in chap. 11 (verses 15-28), are as follows:

> *svādhyāyo brahmacaryaṃ ca dānaṃ yajanam eva ca|*
> *akārpaṇyam anāyāso dayāhiṃsā-kṣamādayaḥ||*
> *jitendriyatvaṃ śaucaṃ ca maṅgalyaṃ bhaktir ucyate|*
> *śaṃkare bhāskare devyāṃ dharmo 'yaṃ mānavaḥ smṛtaḥ||*[14]

This enumeration shows that it contributes much less to Sukeśin's enumeration than chap. 14 does. Another point is to be noted here. At the end of chap. 14 the sages refer to the good of practising one's Svadharma and says that the acceptance of Para-dharma incurs the rage of the Sun-god who always tries to do harm to the sinner. This seems to be an indirect warning to Sukeśin, but he does not seem to take it as such, for we see in chap. 15 that the practice of Varṇāśramadharma (or rather Mānava-dharma) instead of Rākṣasa-dharma incurs the rage of the Sun-god who causes Sukeśin's city to fall down from the sky. All these taken together tend to show that chap. 14 was added to the main story at the time the latter was fabricated.

In chap. 11, we have seen, the sages describe the twelve kinds of Dharma including Rākṣasa-dharma[15]. But Sukeśin is not satisfied with his own Rākṣasa-dharma, and eagerly wants to hear something about Mānava-dharma—a Dharma which is practised even by sages. Such eagerness on the part of Sukeśin is necessary for the development of the story. To satisfy Sukeśin the sages begin with the geography of the earth to give him some idea about the location of the Kumāra-dvīpa before they proceed to describe the customs and usages to be found there, because, they say, men live in all the seven Dvīpas[16], and the laws and customs differ in the different Dvīpas[17]. Towards the end of chap. 11 the sages say that the

[14] Vām 11, 23-24.

[15] *paradārāvamarśitvaṃ pārakyārthe ca lolupa|*
svādhyāyas tryambake bhaktir dharmo 'yaṃ rakṣasaḥ smṛtaḥ|| Vām 11, 26.

[16] Vām 11, 30. [17] Vām 11, 43a.

Puṣkara-dvīpa contains innumerable hells, some of which they mention. This mention of hells prepares the way to the insertion of chap. 12 which deals with Karma-vipāka. It should also be noted here that chaps. 12-14 have their prototypes in the Mārkaṇḍeya-p.; viz., Vām 12 is the reproduction, with various additions and alterations, of Mārk 14 (verses 44 ff.), Vām 13 of Mārk 57, and Vām 14 of Mārk 28 (verses 11-19 and 23 ff.) and 34 (verses 6 ff.). The source of these three chapters being common, it is more probable that they were appropriated at the same time and put into the Vāmana-p. with a view to bringing it on a par with the other Purāṇas of the time, the story of Sukeśin only serving as a means of introducing them.

From the above discussion it appears that chaps. 11-15 of the Vāmana-p. were inserted into it at the same time.

We are now in a position to discuss the date of the addition of Vām 14. In Vām 14, 49b-50a the weekdays Ravi, Maṅgala, Budha, Śukra and Śani are mentioned in such a way as to convince one of the fact that these were familiar at the time of composition of chap. 14. We know that the earliest epigraphic mention of a weekday is found in the Eran inscription of 484 A.D.[18] From the evidence given by Varāhamihira we understand that the weekdays were well-known in his time. In Vām 13, 12 the Turuṣkas are mentioned *(āndhrā dakṣiṇato vīra turuṣkās tvapi cottare).* The Turuṣkas, who are quite different from the Tuṣāras or Tukhāras also mentioned in Vām 13, 41, came to India about the 9th century A.D.[19] So this chapter of the Vāmana-p. is possibly not to be dated earlier than the ninth century A.D. In Vām 12, 48 the Matsya-p. is said to be the chief of all the Purāṇas *(mukhyaṃ purāṇeṣu yathaiva mātsyaṃ).* This is significant. In almost all the lists of the eighteen Purāṇas given in the Mahāpurāṇas the Brahma-p. is regarded as the original one (ādya) and assigned the first place. It is only in the Vāyu (chap. 104) that we find the Matsya-p. occupying the first place and the Brahma-p. being placed much lower in the list. As none of the lists, in which the Brahma-p. is placed first, can reasonably be dated earlier than the fourth century A.D. and as Mat 53 (containing such a list) is to be placed between 550 and 650 A.D., it should be admitted that the custom of regarding the Brahma-p. as the first and foremost of all held ground at least down to the end of the sixth century. It might only be after this time that the Matsya-p. could have begun to be assigned the first place at least by a section of people, if not by all. But when did this happen ?

[18] Fleet, Gupta Inscriptions, pp. 88-89.

[19] It is to be noted that the word *turuṣka* occurs only in those Purāṇas, or parts thereof, which are of comparatively late dates.

The predominance of the Matsya-p., as evidenced by Vām 12, 48 and Vā 104 referred to above, is apparently connected with the high position which the Fish incarnation came to occupy in course of time among the incarnations of Viṣṇu. But when did this incarnation come to occupy such an elevated position ? Let us compare the lists of incarnations and the accounts thereof to see if we can arrive at any solution. In the Mahābhārata the group of the ten principal Prādurbhāvas or Avatāras of later ages seems to be quite unknown. The verse

matsyaḥ kūrmo varāhaś ca narasiṃho 'tha vāmanaḥ|
rāmo rāmaś ca rāmaś ca buddhaḥ kalkīti te daśa||,

which is found in the Kumbhakoṇam edition of the Mahābhārata (XII, 348, 2), is not traceable in the ASB, Bombay and Vaṅga. editions, although it is nearly the same verse as given in a Pallava inscription from which the verse is quoted below. The verses

tataḥ kaliyugasyādau dvijarāja-taruṃ śritaḥ|
bhīṣayā māgadhenaiva dharmarāja-gṛhe vasan||
kāṣāya-vastra-saṃvīto muṇḍitaḥ śukladantavān||
śuddhodana-suto buddho mohayiṣyāmi mānavān||

also, found in the Mokṣa-dharma of the Kumbhakoṇam edition, are not met with in the other editions. So the spurious character and the late origin of these verses are obvious. In the Nārāyaṇīya section of the Śānti-parvan of the Mahābhārata (XII, 339), the manifestations (prādurbhāva) of Nārāyaṇa are enumerated as the Haṃsa, the Tortoise, the Fish, the Boar, the Man-lion, the Dwarf, (Paraśu) Rāma, Rāma Dāśarathi, Sāttvata and Kalki. The lines, which contain this enumeration, seem to have been interpolated later for the following reasons. In Mbh XII, 339, 77 ff. Nārāyaṇa says to Nārada that in future he will take the forms of the Boar, the Man-lion, the twelfth Āditya (i.e., the Dwarf), Rāma of the Bhṛgu family, Rāma Dāśarathi and Sāttvata, and perform various exploits which also he relates to Nārada, adding at the end :

'*kariṣye pralayaṃ ghoram ātma-jñānābhisaṃvṛtam|*
karmāṇyaparimeyāṇi caturmūrtidharo hyaham||
kṛtvā lokān gamiṣyāmi svān ahaṃ brahma-satkṛtam||'

After this is given quite irrelevantly the list of manifestations referred to above, containing the Haṃsa, the Tortoise, the Fish and Kalki, which are not mentioned or even hinted at anywhere in the whole chapter. On the other hand, the Boar, the Man-lion and the Dwarf seem to be regarded, in the majority of cases, as the principal incarnations or manifestations of Viṣṇu. We should also note in this connection that at least in the ASB and Vaṅga. editions of the Mahābhārata there is no such evidence as may indicate that the Buddha came to be regarded as an incarnation before 200 A.D. In Mārk 4 Nārāyaṇa, both as 'saguṇa' and 'nirguṇa', is said to exist in four forms (mūrti) corresponding to the four well-known Vyūhas, viz., (1) Vāsudeva, which is indescribable (anirdeśya), ever-existent, etc., (2) Śeṣa, which supports the world and possesses the quality of darkness (tamoguṇa), (3) a third form called Pradyumna, which is full of the quality of goodness (sattvodrikta), preserves the world and establishes religion, and (4) a fourth form (apparently Aniruddha) which lies on the serpent-bed, has the quality of passion and creates beings. The third form of Nārāyaṇa, the Mārkaṇḍeya-p. further adds, became incarnated as Varāha, Nṛsiṃha, Vāmana and 'innumerable others', and has now become Māthura, i.e., Kṛṣṇa. According to Hv. 1, 41 the manifestations are the Pauṣkaraka the Boar, the Man-lion, the Dwarf, Dattātreya, Jāmadagnya, Rāma, Kṛṣṇa, Veda-vyāsa and Kalki, the last, as stated in the text, being called the tenth. Regarding the Kalki incarnation the Harivaṃśa has :

kalkī viṣṇuyaśā nāma śambhale nāmake dvijaḥ|
sarvaloka-hitārthāya bhūyaś cotpatsyate prabhuḥ||
daśamo bhāvya-saṃpanno yājñavalkya-puraḥsaraḥ|
kṣapayitvā ca tān sarvān bhāvinārthena coditān||
gaṅgā-yamunayor madhye niṣṭhāṃ prāpsyati sānugaḥ||

(Hv I, 41, 164-166a

Here the Kalki incarnation of Viṣṇu is described as future, the purpose of the incarnation being the good of all beings. In Kūr I, 50, Viṣṇu is said to have been born of Ākūti in the Svāyambhuva Manvantara, of Tuṣitā in the Svārociṣa, of Satyā (as Satya) in the Auttama, of Haryā (as Hari) in the Tāmasa, of Saṃkalpā in the Raivata, of Vikuṇṭhā (as Vaikuṇṭha) in the Cākṣuṣa, and of Aditi as Vāmana in the Vaivasvata. Nārāyaṇa, though Nirguṇa, is further said to have been manifested in four (somewhat modified Vyūha) forms due to Guṇa ; viz., (1) Vāsudeva, which is indivisible, beyond the Guṇas, etc., (2) Śiva, also called Kāla, which carries on destruction, (3) Pradyumna, which is full of the quality of goodness (sattvodrikta) and preserves the world, and (4) Aniruddha, also called Brahmā, which creates the world when Nārāyaṇa sleeps with Pradyumna after destruction. Viṣṇu-Nārāyaṇa is also said to be born as Vyāsa to divide the One, i.e., the Veda, into four parts. It should be noted that in its description of the four forms of Nārāyaṇa, the Kūrma-p. has not only been influenced by the Mārkaṇḍeya-p. but has many lines borrowed from the latter.

Brahma-p., chap. 180, which is the reproduction, with some additions, of Mārk 4, 36 ff., describes the four forms of Viṣṇu, the third being said to have become the Boar, the Man-lion, the Dwarf, Jāmadagnya, Dattātreya, Rāma Dāśarathi and 'innumerable others', and the 'present' Māthura. Br 213, which betrays the influence of the Harivaṃśa, enumerates the manifestations as the Boar, the Man-lion, the Dwarf, Dattātreya, Jāmadagnya, Rāma, Māthura, Kalki Viṣṇuyaśas and many others *(ete cānye ca bahavaḥ)*. Regarding Kalki the Brahma-p. says:

'*kalkī viṣṇuyaśā nāma śambhala-grāma-saṃbhavaḥ|*
sarvaloka-hitārthāya bhūyo devo mahāyaśāḥ||'

This verse is a reproduction, with some changes, of Hv I, 41, 164 quoted above. According to the Ahirbudhnya-saṃhitā (5, 50) the principal Vibhavas are thirty-nine in number, in which the Tortoise (called Kamaṭheśvara) occupies the fifteenth, the Boar the sixteenth, the Man-lion the seventeenth, the Fish (ekaśṛṅgatanu[20]) the twenty-eighth, the Dwarf (vāmana-deha) the twenty-ninth, Kṛṣṇa the thirty-fourth, Paraśurāma the thirty-fifth, Rāma Dhanurdhara the thirty-sixth, and Kalki the thirty-eighth place, there being no mention of the Buddha. Regarding Kalki the Saṃhitā says:

'*yo mardayati kalkyākhyo dasyūṃs tiṣya-yugāntajān|*
sūryopari-sthitenaiva mardanena sa gīyate||'

In Bhāg I,3; II, 7; VI, 8 and XI, 4 there are four lists of Avatāras varying in length as well as order. All these lists include the Fish, the Buddha and Kalki. In the third list the Fish occupies the first place, but that is clearly due to chance. The popular idea as to the purposes of the Buddha and Kalki incarnations has not changed in any appreciable degree. Regarding the Buddha incarnation Bhāg I, 3, 24 says:

'*tataḥ kalau saṃpravṛtte saṃmohāya suradviṣām|*
buddho nāmnāñjana-sutaḥ kīkaṭeṣu bhaviṣyati||';

Bhāg II, 7, 37 has

'*devadviṣāṃ nigama-vartmani niṣṭhitānāṃ*
pūrbhir mayena vihitābhir adṛśyaturbhiḥ|
lokān ghnatāṃ mati-vimoham atipralobhaṃ
veṣaṃ vidhāya bahu bhāṣyata aupadharmam||';

[20] In Ag 2, 15 the Fish is called 'ekaśṛṅgadhara'.

and Bhāg VI, 8, 19 has

'* * * * *buddhas tu pāṣaṇḍagaṇa-pramādāt . . . prapātu.*'

With respect to the Kalki incarnation Bhāg I, 3, 25 says:

'*athāsau yuga-saṃdhyāyāṃ dasyu-prāyeṣu rājasu|*
janitā viṣṇuyaśaso nāmnā kalkir jagatpatiḥ||';

Bhāg II, 7, 38 has

'*yarhy ālayeṣv api satāṃ na kathā hareḥ syuḥ*
pāṣaṇḍino dvija-janā vṛṣalā nṛdevāḥ|
svāhā svadhā vaṣaḍ iti sma giro na yatra
śāstā bhaviṣyati kaler bhagavān yugānte||';

and Bhāg VI, 8, 19 has

'*kalkiḥ kaleḥ kāla-malāt prapātu|*'

In Mat 259 and 260 Rāma, the Boar, the Man-lion, the Dwarf, the Fish and the Tortoise are mentioned in connection with the construction of images. These chapters being influenced by and based on Bṛhat-saṃhitā, chap. 58 (*pratimā-lakṣaṇaṃ nāma*), their date cannot be earlier than the sixth century A.D. Mat 54 describes the Nakṣatrapuruṣa-vrata in which the different limbs of Viṣṇu are worshipped with the mention of the names of his different incarnations including the famous ten. The same Vrata is also given in Bṛhat-saṃhitā, chap. 105. A comparison between these two chapters shows that the chapter in the Matsya has not only that in the Bṛhat-saṃhitā as its prototype but makes a distinct advance over the former by introducing the names of the ten Avatāras. The verse containing the name of the Buddha in Mat 47 must be dated much later, for the Vāyu, from which the Matsya has borrowed the chapter, does not contain it. The Pādma Tantra, which is dated earlier than 800 A.D. by Schrader,[21] 'says (I, 2, 31) that of the ten Avatāras the Fish, the Tortoise and the Boar have sprung from Vāsudeva; the Man-lion, Dwarf, Śrīrāma and Paraśurāma from Saṃkarṣaṇa; Balarāma from Pradyumna; and Kṛṣṇa and Kalki from Aniruddha; and it indicates that the other Avatāras (viz., Puruṣa, Satya, Acyuta, Buddha, etc.) are to be distributed in a similar way.'[22] The Viṣvaksena-saṃhitā includes the Buddha and Paraśurāma among the

[21] Schrader, Introduction to the Pāñcarātra and the Ahirbudhnya-saṃhitā, p. 20.
[22] Ibid., p. 48.

secondary Avatāras[23]. A Pallava inscription, dated about the latter half of the seventh century A.D., contains the verse

matsyaḥ kūrmo varāhaś ca nārasiṃho 'tha vāmanaḥ|
rāmo rāmaś ca rāmaś ca buddhaḥ kalkī ca te daśa||[24]

Nammalvar, alias Saint Śaṭagopa, who belonged to the ninth century A.D., gives a hymn which contains 'the conception of the Buddha as an incarnation of Viṣṇu come to delude the Asuras'[25]. According to Gḍ I, 202 *(viṣṇudharmākhya-vidyā-varṇanaṃ nāma)* the different Mūrtis of Viṣṇu are the Matsya, Trivikrama, Vāmana, Narasiṃha, Rāma, Varāha, Nārāyaṇa, Kapila, Datta, Hayagrīva, Makara-dhvaja, Nārada, Kūrma, Dhanvantari, Śeṣa, Yajña, Vyāsa, Buddha and Kalki, the last two being invoked for protection from the Pāṣaṇḍas and the sins (of the Kali age) respectively *(buddhaḥ pāṣaṇḍa-saṃghātāt kalkir avatu kalmaṣāt)*. The nature of the contents of the chapter tends to betray its comparatively late origin[26].

The lists given above are perhaps sufficient to show that popular views regarding the names and numbers of the principal incarnations varied hopelessly before 800 A.D.; that though the group of the ten principal Avatāras with the Fish at the head originated much early, the names of the Avatāras constituting the group often varied; and that the group does not seem to have attained the position of general acceptance before 800 A.D. It also appears from the lists that the mission of the Buddha incarnation was to that time supposed to be the delusion of the Asuras, i.e., Jains and Buddhists, and that of Kalki the extermination of the Pāṣaṇḍins and Dasyus, the removal of 'the dirt of the Kali age', or the good of the people.

Let us now examine some other lists of incarnations and the accounts thereof. The Agni-p. describes, in chaps. 2-16[27], the ten Avatāras of Viṣṇu, viz., Matsya, Kūrma, Varāha, Narasiṃha, Vāmana, Paraśurāma, Rāma, Kṛṣṇa, Buddha and Kalki. Though the Agni-p. believes in the innumerable incarnations of Viṣṇu *(avatārā asaṃkhyātā atītānāgatādayaḥ)*, it lays special stress on the group of ten[28]. About the Buddha incarnation it says that being defeated by the Daityas the gods sought the protection of Viṣṇu who, consequently, was born as Māyāmoha to Śuddhodana and

[23] Ibid., pp. 47-48.

[24] H. Krishna Shastri, The Memoirs of the Archaeological Survey of India, Vol. 26, p. 5.

[25] ABORI, Vol. XIV, 1932-33, pp. 200-201.

[26] See under Garuḍa-purāṇa below.

[27] These chapters are to be assigned to the ninth century A.D. See under Agni-purāṇa.

[28] Cf. Ag 16, 12b-13a.

deluded the Daityas with the result that the latter gave up the Veda-dharma and became Bauddhas. Viṣṇu, in the form of Māyā-moha, next became Ārhata and turned the remaining Daityas into Ārhatas. Thus the Pāṣaṇḍins came into existence. The Agni-p. further adds that at the end of the Kali age there will be an intermixture of castes, the Dasyus will prevail, and the Mlecchas will become kings and eat up the people[29]. Then Kalki, son of Viṣṇu-yaśas, will have Yājñavalkya as his priest, exterminate the Mlecchas and re-establish the distinctions of the four castes. The mention of the Bauddhas and the Ārhatas as Pāṣaṇḍins and, then, of the Mlecchas as kings, shews that by the word *'mleccha'* the Agni means the outlandish dynasties which established kingdoms in India after the death of the Kushan king Vāsudeva. It may also be that by this word the Purāṇa means the Muhammadans who came to India about the 9th century A.D. In Ag 49 the characteristics of the images of the ten incarnations of Viṣṇu have been described. This chapter exhibits a distinct advance over Mat 259 and 260 referred to above in that it adds four incarnations more, viz., Paraśurāma, Balarāma, Buddha and Kalki, to those of the Matsya-p. to make up ten and arranges them in order. Moreover, it replaces Kṛṣṇa by Balarāma. Hence the date of composition of this chapter must be much later than that of Mat 259 and 260. It is highly probable that the date should be placed later than the ninth century A.D.[30] It is to be noted that here also Kalki is described as 'the exterminator of the Mlecchas' (mlecchotsādakara). The Kashmirian polymath Kṣemendra, who flourished in the eleventh century A.D., wrote in 1066 A.D. his Daśāvatāra-carita in which Kṛṣṇa is said to be an incarnation of Viṣṇu[31] and the condition of the earth on the eve of the Kalki incarnation is described as follows:

> *darat-turuṣkāb(ph)agāna-śaka-nandanaiḥ*
> *saṃkocam eṣyati mahī kuṣṭhair iva visarpibhiḥ|*
> *mlecchācchādita-sarvāśā kṛpaṇākrandanādinī*
> *medaḥ-kardaminī kledaṃ raktair yāsyati medinī||*

It is clear that the term 'Mleccha' is used by Kṣemendra to mean especially the Muhammadans who disturbed the peace of India by attacks and massacres. In Var 39-48 ten kinds of Dvādaśī-vrata, named after the ten Avatāras, are described. The very connection of the Vratas with the 'ten incarnations' of Viṣṇu proves their late origin which is further confirmed by the direction *'rūpakāmo yajed buddhaṃ śatrughātāya kalkinam'*[32] pointing to a time when the

[29] *mānuṣān bhakṣayiṣyanti mlecchāḥ pārthiva-rūpiṇaḥ|*
[30] See also under Agni-purāṇa below.
[31] Daśāvatāra-carita, I, 2; I, 10; and VIII, 1 ff. [32] Var 48, 22a.

idea of the people towards the delusive nature of the Buddha incarnation underwent such a change that the Buddha was looked upon as a god conferring beauty. The Padma-p. (Uttara-kh.) describes the first eight of the ten Avatāras in chaps. 258 ff. These chapters bear stamps of very late age. For instance, the Tulasī plant is said to be the wife of Hari. Jayadeva, in his Gītagovinda, mentions the ten Avatāras of Kṛṣṇa and looks upon Kalki as the exterminator of the Mlecchas.

From what has been said above it appears that the group of the ten incarnations of Viṣṇu with the Fish at the head began to attain the state of general acceptance not very much earlier than 800 A.D. And when this group attained such a position, the Fish incarnation also was consolidated in its own place in the group. The Fish thus occupying the first place, at least some people must have looked upon the Purāṇa declared by the Fish (i.e., the Matsya-p.) with the same importance, so much so that in Vām 12 it is called the chief of all Purāṇas. Hence it is highly probable that the Matsya-p. attained such importance not earlier than about the beginning of the ninth century A.D.

Chap. 104 of the Vāyu-p. appears to confirm the above view by including the Bhāgavata and the Ādika-purāṇa in the list of Purāṇas and by naming six systems of philosophy of which the Śākta system is one[33]. The mention of the Bhāgavata-p. shows that the date of composition of the section containing the list, if not of the whole chapter, cannot be earlier than that of the Bhāgavata. The inclusion of the Ādika-p. in the list tends to point to a still later date. That the title 'Ādika' is not used here to mean the Brahma-p., which also is sometimes termed 'Ādi-purāṇa' from the preference it enjoys over other Purāṇas, is clear from the fact that the Brahma-p. also is mentioned in the list. The Ādika-p. mentioned by the Vāyu must, therefore, be identical with the Ādi-upapurāṇa, which alone, besides the Brahma-p., goes by the name 'Ādi-purāṇa'. Alberūnī (about 1030 A.D.) gives two lists of Purāṇas, one of which was dictated to him and the other he copied from the Viṣṇu-p.[34]. The list that was dictated to him consists partly of Mahāpurāṇas and partly of Upapurāṇas such as the Ādi, Narasiṃha, Nanda (Nandi ?), Āditya etc., the first place

[33] *brāhmaṃ śaivaṃ vaiṣṇavaṃ ca sauraṃ śāktaṃ tathārhatam|*
ṣaḍ darśanāni coktāni svabhāva-niyatāni ca|| Vā 104, 16.
Mādhavācārya, in his Bhāṣya on the Parāśara-smṛti (I, i, 305), quotes from the Purāṇa-sāra a verse which names the 'six systems of philosophy of the Bhakti-mārga' as Śaiva, Vaiṣṇava, Śākta, Saura, Vaināyaka and Skānda.

[34] Sachau, Alberūnī's India, I, pp. 130-131.—

being assigned to the Ādi-purāṇa, and the Matsya and Brahma occupying the second and seventeenth places respectively. This list shows that by Alberūnī's time the Upapurāṇa, called Ādi-purāṇa, not only attained the position of being included in the list of the 'eighteen Purāṇas' but became prominent enough to be named first of all. Not only so, the other Upapurāṇas also were regarded so highly that the people did not hesitate to mingle the names of the Upapurāṇas with those of the Mahāpurāṇas to make up the traditional 'eighteen'. But in Vā 104 the Upapurāṇas do not seem to have attained so much prominence as in Alberūnī's days. Of the numerous Upapurāṇas the Ādika only is included in the list but is not assigned the first place. This position of the Ādika-p. seems to point to a time earlier than that of Alberūnī. The mention of Śākta philosophy also tends to assign a similar date to Vā 104. From the fact that the Śākta systems began to appear from a time not very much earlier than about the sixth century A.D.[35], and from the dates of the Śākta Upaniṣads which began to appear not much earlier than the tenth century A.D.[36], it seems that Śākta philosophy attained recognition not earlier than the ninth century A.D. From all this it may be assumed that Vā 104, which places the Matsya-p. first in the list, was written not earlier than the ninth century and not later than the time of Alberūnī. To show that the first place assigned to the Matsya-p. in Vā 104 is not due to mere chance, the Devībhāgavata (I, 3) may be cited as an example. This latter Purāṇa also allows the same preference to the Matsya.

From all the arguments adduced above it may be concluded that Vām 14 was not inserted earlier than the ninth century A.D. As this chapter is drawn upon by Govindānanda in his Varṣakriyā-kaumudī and Śuddhikriyā-kaumudī, by Raghunandana in his Smṛti-tattva, by Narasiṃha Vājapeyin in his Nityācārapradīpa, by Śrīdatta Upādhyāya in his Kṛtyācāra, by Caṇḍeśvara in his Kṛtya-ratnākara, by Mādhavācārya in his Bhāṣya on the Parāśara-smṛti, by Hemādri in his Caturvarga-cintāmaṇi and by Devaṇabhaṭṭa in his Smṛti-candrikā (see App.), its date cannot be placed later than the beginning of the eleventh century A.D. Hence *the date falls either in the ninth or in the tenth century A.D., and most probably in the former.*

The story of Sukeśin, of which chap. 14 forms a vital part, is so closely connected with the other parts of the Purāṇa that *the above date can be taken to be that of composition of almost the entire Purāṇa by the Śiva-worshippers.*

[35] Cf. Farquhar, Outline, pp. 167 ff. [36] Ibid, pp. 266-267.

The present Vāmana, though a comparatively late work, does not seem to have come down to us quite unadulterated. The repetition of the story of the origin of Liṅga-worship in two forms in chaps. 6 and 43 and of the story of the birth and exploits of the Dwarf in chaps. 27-31 and 76-95 shows that some of these chapters must be later additions. But it is very difficult to disconnect them. Whatever of these chapters may have been interpolated, it is sure that the interpolations were made earlier than 1050 A.D., as the quotations from these and other allied chapters show.

The Nāradīya-p., which gives the contents of the Vāmana-p. in chap. 105 of its Pūrva-bhāga, speaks of the two parts of the Purāṇa. The contents of the first part tally fully with those of our printed text. The second part, which is called Bṛhad-vāmana, is said to have consisted of four Saṃhitās,—Māheśvarī, Bhāgavatī, Saurī and Gāṇeśvarī,—each containing 1000 Ślokas. The first of these Saṃhitās was given to Kṛṣṇa and his worshippers, the second to Devī and her incarnations, the third to the Sun-god, and the fourth to Gaṇeśa. The Nāradīya-p. further gives a tradition of succession of the Vāmana-p. According to this tradition the Purāṇa was first imparted by Pulastya to Nārada, who then narrated it to Vyāsa. Lomaharṣaṇa received it from Vyāsa and narrated it to the sages of the Naimiṣa forest.

2. THE LIṄGA-PURĀṆA

The present Liṅga, which consists of two parts—Pūrvārdha and Uttarārdha, seems to be a manual of the Liṅga-worshippers, inculcating the worship of the phallic emblem of Śiva together with five other forms of the god—viz., Īśāna, Aghora, Vāmadeva, Tatpuruṣa and Jāta. The worship of the phallic symbol is extolled even over that of the image of Śiva himself. The violently sectarian character of this Purāṇa is shown by its declaration that a person, who, after hearing the dispraise of Śiva, at once gives up his own life after murdering the censurer, proceeds to the region of Śiva, and that one, who tears out the tongue of a habituated censurer of the god, delivers twentyone generations and attains the same region[37]. In this Purāṇa a Śiva-worshipper is said to be superior to thousands of the worshippers of Viṣṇu and other gods. It further presents Viṣṇu as composing a hymn in honour of Śiva, and Nandin, the active principle of Śiva, as defeating the former god in his Man-lion incarnation.

[37] Lg I, 107, 41-42.

This Purāṇa contains a good number of chapters on Smṛti-topics, mainly religious, viz.,

I, 25-28 ..	on Liṅga-worship,
I, 77-78 ..	on the consecration of a Liṅga,
I, 81 ..	on the Pāśupata-vrata or Śivaliṅga-vrata,
I, 83-84 ..	on the Śaiva Vratas to be observed in the different months,
I, 85, 1-82 ..	on the method of muttering the five-syllabled Mantra,
I, 85, 83-126 ..	on Dīkṣā and Puraścaraṇa,
I, 85, 127 to the end; I, 89 ..	on Sadācāra,
I, 90 ..	on Yati-prāyaścitta,
II, 23-26 ..	on the worship of Śiva,
II, 28-44 ..	on the big donations (mahādāna),
II, 45 ..	on the funeral ceremony of a living being (jīvacchrāddha),
II, 46-49 ..	on the consecration of a Liṅga,
and II, 51 to the end ..	on mystic rites and practices, viz., Vajravāhanikā-vidyā, Mṛtyuñjaya-vidhi, etc.

According to the information given by the Matsya, Skanda and Agni-purāṇa, the Liṅga-p. was declared by Maheśvara in relation to the Āgneya Kalpa, and it consisted of 11000 Ślokas[38]. But in the present Liṅga, whose length is given as 11000 Ślokas and which opens, unlike the earlier Purāṇas, with a list of the names of the holy places visited by Nārada, it is expressly said that the Purāṇa was declared by Brahmā in connection with the Īśāna-kalpa[39]. The interlocution between Śiva and his wife is first referred to by Lomaharṣaṇa as late as in Lg I, 25 in connection with the method of Liṅga-worship.

The above disagreement shows that the present Liṅga-p. is not the earlier one which was noticed by the Matsya, Skanda and Agni. Its apocryphal character is further evidenced by the quotations made from the 'Liṅga-purāṇa' or 'Laiṅga' by many of the commentators and Nibandha-writers. Of these authors, Jīmūtavāhana quotes 18 lines, excepting the repeated ones, in his Kālaviveka; Vijñāneśvara quotes 2 lines in his Mitākṣarā; Aparārka quotes 12 lines in his com.; Madanapāla quotes 10 lines in his Madanapārijāta; Śūlapāṇi quotes 8 lines in his Durgotsava-viveka;

[38] Mat 53, 36-37 and Sk VII, i, 2, 54-56. Ag 272, 14b-15a.
[39] Lg I, 2, 1.

Vācaspatimiśra quotes about 185 lines in his Tīrtha-cintāmaṇi; Raghunandana quotes about 74 lines, excepting the repeated ones, in his Smṛti-tattva; Govindānanda quotes 2 lines in his Śūddhikriyā-kaumudī and 50 lines, excepting the repeated ones, in his Varṣakriyā-kaumudī; and Gadādhara quotes 51 lines in his Kālasāra. But not a single of these numerous quoted lines is found in the present Liṅga-p. This remarkable fact undoubtedly goes against the authenticity of *the present Liṅga, which is most probably the result of a destructive recast to which the earlier Purāṇa was subjected.* How the contents of the earlier Purāṇa were replaced by others in the present one, is shown best by a comparison between chap. 92 on the glorification of Benares in Liṅga I and the numerous verses on the same topic quoted in Vācaspatimiśra's Tīrtha-cintāmaṇi. The earlier Liṅga, however, did not die out immediately after the recast but continued to be drawn upon as an authoritative work by a section of Nibandha-writers including those of even the 16th century A.D., if not later.

The present Liṅga, though an apocryphal one, is certainly not a very late work. Rūpa Gosvāmin, one of the disciples of Caitanya of Navadvīpa, quotes a verse from Liṅga II, 3 in his Haribhakti-rasāmṛtasindhu; Gopālabhaṭṭa quotes a good number of verses from Liṅga II, 2, 4 and 7 in his Haribhaktivilāsa; Narasiṃha Vājapeyin from Liṅga I, 92 in his Nityācārapradīpa; Vidyākara Vājapeyin from Liṅga I, 85 and 94 in his Nityācārapaddhati; Mādhavācārya from Liṅga I, 4, 26, 39, 40 and 89 in his Bhāṣya on the Parāśara-smṛti; Hemādri from Liṅga I, 65 and 81-84 and II, 28-30, 32-40 and 42-45 in his Caturvarga-cintāmaṇi; Ballālasena from Liṅga I, 77 and II, 28 in his Dānasāgara and from Liṅga I, 91 and 100 in his Adbhutasāgara; Devaṇabhaṭṭa from Liṅga I, 26 and 77 in his Smṛti-candrikā; and Vandyaghaṭīya Sarvānanda from Liṅga I, 4 in his Ṭīkāsarvasva (see App.). Moreover, Ballālasena refers to the chapters on 'big donations' occurring in Liṅga II[40]. These evidences

[40] Cf. Dānasāgara, fol. 3b—'*bṛhad api liṅgapurāṇaṃ matsyapurāṇoditair mahādānaiḥ*'.

Though Ballālasena's knowledge of the present Liṅga admits of little doubt, the verses quoted from it in the Dānasāgara may have been interpolated; because on fol. 2a, where Ballāla names only those Epics, Purāṇas and Upapurāṇas which he used in writing the Nibandha, there is no mention of the Liṅga-purāṇa. The corrupt verse

bṛhad api liṅgapurāṇaṃ matsyapurāṇoditair mahādānaiḥ|
avadhārya labdhasāradānanibandhetaranibandham||

given on fol. 3b in connection with the names of the rejected Purāṇas or parts thereof, also tends to show that Ballālasena did not use the Liṅga in his Dānasāgara. (The word '*api*' after '*bṛhat*' seems to suggest that '*avadhīrya*' should be read in place of '*avadhārya*').

adduced by the Nibandha-writers hailing from different parts of India, prove that *the present Liṅga, with its two parts, was written not later than 1000 A.D.* Verses or even entire chapters might have been interpolated later than this time, but the interrelation between the chapters drawn upon by the Nibandha-writers and most of the remaining ones, shows that the great majority of the chapters are to be dated before 1000 A.D. The mention of the names of the planets beginning with the sun[41], of the signs of the zodiac[42], of the Nakṣatras beginning with Aśvinī[43], of the 'Āgama' literature of the Śaivas[44], and of the ten incarnations of Viṣṇu including Kṛṣṇa, the Buddha and Kalki[45], testifies to the fact that *the Purāṇa was not written before 600 A.D.* The genealogical portion also betrays a comparatively late origin of the Purāṇa. About this portion Pargiter says: "The Liṅga account is based on the 'Vāyu version', but adapts to frame its own text. Often it has the same verses, but often also it modifies, curtails, and freely omits, especially incindental and descriptive matter; and it adds occasionally. It also interpolates religious teaching, as where it introduces a long eulogy of Rudra. It however shows traces of the influence of the Matsya version; thus it has the same verses sometimes and ends the Aikṣvāku genealogy with six kings instead of the Vāyu's twentyone just as the Matsya does[46]".

The boundary of India as given in Lg I, 52, 29 (*pūrve kirātās tasyānte paścime yavanāḥ smṛtāḥ*| etc.) should not be taken to give the Purāṇa a very early date, because this verse, which is found to occur in the geographical portions of many of the other Purāṇas also, viz., Vāyu, Brahmāṇḍa, Kūrma, Mārkaṇḍeya etc., is certainly a traditional one.

All of the chapters of the Liṅga-p., which are to be dated earlier than 1000 A.D., do not, however, seem to have been composed at the same time. An examination of the chapters on the method of Liṅga-worship shows that they are to be divided into two groups—one, including Lg I, 25-28, in which Vedic elements prevail and the Vedic Mantras are used frequently, and the other showing the

Besides the present apocryphal Liṅga, Ballālasena seems to have known another spurious Liṅga-p. consisting of 6,000 Ślokas and dealing with Dīkṣā, Pratiṣṭhā, etc. See footnote 131 under Agni-purāṇa.

That more Liṅga-purāṇas than one came into existence at a fairly early date is suggested by our present Liṅga itself when it says:

laiṅgam ekādaśa-vidhaṃ prabhinnaṃ dvāpare yuge

(Lg I, 39, 64a. This line occurs in Skanda VII, i, 2, 101 also. Skanda V, iii, 1, 38 says: *'laiṅgam ekādaśaṃ jñeyaṃ tathaikādaśa saṃkhyayā'*).

41 Lg I, 82, 73-74.

42 Lg I, 82, 75-76.

43 Lg I, 82, 77 ff.

44 Lg I, 85, 35 and II, 55, 25.

45 Lg II, 48, 31-32.

46 Pargiter, AIHT, p. 81.

influence of the Tantras. The chapters of the former group may have been retained from the earlier form of the Purāṇa, and those of the latter seem to have dated from the time of *the recast, which, on account of the Tantric traces, does not seem to have been made earlier than 800 A.D.*

The present Liṅga-p. has a few chapters borrowed from other Purāṇas. For example, Lg I, 89 (on Sadācāra) gives the verses of Vā 16 with further additions, so much so that the former has 122 verses as against the latter's 24; Lg I, 90 (on Yati- prāyaścitta) is almost totally the same as Vā 18; Lg I, 91 (on Ariṣṭa and Oṃkāra-lakṣaṇa) is the same as Vā 19 and 20; Lg I, 40 consists of verses mainly taken from Kūr I, 29 and Mat 144, 48 ff.; and so on. The Liṅga-p. has improved upon the borrowed sections with additions and alterations in such a way that these additions and alterations at once betray its indebtedness.

In this connection we should like to enumerate the Smṛti-topics dealt with in the lost Liṅga-p. The basis of this enumeration is the untraceable quotations made by the Nibandha-writers. These quotations relate to general customs (ācāra), funeral sacrifices, bath during eclipses, vows (viz., Bhrātṛ-dvitīyā, Aśokāṣṭamī, Ekādaśī, Śiva-rātri, Damanaka-caturdaśī and Narasiṃha-caturdaśī), and worship of Śiva, Agni, Durgā (in the autumn), Lakṣmī, Śālagrāma and the spiritual preceptor (guru). The quoted verses on general customs and funeral sacrifices are so small in number that it seems that in the lost Liṅga-p. the chapters on these topics were negligible in comparison with those on the different religious rites.

3. THE VARĀHA-PURĀṆA [47]

The extant Varāha is a comparatively late work. It is rather a manual of prayers and rules mainly for the Viṣṇu-worshippers. That it is not the Varāha-p. which the Matsya, the Skanda and the Agni-purāṇa noticed, can be little doubted. These three Purānas describe the Varāha-p. as follows:

mahāvarāhasya punar māhātmyam adhikṛtya ca|
viṣṇunābhihitaṃ kṣauṇyai tad vāraham ihocyate||
mānavasya prasaṅgena kalpasya muni-sattamāḥ|
caturviṃśat sahasrāṇi tat purāṇam ihocyate||[48]

[47] The Vaṅga. ed. is the same as that in the Bibl. Ind. Ser. There are, of course, slight variations in readings in the two editions.

[48] Mat 53, 38-39 and Sk VII, i, 2, 57-58. Sk reads '*dhanyasya*' for '*kalpasya*' in the third line.

and

caturdaśa-sahasrāṇi vārāhaṃ viṣṇuneritam|
bhūmau varāha-caritaṃ mānavasya pravṛttitaḥ||[49]

According to these descriptions the older Varāha-p. was declared by Viṣṇu and was connected with the Mānava Kalpa, but in the extant Purāṇa of the same title the Boar himself is the narrator and there is no mention of the Mānava Kalpa. Moreover, of the five characteristics of the Purāṇa, there is very little in it. Its account of creation bears the unmistakable stamp of comparatively late age. The Manvantaras and the genealogies of kings and sages have been neglected. The beginning also does not resemble those of the other Purāṇas, there being no mention either of the sacrifice in the Naimiṣa forest or of the sages who request Sūta to narrate the Purāṇas. On the other hand, Sūta reports the interlocution between the Boar and the Earth abruptly and without any introduction.

The extant Varāha-p. consists of four distinct sections: (1) chaps. 1 to 112, (2) chaps. 113 to 192, (3) chaps. 193 to 212, and (4) chaps. 213 to the end[50]. These four sections, which differ from one another in general character and in respect of interlocutors, are most probably the works of different hands hailing from different ages. In the first section (comprising chaps. 1-112), Sūta is the reporter, and the interlocutors are the Boar and the Earth. This section is primarily the work of the Pāñcarātras. Here the highest deity is Nārāyaṇa, and this name of the god is used much more frequently than the names 'Viṣṇu' and 'Hari!'. The names 'Vāsudeva' and 'Kṛṣṇa' are of very rare occurrence. The sectarian Mantra is '*oṃ namo nārāyaṇāya*'[51], and there is not even a single mention of the Mantra '*oṃ namo bhagavate vāsudevāya*'. In this section importance is given to everything Pāñcarātra. The gifts made to the Pāñcarātra Ācāryas are said to be productive of immense good (Var 50, 16). The study of the Pāñcarātra Saṃhitās and the observance of the rules of the Pāñcarātras are recommended, next to the Vedas, as the means of realising Viṣṇu-Brahma. Viṣṇu is brought in to say:

"*pauruṣaṃ sūktam āsthāya ye yajanti dvijāśu māṃ|*
te māṃ prāpsyanti satataṃ saṃhitādhyayanena ca||

[49] Ag 272, 16.

[50] Haraprasad Shastri wrongly divides the contents of the Bibl. Ind. ed. of the Varāha-p. into 3 sections: (1) from chap. 1 to 112, (2) from 113 to 192, and (3) from 193 to the end. See, Shastri, Cat. of Sans. Mss, ASB, Vol. V, Preface, pp. clxv-clxvi.

[51] Var 37, 21 and 31; 49, 31.

alābhe veda-śāstrāṇāṃ pañcarātroditena hi|
mārgeṇa māṃ yajante ye te māṃ prāpsyanti mānavāḥ||[52]

Though in this section Śiva, Brahmā and Viṣṇu are said to be not different from one another, it is Nārāyaṇa (also called Viṣṇu) who is the highest god, and all other gods, including Brahmā and Śiva, are said to be born of him[53]. Rudra himself acknowledges the superiority of Nārāyaṇa and describes the latter as '*sakala-vidyāvabodhita-paramātma-svarūpī vigata-kalmaṣaḥ paramāṇur acintyātmā nārāyaṇaḥ sakala-lokāloka-vyāpī* . . . . . .'[54]. The Boar also describes Nārāyaṇa as 'śuddha', 'sarva-gata', 'nitya', 'vyoma-rūpa', 'sanātana' and 'bhāvābhāva-nirmukta'[55] and says that even gods cannot see his supreme form (*paramaṃ rūpam*—Var 4, 4). Nārāyaṇa is further identified definitely with 'Puruṣa of the Vedānta'[56] and the supreme Brahma of the Veda and other holy scriptures[57]. Inspite of this identification, a distinction is made between Nārāyaṇa- or Viṣṇu-Brahma and the inferior Viṣṇu of the Trinity. The latter is born of the former and is incarnated on earth (Var 73, 47).

This section was written with a view to popularising the Pāñcarātra system which was losing popular favour in Northern India[58]. It was mainly directed against the antagonistic non-Vedic Pāśupatas (i.e., the Āgamic Śaivas) who were growing in number[59] most probably at the cost of the Pāñcarātras[60]. Here Rudra is brought in to denounce the non-Vedic Pāśupatas (also called Raudras) as well as their scriptures. The former are blamed as 'given to mean and sinful acts', 'addicted to wine, meat and women' and the like (Var 71, 58), and the latter are called 'veda-bāhya' and 'tāmasa' and are said to be meant for deluding and degrading the people (*mohārthaṃ*—Var 70, 41 ; *patana-kāraṇaṃ*—Var 70, 42).

The way in which this section ends, shows that originally it was not continued further and that it formed a distinct work by itself. Towards its end, the Boar says to the Earth : "Thus, O beautiful

[52] Var 66, 10-11.

[53] Var 17, 23-25 ; 90, 3 ; and so on.

[54] Var 74, 5.

[55] Var 6, 15.

[56] *evaṃ vedānta-puruṣaḥ prokto nārāyaṇātmakaḥ|* Var 17, 73.
In the Śatapatha-brāhmaṇa also Nārāyaṇa is identified with Puruṣa and is said to be the author of the Puruṣa-sūkta of the Ṛg-veda. See, Bhandarkar, Vaiṣṇavism etc., p. 31.

[57] Var 39, 16.

[58] Cf. *yugāni triṇi bahavo mām upaiṣyanti mānavāḥ|*
antye yuge praviralā bhaviṣyanti madāśrayāḥ|| Var 70, 34b-35a.

[59] Cf. *asaṃkhyātās tu te raudrā bhavitāro mahītale.* Var 71, 57.

[60] Cf. *kalau mat-kṛta-mārgeṇa bahu-rūpeṇa tāmasaiḥ|*
ijyate dveṣa-buddhyā sa paramātmā janārdanaḥ|| Var 70, 25.

lady, I have narrated to you the sanctifying and all-giving Saṃhitā named after the Boar" (*varāhākhyā saṃhitā*—112, 63), and then gives two traditions of the rise and circulation of the Purāṇa-saṃhitā. According to one of these traditions, the Saṃhitā arose from the Omniscient in a previous Kalpa and was learnt by Brahmā, who then gave it to his son Pulastya. Pulastya handed it down to Bhārgava Rāma, Bhārgava Rāma to his own disciple Ugra, and Ugra to Manu. According to the other tradition, the Boar received the Saṃhitā from the Omniscient in the 'present Kalpa' and gave it to the Earth. The Saṃhitā would then pass through the sages Kapila and others and reach Vyāsa from whom Lomaharṣaṇa would get it and declare it to his own disciple Śaunaka. The Boar next names the eighteen Mahāpurāṇas and finishes by glorifying the study, hearing, preservation and worship of the 'Śāstra named Vārāha'.

In the second section (extending over chapters 113 to 192) Sūta is the general reporter of what the Earth said to Sanatkumāra and others after she had been raised by the Boar. In this section Sanatkumāra, son of Brahmā, asks the Earth to tell him what strange things she experienced while she was upheld by the Boar and what the latter told her. Consequently, the Earth narrates the interlocation between herself and the Boar to Sanatkumāra and the other sages invited by him. Thus, besides Sūta, there are two sets of interlocutors in this section: (1) Sanatkumāra and the Earth, and (2) the Boar and the Earth[61].

Unlike the first, this section bears a distinct Bhāgavata stamp and is meant for guiding the Bhāgavatas especially in their religious observances. In this section the Viṣṇu-worshippers are termed 'Bhāgavata', and this word is used much more frequently than the generic term 'Vaiṣṇava'. The secret Dharma proclaimed by the Boar is to be disclosed only to a sincere Bhāgavata (Var 117, 47); Viṣṇu accepts those things which are preferred by the Bhāgavatas (Var 119, 10); the Bhāgavatas are to be honoured at the end of the worship of Viṣṇu (Var 124, 10); the pure Bhāgavatas are always to be visited and honoured by the people (Var 125, 168); in initiation the Bhāgavata preceptor and other Bhāgavatas are to be honoured (chaps. 127-128); and so forth. Though the name 'Nārāyaṇa' for

It is to be noted that the scriptures of the non-Vedic Pāśupatas are condemned as 'tāmasa', and that Nārāyaṇa and Śiva are regarded as one. Therefore, those, who become non-Vedic Pāśupatas and decry Nārāyaṇa, really worship the latter through the spirit of hostility (dveṣa-buddhi).

[61] Haraprasad Shastri wrongly gives the sets of interlocutors in this section as: (1) Sauti and the Ṛsis, (2) Sanatkumāra and the Ṛsis, and (3) the Boar and the Earth. See, Shastri, Cat. of Sans. Mss, ASB, Vol. V, Preface, p. clxvi.

the highest god is not rarely used, the name 'Viṣṇu' is more frequent here than in the first section. The word 'Vāsudeva' also is used at times[62]. This section is named 'Bhagavacchāstra' in the colophons of almost all the chapters, and its contents are called 'Bhagavat-prokta-dharma' or 'Viṣṇu-prokta-dharma'[63]. Though the sectarian Mantra *'namo nārāyaṇāya'* is of more frequent occurrence, the Mantra *'oṃ namo vāsudevāya'* also is found to occur[64].

In the third section (chaps. 193-212) Sūta is the reporter as usual, the interlocutors being the king Janamejaya and the sage Vaiśampāyana[65]. After the twelve-year sacrifice is preformed, the former expiates the murder of 'the Brāhman' and approaches the latter to hear about the results of actions (Karma-vipāka) and the region of Yama. Consequently, Vaiśampāyana narrates the story of Nāciketa in which the latter speaks to his father and other sages about his visit to, and experience of, the realm of Yama.

This third section, named Dharma-saṃhitā (Var 212, 1), constitutes a distinct unit by itself. It does not seem to be connected with the chapters of the first or the second section. The line '*aśvamedhe tathā vṛtte rājā vai janamejayaḥ*' towards the beginning of this section proves its isolated character, because in the preceding sections nothing is said about king Janamejaya or his horse-sacrifice. It is highly probable that these chapters were taken from some other source in which the story of Janamejaya was narrated. It is to be noted that though in chaps. 211-212 the method of Viṣṇu-worship is given, the other chapters of this section remarkably lack the characteristics found in the first and second sections.

The contents of the fourth section (chaps. 213 to the end) are reported by Sūta as an interlocution between Sanatkumāra and Brahmā. This section is strictly Śaiva. It treats of the origin and glorification of Uttara Gokarṇa and other holy places in Nepal, which are sacred to Śiva. In connection with these places, Śiva also is glorified. This section was added most probably by an inhabitant of Nepal who wanted to glorify Uttara Gokarṇa in Nepal over Dakṣiṇa Gokarṇa (in Mathurā ?). The former is said to contain the greater part of the body of Śiva and to be more sacred than even Prabhāsa, Prayāga, Naimiṣāraṇya, Puṣkara and Kurukṣetra. There is also mention of the Kṣatriya kings of the Solar race who took possession of the kingdom of Nepal from the

[62] Cf Var 129, 3 and 51-52; 148, 10; and so on.

[63] Var 113, 5 and 122, 89. —[64] Cf. Var 123, 32; 182, 9.

[65] Here also Haraprasad Shastri wrongly gives the prominent interlocutors as (1) Lomaharṣaṇa and Janamejaya and (2) Sanatkumāra and Brahmā. See, Shastri, Cat. of Sans. Mss, ASB, Vol. V, Preface, p. clxvi.

Mlecchas, established the Brahmanical religion and popularised the Liṅga-worship (Var 215, 42-46).

From what has been said above it is clear that the four sections of the Varāha-p. have different characteristics and are, therefore, to be ascribed to different authors. In these four sections themselves, again, there are chapters and verses which are later interpolations. Before we proceed to discuss the dates of these different sections, we shall try to find out these interpolated portions, especially those in the first two sections.

In the first section, chaps. 90-97 and 99-112 (verses 1-62) seem to have been added later. Of these, chaps. 90-96, on the origin, exploits and fundamental unity of the three Śaktis,—Brāhmī, Vaiṣṇavī and Raudrī,—are distinctly Śākta documents. Chap. 97 has been inserted by the Śaivas to show the origin of the Rudravrata (also called the Vābhravya- or Śuddhaśaiva-vrata) and to establish the sacredness of the Pāśupata-śāstra. It is clearly a protest made against chaps. 70-71, in which the Rudravrata and the Pāśupata-śāstra have been condemned by the Pāñcarātras. Chap. 99 refers to the Vaiṣṇavī Śakti who killed the demon Mahiṣa on the Mandara hills. So, this chap. cannot possibly be earlier than the chapters (90-96) on the Śaktis. Chapters 99 (verses 54 ff.) to 112 (verses 1-62), on different kinds of gifts, have been introduced incoherently. As Var 99, 54b-93 and 112, 53-59 tally respectively with Padma-p. (Sṛṣṭi-kh.) 34, verses 333-372 and 378-384, it is probable that some one took these portions from the Padma-p. (Sṛṣṭi-kh.), developed them with further additions and then inserted the whole into the Varāha-p. That such has been the case with these chapters on gifts seems to be shown by the fact that though in Var 99, 82 the priest of the hungry king Vinītāśva advises the latter to make gifts of Tila-dhenu, Jala-dhenu, Ghṛta-dhenu, Dhenu and Rasa-dhenu for getting rid of hunger, he is found to describe the methods of making many other gifts in chaps. 102-112.

The remaining chapters of the first section may be taken to be contemporaneous, for they are closely interrelated; viz., Var 10, 44 and 50, in which it is said that all informations about Indra and the two demons Vidyut and Suvidyut would be given later, point to chap. 16; Var 11, 112 points to chaps. 17 and 36 (verses 1-8) on the attainment of kingship by the warriors born of the gem given by Viṣṇu to the sage Gauramukha; Var 17, 23-26, referring to the origin of all the gods from Nārāyaṇa, point to chaps. 18-34; and so on.

In the second section (chaps. 113-192), chaps. 140-151 (on the holy places and the duties of women under impurity) and

152-180 (on Mathurā) seem to have been interpolated. Though Kokāmukha, a place sacred to the Boar, is already glorified in chap. 122, there is no reason why it should be repeated by the same author as late as in chap. 140. That chap. 122 was already there when chap. 140 was added is certain, because in Var 140, 4 the Boar refers to Kokāmukha as already described (*tava kokāmukhaṃ nāma yan mayā pūrva-bhāṣitam*). There are other reasons why chaps. 140-151 can be taken as spurious. Some of the Tīrtha-māhātmyas in these chapters are told in the form of predictions; the stories do not resemble those in chaps. 122 (on Kokāmukha), 125-126 (on Kubjāmraka) and 137-138 (on Saukara-kṣetra); the line '*prabhātāyāṃ tu śarvaryām udite tu divākare*' or '*vyatītāyāṃ tu śarvaryām udite ca divākare*' which occurs often in other chapters not excepting even the chapters on Kokāmukha, Kubjāmraka and Saukara-kṣetra, and which, consequently, seems to be a favourite expression of the author of this section of the Purāṇa, is not found in chaps. 140-151; and there is no mention of the duties of women under menstruation in chap. 114 in which the Earth mentions the topics on which the Boar is to speak to her. In chaps. 140-151, again, there are some passages which appear to have been added still later. In Var 140, 4-5 the Boar names the three places Kokāmukha, Vadarī and Lohārgala, which he does not leave. Now, the Boar speaks on Kokāmukha and Vadarī in chaps. 140 and 141 respectively, but Lohārgala is taken up as late as in chap. 151. Hence it is highly probable that the intervening chaps. 142-150 are later than chaps. 140-141 and 151.

Chaps. 152-180 (on Mathurā-māhātmya) are ascribed by scholars to Sanātana, a disciple of Caitanya of Navadvīpa[66]. Verse 26 of Var 152 is found quoted in the Haribhaktivilāsa of Gopālabhaṭṭa, a contemporary of Sanātana and disciple of Caitanya, with the definite mention that the verse is taken from 'the Mathurā-māhātmya of the Varāha-p'[67]. That these chapters on Mathurā-māhātmya are later than the other chapters on holy places in the second section can be little doubted; because the story of the Brahma-rākṣasa in chap. 155 is certainly later than that in chap. 139; the performance of Śrāddha and the offer of rice-balls to the patriarchs in the holy places in Mathurā are highly spoken of in these chapters only; and the name 'Kṛṣṇa', which is rare in other chapters, is used more than once.

[66] Farquhar, Outline, pp. 309-310.

[67] Haribhaktivilāsa, p. 687. It is believed that the Haribhaktivilāsa was composed by Sanātana but was attributed to Gopālabhaṭṭa, another disciple of Caitanya.

It is difficult to detect the interpolated portions, if any, in the third and fourth sections. These two sections are certainly later than the original chapters in the first two sections.

We are now in a position to discuss the dates of the different chapters of this Purāṇa. Let us begin with the first section. The famous list of the ten incarnations of Viṣṇu[68] given in chaps. 4 (verse 2), 48 (verses 17-22) and 55 (verses 35-37), none of which can be proved to be spurious, shows that this list, including the Buddha, was well-known at the time when the first section was composed. If the Buddha came to be regarded as an incarnation of Viṣṇu about 550 A.D., then the date of this section of the Varāha-p. cannot reasonably be placed earlier than 650 A.D. From the description of the ten Vratas named after the ten incarnations of Viṣṇu, we understand that the Buddha was not only accepted as an incarnation of Viṣṇu but was popularly worshipped by the Pāñcarātras. Moreover, the idea of the people regarding the delusive nature of the Buddha was forgotten at least by a section of people who worshipped him for attaining physical beauty (*rūpakāmo yajed buddhaṃ*—Var 48, 22). Hence the date of composition of the first section should be placed lower still. A comparison between the stories of the sage Gautama in Kūr I, 16, 95 ff. and Var 71 proves the earlier origin of the story in the former Purāṇa. This earlier date of the Kūrma-p. is supported by another evidence. In the Kūrma-p. (I, 25) the Pāśupatas introduce a story that Viṣṇu (in the form of Kṛṣṇa) worshipped Śiva for a son. But in the Varāha-p. (73, 40-50) the Pāñcarātras say that Śiva first worshipped Nārāyaṇa who, at the former's prayer, granted the boon that he would worship Śiva for a favour. Thus the attempt of the Pāśupatas to raise Śiva over Viṣṇu is baffled by the Pāñcarātras. That the author of the first section of the Varāha-p. was acquainted with the Kūrma-p. is shown by the verses common to the chapters narrating the stories of Gautama in the two Purāṇas. Hence it is sure that the first section of the Varāha-p. was written after the Kūrma-p. had been recast by the Pāśupatas. As this recast was made towards the beginning of the 8th century A.D., the date of the first section of the Varāha-p. cannot be placed earlier than the middle of that century. Thus we get the upper limit.

Gopālabhaṭṭa quotes verses 7-52 of Var 99 in his Haribhaktivilāsa. This chapter appearing to be spurious, the date of the original chapters of the first section of the Varāha-p. should not

[68] Matsya, Kūrma, Varāha, Narasiṃha, Vāmana, (Paraśu-) Rāma, Rāma (Dāśarathi), Kṛṣṇa, Buddha and Kalki.

be placed later than 1400 A.D. Again, Vidyākara Vājapeyin quotes three verses from Var 66 and 70 in his Nityācārapaddhati; Vācaspatimiśra has a good number of verses from chap. 7 in his Tīrtha-cintāmaṇi; Śūlapāṇi has one verse from chap. 62 in his Vratakāla-viveka; Caṇḍeśvara quotes the entire chapters 40, 42 and 58 and also a large number of verses from chaps. 39 and 41 in his Kṛtya-ratnākara; Hemādri draws profusely upon chaps. 13, 14, 31, 32, 34, 37, 39-50, 55-65, 99, 109 and 112 in his Caturvarga-cintāmaṇi; Aparārka quotes a considerable number of verses from chaps. 13, 66, 70, 71 and 112 in his com. on Yāj; and Jīmūtavāhana draws upon chaps. 28-30 in his Kālaviveka (see App.). Hence the date of the original chapters of the first section of the Varāha-p. cannot be placed later than 1000 A.D. As in the Rudra-gītā of the Varāha-p. the words 'raudra' and 'pāśupata' have been used to mean the Āgamic Śaivas and their scriptures, these chapters should not be placed later than the beginning of the 9th century A.D., because the distinctive terms 'Śaiva' and 'Āgama' were well-known in the 9th century A.D.[69]

Thus the date of the original chapters of the first section of the Varāha-p. falls between the middle of the 8th and the beginning of the 9th century A.D., i.e., about 800 A.D.

As Hemādri has verses 82-83 and 85-88 from chap. 99 and verses 31-40 from chap. 112 and as Aparārka quotes verses 31-40 from chap. 112, the spurious chapters (Var 99, 54 to Var 112, 62) on gifts cannot be dated later than 1100 A.D. As Gopālabhaṭṭa quotes verses 7-52 from chap. 99 and as in chap. 99 there is mention of the Vaiṣṇavī Śakti who killed Mahiṣa on the Mandara hills, chaps. 90-96 (on the three Śaktis) and 99 (verses 1-52) should not be placed later than 1400 A.D. The lower limit of the date of chap. 97 is not known.

Let us now take up the second section. The use of the pronoun '*tena*' for the Boar in the very opening verse (*sa tena sāntvitāyāṃ vai pṛthivyāṃ yaḥ samāgataḥ*| etc.) of this section presupposes the chapters of the first. Therefore this section, which is the work of a different hand, is certainly later than 800 A.D. As Gopālabhaṭṭa quotes verses from chaps. 119, 128, 129, 131, 139 and 152 in his Haribhaktivilāsa, Govindānanda from chaps. 187, 188 and 190 in his Śrāddhakriyā-kaumudī, Dānakriyā-kaumudī and Śuddhikriyā-kaumudī, Śūlapāṇi from chap. 116 in his Prāyaścitta-viveka, Mādhavācārya from chap. 190 in his Bhāṣya on the Parāśara-smṛti, Madanapāla from chaps. 188 and 190 in his Madana-pārijāta, Caṇḍeśvara from chaps. 116 and 139 in his Kṛtya-ratnākara, Ānandatīrtha Madhva from chap. 70 in his Brahmasūtra-bhāṣya,

[69] See under Kūrma-purāṇa above.

Hemādri from chaps. 116, 139, 188 and 190 in his Caturvarga-cintāmaṇi, Devaṇabhaṭṭa from chap. 190 in his Smṛti-candrikā, Aniruddhabhaṭṭa from chap. 187 in his Hāralatā and Pitṛ-dayitā, and Aparārka from chaps. 188 and 190 in his com.[70], it is sure that the original chapters of this section were composed not later than 1000 A.D.

As chaps. 140-151 are earlier than the chapters on Mathurā-māhātmya, the lower limit of the date of the former is to be placed about 1500 A.D. No Nibandha-writer having been found to draw upon them, it is difficult to say anything more accurately.

As to the chapters on Mathurā-māhātmya, we have seen that they are later than the spurious chaps. 140-151 but earlier than the date of composition of the Haribhaktivilāsa.

The third section, which is certainly later than the original chapters of the preceding sections, was added to the Varāha-p. earlier than 1100 A.D., because Mādhavācārya quotes a verse from chap. 202 in his com. on the Parāśara-smṛti, Śrīdatta Upādhyāya quotes verses from chaps. 210-211 in his Kṛtyācāra, Caṇḍeśvara from chap. 211 in his Kṛtya-ratnākara, Hemādri from chap. 211 in his Caturvarga-cintāmaṇi, and Ballālasena from chaps. 205-207 in his Dānasāgara (see App.). Hence the date of this section is to be placed between 900 and 1100 A.D.

The date of the fourth section is not known. No Nibandha-writer has been found to draw upon it. It does not seem to have been added to the Varāha-p. earlier than 1100 A.D.

The results of the above analysis are as follows:

I. First section (comprising chaps. 1-112)

(a) Original

Chaps. 1-89 and 98	..	*C.* 800 A.D.

(b) Interpolated

Chaps. 90-96, and 99 (verses 1-52)	..	Not later than 1400 A.D.
Chap. 97	..	Date not known.
Chap. 99 (verses 53 to the end); Chaps. 100-111; and Chap. 112 (verses 1-62).	..	Not later than 1100 A.D

[70] See App.

II. Second section (comprising chaps. 113-192)		
(a) Original		
Chaps. 113-139 and 181-192	..	800-1000 A.D. (later than the original chapters in the first section).
(b) Interpolated		
Chaps. 140-151	..	Not later than 1500 A.D.
Chaps. 152-180	..	Later than chaps. 140-151 but not later than the date of composition of the Haribhaktivilāsa.
III. Third section		
Chaps. 193-212	..	Between 900 and 1100 A.D.
IV. Fourth section		
Chaps. 213 to the end ..	..	Not known; probably not earlier than 1100 A.D.

Besides the four sections of which we have spoken above, the present Varāha contained a fifth section which has been lost. The Nāradīya-p. (I, 103) divides the 'Varāha-p.' into two parts (bhāga)—Pūrva and Uttara, and lays down their contents. According to the Nāradīya, the Uttara-bhāga, in which the interlocutors were Pulastya and king Kuru, treated of Dharmas, Tīrtha-māhātmyas and Puṣkara[71]. Though the contents of the Pūrva-bhāga agree fully with those of the extant Varāha-p., the Uttara-bhāga is not found at all in the latter. There are, however, references in chap. 217 which show that the contents of the Uttara-bhāga followed this chapter. In Var 217, 1-6 Sanatkumāra enumerates the topics already spoken on by Brahmā and requests the latter to tell him about the origin of Tīrthas. Brahmā, consequently, refers Sanatkumāra to Pulastya who, Brahmā says, would speak on Tīrthas to Kuru-rāja and the sages.

[71] *uttare pravibhāge tu pulastya-kururājayoḥ|*
saṃvāde sarva-tīrthānāṃ māhātmyaṃ vistarāt pṛthak||
aśeṣa-dharmāś cākhyātāḥ pauṣkaraṃ puṇya-parva ca|
Nār I, 103, 13-14a.

Though it is difficult to find the provenance of the different sections of the present Varāha-p., we are sure that the first three sections of the present Varāha were composed in Northern India, for almost all of the numerous holy places named in these sections belong to this part of the country. Had the authors of these sections been the inhabitants of Southern India, they would have never ignored the holy places in their own part of the country. The fourth section, which deals with the holy places in Nepal, was most probably composed by an inhabitant of that place.

The authors of at least the first two sections of the Varāha-p. appear to have consulted other works before composing these sections. In Var 2, 2b the contents of this Purāṇa are said to have been derived from 'all Śāstras', and in Var 148, 20 this Purāṇa is said to be the essence of all Śāstras[72]. The literal agreement between Var 13 (verses 33 to the end) and 14 (verses 1-50, except 1 and 8a) and Viṣ III, 14 (verses 4 to the end) and 15 (1 to the end, except 1a, 8b-10, 22-23a and 38) shows that the author of the first section borrowed these common portions from the Viṣṇu-p. The story of Kṛṣṇa's curse on Śāmba and the latter's worship of the Sun (Var 177) is based on Bhav I, 73 ff. The latter Purāṇa is mentioned twice in Var 177.

4. THE PADMA-PURĀṆA

The present Padma, which is the result of several recasts, has come down to us in two distinct recensions—North Indian (Bengal) and South Indian. In Bengal Mss the Purāṇa is found to consist of five Khaṇḍas or books arranged in the following order —(1) Sṛṣṭi, (2) Bhūmi, (3) Svarga, (4) Pātāla and (5) Uttara. No edition of the Bengal recension has been published. The South Indian recension has been published by the Ānandāśrama and the Veṅkaṭeśvara Press. In both these editions the Purāṇa

[72] *kathayāmi purāṇasya viṣayaṃ sarva-śāstrataḥ|*
and
yathā ca mathyamānād vai dadhnaś coddhriyate ghṛtam|
evaṃ sarveṣu śāstreṣu vārāhaṃ ghṛta-saṃmitam||

It should be noted that the opening verse
triḥ-sapta-ṣaṭ-kṣiti-mite nṛpa-vikramasya
kāle gate bhagavato hari-bodhanasya|
viśveśvareṇa saha mādhavabhaṭṭa-nāmnā
kāśyāṃ varāha-kathitaṃ likhitaṃ purāṇam||
of chap. 218 in the Bibl. Ind. ed. of the Varāha-p. cannot be made the basis for any chronological deduction regarding the Purāṇa. It is merely a post-colophon statement of the scribe.

is found to consist of six Khaṇḍas, viz., (1) Ādi, (2) Bhūmi, (3) Brahma, (4) Pātāla, (5) Sṛṣṭi (also called Prakriyā) and (6) Uttara in the AnSS ed., and (1) Sṛṣṭi, (2) Bhūmi, (3) Svarga, (4) Brahma, (5) Pātāla and (6) Uttara in the Veṅk. ed. The Ādi-kh. in the former edition is the same as the 'Svarga-khaṇḍa' in the latter. Though in this so-called 'Svarga-khaṇḍa' (1, 23-24) the six Khaṇḍas have been enumerated in the same order and with the same titles as in the AnSS ed., the arrangement and titles of the Khaṇḍas in the Veṅk. edition are intended most probably for making the Purāṇa conform as far as possible to the old tradition.

That originally the Padma-p. consisted of five Khaṇḍas is evidenced not only by the Bengal Mss, which invariably give the number of the Khaṇḍas as five and arrange them in the same order as given above, but also by the printed editions themselves. In almost all places of the latter, except especially in the Ādi or the so-called 'Svarga', the enumeration of the Khaṇḍas is exactly the same as in Bengal Mss. In some Mss of the Ādi even, the titles of the five Khaṇḍas are found in place of those of the six[73].

The Bengal recension which, on account of the number, arrangement and contents of the Khaṇḍas, is often more reliable than the South Indian one, does not, however, represent the Padma-p. in its original form. In the Sṛṣṭi-kh. (1, 54-60) the contents of the five Parvans, corresponding to the five Khaṇḍas, are given as follows: the first, called Pauṣkara, treating of creation by Brahmā; the second, called Tīrtha-parvan, on mountains, islands and oceans; the third (called Svarga in the Bengal Mss of the Sṛṣṭi-kh.), on kings who gave rich sacrificial gifts; the fourth, on the genealogies of kings; and the fifth, on salvation. The topics, enumerated at the beginning of the Pātāla-kh. as already dealt with in the Khaṇḍas preceding it, agree with the above mentioned contents of the first three Khaṇḍas (see under Pātāla-khaṇḍa below). At the very outset of the Bengal Mss of the Svarga-kh. also, Sūta refers to the geography of the earth as already described, making no mention of the other topics dealt with in the preceding Bhūmi-kh[74]. From these references it can

[73] Ādi-kh., p. 2, footnotes 1 and 2

[74] Cf., for example, Ms No. 1625 of the Svarga-kh. in the D.U. Mss Lib. This Ms begins as follows:
sūta uvāca —
śeṣa-bhāṣitam ākarṇya tathā bhūgola-varṇanam|
pitā me punar āpṛcchat praṇato bādarāyaṇam||
sa niśamya tu bhūgolaṃ munir vātsyāyanaḥ punaḥ|
kim apṛcchac cheṣanāgaṃ tad bhavān vaktum arhati||
&c. &c.

be understood that the Bhūmi-kh., in its earlier form, treated mainly of the geography of the earth. It had probably also chapters on holy places from which it could derive its name. But the present Bhūmi-kh. of the Bengal recension is practically a book of legends having only four chapters on geography towards the end. Similar also is the case with the other Khaṇḍas, very small portions of which can claim to be original.

We shall now examine the different Khaṇḍas.

(1) ĀDI-KHAṆḌA. This Khaṇḍa, which is purely Vaiṣṇava, begins with a short account of the creation of the universe. It then passes on to the geography of the earth, deals with the glories of various holy places and rivers, and ends with a few chapters on Viṣṇu-bhakti and the duties of the members of the different castes in the different stages of their life.

This Khaṇḍa has a good number of chapters in common with some of the other Purāṇas; viz.,

Padma-p. (Ādi-kh.)	13, 2 ff.	=	Matsya-p. 186, 6b ff.
„	14-21	=	„ 187-194 respectively.
„	30	=	Padma-p. (Uttara-kh.) 243, 1-42.
„	31	=	„ „ 243, 43-96b; 244, 67-88a; and 245.
„	33, 3 ff.	=	Kūrma-p. I, 30, 16 ff.
„	34	=	„ I, 31, 3 ff.
„	35	=	„ I, 32, 1b ff.
„	36, 1b ff.	=	„ I, 33, 20 ff.
„	37,2 ff.	=	„ I, 34 2-19.
„	40, 15 ff.	=	Matsya-p. 103, 1b ff.
„	41-48	=	„ 104-111 respectively.
„	49	=	„ 112, 1-17.
„	51, 5 ff.	=	Kūrma-p. II, 12.
„	52-56	=	„ II, 13-17 respectively.
„	57-60	=	„ II, 26-29 „

It can be little doubted that as regards these common chapters the Ādi-kh. is the borrower. In order to establish the indebtedness of the Ādi we may compare, for example, the readings and contents of Ādi-kh. 51-60 with those of Kūr II, 12-17 and 26-29 and of chapters I-III of the Uśanas-saṃhitā.

(a) Uś.-saṃ. II, 1a ..	*snātvā ca tathā rathyopasarpaṇe.*
Kūr II, 13, 1a ..	Veṅk. ed.—*suptvā ca snātvā rathyopasarpaṇe* (v. l. '*rathyāvasarpaṇe*'). Vaṅga. ed.—*suptvā ca snātvā rathyāvasarpaṇe.*
Pd (Ādi) 52, 1a ..	*suptā ca snātvā rathyāvasarpaṇe.*
(b) Uś.-saṃ. II, 2b ..	*tathā cādhyayanārambhe.*
Kūr II, 13, 2b ..	Veṅk. ed.—*ṣṭhīvitvādhyayanārambhe.* Vaṅga. ed.—same as in the Veṅk. ed.
Pd (Ādi) 52, 2b ..	same as in the Kūrma-p.
(c) Uś.-saṃ. II, 3a ..	*samāgamya.*
Kūr II, 13, 3a ..	Veṅk. ed.—*samāgamya.* Vaṅga. ed.—*samākramya.*
Pd (Ādi) 52, 3a ..	*samākramya.*
(d) Uś.-saṃ. II, 3b ..	*ācānte cācamet.*
Kūr II, 13, 3b ..	Veṅk. ed.—*ācānto 'pyācamet.* Vaṅga. ed.—same as in the Veṅk. ed.
Pd (Ādi) 52, 3b ..	same as in the Kūrma-p.
(e) Uś.-saṃ. II, 5a ..	*aśrupāte tathācāme ahitasya . . .*
Kūr II, 13, 5a ..	Veṅk. ed.—*ācāmed aśrupāte vā lohitasya . . . . .* Vaṅga. ed.—same as in the Veṅk. ed.
Pd (Ādi) 52, 5a ..	same as in the Kūrma-p.
(f) Uś.-saṃ. II. 6a ..	*spṛṣṭvā . . . . . athānyataḥ.*
Kūr II, 13, 6a ..	Veṅk. ed.—*suptvā . . . . athāvyayaḥ* (v. l. '*athānyataḥ*'). Vaṅga. ed.—*suptvā . . . . athānyataḥ.*
Pd (Ādi) 52, 6a ..	*āgato vā 'camet suptvā sakṛt sakṛd athānyataḥ.*
(g) Uś.-saṃ. II, 7a ..	*nṝṇām athāśmanaḥ . . . . nīviṃ viparidhāya ca.*
Kūr II, 13, 7a ..	Veṅk. ed.—*strīṇām athātmanaḥ . . . . nīviṃ vā paridhāya ca* (v. l. '*strīṇām athātma-saṃsparśe* etc'.). Vaṅga. ed.—. . . . *nīliṃ vā . . .*
Pd (Ādi) 52, 7a ..	*strīṇām athātma-saṃsparśe nīliṃ vā paridhāya ca. ..*
&c.	&c.

Scores of similar examples may be given, but it is needless to multiply them. The few examples given above are sufficient to show that the Ādi-kh. follows much more the Kūrma-p. than the Uśanas-saṃhitā. Of course, in a few cases the Ādi-kh. has readings which are found not in the Kūrma-p. but in the Uśanas-saṃhitā. This can be explained by presuming that the Ms of the Kūrma-p., from which the chapters of the Ādi-kh. were derived, had better readings than the Mss on which the printed editions are based. As regards the few cases wherein the Ādi-kh. agrees neither with the Kūrma-p. nor with the Uśanas-saṃhitā, the scribes of the Mss are probably responsible.

In Ādi-kh., chap. 50, Sūta refers to Karma-yoga, the practice of which alone, he says, can please Viṣṇu, and in chap. 51 he proceeds, at the request of the sages, to describe it to them. Thus the unknown interpolator creates an opportunity for himself to insert some of the chapters of the Kūrma-p. In doing so, he has tried to efface the Śaiva stamp which these chapters bear. Thus in a few places the names of Śiva have been replaced conveniently by those of Viṣṇu[75], while in many other places the names of the god have been retained intact[76]. In Ādi-kh. 60, 32 ff. meditation on Śiva is emphasised; and he, not Viṣṇu, is identified with the supreme Brahma in the same words as in Kūr II, 29, 37 ff.

A comparison of contents of the above mentioned chapters of the Uśanas-saṃhitā, the Kūrma-p. and the Padma-p. (Ādi-kh.) also shows that the Ādi-kh. borrowed the Smṛti-chapters from the Kūrma-p. Chapters I-IX of the Uśanas-saṃhitā are found, with some variations in the numbers of verses, in Kūr II, 12-15, 19-23, and 30-33. The intervening chapters, i.e., Kūr II, 16-18 and 24-29, were probably added at the time the incorporation was made, or after it. The Ādi-kh. takes some of the chapters common to the Uśanas-saṃhitā and the Kūrma-p. and some of those which are found only in the latter. For example, of Kūr II, 12-15, 19-23 and 30-33 the Ādi takes chaps. 12-15 only, and of Kūr II, 16-18 and 24-29 it takes chaps. 16-17 and 26-29, leaving out those chapters which treat of funeral ceremonies, penances, impurity, sacrifices, means of livelihood, daily duties and rules of diet. This shows that the Ādi-kh. used the Kūrma-p. as its source and not *vice versa*. Had the Kūrma-p. been the borrower, it would have been necessary for it to compare the contents of the Uśanas-saṃhitā with those of the Ādi-kh. and

[75] Viz., Ādi-kh. 54, 35b where '*mahādeva*' of the Kūr has been replaced by '*hṛṣīkeśa*'; Ādi 57, 26b has '*keśavaṃ*' for '*śaṃkaraṃ*' of the Kūr; Ādi 57, 27a reads '*viṣṇur hṛṣīkeśaḥ*' for '*somo mahādevaḥ*' of the Kūr; and so on.

[76] Viz., Ādi 60 ,11b; 60, 20a; 57, 28a, 30a and 31b; and so forth.

to accept some chapters from the one and some from the other, while supplementing the borrowed chapters with those of its own composition. Such a case seems to be improbable, especially when we take into consideration the other arguments given above. As regards the few additional verses in some of the chapters common to the Kūrma-p. and the Ādi-kh., it is clear that at least some of them were added later. For example, Kūr II, 14, 57b-61a, which describe the method of Gāyatrī-uddhāra after the manner of the Tantriks, are to be found neither in the Ādi nor in the Veṅk. ed. of the Kūrma-p. The other such extra verses might have either been later additions to the Kūrma-p. or been lost from the Ādi in course of time.

As to the other chapters common to the Ādi-kh. on the one hand and the Matsya, Padma (Uttara-kh.) and Kūrma-p. on the other, it may similarly be proved that the Ādi-kh. is the borrower. Now, Mat 103-112 are to be dated between 850 and 1250 A.D.; Mat 186-194 are to be placed later than 800 A.D.[77]; Kūr I, 30-34 are to be dated between 700 and 1150 A.D., and most probably between 700 and 800 A.D.; and Kūr II, 12-17 and 26-29 were added between 700 and 800 A.D.[78] Hence the date of composition, or rather compilation, of *the Ādi-kh. cannot reasonably be placed before* 950 *A.D.* As its contents have been included in those of the so-called 'Svarga-khaṇḍa' given in the Nāradīya-p. (I, 39, 14-19a), *it should not be dated later than* 1400 *A.D.*

Though the large majority of the verses quoted by Gopālabhaṭṭa from the Devadūta-vikuṇḍala-saṃvāda (interlocution between Devadūta and Vikuṇḍala) of the 'Pādma', and only a few of the verses quoted from the same Purāṇa in Vācaspatimiśra's Tīrthacintāmaṇi, are traceable in the Ādi-khaṇḍa (chapters 31 and 43 respectively), it is highly probable that these two authors took these verses from the Uttara-kh. (chaps. 243-246) wherein the entire chapter 31 and a few verses, including most of the quoted ones, of chap. 43 of the Ādi-kh. are found.

That part of the Padma-p. which has been published by the Vaṅgavāsī Press, Calcutta, under the title 'Svarga-khaṇḍa' is nothing but the combination of the Ādi- and the Brahma-kh. as found in the AnSS ed. The main differences, besides those in readings, between these two editions are that Ādi-kh. (AnSS ed.) 1, 18 to the end, which contain the names of the six Khaṇḍas (viz., Ādi, Bhūmi, Brahma etc.) and which describe how the Padma-p. was inherited by Sūta from Hari through Brahmā, Nārada and Vyāsa, and the entire chapter 24 of the Brahma-kh. are not found in the Vaṅga. ed.

[77] See under Matsya-purāṇa. [78] See under Kūrma-purāṇa.

Ādi-kh. 2, 1a reads '*ādi-sargam ahaṃ tāvat* etc'., while the so-called Svarga-kh. (1, 18a) reads '*adya svargam ahaṃ* etc.' The 'Svarga-kh.' in the Veṅk. ed. also gives the names of the six Khaṇḍas beginning with the Ādi and reads '*ādi-sargaṃ* etc'. Yet it is called 'Svarga-khaṇḍa'. The facts that in some Mss the Ādi- and the Brahma-kh. are combined under the title 'Svarga-khaṇḍa' and that the contents of the 'Svarga-khaṇḍa' given in Nār I, 93, 14-19a are the same as those of the Ādi- and the Brahma-kh., show that there was a confusion of the Ādi and Brahma with the real Svarga-khaṇḍa perhaps on account of the reading '*adya svargaṃ* etc'. in some Mss of the Ādi.

(2) BHŪMI-KHAṆḌA. [79]. It has already been said that the Bhūmi-kh., in its earlier form, treated mainly of geography—a topic which is totally wanting in our present edition. Our Bhūmi has become entirely a book of legends. These legends have been introduced in order to prove the sanctity of various holy places and to show how Prahlāda, though a demon, became so great a devotee of Viṣṇu, and why a teacher, a father or a chaste and devoted wife is called a Tīrtha. In connection with these legends and glorifications, the duties of the Āśramas have been treated of in chap. 59, gifts in chaps. 39 and 40, duties of women in chap. 41, holy places in chaps. 90 and 92, and Vrata in chap. 87.

The present Bhūmi does not seem to have come from an early date. At the very beginning of this Khaṇḍa the sages refer to the 'Purāṇas' in which Prahlāda has been said to have pleased Keśava

[79] The AnSS ed. is almost the same as the Vaṅga. ed., the main differences, besides those in readings, being that the chapters in the latter edition have often a few additional verses. There are also variations in the numbers of chapters, though the contents are the same; viz.,

AnSS ed.		Vaṅga. ed.
Chaps. 1-14	=	Chaps. 1-14 respectively.
Chap. 15	=	Chaps. 15-16.
Chaps. 16-37	=	Chaps. 17-38 respectively.
Chaps. 38-39	=	Chap. 39.
Chaps. 40 to the end	=	Chaps. 40 to the end respectively.

The Veṅk. ed. also is generally the same as the AnSS ed. Like the latter it consists of 125 chapters which correspond to those in the latter ed.

The contents of the Bhūmi-kh., as found in the Bengal recension, are more variegated than those of the AnSS ed. Chaps. 1-120 of this recension (see Ms No. 1622, D.U. Mss Lib.) are in general agreement with the chapters of the AnSS edition; chaps. 121-127 deal with the Sthāvara-tīrtha; chaps. 128-131 with Bhūgola-varṇana; chap. 132 with Purāṇa-mahima-varṇana; and chap. 133 with Viṣayānu-krama. Chaps. 121 to the end of the Ms are not found in the AnSS edition.

even at the age of five; and they ask Sūta why, during the war between the gods and demons, this Prahlāda fought with Vāsudeva and was ultimately killed and absorbed by the latter. In answer to this question, Sūta tells them the legends of Somaśarman. The above reference to the age and conduct of Prahlāda betrays an acquaintance of the author of the Bhūmi-kh. with the Bhāgavata-p., in which alone the legend of Prahlāda has been told with the express mention of his age[80]. Therefore, the date of the Bhūmi-kh. cannot possibly be earlier than the beginning of the seventh century A.D. This limit is supported by the mention of the Buddha among the incarnations of Viṣṇu in Bhūmi-kh. 18, 66. We have seen that the Buddha began to be regarded as such probably from about 550 A.D. (see under Matsya-p.). Further, in Bhūmi 78 the 'Turuṣkas' have been mentioned as Mlecchas, who have no lock of hair left on the crown of their head (śikhāvihīna), kill cows and Brāhmans, fall easy prey to appetite, have itches, do not tuck the hem of their lower garment into the waistband (mukta-kaccha), are of furious temperament, are habituated adulterers, eat everything without discrimination, marry girls of their own Gotras, and are guilty of similar other vices. The mention of the 'Turuṣkas' and the way in which they are described, mean undoubtedly the Muhammadans who came to India about the ninth century A.D. Hence the date of *the Bhūmi-kh. cannot reasonably be placed earlier than* 900 *A.D.* Such a late date is supported not only by the importance given to the Tulasī plant and by the mention of a wife as a Tīrtha but also by the fact that none of the numerous verses quoted from the 'Padma-p.' or 'Pādma' in Devaṇabhaṭṭa's Smṛti-candrikā, Aparārka's com. on Yāj., Aniruddhabhaṭṭa's Hāralatā, Jīmūtavāhana's Kāla-viveka, Hemādri's Caturvarga-cintāmaṇi, Madanapāla's Madana-pārijāta, Vācaspatimiśra's Tīrtha-cintāmaṇi, Mādhavācārya's com. on the Parāśara-smṛti, Vidyākara Vājapeyin's Nityācārapaddhati, Śūlapāṇi's Dīpakalikā, Vratakāla-viveka, Prāyaścitta-viveka and Śrāddha-viveka, Caṇḍeśvara's Kṛtya-ratnākara, Śrīdatta Upādhyāya's Kṛtyācāra, Govindānanda's Varṣakriyā-kaumudī, and Raghunandana's Smṛti-tattva, is traceable in this Khaṇḍa.

The Bhūmi-kh., which is presumably a work of the Bhāgavatas[81], was written most probably somewhere about the river Narmadā, because this river, which is also called Revā[82], has been

[80] Bhāg VII, 5, 36 (*pañca-hāyanaḥ*).

In the Viṣṇu-p. also the story of Prahlāda is given, but there is no express mention of his age.

[81] Cf. Bhūmi-kh. 98, 39, wherein the Bhāgavata Mantra '*oṃ namo bhagavate vāsudevāya*' has been given.

glorified more than once and declared to have a sanctifying power much greater than that of even the Gaṅgā, Sindhu etc[83].

(3) BRAHMA-KHAṆḌA. This Khaṇḍa, in which the interlocutors are Sūta and Śaunaka, occupies the third place in our edition of the Padma-p. But its real position seems to have been immediately after the Ādi-kh., for Śaunaka, who appears in this Khaṇḍa without even a single word of introduction, is introduced first at the beginning of the Ādi-kh. but is not found in the Bhūmi-kh. which intervenes between the Ādi and the Brahma.

The Brahma-khaṇḍa is a short one consisting of 26 chapters only. It is concerned with the description of Vaiṣṇava feasts and festivals. Thus, it treats of the merits of besmearing a Viṣṇu-temple with cowdung and of burning a lamp there at night, the observances during the month of Kārttika, the Jayantī-vrata, the Guruvāra-vrata, the birthday festivals of Rādhā and Kṛṣṇa, the Ekādaśī-vrata, the worship of Viṣṇu on the fullmoon day, and the offer of various things to Viṣṇu. The merits of observing these festivals have been illustrated with various stories. In connection with the birthday festival of Rādhā, the story of the churning of the ocean has been narrated.

This Khaṇḍa comes undoubtedly from a very late date. It speaks highly of the gifts of lamps to the shrines of Viṣṇu. The birthday festival of Rādhā has been treated of in chap. 7 and referred to in other places. The Tulasī plant has been glorified in chap. 22 and called the 'wife of Hari' in chap. 10. Brāhmaṇa-māhātmya has been dealt with in chap. 14, wherein Sūta says: "O best of the twice-born, a Brāhman is superior to (the members of) all castes. He is known to be a prop of all the gods, and is (identical with) the lord Nārāyaṇa. . . . . . The man who licks a particle of water sticking to the foot of a Brāhman, gets rid of all sins (arising out) of the murder of Brāhmans, etc. . . . . By serving the feet of a twice-born a sonless woman is gifted with a son, and one, who brings forth dead children, bears living ones. The holy places existing in the universe are found in a sea, and those in the latter exist at the feet of a twice-born". All these are unmistakable stamps of a very late age. The inscriptional evidences show that the gifts of lamps to shrines became popular in southern India from about the end of the ninth century A.D.[84].

[82] See Pd (Bhūmi-kh.) 92, 32; Devī-p. (Vaṅga. ed.) 37, 41; Sk V, iii (Revā-kh.) 5, 7; Eggeling, Ind. off. Cat., VI, p. 1303; and so on.

[83] Bhūmi-kh. 92.

[84] Ep. Ind., III, 1894-5, pp. 281 and 284; V, pp. 42-44 and 104-106; VII, 1902-3, pp. 133 ff. and 138 ff.; and so on. JASB, Vol. LXXII, 1903, p. 120.

The birthday festival of Rādhā also indicates the late origin of the Khaṇḍa, there being no mention of the Rādhā-cult in the Mahābhārata, Rāmāyaṇa, Harivaṃśa and the earlier Purāṇas. 'Nimbārka, probably in the 12th century, regards Rādhā as the eternal consort of Kṛṣṇa, who, in his view, is not merely an incarnation of Viṣṇu, but the eternal Brahma. It was not until the 16th century that the sect of the Rādhāvallabhins, who attach great importance to the worship of Rādhā as Śakti, arose'[85]. The use of the Tulasī leaves in Viṣṇu-worship, the deification of the plant, and the undue glorification of Brāhmans also point to a late date which is further supported by the fact that none of the Nibandha-writers are found to name or draw upon this Khaṇḍa. Its contents are, however, included in those of the so-called 'Svarga-khaṇḍa' given in the Nāradīya-p. Hence *its date cannot be placed later than 1400 A.D.*

(4) PĀTĀLA-KHAṆḌA. [86]. This Khaṇḍa begins with Śeṣa and Vātsyāyana as interlocutors, their interlocution being reported by Sūta to the sages.

At the very outset of this Khaṇḍa, the sages mention the Svarga-kh. as already listened to[87]. This shows that the Pātāla-kh. was preceded immediately by the Svarga-kh. and not by the Brahma-kh. as in the printed editions. That this Svarga-kh. is

[85] Winternitz, Ind. Lit., Vol. I, p. 568, footnote 3. Also Grierson, ERE, X, pp. 559 ff. Farquhar, Outline, p. 318.

[86] Though the AnSS ed. has 113 chapters in place of only 72 of the Vaṅga. ed., their contents are in general the same. The cause of such variation in the numbers of chapters is that a good number of chapters of the Vaṅga. ed. have each been broken up into two or more chapters in the AnSS ed. The readings in the two editions agree closely, but the chapters in the Vaṅga. ed. have sometimes a few more verses than those in the AnSS ed.

The Veṅk. ed. of the Pātāla-kh. contains 117 chapters, but its contents are on the whole the same as those of the Vaṅga. and AnSS editions.

The Pātāla-kh. of the Bengal recension differs considerably from the printed editions. In Ms No. 1623 (D. U. Mss Lib.) there are practically four groups of chapters. Of these, chaps. 1-28, constituting the first group, deal with the description of the subterranean regions, the story of killing the demon Tripura, the legends of the kings of the Solar race, and especially the Rāma-legend. These chapters are not found in the printed editions. Chaps. 29-96, forming the second group, tally generally with chaps. 1-68 of the AnSS ed. Chaps. 97-99, constituting the third group, deal with the descendants of Rāma and with the glories of the Bhāgavata-p., and are not found in the printed editions. Chaps. 100 to the end of the fourth group describe the Kṛṣṇa-legend and have their parallels in the printed editions.

[87] *śrutaṃ sarvaṃ mahābhāga svarga-khaṇḍaṃ manoharam|*

Pātāla 1, 2.

not the same as the 'Svarga-khaṇḍa' of the Vaṅga. and Veṅk. editions is shown by Vātsyāyana's enumeration of the topics dealt with in those parts of the Padma-p. which preceded the Pātāla-khaṇḍa. These topics are: accounts of creation, destruction etc. of the world; geography of the earth and the universe; the solar system; stories of kings; stories of the kings of the Solar race; and the story of Rāma and his horse-sacrifice. Of these, the accounts of creation, destruction etc. are to be found in the Sṛṣṭi-kh.; geography was dealt with in the Bhūmi-kh.; and the accounts of the solar system and stories of kings occur in the Svarga-kh. of the Bengal recension.

The Pātāla-kh. consists of three distinct parts, viz.,

(A) chaps. 1-68—on Rāma's return from Laṅkā and celebration of the horse-sacrifice,

(B) chaps. 69-99—on Kṛṣṇa-carita, including Vaiśākha-māhātmya,

and (C) chaps. 100 to the end—on Rāma's life after the horse-sacrifice.

These three parts are quite unconnected and distinct in character, and deserve separate consideration.

(A) Chaps. 1-98. This portion of the Purāṇa is avowedly Rāmaite. It deifies Rāma and conceives him as Viṣṇu incarnate. Sītā is identified with Lakṣmī. The utterance of Rāma's name is said to be extremely sanctifying and capable of conferring final release.

In this portion there are a few chapters on Smṛti-matter; viz., chap. 9 (verses 40-63) deals with Varṇāśramadharma, chaps. 17-22 with holy places, and chap. 48 (verses 4-69) with the results of actions. These chapters and verses are found in the Bengal Mss also.

Pātāla-kh. 1-68 do not seem to be of very early origin. The fact that in the Bengal Mss of this Khaṇḍa the first twentyeight chapters end with the passing of Rāma to heaven, indicates that the portion dealing with Rāma's celebration of the horse-sacrifice is the work of a different hand. Otherwise, the story of the sacrifice would have preceded that of Rāma's climbing the heaven. Now, from the mention of the Bhāgavata-p. in Pātāla 10, 65 it seems that chaps. 1-68 were written later than the end of the sixth century A.D. The occurrence of the name of the Tulasī plant in more places than one and the reference to its worship, tend to assign a much later date to the chapters. It is highly probable that these chapters were added to the Pātāla-kh. after the Muhammadans had come to India, because in Pātāla 33, 43 people are advised not to drink water from the wells of the Mlecchas. It is noteworthy in this connection that none of the verses quoted by the early Nibandha-writers from the Padma-p. is found in the present Pātāla-kh.

In chap. 66 the Rāmāyaṇa is said to consist of six Kāṇḍas—Bāla, Āraṇyaka, Kiṣkindhyā, Sundara, Yuddha and Uttara. The contents of each of these Kāṇḍas have also been given. The mention of the 'six Kāṇḍas' of the Rāmāyaṇa should not be taken to assign Pātāla 1-68 to an early date, because the Bāla-kāṇḍa includes the contents of the Ayodhyā-kāṇḍa also.

(B) Chaps. 69-99. This portion, in which Sūta reports to the sages the interlocution between Śiva and Pārvatī on Kṛṣṇa-carita, was certainly added later. At the beginning of the Pātāla-kh. Vātsyāyana requests Śeṣa to tell him elaborately about the celebration of the Aśvamedha sacrifice by Rāma, no mention being made of Kṛṣṇa-carita.

In this portion Kṛṣṇa and Rādhā have been glorified. Here Kṛṣṇa has sometimes been identified with the supreme Brahma. He is Viṣṇu incarnate. His worship frees the worshipper of all sins and gives him final release. Rādhā is called Kṛṣṇa's Śakti. She is the 'avyayā mūla-prakṛti', of which Durgā and other goddesses are infinitesimal parts. "Millions of Viṣṇus are born of the dust of her feet". Vṛndāvana, the place of the love adventures of Kṛṣṇa, Rādhā and other Gopīs, is highly praised. It is said: "Vṛndāvana is the most secret place in the world. It is holy and beautiful. It is the imperishable, blissful and eternal place of Govinda. It is not separate from his body and is the prop of the bliss of experiencing the supreme Brahma". By these and similar other extravagant expressions Vṛndāvana has been equalled with the eternal abode of Viṣṇu.

Besides the stories and praises of gods and goddesses, there are a few chapters on Smṛti-topics; viz., chaps. 78-79 deal with the worship of Śālagrāma, chap. 80 with the worship of Viṣṇu, chaps. 81-82 with initiation, and chaps. 84-99 with the Vratas in the month of Vaiśākha.

Pātāla-kh. 69-99 seem to have come from a very late date. In connection with the description of Vṛndāvana, mention is made of the 'stealing of clothes' by Kṛṣṇa and the worship of the goddess Kātyāyanī by the Gopīs. This mention betrays the acquaintance of the author of these chapters with the Bhāgavata-p. Further, in these chapters there are numerous traces of a developed Rādhā-cult. Indications of Tantricism here are also not negligible. The 'Tantras' and 'Āgamas' have been mentioned as authorities more than once; the Tantric Yantra has been recognised as one of the mediums of worship (Pātāla 79, 1); and the use of the Tantric formulae, Nyāsa, Mudrā etc. has been ordained. The method of the worship (sādhana) of Kṛṣṇa, as laid down in chap. 83, wants that the worshipper should always consider himself a maiden fit for cohabitation with Kṛṣṇa. These facts considered together show that Pātāla-kh. 69-99 are most probably to be dated not earlier than 900 A.D. These chapters are, of course, not later than 1400 A.D., for Gopālabhaṭṭa quotes numerous verses from chaps. 84-94 and 96 in his Haribhaktivilāsa (see App.), and the contents of these chapters are given in Nāradīya-p. I, 93.

(C) Chaps. 100 to the end. This portion, in which the interlocution between Śaṃkara (i.e., Śiva) and Rāma is reported by Sūta to the sages, was undoubtedly written by the Liṅga-worshippers. Though here the unity of Śiva and Viṣṇu in the form of Rāma is recognised and also often asserted, it is Śiva who is assigned a higher place. The Śaiva character of this portion is best shown by the facts that the method of Liṅga-worship has been given elaborately at several places and the glories of the ashes (bhasma) have been sung in many of the chapters.

In this portion chaps. 101 and 113 deal with funeral ceremonies, chap. 102 with the duties of women, chaps. 101, 105 and 110 with Liṅga-worship, chap. 108 with Vrata, and chap. 110 with Yuga-dharma.

The date of this portion of the Pātāla-kh. cannot be placed earlier than 800 A.D. In chap. 102, verses 1-2, the Kūrma-p. has been mentioned as conferring devotion to Śiva; and in Pātāla 110, 483 this Purāṇa has been prescribed to be read, because it preaches the unity of Śiva and Viṣṇu. Such a character of the Kūrma-p. and its prescription by the Liṅga-worshippers point to its Pāśupata character. As this portion does not seem to be earlier than chaps. 1-68, it should be dated later than 900 A.D.

In Pātāla-kh. 100, 44-50 the method of writing a few syllables is described in connection with copying the Purāṇas for the enhancement of one's religious merits. But this description should not be taken as basis for determining the date of Pātāla-kh. 100 to the end.

(5) SṚṢṬI-KHAṆḌA.[88]. This Khaṇḍa, which is assigned the fifth place in our edition, is really the first of the set. This position of the Khaṇḍa is betrayed by the mode of its beginning as well as by the sequence and contents of the five Parvans given in chap. 1.

This Khaṇḍa, as we have it now, can be rightly divided into two parts:

(1) chaps. 1-43 (verses 1-97)

and (2) chaps. 43 (verses 98 ff.) to the end.

It will be seen hereinafter that the chapters of the second part were added to the Sṛṣṭi-kh. after the Muhammadans had established kingdoms in India. Hence the chapters of the first part, which are of earlier date, are examined first.

[88] The Sṛṣṭi-khaṇḍa in Bengal Mss. consists only of 46 (or according to Aufrecht, 45) chapters. The corresponding chapters in a Bengal Ms. (No. 1621, D. U. Mss Lib.) of this Khaṇḍa and the AnSS ed. are given below:

Ms of Sṛṣṭi-kh.		AnSS ed.	Ms of Sṛṣṭi-kh.		AnSS ed.
Chaps. 1-22	=	Chaps. 1-22 respectively.	Chaps. 37-38	=	Chaps. 35-36 respectively.
Chap. 23	=	„ 23, and 24, 1-63.	Chap. 39	=	„ 37, and 38,1.
Chaps. 24-27	=	Chap. 24, 64-277.	„ 40	=	Chap. 38, 2 to the end.
Chap. 28	=	„ 25, 8b to the end.	„ 41	=	„ 39 (especially except verses 15-31 and 95-96).
Chap. 29	=	Chaps. 26-27.	Chaps. 42-43	=	„ 40, 1-439a.
Chaps. 30-35	=	„ 28-33 respectively.	Chap. 44 (especially except verses 1-32)	=	„ 40, 439b to the end.
Chap. 36	=	Chap. 34 (especially except verses 156-165).			„ 41, 1-106.
			Cf. chaps. 45-46 with		chaps. 42-43.

The numbers of verses in these corresponding chapters very seldom agree. It is noteworthy that as regards the chapters borrowed from the Matsya-p. the Ms is at times more true to its original than the printed edition which appears to have undergone additions and losses.

The contents of the Vaṅga. ed. of the Sṛṣṭi-kh. are in general agreement with those of the AnSS ed. except in that chaps. 80 and 81 (on the worship of the Moon and the Mars) in the former edition are not found in the latter, and chaps. 30 and 31, 1-8 (on the origin and exploits of the goddess Kṣemaṅkarī) in the latter edition are not found in the former. There are, of course, differences in readings and numbers of verses in the corresponding chapters.

The Veṅk. ed. of this Khaṇḍa does not contain the story of Kṣemaṅkarī. It resembles much the Vaṅga, ed.

A careful study of the chapters of the first part shows that they should be divided again into several groups; viz.,

group 1—chapters 1-18, 29 and 31 (verses 76 to the end);
group 2—chapters 19-28, 32-42 and 43 (verses 1-97);
group 3—chapter 31 (verses 8b-75); also others like chap. 20, verses 139b-143a;
and group 4—chapters 30 and 31 (verses 1-8a).

The chapters of group 1, which begins with a verse extolling the holy waters of Puṣkara and mentioning Brahmā and the Vipras, constitute the nucleus of the present Sṛṣṭi-kh. This section of the Khaṇḍa was written, or rather compiled, by the Brahmā-worshippers. It contains an interesting story which is important in that it throws light on the contemporary state of Brahmā-worship as well as on the motive with which the Brahmā-worshippers set to write this part of the work. The story says that once Brahmā instituted at Puṣkara a pompous sacrifice which was attended and contributed to by all the gods. When everything was ready and the time for initiation was drawing near, a priest invited Sāvitrī, wife of Brahmā, to come to the sacrificial hall. But Sāvitrī was engaged in managing household affairs. She declined to go until her work was finished and the goddesses turned up to accompany her. The priest, therefore, returned to Brahmā and told him what Sāvitrī had said. Brahmā was angry and asked Indra to procure a second wife for him. Consequently, Indra brought in Gāyatrī, an Ābhīra girl. Then Sāvitrī came to the place in company with the goddesses and found Gāyatrī. She got angry and cursed Brahmā saying that the people would not worship him at any time throughout the whole year except only once in the month of Kārttika[89]. She also cursed Gāyatrī and the gods and goddesses present, and went away. Then, Gāyatrī rose up and gave a boon to Brahmā that those people, who would worship him, would have enough of worldly prosperity in this life and attain final emancipation in the end[90]. She granted boons to the other gods and goddesses also.

The above story shows that the motive of the Brahmā-worshippers was to revive Brahmāism which was in a decadent state. Many of the worshippers of Brahmā accepted Śaivism[91], and the worship of the god was growing obsolete. The Brahmā-worshippers, therefore, fabricated stories to extol Brahmā and his worship and to explain away the growing unpopularity of the

[89] Sṛṣṭi-kh. 17, 152-153. [90] Sṛṣṭi-kh. 17, 260-261.

[91] Cf. Sṛṣṭi-kh. 14, 133a—'*koṭyāḥ śataṃ tu viprāṇām uddhartāsi mahādyute*'—addressed by Brahmā to Śiva. 'Vipras' are the worshippers of Brahmā.

worship of the god by ascribing it to the curse of Sāvitrī. They also borrowed a number of chapters from the Matsya and the Viṣṇu-p. In these chapters they subsituted the names of other gods with those of Brahmā and made similar other changes in order that these borrowed chapters might serve their sectarian end. The chapters borrowed from the Matsya-p. have already been enumerated (see under Matsya-p.). Those taken from the Viṣṇu-p. are given below.

Padma-p. (Sṛṣṭi-kh.)		Viṣṇu-p.
2, 83 to the end (except a few lines)	=	I, 2, verses 10-13a, 14b, 33b and 34 to the end.
3, 1-20a	=	I, 3 (except a good number of verses).
3, 20b-52	=	I, 4 (except a good number of verses).
3, 53-116	=	I, 5, 4b to the end.
3, 117-155a	=	I, 6.
3, 155b-188a	=	I, 7.
3, 188b to the end	=	I, 8, 1-13.
4, 1 and 4-83a	=	I, 8, 14; and I, 9, 1-38a, 66b and 76-113a.
13, 348-349a, 350b, 352-363 and 364b-376.	=	III, 17, 41-42a; and III, 18, 1a, 2-6a, 7-17, 19 and 23-29.

[These corresponding chapters differ more or less in the numbers of verses. The Vaṅga. ed. is often more faithful to its original than the AnSS ed.]

The chapters in group 2 are different from those in group 1 in general character, some being Vaiṣṇava, some Rāmaite and some Śaiva. A good number of these chapters have been borrowed from the Matsya-p., but they do not show any traces of the attempt of the Brahmā-worshippers to adapt them to their own purpose. Hence it can be little doubted that the chapters of the second group were added to the Sṛṣṭi-kh. by some people other than the Brahmā-worshippers. These chapters, being rooted in those of group 1 and frequently referring to the events and stories in the latter, are certainly later in date. Their comparatively late date is further established by the story of king Śveta (in Sṛṣṭi-kh. 33, 85 ff.) which is different from that in chap. 31 (verses 104 ff.) of the first group.

The portions of chapters constituting the third group are the works of those Brahmā-worshippers who were influenced by Tantricism, for the method of Brāhmī initiation (dīkṣā) described in Sṛṣṭi-kh. 31, 8b-75 is highly Tantric. This method of initiation stands in great contrast with that briefly described in chap. 15 (verses 96 ff.) of group 1. This latter form of initiation is to be carried out 'after the Vedic method' (*vedoktena vidhānena*), and it is free from Tantric influence. The fact that there is no Tantric element either in the above mentioned chapter or in others proves the comparatively late date of the sections in the third group. The occurrence of some of these sections in the chapters of group 2, shows that the former are later than the latter.

The chapters forming the fourth group deal with the origin and exploits of Kṣemaṅkarī, a Śākta deity on the Puṣkara hills. They are, therefore, the works of a Śākta hand. Their absence from the Vaṅga. and Veṅk. editions tends to prove their comparatively recent origin.

From the above discussion about the different groups of chapters constituting the first part it follows that *the Sṛṣṭi-kh. was first written, or compiled, by the Brahmā-worshippers; it was then taken up by some non-Brāhmas who added to it many new chapters; next, the Tantric Brāhmas interpolated some verses or groups of verses; and last of all the Śāktas made further additions.*

As to the dates of these chapters it can be said that those of group 1 were written most probably not earlier than 600 A.D. Those chapters (viz., 16-22) of the Matsya-p., which have been borrowed in this group, cannot reasonably be dated earlier than 400 A.D. (see under Matsya-p.), Moreover, the decadent state of Brahmāism which is indicated by the chapters of this group, points to a period later than that of Varāhamihira, during whose time the Brahmā-sect was still a living one. Therefore, 600 A.D. may be taken to be the upper limit of the date of the chapters of the aforesaid group. As verses have been quoted from chap. 10 in the Smṛti-tattva of Raghunandana, from chap. 15 in the Kṛtyācāra of Śrīdatta Upādhyāya, from chap. 31 in the Kṛtya-ratnākara of Caṇḍeśvara, from chaps. 9, 10, 17 and 31 in the Caturvarga-cintāmaṇi of Hemādri, from chaps. 10, 15 and 31 in the Dānasāgara of Ballālasena, from chap. 7 in the Smṛti-candrikā of Devaṇabhaṭṭa, from chap. 10 in the Hāralatā of Aniruddha-bhaṭṭa, and from chaps. 8 and 31 in Aparārka's com. on Yāj. (see App.), it is sure that the chapters of the first group were written earlier than 950 A.D. Again, the date of the chapters of the second group also cannot be placed later than 950 A.D., because

Raghunandana quotes a number of verses from chap. 20 in his Smṛti-tattva, Vidyākara Vājapeyin from the same chapter in his Nityācārapaddhati, Mādhavācārya from chap. 27 in his com. on the Parāśara-smṛti, Śrīdatta Upādhyāya from chap. 20 in his Kṛtyācāra, Hemādri from chaps. 20-24 and 27-28 in his Caturvarga-cintāmaṇi, Ballālasena from chaps. 37 and 42 in his Adbhutasāgara[92], Aparārka from chap. 20 in his com. on Yāj., and Jīmūtavāhana from chap. 27 in his Kālaviveka (see App.). Therefore, the chapters constituting the first and second groups are to be dated between 600 and 950 A.D. If a gap of at least 50 years be allowed between the dates of the chapters of the two groups, then *the chapters of the first group should be dated between 600 and 750 A.D., and those of the second between 800 and 950 A.D. It is, however, highly probable that the former were put into the Sṛṣṭi-kh. in the latter half of the seventh and the latter in the former half of the eighth century A.D.*

The chapters of the third and fourth groups, being later than those of the first two, cannot reasonably be dated earlier than about 850 A.D. As no Nibandha-writer has been found to draw upon them, it is difficult to say anything about the lower limit.

Chapters 43 (verses 98 ff.) to the end, which, according to our division, form the second part of the work, are not found in the Bengal Mss. So their comparatively late date can be well understood. These chapters were written and added to the Sṛṣṭi-kh. after the Muhammadans had established kingdoms in India. These foreigners have been called kings[93] and scornfully described more than once under the names 'Turuṣka', 'Mleccha' and 'Yavana'[94]. The descriptions are undoubtedly aimed at the Muhammadans who 'polluted' the society and the land of the Hindus by their contact and slaughter of cows. Hence the date of composition of this part of the Sṛṣṭi-kh. can by no means be placed earlier than 1000 A.D. Such a late date is supported by the contents also, which are replete with Tantric elements. The Āgamas have many times been mentioned as authorities along with the Vedas and the Purāṇas; the Tulasī plant has been glorified in highly extravagant language; and so on. As Hemādri quotes

92 In connection with the quotations the following stories of the Padma-p. have been mentioned in the Adbhutasāgara:

(i) Hiraṇyakaśipu-vadha (Adbhs, pp. 20, 23, 50 etc.);
(ii) Tārakāmaya yuddha (Adbhs, pp. 319, 332 etc.);
(iii) Deva-parājaya (Adbhs, p. 409).

These stories occur in the Sṛṣṭi-kh.

93 Sṛṣṭi-kh. 74, 51—*nṛpā mlecchāḥ.*

94 Ibid., 44, 71-78; 58, 91-92 and 94; and 74.

verses from chap. 47 in his Caturvarga-cintāmaṇi, at least some of the chapters of this part of the Sṛṣṭi-kh. must be dated earlier than 1200 A.D.

The Sṛṣṭi-kh., with its latest additions, were, however, practically complete before 1400 A.D., because the contents of this Khaṇḍa given in Nār I, 93 are exactly the same as those of our edition. Isolated verses might, of course, have been inserted here and there in this Khaṇḍa even after 1400 A.D., but those are not many and important.

(6) UTTARA-KHAṆḌA.[95] This Khaṇḍa is a conglomeration of legends and glorifications, some of which appear as independent works in Mss[96]. It also contains a few chapters on marriage, gifts, worship, vows, and the duties of the castes and Āśramas.

Inspite of its big volume, this Khaṇḍa does not seem to contain even a single chapter which can claim an early origin. On the other hand, stamps of late age are discernible at every step. For instance, the famous list of the ten incarnations of Viṣṇu including the Buddha and Kalki occurs in more places than one[97], showing its well established character. The Tulasī plant is not only mentioned and glorified in the majority of the chapters but also deified. A Vrata called the Tulasī-trirātri-vrata is narrated, and long stories about the origin of the goddess Tulasī are given. The Bhāgavata-p. is mentioned in chap. 63, verse 55 and glorified in chaps. 190 ff. The worship of the five deities (pañcāyatana-pūjā) of the Smārtas is referred to in one place (viz., Uttara-kh.

95 The Ms (No. 1624, D.U.Mss Lib.) of the Uttara-kh. does not always agree with the AnSS ed. The arrangement of its chapters is quite different, and it contains a few chapters which are not found in the printed ed. In the common chapters also there are differences in readings, numbers of verses, and interlocutors.

This Ms has preserved the marks of the interfering hands of the Rādhāvallabhins and the followers of Madhva and Rāmānuja. For instance, in chap. 106 the sect-mark of the Rādhāvallabhins is mentioned more than once; in chaps. 162-163 the worship of Rādhā is treated of; in chap. 101 the four Vaiṣṇava sects including Śrī and Mādhvī are mentioned (*ataḥ kalau bhaviṣyanti catvāraḥ sampradāyinaḥ| śrī-mādhvī-rudra-sanakā vaiṣṇavāḥ kṣiti-pāvanāḥ||*); and in chap. 78 there is mention of the method of initiation introduced by Rāmānuja (*śrīmad-rāmānuja-dīkṣā-vidhānaṃ vidhi-pūrvakam| kathitaṃ . . . . . .||*).

96 For example, independent Mss of the Bhāgavata-māhātmya and Māgha-māhātmya are sometimes found. These Māhātmyas, however, derive their authority from the Padma-p.

97 Uttara-kh. 31, 13-14; 68, 51; 72, 27; 72, 279 and 283; 76, 9-11; and 257, 40-41.

90, 63) and included among the daily duties of the people in another (viz., Uttara-kh. 233, 41). The Kūrma-p. is included among the Tāmasa Purāṇas glorifying Śiva in Uttara-kh. 263, 81. There are also marks of Tantric influence, so much so that the Tantras and Āgamas are regarded as authorities and Tantric Mantras are prescribed.

The above internal evidences, considered together, show that the *Uttara-kh. can scarcely be earlier than 900 A.D.* This late date of the Khaṇḍa seems to be supported by the fact that none of the verses quoted in the early Nibandhas from the 'Padma-p.' or 'Pādma' is traceable in it.

That the Uttara-kh. is not a unified work scarcely requires any evidence to prove. The appearance of some of its parts in independent Mss shows that these parts did not originally belong to the Khaṇḍa. Further, in the marginal notes in a Ms of the Yathārtha-mañjarī[98] it is written that according to a Purāṇācārya named Narasiṃha Ṭhakkura, Madhvācārya wrote three hundred verses on the denouncement of the ashes and the Rudrākṣas and added them to the Uttara-khaṇḍa[99]. Though the absence of such verses subjects the above information to doubts, there is a chapter (263) which seems to have been interpolated by some person belonging to the Śrī or Mādhva sect. In this chapter the Pāṣaṇḍins, including especially the Śiva-worshippers, have been described and the Māyā-vāda (of Śaṃkarācārya) has been denounced as Pracchanna Bauddha (i.e., Buddhist in disguise). This chapter, however, cannot be dated later than 1500 A.D., because Vijñāna Bhikṣu (middle of the 16th century) quotes in his Sāṃkhyapravacana-bhāṣya those verses from this chapter which contain the above mentioned denouncement (see App.).

Though the Uttara-kh. was open to additions and modifications down to a very recent date[100], it seems to have attained practically its present contents earlier than 1500 A.D. Vācaspatimiśra, Govindānanda, Raghunandana, Gopālabhaṭṭa and Vijñāna Bhikṣu quote verses from some of the chapters of this Khaṇḍa (see App.);

[98] Ms No. 4093, dated 1734 Śaka, D.U.Mss Lib. The author is Śrītīrtha-svāmin, or Rāmānanda-tīrtha according to R. L. Mitra's Notices of Sanskrit Mss, L. 1017.

[99] *tarhi pādmīya-dvitīyottara-khaṇḍe yad bhasma-rudrākṣa-nindā tat-khaṇḍīya-triśata-ślokānāṃ madhvācārya-kṛtatvaṃ purāṇācārya-narasiṃha-ṭhakkureṇa likhitam* . . . . . Yathārtha-mañjarī, fol. 5b.
asminn eva khaṇḍe kalau śiva-pūjāyām abhiśāpo likhitaḥ|
ataḥ pūrvāparāsaṃlagnatvād asmin khaṇḍe triśata-ślokā
madhvācārya-kṛtā iti narasiṃhena likhitam.—Yathārtha-mañjarī, fol. 67b.

[100] This is best shown by the untraceable quoted verses and by a comparison between the printed text of the Uttara-kh. and that preserved in Bengal Mss.

the contents of the 'Uttara-khaṇḍa' as given in Nār I, 93 seem to tally with those of the AnSS ed.; and there is a Ms[101] of the Māgha-māhātmya which is dated 1311 Śaka.

5. THE BṚHANNĀRADĪYA AND THE NĀRADĪYA PURĀṆA.

As these two Purāṇas are closely interrelated and as either of them has sometimes been taken to be the original Nāradīya Purāṇa[102], it is necessary to examine them in order to understand their true character.

The Bṛhannāradīya[103] is purely a sectarian work lacking all the characteristics of a Mahāpurāṇa. It describes the Vaiṣṇava feasts and ceremonies illustrated by various legends and contains chapters on the glorification of the Ganges, the duties of the castes and Āśramas, the funeral sacrifices and expiations, and so forth. It is preeminently a work on Viṣṇu-bhakti (devotion to Viṣṇu) which is said to have ten gradations, viz., Tāmasādhamā, Tāmasa-madhyamā, Tāmasottamā, Rājasādhamā, Rājasa-madhyamā, Rāja-sottamā, Sāttvikādhamā, Sāttvika-madhyamā, Sāttvikottamā and Uttamottamā[104]. This Bhakti is repeatedly declared by the Purāṇa to be the only means of salvation.

The title 'Bṛhannārada' or 'Bṛhannāradīya' given to the work both in the body of the chapters[105] and the colophons shows that it is not the original Nāradīya P., the words 'bṛhat', 'vṛddha' etc. being found to be prefixed to the titles of comparatively late works only. It should not be held that the Bṛhannāradīya P. 'is generally so called to distinguish it from the Nārada—or Nāradīya—Upapurāṇa'[106], for, we shall see below, the present Nāradīya P. was composed, or rather compiled, after the Bṛhannāradīya mainly with the chapters of the latter. That the Bṛhannāradīya is not

[101] No. 931, D. U. Mss Lib. This Ms was brought to my notice by Mr. Subodh Chandra Banerjee, M.A., of the Dacca University Mss Library.

[102] Cf. Haraprasad Shastri, Cat. of Sans. Mss, ASB, Vol. V, Preface, pp. cxxxv-cxliii. Winternitz, Ind. Lit., I, p, 557. Viśvakoṣa (a Bengali Encyclopaedia), edited by Nagendra Nath Basu, Vol. XI, p. 627.

[103] The Vaṅga. ed. is generally the same as the ASB ed. Both consist of 38 chapters. There are, of course, occasional variations in readings and numbers of verses in the corresponding chapters.

[104] Bnār 14, 195-207.

[105] Bnār 1, 36—*purāṇaṃ nāradīyākhyaṃ bṛhad vedārtha-sammitam*; 1, 66 — . . . . *bṛhannārada-nāmadheyaṃ . . . purāṇam*; and 38, 132— . . . . *bṛhannārada-saṃjñitam*.

[106] Winternitz, Ind. Lit., I, p. 557.

the original Nāradīya P. but only an Upapurāṇa, is established by other evidences also. The Matsya (53, 23), the Skanda (VII, i, 2, 43) and the Agni-p. (272, 8) describe the Nāradīya P. as follows :

> "*yatrāha nārado dharmān bṛhatkalpāśritān iha|*
> *pañcaviṃśa* (Ag reads *pañcaviṃśat*) *sahasrāṇi nāradīyaṃ tad ucyate||*"

According to this description the Nāradīya P. was declared by the sage Nārada in relation to the Bṛhat Kalpa. But in the Bṛhannāradīya, though Nārada is found to speak to Sanatkumāra, there is no mention of the Bṛhat Kalpa, Moreover, the Bṛhaddharma-p. (I, 25, 23) includes this Purāṇa among the Upapurāṇas. The references to and quotations from this Purāṇa in the Smṛti-works also show that it was known to them as Bṛhannāradīya and not as Nāradīya P.

The date of the Bṛhannāradīya can be ascertained within narrow limits. In the D. U. Mss Lib. there is a Ms (No. 1667) of this Purāṇa which is dated 1578 Śaka (= 1656 A.D.). This Ms tallying fully with the printed edition, the Bṛhannāradīya must be earlier than the beginning of the seventeenth century A.D. As Gopālabhaṭṭa quotes verses from chaps. 1-6, 11, 13, 18, 21, 23, 28, 32, 34, 35, 37 and 38 in his Haribhaktivilāsa, Govindānanda from chaps. 7, 14 and 25-27 in his Śuddhikriyā-kaumudī, Varṣakriyā-kaumudī and Śrāddhakriyā-kaumudī, Raghunandana from chaps. 7, 14, 22 and 24 in his Smṛti-tattva, and Śūlapāṇi from chap. 16 in his Vratakāla-viveka, the Bṛhannāradīya can by no means be placed later than 1350 A.D. Further, we shall see below that the present Nāradīya P., in which the chapters of the Bṛhannāradīya form the main section, was compiled not later than the end of the tenth century A.D. If a period of at least 50 years be allowed to intervene between the dates of the Bṛhannāradīya and the present Nāradīya, then the date of the former cannot be placed later than 950 A.D. Thus we get the lower limit. Again, in the Bṛhannāradīya Viṣṇu's Śakti, which permeates the whole world and effects its creation, preservation and destruction[107], is said to be known as Lakṣmī, Umā, Durgā, Bhāratī, Bhadrakālī etc.[108]. She is the Prakṛti and the illusion (Māyā) which subjects the creatures to rebirths[109]. Such a developed Śakti theory points to a date not earlier than about 550 A.D., for, though in the Jayākhya-saṃhitā, which is dated about 450 A.D., Lakṣmī, Jayā, Kīrti and Māyā are called

[107] Bnār 3, 6, 10 and 16. [108] Bnār 3, 13 ff.
[109] Bnār 3, 9 and 15.

Viṣṇu's Śakti, they play no part in creation. The reference, in Bnār 2, 44, to the story of Ajāmila's attainment of the highest region by singing the glory of Viṣṇu seems to betray an acquaintance of the author of the Bṛhannāradīya with the Bhāgavata-p. The doctrine of nonduality (Advaita) and illusion (Māyā), summarily referred to in Bnār 31, 57 ff., shows that the Purāṇa cannot possibly be earlier than Śaṃkarācārya. Hence *the date of composition of the Bṛhannāradīya falls between 850 and 950 A.D., and it is probable that the Purāṇa was composed sometime about the middle of the 9th century. As there is nothing which goes against the integrity of the Purāṇa, the above date may be taken to be that of the entire work.*

The Bṛhannāradīya, which, on account of its lengthy glorification of the river Ganges and its recognition of Prayāga and Benares as the best of all holy places[110], appears to have been written in Northern India, is a work of the Bhāgavata Vaiṣṇavas. In it the highest deity is Mahāviṣṇu, who becomes Brahmā, the inferior Viṣṇu, and Śiva through the three Guṇas—Sattva, Rajas and Tamas respectively[111]; the names used to mean the god of the Bhāgavatas are 'Viṣṇu' and 'Nārāyaṇa', the name 'Kṛṣṇa' being rare; and the sectarian Mantra is '*oṃ namo nārāyaṇāya*'. It is tolerant of Śaivism and declares: "The man, who differentiates between Hari, Śaṃkara and Brahmā, remains in hell as long as the moon and stars exist"[112].

Let us now pass on to the Nāradīya P. It is divided into two parts (bhāga)—the former (Pūrva), consisting of 125 chapters, and the latter (Uttara), of 82 chapters. The former part, again, is subdivided into four subsections called Pādas. The lengths of these Pādas are as follows:

	(1) first Pāda	.. ..	chaps. 1-41,
	(2) second Pāda	.. ..	chaps. 42-62,
	(3) third Pāda	.. ..	chaps. 63-91,
and	(4) fourth Pāda	.. ..	chaps. 92-125.

Though, as usual, the Nāradīya P. is declared by Sūta to the sages, the speakers in the different sections differ; viz., in the four Pādas of the Pūrva-bhāga Sanaka, Sanandana, Sanatkumāra and Sanātana speak respectively to Nārada, and in the Uttara-bhāga Vasiṣṭha speaks to Māndhātṛ.

The present Nāradīya P. is not the earlier Nāradīya noticed by the Matsya, Skanda and Agni. According to these three Purāṇas the Nāradīya was declared by Nārada in relation to the Bṛhat Kalpa.

110 Bnār 6, 9 and 37.

111 Bnār 3, 2.

112 Bnār 3, 45.

In the present Nāradīya, however, Nārada is not the speaker but the hearer, and there is no mention of the Bṛhat Kalpa. The word *bṛhadupākhyāna,* which is used, abruptly and without any reference to the Bṛhat Kalpa, in the colophons of the majority of chapters in Nār I, does not occur in the colophons of Nār I, 1-41 which constitute the main part of the work[113]. So, this word cannot be used to establish that the present Nāradīya P. is the earlier one. Moreover, Nār I, 1-41 are generally the same as Bnār, chapters 1 to the end, though there are variations in readings and numbers of verses. As regards these common chapters, the Nāradīya P. seems to be the borrower, for this is indicated by the fact that though necessary changes have been made in the borrowed chapters of the Nāradīya P., and the word *bṛhat* used in the Bṛhannāradīya (1, 36 and 66) as a prefix to the title of the Purāṇa has been replaced by *'etat'* and *'idaṃ'* in the corresponding verses (viz., I, 1, 36 and 64) of the Nāradīya P. obviously in order to adapt the chapters of the Bṛhannāradīya to the title and interlocutor of the Nāradīya, the Purāṇa is still called 'Bṛhannāradīya' in the colophons of the chapters of all the sections. The occurrence of this word in the colophons shows that inspite of fresh additions and the new title, the people did not forget the real character of the so-called Nāradīya P. As to Nār I, 42-125, it will be seen below that they are comparatively late additions. Though the Uttara-bhāga derives its authority from, and is attached to, the present Nāradīya, it is really an independent work. It is for this reason that this Bhāga differs in general character from Nār I, 1-41 and is sometimes found to appear in Mss as an independent text.

From the above discussion it follows that the present Nāradīya is not the earlier one and that the chapters of the Bṛhannāradīya were added to by others and given the title 'Nāradīya Purāṇa'. So it is undoubtedly an Upapurāṇa. The title of the work need not be taken to go against its apocryphal character, because Upapurāṇas bearing the titles of Mahāpurāṇas are not very rare in the Purāṇic literature. The Kūrma-p. (I, 1, 18), Garuḍa-p. (I, 227, 19), Devībhāgavata (I, 3, 14) and Bṛhaddharma-p. (I, 25, 23) include a 'Nāradīya P.' among the Upapurāṇas. It is not known whether the present Nāradīya is identical with that mentioned by these Purāṇas.

Let us now proceed to discuss the dates of the different sections of the present Nāradīya P. As Gopālabhaṭṭa quotes verses from chaps. 2, 3, 6, 10, 22, 24, 31 and 38 of Nār II in his Haribhakti-

[113] Haraprasad Shastri wrongly says that the word '*bṛhadupākhyāna*' is found in every colophon. See, Shastri, Cat. of Sans. Mss. ASB, Vol. V, Preface, p. cxxxv.

vilāsa, Gadādhara from chap. 23 of Nār I and chaps. 1, 2, 22, and 31 of Nār II. in his Kālasāra, Raghunandana from chaps. 13, 27 and 30 of Nār I and chaps. 1, 2, 22, 24 and 38 of Nār II in his Smṛti-tattva, Govindānanda from chap. 28 of Nār I in his Śrāddhakriyā-kaumudī, Vācaspatimiśra from chaps. 38 and 39 of Nār II in his Tīrtha-cintāmaṇi, Madanapāla from chap. 2 of Nār II in his Madana-pārijāta, Mādhavācārya from chap. 7 of Nār I and chaps. 7, 23, 27 and 31 of Nār II in his com. on the Parāśara-smṛti, Hemādri from chaps. 23 and 25 of Nār I and chaps. 1-3, 22, 24 and 31 of Nār II in his Caturvarga-cintāmaṇi, and Devaṇabhaṭṭa from chaps. 1, 2, 23, 31 and 37 of Nār II in his Smṛti-candrikā[114], and as Gopālabhaṭṭa refers to the interlocutions between (1) Mohinī and king Rukmāṅgada and (2) the sage Vāmadeva and Rukmāṅgada in his Hari-bhaktivilāsa (pp. 386, 519 and 1034), Hemādri mentions Māṃdhātṛ, Vasiṣṭha, Mohinī and Rukmāṅgada as speakers in his Caturvarga-cintāmaṇi (Vol. II, part ii, pp. 772-5 etc.) and Devaṇabhaṭṭa mentions Mohinī and Vasiṣṭha as speakers in his Smṛti-candrikā (Vol. IV, pp. 65, 68 and 121), it is sure that the first Pāda of the Pūrva-bhāga and the story of king Rukmāṅgada and his wife Mohinī in the Uttara-bhāga (chaps. 1-37) were combined under the title 'Nāradīya P.' earlier than 1100 A.D. The verses quoted by the above mentioned Smṛti-writers from the 'Nāradīya P.' and traced in the present Nāradīya prove that these Smṛti-writers, hailing from different parts of India, draw only upon the present apocryphal Nāradīya[115], and that the real Nāradīya was generally superseded by the present one even as early as the beginning of the twelfth century A.D. As the attainment of such circulated importance by the present Nāradīya could not be possible in a short time, *the Purāṇa should be dated not later than the end of the tenth century.* The Bṛhannāradīya being earlier than the present Nāradīya, *the latter cannot be placed earlier than the last quarter of the ninth century A.D.*

The above date is not the date of all sections of the Nāradīya P., for chaps. 42-125 of the Pūrva-bhāga and chaps. 38-82 of the Uttara-bhāga bear stamps of comparatively late dates. In the former chapters the interlocutors differ from those of the remaining ones, and there is a breach here in the tone of Bhakti that permeates Nār I, 1-41. There are also traces of a fully developed Rādhā

[114] See App.

[115] By his statement that he did not draw upon the Nāradīya P. because it did not contain any chapter on gift, Ballālasena means most probably the present Nāradīya in which there is no chapter on gifts. Cf. Dānasāgara, fol. 3b—*bhāgavataṃ ca purāṇaṃ brahmāṇḍaṃ caiva nāradīyaṃ ca| dāna-vidhi-śūnyam etat trayam iha na niban(? d)dham avadhārya||.*

cult. In Nār I, 83 Rādhā is called the Mūla-prakṛti. She is described as 'nirguṇā', 'nityā', 'sarvādyā', 'tejomaṇḍala-madhyasthā', 'dṛśyādṛśya-svarūpiṇī' etc., and is said to be inseparably connected with Kṛṣṇa who is called Paramātman and of whom Nārāyaṇa, Śiva and the other Kṛṣṇa, 'the lord of the Gopikās', are born. The goddesses like Mahālakṣmī, Durgā, Sarasvatī and others are said to be the partial incarnations (aṃśāvatāra) of Rādhā. In Nār I, 88 the formation of the Tantric Mantras of Rādhā and the Tantric method of her worship have been laid down. The contents of the eighteen Mahāpurāṇas, as given in Nār I, 92-109, tally fully with those of almost all the present ones. So these chapters could not have been written before these Purāṇas attained practically their present form. The late age of Nār I, 42-125 seems further to be evidenced by the fact that none of the numerous Smṛti-writers has been found to quote even a single line from them. Chapters 38 ff. of the Uttara-bhāga deal with the glories of the river Ganges and the holy places Kāśī, Puruṣottama etc. These chapters are comparatively late additions and are generally derived from other sources. For instance, Nār II, 52-61 have many verses in common with Brahma-p. 28 and 45 ff. Their comparatively late date is further evidenced by the fact that though in Pūrva-bhāga chap. 125 (verse 26) the Nāradīya is said to have four Pādas, in Uttara-bhāga chap. 82 (verse 41) it is said to consist of five Pādas. All of the chapters 38-82 of Nār II, however, are not very late additions. The quotations made by Gopālabhaṭṭa, Raghunandana and Vācaspatimiśra from chaps. 38 and 39 of Nār II prove that at least chaps. 38-43 on the Ganges are earlier than Vācaspatimiśra.

The result of the above analysis, so far as it relates to the Nāradīya P., is as follows:

Nār I, 1-41	..	*C.* 875-1000 A.D.
Nār I, 42-125	..	Comparatively late.
Nār II, 1-37	..	*C.* 875-1000 A.D.
Nār II, 38-82	..	Comparatively late. At least Nār II, 38-43 are earlier than Vācaspatimiśra.

On the evidences of the grammatical tradition, the treatment of the three branches of Jyotiṣa, and the attribution of the five Kalpas of the Atharva-veda to all the Śākhās of all the Vedas, Haraprasad Shastri brings down the date of the Nāradīya P. to 700-800 A.D.[116]. We cannot understand why he does not put the date of the Purāṇa lower still, though there is no evidence to push up the lower limit of the date to such an early period as 800 A.D. The only argument

[116] Haraprasad Shastri, Cat. of Sans. Mss, ASB, Vol. V, Preface, pp. cxxxvii-cxxxviii.

he adduces in this regard is the inclusion of Vindu among the Pāśas. He says that as the Nāradīya P., in its description of the Śaiva system of philosophy, admits Vindu as one of the subdivisions of Pāśas or bondages, it is earlier than the Sarvadarsana-saṃgraha which does not recognise Vindu[117]. This argument becomes untenable when we consider that many of the chapters 42-125 of the Pūrva-bhāga are either derived from or based on those of other works, and that the contents of chaps. 63-91, which are said to constitute the 'Mahātantra'[118], are the summary of those of the Tantras of different sects[119]. Therefore the inclusion of Vindu among the Pāśas cannot go against the late date of Nār I, 42-125.

The present Nāradīya is more a compilation than an original work. In many places of the Purāṇa itself[120] it is called a 'Saṃhitā' and really so, for many of the chapters are found to tally with those occurring in other works. For example, there are verses common to Nār I, 43 (verses 50 ff.) and Padma-p. (Svarga-kh.[121]) chaps. 25 and 26; Nār I, 48 (verses 14 ff.) and 49 agree almost literally with Viṣ II, 13 (verses 13 ff.) to 16; many verses are found common to Nār II, 52-61 and Brahma-p. 28 and 45 ff.; and so forth.

A good number of verses, quoted by the Smṛti-writers from the Nāradīya P. but not found in the present Nāradīya, shows that in the earlier form of the Purāṇa there were many verses which have been lost in the printed edition. The 'Nāradīya P.' drawn upon by Jīmūtavāhana does not seem to be the same as the present Nāradīya because of the facts that none of the 47 lines quoted by him from the 'Nāradīya P.' in his Kālaviveka is traceable in the present Nāradīya, and that the interlocutions between (1) Markaṇḍeya and Viṣṇu and (2) Vaiśya and Bhikṣu, which he mentions as having occurred in the 'Nāradīya P.', are not found in the present edition. It is, therefore, highly probable that Jīmūtavāhana used a different recension of the Nāradīya P., if not the earlier or original one.

[117] Ibid., pp. cxlii-cxliii.

[118] Cf. *mahātantre samuddiṣṭaṃ pasupāśa-vimokṣaṇam*|—Nar I, 97, 5; *tripadārthaṃ catuṣpādaṃ mahātantraṃ pracakṣate*|—Nār I, 63, 13; *mahātantraṃ tvayā proktaṃ sarva-tantrottamottamam*| —Nār I, 92, 2.

[119] Cf. *tantroktaṃ vada sarvajña tvām ahaṃ śaraṇaṃ gataḥ*|
śaktes tantrāṇy anekāni śivoktāni munīśvara||
yāni tat-sāram uddhṛtya sākalyenābhidhehi naḥ|
Nār I, 83, 7-8. Also cf. Nār I, 83, 5 and I, 76, 6.

[120] Viz., Nār II, 82, verses 34, 35, 40, 44 etc; I, 62, 77 and 79.

[121] Ms No. 1625, D. U. Mss Lib.

6. THE AGNI-PURĀṆA.[122]

The Matsya and the Skanda-p. notice the 'Agni-purāṇa' as follows:

> "That Purāṇa which describes the occurrences of the Īśāna-kalpa and was related by Agni to Vaśiṣṭha is called the Āgneya"[123].

But in the present Agni-p., though Agni is found to speak to Vaśiṣṭha, there is no mention of the Īśāna-kalpa. On the other hand, the Vārāha Kalpa has been mentioned in connection with the Tortoise incarnation of Viṣṇu (see Ag 2, 17). This disagreement between the description in the Matsya and the Skanda-p. and the contents of the present Agni shows that the latter is not the earlier Agni-p. which was noticed by these two Purāṇas. This apocryphal character of the present Agni is further evidenced by the verses quoted from the 'Agni-purāṇa' or 'Āgneya' in the Smṛti-Nibandhas but not found in the present Agni. The express mention of Vaśiṣṭha and king Ambarīṣa as interlocutors[124], and the occurrence of the words 'kuru-śārdūla', 'vīra', 'rājan', 'nṛpa', 'rājendra' etc. in the vocative case in many of the quoted passages[125], prove that in the original (or rather earlier) Agni-purāṇa Vaśiṣṭha spoke to king Ambarīṣa at least on the various topics on Dharma. Moreover, in one of the verses quoted from the 'Āgneya-P.' in the Tīrtha-cintāmaṇi Sūrya is mentioned as the speaker, and in another Viṣṇu speaks to Gaṅgā (cf. Tīrtha-cintāmaṇi, pp. 206 and 263). In the present Agni-p., however, there is no interlocution between Vaśiṣṭha and king Ambarīṣa or between Viṣṇu and Gaṅgā, and there is also no chapter in which

[122] The Vaṅga. ed. is chapter by chapter the same as the AnSS ed. There are, of course, occasional variations in readings and numbers of verses in the corresponding chapters.

[123] *yat tad īśānakaṃ kalpaṃ vṛttāntam adhikṛtya ca|*
vaśiṣṭhāyāgninā proktam āgneyaṃ tat pracakṣate||

Mat 53, 28 and Sk VII, i, 2, 47. The latter reads *'īśāna-kalpasya'* in the first line.

In Ag 272, which is an abridgment of Mat 53 and not of Nār I, 92-109 as Haraprasad Shastri holds, the reference to the Īśāna-kalpa has been left out obviously with a view to adapting the description to the present Agni.

[124] Cf. Dānasāgara, fol. 253a and 96a-97b; and Kṛtya-ratnākara, fol. 189b.

[125] Cf. Dānasāgara, fol. 96a-97b, 99a-b, 100a-b, etc.;
Caturvarga-cintāmaṇi, I, pp. 527 and 978, II, pp. 1136 ff. and so on;
Kṛtya-ratnākara, fol. 189b; Dānakriyā-kaumudī, p. 57;
Haribhaktivilāsa, p. 752; Smṛti-tattva I, 411 and II, 286;
Kālasāra, pp. 70, 126 and 602; and so on.

Sūrya is the speaker. The above facts, considered together, prove definitely that the present Agni-p. is not the earlier one[126].

From a comparison between the present Agni-p. and the verses quoted in the Nibandhas from the earlier Agni we understand that the former is the result of a destructive recast to which the latter was subjected. How in this recast the form of the older Purāṇa was changed is best exemplified by a comparison between a long passage, or rather an entire chapter, quoted from the 'Agni-p.' in the Dānasāgara (fol. 96a-97b) and chap. 210 of the present Agni. In the quoted passage Vaśiṣṭha is found to speak to the king (Ambarīṣa) on Guḍadhenu-dāna (gift of a cow made of raw sugar); but in the said chapter of the present Agni, though all the marks proving the interlocution between Vaśiṣṭha and the king have been eliminated, many verses have been retained; viz., Ag 210, verses 13b-17a, 19-21, 22b, 23 and 25-29a tally with some of the verses quoted in the Dānasāgara (fol. 96a-97b). The above comparison further shows that the present Agni-p. is not a new work from beginning to end but has retained fragments of chapters and isolated verses from the earlier Purāṇa. It is for this reason that a few of the numerous quoted verses are found in the present Agni with variations in readings and arrangement of lines.

The present Agni-p., though an apocryphal and comparatively late work, does not seem to have come down to us quite unadulterated. *There are evidences to show that some of its chapters, viz., 21-106, 263-272 and 317-326, are in all probability later interpolations.* In Ag 1 the essence of all knowledge (vidyā-sāra) is proposed to be given. This knowledge is divided into two classes—Parā and Aparā. The Parā Vidyā is that with which the supreme Brahma is attained, and the Aparā Vidyā consists of the four Vedas, the six Vedāṅgas (Śikṣā, Kalpa, Vyākaraṇa, Nirukta, Chandas and Jyotiṣa), Abhidhāna, Mīmāṃsā, Dharmaśāstra, Purāṇa,Nyāya, Vaidyaka, Gāndharva, Dhanurveda and Arthaśāstra. It is to be noticed that in the above enumeration there is mention neither of the Pāñcarātra Saṃhitās, of which, as we shall see below, some of the interpolated chapters of the present Agni-p. seem to be summaries, nor of the methods of the worship of different gods dealt with in these chapters. Again, in chap. 20 Agni speaks of the nine kinds of creation, refers to the story of Satī's birth as the daughter of Himālaya, and ends with the verse

'ṛṣibhyo nāradādyuktāḥ pūjāḥ snānādi-pūrvikāḥ|
svāyaṃbhuvādyās tāḥ kṛtvā viṣṇvāder bhukti-muktidāḥ||'

[126] Dr. S. K. De also expressly calls it 'apocryphal'. See De, Sanskrit Poetics, Vol. I, p. 102.

This verse, which serves as an introduction to chaps. 21-106 on the Tantric worship of Viṣṇu, Śiva, Gaṇeśa, Sūrya and Gaurī, is so irrelevant and abrupt that it proves the spurious character of these chapters. Their comparatively late date is further established by the fact that though in chaps. 12-15 Kṛṣṇa is the eighth of the ten incarnations of Viṣṇu, in chap. 49 (verse 6) it is Haladhara who occupies his place. From the lists of the ten incarnations of Viṣṇu we know that the substitution of Kṛṣṇa by Haladhara is of much later date. Of these interpolated chapters (21-106), the first 49 (i.e., chaps. 21-70 on Viṣṇu-worship, Viṣṇu-dīkṣā, installation of the images of Viṣṇu, and so forth) are most probably summaries of one or more of the Pāñcarātra Saṃhitās, for some of the verses quoted in Gopālabhaṭṭa's Haribhaktivilāsa from the Hayaśīrṣa-pañcarātra have their parallels in Ag 39-70 ascribed to Hayagrīva. For example, Ag 41, 3 (*iṣṭakāś ca supakvāḥ syuḥ*) resembles the quotation from the Hayaśīrṣa-pañcarātra in Haribhaktivilāsa, p. 1315. Ag 71-106 (on Pañcāyatana-pūjā), again, seem to be later than Ag 21-70. The last verse

> *skandāyeśo yathā prāha pratiṣṭhādyaṃ tathā śṛṇu |*
> *sūryeśa-gaṇa-śaktyādeḥ parivārasya vai hareḥ||*

of chap. 70, that introduces chaps. 71-106 declared by Īśvara (i.e., Śiva), is also abrupt and irrelevant. This introductory verse being ascribed to Hayagrīva, *it is highly probable that chaps. 71-106 are later than chaps. 21-70.* In Ag 259, 1 Agni proposes to report what Puṣkara said to Rāma on 'ṛg-yajuḥ-sāmātharva-vidhāna'. Consequently chaps. 259 (verses 2 ff.) to 262, ascribed to Puṣkara, deal with Ṛg-, Yajuḥ-, Sāma- and Atharva-vidhāna. But the speaker is found to speak further on omens, worship, bath etc., almost all of which are imbued with Tantric elements. This continued portion (i.e., chaps. 263-272) of Puṣkara's speech is most probably spurious. The word *bhūyaḥ* in the line *'bhūyaḥ skandāya yān āha mantrān īśaś ca tān vade'* (Ag 316, 5) which introduces chaps. 317-326 ascribed to Īśvara, presupposes chaps. 71-106 in which Īśvara speaks to Skanda. Therefore, *at least chaps. 317-326 cannot be earlier than chaps. 71-106.* Among the remaining chapters there may be some which are spurious, but it is almost impossible to detect them.

From the first chapter of the present Agni we understand that the compiler of this Purāṇa had the deliberate intention of making the work a sort of a cyclopaedia in miniature. With this end in view he summarised the contents of some works, viz., the Rāmāyaṇa, the Mahābhārata, the Harivaṃśa, the section on Gayā-māhātmya in the Vāyu-p., the Sūtras of Piṅgala with a commentary, the Amarakośa[127], the Yuddha-jayārṇava[128], the Hastyāyurveda of Pālakāpya, etc., and incorporated verses or entire chapters of other works, viz., the Nārada-smṛti[129], the Yājñavalkya-smṛti and the Viṣṇu-p.[130]. Hence it can be little dubted that the chapters on the different branches of learning belonged to the *present* Agni-p. in its earliest form, and that they were put together to constitute the Purāṇa at the same time. That of these chapters at least those on Bhuvana-koṣa, Yoga and Brahma-jñāna are contemporaneous, is further established by Ag 107, 12b-13a (*bharate datta-lakṣmīkaḥ śālagrāme hariṃ gataḥ| sa yogī yoga-prastāve vakṣye taccaritaṃ punaḥ||*) containing an unmistakable reference to chap. 380 wherein the story of Bharata is given in connection with Yoga and the knowledge of Brahma. From all these we can safely hold that the date of compilation of the present Agni is the same as that of the summaries and incorporations. Now, in course of enumerating those Purāṇas, or parts thereof, which he rejected as compiled, unauthoritative or influenced by Tantricism, Ballālasena names in his Dānasāgara a few spurious Purāṇas including the 'Āgneya' and the 'Tārkṣya' and enumerates their contents which agree remarkably with those of the present Agni and Garuḍa[131]. So the present Agni, in which the great majority of the numerous verses quoted in the Dānasāgara from

[127] Haraprasad Shastri, Cat. of Sans. Mss, ASB, Vol. V, Preface, pp. cxlvii-cxlviii and cl. Wilson, Essays, Vol. I, pp. 89-90.

[128] Ag 123-149 are certainly the summary of the Yuddha-jayārṇava—a work drawn upon by Narapati (the author of the Svarodaya), Raghunandana and others, because we have found that some of the lines quoted from the Yuddha-jayārṇava in the Smṛti-tattva resemble some lines in the above mentioned chapters of the Agni-p. For instance, the line '*yasminnṛkṣe sthito bhānus tadādi trīṇi mastake*' quoted from the Yuddha-jayārṇava in Smṛti-tattva I, p. 642 may be compared with Ag 126, 1b—'*yasminnṛkṣe bhavet sūryas tadādau trīṇi mūrdhani*'. Moreover, in Ag 123, 1 Agni proposes to give the substance of the Yuddha-jayārṇava (*vakṣye . . . . sāraṃ yuddha-jayārṇave*). This substance, however, does not seem to be very true to the original but appears to have innovations.

[129] Kane, Hist. of Dhs., Vol. I, p. 173.

[130] Ag 380 has numerous verses in common with Viṣ II, 13, verses 13 ff.

[131] Dānasāgara, fol. 3b-4a—

tārkṣyaṃ purāṇam aparaṃ brāhmam āgneyam eva ca|
trayoviṃśati-sāhasryaṃ purāṇam api vaiṣṇavam||
ṣaṭ-sāhasra-mitaṃ liṅgaṃ purāṇam aparaṃ tathā|
dīkṣā-pratiṣṭhā-pāṣaṇḍa-mukti-ratna-parīkṣaṇaiḥ||
mṛṣā-vaṃśānucaritaiḥ koṣa-vyākaraṇādibhiḥ|
asaṅgata-kathā-bandha-paraspara-virodhitaḥ||
tan mīna-ketanādīnāṃ bhaṇḍa-pāṣaṇḍa-liṅgināṃ|
loka-vañcanam ālokya sarvam evāvar(? dh)īritam||

an 'Agni-p.' is not traceable, must be the same as Ballālasena's spurious 'Āgneya' and consequently be earlier than 1100 A.D. P. V. Kane compares the text of the Vyavahāra section of the Yājñavalkya-smṛti found in the Agni-p. (chap. 253, verse 32 to chap. 258) with those used by the commentators Viśvarūpa and Vijñāneśvara and comes to the conclusion 'that the text of Yāj. preserved in the Agni-purāṇa is intermediate between the text of Viśvarūpa and that of the Mitākṣarā'. He further adds: "As Viśvarūpa flourished about 800-825 A.D., the Agni-purāṇa represents a text of Yāj. current somewhat later, i.e., about 900 A.D."[132] As to the Alaṃkāra-section of the Agni, Kane is of opinion that as the extant Agni quotes Daṇḍin and Bhāmaha and knew the theory of Dhvani, it was composed about 900 A.D.[133] S. K. De differs from Kane and assigns this section to the beginning of the ninth century A.D.[134] Inspite of these differences of opinions, there can be no serious objection if we hold that *the present Agni-p. was compiled some time during the ninth century*[135]. Haraprasad Shastri also places the date of the Purāṇa between 800 and 900 A.D.[136] This general date seems to be supported by other evidences also. Tantricism in the sections on astronomy and medicine, which have been mentioned among the different branches of the Aparā Vidyā, shows that the date of the Agni-p. cannot possibly be earlier than 800 A.D., because from an examination of the Matsya, Varāha

It is to be noted that though Ballālasena expressly says that he rejected the 'Tārkṣya', 'Brāhma', 'Āgneya', 'Vaiṣṇava' and 'Liṅga' as spurious and deceptive, he draws considerably upon a Brahma-, an Agni- and a Viṣṇu-purāṇa in his Dānasāgara and includes them in the list of the Purāṇas used in writing the digest (see Dānasāgara, fol. 2a). So, it is sure that he knew another set of Purāṇas which he considered genuine. The word *apara* used in the above verses is important in this connection.

132 Kane, Hist. of Dhs., Vol. I, p. 172.

133 Kane, History of Sanskrit Poetics, pp. II-V, and Hist. of Dhs., Vol. I, p. 172.

134 S. K. De, Sanskrit Poetics, Vol. I, p. 104. Also see De in JRAS, 1923 (Part IV, October), pp. 537-549.

135 In IHQ Vol. X, 1934, pp. 767 ff. an attempt has been made by V. Rāghavan to prove the indebtedness of the Alaṃkāra-section of the Agni-p. to the works of Bhoja and thus to assign the Purāṇa to a post-Bhoja date. But this date cannot be finally accepted until further and more definite proofs have been adduced in its favour.

See also Poona Orientalists, Vol. II, April, 1937, pp. 15-17 for S. K. De's notes on V. Rāghavan's views.

Wilson's view that the present Agni is probably to be placed anterior to the eighth and ninth centuries A.D., hardly deserves any attention. See, Wilson, Essays, Vol. I, p. 90.

136 Haraprasad Shastri, Cat. of Sans. Mss. ASB, Vol. V, Preface, p. cli.

and other Purāṇas we understand that the Tantric elements began to be absorbed appreciably by the Purāṇas not earlier than about 800 A.D. Again, the majority of the verses quoted by Govindānanda in his Dānakriyā-kaumudī (but not in his other works) from the Agni-p. are found in the present Agni (see App.). Moreover, the verses on Guḍadhenu-dāna quoted in the Dānakriyā-kaumudī (pp. 58-61), though agreeing remarkably with Ag 210, 10b-31a, differ from the passage on the same topic quoted in Ballālasena's Dānasāgara (fol. 96a-97b). It is, therefore, sure that at least the verses on Guḍadhenu-dāna, from which Vasiṣṭha and Ambarīṣa have been eliminated, were taken by Govindānanda from the present Agni. Hence the present Agni must be dated not later than 1500 A.D. According to Haraprasad Shastri 'the eight chapters on Prosody in the Agni-p. is the summary of the Sūtras of Piṅgala with a commentary. That commentary is controverted by Halāyudha in the second half of the tenth century without naming its author. So the Agni would come some considerable time before Halāyudha. Had Halāyudha's commentary been known to the author he would certainly have given the summary of this most popular commentary and not an obscure predecessor of it[137]'.

The present Agni is originally a work of the Pāñcarātras. It proposes to deal with Brahma which is identified with Viṣṇu (cf. Ag 1, 9-11). It is for this reason that Viṣṇu's incarnations are narrated at the very outset. In other non-spurious chapters also it is Viṣṇu who is identified with Brahma and whose worship is preached. As examples, the chapters on Yoga and Brahma-vijñāna may be referred to. The Purāṇa has sometimes been taken to be a manual of the Bhāgavata priests[138]. But such a character cannot be attributed to the *present* Purāṇa in its original form, because the Bhāgavata characteristics are found only in those chapters which, we have seen, are in all probability later additions.

It is difficult to say where the present Agni was first compiled. The view of Haraprasad Shastri that it was compiled in Bengal or Behar is based on evidences contained in those chapters of the Purāṇa which appear to be spurious.

Besides the extant Agni-p., Mss have been found of another work called 'Vahni-purāṇa' [139]. This Vahni-purāṇa, which is quite different from the present Agni, contains no mention of the Īśāna-kalpa or of the interlocution between Agni and Vaśiṣṭha. Though it contains an interlocution between 'Deva and Ambarīṣa[140]', there

[137] Haraprasad Shastri, Cat. of Sans. Mss, ASB, Vol. V, Preface, p. cl.

[138] Farquhar, Outline, p. 179.

[139] Eggeling, India Office Catalogue, Part VI, pp. 1294 ff.

[140] Ibid, p. 1295.

is none between Vaśiṣṭha and king Ambarīṣa as in the Agni drawn upon by the Nibandha-writers. Therefore, it is certainly not the earlier Agni which was known to these authors, though it seems to have been based on the latter. Whether it is the same as the 'Vahni-purāṇa' drawn upon by the Nibandha-writers like Devaṇabhaṭṭa, Hemādri, Mādhavāvārya, Gopālabhaṭṭa and Gadādhara, cannot be asserted until the quoted verses have been traced in it. That sometimes the 'Agni-purāṇa' was confused with the 'Vahni-purāṇa' is shown by the reading '*Agni-purāṇa*' in one Ms of Mādhavācārya's com. on the Parāśara-smṛti for '*Vahni-purāṇa*' in others[141]. But such rare variations should not be made the basis of the statement that it was the real Agni which was also called 'Vahni-purāṇa'.

In this connection a few words regarding the contents of the earlier Agni-purāṇa may be said here on the basis of the quotations made from it in the Nibandhas. These quotations show that the Purāṇa dealt, among other topics, with Adbhuta-śānti (see Adbhs.), different kinds of gifts (see Dānasāgara), dedication of tanks and gardens, impurity due to births and deaths, funeral sacrifices, penances, fasts and worships on different Tithis, bathing and worship of Viṣṇu, selection and worship of Śālagrāma, and bath in the Ganges Regarding the stories occurring in it Ballālasena's Adbhutasāgara and Gopālabhaṭṭa's Haribhaktivilāsa supply us with valuable information not only by quoting verses from the 'Agni-p.' or 'Āgneya' but also by referring to the topics or stories contained in the chapters from which the verses were drawn. From these quotations and references we understand that the Purāṇa contained a long story of Vāmanotpatti and Hiraṇyakaśipu-vadha dealt with most probably in more chapters than one[142]. It also contained the long story of the Rāmāyaṇa, because there is mention of the blind sage's 'lament for his son killed by Daśaratha'[143], of Rāvaṇa's fight with Indra and the latter's defeat[144], and of Trijaṭā's detailed dream about the fate of Rāvaṇa and his capital[145]. The quoted verses further show that the chapter or chapters dealing with Hiraṇyakaśipu-vadha had a large number of verses, if not all, in common with Mat 161-3, Pd (Sṛṣṭi-kh.) 42 and Hv III, 41-47[146], and that the section on Trijaṭā-svapna had many verses in common with the Rāmāyaṇa[147].

141 See Mādhavācārya's com. on the Parāśara-smṛti, Vol. I, Part i, p. 178.
142 See Adbhs, p. 708; and pp. 19, 50, 320 etc.
143 See Haribhaktivilāsa, p. 943—*agnipurāṇe daśaratha-hata-putra-vipralāpe* etc.
144 Adbhs, pp. 23, 657 etc.
145 Ibid., pp. 500, 501 etc.
146 Ibid., pp. 50-51, 320, 378, 412 etc.
147 Ibid., pp. 512, 513 etc.

7. THE GARUḌA-PURĀṆA. [148]

The title of the present Garuḍa-purāṇa is due to the story that Garuḍa once worshipped Viṣṇu and received a boon from the latter that he would become the author of a Purāṇa-saṃhitā. Consequenty, Garuḍa spoke out the Garuḍa-purāṇa to Kaśyapa. Viṣṇu then imparted it to Rudra, Brahmā and other gods; Brahmā to Vyāsa, Dakṣa and others; Vyāsa to Sūta; and Sūta to the sages Śaunaka and others in the Naimiṣa forest (see Gḍ I, 2).

This Purāṇa, which consists of two Khaṇḍas— Pūrva and Uttara, is a work of cyclopaedic character containing almost everything of general interest. Thus in the Pūrva-khaṇḍa there are chapters on almost all the five themes of the Purāṇa as well as on astronomy, astrology, testing of gems (ratna-parīkṣā), omina and portenta, chiromancy, medicine, metrics, grammar, politics (nīti), various Smṛti-topics, details of the worship of different deities, vows (vrata), initiation, holy places, Yoga, knowledge of the supreme Brahma, and the stories of the Rāmāyaṇa, Mahābhārata and Harivaṃśa. The Uttara-khaṇḍa is a voluminous but quite unsystematic work and 'treats of everything connected with death, the dead and the beyond. In motley confusion and with many repetitions, we find doctrines on the fate of the soul after death, Karman, rebirth and release from brith, on desire as the cause of Saṃsāra, on omens of death, the path of Yama, the fate of the Pretas - - - - -, the torments of the hells, and the Pretas as causing evil omens and dreams'. Of these two Khaṇḍas the first consists mainly of the

[148] Jīvānanda Vidyāsāgara's ed. of the Gḍ differs much from the Vaṅga. ed. The corresponding chapters in the Pūrva-khaṇḍas of the two editions are the following:

Jīvānanda's ed.		Vaṅga. ed.	Jīvānanda's ed.		Vaṅga. ed.
I, 1-132	=	I, 1-132 respectively;	I, 192-204	=	I, 198-210 respectively;
133	=	133-134;	205-221	=	217-233 respectively;
134	=	135;	222	=	234-235;
135	=	136-139;	223-228	=	236-241 respectively;
136-191	=	140-195 respectively;	229	=	242-243.

Chaps. 196-197 and 211-216 of the Vaṅga. ed. are not found in Jīvānanda's ed. There are also numerous variations in readings and numbers of verses in the corresponding chapters. The Uttara-khaṇḍa of this Purāṇa varies so hopelessly in the two editions that it is impossible to note the variations here.

The difference between the Vaṅga. and Veṅk. editions is also not negligible; for Gḍ I, 235 (on the glories of Viṣṇu) of the Vaṅga. ed. is not found in the Veṅk. ed., and Gḍ I, 239-240 (on Brahma-gītā) of the latter ed. are not found in the former. As regards the remaining chapters of the Pūrva-khaṇḍas in the two editions, there are occasional variations in readings and numbers of verses.

The differences between the Uttara-khaṇḍas in the two editions are too numerous to be noted here.

incorporation of entire chapters and isolated verses of some of the standard works on the different branches of learning. It also gives summaries of some other works. Of these different sources used by the Garuḍa-p. some have already been pointed out by scholars. These are the Yājñavalkya-smṛti, Manu-smṛti, Parāśara-smṛti, Bṛhat-saṃhitā, Kalāpa Vyākaraṇa with Kātyāyana's additional chapter on verbal derivations, Aṣṭāṅgahṛdaya-saṃhitā of Vāgbhaṭa II, Aśva-cikitsā of Nakula, and Cāṇakya-rājanītiśāstra of Bhoja[149]. Besides these, the Garuḍa-p. is found to have chapters and verses in common with other Purāṇas also; viz.,

> Gḍ I, 1, 14-34a, in which the 21 incarnations of Vāsudeva have been enumerated, agree almost literally with Bhāg I, 3, 6-26a; Gḍ I, 49, 2-30, I, 50, 1-79 (except 50a and 66b) and I, 51, 1 to the end are all found in Kūr I, 2, II, 18 and II, 26 respectively; Gḍ I, 50, 81-82 = Kūr II, 23, 1 and 13; Gḍ I, 51, 3 = Kūr II, 25, 2; Gḍ I, 52 (except 2b) = Kūr II, 30 and 32-33; Gḍ I, 227, 14-20 = Kūr I, 1, 12-20; a few verses are common to Gḍ I, 82-86 and Vā 105 ff. (on Gayā-māhātmya); Gḍ I, 88-90 = Mārk 95-98.

That as regards these common portions the Garuḍa is the borrower can be little doubted. Its late origin, its careless omission of numerous verses from the incorporated chapters, and its summarization of chapters which come from early dates—all go against its originality.

The contents of the present Garuḍa do not conform to the description of the 'Gāruḍa' given in the Matsya, the Skanda and the Agni-purāṇa, according to which the Garuḍa-p. was declared by Kṛṣṇa (or Viṣṇu according to the Agni) in connection with the origin of Garuḍa from the cosmic egg (viśvāṇḍa) in the Gāruḍa Kalpa[150]. In the extant Garuḍa, though Viṣṇu is the narrator, there is no mention of the Gāruḍa Kalpa or of the origin of Garuḍa from the cosmic egg. This disagreement, and the absence of the verses quoted by the early authors like Ānandatīrtha Madhva,

[149] IHQ, Vol. VI, 1930, pp. 555-558. Haraprasad Shastri, Cat. of Sans. Mss, ASB, Vol. V, Preface, pp. cxcii-cxciii. Kane, Hist. of Dhs., Vol. I, pp. 175 and 191.

[150] Cf. *yadā ca gāruḍe kalpe viśvāṇḍād garuḍodbhavam|*
adhikṛtyābravīt kṛṣṇo gāruḍaṃ tad ihocyate||

Mat 53, 52 and Sk VII, i, 2, 72. The latter reads '*vā*' for '*ca*' and '*garuḍo 'bhavat*' for '*garuḍodbhavam*' in the first line.

gāruḍaṃ cāṣṭasāhasraṃ viṣṇūktaṃ tārkṣya-kalpake|
viśvāṇḍād garuḍotpattiṃ tad dadyāddhema-haṃsavat||

Ag 272, 21b-22a.

Devaṇabhaṭṭa, Hemādri[151], Mādhavācārya and Śūlapāṇi, show that the present Garuḍa is not the earlier one noticed by the Matsya, Skanda and Agni-purāṇa and drawn upon by the said authors.

The date of the extant Garuḍa can be ascertained within narrow limits. Rūpa Gosvāmin, a disciple of Caitanya of Navadvīpa, quotes a verse from Gḍ I, 232 in his Haribhaktirasāmṛtasindhu; Gopālabhaṭṭa quotes a good number of verses from Gḍ I, 66, 221, 231, 232, 235 and 239 in his Haribhaktivilāsa; Gadādhara from Gḍ I, 52, 127 and 133 in his Kālasāra; Govindānanda from Gḍ I, 31, 84 (Gayā-māhātmya), 123-125, 127-129, 131, 140, 217, 222 and 224 in his Varṣakriyā-kaumudī, Śuddhikriyā-kaumudī and Śrāddhakriyā-kaumudī; Raghunandana from Gḍ I, 68 (ratna-parīkṣā), 110 (nīti-sāra), 124, 129, 131, 133, 172 (Āyurveda), 173 (Āyurveda), 217 and 221 in his Smṛti-tattva; and Vācaspatimiśra from Gḍ I, 82 (Gayā-māhātmya) and 84 (Gayā-māhātmya) in his Tīrtha-cintāmaṇi (see App.). These quotations show that the present Garuḍa-p. came into being earlier than 1400 A.D. In his Dānasāgara Ballālasena mentions a spurious 'Tārkṣya' (i.e., Gāruḍa) Purāṇa which, as the enumeration of its contents shows, is the same as our present Garuḍa. So, our Garuḍa-p. must be earlier than 1100 A.D.[152] Kane compares the text of the Yājñavalkya-smṛti preserved in the Garuḍa-p. with those used by Viśvarūpa and Vijñāneśvara and comes to the conclusion that 'the Garuḍa-purāṇa represents a stage intermediate between Viśvarūpa and Vijñāneśvara'[153]. Therefore the date of the Garuḍa-p. falls between 800 and 1000 A.D. Again, as the Garuḍa has verses from those portions of the Kūrma-p. which were added by the Pāśupatas between 700 and 800 A.D., and as Vagbhaṭa II, the author of the Aṣṭāṅgahṛdaya-saṃhitā, lived between the 8th and 9th centuries A.D.[154], the Garuḍa-p.

[151] Numerous extracts, large and small, have been quoted from a 'Gāruḍa-p.' or 'Garuḍa-p.' on the classification of gifts, limitations on the acceptance of gifts, proper time and place for making gifts, erection of a pandal for the purpose, different varieties of gifts (viz., Tulāpuruṣa-dāna, Suvarṇa-vṛṣa-dāna, Rūpya-vṛṣa-dāna, Vidyā-dāna, Veda-dāna, Śvetāśva-dāna, Gaja-dāna, Ratha-dāna, Kanyā-dāna, etc. etc.), praise of 'tapas' which is practised through Vratas, results of Vratas, different kinds of Vratas (viz., Vidyā-pratipad-vrata, Vidyā-vrata, Śānti-vrata, Saubhāgya-vrata, Śrīpañcamī-vrata, Sudarśana-ṣaṣṭhī-vrata, Maṅgalya-vrata, Narasiṃha-vrata, Gopāla-navamī-vrata, Ārogya-vrata, Gāyatrī-vrata, Āyur-vrata and Kāñcanapurī-vrata), funeral sacrifices, Ekādaśī and Dvādaśī; and in some of these extracts Sanatkumāra is mentioned as speaking to a king (addressed as '*pārthiva*', '*rājan*' etc., cf. Caturvarga-cintāmaṇi I, pp. 215, 489-491, etc.) or to Bharadvāja (cf. Caturvarga-cintāmaṇi, II, i, pp. 338-341, 386-9, 465-471 etc.; II, ii, pp. 62-3, 227-9, etc.).

[152] See Dānasāgara, fol. 3b-4a. See also footnote 131 under Agni-p.

[153] Kane, Hist. of Dhs., Vol. I, p. 175.

[154] Hoernle, Medicine of Ancient India, Part 1, pp. 11-13. JRAS, 1909, p. 882.

cannot be earlier than about the middle of the 9th century. *It is, therefore, highly probable that the extant Garuḍa was compiled between 850 and 1000 A.D. A comparison between the Garuḍa and the extant Agni tends to show that the former was modelled on the latter. So the Garuḍa-p. should be dated in the 10th century A.D.* This date is not, however, applicable to all the chapters of the Garuḍa. *The Uttara-khaṇḍa,* inspite of its having Viṣṇu and Garuḍa as interlocutors, *is undoubtedly a later addition.* It is a distinct work by itself, having a fresh beginning. In the enumeration of contents given in Gḍ I, 3 there is no mention of the topics dealt with in the Uttara-khaṇḍa. Moreover, no Nibandha-writer has been found to draw upon this Khaṇḍa. In the Hari-bhaktivilāsa (p. 940) there is mention of an interlocution between the Bhagavat and Garuḍa, but the verse, which is ascribed to them, is not found in the Uttara-khaṇḍa. The other verses also[155], in which Garuḍa has been addressed as *'khaga', 'pakṣīndra'* etc., are not found in this Khaṇḍa. Hence the spurious character of this Khaṇḍa is undeniable. Besides this Khaṇḍa, *there are chapters in the Pūrva-khaṇḍa which appear to be spurious. These are especially chapters 146-149 and 202.* Of these, the former deal with the incarnations of Viṣṇu and, in connection with them, narrate the stories of the Rāmāyaṇa, Mahābhārata and Harivaṃśa, none of which has been referred to in the synopsis of contents given in Gḍ I, 3. The number of incarnations named in these chapters is only ten, and 'Vāmana' is replaced by 'Dhanvantari' which is assigned the third place. This number is in entire disagreement with that given in chap. 1, wherein 21 incarnations are named and which was certainly not added later. Again, in chap. 202 the number of Viṣṇu's incarnations named is seventeen, and among them there are four names, viz., Rāma, Hayagrīva, Makaradhvaja and Nāga, which are not found in chap. 1. These varying lists of incarnations cannot be ascribed to one hand. Hence the chapters under discussion cannot but be spurious. Besides these chapters, there are possibly others which are spurious, but it is very difficult to detect them.

The extant Garuḍa-p., though a comparatively late work, does not seem to have come down to us in its original form. Many chapters and verses, which once occurred in this apocryphal Garuḍa, are not found in it at present. In the synopsis of contents in Gḍ I, 3, there is mention of 'Vyavahāra', but in the present form of the Purāṇa there is no chapter on this topic. This

[155] Viz., those in Madana-pārijāta, pp. 302-303; Smṛti-tattva I, 147; Haribhakti-vilāsa, pp. 333, 334, 362, 460, 465 etc.

Vyavahāra-section, which is now missing, was taken most probably from the Yājñavalkya-smṛti, because, though the Garuḍa appropriates a large number of sections from the first and third chapters of the Yājñavalkya-smṛti, the chapter on Vyavahāra is remarkably absent from the Purāṇa. The Haribhaktivilāsa mentions the interlocutions between (1) Nārada and king Dhundhumāra[156], (2) Śuka and king Ambarīṣa[157], and (3) Nārada and Indra[158]. The occasional occurrence of the words *narādhipa, viśāṃpati* etc. in the vocative case[159] in the verses quoted by other Nibandha-writers also shows that the above mentioned interlocutions were not unknown to them. None of these interlocutions is, however, found in the present Garuḍa. Besides these, a large number of verses quoted by those Nibandhakāras who used the apocryphal Garuḍa, is not found in our present Garuḍa.

The extant Garuḍa is avowedly a Vaiṣṇava Purāṇa. It was compiled with a view to glorifying Viṣṇu and preaching his worship[160]. It is for this reason that in numerous places in the Purāṇa Viṣṇu, and not any other god, is identified with the supreme Brahma, and more attention is paid to his worship. The methods of the worship of Śiva, Durgā, Gaṇeśa and Sūrya also are found in this Purāṇa, but these deities are never given so much importance as Viṣṇu. On the other hand, they are said to be Viṣṇu's attendant deities[161]. It is perhaps for this reason that the details of their worship have been included in this Purāṇa.

From the evidences given by the Purāṇas[162] and the Nibandha-writers we understand that the Garuḍa-p. was also sometimes called 'Tārkṣya', 'Vainateya' or 'Sauparṇa'. Among the Mahāpurāṇas mentioned in the Dānasāgara we find the name 'Tārkṣya' and not 'Garuḍa'. The quotations made by the Nibandha-writers under the names 'Tārkṣya' 'Vainateya' and 'Sauparṇa' are not, however, found in the extant Garuḍa.

8. THE BRAHMA-PURĀṆA. [163].

It is a general belief that the present Brahma-p is the original one, the peculiarity being that it has suffered through additions

[156] Haribhaktivilāsa, p. 322. [157] Ibid., p. 678. [158] Ibid., p. 882.

[159] See, for example, Smṛti-tattva I, p. 148 and II, pp. 567-569.

[160] Cf. Gḍ I, 1, 11a—*purāṇaṃ gāruḍaṃ vakṣye sāraṃ viṣṇu-kathāśrayam.*

[161] Cf. Gḍ I, 6, 70—'*sūryādi-parivāreṇa manvādyā ījire harim*'. This line is introductory to chaps. 7 ff. on the worship of Śiva, Durgā and others.

[162] Cf. Bhāg XII, 13, 8 and Vā 104, 8.

[163] The AnSS ed. is chapter by chapter the same as the Vaṅga. ed. There are occasional variations in readings and numbers of verses in the corresponding chapters, but these variations are not many and important for our purpose.

and losses. This belief is at the base of almost all statements that have been made so long by scholars about its date and authoritativeness. From an examination of the Purāṇas and the Smṛti-Nibandhas, however, it has been found that the present Brahma-p. is not the original one but is merely an Upapurāṇa of the same title and that it was known as such even as late as in the sixteenth century A.D., if not later.

Almost all the Nibandha-writers have profusely drawn upon the 'Brahma-p.' or 'Brāhma' which was, therefore, one of the most authoritative works in the whole range of Purāṇic literature. But, curiously enough, not a single of the numerous quotations made by Jīmūtavāhana, Aparārka, Haradatta (the commentator of the Gautama-dharmasūtra), Aniruddhabhaṭṭa, Ballālasena, Devaṇabhaṭṭa, Kullūkabhaṭṭa, Madanapāla, Śrīdatta Upādhyāya, Caṇḍeśvara, Rudradhara and many others, is traceable in the present Brahma-p. This is significant and undoubtedly goes against the authenticity of this Purāṇa. Definite information, however, about the apocryphal character of the present Brahma is supplied to us by Narasiṃha Vājapeyin, a Nibandha-writer of Orissa. Speaking on the authenticity of the two Purāṇas entitled 'Brahma-purāṇa', he says in his Nityācārapradīpa (p. 19):

> "*brahmapurāṇaṃ ca kalpatarau yad-vākyāny ādṛtāni, tad-vyatiriktaṃ brahmapurāṇaṃ puruṣottama-māhātmyopabṛṃhitaṃ hemādryādinibandha-parigṛhītaṃ śiṣṭa-parigrahād eva pramāṇaṃ, tad apy upapurāṇāntargatam eva*".

Thus he clearly distinguishes between the two Brahma-purāṇas—one, a Mahāpurāṇa, and the other, an Upapurāṇa. His definite mention of the Puruṣottama-māhātmya as occurring in the Upapurāṇa proves the apocryphal character of the extant Brahma-p., in which there are chapters on this Māhātmya. Its apocryphal character is further established by the fact that though Narasiṃha Vājapeyin was certainly acquainted with the present Brahma-p., none of the numerous quotations made by him from the 'Brahma-purāṇa' in his Nityācārapradīpa is traceable in it. It cannot be argued that the Smṛti-chapters of the present apocryphal Brahma-p. date from a time later than that of the Nibandha-writer, because there is a Ms (No. 2337) of this Purāṇa in the D. U. Mss Lib. which is dated 1616 Śaka (= 1694 A.D.) and which tallies almost literally with the present editions. The evidences of the Purāṇas also go against the authenticity of the present Brahma. According to the Matsya, the Skanda and the Agni-purāṇa Brahmā and Marīci are the interlocutors in the original (or rather earlier)

Brahma-p.[164], but in the present Brahma we find Brahmā and Dakṣa. All these facts establish the apocryphal character of the present Brahma-p. The title of the work should not be taken as a point in favour of its authenticity. The lists of Upapurāṇas contained in some of the Mahāpurāṇas show that there were Upapurāṇas bearing the titles of Mahāpurāṇas. For example, Kūr I, 1, 17-20 name the Skanda, Vāmana, Brahmāṇḍa and Nāradīya Upapurāṇas.

Though the present apocryphal Brahma-p. is a voluminous work, there is little which it can claim as its own. It is a late conglomeration of chapters mainly borrowed from other sources such as the Viṣṇu-p., Mārkaṇḍeya-p., Vāyu-p., Mahābhārata and Harivaṃśa, as the following list will show.

Br 1 (verses 21-30)	=	Viṣ I, 2, 1-8.
„ 1 (verses 31 to the end)	=	Hv I, 1, 19 to the end.
„ 2-5	=	„ I, 2-7.
„ 6-8	=	„ I, 9-15.
„ 9	=	„ I, 25.
„ 10	=	„ I, 26 (verses 1-11 and 48-49); and „ I, 27.
„ 11-17	=	„ I, 28-39.
„ 18 (except verses 1-6); „ 19-24	=	Viṣ II, 2-7 and 9.
„ 27 (verses 10 to the end)	=	Mārk 57 (except verses 1b, 50-52a and 64b).
„ 39-40	=	Vā 30 (verses 79 to the end).

Brahma-p. 70, 12 to chap. 175 deal with Gautamī-māhātmya which constituted an independent work by itself.

Br 179 (except verses 1-10 and 66-75)	=	Hv I, 40, 8 to the end (except verses 41b-43a, 46b, 56a, 64 and 66a).
„ 180, 1-5 (except 3a)	=	Mārk 4, 36-40a.

[164] *brahmaṇābhihitaṃ pūrvaṃ yāvanmātraṃ marīcaye|*
brāhmaṃ tridaśasāhasraṃ purāṇaṃ parikīrtyate||

Mat 53, 12b-13a; and Sk VII, i, 2, 28. Sk reads *'tad daśasāhasram'* for *'tridaśa-sāhasraṃ'*, and *'tad ihocyate'* for *'parikīrtyate'* in the second line. Ag 272, 1 agrees with the Matsya in the first line but differs in the second, which runs as follows:

lakṣārdhārdhaṃ tu tad brāhmaṃ likhitvā saṃpradāpayet'.

Br	180, 6-13	= Viṣ	I, 2, 1-8.
,,	180, 14 to the end (except 29-38 and 42a)	= Mārk	4, 40b to the end.
,,	181 (5 ff.)—212	= Viṣ	V, 1 to the end (except V, 1, 1-11).
,,	213, 3-9	= Hv	I, 40, 1-7.
,,	213, 10 to the end (except 21b-22a, 131a, 164 and 171)	= ,,	I, 41 (except 12b-c, 15b-19, 21a, 22b, 28c, 49b, 55, 58a, 59, 83a, 111b, 138, 151b, 161-163, and 165-169).

Br 217 has many verses in common with Mārk 15.

Br	220, 22-29	= Mārk	32, 1-8.
,,	220, 33-42	= ,,	33, 8b to the end.
,,	220, 69-82a	= ,,	30, 12 to the end (except 19b).
,,	220, 82b-99	= ,,	31, 1-8.
,,	220, 101b	= ,,	31, 23b.
,,	220, 102a	= ,,	31, 25a.
,,	220, 105-110a	= ,,	31, 30-34.
,,	220, 110b-120a	= ,,	32, 28-37.
,,	221, 1-109a (except 59b, 77b, 84 and 85b)	= ,,	34 (except 17b, 30b, 42b, 68-69a, 74a, 76b-77, 81a, 85b, 88-90a, 92a, 93 and 102-103a).
,,	221, 109b-165a	= ,,	35 (except 8b, 33b and 55a).
,,	222, 1-21	= Viṣ	III, 8, 20 to the end.
,,	222, 22 to the end (except verses 51-52)	= ,,	III, 9.
,,	230, 1 to the end	= ,,	VI, 1-2.
,,	232, 1 to the end	= ,,	VI, 3.
,,	233, 1 to the end	= ,,	VI, 4 (except 15b and 49b).
,,	234 (except 69b)	= ,,	VI, 5 (except 52-54, 69-78a and 81a).

Br 236	=	Mbh XII (Śānti-parvan), 238-239 (= ASB ed. 239-240; Bombay ed. 240-241).
„ 237	=	„ „ „ 240 and 245-247 (= ASB ed. 241 and 246-248; Bombay ed. 242 and 247-248).
„ 238	=	„ „ „ 248-249 and 273 (= ASB ed. 249-250 and 275 Bombay ed. 249-250 and 274).
„ 239-241	=	„ „ „ 300-302 respectively (= ASB ed. 302-304; Bombay ed. 300-302).
„ 242	=	„ „ „ 303-304 .(= ASB ed. 305-306; Bombay ed. 303-304).
„ 243	=	„ „ „ 305-306 (= ASB ed. 307-308; Bombay ed. 305-306).
„ 244-245	=	„ „ „ 307-308 rspectively (= ASB ed. 309-310; Bombay ed. 307-308)[165].

That, as regards these common chapters, the apocryphal Brahma-p. is the borrower, requires no evidence to prove. The quotations made by the early authors from the Viṣṇu, Mārkaṇḍeya and Vāyu-p. show that the chapters borrowed by the Brahma-p. have been occurring in these Purāṇas from a time earlier than that of compilation of the present Brahma. As to the chapters common to the Brahma-p. and the Harivaṃśa, a comparison of the portions common to the

[165] Br 236-245 on Sāṃkhya and Yoga were traced by F. Otto Schrader in the Śānti-parvan of the Mbh and published in the Indian Culture (Vol. II, 1935-36, pp. 592-3) as a note on my article on 'The Apocryphal Brahma-Purāṇa' which appeared in the same journal.

Vāyu, Harivaṃśa and Brahma[166] proves the indebtedness of the Brahma to the Harivaṃśa. In these common portions the Brahma follows more the Harivaṃśa in its readings and extra verses than the Vāyu. The portions common to the Vāyu and the Harivaṃśa, and the references in the latter to the names of the great sages and the ten sons of Tāmasa Manu as declared by Vāyu (*vāyu-proktāḥ* —Hv I, 7, 13 and 25), tend to show that the Harivaṃśa had the Vāyu-p. as one of its sources. Pargiter also doubts the Harivaṃśa version of the dynastic account to be a revision of that of the Vāyu and says that 'it is manifestly later than the 'Vāyu version' [167].' As to the chapters common to the Brahma-p. and the Mahābhārata, the priority of those of the latter is unquestionable.

We have given above the list of chapters that have been borrowed by the Brahma-p. from different sources. If these chapters are left out of consideration, those which remain untraced are unimportant and small in number. They are as follows:

Br	1 (verses 1-20)	— Introductory verses.
„	18 (verses 1-6)	— Enumeration of the topics treated of in chaps. 1-17.
„	25	— Names of holy places.
„	26	— For introducing chap. 27 on geography.
„	27 (verses 1-10)	
„	28-38	— Gods and holy places in Orissa.
„	41-70 (1-11)	
„	176-178	
„	214-215	— On hells.
„	216-217 (partly)	— On the results of actions done (karma-vipāka).
„	218	
„	219	— On Śrāddha.
„	220 (verses 1-21, 30-32, 43-68, 100-101a, 102b-104, 120b-212).	
„	223-225	— On Karma-vipāka.
„	226-229	— On the worship of Viṣṇu.
„	231	— Accounts of the Dvāpara and the future ages.

166 Viz., Vā 62, 72b-98, Hv I, 2, 7-27 and Br 2, 7-28a; Vā 62, 99-193, Hv I, 4, 26 ff. to I, 6, 44a and Br 4, 19-110; Vā 63, 1-11, Hv I, 6, 44b-54 and Br 4, 111-122.

167 Pargiter, AIHT, pp. 78-79.

Br 235 — For introducing chaps. 236-245 on Sāṃkhya and Yoga.
„ 246 — On Purāṇa-māhātmya, etc.

Besides these, there may be found even in the borrowed chapters verses which are not traceable in the originals. These verses do not contain anything important for our purpose, nor do they shed any light on the date of composition of the present Brahma-p. Therefore, they may be neglected.

The apocryphal Brahma-p., with its borrowed and non-borrowed chapters, does not seem to have been composed, or rather compiled, earlier than the beginning of the tenth century A.D. Had it been composed earlier, it should have been drawn upon, or at least referred to, by the Nibandha-writers earlier than the middle of the 13th century A.D.[168] It is not that the early Nibandha-writers did not believe in the authoritativeness of the Upapurāṇas. The numerous verses quoted by them from a good number of such works[169] show that they gave almost the same importance to the Upapurāṇas and the Mahāpurāṇas as sources of Dharma. Even after the middle of the 13th century this apocryphal Brahma-p. began to be regarded as an authority only by a comparatively small section of writers consisting mainly of Hemādri, Śūlapāṇi, Vācaspatimiśra and Govindānanda. Each of them quotes a good number of verses from the present Brahma-p. Of the very numerous quotations made by Raghunandana in his Smṛti-tattva from the 'Brahma-p.' some are found in those chapters of the extant Brahma which deal with the holy places in Orissa. Raghunandana draws upon the extant Brahma-p. in his Yātrā-tattva also. These quotations made in relation to the worship of the Sun, Śiva and god Puruṣottama, and the expression '*brahma-*

[168] In Dānasāgara, fol. 4a there is mention of a few spurious Purāṇas including the 'Brāhma' with a general statement of their contents. But as these contents do not agree even partially with those of our extant Brahma, it is highly probable, if not sure, that the spurious 'Brāhma' of the Dānasāgara was different from our present Brahma.

R. L. Mitra describes a Brahma-p. which consists of two Khaṇḍas,—Pūrva and Uttara, and is quite different from our present Brahma. As it mentions the history of Rādhā, her worship, Tulasī's marriage with Śaṅkhacūḍa, the history of Manasā, etc., it must be a very late work. See, Mitra, A Catalogue of Sanskrit Mss in the Library of His Highness the Mahārājā of Bikaner, pp. 187-9.

[169] Viz., Ādi-p. (not the Brahma-p. which also is sometimes called 'Ādi-p.'), Āditya-p., Nṛsiṃha-p., Kālikā-p, Nandi-p., Nandikeśvara, Devī-p., Saura-p., Saura-dharmottara, Bhaviṣyottara, Viṣṇu-rahasya, Viṣṇu-dharma, Viṣṇu-dharmottara, Viṣṇu-dharmottarāmṛta, Bṛhad-viṣṇudharma, Śiva-rahasya, Śiva-dharmottara, Bhagavatī-p., Śāmba-p. and so forth.

purāṇokta-mārkaṇḍeya-hrade pradyumna-sarovare samudra-rūpādi-tīrtha-bhedādau etc.' in Smṛti-tattva I, p. 366 show that though Raghunandana used mainly the original (or rather earlier) Brahma-p., he must have quoted verses from the apocryphal Purāṇa also. From all this it is highly probable that the *present Brahma-p. is to be dated not earlier than the beginning of the tenth century A.D. As Hemādri, Śūlapāṇi, Vācaspatimiśra, Govindānanda and Raghunandana quote verses from it, it cannot be later than 1200 A.D.*[170]

Let us now pass on to the different chapters. Chap. 25 gives a long list of the names of holy places chiefly of Northern India. Though it mentions the Virajā-tīrtha and the Indradyumna-saras, the names of Puruṣottama-kṣetra and Ekāmra-kṣetra are conspicuous by their absence. Moreover, this chapter is wholly unconnected with those preceding and following it. So it seems to have been interpolated by some one living outside Orissa.

Chap. 26 is meant for serving as an introduction to chap. 27 dealing with the geography of India. It was, therefore, written at the time when chap. 27 was borrowed from the Mārkaṇḍeya-p.

Chaps. 28-70 and 176-178, on the holy places in Orissa, should be considered in four groups :

(1) chaps. 28 (1-8), 42 (35 to the end), 43-69, 70 (1-11), and 176-178 on Puruṣottama-kṣetra or Puri sacred to Viṣṇu ;
(2) chaps. 28 (9 ff.)—33 on Koṇārka sacred to the Sun-god ;
(3) chaps. 34-41 on Ekāmra-kṣetra or Bhuvaneśvara sacred to Śiva ; and
(4) chap. 42 (1-34) on Virajā-kṣetra or Jajpore sacred to Devī.

Of these four groups of chapters, those belonging to group (1) were written first of all. The chapters of the remaining three groups were interpolated later. The reference to the quarrel between the Śaivas and the Bhāgavatas, and the avowedly sectarian character of the chapters of the different groups, prove that they were written by different hands.

The determination of the date of composition of the chapters on Puruṣottamakṣetra-māhātmya is rather difficult. They could

170 In his Essays, Vol. I, p. 18, Wilson opines that our present Brahma-p. 'was composed in the course of the thirteenth or fourteenth century'. But this opinion is open to serious doubts, because, even if the Purāṇa was compiled towards the beginning of the thirteenth century, it could hardly be expected to reach Hemādri, an inhabitant of Devagiri in Hyderabad, and to attain the position of an authoritative Purāṇa within fifty years of its compilation.

171 Br 56, 65 and 72-73.

not have possibly been written earlier than the end of the 9th century A.D., because there is mention of the Śiva-temple at the side of the Mārkaṇḍeya lake[171]. This temple was built in 820 A.D. by Kuṇḍala-keśarin, king of Orissa. Again, the expensive stone temple, which the mythical king Indradyumna is said to have built at Puruṣottama-kṣetra, may be indentical with that built by Ananta-varman Coḍagaṅga (Śaka 998-1069), one of the eastern Gaṅga kings of Orissa. He was 'a good patron of religious works and charities', and 'under his orders was built the great temple of Jagannātha at Puri'[172]. We cannot, however, put much stress on this supposition, because it is not known definitely that there was no Viṣṇu-temple at Puri before the time of Ananta-varman Coḍagaṅga. That the chapters on Puruṣottama-kṣetra were incorporated into the present Brahma not later than the middle of the 12th century A.D. is certain, because these chapters are earlier than those on Koṇārka, Ekāmra-kṣetra and Virajā-kṣetra and many of these chapters are drawn upon by Vācaspatimiśra in his Tīrtha-cintāmaṇi, by Śūlapāṇi in his Dolayātrā-viveka and Rāsayātrā-viveka, and by Hemādri in his Caturvarga-cintāmaṇi.

The story of Kaṇḍu in Br 178 seems to have been added later than chaps. 176-177. This story is told by Vyāsa, whereas in all other chapters on Orissa Brahmā is the speaker. Moreover, the story is inserted all on a sudden without any previous hint. The story that there had been at Puruṣottama an image of Viṣṇu made of sapphire and that it had been buried in golden sand by the god himself before Indradyumna went to the place, is most probably fabricated to give the place an air of greater sanctity and antiquity. A similar attempt was also made with respect to the image. It is said that the image was first constructed by Viśvakarman at the command of Viṣṇu. It was then taken to heaven by Indra, thence to Laṅkā by Rāvaṇa, and from Laṅkā to Ayodhyā by Rāma. It was then given to the lord of oceans who, 'for some reason', placed it at Puruṣottama (cf. chap. 176). The honest motive underlying this story is obvious.

The chapters on Koṇārka, Ekāmra-kṣetra and Virajā-kṣetra must be earlier than 1200 A.D., because some of these chapters have been drawn upon in the Caturvarga-cintāmaṇi by Hemādri who lived far away from Orissa, the original home of these chapters, as well as by Vācaspatimiśra in his Tīrtha-cintāmaṇi. As to the upper limit of the date of these chapters, it may be said that as they are later than the chapters on Puruṣottama-kṣetra, they cannot possibly be earlier than 950 A.D. By their mention of a Sun-temple

[171] Br 56, 65 and 72-73. [172] JASB, Vol. LXXII, 1903, p. 110.

at Koṇārka in Br 28, 46-7, they may appear to be later than 1240 A.D.; but it is extremely difficult to prove that the Sun-temple mentioned by the Brahma-p. is the same as that built between 1240 and 1251 A.D.[173] by Narasiṃhadeva I of the Gaṅga dynasty of Orissa. Even if the two Sun-temples mentioned above were taken to be identical, we could hardly expect chapters to have been written on the glories of the temple and to have reached Hemādri within only a quarter of a century after the construction of the temple. It is therefore highly probable that there was already an ancient Sun-temple at Koṇārka before 1240 A.D., and Narasiṃhadeva I either built another which has superseded the ancient temple in its fame and glory or rebuilt the ancient one which can be expected to have been in a dilapidated condition.

Chaps. 214-215 on hells and chaps. 216-218 on Karma-vipāka are probably of the same date as that of compilation of the present Brahma. They cannot be later than 1500 A.D., because Govindānanda quotes verses from chaps. 216 and 218 in his Dānakriyā-kaumudī (see App.). Many verses of these chapters seem to be in common with those in the original Brahma-p., because, of the numerous quotations made by Mādhavācārya, only a few are found in chaps. 214, 215 and 217 of the present Brahma. As none of the quotations made by him on general customs, impurity, funeral sacrifices and penance is found in the present Brahma-p. though it contains chapters on most of these topics, it is sure that Mādhava used the real Brahma and not the present apocryphal one.

Chaps. 219-222 (on funeral sacrifices, customs, duties of the castes and Āśramas, and impurity due to births and deaths) should be dated earlier than 1200 A.D., because Govindānanda quotes numerous verses from chaps. 219-221 in his Śrāddhakriyā-kaumudī and Hemādri draws upon these chapters in his Caturvarga-cintāmaṇi[174]. These chapters (219-222) most probably come from the same date as that of compilation of the present Brahma.

The date of chaps. 223-231, dealing with Karma-vipāka, Viṣṇu-worship etc., is not known definitely. They may have come from the same date as that of compilation of the present Brahma.

[173] According to an inscription discovered at Śrīkūrmam in Orissa, a person named Sāhasa-malla made a grant at the Sun-temple during the reign of Narasiṃhadeva I in 1251 A.D. So, this temple must have been built earlier than 1251 A.D.

[174] Hemādri and Govindānanda draw not only upon the present apocryphal Brahma-p. but also upon the earlier Brahma. It is for this reason that many of the quotations made by Hemādri in his Caturvarga-cintāmaṇi and by Govindānanda in his Dānakriyā-kaumudī and Śrāddhakriyā-kaumudī and all of the numerous quotations made by the latter in his Śuddhikriyā-kaumudī and Varṣakriyā-kaumudī are absent from the present Brahma-p.

Chaps. 235 and 246, attached to chaps. 236-245 on Sāṃkhya and Yoga, were most probably added by the compiler. In some Mss of the present Brahma these chapters are not found at all[175].

The Gautamī-māhātmya (chaps. 70-175), which was certainly composed by somebody living about the river Godāvarī, is a distinct 'work' (*pustakaṃ*) by itself. It is called a 'highly meritorious Purāṇa' declared by Brahmā (cf. Br 175, 78 and 87). The place which it occupies in the Brahma-p. was not meant for it, because it divides the chapters on Puruṣottamakṣetra-māhātmya. The way in which chap. 176 opens, shows that it immediately followed chap. 69. Moreover, in chap. 176 there is no hint from which we may conclude that the Māhātmya was there. In Br 179, 2 the sages refer to Bhāratavarṣa (chap. 27) and Puruṣottama-kṣetra, of which, they say, Vyāsa told them elaborately, but they do not mention the Gautamī-māhātmya which also precedes chap. 179 in our edition. So, it is clear that the Māhātmya was not originally there. In the Veṅk. ed. it is placed at the end. This Māhātmya was attached to the Brahma-p. later than the chapters on Orissa, for the Nāradīya-p. (I, 92), which gives the contents of the present Brahma-p. including the Māhātmyas of Puruṣottama-kṣetra and Ekāmra-kṣetra, does not mention the Gautamī-māhātmya.

The Gautamī-māhātmya does not seem to have been composed earlier than the tenth century A.D. The story of Gautama's bringing the Godāvarī (i.e., Gautamī) is undoubtedly later than those in Kūr I, 16, 95-123 and Var 71. The story of Bhagīratha (Br 78) also is of very late origin. As no author has been found to draw upon this Māhātmya, it is impossible to say anything definitely.

The results of the above analysis are as follows:

(1) Date of compilation	—Not earlier than the beginning of the tenth century A.D. and not later than 1200 A.D.
(2) Chaps. 214-218	—Not later than 1500 A.D. Probably of the same date as that of compilation of the Purāṇa.
„ 219-222	—Not later than 1200 A.D. Most probably of the same date as that of compilation of the Purāṇa.
„ 223-231	—Not known. May have come from the same date as that of compilation.

175 Haraprasad Shastri, Cat. of Sans. Mss, ASB, Vol. V, Preface, p. xcvii.

Chaps. 235 and 246	—Most probably added by the compiler.
(3) „ 70-175	—Most probably earlier than the tenth century A.D.

(4) Interpolations :

Chap. 25	—Comparatively late.
Chap 28 (1-8) 42 (35 to the end), 43-69, 70 (1-11) and 176-177	— Most probably not earlier than the end of the 9th century ; certainly not later than the middle of the 12th century.
Chap. 178	—Later than the chaps. of the immediately preceding group.
Chaps. 28 (9 ff.)—33; „ 34-41 ; Chap. 42 (1-34)	— *C.* Between 950 and 1200 A.D.

Though a comparatively late work, the present Brahma-p. has not escaped additions and alterations. Some of its chapters have been lost. Vācaspatimiśra's numerous quotations on Avimukta-kṣetra-māhātmya show that the apocryphal Brahma-p. once contained a good number of chapters on this Māhātmya. The Nāradīya-p. gives a list of contents of the apocryphal Brahma-p. This list includes the story of Rāma which is not found in the printed editions.

Excepting the chapters on Koṇārka, Ekāmra-kṣetra and Virajā-kṣetra, the present Brahma-p. is Vaiṣṇava from beginning to end. There can be no doubt, therefore, about the Vaiṣṇava authorship of the Purāṇa.

In this connection we should like to say a few words about the Smṛti-contents of the original (or rather earlier) Brahma-p. which seems to have been lost. It has already been said that this Purāṇa was regarded as one of the most authoritative works in the whole range of Purāṇic literature. The quotations made by the Nibandha-writers show that it was a rich store of Smṛti materials. The multifarious Smṛti-topics, dealt with in this Purāṇa, appear to have been the following : (a) the duties of the Āśramas, (b) general customs and daily duties (āhnika), (c) eatables and non-eatables, (d) rules of diet, (e) purification of things, (f) purification of the body, (g) funeral sacrifices, (h) impurity, (i) bath, (j) gifts, (k) duties of women, (l) different kinds of sins, (m) penances, (n) vows (vrata), and (o) observances in the different months (māsa-kṛtya). This list is based on the quotations made by Jīmūtavāhana, Devaṇabhaṭṭa, Aniruddhabhaṭṭa, Ballālasena, Aparārka, Haradatta, Hemādri, Kullūkabhaṭṭa, Madanapāla, Mādhavācārya, Caṇḍeśvara, Raghunandana, Narasiṃha Vājapeyin, and others.

9. THE SKANDA-PURĀṆA.[176]

The present Skanda consists of seven Khaṇḍas or books— Māheśvara, Viṣṇu, Brahma, Kāśī, Āvantya, Nāgara and Prabhāsa. The Māheśvara-khaṇḍa consists of the Kedāra-kh., Kumārikā-kh. and Aruṇācala-māhātmya (the third being divided into two parts—Pūrvārdha and Uttarārdha); the Viṣṇu-khaṇḍa, of the Māhātmyas of Veṅkaṭācala, Puruṣottamakṣetra[177], Vadarikāśrama, Kārttika-māsa, Mārgaśīrṣa-māsa, Bhāgavata, Vaiśākha-māsa and Ayodhyā; the Brahma-khaṇḍa, of Setumāhātmya, Dharmāraṇya-kh. and Uttara-kh.; the Kāśī-khaṇḍa, of two parts called Pūrvārdha and Uttarārdha; the Āvantya-khaṇḍa, of Avantīkṣetra-māhātmya, Caturaśīti-liṅga-māhātmya and Revā-kh.[178]; and the Prabhāsa-

[176] The Vaṅga. ed. of the Skanda-p. is generally the same as the Veṅk. ed., the most notable differences between the two being as follows:

Vaṅga. ed.		Veṅk. ed.
II, ii (Puruṣottamakṣetra-māhātmya), 40	=	II, ii, 40-41.
II, ii, 41, verses 1-36	=	II, ii, 42.
II, ii, 41, verses 37 ff.	—	Not found in the Veṅk. ed.
II, ii, 42-43	=	II, ii, 43-44 respectively.
II, ii, 44	=	II, ii, 45-46.
II, ii, 45	=	II, ii, 47-48.
II, ii, 46-56; II, ii, 57, verses 1-41	—	Not found in the Veṅk. ed.
II, ii, 57, verses 42 to the end	=	II, ii, 49.
V, iii (Revā-kh.), 233-6 (on the worship of Satya-narayaṇa)	—	Not found in the Veṅk. ed.

Besides these, there are other minor differences which need not be mentioned here.

The above differences between the two editions are explained by the editor of the Vaṅga. ed. of the Purāṇa by saying that he took the Veṅk. ed. as the basis and added to it the additional chapters and verses he found in those Bengal Mss of the respective Khaṇḍas which he used for his edition (see Preface to the Vaṅga. ed. of the Skanda-p., pp. 10-11).

[177] The Vaṅga. ed. of the Utkala-kh. is the same as the Puruṣottama-kṣetra-māhātmya occurring in the Viṣṇu-kh. of the Vaṅga. ed. of the Skanda-p.

Of the four Mss of the Puruṣottamakṣetra-māhātmya described by Eggeling in his Ind. Off. Cat., Part VI, pp. 1325-29, three consist of 45 chapters each and one of 61 chapters, whereas the Vaṅga. ed. has 57 chapters.

For the differences between the versions of this Māhātmya as occurring in the Vaṅga. and Veṅk. editions, see footnote 176.

[178] The Revā-kh., described by Eggeling in his Ind. Off. Cat., Part VI, pp. 1360-62, seems to be much shorter than the printed text.

khaṇḍa, of Prabhāsakṣetra-māhātmya, Vastrāpathakṣetra-māhātmya, Arvuda-kh. and Dvārakā-māhātmya.

Though the above division of the Skanda is supported by the Nāradīya-p.[179], its real division seems to have been into six Saṃhitās with further subdivisions. According to the Hālāsya-māhātmya of the Agastya-saṃhitā (i.e., Śāṃkarī Saṃhitā)[180] of the Skanda-p., the Skanda consisted of six Saṃhitās, viz., Sanatkumāra-saṃhitā, Sūta-saṃhitā, Śāṃkarī Saṃhitā, Vaiṣṇavī Saṃhitā, Brāhmī Saṃhitā and Saura-saṃhitā, and of fifty Khaṇḍas[181]. The Saṃbhava-kāṇḍa, which is one of the seven Kāṇḍas constituting the Śivarahasya-kh. of the Śaṃkara-saṃhitā of the Skanda-p., similarly divides the Skanda but transposes the Brāhmī and the Śāṃkarī Saṃhitā. It further gives the lengths of the Saṃhitās as follows.

(1) Sanatkumāra-saṃhitā consisting of 55,000 Ślokas or Granthas, (2) Sūta-saṃhitā, of 6,000 Ślokas, (3) Brāhmī Saṃhitā, of 3,000 Ślokas, (4) Vaiṣṇavī Saṃhitā, of 5,000 Ślokas, (5) Śāṃkarī Saṃhitā, of 30,000 Ślokas, and (6) Saurī Saṃhitā, of 1,000 Ślokas[182].

In some Mss the Revā-kh. claims to be a section of the Uttara-kh. of the Vāyu-p. (see, Eggeling, *op. cit.*, Part VI, pp. 1302 ff.). This claim seems to be supported by the Revā-kh. as found in the printed Skanda-p. Cf. Sk V, iii, 5, 16 and 229, 1.

[179] Nār I, 104.

Though the contents of the different Khaṇḍas, as given by the Nāradīya, agree generally with those of the respective Khaṇḍas of the Veṅk. ed. of the Skanda, the Mathurā-māhātmya and the Māgha-māhātmya, which, according to the Nāradīya, formed parts of the Viṣṇu-kh., are not found in the printed Viṣṇu-kh.

According to Saura-p. (AnSS ed.) 9, 10, the Skanda was a very voluminous work consisting of eight Khaṇḍas.

According to the Prabhāsa-kh. (i, 2, 102-106) the Skanda-p. consisted of seven parts (bhāga); viz., (i) the first, called Māheśvara, on Skanda-māhātmya, (ii) the second, called Vaiṣṇava, (iii) the third on the Māhātmya of Brahmā, (iv) the fourth on Kāśī-māhātmya, (v) the fifth on the Māhātmyas of Revā and Ujjayinī, (vi) the sixth, called Nāgara, on Tīrtha-māhātmya, and (vii) the seventh, called Prābhāsika, on Prabhāsakṣetra-māhātmya, Tīrtha-māhātmya and the Māhātmyas of Śaṃkara and other gods.

Sk V, iii, 1, 40 also speaks of the seven parts (khaṇḍa) of the Skanda-p.

The above division of the Skanda into seven Khaṇḍas seems to be late; but it is certainly not later than 1600 A.D., because Mitra Miśra quotes the above mentioned verses of the Prabhāsa-kh. in his Vīramitrodaya (Paribhāṣā-prakāśa, p. 13) by expressly naming the Khaṇḍa as the source.

[180] According to the Hālāsya-māhātmya, the Agastya-saṃhitā, to which this Māhātmya belongs, is the same as the Śāṃkarī Saṃhitā of the Skanda-p. See, Eggeling, *op. cit.*, Part VI. pp. 1320 ff.

An 'Agastya-saṃhitā' is drawn upon in the Caturvarga-cintāmaṇi (Vol. II, Part i, pp. 941-946).

[181] Eggeling, *op. cit.*, Part VI, pp. 1320-21. [182] Ibid., pp. 1363-4.

In its Śiva-māhātmya-khaṇḍa the Sūta-saṃhitā, which is furnished with Mādhavācārya's commentary entitled Sūta-saṃhitā-tātparya-dīpikā, divides and subdivides the Skanda-p. in the same way as the Hālāsya-māhātmya but differs from the Saṃbhava-kāṇḍa as regards the lengths of the six Saṃhitās which are as follows :

> (1) Sanatkumāra-saṃhitā, of 36,000 Granthas, (2) Sūta-saṃhitā, of 6,000 Granthas, (3) Śāṃkarī Saṃhitā, of 30,000 Granthas, (4) Vaiṣṇavī Saṃhitā, of 5,000 Granthas, (5) Brāhmī Saṃhitā, of 3,000 Granthas, and (6) Saura-saṃhitā, of 6,000 Granthas.

Thus the total number of Granthas is 86,000, though it is expressly said that the Skanda-p. consists of one lac of Granthas[183]. The Saura-saṃhitā also says that the Skanda-p. consisted of six Saṃhitās and fifty Khaṇḍas, and that the Saura-saṃhitā, which was the last, contained 1,000 Granthas[184].

More detailed, though slightly different, information about the divisions and subdivisions of the Skanda-p. is supplied by the Kālikā-kh. belonging to the Sanatkumāra-saṃhitā[185]. According to this Khaṇḍa, the Skanda was divided into six Saṃhitās and fifty Khaṇḍas. Of these six Saṃhitās, the first, called Sanatkumāra-saṃhitā, consisted of 25 Khaṇḍas[186], 10,000 chapters and 50,000

[183] Ibid., p. 1378. [184] Ibid., p. 1382.

[185] Shastri and Gui, Cat. of Sans. Mss, Cal. Sans. Coll., Vol. IV, No. 285.

The Kālikā-kh. contains many legends about Śiva and prayers addressed to that god, describes the origin of 500 rivers, and gives an account of the different castes and orders and their duties. It describes also the manners and customs of different parts of India. A geographical account of the world is also attempted.

This Kālikā-kh. consists of 100 chapters, and the date of the Ms is Śaka 1718. (A 'Kālikā-kh.' is drawn upon in Caturvarga-cintāmaṇi, Vol. III, Part i, p. 1206).

[186] The names of these Khaṇḍas, as given in the Kālikā-kh., are as follows;

(1) Kṣetra-kh., dealing elaborately with different places holy to Śiva, Viṣṇu and other gods;
(2) Tīrtha-kh., dealing with various holy places, the pious acts to be done there, the stories of the origin of these places, and so forth;
(3) Kāśī-kh., on the glories of Benares;
(4) Sahyādri-kh., containing the glories of Sahyādri and Setubhūpāla (?), and the account of Candanāpīṭha; (see also footnote 198 below);
(5) Himācala-kh., on the glories of the lord of the world (viśveśa);
(6) Malayācala-kh., describing the worship of Śiva (śiva-pūjopavarṇana);
(7) Vindhyādri-kh., on Viśveśa-mahimā;
(8) Mokṣa-kh., on Mokṣa-dharma;
(9) Prabhāsa-kh., on Dharma and the glories of Prabhāsa;
(10) Puṣkara-kh.;
(11) Nāgara-kh.;
(12) Narmadā-kh., on the stories of the Narmadā;
(13) Śrīśaila-kh., on the glories of Śrīśaila;

Ślokas; the second, called Sūta-saṃhitā, consisted of four parts[187] and 76 chapters; the third, called Śaṃkara-saṃhitā, was divided into 21 parts[188] and 2,000 chapters; the fourth, called Vaiṣṇavī Saṃhitā, contained 300 chapters; the fifth, called Brāhmī Saṃhitā, consisted of 3,000 Ślokas; and the sixth, called Saura-saṃhitā, contained 60,000 Ślokas.

That the above division of the Skanda-p. into Saṃhitās is not fictitious, is proved by the fact that some of the Saṃhitās still exist, partly or wholly, in Mss. For example, the Sanatkumāra-saṃhitā[189], the Śāṃkarī Saṃhitā[190], the Sūta-saṃhitā[191] and the

(14) Avanti-kh., on Avanti-mahimā;
(15) Gaurī-kh., on Gaurī's attainment of the fruit of her penance, and the method of Gaurī-vrata; (a Gaurī-kāṇḍa is drawn upon in the Prāyaścitta-khaṇḍa claiming to be a part of the Caturvarga-cintāmaṇi of Hemādri);
(16) Kurukṣetra-kh., on the glories of Kurukṣetra, and the gifts to be made there on the occasion of the solar eclipse;
(17) Kedāra-kh., on the birth of Śiva;
(18) Haridvāra-kh., on Haridvāra-praśaṃsā;
(19) Setumāhātmya-kh., on Setutīrtha-praśaṃsā;
(20) Kālikā- or Kālī-kh., on the praise of and legends about Śiva, and prayers to the god;
(21) Vratopākhyāna-kh., on vows and stories relating to Śiva;
(22) Nadī-kh., on the origin of 500 rivers;
(23) Dharma-kh., on the duties of the castes and orders;
(24) Deśa-kh., on Deśadharmānukathana and Deśavidhikrama;
and (25) Varṣa-kh., on the division of the earth into Dvīpas and Varṣas.

Shastri and Gui, Cat. of Sans. Mss, Cal. Sans. Coll., Vol. IV, No. 285. Unfortunately for us, the verses containing the names and extents of the divisions and subdivisions of the remaining five Saṃhitās are not given in the Catalogue. A very short account of these Saṃhitās is, however, given in the description of the Ms. See footnote 185 above.

[187] Eggeling, in his Ind. Off. Cat., Part VI, pp. 1377 ff., describes a complete Sūta-saṃhitā furnished with Mādhavācārya's commentary named Sūta-saṃhitā-tātparya-dīpikā and consisting of four Khaṇḍas, viz., Śivamāhātmya-kh., Jñāna-yoga-kh., Mukti-kh. and Yajñavaibhava-kh. The last of these Khaṇḍas is subdivided into two sections called Adhobhāga and Uparibhāga, the latter being further subdivided into Brahma-gītā and Sūta-gītā. See also, Shastri, Cat. of Sans. Mss, ASB, V, Nos. 3848-60; Shastri and Gui, Cat. of Sans. Mss, Cal. Sans. Coll., IV, Nos. 229 and 242.

[188] According to the Sambhava-kāṇḍa, the Śāṃkarī Saṃhitā consisted of 12 Khaṇḍas. See, Eggeling, Ind. Off. Cat., Part VI, p. 1364.

[189] Eggeling, Ind. Off. Cat., Part VI, pp. 1365 ff. On pp. 1409-10 of the Catalogue, Eggeling describes a fragment of a Sanatkumāra-saṃhitā which, on account of the treatment of the worship of Rādhā, seems to be of very late origin.

[190] Eggeling, Ind. Off. Cat., Part VI, pp. 1320 ff. and 1362 ff.; Shastri, Cat. of Sans. Mss, ASB, V, Nos. 3864A-65; Shastri and Gui, *op. cit.*, IV, No. 241 (Sambhava-kāṇḍa).

[191] Eggeling, *op. cit.*, VI, pp. 1370 ff. and 1377 ff. The Sūta-saṃhitā, with Mādhavācārya's com., has been published by the Ānandāśrama Press, Poona.

Saura-saṃhitā[192] may be named. Mādhavācārya's commentary on the Sūta-saṃhitā proves that the above division of the Skanda into six Saṃhitās must have been made much earlier than 1300 A.D.

Besides the different Khaṇḍas mentioned above, there were many others which claimed to be parts of the Skanda-p. Some of these Khaṇḍas are available in Mss partly or wholly, viz., Ambikā-kh.[193], Tāpī-kh.[194], Kanakādri-kh.[195], Bhīma-kh.[196], Śiva-rahasya-kh.[197], Sahyādri-kh.[198], Bṛhadbrahmottara-kh.[199], Parvata-kh.[200], Ayodhyā-kh.[201], Mathurā-kh.[202], Pātāla-kh.[203], Nirvāṇa-kh.[204], Umā-kh.[205], Paraśurāma-kh.[206], Bhū-kh.[207], Himavat-kh.[208], and so on. There is also mention of a Pauṇḍra-kh. in the Dānasāgara (fol. 3b), of a Mahākāla-khaṇḍa in the Caturvarga-cintāmaṇi (Vol. II, Part ii, p. 151 and Vol. III, Part i, p. 1098), and of a Camatkāra-kh. in the Caturvarga-cintāmaṇi (Vol. III, Part i,

192 Eggeling, *op. cit.*, VI, pp. 1382-83.

193 Ibid., pp. 1321 ff. Shastri, Cat. of Sans. Mss, ASB, V, Nos. 3921-22.

194 Shastri and Gui, *op. cit.*, IV, No. 294.

195 Is it the same as the Sahyādri-kh.? See, Eggeling, *op. cit.*, VI, p. 1329. Shastri and Gui, *op. cit.*, IV, No. 244.

196 Eggeling, *op. cit.*, VI, pp. 1357-58.

197 This Khaṇḍa belongs to the Śaṃkara-saṃhitā and consists of 7 Kāṇḍas, viz., Saṃbhava, Āsura, Vīra-māhendra, Yuddha, Deva, Dakṣa and Upadeśa. See, Eggeling, Ind. Off. Cat., VI, pp. 1362-65; Shastri, Cat. of Sans. Mss, ASB, V, Nos. 3864A-65. Also Shastri and Gui, *op. cit.*, IV, Nos. 281, 282, 288 and 291-3 for separate Mss of the Kāṇḍas.

198 It belongs to the Sanatkumāra-saṃhitā. Eggeling, *op. cit.*, VI, pp. 1369 ff.; Shastri, *op. cit.*, V, Nos. 3930-32; Shastri and Gui, *op. cit.*, IV, No. 249. See also footnote 186 above. A 'Sahya- (v.l. Satya-) khaṇḍa' is drawn upon in Kālanirṇaya, p. 290; and a 'Sahyādri-khaṇḍa' is drawn upon in Caturvarga-cintāmaṇi, Vol. III (Pariśeṣa-kh.), Part i, p. 718 and Part ii, pp. 305 and 306.

199 It begins with the same verses as the Brahmottara-kh. of the printed Skanda and seems to have the same contents. See, Aufrecht, Bod. Cat., No. 126.

200 Eggeling, *op. cit.*, VI, p. 1353.

201 Shastri, *op. cit.*, V, No. 3925. This Khaṇḍa is different from the Ayodhyā-māhātmya of the printed Viṣṇu-kh.

202 Shastri, *op. cit.*, V, No. 3926.

203 Shastri and Gui, *op. cit.*, IV, Nos. 228-9.

204 Shastri, *op. cit.*, V, No. 3927; Shastri and Gui, *op. cit.*, IV, No. 290.

205 Shastri and Gui, *op. cit.*, IV, No. 284.

206 Shastri, *op. cit.*, V, Nos. 3928-29.

207 Shastri, *op. cit.*, V, No. 3933 (Śambhalagrāma-māhātmya); Shastri and Gui, *op. cit.*, IV, No. 231 (on the shrines in and about Sambhalpur); Eggeling, *op. cit.*, VI, p. 1358 (No. 3667). Is it the same as the Mahī-kh. named and drawn upon in the Haribhaktivilāsa, p. 897?

208 Shastri and Gui, *op. cit.*, IV, No. 253. Is it the same as the Himācala-kh. which is one of the 25 Khaṇḍas constituting the Sanatkumāra-saṃhitā?

pp. 357, 360, 650, 676, 698, 706-7 and so on), Madana-pārijāta (p. 310) and Mādhavācārya's commentary on the Parāśara-smṛti (II, ii, pp. 220-221). Though no Ms of the Pauṇḍra-kh. has yet come to light, Mss have been found of a Karatoyā-māhātmya[209] which consists of two parts—Pauṇḍrakṣetra-māhātmya (verses 1-60) and Karatoyā-māhātmya (verses 61-85), and is said in the colophons to have formed part of the last (or latter) part of the Pauṇḍra-kh. (uttara-pauṇḍra-khaṇḍa). Besides the colophons, the Māhātmya itself contains indications which show that it was not an isolated booklet deriving authority from the Pauṇḍra-kh. but formed a chapter of a bigger work dealing, among other things, with topics on the Pauṇḍra-kṣetra as well as with the results of bathing in the river Karatoyā[210].

The Camatkāra-kh. seems to have been preserved partially, with changes and modifications, in the Nāgara-kh. which contains a number of chapters on a king named Camatkāra and a town named after him. Two of the lines quoted by Hemādri from a 'Camatkāra-kh.' are found in chap. 20 of the Nāgara-kh.

From the above accounts of the divisions and subdivisions of the Skanda it is evident that the Purāṇa grew up into a huge bulk

209 Ms No. 1434, D. U. Mss Lib. It is a complete Ms consisting of 4 folios and dated Śaka 1784. The Māhātmya was published in 1298 B.S. (= 1891 A.D.) with a Bengali translation by Pandit Rāja Candra Nyāyapañcānana. It has also been printed in Prabhas Chandra Sen's Mahāsthāna and its Environments (pub. by the Varendra Research Society, Rajshahi, 1929), pp. 25-8.

From the use of the words *'etat'*, *'atra'* etc. to mean the Pauṇḍra-kṣetra and from the way in which the Karatoyā and the Karatoyā-tīrtha have been respected and glorified over all other rivers and holy places, it seems that it was composed by one living at or near about Mahāsthāna in Pauṇḍra-vardhana. There is also a linguistic peculiarity in the word *'taddhāre'* (meaning 'to her') in verse 74 showing the Bengali origin of the Māhātmya.

The metres used in this Māhātmya are the Vasantatilakā, Mandākrāntā, Śārdūla-vikrīḍita, Upajāti, and Śloka (in the majority of the verses).

210 For instance, at the very beginning of the Māhātmya Pārvatī asks Śiva saying:

"*aparaṃ kathyatāṃ deva nadīnāṃ ca viśeṣataḥ|*
pauṇḍra-kṣetrasya māhātmyaṃ na śrutaṃ vistarāt prabho||
. . . ."

To this Śiva answers:

". . . . .
puraiva kathitaṃ sarvaṃ pauṇḍrasya ca sureśvari|
tatraiva kathitaṃ tubhyaṃ karatoyā-phalaṃ yathā||"

and then goes on narrating the Māhātmyas as declared by Bhārgava.

Note the abrupt beginning and the words *'aparaṃ'*, *'puraiva'* and *'tatraiva'* used in the above verses. Note also the nonmention of the occasion on which the interlocution between Śiva and Pārvatī took place.

with the addition of parts which could never come from the same hand[211] or belong to the same age, and that the Khaṇḍas, which now constitute the printed Skanda, belonged originally to one or other of the Saṃhitās[212].

Though the Khaṇḍas of the printed Skanda are thus derived from the Saṃhitās and the names of some of them are mentioned in the comparatively early Nibandhas[213], they can seldom claim to have come in their *entirety* from a very early date. A careful examination of their contents and the frequent Tantric traces found in them seem to show that they were subjected to revisions and emendations at times. During these revisions, some of the older portions were rejected and some were retained with modifications, while many new chapters and verses were added. It is most probably for this reason that of about 750 lines quoted by Vijñāneśvara, Jīmūtavāhana (in his Kālaviveka), Aparārka, Ballālasena (in his Dānasāgara and Adbhutasāgara), Devaṇabhaṭṭa, Mādhavācārya (in his Kālanirṇaya and com. on the Parāśara-smṛti), Madanapāla and Śūlapāṇi (in his Vratakāla-viveka, Rāsayātrā-viveka, Dīpa-kalikā and Dolayātrā-viveka) from a 'Skanda-p.' or 'Skānda' without any special mention of the names of the Khaṇḍas from which these lines were drawn, only about 137 are found in the Viṣṇu-kh., Kāśī-kh., Nāgara-kh. and Prabhāsa-kh. of the printed Skanda[214]. Hemādri also quotes hundreds of verses

[211] While speaking of the spurious Purāṇas in his Dānasāgara, Ballālasena remarks that due to its wide circulation the Skanda-p. existed in more parts than one, and that three of its parts dealt with the accounts of Pauṇḍra, Revā and Avanti, thus seeming to include these three parts among the spurious Purāṇas. Cf. Dānasāgara, fol. 3b—*pracarad-rūpataḥ skanda-purāṇaikāṃśato 'dhikam| yat-khaṇḍa-tritayaṃ pauṇḍra-revāvanti-kathāśrayam||*

[212] For instance, the Kāśī-kh., Avanti-kh., Nāgara-kh., Prabhāsa-kh., Revā-kh. (forming part of the printed Āvantya-kh.), Kedāra-kh. (forming part of the printed Māheśvara-kh.) and Setumāhātmya-kh. (forming part of the printed Brahma-kh.) really belonged to the Sanatkumāra-saṃhitā. See footnote 186 above.

[213] The Nāgara-kh. is mentioned in the Smṛti-candrikā, Caturvarga-cintāmaṇi, Mādhavācārya's com. on the Parāśara-smṛti, Kālanirṇaya (of Mādhavācārya), Vratakāla-viveka (of Śūlapāṇi), etc.; the Revā-kh. is mentioned in the Caturvarga-cintāmaṇi, Mādhavācārya's com. on the Parāśara-smṛti, Dānasāgara, etc.; the Avanti-kh. is mentioned in the Dānasāgara; the Prabhāsa-kh. is mentioned in the Caturvarga-cintāmaṇi, Mādhavācārya's com. on the Parāśara-smṛti, Kālanirṇaya, etc.; and so on. (See App.).

[214] Of these numerous quoted lines, the Mitākṣarā has 1 which is not found in the present Skanda; the Kālaviveka has 28, of which only 4 are found in Prabhāsa-kh. i, 208; Aparārka's com. has 40, of which only 2 are found in

from this Purāṇa in his Caturvarga-cintāmaṇi, and a good number of these quoted verses is found in the extant Skanda. (See App. for the traced lines).

Besides the quoted lines mentioned above, there are also others which have been quoted by the Smṛti-writers with the special mention of the names of the Khaṇḍas or Māhātmyas from which these lines were drawn. For instance, from a 'Kāśī-kh.', the Vidhāna-pārijāta (Vol. I) has 132 lines, almost all of which are found in chap. 37 of Kāśī-kh. i; Raghunandana's Smṛti-tattva has 22 lines, of which 18 are found in chaps. 4 and 35 of Kāśī-kh. i; Govindānanda's Śrāddhakriyā-kaumudī, Śuddhikriyā-kaumudī and Varṣakriyā-kaumudī have 59 lines, of which 48 are found in chaps. 4, 27, 35, 38 and 40 of Kāśī-kh. i; Vācaspatimiśra's Tīrtha-cintāmaṇi has 56 lines, of which 51 are found in chap. 59 of Kāśī-kh. ii; and Hemādri's Caturvarga-cintāmaṇi has 42 lines, none of which is found in the printed Kāśī-kh. From an 'Avanti-kh.', Mādhavācārya's Kālanirṇaya has 2 lines, none of which is found in the printed Āvantya-kh. From a 'Revā-kh.', Mādhavācārya's commentary on the Parāśara-smṛti has 27 lines, of which 9 are found in chap. 159 of Sk V, iii (Revā-kh.); and Hemādri's Caturvarga-cintāmaṇi has 81 lines, none of which is found in the printed Revā-kh. From a 'Nāgara-kh.', Raghunandana's Smṛti-tattva has 10 lines (except the repeated ones), of which 5 are found in chaps. 216 and 266 of the present Nāgara-kh.; Śūlapāṇi's Vratakāla-viveka has 2 lines, which are not found in our printed Nāgara; Mādhavācārya's Kālanirṇaya and his commentary on the Parāśara-smṛti have 32 lines, of which 15 are found in chaps. 216, 217 and 266 of the Nāgara-kh.; Hemādri's Caturvarga-cintāmaṇi has a few hundreds of lines, the majority of which is found in Nāgara-kh., chaps. 162, 177, 178, 215-222, 266 etc.; and Devaṇabhaṭṭa's Smṛti-candrikā has 8 lines, one of which is found in our

Prabhāsa-kh. i, 208; the Dānasāgara has 136 and the Adbhs. has 29, none of these lines being found in the present Skanda; the Smṛti-candrikā has 54, none of which is found in the present Skanda; the Kālanirṇaya has 203, of which 6 are found in Nāgara-kh., chap. 266, and 4 in Prabhāsa-kh. i, 19; Mādhavācārya's com. on the Parāśara-smṛti has 72, of which only 7 are found in Prabhāsa-kh. i, 207; the Madana-pārijāta has 47, of which 25 are found in Kāśī-kh. i. 4; the Vratakāla-viveka has 6, of which 2 occur in Kāśī-kh. ii, 84; the Rāsayātrā-viveka has 37, none of which is found in our present Skanda; the Dīpa-kalikā has 8, of which 2 occur in Sk V, iii, 209, VI, 21, VI, 37, etc.; and the Dolayātrā-viveka has 85, all of which occur in Viṣṇu-kh. ii (Puruṣottamakṣetra-māhātmya), 42. The Smṛti-tattva also quotes, from a 'Skanda-p.' or 'Skānda,' verses which are sometimes found in the Puruṣottamakṣetra-māhātmya and other parts of the present Skanda. (See App.)

printed Nāgara. From a 'Prabhāsa-kh.', Raghunandana's Smṛti-tattva has 6 lines (except the repeated ones), all of which are found in chaps. 19 and 205 of Sk VII (Prabhāsa-kh.), i; Hemādri's Caturvarga-cintāmaṇi has a few hundreds of lines, the majority of which is found in Prabhāsa-kh. i, chaps. 19, 205-208 and 336; and Mādhavācārya's Kālanirṇaya and his commentary on the Parāśara-smṛti have 11 lines, of which 3 are found in chap. 205 of Sk VII, i. From 'chap. 29 of the Puruṣottama-māhātmya' Śūlapāṇi's Dolayātrā-viveka (fol. 3b) has a few lines, one of which is found in chap. 29 of the present Puruṣottamakṣetra-māhātmya. From a 'Camatkāra-kh.', Mādhavācārya quotes 22 lines in his commentary on the Parāśara-smṛti and Madanapāla has 2 lines in his Madana-pārijāta, but none of these lines is found in those chapters of the Nāgara-kh. which contain stories of a king named Camatkāra and of a town named after him. Of the 143 lines quoted by Hemādri from the 'Camatkāra-kh.', only two are found in the Nāgara-kh. (chap. 20).

The above informations regarding the different Khaṇḍas of the present Skanda show that at least some of these Khaṇḍas contain Smṛti-chapters which are fairly old. For instance, the Puruṣottama-kṣetra-māhātmya contains chapters which must be dated earlier than 1300 A.D.; the Kāśī-kh. has chapters (especially i, 4, 35 and 38) which are older than 1300 A.D.[215]; the Revā-kh. contains chapters (especially chap. 159) which are earlier than 1300 A.D.; the Nāgara-kh. contains chapters (especially chaps. 177, 178, 215-222 and 266) which are earlier than 1200 A.D.; and the Prabhāsa-kh. has chapters, of which some (especially chaps. 19, 205-207 and 336 of Prabhāsa-kh. i) are earlier than 1200 A.D. and some (especially chap. 208 of Prabhāsa-kh. i) are earlier than 1050 A.D. (See App.).

As to the upper limit of the date of the present Skanda, it can be said that *there seems to be little in it which can be dated earlier than 700 A.D.* At least, the frequent Tantric traces tend to create such an impression[216].

[215] The Bengali encyclopædia Viśvakoṣa (Vol. XI, p. 565) informs us that in the Viśvakoṣa Office there is a Ms of the Kāśī-kh. which is dated 933 Śaka. As it has not been possible for us to compare the contents of this Ms with those of the printed Kāśī-kh., we cannot say definitely how far the latter contains older materials.

[216] Tantric elements began to be absorbed by the Skanda-p. even earlier than 1100 A.D. Cf. the verses quoted from the 'Skanda-p.' in Aparārka's com., p. 295 (*oṃ hrīṃ namo bhagavati . . . . huṃ kuru huṃ kuru . . . . svāhā| iti dhenu-karṇa-japaḥ*) and Kālanirṇaya, p. 289 (*āgamokta-vidhiṃ kṛtvā* etc.).

Though the present Skanda is merely a part of the bigger one, it is by no means a small work. So, for want of sufficient space, a detailed analysis of its contents has not been attempted here.

10. THE BRAHMAVAIVARTA-PURĀṆA

This voluminous work, which consists of four parts, viz., (I) Brahma-kh., (II) Prakṛti-kh., (III) Gaṇapati-kh., and (IV) Kṛṣṇa-janma-kh., glorifies Kṛṣṇa and identifies him with the supreme Brahma. It seems to have been meant for preaching the worship of Kṛṣṇa and Rādhā. It contains, besides numerous legends and glorifications, a good number of chapters on Smṛti-matter; viz., Bv I, 10 on the mixed castes; II, 9 on gifts; II, 10, 22-23, 39, 43-46, 55 and 65 and III, 13, 19 and 32 on worship; II, 24-27, 29-33 and 52 on hells and the results of actions done; II, 54 and IV, 21 on the worship and glorification of the Brāhmans; III, 3-4 and IV, 8, 16, 26 and 27 on Vratas; and IV, 83-84 on Varṇāśramadharma and the duties of women.

A perusal of the Brahmavaivarta-p. shows that it is one of the latest of the extant Purāṇic works. Jogesh Chandra Roy has carefully examined this Purāṇa and come to the conclusion that *it was first composed most probably in the 8th century A.D. From about the 10th century it began to be changed by the interfering hands of the Bengal authors who recast it to its present form and contents in the sixteenth century.* Inspite of this late recast, there are portions which have been retained from an earlier form of the Purāṇa[217].

The above view of J. C. Roy is supported by the quotations made by the Nibandha-writers from a 'Brahmavaivarta-p.' Of about 1500 lines quoted from this Purāṇa in the Smṛti-candrikā[218], Caturvarga-cintāmaṇi (including the Prāyaścitta-khaṇḍa ascribed to Hemādri), Kālanirṇaya (of Mādhavācārya), Vratakāla-viveka, Rāsayātrā-viveka, Smṛti-tattva, Kālasāra, Varṣakriyā-kaumudī and Haribhaktivilāsa, only about 30 (except the repeated ones) are found in Bv IV, 8 and 26 dealing with the Janmāṣṭamī-vrata and the Ekādaśī-vrata respectively (see App.). The absence of the remaining verses from the present Brahmavaivarta shows that the Purāṇa with its present contents was not known to the writers of even the sixteenth century A.D., and that all the Smṛti-chapters, except IV, 8 and 26, are very late additions.

[217] Bhāratavarṣa (a Bengali Journal), 1337 B. S., Āṣāḍha, pp. 94-104. Wilson holds that the Purāṇa 'was compiled subsequent to the Muhammadan invasion'. See, Wilson, Essays, Vol. I, p. 120.

[218] In this work the Purāṇa is named Brahmakaivarta. This Purāṇa seems to be different from the Brahmakaivarta-p. current in Southern India.

The fact that none of the early Nibandha-writers, except Devaṇabhaṭṭa, is found to draw upon the 'Brahmavaivarta-p.', which, as the quotations made by the comparatively late Nibandha-writers show, was a rich store of Smṛti materials mainly religious, proves the comparative unpopularity of the Purāṇa with these early authors.

The statement that the present Brahmavaivarta was first composed most probably in the 8th century A.D., should not be taken to mean that there was no Purāṇa named Brahmavaivarta before that century. From the consideration of the oldness of the dictum that there were eighteen Mahāpurāṇas, it seems highly probable that before 700 A.D. there existed a Brahmavaivarta which is now lost.

11. THE BHAVIṢYA-PURĀṆA

Regarding the contents of the Bhaviṣya-p. the Matsya informs us that, in relation to the Aghora-kalpa, Brahmā spoke out to Manu the Purāṇa which dealt with the glories of the Sun, and that it contained 14,500 verses[219]. The information supplied by the Agni-p. differs slightly from that of the Matsya. According to this Purāṇa the Bhaviṣya, which originated from the Sun (sūrya-saṃbhava), was declared by Bhava to Manu, and its extent was 14,000 Ślokas[220]. More detailed information, though of considerably late date, in the same direction is contained in Nāradīya-p. I, 100, wherein it is said that once Manu enquired of Brahmā about Dharma. Accordingly, the latter spoke out the Bhaviṣya-p. in relation to the Aghora-kalpa. This Purāṇa was then divided by Vyāsa into five Parvans, viz., Brāhma, Vaiṣṇava, Śaiva, Saura and Pratisarga. The contents of all these Parvans are also given. About the Brāhma Parvan it is said that it began as an interlocution between Sūta and Śaunaka, and that it was mainly a book on the Sun (āditya-carita-prāya).[221]

219 *yatrādhikṛtya māhātmyam ādityasya caturmukhaḥ|*
aghora-kalpa-vṛttānta-prasaṅgena jagat-sthitim|
manave kathayāmāsa bhūta-grāmasya lakṣaṇam||
caturdaśa sahasrāṇi tathā pañca śatāni ca|
bhaviṣya-carita-prāyaṃ bhaviṣyaṃ tad ihocyate|| Mat 53, 30-31.
These verses are the same as Sk VII, i, 2, 49-50, the difference being that the Skanda reads *'jagat-patiḥ'* for *'jagat-sthitim'*.

220 Ag 272, 12.

221 Nār I, 100.
The contents of the 'Brāhma Parvan', as described by the Nāradīya, agree much with those of our present Brāhma which also is 'āditya-carita-prāya', contains various stories about the Sun, deals with creation etc.

From these informations we learn that the Bhaviṣya was narrated in relation to the Aghora-kalpa mainly as an interlocution between Brahmā and Manu, that it consisted of five Parvans, and that the Brāhma Parvan, which dealt primarily with the Sun, began as an interlocution between Sūta and Śaunaka. The printed Bhaviṣya, on the other hand, does not contain any interlocution between Brahmā and Manu; it is divided into four Parvans, viz., Brāhma, Madhyama, Pratisarga and Uttara[222]; there is no mention of the Aghora-kalpa; and though the Brāhma Parvan contains a good number of chapters on the Sun and his worship, it does not begin with the conversation between Sūta and Śaunaka. These

in chap. 2, is the essence of the Śāstras (cf. chap. 2, verses 5 ff.), treats of the sacraments in chaps. 3 ff. and of the Tithi-kalpas (i.e., rites and duties due on different lunar days) up to the Saptamī-kalpa in chaps. 17 ff., and so on.

222 According to Saura-p. (AnSS ed.) 9,8 and Sk V, iii (Revā-kh.), 1, 34b-35a also, the Bhaviṣya consists of four Parvans.

Just as in the case of the numbers of Parvans, there are remarkable differences in their lengths also. Haraprasad Shastri describes a Ms of a 'Bhaviṣya-p.' consisting of five Parvans—Brāhma, Vaiṣṇava, Śaiva, Tvāṣṭra (i.e., Saura) and Pratisarga and dealing with the Kalpas (rites and ceremonies) due on different Tithis (lunar days), with the stories of Rudra and the Sun, and so forth (see, Shāstri, Cat. of Sans. Mss, ASB, Vol. V, No. 3738). The description shows that (1) the Brāhma Parvan ends with the Pratipat-kalpa, the interlocutors being Śatānīka and Sumantu; (2) the Viṣṇu-parvan deals with all the remaining Tithi-kalpas, has the same principal interlocutors as in the Brāhma Parvan, and consists of 31 chapters; (3) the Rudra-parvan has the same interlocutors, deals with the origin of Rudra, Datta and others, and consists of 3 chapters; (4) the Tvaṣṭṛ-parvan has Śatānīka as one of the interlocutors, contains a Sūrya-śuka-saṃvāda, and deals with the story of the marriage of the Sun with Saṃjñā, Śuka's going to the solar region (sūrya-maṇḍala), and so on; and (5) the Pratisarga-parvan begins with the Sun as an interlocutor, contains a Sūrya-śuka-saṃvāda, and ends with the return of Śuka from the solar region.

Mss of the Bhaviṣya-p. described by Eggeling (Ind. Off. Cat., Part VI, No. 3447) and Aufrecht (Bodleian Catalogue, No. 75) extend upto the Saptamī-kalpa, and almost all their contents occur in the Brāhma Parvan of our printed Bhaviṣya (see Bhav I, 2 ff.). These Mss deal, among other things, with the stories of the Bhojakas and their origin from the Magas of the Śāka-dvīpa and are 'āditya-carita-prāya'. So they seem to have much in common with the Brāhma Parvan of the Bhaviṣya described in the Nāradīya-p., according to which this Parvan also extended up to the Saptamī-kalpa and was 'āditya-carita-prāya'.

Another Ms. of the Bhaviṣya divides the Purāṇa into two Bhāgas—Pūrva and Upari, the former consisting of the Brāhma and Vaiṣṇava Parvans and extending up to the Navamī-kalpa, and the latter containing the Madhyama-tantra composed of four parts (bhāga). This Madhyama-tantra has many chapters and verses in common with the Madhyama

disagreements show that at least the major portion of the present Bhaviṣya does not represent the earlier one known to and noticed by the Matsya, Agni and Nāradīya-p.[223] As a matter of fact, the three Parvans—Madhyama, Pratisarga and Uttara—are comparatively late appendages. Of these three, the Madhyama Parvan, which is not mentioned in Bhav I, 2, 2-3 speaking of five Parvans, viz., Brāhma, Vaiṣṇava, Śaiva, Tvāṣṭra and Pratisarga, is full of Tantric elements, recognises the authority of the Tantras, and mentions the Yāmalas, Ḍāmaras etc. Moreover, none of the numerous verses quoted from the 'Bhaviṣya-p.' or 'Bhaviṣya' by the comparatively early commentators and Nibandha-writers like Bhavadeva, Jīmūtavāhana, Vijñāneśvara, Aparārka, Devaṇabhaṭṭa, Ballālasena, Aniruddhabhaṭṭa, Hemādri, Madanapāla, Mādhavācārya and Śūlapāṇi is found to occur in this Parvan though it is full of Smṛti materials. So, it can hardly claim to have come from an early date[224]. The Pratisarga-parvan, though nominally mentioned in Bhav I, 2, 2-3, is practically a new work. It narrates stories about Adam, Noah, Yākuta and others, and speaks of Taimurlong, Nadir Shah and Akbar with their descendants. It gives the story of Jayacandra and Pṛthvīrāja, preaches the glories of the worship of Satya-nārāyaṇa, and fabricates myths about the births of Varāhamihira, Śaṃkarācārya, Rāmānuja, Nimbārka, Madhva, Jayadeva, Viṣṇusvāmin, Bhaṭṭojidīkṣita, Ānandagiri, Kṛṣṇa-caitanya, Nityānanda, Kabīra, Nānaka, Ruidāsa, and others. It even knows the British rule in India and names Calcutta and the Parliament (aṣṭa-kauśalya). Thus its contents betray its late date[225]. The

Parvan of our printed Bhaviṣya (see, Shastri, Cat. of Sans. Mss, ASB, Vol. V, No. 3740; and Notices of Sanskrit Mss, Second Series, Vol. II, No. 151).

Yet another Ms of the same Purāṇa speaks of three parts (khaṇḍa)—Vaiṣṇava, Śiva and Śakti, and gives the lives even of Jīva Gosvāmin and other followers of Caitanya. It thus resembles the Pratisarga-parvan of our printed Bhaviṣya (see, Shastri and Gui, *op. cit.*, Vol. IV, No. 176).

223 According to the Nāradīya-p. (I, 100, 13) the Bhaviṣya known to it consisted of 14,000 Ślokas. So, it was a much shorter work than our printed Bhaviṣya.

224 Though the Madhyama Parvan is generally a late work, it contains chapters and verses which must be dated earlier than 1500 A.D.; because, of the verses quoted by Raghunandana in his Smṛti-tattva II, pp. 286-7 from the 'bhaviṣyapurāṇīya-madhyatantra-ṣaṣṭhādhyāya' and on p. 509 from 'the ninth chapter of the third part' of the same Purāṇa (cf. *iti bhaviṣya-purāṇe tṛtīya-bhāge navamo 'dhyāyaḥ*), those on p. 509 are found to tally with Bhav II (Madhyama Parvan), iii (Tṛtīya Bhāga), chap. 18, verses 1 and 4-10 (the lines '*tathā jambu*', '*eteṣāṃ valkala-rasaḥ*' and '*kuśa-valmīka-saṃbhūtaṃ*' being not found).

225 According to the Nāradīya-p. (I, 100, 10) the Pratisarga-parvan known to it contained various legends (*nānākhyāna-samanvitaṃ*). In the printed

Uttara Parvan, which calls itself a distinct 'Purāṇa named Bhaviṣyottara' [226] and is generally the same as the 'Bhaviṣyottara-p.' known to Aparārka, Hemādri, Mādhavācārya and others, contains chapters and verses which must be dated earlier than 1100 A.D. Its distinct character is further established by the fact that none of the verses quoted from the 'Bhaviṣya-p.' or 'Bhaviṣya' by the commentators and Nibandha-writers except Hemādri is found in this Parvan, though it is full of various Smṛti matters[227]. The few cases, in which the verses quoted by Hemādri from the 'Bhaviṣya-p.' are found in the Uttara Parvan, must be due to the confusion between the titles 'Bhaviṣya' and 'Bhaviṣyottara'. (Cf., for instance, Caturvarga-cintāmaṇi, II, i, pp. 604-5, 669-671 and 705-717, and II, ii, 526-7, wherein verses, though really belonging to the 'Bhaviṣya-p.', have been ascribed to the 'Bhaviṣyottara'. See also App.).

Different, however, is the case with the Brāhma Parvan, in which a good number of the quoted verses is traceable. Thus, some of the verses quoted from the 'Bhaviṣya-p.' in the Mitākṣarā (on Yāj.), Kālaviveka, Aparārka's com. on Yāj., Dānasāgara, Smṛticandrikā, Caturvarga-cintāmaṇi, Mādhavācārya's com. on the Parāśara-smṛti, Madana-pārijāta and Kullūkabhaṭṭa's com. on the Manu-smṛti are found in Bhav I, chaps. 2, 3, 4, 18, 19, 21, 22, 31, 32, 36-39, 46, 47, 51, 55-59, 64, 65, 68-70, 81-83, 86, 89, 90, 91 93, 96--101, 103, 104-106, 108-112, 118, 165-170, 172, 181, 183, 184, 186, 197, 208, 209, 212-214 and so forth (see App.). Therefore, it is sure that the major portion of the present Brāhma Parvan can rightly claim an early origin. Now the question is whether this Brāhma Parvan is the same as that of the Bhaviṣya known to the Matsya, Agni and Nāradīya. We have seen from the Matsya and the Nāradīya that the Brāhma Parvan of the earlier Purāṇa began as an interlocution between Sūta and Śaunaka, and that the Purāṇa was first declared by Brahmā to Manu. In the extant Brāhma Parvan, on the other hand, there is mention neither of Sūta and Śaunaka nor of Brahmā and Manu. It begins, unlike the other Parvans, with the story of king Śatānīka, who, being advised by the sages, asks Vyāsa to speak on Dharmaśāstra.

Pratisarga-parvan also we find nothing but a number of mythical stories. But this coincidence must not be taken to assign the present Pratisarga-parvan to an early date, because Nār I, 92-109, which give the contents of the Mahāpurāṇas, are of a considerably late date.

226 Cf. Bhav IV, 207, 10b—*khyātaṃ bhaviṣyottara-nāmadheyaṃ mayā purāṇaṃ tava sauhṛdena.*

227 More detailed information regarding the so-called Uttara Parvan will be given in our 'Studies in the Upapurāṇas'.

Vyāsa refers the king to his pupil Sumantu who is to speak on Dharma matters. Sumantu, therefore, first names the authors of the Dharmaśāstras, viz., Manu, Viṣṇu, Yama, Aṅgiras and fourteen others, and goes on answering the questions put to him by Śatānīka.

The above disagreements show that the extant Brāhma Parvan is the result of a recast to which its prototype was subjected. In this recast the general form of the Parvan was changed and many chapters were discarded[228]. It is most probably for this reason that numerous quoted verses, especially on vows and penances, are not found in the extant Brāhma Parvan.

The Brāhma Parvan calls itself a Dharmaśāstra in which Śrauta and Smārta Dharma has been described[229]. The topics dealt with in it are multifarious. In chaps. 1-46 it treats of the duties of the castes and Āśramas, the sacraments, the duties of women, the good and bad signs of men, women and kings, and the method of worshipping Brahmā, Gaṇeśa, Skanda and the Snakes on different Tithis; and chaps. 47-215 are devoted to the numerous solar vows, the glories of the Sun, and the origin of the Bhojakas from the Magas brought to India by Śāmba from the Śāka-dvīpa and married to the girls of the Bhoja family. This Parvan has taken a few verses from the Bṛhat-saṃhitā of Varāha-mihira without naming the source[230]. It refers frequently to Manu[231] and has numerous verses in common with the Manu-smṛti. Sometimes it expands the ideas contained in the verses of Manu. Aparārka and Kullūkabhaṭṭa are, therefore, justified in saying that

[228] About the Bhaviṣya-p. the Dānasāgara (fol. 3b) says:
saptamyavadhi purāṇaṃ bhaviṣyam api saṃgṛhītam atiyatnāt|
tyaktvāṣṭamī-navamyoḥ (° myau ?) kanyau ((kalau ?) pāṣaṇḍibhir grastau (° ste ?)||

This remark shows that the Bhaviṣya-p. known to Ballālasena dealt, among other topics, with the different Tithi-kalpas up to the Navamī-kalpa. In his Caturvarga-cintāmaṇi Hemādri quotes numerous verses from the 'Bhaviṣya-p.' on the Aṣṭamī-, Navamī- and other Tithi-kalpas. But in our printed Bhaviṣya there is no chapter on the Aṣṭamī- or Navamī-kalpa. According to Nār I, 100, 9 the Tithi-kalpas beginning with the Aṣṭamī-kalpa were dealt with in the Vaiṣṇava Parvan.

The present Brāhma Parvan has not only suffered through losses but has also gained by incorporation. For instance, it includes the major portion of the Sāmba-p. (cf. Bhav I, 72 ff. and Sāmba-p., Veṅk. ed., chaps. 3 ff.).

[229] Bhav I, 1, 71 and 75.

[230] Bhav I, 130, 27 ff. (= Bṛhat-saṃhitā 56, 20 ff.),
I, 132, 26 ff. (= Bṛhat-saṃhitā, chap. 58, verses 48, 47b, 50-52 and 41-42), and
I, 137, 4 ff. (= Bṛhat-saṃhitā 60, 14 ff.).

[231] Cf. Bhav I, 2, 114; I, 3, 10; I, 4, 23 and 141; and so on.

the Bhaviṣya-p. expounds the passages of the Manu-smṛti[232]. This indebtedness to Manu is not, however, peculiar with the Bhaviṣya only. Most of the other Purāṇas often refer to Manu as an authority and have verses in common with the work of the great law-giver[233].

The determination of the date of composition of the earlier portions of the extant Brāhma Parvan is very difficult, there being no sufficient evidence on which we may base our conclusion. It is, however, possible to form an idea of the upper limit of the date of especially the Smṛti-chapters. An examination of these chapters as well as of the untraceable verses quoted in the Nibandhas shows that they were composed at a time when the names of the zodiacal signs and the weekdays were well known and widely used[234]. The Nakṣatras have been mentioned in the order from Kṛttikā to Bharaṇī in one place (viz., Bhav I, 179, 1-10) and from Aśvinī to Revatī in another (viz., Bhav I, 102, 47-71). The chapters in which the Nakṣatras have been named are closely connected with the preceding and the following ones, in some of which the verses quoted by the Nibandha-writers have been traced. These chapters, therefore, cannot be taken as dating later than the adjacent ones. Now, the orders of the Nakṣatras and the popularity of the names of the Rāśis and the weekdays show that the upper limit of the date of composition of the Smṛti-chapters should be placed about 500 A.D., because from 550 A.D. the order of the Nakṣatras from Aśvinī to Revatī atained a state of general acceptance. If the chapters containing verses from the Bṛhat-saṃhitā are not later additions, this limit should be placed later than 550 A.D. As we are not sure about the real character of these chapters, we shall have to remain satisfied with 500 A.D. as the upper limit.

In the extant Brāhma Parvan there are certainly some interpolated chapters which seem to include those influenced by Tantricism, because chapters dealing with the same topics but free from Tantricism are also found to occur. The chapters, in which Tantric influence is very conspicuous, are the following:

I, 16 (verses 35 ff.) to I, 18—on Brahmā-worship;
I, 29-30 —on Gaṇeśa-worship;
I, 49, 199-200, 205-206 and 211-215—on Sun-worship.

232 Cf. Aparārka's com. on Yāj., pp. 1071 and 1076; and Kullūka's com. on Manu XI, 73, 74, 76 and 101.

233 See my article in Indian Culture, Vol. I, 1935, pp. 587-614.

234 Cf. Bhav I, 102, 76; I, 179, 12-13; I, 81, 2 and 16; I, 84, 1-2; I, 90, 1; and so forth. Kālaviveka, pp. 194-195, 300, 301-302, 420 and 492.

Some of these chapters must be dated earlier than 1200 A.D. (see App.). The rest might have been interpolated at the time of appending the other Parvans which also are replete with Tantricism.

A few words may be said here on the Smṛti-contents of that Bhaviṣya-p. which was used by the Nibandhakāras. From the quotations we understand that in this Bhaviṣya-p. there were some Smṛti-chapters in which the interlocutors were Sumantu and a king (Śatānīka?) of the Kuru family[235]. There were also some more chapters in which Īśvara spoke to Guha (i.e., Kārttikeya) on penances.[236] This interlocution between Īśvara and Guha is not found in the present Bhaviṣya. From the quoted verses we understand further that the chapters on penances were based on the works of Parāśara, Śaṃkha, Vasiṣṭha, Manu and Gautama who are mentioned as authorities in the quoted verses[237].

[235] Cf. Mitākṣarā on Yāj. III, 6; Aparārka's com., pp. 15, 39 and 563; Kālaviveka, pp. 302 and 413; and so on.

[236] Cf. Aparārka's com., pp. 1067-1069; Bhavadeva's Prāyaścitta-prakaraṇa, p. 17; Kullūka's com. on Manu XI, 78; and so on.

[237] Cf. Aparārka's com., pp. 1061-1062, 1067, 1071 and 1075; and Kullūka's com. on Manu XI, 91 and 147.

CHAPTER IV

A CHRONOLOGICAL TABLE OF THE PURĀṆIC CHAPTERS ON HINDU RITES AND CUSTOMS

In the previous two chapters the Purāṇas have been carefully analysed in order to find out the genuine and the interpolated Smṛti-chapters and to determine the dates of their composition. The results of this analysis, *so far as they relate to the Smṛti-chapters,* are given below in a tabular form.

1. Mārkaṇḍeya-purāṇa.

Chaps. 12 and 14	—on hells.	
Chap. 15	—on the results of actions done.	—Some time about the 3rd or 4th century A.D. Most probably in the 3rd century. (Chaps. 15, 28-29, 30-33 (1-7), 34, 35)
Chaps. 28-29	—on the duties of the castes and Āśramas.	
„ 30-33 (1-7)	—on funeral sacrifices.	
Chap. 34	—on customs in general.	
„ 35	—on eatables and non-eatables.	
„ 33 (8 to the end)	—on funeral sacrifices.	—Not later than the beginning of the 5th century A.D. but later than the above chapters.

2. Vāyu-purāṇa.

Chaps. 57-59	—on Yuga-dharma.	—*C.* Between 200 and 275 A.D.
„ 73-83 (except verses 14-42 of chap. 82);	—on funeral sacrifices, impurity, and purification of things.	—*C.* 200-500 A.D. Probably in the middle of the 3rd century.

Chaps. 16-17	—on the duties of the Āśramas.	—Probably after 400 A.D., but certainly earlier than 1300 A.D.
Chap. 18	—on penances for the mendicants (yati).	
„ 101	—on hells and results of actions done.	—Not known. May have come from the same date as chaps. 57-59.
Chaps. 105-112	—on the glorification of Gayā.	—Added later. Certainly earlier than 1400 A.D.
Chap. 82 (14-42)	—on the results of performing funeral sacrifices in the holy places such as Gayā, Brahma-kuṇḍa, etc.	—Added later.

3. Brahmāṇḍa-purāṇa.

II, 29-32	—on Yuga-dharma.	—*C*. Between 200 and 275 A.D.
III, 10 (verses 52 ff.) to III, 23	—on funeral sacrifices, impurity, and purification of things.	—*C*. 200-500 A.D. Probably in the middle of the 3rd century A.D.
IV, 2	—on hells and results of actions done.	—Not known. May belong to 200-275 A.D.

4. Viṣṇu-purāṇa.

II, 6 VI, 5	—on hells.	—*C*. Between 100 and 350 A.D. Most probably in the last quarter of the 3rd or the first quarter of the 4th century A.D.
III, 8-16	—on the duties of the çastes and Āśramas, customs in general, impurity, and funeral sacrifices.	
VI, 1-2	—on Yuga-dharma and the results of actions done.	

5. Matsya-purāṇa.

Chap. 7 (37-49)	—on the duties of women.	—Not later than 950 A.D. Most probably as old as the date of composition, or rather compilation, of the extant Matsya.
Chaps. 16-22	—on funeral sacrifices.	—*C*. 400-850 A.D. Probably between 550 and 650 A.D.
„ 142 and 144-145	—on Yuga-dharma.	—(Most probably) of the same date as that of composition of the extant Matsya.
Chap. 53	—on gifts.	—*C*. 550-650 A.D.
Chaps. 54-57	—on vows (vrata).	
Chap. 61	—on vow.	
„ 68	—on bath.	
Chaps. 83-92	—on gifts.	
Chaps. 58-59	—on consecration.	—*C*. 550-650 A.D. (Later than the chapters of the just preceding group).
Chap. 60	—on vow.	
Chaps. 62-64	—on vows.	
Chap. 66	—on vow.	
„ 67	—on bath.	
Chaps. 69-72	—on vows.	
„ 74-75	—on vows.	
„ 77-80	—on vows.	
Chap. 81	—on vow.	
„ 82	—on gifts.	
Chaps. 274-289	—on gifts.	—*C*. 550-650 A.D.
„ 258-263	—on Pratimā-lakṣaṇa.	—*C*. 550-650 A.D.
„ 264-270	—on consecration and Vāstu.	
„ 205-206	—on gifts.	—*C*. 400-1100 A.D. Probably 550-650 A.D.
Chap. 207	—on dedication (utsarga).	
„ 76	—on vow.	—*C*. 650-950 A.D.
Chaps. 95-96 „ 97-101	—on vows.	—*C*. 600-900 A.D. Chaps. 95-96 are earlier than chaps. 97-101.

Chap. 7 (6-30)	—on vow.	—Interpolated? Most probably not later than 900 A.D.
„ 102	—on bath.	—*C.* 650-950 A.D.
Chaps. 215-243	—on the duties of kings, law (vyavahāra), penances, sacrifices to the planets and the methods of their pacification.	—*C.* 650-1000 A.D.
„ 252-257	—on Vāstu.	
„ 93-94	—on sacrifices to the planets and the methods of their pacification.	—*C.* 650-1000 A.D.
„ 180-185	—on holy places.	—*C.* 700-1075 A.D.
Chap. 165	—on Yuga-dharma.	—Probably not later than 950 A.D.
Chaps. 103-112	—on holy places.	—*C.* 850-1250 A.D.
Chap. 13 (10 to the end)	—on holy places.	—Late interpolation.
„ 65	—on vow.	—Uncertain. Surely very late.
„ 73	—on vow.	
„ 39	—on hells.	—Late, but uncertain.
„ 40	—on the duties of the Āśramas.	
Chaps. 186-194	—on holy places.	—Very late. (Later than 800 A.D.).

6. Bhāgavata-purāṇa.

III, 30	—on the results of actions.	—*C.* Sixth century A.D. Probably in the former half of this century.
VII, 11-13 XI, 17-18	—on the duties of the castes and Āśramas.	
VII, 14-15	—on funeral sacrifices and holy places.	

23

7. Kūrma-purāṇa.

Chapters	Subject	Date
I, 2, verses 36-75, and I, 3	—on the duties of the castes and Āśramas.	—*C*. 550-650 A.D.
II, 12-13, II, 14 (except verses 57b-61a), II, 15, II, 19, II, 24-25 and 27-29,	—on the duties of the castes and Āśramas.	—*C*. 700-800 A.D. Most probably at the beginning of the 8th century.
II, 16	—on customs in general.	
II, 17	—on eatables and non-eatables.	
II, 18-19	—on daily duties.	
II, 20-22	—on funeral sacrifices.	
II, 23	—on impurity.	
II, 26	—on gift.	
II, 30 and 32-33	—on penances.	
I, 28	—on Yuga-dharma.	—*C*. 700-1400 A.D. Probably 700-800 A.D.
I, 29	—on the nature of the Kali age.	
I, 30-34	—on holy places.	—*C*. 700-1150 A.D. Probably 700-800 A.D.
II, 34-42	—on holy places.	—*C*. 750-1250 A.D., or rather 800-1250 A.D.
I, 35-38	—on holy places.	—*C*. 750-1200 A.D., or rather 800-1200 A.D.
I, 2, verses 76-87	—on the duties of the castes and Āśramas.	—Interpolated much later.
II, 14, verses 57b-61a	—on Gāyatrī-uddhāra.	—Very late interpolation.
II, 31	—on holy places.	—Interpolated much later.

8. Vāmana-purāṇa.

Chap. 11	—on hells.	—*C.* 9th or 10th century A.D. Most probably in the former.
„ 12	—on the results of actions.	
„ 14	—on the duties of the castes and Āśramas, customs in general, eatables and non-eatables, purification of the body and things, and impurity due to births and deaths.	
„ 80	—on vow.	—Earlier than 1050 A.D. May belong to the 9th or the 10th century.
„ 95	—on the worship of Viṣṇu.	

9. Liṅga-purāṇa.

I, 25-28	—on Liṅga-worship.	—*C.* Between 600 and 1000 A.D. Most probably 600-800 A.D.
I, 77-78	—on the consecration of a Liṅga.	—*C.* Between 600 and 1000 A.D. Most probably 800-1000 A.D.
I, 81	—on Pāśupata-vrata or Śiva-liṅga-vrata.	
I, 83-84	—on Śaiva Vratas to be observed in the different months.	
I, 85, 1-82	—on the method of muttering the five-syllabled Mantra.	
I, 85, 83-126	—on Dīkṣā and Puraścaraṇa.	
I, 85, 127 to the end; I, 89	—on customs in general.	
I, 90	—on penances for Yatis.	

II, 23-26	—on Śiva-worship.	*C.* Between 600 and 1000 A.D. Most probably 800-1000 A.D.
II, 28-44	— on great gifts.	
II, 45	—on funeral sacrifices for living persons.	
II, 46-49	—on consecrating the Liṅga.	
II, 51 to the end	— on mystic rites and practices.	

10. Varāha-purāṇa.

Chaps. 13-14	—on funeral sacrifices.	—*C.* 800 A.D.
„ 19-35	—on Tithis.	
Chap. 37	—on worship.	
Chaps. 38-65	—on vows.	
Chap. 68	—on Yuga-dharma and penances.	
Chaps. 115-120, „ 123-124	—on worship.	—*C.* Between 800 and 1000 A.D. Later than the former chapters.
Chap. 126	—on holy places.	
Chaps. 127-129	—on initiation.	
„ 130-136	—on penances.	
„ 137-139	—on holy places.	—*C.* Between 800 and 1000 A.D. Later than the chapters of the first group.
„ 181-186	—on consecration.	— „ „
„ 187-192	—on funeral sacrifices.	
„ 198-206	—on hells and results of actions.	—Between 900 and 1100 A.D.
Chap. 207	—on gifts.	— „ „
Chaps. 208-209	—on the duties of women.	— „ „
„ 140-151	—on holy places.	—Interpolated. Not later than 1500 A.D.
„ 152-180	— on holy places.	—Later than chapters 140-151, but not later than the Haribhaktivilāsa.
Chap. 99 (1-52)	—on worship.	—Not later than 1400 A.D.

Chap. 99 (53 ff.), Chaps. 100-111, Chap. 112 (1-62)	—on worship and gifts.	—Not later than 1100 A.D.
Chaps. 213-216	—on holy places.	—Not known. Interpolated late; probably not earlier than 1100 A.D.

11. Padma-purāṇa

(a) Ādi-khaṇḍa.

Chaps. 11-30, Chap. 32 and Chaps. 33-49	—on holy places.	—*C.* Between 950 and 1400 A.D.
Chap. 31	—on the glories of Śālagrāma.	
Chaps. 51-54; and „ 58-60	—on the duties of the castes and Āśramas.	
Chap. 55	– on customs in general.	
„ 56	—on eatables and non-eatables.	
„ 57	—on gifts.	

(b) Bhūmi-khaṇḍa.

Chaps. 39-40	—on gifts.	—*C.* Between 900 and 1400 A.D.
Chap. 41	—on the duties of women.	
„ 59	—on the duties of the Āśramas.	
„ 87	—on vows.	
Chaps. 90 and 92	—on holy places.	

(c) Brahma-khaṇḍa.

Chaps. 1 to the end	—on vows, worship, besmearing the temple with cow-dung, glories of Brāhmans, religious observances in different months, etc.	— Very late. Most probably of the same date as that of the chapters of the Ādi-kh.

(d) Pātāla-khaṇḍa.

Chap. 9 (40-63)	—on the duties of the castes and Āśramas.	—Later than the sixth century A.D. Most probably later than the time of the advent of the Muhammadans. But earlier than 1400 A.D.
Chaps. 17-22	—on holy places.	
Chap. 48 (4-69)	—on the results of actions.	
Chaps. 78-79	—on the worship of Śālagrāma.	—Most probably not earlier than 900 A.D. Certainly earlier than 1400 A.D.
Chap. 80	—on Viṣṇu-worship.	
Chaps. 81-82	—on initiation.	
„ 84-99	—on vows.	
Chap. 102	—on the duties of women.	—Not earlier than 800 A.D. Most probably later than 900 A.D., but earlier than 1400 A.D.
Chaps. 101, 105 and 110	—on funeral sacrifices, Liṅga-worship and Yuga-dharma	
Chap. 108	—on vows.	
„ 113	—on funeral sacrifices.	

(e) Sṛṣṭi-khaṇḍa.

(As to those chapters which were borrowed by the Sṛṣṭi-kh. from the Matsya-p., the dates given below are those of their incorporation into the Sṛṣṭi-kh.).

Chap. 7 (8-30)	—on vow.	—*C* 600-750 A.D. Most probably in the latter half of the 7th century.
„ 7 (39-50)	—on the duties of women.	
„ 9 (73 to the end); Chaps. 10-11	—on funeral sacrifices.	
Chap. 15 (96-158)	—on initiation and the duties of the Brahmā-worshippers.	
„ 15 (161 to the end)	—on the duties of the castes and Āśramas.	

Chap. 17 (188-259)	—on holy places and Brahmā-worship.	—*C.* 600-750 A.D. Most probably in the latter half of the 7th century.
„ 29	—on holy places.	
„ 31 (76 to the end)	—on vows and gifts.	
Chaps. 20-25	—on vows, gifts, bath and consecration.	—*C.* Between 800 and 950 A.D. Most probably in the former half of the 8th century.
„ 27-28	—on holy places and results of actions.	
Chap. 36 (28-51)	—on Yuga-dharma.	
„ 31 (8-75)	—on Brāhmī initiation.	—*C.* Between 850 and 1400 A.D.
„ 43 (99 to the end)	—on the glories of Brāhmans, the characteristics of the Gāyatrī and its muttering, Prāṇāyāma, Nyāsa, etc.	—*C.* Between 1000 and 1400 A.D. Some of the chapters, of which chap. 47 is one, of this group must be dated earlier than 1200 A.D.
„ 44	—on bad Brāhmans.	
„ 45 (61 to the end)	—on the glories of Brāhmans and the means of their livelihood, Pātakas, and gift.	
„ 46	—on customs in general and purification of things.	
„ 47	—on the duties of women, and funeral sacrifices.	
„ 49	—on the duties of a wife, and giving away (in marriage) of the daughter.	
„ 54	—on the merits of digging tanks.	
„ 55	—on the merits of dedicating trees, gardens and water reservoirs.	

Chaps. 56-57	—on constructing dams, digging ponds, making gifts, worshipping Viṣṇu and other gods, erecting temples, and so forth.	—*C.* Between 1000 and 1400 A.D. Some of the chapters, of which chap. 47 is one, of this group must be dated earlier than 1200 A.D.
Chap. 58	—on vows, glories of the Tulasī plant, etc.	
„ 59	—on the glories of the Tulasī plant.	
„ 60	—on the glories of the Ganges.	
Chaps. 61-62	—on the worship of Gaṇeśa.	
„ 75-76	—on vows.	
„ 78 to the end	—on the methods of worshipping the planets and Devī.	

(f) Uttara-khaṇḍa.

Chapters on marriage, gifts, vows, worship, duties of the castes and Āśramas, and holy places.	—Late. Most probably not earlier than 900 A.D. Major portion earlier than 1500 A.D.

12. Bṛhannāradīya and Nāradīya Purāṇas.

(a) Chapters of the Bnār dealing with the duties of the castes and Āśramas, funeral sacrifices, penances, holy places, vows, etc.	—Most probably between 850 and 950 A.D.; probably some time about the middle of the 9th century.

(b) Nāradīya P.

(As to those chapters of the Nāradīya which were borrowed from the Bnār, the date given below is that of their incorporation into the Nāradīya).

I, 12	—on holy places.	
I, 13	—on building temples, digging ponds and making various kinds of gifts.	—C. 875-1000 A.D.

I, 14	—on the duties of the castes and Āśramas, sins (pātaka), penances and funeral sacrifices.	—*C.* 875-1000 A.D.
I, 17-23	—on vows.	
I, 24-30	—on customs, duties of the castes and Āśramas, funeral sacrifices, penances, Tithis, great sins (mahāpātaka), minor sins, etc.	
I, 31-32	—on the duties of the castes and Āśramas.	
II, 1-37	—on the glories of vows.	
I, 43	—on the duties of the castes and Āśramas.	—Late interpolations. At least Nār II, 38-43 on Gaṅgā-māhātmya are earlier than Vācaspatimiśra.
I, 64-68 I, 82-91	—on initiation, the method of muttering the Mantra, and worship.	
I, 110-124	—on various kinds of vows.	
II, 39 to the end	—on the glories of holy places.	

13. Agni-Purāṇa.

(a) The Smṛti-chapters which are original to the Agni-p. (except those chapters which are borrowed from earlier sources)	—on holy places, funeral sacrifices, worship of various deities, duties of the castes and Āśramas, marriage, customs in general, purification of things, impurity, sacrifices to the planets, sins, penances, vows, hells, gifts, duties of kings, etc.	—During the 9th century A.D.

(b) Interpolated chapters.

Chaps. 21-106, „ 263-272, and „ 317-326 (There may be a few more chapters, but they cannot be separated).	—on worship, bath, maintenance of the fire, performance of Mudrās, initiation, sacraments, building temples, consecration of images and books, Vāstu, etc.	—Later than the chapters mentioned above.

14. Garuḍa-purāṇa.

(a) Smṛti-chapters in the Pūrva-kh. (except those borrowed from the Yājñavalkya-smṛti and the Parāśara-smṛti).	—on various kinds of worship, initiation, Nyāsa, investiture with the sacred thread, consecration of images, daily duties, gifts, penances, vows, bath, funeral sacrifices, Yuga-dharma, Saṃdhyā, etc.	—During the 10th century A.D.
(b) Smṛti-chapters of the Uttara-kh.	—on hells, method of burning a man made of straw, impurity, funeral sacrifices, gifts, etc.	—Later than the chapters of the Pūrva-kh.

15. Brahma-purāṇa.

The date of composition, or rather compilation, of the Brahma-purāṇa.		—*C.* Between 900 and 1200 A.D.
Chap. 25	—on holy places.	—Spurious.
Chaps. 28 (1-8), 42 (35 to the end), 43-69, 70 (1-11) and 176-177.	—on bath and holy places.	—*C.* Between 900 and 1150 A.D. Earlier than the chaps. of the next group.

Chap. 28 (9 to the end), Chaps. 29-41 and Chap. 42 (1-34)	—on holy places.	—*C.* Between 950 and 1200 A.D.
Chaps. 214-218	—on hells and results of actions.	—Not later than 1500 A.D. Probably of the same date as that of composition of the present Brahma.
,, 219-222	—on funeral sacrifices, customs, impurity and the duties of the castes and Āśramas.	—Earlier than 1200 A.D.
Chaps. 223-231	—on marriage, holy places, worship, Yuga-dharma, and results of actions.	—Not known definitely. May have come from the same date as that of compilation of the present Brahma.
,, 70-175	—on holy places.	—Not known. Probably not earlier than the 10th century A.D.

16. Skanda-purāṇa.

Smṛti-chapters of the Sk.	—Generally late. There are, of course, a few chapters which are to be dated earlier than 1050 A.D. For further details, see under Skanda-p. (Chap. III, section 9).

17. Brahmavaivarta-purāṇa.

IV, 8	—on the Janmāṣṭamī-vrata.	—*C.* Between the 8th and the beginning of the 14th century A.D.
IV, 26	—on the Ekādaśī-vrata.	

Other chapters	—*C.* Between the 10th and the 16th century A.D.

18. Bhaviṣya-purāṇa.

Smṛti--chapters of the Bhaviṣya	—on the duties of the castes and Āśramas, duties of women, customs, marriage, worship, vows, initiation etc.	—Not earlier than 500 A.D.

Of these,

Bhav I, chaps.	21, 31, 32, 36, 37, 39, 46, 81, 96-101 and 106.	—Not later than 1000 A.D.
Bhav I, chaps.	3, 4, 64, 65, 93, 103, 118, 181, 184 and 186.	—Not later than 1075 A.D.
Bhav I, chaps.	2, 18, 19, 22, 38, 47, 51, 55-59, 68-70, 82, 83, 86, 89-91, 104, 105, 108-112, 165-170, 172, 183, 197, 208, 209, 212-214, and so on.	—Not later than 1200 A.D.

The lower limits of the dates of the remaining chapters are not known.

The above table will show that the Purāṇas began to incorporate Smṛti-matter from about 200 A.D., and that there were two main stages in the development of the Purāṇic Smṛti materials. In the first stage, which covered a period ranging approximately from the beginning of the third to the end of the fifth century A.D., the Purāṇas dealt only with those topics on Hindu rites and customs which formed the subject-matter of the early Smṛti Saṃhitās such as those of Manu and Yājñavalkya.[1] But in the second stage, which began from about the beginning of the sixth century A.D.,

[1] These topics are: Varṇāśrama-dharma, Ācāra, Āhnika, Bhakṣyābhakṣya, Vivāha, Aśauca, Śrāddha, Dravya-śuddhi, Pātaka, Prāyaścitta, Naraka, Karma-vipāka and Yuga-dharma.

we are astonished to find a well marked improvement on the varieties of the Smṛti-topics. In this stage the new topics added relate mainly to various kinds of gifts, initiation, sacrifices to the planets and their pacification, Homa, consecration (pratiṣṭhā) of images etc., Saṃdhyā, glorification of Brāhmans and their worship, glorification of holy places, Tithis, Utsarga, Vrata and Pūjā. These topics are found neither in the works of Manu and Yāj.[2] nor in the Purāṇas, or portions thereof, which were written earlier than about the beginning of the sixth century A.D.

[2] The Yājñavalkya-smṛti contains verses on Vināyaka-pūjā and Graha-śānti.

PART II

CHAPTER I

THE HINDU SOCIETY BEFORE 200 A. D., AND THE PURĀṆIC RITES AND CUSTOMS IN THE FIRST STAGE OF THEIR DEVELOPMENT

It has already been said that the Purāṇas, which dealt originally with the five topics only, have now grown up to be encyclopædic works by incorporating chapters not only on religious and social matters but also on law, politics, poetics, grammar, medicine, music, dancing and sculpture, and that there were two main stages in the development of the Purāṇic rites and customs. Hence the question naturally arises as to what led to such a remarkable change in the form and character of the Purāṇas, and determined the stages in the development of their Smṛti materials. To answer this we shall have to review briefly the early religious movements and the foreign invasions and occupations, and their effect on Brahmanical society. This discussion will, on the one hand, help us to find an explanation as to the present form of the Purāṇas, and, on the other, explain the nature of their Smṛti-contents.

Ancient India saw the rise of various religious movements which may be classified, according to their relation to the Vedic (comprising Śrauta and Smārta), as anti-Vedic (viz., Jainism, Ājīvakism and Buddhism), semi-Vedic (consisting primarily of Vaiṣṇavism, Śaivism and Brahmāism), and non-Vedic (viz., Śāktism). Besides the staunch followers of these religions, there was another class of people who were rather of a mixed type. On the one hand, they had high regard for the sectarian gods and looked upon their worship as the means of attaining salvation; on the other, they valued much the practice of the rules of the Varṇāśramadharma, and regarded the Vedas as the highest authority. We shall see hereinafter that the Purāṇic Dharma originated with this last-mentioned class of people.

The Brahmanical religion, rooted in the Vedas, allowed the highest place to the Brāhmans in society. In the Ṛg-veda, the Brāhmans are said to have sprung from the mouth of Puruṣa (the

Primeval Being). They formed the intellectual class among the Aryans, and commanded,—at least claimed for themselves,—the highest respect. Their duties were the performance of sacrifices, the study of the Vedas, and making gifts, and they depended, for maintenance, upon the liberality of kings and others received mainly in the forms of priestly fees and gifts. They enjoyed allowances and preferences even in the courts of justice. In marriage, inheritance etc. also, the Brāhmans enjoyed greater privileges than the other classes. The Kṣatriyas and the Vaiśyas had their prescribed duties which they were required to perform. The Śūdras were to serve the twice-born, who claimed absolute right over the earnings of their respective slaves.[1] Such a state of Brahmanism continued, more or less smoothly, for a time until there arose many new religious systems, some of which were clear protests against the position of the Brāhmans and the authority of the Vedas, while others also were not very favourable to the Varṇāśramadharma. The rise and propagation of these rival faiths proved very fatal to the sacrificial religion of the Vedas which was already on the decline. We find that long before the time of Manu the Śrauta rites were gradually becoming obsolete and the orthodox Vedic religionists were turning Smārtas.

Probably long before the time of Gautama Buddha there were revolts against the Brahmanical doctrines. The Suttanipāta, in one of its sections named Mahāvagga,[2] mentions sixtythree different philosophical schools—probably all of them non-Brahmanical—existing at the time of the Buddha; and there are passages in Jain literature exhibiting a far larger number of such heretical doctrines.[3] Of the teachers of these anti-Vedic religious systems the names of Vardhamāna Mahāvīra, Gosāla Maṅkhaliputta and Gautama Buddha are too well known to be overlooked, and these three non-Brahmanical teachers were the most formidable enemies of Brahmanism.

Mahāvīra, the son of a nobleman of Vaiśāli, practised severe austerity and became the founder, or rather the reformer, of the Jain church. According to Jain traditions Mahāvīra was immediately preceded by Pārśva, the 23rd Tīrthaṅkara. Professor Jacobi and others hold that this Pārśva was the real founder of Jainism. For want of information, literary or otherwise, we are not sure what the teachings of Pārśva were, and in what respects Mahāvīra differed from his predecessor. 'We are told that Pārśva enjoined on his followers four great vows, viz., not to injure life, to

[1] Gautama-dharmasūtra X, 65—*tadartho 'sya nicayaḥ syāt.*

[2] S. B. E., Vol. X, 2, p. 93.

[3] CHI, Vol. I, p. 150.

be truthful, not to steal and to possess no property, while Mahāvīra added a fifth requisition, viz., that of chastity. Pārśva allowed his disciples to wear an upper and an under garment. Mahāvīra, on his part, followed the more rigid rule which obliged the ascetic to be completely naked'.[4] Over and above these, Mahāvīra valued most the fourth stage of life and recommended it to his followers. These teachings of Pārśva and Mahāvīra were largely antagonistic to the ideas and tenets of Brahmanism. Moreover, the Jains did not recognise the authority of the Vedas. They had little faith in caste distinctions and in the Brahmanical rites and duties.

During the lifetime of Mahāvīra the spread of Jainism was rather limited. Though 'there seems to be little doubt that the Jains have more claim to include the parricide king (Ajātaśatru) amongst their converts than the Buddhists'[5], Jainism does not seem generally to have overstepped the boundaries of the kingdoms of Magadha and Aṅga where the great teacher principally dwelt. After the death of Mahāvīra about 468 B.C.,[6] his followers and successors succeeded in popularising the faith to a much greater degree, so that it did not fail to gain the support of kings as well as commoners. From the evidence of the legendary tales related by Jain writers, of whom Hemacandra is the most important, it seems that Udāyin, the successor of Ajātaśatru, was a great champion of the faith. He was so partial to the Jains that his partiality turned out to be the very cause of his death.[7] From the fact that the Jains do not condemn the Nandas like the Buddhists, it seems that the Nanda kings were not unfavourably disposed towards Jainism. The Jain tradition tells us that the Nanda kings had a line of Jain ministers of whom Kalpaka was the first. This Kalpaka was made to accept the ministership against his will, and with his help the Nanda king uprooted the Kṣatriya rulers from the face of the earth.[8] From all this we are tempted to suppose that the Nanda kings were Jains.[9] This supposition is strengthened by the Hāthīgumphā inscription of Khāravela, wherein *Nanda-rāja* is found connected with an idol of the first Jina.[10] From the evidence of this inscription we know that Khāravela was a strong upholder

[4] Ibid., Vol. I, p. 154. Also see S.B.E., Vol. XLV, p. 121, and Dr. Hoernle in ERE, Vol. I, p. 264.

[5] CHI, Vol. I, p. 161.

[6] Ibid., Vol. I, p. 156. [7] Ibid., Vol. I, p. 164.

[8] Āvaśyaka-sūtra, edited by Haribhadrasūri, Benares, 1905, pp. 691-693.

[9] Smith, JRAS, 1918, p. 546—"I may mention that I had come independently to the opinion that the Nandas were jains"

[10] Ind. Ant., Vol. XLIII, 1914, p. 173.

of the Jain religion.[11] According to Jain literary tradition, Samprati, a grandson of Aśoka, was a staunch Jain. He reigned probably in Ujjain, which, as the later Jain authors say, came to be regarded as one of the most important centres of Jainism even before the death of Aśoka. The numerous Mathurā inscriptions, discovered by Cunningham and Führer, show that in the period ranging from about the middle of the second century B.C. to the end of the Kushan rule Jainism was firmly established in Mathurā where there grew up 'a widespread and firmly established Jain community, strongly supported by pious lay devotees, and very zealous in the consecration and worship of images and shrines devoted to Mahāvīra and his predecessors.'[12]

Mahāvīra had a great rival in Gosāla Maṅkhaliputta, who lived with him for six years and practised austerities. At last they were separated by a dispute, and Gosāla soon set up a new religious system of his own. His followers were called Ājīvakas, and his teachings resembled much those of Mahāvīra. He made Śrāvastī his head quarters, and came to have, in course of time, a grand following there.[13] The Jains tell us that Gosāla was not very strict about moral matters.

Want of sufficient evidence, literary or otherwise, leaves us in darkness as to the spread and popularity of the system. It is mainly from the Jain works that we gather scrappy accounts about the Ājīvakas. The way in which the Jain authors attack Gosāla in their works, shows that the Ājīvakas formed a powerful sect which arrested the spread of Jainism. That the Ājīvaka sect continued to exist during the reigns of Aśoka and his successors is shown by a few inscriptions. The three cave inscriptions of Aśoka at Barābar in the Gayā district[14] record the dedication of cave dwellings for the use of the Ājīvakas who 'went about naked, and were noted for ascetic practices of the most rigorous kind.'[15] Another inscription of Aśoka names the Ājīvakas along with the Buddhists, Brāhmans and others.[16] Daśaratha, a grandson of Aśoka, is known from three inscriptions to have bestowed on the Ājīvaka sect caves in the Nāgārjuna hills.[17] These evidences show that the Ājīvaka sect did not lose hold on the society, but commanded respect even of kings.

The third great heretical system is Buddhism preached by Gautama Buddha, who also, like Mahāvīra and Gosāla Maṅkhaliputta, was a non-Brāhman and preached a system which was in

[11] JBORS, Vol. IV, 1918, pp. 364-404.
[12] CHI, Vol. I, p. 167.
[13] Ibid., Vol. I, p. 162.
[14] Corp. Inscr. Ind., Vol. I, pp. 181-182.
[15] Smith, EHI, p. 177.
[16] Corp. Inscr. Ind., Vol. I, p. 131.
[17] Ibid., Vol. I, pp. 103-104 and 134-136.

every way detrimental to the interests of Brahmanism. The Buddhists, especially those who entered the Saṅgha, practised Ahiṃsā, did not regard the Vedas and the Brāhmans, ignored the Vedic gods, did not recognise caste distinctions, and cared little for the Varṇāśramadharma. In their opinion Śrāddha was a mere policy of the Brāhmans. These and similar other ideas and practices made the Buddhists the bitterest enemies of Brahmanism.

Buddhism had found great patrons in kings of whom Aśoka and Kaniṣka are the most important. Aśoka was a non-Brāhman, and a 'Śūdra' according to the Purāṇas. He did his best to popularise Buddhism in India and abroad, and looked upon the Buddhist monks with special favour. In his time the Buddhists increased overwhelmingly in number mainly at the cost of the followers of Brahmanism. Aśoka himself says: "The gods who were worshipped as true divinities in India have been rendered false..........by my zeal." After the downfall of the Mauryas, there was a Brahmanic revival under the Śuṅgas, but the impetus which Buddhism received from Aśoka was not to be stopped. The inscriptions of the reign of the early Āndhras show that Buddhism was in a flourishing condition at that period.[18] The rule of the Kushan kings also was very favourable to Buddhism. According to the Rāja-taraṅgiṇī, "These kings who were given to acts of piety, though descended from the Turuṣka race, built at Śuṣkaletra and other places Maṭhas, Caityas, and similar (structures). During the powerful reign of these (kings) the land of Kāśmīra was, to a great extent, in the possession of the Bauddhas, who by (practising) the law of religious mendicancy (pravrajyā) had acquired great renown[19]". 'The general prevalence of Buddhism in Northern India, including Kasmir, Afghanistan, and Suwat, during the two centuries immediately preceding and the two next following the Christian era, is simply attested by the numerous remains of Buddhist monuments erected during that period, and a multitude of inscriptions, which are almost all either Buddhist or Jain.'[20]

We have seen above the nature and spread of the three great heresies. We shall now direct our attention to two other religious movements, viz., Vaiṣṇavism and Śaivism. Materials for the reconstruction of the early history of these religions are so meagre that we cannot say definitely how these systems grew up and what contributions the Aryans and the non-Aryans made to their growth.

[18] Ind. Ant., Vol. XLVIII, 1919, pp. 77 ff.

[19] Stein, Kalhan's Chronicle of the Kings of Kasmir, Vol. I, p. 31.

[20] Smith, EHI, p. 318.

The earliest records of Vaiṣṇavism and Śaivism are contained in the Mahābhārata; but even there these systems do not seem to appear in their true character, because 'the priests have preserved for us, not so much the opinions the people actually held, as the opinions the priests wished them to hold'[21]. It is, therefore, quite probable that in the present Mahābhārata, which is practically a work of those who believed in the Vedas and the caste and Āśrama rules, and in which the attempt at popularising the Vedas and the Varṇāśramadharma and elevating the position of the Brāhmans is clearly discernible, the forms of Vaiṣṇavism and Śaivism have been influenced by the ideas and motives of its authors.

The term Vaiṣṇavism is very comprehensive in its denotation; but the modern Vaiṣṇavas consist generally of the Pāñcarātras and the Bhāgavatas. These two sections, though originally different[22], are designated by the generic term *Vaiṣṇava* on account of the identification of their respective sectarian deities with Viṣṇu.

The earliest document of the Pāñcarātras is the Nārāyaṇīya section of the Mahābhārata (XII, 335-351). Here we are told that there were seven Citra-śikhaṇḍin Ṛṣis who proclaimed, on the mount Meru, a Śāstra which was on a par (sammita) with the four Vedas[23]. This Śāstra contained one lac of verses, and it was meant for the populace[24]. As it was to direct them both in activity (pravṛtti) and inactivity (nivṛtti), it was *made consistent* with the four Vedas[25]. We do not know for certain whether there was really any ancient Pāñcarātra work ascribed to the seven Citra-śikhaṇḍin Ṛṣis, but the very reference to making the scripture, which was meant for the commoners, conform to the four Vedas, is important in that it implies the originally non-Vedic, if not also anti-Vedic, character of the ideas and practices of the Pāñcarātra system. The Mahābhārata itself admits that the Pāñcarātra system is different from the Vedic, for it says: "Know, O saintly king, the Sāṃkhya, the Yoga, the Pāñcarātra, the Vedas and the Pāśupata as knowledges holding different views"[26]. It has been held that the above mentioned scripture compiled by the seven Citra-śikhaṇḍin Ṛṣis was the forerunner of the Pāñcarātra Saṃhitās[27]. But this view seems to

[21] Rhys Davids, Buddhist India, p. 210. Cf. also Richard Fick, Social Organisation in North-east India in Buddha s time, p. 14.

[22] IHQ, VI, 1930, pp. 315 ff. and 437 ff.; VII, 1931, pp. 93 ff., 343 ff. and 735 ff.; and VIII, 1932, pp. 64 ff. Bhandarkar, Vaiṣṇavism etc., pp. 30 ff.

[23] Mbh XII, 335, 27b-29a.

[24] Cf. *loka-tantrasya kṛtsnasya yasmād dharmaḥ pravartate*|Mbh XII, 335, 39; also Mbh XII, 335, 29a—*loka-dharmam anuttamam.*

[25] Mbh XII, 335, 40.

[26] Ibid., XII, 349, 1 and 64.

[27] Farquhar, Outline, p. 98.

be untenable because of the fact that, as we shall see afterwards, the prescriptions of the early Saṃhitās of this sect are not at all favourable to the Varṇāśramadharma and the authority of the Vedas. On the other hand, the influence of the Varṇāśramadharma on the Saṃhitās increases with their comparatively late dates. It seems, therefore, that the original non-Vedic as well as anti-Vedic ideas of the Pāñcarātras were permeated through the Saṃhitās while the idea of reconciling the scripture of the seven Ṛṣis with the Vedas found its later expression in the epics and the Purāṇas.

Of the early character of Bhāgavatism we can scarcely say anything definitely. That this system also was not, in its real character, very favourably inclined towards the Varṇāśramadharma and the Brāhmans, seems to be suggested by the facts that the Vṛṣṇis, among whom Kṛṣṇa was born, were noted for their irreverent attitude towards the Brāhmans[28], and that the casteless foreigners were freely admitted into the Bhāgavata fold. The Besnagar inscription[29] of the second century B.C. mentions Heliodoros, an ambassador of the Greek king Antialkidas, as a Bhāgavata. The inscription further tells us that this Heliodoros erected, in honour of Vāsudeva, a flagstaff on the top of which there was an image of Garuḍa. The Bhāgavata-purāṇa (II, 4, 18) also refers to the acceptance of Vaiṣṇavism by the foreigners :

kirāta-hūṇāndhra-pulinda-pukvasā
ābhīra-suhmā yavanāḥ khaśādayaḥ|
ye 'nye ca pāpā yad-upāśrayāśrayāḥ
śudhyanti tasmai prabhaviṣṇave namaḥ||

We should note that these casteless foreign races were held in great contempt by the Purāṇic Brāhmans who called them 'sinners'[30], 'Mlecchas'[31] and 'inimical to Brahmanism'[32], and that the authors of the Purāṇas always warned the people against disclosing the contents of these 'holy books' to such people[33]. The admittance of the casteless foreigners into the Vaiṣṇava fold, and the encouragement to Saṃnyāsa for the practice of Yoga[34], as contrasted with the conservative and orthodox views of the Purāṇas, tend to show that the character of Vaiṣṇavism, which

28 Arthaśāstra of Kauṭilya, text, edited by R. Shama Sastry, p. 12; Cowell's Jātaka, Vol. IV, pp. 55-56 and Vol. V, p. 138.

29 Luders, Inscription No. 669, Ep. Ind., X, 1909-10, Appendix.

30 Bhāg II, 4, 18 and II, 7, 46.

31 Viṣ V, 38, 28.

32 Viṣ IV, 24, 18—*abrahmaṇyān.*

33 Cf. Vā 103, 69b-70.

34 Cf. Arthaśāstra of Kauṭilya, text, p. 403 wherein there is mention of spies, disguised as ascetics with shaved head or braided hair, and pretending to be the worshippers of god Saṃkarṣaṇa. Megasthenes calls the worshippers of Śiva and Kṛṣṇa 'philosophers'. Cf. McCrindle, Ancient India, p. 97.

was accepted by these foreigners, must have been against the Varṇāśramadharma and, therefore, a menace to it. From the position of women and Śūdras in the Vaiṣṇavism of the epics and the Purāṇas it seems that in popular Vaiṣṇavism also initiation was open to them, and they were allowed to worship Viṣṇu themselves.

Inscriptions and authors of the pre-Christian era testify to the early spread and popularity of Vaiṣṇavism. Pāṇini (IV, 3, 95 and 98) speaks of the formation of the word '*vāsudevaka*' to mean 'a person the object of whose Bhakti is Vāsudeva'. Megasthenes, who lived in the court of Candragupta Maurya, informs us that the worship of Viṣṇu (under the form of Kṛṣṇa) was very popular especially among the Śūrasenas[35]. In Kauṭilya's Arthaśāstra (text, p. 403) there is mention of the worshippers of god Saṃkarṣaṇa. Patañjali, in his Mahābhāṣya (on Pāṇini IV, 3, 98), mentions '*vāsudeva-vargyaḥ*' and '*vāsudeva-varginaḥ*' (i.e., the followers of Vāsudeva), and regards Kṛṣṇa Vāsudeva as a divine being rather than a mere Kṣatriya[36]. In the Ghoṣuṇḍi Stone Inscription[37] of the pre-Christian era there is a clear reference to the worship of Saṃkarṣaṇa and Vāsudeva. The Nānāghāṭ Cave Inscription[38] begins with an invocation of several gods including Saṃkarṣaṇa and Vāsudeva. The name 'Vāsudeva' was very popular with the Indians as well as the foreigners. The Peshāwar Museum Inscription (No. 21) names a Brāhman Vāsudeva, son of Indradeva and resident of Obhara, who caused a well to be dug[39]. The ninth king of the Śuṅga dynasty was named Bhāgavata, and the founder of the Kāṇva dynasty was named Vāsudeva. Vāsudeva was also the name of the successor of the Kushan king Huviṣka. These evidences sufficiently prove the spread and popularity of Vaiṣṇavism. If the suggestion that the Ghoṣuṇḍi Stone Inscription belongs to the Kāṇva dynasty[40] is accepted, then it becomes evident that Vaiṣṇavism 'found favour not only with the foreigners such as the Śakas, Yavanas etc., but also with the Vedic Aryans of the royal family like the Kāṇvas, from an early date'.

The early character of Śaivism also does not seem to have been very favourable to the Varṇāśramadharma and the authority

[35] McCrindle, Ancient India, p. 201. CHI, Vol. I, pp. 408 and 485.

[36] Ind. Ant.,Vol. III, 1874, pp. 14-16.

[37] Ind. Ant., Vol. LXI, 1932, p. 203. Also see JASB, Vol. 56, i, 1887, pp 74 ff; Memoirs No. 4 of the ASI, 1920, p. 119; Ep. Ind., XVI, 1921-2, pp. 25 ff; IHQ, Vol. IX, 1933, pp. 795 ff.

[38] Luders, Inscription No. 1112, Ep. Ind., X, 1909-10, Appendix, p. 121.

[39] Corp. Inscr. Ind., Vol. II, part 1, p. 157.

[40] IHQ, IX, 1933, pp. 795-799.

of the Vedas. This irreverent character of Śaivism seems to be hinted at in a dialogue between Dakṣa and Śiva in the Mahābhārata, in which the latter says that in ancient times he formulated the Pāśupata system which was 'contradictory to, though in a very few cases agreeing with, the rules of the Varṇāśramadharma' and which was 'denounced by the unwise'[41]. It is perhaps on account of their characteristic non-Brahmanical ideas and practices that the worshippers of Śiva (originally called Pāśupatas) have been looked down upon by the Smṛti-writers. The Smṛti-candrikā (II, 310) quotes from the Ṣaṭtriṃśan-mata three lines which run as follows :

bauddhān pāśupatāñ jainān lokāyatika-kāpilān|
vikarmasthān dvijān spṛṣṭvā sacelo jalam āviśet||
kāpālikāṃs tu saṃspṛśya prāṇāyāmo 'dhiko mataḥ|

'A man should bathe with all his clothes on if he chances to touch the Bauddhas, the Pāśupatas, the Jainas, the Lokāyatikas, the Kāpilas, and those Brāhmans who have taken up the duties not meant for them. But if he touches the Kāpālikas, he should perform Prāṇāyāma in addition'. There is another verse quoted in the same work (II, 311), which says: "One should bathe with the garments on after touching the Śaivas, the Pāśupatas, the Lokāyatikas, the Nāstikas, the Brāhmans who have taken up the duties not meant for them, and the Śūdras". The Kāpālikas, Sāttvatas, Bauddhas, Jainas and others are called '*durācārāḥ śaucācāra-bahiṣkṛtāḥ*' in a passage quoted by Aparārka (com., p. 143) from the Brahmāṇḍa-p., and are classed by him with the

41 * * * * * o

vedāt ṣaḍaṅgād uddhṛtya sāṃkhya-yogāc ca yuktitaḥ|

* * * * * *

apūrvaṃ sarvatobhadraṃ viśvatomukham avyayam|
abdair daśārdha-saṃyuktaṃ gūḍham aprājña-ninditam||
varṇāśrama-kṛtair dharmair viparītaṃ kvacit samam|
gatāṃ tair adhyavasitam atyāśramam idaṃ vratam||
mayā pāśupataṃ dakṣa śubham utpāditaṃ purā|

* * * * * * *

Mbh XII, 284, 121-124a.

These verses are found quoted in Aparārka's com. on Yāj. (pp. 17-18). The readings given by Aparārka are sometimes different and also perhaps better; viz., he reads '*śaktitaḥ*' for '*yuktitaḥ*', '*arthair daśārdhaiḥ saṃyuktaṃ*' for '*abdair daśārdha-saṃyuktaṃ*', *śatāntaiḥ*' for '*gatāṃ taiḥ*', '*anyāśramaṃ*' for '*atyāśramaṃ*', '*smṛtaṃ*' for '*vrataṃ*', '*pūrvaṃ*' for '*dakṣa*', and '*yogaṃ*' for '*śubhaṃ*'.

These verses are also found, with variations in readings, in Lg II, 20, 9-11; Vā 30, 293-295; Br 40, 108-110; etc.

outcasts (*patita*—com., p. 143). Examples of such hatred borne towards the Śiva-worshippers, and especially the Kāpālikas, are not rare in Sanskrit literature. The main causes of this hatred seem to be the peculiar manners and customs of these sectaries. The Pāśupatas used to remain completely naked or with a piece of rag (kaupīna) on[42], bear awkward signs, hold a torch in the hand, laugh, sing, dance, shout, make amorous gestures and do similar other acts. They besmeared their bodies with ashes, and used to live in the cemeteries. They cared little for the caste and Āśrama rules, and admitted the casteless foreigners into their fold. The Śūdras and women were allowed to have Dīkṣā and to worship the deity. The dress and manners of the Kāpālikas were much more repulsive. Their sacred thread was made of hair, their rosaries consisted of human bones, they held in their hands skulls which were besmeared with blood, and they wore matted hair which they ornamented with pieces of bones[43]. By these and similar other repulsive acts they could not but excite the hatred of at least the members of the Brahmanical fold. There was another reason why the Śiva-worshippers were not in good grace of those who believed in the Varṇāśramadharma. It was that they, like the Pāñcarātras, laid special stress on Saṃnyāsa for the practice of Yoga, and thus encouraged the breach of order and discipline in society.

From early times the worship of Śiva became very popular. The inscriptions and early authors give ample evidence in this direction. "A round copper seal, measuring 1·35 × 1·35 inches, with two rings on the back, was found at Sirkap in the year 1914-5. It shows the figure of Śiva with trident in left hand and club in right . . . . ."[44]. Patañjali, in his Mahābhāṣya, mentions the Śiva-bhāgavatas, devotees of Śiva, and speaks of the stress they lay on the worship of images[45]. Megasthenes speaks of the popularity of the worship of Śiva especially in the hill regions, and compares Candragupta's hunting expedition to the processions of Dionysus (i.e., Śiva). Aśoka is said to have been a devotee of Śiva in his early life[46]. 'The Śaka and Kushan kings who reigned from the first century B.C. to the third century A.D. were usually Śivaites or Buddhists and were, with a few exceptions, not well disposed towards the religion of Vāsudeva'[47]. The Kushan king Kadphises II (78-110 A.D.) was so ardent a worshipper of Śiva

[42] Kūr I, 33, 8; II, 37, 100; etc.

[43] Var 97, 13-14 and 20. Bṛhat-saṃhitā, p. 61.

[44] Corp. Inscr. Ind., Vol. II, part 1, p. 102.

[45] Mahābhāṣya on Pāṇini V, 2, 76.

[46] Smith, EHI, p. 185.

[47] H. C. Roy Choudhury, Early History of the Vaiṣṇava sect, p. 100.

that he had a picture of the god stamped on his coins.[48] Among the forms of deities stamped on the coins of Huviṣka, there is the figure of the 'Phallic Śiva' [49]. Vāsudeva (182-220 A.D.), another Kushan king, was a worshipper of Śiva[50]. The above instances amply testify to the spread and popularity of Śiva-worship in ancient India. The popularity of the worship of this god is further proved by the fact that in numerous cases the names of kings and commoners are found connected with that of Śiva. The Shahdaur Inscription names one renowned, rich, and wealthy Śiva-rakṣita (protected by Śiva; cf. 'Buddha-rakṣita') who made a donation of ten thousand Kārṣāpaṇas[51]. The Bīmarān Vase Inscription mentions one Śiva-rakṣita, 'the Mūjavat scion' [52]. A seal inscription discovered in the Punjab belongs to 'Śivasena, the Kṣatrapa in the town of Abhisāraprastha' [53]. A cave inscription at Nasik refers itself to the reign of the Ābhīra king Īśvarasena, son of Śivadatta[54]. It is needless to multiply examples.

Before we proceed further let us have a short pause here to enquire into the ideas, rites and customs of the followers of early Vaiṣṇavism and Śaivism. We have said above that the original character of these two religions was most probably non-Brahmanical. By this it is not meant that those who worshipped Viṣṇu and Śiva were all influenced by non-Brahmanical ideas and practices and violated the Brahmanical rules of castes and stages. What we mean to say is that these two religions in their popular character were imbued with non-Brahmanical ideas and practices. On the other hand, it seems that among the early worshippers of these two deities there was one section of people who, though won over to the worship of these deities, looked upon the Vedas as authorities, attached great importance to the Varṇāśramadharma and the Smṛti rules, and did not like to give them up. We shall call them Smārta-Vaiṣṇavas and Smārta-Śaivas. The Jayākhya-saṃhitā mentions such Smārta adherents to the Pāñcarātra system. It divides the Pāñcarātra Vaiṣṇavas into three groups, with further subdivisions, according to the extent of their renunciation (saṃnyāsa), the nature of their attachment to the sect, and their method of worshipping Viṣṇu. The first group consists of the Yatis, Ekāntins, Vaikhānasas, Karmasāttvatas and Śikhins; the second group, of the Āptas (i.e., those who join the order wholeheartedly),

48 Smith, EHI, p. 318; Cunningham, Coins of the Indo-Scythians, part III, p. 8.
49 Cunningham, Coins of the Indo-Scythians, part III, p. 101.
50 Ibid., p. 11.
51 Corp. Inscr. Ind., Vol. II, part 1, pp. 16-17.
52 Ibid., p. 52.
53 Ibid., p. 103.
54 Ep. Ind., VIII, 1905-6, p. 88. Ind. Ant., Vol. XLVII. 1918, p. 156.

Anāptas, Ārambhins and Sampravartins; and the third group, of the Yogins, Japa-niṣṭhas, Tāpasas, Śāstrajñas and Śāstra-dhārakas. The Anāptas, Ārambhins and Sampravartins are defined as follows:

varṇa-dharmam anujjhitya hy āptādiṣṭena karmaṇā|
yajanti śraddhayā devam anāptās te prakīrtitāḥ||
vinā tenārtha-siddhyartham viśvātmānam yajanti ye|
ārambhiṇas te boddhavyā vaiṣṇavā brāhmaṇādayaḥ||
śraddhayā ye pravartante svayam sampūjane hareḥ|
amārgeṇa tu viprendra viddhi tān sampravartinaḥ||

'Those, who do not give up the duties imposed on them by their castes but worship the god with devotion (śraddhā) with acts prescribed by the Āptas, are called Anāptas. The Vaiṣṇava Brāhmans and others who, without caring for it (i.e., the instruction of the Āptas), worship the universal soul for the attainment of the desired objects, are called Ārambhins. O best of Brāhmans, know those people as Sampravartins who, out of Śraddhā, of themselves set to worship Hari in a wrong way'[55]. Probably among the Śiva-worshippers also there were adherents of the types of these Anāptas, Ārambhins and Sampravartins mentioned above. It is undoubtedly these types of Brāhman adherents to Vaiṣṇavism and Śaivism to whom the composite character of Purāṇic Hinduism was originally due, and who were also the authors of the present Purāṇas; because these works exhibit, on the one hand, the sectarian zeal in glorifying the respective deities, and, on the other, try to establish the Varṇāśramadharma and the authority of the Vedas.

Besides the Vaiṣṇavas and the Śaivas there grew up in ancient India another sect which inculcated the worship of Brahmā. Of the early history and character of this Brahmā-sect we know almost nothing. The accounts which we find in the Mārkaṇḍeya-purāṇa and the Padma-purāṇa (Sṛṣṭi-kh.) are of comparatively late dates. Though from these accounts we cannot form any clear idea of the early character of the sect, one thing seems to be clear to us. It is that the Brahmā-sect attached great importance to asceticism for the realisation of Brahmā, the supreme Brahma.

The different sects and systems of religion that we have just reviewed created an atmosphere which did not in an orthodox way conform to Vedic or Brahmanical ideas. This atmosphere was further disturbed by the advent of the casteless foreigners such as the Greeks, Śakas, Pahlavas, Kushans, Ābhīras and others, who founded extensive kingdoms and settled in this country. Though

[55] Jayākhya-saṃhitā, XXII, 34b-37a.

these foreigners accepted Buddhism, Śaivism or Vaiṣṇavism and were soon Indianised, their anti-Brahmanic manners and customs could not but influence the people, especially their co-religionists. Most of these alien tribes being originally nomadic, they can be expected to have had a variable standard of morality which also certainly affected the people.

Further trouble was created to the Brāhmans by the political supremacy of the non-Kṣatriyas, or rather Śūdras as the Purāṇas hold, under the Nandas, the Mauryas and probably also the Āndhras[56]. The Brāhmans always emphasised the low social status of the Śūdras and reduced them to servitude. In religious life also the latter enjoyed little privilege and freedom. It is natural, therefore, that these down-trodden Śūdras should have revolted against the Brāhmans when they had political power in their hand. How these powerful Śūdras behaved with the Brāhmans, we shall see later on.

[56] The way in which the land of the Āndhras was looked down upon by the Aryans shows that the inhabitants of this place could never claim a position better than that of the Śūdras. About the origin of the people of Southern India Baudhāyana says: "Those people are of mixed origin, who are inhabitants of Avantī, Aṅga, Magadha, Surāṣṭra, Dakṣiṇāpatha, Upāvṛt, Sindhu and Sauvīra" (Baudhāyana-dharmasūtra I, 1, 29). The land of the Āndhras and others lay outside the pale of Āryāvarta, beyond which, as Manu says, lived the Mlecchas. It was for this reason that the orthodox Brahmanists deemed it sinful to go to these parts of India. Vyāsa says: "One should shun the lands of the Aṅgas, Vaṅgas, Āndhras and other Mleccha tribes, and also those tracts of land where there are no antelopes". (See Smṛti-candrikā I, p. 22). Devala, quoted in the Mitākṣarā (on Yāj. III, 292), says: "By going to Sindhu, Sauvīra, Surāṣṭra, the frontier provinces, Aṅga, Vaṅga, Kaliṅga and Andhra, one deserves to be purified again". Similar other passages, quoted in the Smṛti-candrikā (I, pp. 22-23 and 24) from the Ādi- and the Skanda-purāṇa, show that the twice-born, who went to these countries except in times of distress, were looked upon as fallen from their castes (patita). As to the origin of the Āndhras, the twice-born had a low opinion. According to Manu their origin is as follows:— The issue of a Brāhman on his wedded Śūdra wife is known as a Niṣāda (Manu X, 8), and that of a Vaiśya on a Brāhman woman is a Vaideha (Manu X, 11). Again, the issue of a Niṣāda father and a Vaideha mother is a Kārāvara, and that of a Vaideha father on a Kārāvara mother is an Āndhra (Manu X, 36). This idea about the origin of the Āndhras shows that they could not claim a status better than that of the Śūdras. The Bhāgavata-purāṇa (XII, 1, 20) calls the founder of the Āndhra dynasty a Vṛṣala i.e., Śūdra:

hatvā kāṇvaṃ suśarmāṇaṃ tad-bhṛtyo vṛṣalo balī|
gāṃ bhokṣaty andhra-jātīyaḥ kañcit kālam asattamaḥ||

'After murdering Suśarman of the Kāṇva dynasty, his servant, a powerful and most wicked Vṛṣala of the Āndhra race, will enjoy the earth for some time'.

We have enumerated above all the forces that, acting simultaneously, produced a state of society which was favourable neither to the propagation of Brahmanical ideas nor to the orthodox Brāhmans. An account of this social disorder can be gathered from the early Buddhist literature and the Purāṇas. In the latter treatises there are chapters on the description of the Kali age which can reasonably be taken to give an account of the Hindu society during the period ranging from the time of the prevalence of Buddhism and Jainism (i.e., from the reign of the Nandas) to the end of the Āndhra rule in western India. As these chapters speak of 'many Śūdra kings' who ruled in the Kali age and encouraged the spread of Buddhism and Jainism[57], and as in the Purāṇas Mahāpadma Nanda is called the first Śūdra monarch[58], it must be admitted that they point to a period covering roughly the reigns of the Nandas and the Mauryas who, with a very few exceptions, were supporters of the heresies. The references in these chapters to the performance of horse-sacrifices by the Śūdra kings[59] seem to point to the rule of the Āndhra dynasty, the founder of which is called a Vṛṣala by the Bhāgavata-purāṇa. From the evidence of inscriptions we know that the Āndhra kings performed many sacrifices, including the Aśvamedha and the Gavāmayana[60]. During his excavations at Besnagar D. R. Bhandarkar discovered a sacrificial hall (yajña-śālā) and near it a seal inscription which reads as follows:

L. 1. *ṭimitra-dātṛsya [sa]—ho(tā) =*
L. 2. *p(o)tā-maṃtra-sajana [? i].*

On this inscription he made the following remarks: "The meaning of this legend, as just remarked, is not clear, but the words *hotā, potā* and *maṃtra,* which are technical to sacrificial literature, indicate that the sealing is really connected with the Yajña-śālā. And the import of the legend appears to be: 'Of the donor Ṭimitra accompanied by the Hotā, Potā, Hymn-kinsmen and ....' Timitra doubtless is the name of an individual, and seems to be the Sanskritised form of the Greek Demetrius. And it appears that this Greek personage called Demetrius was the *dātā* or *yajamāna* who instituted the sacrifice. The performance of a Brahmanic

57 Mat 144, 40 and 43; Vā 58, 40; Bḍ II, 31, 41; Kūr I, 29, 7; and so on.

58 Mat 272, 17b-18a; Vā 90, 320b-327a; Bḍ III, 74, 139b-140a; and Viṣ IV, 24, 4-5. Also Bhāg XII, 1, 7-8.

59 *yajanti hy aśvamedhaiś ca rājānaḥ śūdra-yonayaḥ*|—Mat 144, 43a.
yajante cāśvamedhena rājānaḥ śūdra-yonayaḥ| —Bḍ II, 31, 67b.
Vā 58, 67a wrongly reads '*nāśvamedhena*' for '*cāśvamedhena*' of the Brahmāṇḍa.

60 Ind. Ant., Vol. XLVIII, 1919, p. 77.

sacrifice by a Greek is not a thing that needs surprise us, because we know that many Greeks like other foreign people, such as Śakas and Pahlavas, became Buddhists or Hindus. Nay, at Vidiśā itself, as evidenced from an inscription incised on the Kham Bābā pillar, we have an instance of a Greek ambassador Heliodora (Heliodoros) calling himself a Bhāgavata or a devotee of Vāsudeva"[61]. From this remark it seems that the Greek Demetrius performed a sacrifice, but this sacrifice could not be meant by the lines of the Purāṇas referred to above, because the Greeks are always called Yavanas and not Śūdras. That the Purāṇic chapters on the description of the Kali age point to the period mentioned above is further shown by the Viṣṇu-purāṇa which describes the full swing of Kali (kali-vṛddhi) as follows:

"Whenever there is noticed an increase (in the number) of the heretics, then, Oh Maitreya, should the full swing of Kali be estimated by the wise. Whenever there is a decrease in the number of the good who follow the path of the Vedas, and the efforts of those who cultivate Dharma relax, then, Maitreya, the predominance of Kali should be guessed by the learned. Whenever Puruṣottama, the god of sacrifices, becomes no longer the object of these (i.e., sacrifices), then the force of Kali should be understood. When the people do not show respect to the sayings of the Vedas but are inclined towards the heretics, then, Oh best of the twice-born, the augmented influence of the Kali age should be inferred"[62].

This description points undoubtedly to the prevalence of Jainism, and especially of Buddhism, which became very powerful from the time of Aśoka Maurya. The other Purāṇas also ascribe the social disorder more to the heretics, viz., the Buddhists, Jains and Kāpālikas[63], than to anything else. From all that has been said above it becomes evident that the Purāṇic chapters on the Kali age are the records of the state of society during the period with which we are concerned here. The numerous verses found common to these chapters show that these are derived from a common source which must be very old. This source is probably to be traced in a tradition, for the origin of which the turmoil in society caused by the forces enumerated above should be held responsible. Now, the question may arise as to the real historical value of these chapters. Though the accounts contained in these chapters may appear to us rather hyperbolical, we should not set them aside as historically worthless. The authors of the present Purāṇas being Brāhmans, it is not expected that the picture, they themselves present

[61] ASI, Annual Report, 1914-15, pp. 77-78. [62] Viṣ VI, 1, 44-47.

[63] Kūr I, 29, 13; Mat 144, 40; Vā 58, 64; and Bd II, 31, 65.

before us, of their own degradation and humiliation on the one hand and the rise of the servile Śūdras on the other, should be totally false. Moreover, many of the statements of the Purāṇas can be supported by those contained in the inscriptions and the early Buddhist literature. Even if their statements could not have been thus supported, their value would have still remained, for, with all their exaggerations, they record the apprehension created in the minds of the Brāhmans by the rise of the heresies.

Let us now see what information the Purāṇic chapters supply of the state of society during the said period. For this purpose we shall look, as our sources, generally to the verses common to the chapters on the description of the Kali-yuga in the following Purāṇas, viz., the Vāyu (chap. 58), Brahmāṇḍa (II, 31), Matsya (chap. 144), Bhāgavata (XII, 2), Viṣṇu (VI, 1) and Kūrma (1, 29), because these Purāṇas come from comparatively early dates. These chapters give us the picture of a society in which the people often neglected the caste and Āśrama rules, and were influenced by the non-Brahmanical and anti-Brahmanical ideas and beliefs. The spread of the heresies told upon the people to such an extent that the members of all the four castes and Āśramas were affected more or less. The people did not often like to observe the rules of castes and to carry into execution the duties enjoined by the Ṛg-, the Sāma- and the Yajur-veda[64]. Their mind was always occupied with the thoughts of money, and they did not hesitate to adopt unfair means to acquire it[65]. The twice-born gave up the study of the Vedas and the performance of sacrifices[66] which were reserved for the 'foolish'[67]. They forsook their own Dharma, became wandering mendicants 'in hundreds and thousands', and worshipped gods with popular songs, but could not attain the supreme Brahma[68]. They neglected the rules of Snāna, Homa, Japa, Dāna etc., and spoke ill of the Brāhmans, the Vedas, the Dharmaśāstras and the Purāṇas[69]. They performed various acts on the authority of the non-Vedic works, lost all attraction for their own duties, cared little for the rules of conduct, mixed with the heretics, and became professional beggars[70]. They alarmed the people with their bad ambitions, bad education, bad customs and bad earnings[71]. On account of the spread of Buddhism and Jainism, the supremacy

[64] Viṣ VI, 1, 10 and 49. [65] Ibid, VI, 1, 20a and 21b.

[66] Vā 58, 38; Bḍ II, 31, 39a; Mat 144, 38a; and Kūr I, 29, 5a.

[67] Kūr I, 29, 5b.

[68] Kūr I, 29, 23b-24; Vā 58, 50a; Bḍ II, 31, 51b.

[69] Kūr I, 29, 8-9 and Viṣ VI, 1, 32b.

[70] Kūr I, 29, 10-11; Vā 58, 52a; Bḍ II, 31, 53b and 54b.

[71] Kūr I, 29, 4; Mat 144, 35b-36a; Vā 58, 36; Bḍ II, 31, 36.

of the Brāhmans was often questioned. Men of all degrees pretended to be equal with the Brāhmans[72] and defied their authority[73] They did not care for the directions of the Brāhmans in fasting, observing vows and making gifts, but were guided by their own *a priori* speculations[74]. The Vaiśyas gave up trade and agriculture, and earned their livelihood by servitude or the exercise of mechanical arts[75]. In this way the pure Kṣatriyas and Vaiśyas were almost extinct[76], and the prevailing caste was the Śūdra[77]. The Purāṇas further say that in the Kali age the majority of kings were Śūdras[78]. This political supremacy of the Śūdras made their position felt by the members of the higher castes. The Purānas give interesting accounts of this elevated position of the Śūdras. The Kūrma-p. says: "The foolish (Śūdra) commoners drive away the Brāhmans when the latter are found occupying seats, and the Śūdra officers of state beat them. The Śūdras occupy better seats in the midst of Brāhmans, and the kings insult the latter. The Brāhmans, who are less educated in the Vedas and are less fortunate and powerful, honour the Śūdras with flowers, decoratives and other auspicious things. Though thus honoured, the Śūdras do not care to favour the Brāhmans even with a kind glance. The Brāhmans do not venture to enter the houses of the Śūdras, but stand at the gates for an opportunity to pay respect to them. The Brāhmans, who depend upon the Śūdras for their livelihood, surround them, when they are seated in vehicles, with a view to honouring them with praises, and teach them the Vedas. Thus even the best of Brāhmans fare against the directions of the Vedas, turn non-believers, and sell the fruit of their penance and sacrifices"[79]. The Śūdras, who had knowledge of Dharma and Artha, read the Vedas, and the Śūdra monarchs performed horse-sacrifices[80]. The Brāhmans became spiritually connected with the Śūdras who claimed equality of status as regards bed, seat and dining[81]. In religion also the Śūdras exhibited abnormal zeal. Naturally the Śūdras had a special attraction for Buddhism, because it denounced caste system and

[72] Viṣ VI, 1, 23a.
[73] Viṣ VI, 1, 49.
[74] Viṣ VI, 1, 15.
[75] Viṣ VI, 1, 36.
[76] Mat 144, 38b; Vā 58, 38c; Bd II, 31, 39b.
[77] Viṣ VI, 1, 51b—*śūdra-prāyās tathā varṇā bhaviṣyanti kalau yuge.* Also Mat 144, 78b; Bhāg XII, 2, 14a.
[78] Mat 144, 40a; Vā 58, 40a; and so on.
[79] Kūr I, 29, 17-23.
[80] Mat 144, 42-43; Bd II, 31, 67; Vā 58, 66b-67a. The Vāyu has wrong readings.
[81] Mat 144, 39; Vā 58, 39; Bd II, 31, 40; Kūr I, 29, 6.

challenged the supremacy of the Brāhmans. They were further encouraged by the acceptance of Buddhism and Jainism by the kings who belonged to their own caste, the result being that many of them became Buddhist monks and began to preach Buddhism. The Vāyu-(58, 59) and the Brahmāṇḍa-p. (II, 31, 59b-60a) say: "With white teeth, eyes brought under control, heads shaved and red clothes on, the Śūdras will perform religious deeds"[82].

Besides the above causes of disturbance, there were also others which seemed to destroy social peace and order. Kings turned robbers, and the officers lost all sympathy for their masters[83]. There was a great spread of Śaivism with the result that in the country buildings and squares were marked with tridents, and women used these to tie their hair[84]. Some people put on red clothes, some became Nirgranthas, some turned Kāpālikas, some sold the Vedas, and some sold the Tīrthas[85]. Women used to abandon their poor husbands and go to the rich[86]. They became prone to enjoyment, were lax about moral character[87], and disobeyed their husbands[88]. They were selfish, remained unclean and told lies[89]. They were wicked, and always hankered after union with wicked people[90]. The life and property of the people were made insecure by a remarkable increase of petty thieves, burglars and robbers[91]. Murder of children, women and heroes, slaughter of cows, abortion, cheating, misery, diseases, devastation etc. prevailed[92] and vitiated the atmosphere.

Thus the Purāṇas give a dismal picture of the troubles of the Kali age. In spite of obvious exaggeration, this description refers to the disintegration of the social fabric, on account of the vigour of Buddhism from the time of Aśoka Maurya, the position of the Śūdras as kings and perhaps also as high state officers, and the settlement of the immoral and casteless nomads, viz., Śakas, Pahlavas and Ābhīras.

The picture of the Hindu society, which the Jātakas present, is in many respects similar to that found in the Purāṇas. A study of the Jātakas creates in us the impression that 'the world of India

[82] Also cf. Kūr I, 29, 13 which reads '*añjitākṣāḥ*'.
[83] Vā 58, 42; Bḍ II, 31, 43; Viṣ VI, 1, 34.
[84] Kūr I, 29, 12; Bḍ (II, 31, 50) reads '*śiva-śūlā dvijās tathā*'.
[85] Vā 58, 64b-65a; Bḍ II, 31, 65; Kūr I, 29, 16; and Mat 144, 40b.
[86] Viṣ VI, 1, 18.
[87] Viṣ VI, 1, 21.
[88] Viṣ VI, 1, 29b.
[89] Viṣ VI, 1, 30.
[90] Viṣ VI, 1, 31.
[91] Vā 58, 60; Bḍ II, 31, 60b-61a; Kūr I, 29, 14.
[92] Mat 144, 43-46; Vā 58, 67-69; Bd II, 31, 68-70; Kūr I, 29, 15.

was one in which the ancient priestly caste had lost its authority, that nobles and merchants were more regarded than Brāhmans'[93], and that the people, not excepting even the Brāhmans, often did not care to set much store by the Brahmanical rules of castes and Āśramas[94]. The Brāhmans were often found to follow professions which were against the prescriptions of the 'lawbooks'. Thus, for earning their livelihood, they became caravan-guards, agriculturists, goatherds and cowherds, hawkers, carpenters, snake-charmers, hunters, carriage-drivers, wheelwrights, archers or weavers, without incurring any social stigma. Sometimes they mastered, or pretended to be masters of, astrology, palmistry, magic etc., for earning money. The Brāhmans, who were employed as state officials, were sometimes found guilty of misconduct for the sake of money[95]. There are indications in the Jātakas that among the Kṣatriyas and the middle classes also the pursuance of the hereditary profession was not compulsory, and the change of vocations was of common occurrence[96].

In the India of the Jātakas the gulf between the different castes was narrowed to a great extent. There are many instances in which the members of different castes—princes, Brāhmans, Śreṣṭhins—are found to form friendship, to interdine, to intermarry and to send their sons to the same teacher, there being no reflection passed on them for doing so[97]. That such contamination of castes was in progress in the early centuries of the Christian era is also evidenced by the Nasik inscription of Rājā Vasiṣṭhīputra Śrī Pulumāyī in which he is said to have 'stopped the contamination of the four Varṇas' (*viṇivatita-cātuvaṇa-sakarasa*)[98].

Buddhism encouraged Pravrajyā (wandering mendicancy) for the attainment of Nirvāṇa, and, as a result, the order of the four stages of life was often violated. The Jātakas contain numerous examples of Kṣatriyas and Brāhmans who turned wandering mendicants immediately after studentship[99]. The people believed that the whole family was sanctified if any of its members accepted Pravrajyā, and consequently parents and relatives sometimes

93 CHI, Vol. I, p. 221. Fick, Social Organisation, pp. 89 ff. Cf. also Viṣ VI, 1, 19.

94 CHI, Vol. I, p. 210.

95 Ibid., Vol. I, pp. 203-204 and 209.

Isan Chandra Ghosh, Jātaka, Vol. II, Upakramaṇikā, pp. 11-12. Rhys Davids, Buddhist India, pp. 56-57.

96 Rhys Davids, Buddhist India, pp. 56 ff. CHI, Vol. I, p. 210.

97 CHI, Vol. I, p. 209.

98 Ep. Ind., VIII, 1905-1906, pp. 60-61.

99 See Samṛddhi-jātaka—Fausböll, No. 167; Lomaśa-kāśyapa-jātaka—Fausböll, No. 433; Kṛṣṇa-jātaka—Fausböll, No. 440; and Śoṇananda-jātaka—Fausböll, No. 532.

instigated their wards to become wandering mendicants[100]. The wandering life was not restricted among the Brāhmaṇs and the Kṣatriyas. People of other castes also were equally free to accept it. The Bodhisattva in the Kalyāṇadharma-jātaka (Fausbôll, No. 171) was a Śreṣṭhin of Benares; Kuddāla-paṇḍita in the Kuddāla-jātaka (Fausbôll, No. 70) was a Parṇika; Mātaṅga in the Mātaṅga-jātaka (Fausbôll, No. 497), and Citta and Saṃbhūta in the Citta-saṃbhūta-jātaka (Fausbôll, No. 498) were Caṇḍālas; and Dukūlaka in the Śyāma-jātaka (Fausbôll, No. 540) was a Niṣāda.

Buddhism allowed more freedom to women especially in religious matters, and thus became instrumental to their advancement. The attractive power of Buddha's Dhamma was felt as well by women as by men. With the hope of better rebirth, or the total annihilation of it, the former often renounced the world and accepted the more rigorous life of the Bhikkhunis[101]. We should mention here that the Śvetāmbara Jains also gave women admission into their order. This is shown especially by the frequent mention of nuns in the Mathurā inscriptions. The freedom which Buddhism and Jainism thus allowed to women could not but make them have, at least in a good number of cases, a far greater attraction for these two faiths than for Hinduism.

About the conduct of the Śūdras we know little from Buddhist literature. That a strained relation existed between them and the Brāhmans during this period, is evident from Manu who says: "Let (the first part of) a Brāhman's name (denote something) auspicious, a Kṣatriya's be connected with power, and a Vaiśya's with wealth, but a Śūdra's (express something) contemptible"[102]. The selection of such a name for the Śūdra seems to be the outcome of great enmity and deep hatred.

We have given above the accounts of Indian society as gathered from two opposite sources—one Purāṇic and the other Buddhistic. The similarity between the two accounts is very great. In numerous cases what the Purāṇas formulate, the Jātakas seem to illustrate. This striking agreement between the two accounts proves that they are not so much imaginary as we may take them to be, but have some historical value. These accounts show that the authority of the Vedas was often not recognised, the Varṇāśramadharma was neglected, and there was a remarkable increase in the number of Saṃnyāsins and Parivrājakas. The

[100] See Cullaśreṣṭhi-jātaka—Fausbôll, No. 4; Aśāta-mantra-jātaka—Fausbôll, No. 61; and Saṃstava-jātaka—Fausbôll, No. 162.

[101] Bimala Charan Law, Women in Buddhist Literature, pp. 66 ff.

[102] Manu-smṛti II, 31.

social position of the orthodox Brāhmans was much lowered, and there was a gradual decrease in their numerical strength, many of them being influenced by the non-Brahmanical ideas and practices. The Śūdras became defiant of the upper three castes, and often went out of the Hindu fold to the great disadvantage of their co-religionists, especially the Brāhmans. Women became prone to demoralisation, and many of them took up the wandering life and thus created disadvantages to their families. In short, the condition of Brahmanism became very insecure. Consequently, the Brahmanists felt it necessary to make an attempt to re-establish the Varṇāśramadharma, the authority of the Vedas, and the moral rules among women, Śūdras, and those members of the upper three castes who, being influenced by the faiths other than Brahmanism, disregarded the Vedas and violated the rules of the Varṇāśramadharma. This attempt seems to have been made by two sections of people in two different ways, viz., by the orthodox Brahmanists who first began to preach the performance of Gṛhya rites through Smṛti works, and by the more numerous Smārta-Vaiṣṇavas and Smārta-Śaivas who introduced Smṛti materials into the Mahābhārata and the Purāṇas to preach Vaiṣṇavism and Śaivism as against the heretical religions and also to establish the Varṇāśramadharma, the authority of the Vedas, and the moral rules not only among the Vaiṣṇavas and the Śaivas but also among others. That this intention was at the base of the introduction of Smṛti-matter into the Mahābhārata and the Purāṇas is evidenced by the Purāṇas themselves. The Bhāgavata-p. says: "Women, Śūdras and the mean twice-born are unfit for hearing the Vedas, and are, therefore, ignorant of performing, in this world, the good (in the shape of) work; for this reason, the sage, by (his) grace, compiled the legend of Bhārata, with a view that their good in this behalf may be effected"[103]; and "Verily, pretending (to compile) the Bhārata, I have pointed out the meaning of the Vedas, and in which (said Bhārata) can surely be found the meaning of (all those subjects of which) Dharma is the first, even by women, Śūdras and others"[104]. The Devībhāgavata says: "Women, Śūdras and the mean twice-born (dvija-bandhu) are not entitled to hear the Vedas; it is only for their good that the Purāṇas have been written"[105]. The contents of the Mahābhārata and the earlier Purāṇas (viz., Mārkaṇḍeya, Vāyu, Brahmāṇḍa and Viṣṇu) as compared with those of the later Purāṇas seem also to betray such a motive of their authors. It

103 Bhāg I, 4, 25.

104 Bhāg I, 4, 29.

105 Dbh I, 3, 21.

should be noted here that this attempt of the Smārta devotees of the different gods to preach their respective faiths with a view to establishing the Varṇāśramadharma and the authority of the Vedas was responsible for giving rise to Purāṇic Vaiṣṇavism, Śaivism, Brahmāism, Śāktism etc. as distinct from their popular prototypes[106].

[106] By popular Vaiṣṇavism, Śaivism and Brahmāism we mean those types of these religions which were current among the common people, were regardless of the Brahmanical rules of castes and stages, and imbibed Tantric practices. Popular Śāktism is the Śāktism of the Tantras.

CHAPTER II

THE HINDU SOCIETY FROM THE 3RD TO THE 6TH CENTURY A.D., AND THE PURĀṆIC RITES AND CUSTOMS IN THE SECOND STAGE OF THEIR DEVELOPMENT

When the Brahmanists and the Smārta sectaries began their attempts to re-establish the Varṇāśramadharma, the authority of the Vedas, and the moral rules, they were confronted by a fresh set of troubles which were no less vigorous than those already mentioned. These troubles were caused by the foreign invasions from the north-west and by the spread and popularity of Trantricism.

After the reign of the Kushan king Vāsudeva, Northern India, excluding the Punjab, entered upon one of the darkest periods of her history. This period extended from the downfall of the Kushan and Āndhra dynasties, about 220 or 230 A.D., to the rise of the Imperial Guptas[1]. 'The period evidently was one of extreme confusion associated with foreign invasions from the north-west, which is reflected in the muddled statements of the Purāṇas concerning the Ābhīras, Gardabhilas, Śakas, Yavanas, Bāhlīkas and other outlandish dynasties named as the successors of the Āndhras. The dynastics thus enumerated clearly were to a large extent contemporary with one another, not consecutive, and none of them could claim paramount rank'[2]. The accounts of the foreign invaders contained in the Purāṇas seem, at times, to-be supported by the inscriptions. A Nasik inscription[3] of the Ābhīra king Īśvarasena, son of Śivadatta, shows that in Mahārāṣṭra 'the Āndhras were succeeded by a dynasty of the Ābhīras'[4]. In the

[1] Smith, EHI, p. 292.

[2] Ibid., p. 290. Also cf. Rapson, Cat. of Ind. Coins in the Brit. Mus., Introduction, p. 45.

[3] Ep. Ind., VIII, 1905-6, p. 88.

[4] Rapson, *op. cit.*, Introduction, p. 44. D. R. Bhandarkar in Ind. Ant., Vol. XLVII, 1918, p. 156.

inscription Śivadatta is not called a king; so it seems that Īśvarasena was an upstart. This Īśvarasena has been identified with a king named Īśvaradatta, whose coins have been found in Malwa, Gujrat and Kathiawar, and who is looked upon as an Ābhīra intruder[5]. Īśvaradatta has been assigned by D. R. Bhandarkar to A.D. 188-190[6]. That the Ābhīras became powerful about this time is also shown by the Gunda inscription of Rudrasiṃha I (about 180 A.D.) which 'records a donation made at the village of Rasopadra by the Ābhīra General (senāpati) Rudrabhūti, son of General Bāhaka'[7].

The conduct of the foreign invaders and the disturbance they created in society are described in the Purāṇas, viz., Vāyu (99, 387-412), Brahmāṇḍa (III, 74, 190-214), Matsya (273, 25-33), Viṣṇu (IV, 24, 18-25) and Bhāgavata (XII, 1, 38-41). In order to acquaint ourselves with the nature of these Purāṇic descriptions we give below the translation of Viṣ IV, 24, 18-25.

"These will all be contemporary monarchs reigning over the earth; kings of churlish spirit, violent temper, and ever addicted to falsehood and unrighteousness. They will inflict death on women, children and cows; they will seize upon the property of others; they will be of limited power, and will, for the most part, rapidly rise and fall; their lives will be short, their desires insatiable; and they will display but little Dharma. The people of various countries will intermingle with them and follow their example; and the barbarians, being powerful under the patronage of princes, and the purer tribes, acting in a contrary manner (*viparyayena vartamānāḥ*), will destroy the people. Wealth and piety will decrease day by day, until the world will be wholly depraved. Then property alone will confer rank; wealth will be the only source of Dharma; passion will be the sole bond of union between the sexes; falsehood will be the only means of success in litigation; and women will be objects merely of sexual gratification. The Earth will be venerated but for her mineral treasures; the Brahmanical thread will constitute a Brāhman; external types will be the only distinctions of the several orders of life; dishonesty will be the (universal) means of subsistence; weakness will be the cause of dependence; menace and presumption will be substituted for learning; liberality will constitute Dharma; simple ablution will be purification; mutual assent will be marriage; fine clothes will be dignity; and water or a temple afar off will be

[5] Rapson, *op. cit.*, Introduction, pp. 133-136. Ind. Ant., Vol. XLVII, 1918, p. 156. JRAS, 1890, p. 657.

[6] ASI, Annual Report, 1913-14, p. 230.

[7] Ind. Ant., Vol. X, 1881, p. 157.

esteemed as a holy place (tīrtha). Amidst all castes, he who is the strongest will reign over a principality thus vitiated by many faults. The people, unable to bear the heavy burdens imposed upon them by their avaricious sovereigns, will take refuge amongst the valleys of the mountains, and will be glad to feed upon (wild) honey, herbs, roots, fruits, leaves and flowers; their only convering will be the bark of trees; and they will be exposed to the cold, and wind, and sun, and rain. No man's life will exceed three and twenty years. Thus, in the Kali age, shall decay constantly proceed, until the human race approaches its annihilation".

Such is the description given by the Purāṇas. What we specially gather from this description is that, as a result of political unrest and of the intercourse of the people with casteless and immoral foreigners, famine and pestilence broke out, people became regardless of the Śrauta and Smārta Dharma, and immorality spread. Though exaggeration is not at all impossible in the Purāṇic descriptions, the numerous verses found common in those portions of the Purāṇas which deal with the evils of the foreign invasions show that they are not purely the productions of the fanciful brains of later interpolators but are derived from a common source which must be very old, and that the people believed deeply in the truth of this source.

After this period of anarchy had been over, light again dawned with the rise of the imperial Guptas. Under these powerful Hindu monarchs the people lived happily and peacefully, Brahmanical Hinduism was restored to popular favour, and the condition of the Brāhmans was improved both socially and economically. The period of the Guptas can be called a golden age for the Brāhmans, but that golden age also was destined to have its end. The decline of the Gupta power was followed by the irruption of the casteless and savage nomads, known as the Hūṇas, under the leadership of Toramāṇa, who became the ruler of Malwa. After his death about 502 A.D., he was succeeded by his son Mihiragula, who was too notorious for his implacable cruelty. That at least during the time of the decline of the Gupta power and the reigns of the Hūṇa sovereigns the Brahmanical rules of conduct were disregarded, is proved by the Mandasor stone pillar inscription of Yaśodharman[8], which says:

"(Line 2).—He, to whose arm, as if (to the arm) of (the god) Śārṅgapāṇi, ... the earth betook itself (for succour), when *it was afflicted by kings of the present age*, who manifested pride; who were cruel through want of proper training; who, from

[8] Fleet, Gupta Inscriptions, pp. 146-148.

delusion, *transgressed the path of good conduct (laṅghitācāra-mārgair mohāt ....); * (and) *who were destitute of virtuous delights* :—

(Line 3).—He who, in *this age which is the ravisher of good behaviour* .... not associating with other *kings who adopted a reprehensible course of conduct (nindyācāreṣu yo 'smin vinayamuṣi yuge kalpanā-mātra-vṛttyā rājasv anyeṣu* ....) ...."

A further indication in this direction is contained in the Betul inscription (dated 518-519 A.D.) of Mahārāja Saṃkṣobha wherein he is said to have been intent upon establishing the religious duties of the castes and the different periods of life *(varṇāśramadharma-sthāpanābhiratena)*[9].

After the defeat of Mihiragula by Yaśodharman about 528 A.D., India enjoyed 'almost complete immunity from foreign attack for nearly five centuries' [10], after which the Muhammadans disturbed the peace of the country with invasions and occupations. With these, however, we are not concerned here.

We have seen how, after the end of the Kushan rule with the death of Vāsudeva, the position of the Brahmanical religion and the Brāhmans was made insecure by the foreign monarchies. We shall now turn our attention to the other more dangerous source of trouble, viz., Tantricism.

It is not yet definitely known how and when Tantricism arose, but that it is of considerable antiquity cannot be denied. It is purely of non-Vedic origin. Its ideas and practices also are non-Vedic. In its early character it does not seem to have recognised the Varṇāśramadharma and the authority of the Vedas, though in later times it could not totally ignore these.

From about the beginning of the fifth century A.D., if not earlier, the Vaiṣṇavas, and probably also the Śaivas, came to be influenced by Tantricism. The extant Saṃhitās of the Pāñcarātras are perhaps the earliest available records of this influence. How dangerously the Tantric ideas and practices influenced the Pāñcarātras we shall see from an examination of the contents of the Jayākhya-saṃhitā which has been assigned by B. Bhattacharya to about 450 A.D. on the strength of doctrinal and palaeographical evidences[11].

The Jayākhya-saṃhitā is looked upon 'by the Vaiṣṇavas as one of the three most ancient and most authoritative works of the Pāñcarātra Āgama', the other two being the Sāttvata- and the

[9] Ep. Ind., VIII, 1905-6, pp. 287-288. [10] Smith, EHI, p. 341.

[11] Jayākhya-saṃhitā, Foreword, pp. 26-34.

Pauṣkara-saṃhitā. It is divided into 33 Paṭalas, or chapters, dealing with creation, dissertations on the Mantras, oblations to Fire (agni-kārya), initiation, consecration of images or pictures, investiture with the sacred thread (pavitrāropaṇa), the different types of Vaiṣṇavas and their characteristics, funeral ceremony, cremation of the dead, penances, attainment of supernatural powers by muttering spells, and Yoga. All these rites and practices, not excepting even those which are Vedic in origin, are highly imbued with Tantric elements. The method of bath (Paṭala IX), without which none is entitled to take part in any religious rite, is full of Tantric practices. The Tantric spell, called Astra-mantra, is to be used in procuring bathing soil, in sanctifying that part of the river-bank where the soil is kept, in consecrating the sacred thread, in taking lumps of mud which are thrown in all directions to allay the impediments of bath, and so on. Mantra-nyāsa and Mudrās are to be performed with a view to sanctifying the water which, flowing or stagnant, may have been polluted by insects. The Mūla-mantra is to be used in purifying a lump of mud which is then to be thrown into water in order to bring there the holy places, viz., Prayāga, Cakra-tīrtha, Prabhāsa, Puṣkara etc., and the holy waters of the Gaṅgā and the Yamunā. Towards the end of the bath the man is to sit in water, practise Prāṇāyāma accompanied with the performance of Mudrās, meditate on the deity, and give libations to the patriarchs. After bath he is to put on dry clothes and offer libations of water to the gods, sages etc. This method of bath is called Audaka-snāna, i.e., bath in water. In the Mantra-snāna (i.e., bath with the spell) also Nyāsas and Mudrās are to be performed.

After the bath is over, the man is to practise Samādhi (Paṭala X) and Mantra-nyāsa (Paṭala XI), the latter requiring the performance of the Mudrā also.

Then comes the worship of Viṣṇu which consists of the Mānasa-yāga (mental worship—Paṭala XII), Bāhya-yāga (external worship —Paṭala XIII), Japa (muttering of the Mantra—Paṭala XIV) and Agni-kārya (oblations to Fire—Paṭala XV). The mental worship has many Tantric elements, viz., Mantra-nyāsa, Mudrā etc. The method of external worship also is highly Tantric. It abounds in Tantric Mantras, Yantras, Maṇḍalas, Nyāsas, Mudrās, Bhūta-śuddhi etc. There is no necessity of making gifts or paying priestly fees to Brāhmans. The Agni-kārya, in which Viṣṇu is worshipped on fire and which is sometimes called Homa, is much more of a Tantric than Vedic character. It consists of various operations, viz., Kuṇḍa-saṃskāra, Mekhalā-pūjana etc., which require the citation of Tantric Mantras (Mūla-mantra, Astra-Mantra, Hṛdaya-mantra,

Kavaca-mantra, Netra-mantra, etc.) and the performance of Mudrās. The whole procedure is peculiar, and has not much similiarity with its Vedic prototype. It is noteworthy that no Vedic Mantra, except the syllable 'Oṃ', is used throughout the whole function.

The method of initiation, described in Paṭalas XVI-XIX, is purely Tantric. It consists of parts which have been derived from, or influenced by, the Tantras. It is open to all the members of the four castes, not even excepting women and children. In this form of initiation the position of the spiritual preceptor is not the monopoly of Brāhmans. It is true that Brāhman preceptors are generally preferred, but where such preceptors are not available, worthy people of the other three castes also are allowed to act as such for those belonging to their own respective castes or to those inferior to their own.

The methods of Devatā-pratiṣṭhā and Pavitrāropaṇa, which are dealt with in Paṭalas XX and XXI, have also many Tantric elements.

The method of Śrāddha (Paṭala XXIII), though Vedic in origin, is, as found in the Jayākhya, much less Vedic than Tantric. The firm belief of the Pāñcarātras in the magic power of the Tantric spells and practices, and their great devotion to Viṣṇu have found their way even into this Vedic rite. Consequently, the procedures have been changed without caring for the directions of the Vedic authorities; some innovations have been made; citations of Tantric formulae instead of the Vedic ones, and the performance of Mudrās and Nyāsas are required at every step; the patriarchs are to be meditated upon as identical with the Vyūha-forms (Pradyumna, Aniruddha, Saṃkarṣaṇa and Vāsudeva) of Viṣṇu and worshipped; and so on. Only the Pāñcarātra Vaiṣṇavas are to be invited in the ceremony, and gifts are to be made to them only.

Paṭala XXIV, which deals with the cremation of a dead body, exhibits Tantric influence in the worship which is required before cremation and in the rites ancillary to it. It does not involve making gifts to anybody.

In Prāyaścitta (Paṭala XXV) the Pāñcarātras are not at all guided by the authorities of the Vedic schools. While the Vedic Aryans subject themselves to severe punishments and self-torture to atone for the crimes committed, the Pāñcarātras take recourse, for purification in all cases, to the magic power of the sectarian Mantras, so deep-rooted their belief in these Mantras is. Whatever heinous crimes a Vaiṣṇava may commit, he is sure to be free from sin, according to the Pāñcarātras, by muttering a sectarian Mantra, the peculiarity being that the nature of the Mantra and the number of mutterings differ with the nature of the crime. In some cases, of course, the Pāñcarātras are found to perform Homa and observe certain rules about food and bath while muttering the Mantras, but these rules are nothing in comparison with the strictness of those of the Brahmanical lawbooks. Let us cite one example or two for the sake of comparison. In the case of adultery with the wife of one's Guru,—a crime which is included in the Mahāpātakas or great sins by the Vedic lawgivers,—Gautama says: "One, who has defiled the bed of his Guru, shall lie on a heated bed of iron. Or (he) shall embrace the iron image of a woman glowing with heat. Or (he) shall cut off his generative organ together with testicles, hold these in his hands, and walk straight towards the south-west till his body collapses. If dead, (he) becomes pure"[12]. According to the Jayākhya-saṃhitā (XXV, 31-35), a Pāñcarātra Vaiṣṇava, who is guilty of this crime, is to mutter the Nṛsiṃha-mantra, the number of mutterings varying as the crime is voluntary or otherwise. He is also to live on alms and remain silent during the muttering. After the muttering is over, he is to perform Yāga (i.e., worship) and Homa. Again, in the case of the murder of a Brāhman Gautama ordains: "The murderer of a Brāhman shall fall, (after being) emaciated, thrice into a fire. Or (he) shall be the target for armed men in a battle. Or, remaining chaste, he may, during twelve years, enter the village for the purpose of begging, carrying a staff and a skull in his hand, and proclaiming his deed. If he meets an Ārya, he shall step out of the road. Standing by day, sitting at night, and bathing in the morning, at noon, and in the evening, he may be purified (after twelve years). Or by saving the life of a Brāhman. Or if he is, at least, thrice vanquished in (trying to recover) the property (of a Brāhman) stolen (by robbers). Or by bathing (with the priests) at (the end of) a horse-sacrifice. Or at (the end of) any other (Vedic) sacrifice, provided that an Agniṣṭut (sacrifice) forms part of it"[13]. But the Jayākhya-saṃhitā (XXV, 23-26a) says in such a case: "By murdering a Brāhman voluntarily, (the sinner) should mutter the Siṃha-mantra untiringly and incessantly for two years, take a small quantity of food procured without asking for it, bathe thrice (daily), and perform Nyāsas. After the expiry of two years, (he) should go to a holy place or a temple and practise the vows Kṛcchra, Cāndrāyaṇa etc. according to his capacity. When the vows are over, (he) should be initiated again after the Navanābha (fashion). He should give away all his belongings to his preceptor and, with the latter's permission, to the devotees (of

[12] Gaut. XXIII, 8-11. [13] Ibid., XXII, 2-10.

Viṣṇu)". In penances no gifts are to be made to Brāhmans—priests or otherwise. In the three cases, viz., the wilful murder of a Brāhman, the killing of a cow, and the commission of mistakes in citing the Mantra during worship etc., where gifts are ordained, the recipients are not Brāhmans. In the first case, the sinner is to give away all his belongings to his preceptor and, with the latter's permission, to other Vaiṣṇavas; in the second, he is to give two cows to his preceptor; and in the third, he is to make twelve kinds of gifts (cows, food, gold, gems etc.) to twelve Ācāryas.

The Jayākhya-saṃhitā ignores priesthood and gifts to non-Pāñcarātra Brāhmans. If the help and co-operation of anybody are needed, he is the preceptor, and to the preceptor the gifts often go. The other recipients of gifts are the Ācāryas, Yatis, Āptas, Ekāntins, Vaikhānasas, etc.—all belonging to the Pāñcarātra sect. In Śrāddha the Pāñcarātras only are invited, and gifts are made to them only. Generally gifts do not form part of penances. In the three cases where gifts are ordained, the recipients are, as we have seen above, the preceptors or the Ācāryas. The method of consecration of an image (Paṭala XX) requires that at the beginning four Ācāryas or Sādhakas are to be honoured with cloth etc. During consecration, the Brāhmans (probably of the Pāñcarātra sect) are to be called upon to cite verses from the four Vedas, and the preceptor, the Yatis, the Āptas, the Ekāntins and others also are to be invited to attend. All these people are to be honoured with scents, flowers, food, priestly fees, etc. In Pavitrāropaṇa (Paṭala XXI), the preceptor, who is said to be like Viṣṇu, is to be honoured with fees, food and drink, and gifts are to be made to the Vaiṣṇavas, viz., the Yatis, Āptas, Vaikhānasas and others, there being made no distinction of castes but the merits of making gifts increasing as the caste is higher. By gifts of land, money, houses etc. made to the Vaikhānasas, Karma-sāttvatas, Śikhins and householders—all belonging to the Pāñcarātra sect—for the worship of Viṣṇu, the donor is said to attain final release or to repair to the place of the Bhagavat (Jayākhya XXII, 19-22).

The Pāñcarātras attach more importance to their own sectarian scriptures than to the Vedas. If they are required to read anything with devotion, it is the Pāñcarātra Saṃhitās, because their aim is to gain knowledge of Vāsudeva, the 'final Truth'. The Jayākhya (I, 13-14) says: "In case the final Truth remains unknown, there can be no permanent residence in heaven—not to speak of freedom from bondage—through (the) mere (performance of) sacrifices, mastering the Vedas, (making) gifts, working, or observing various vows such as the Cāndrāyaṇa etc." The study of the Vedas is meant by the Pāñcarātras for a mere acquaintance with the contents of these works. Aparārka quotes a passage from a Pāñcarātra Saṃhitā to show that the Pāñcarātras read the Vedas for mere knowledge[14].

A strong belief in the magic power of the Tantric Mantras permeates the whole of the Jayākhya-saṃhitā. Long chapters have been devoted to dissertations on these. It is difficult to find out any Mantra which is not Tantric. These Tantric Mantras are believed to have the power of conferring Bhukti (enjoyment) and Mukti (final release)[15]. This belief is at the basis of the use of some Mantras for Vaśīkaraṇa, Māraṇa, etc., and for the different kinds of Sādhana (viz., Yakṣiṇī-sādhana, Gulikā-sādhana etc.,), and for attaining Brahma which is called 'mantra-mūrti'.

The above analysis of the contents of the Jayākhya-saṃhitā clearly shows the non-Brahmanical character of the ideas, rites and practices of the Pāñcarātras of the Saṃhitās. The contents of other Saṃhitās also are in general agreement with those of the Jayākhya.

It is not yet known when the Śaivas began to be influenced by Tantricism and to produce the Āgamas. That the Tantric influence began to be imbibed by them quite early cannot be denied. None of the Śaiva Āgamas of this period being yet available to us *in toto,* we are almost in total darkness about their contents[16]. We shall, therefore, have to look to other sources for information about these Āgamic Śaivas who are distinct from the Pāśupatas. There is a story in the Bengal Mss of the Padmapurāṇa[17], according to which Citrasena, a descendant of the Lunar race and king of the land of the Drāviḍas, was at first a man of virtue and performed many sacrifices, but was afterwards converted by the Śaivas to their faith. In this story the Śaivas are described as 'veda-bāhya' and 'pāṣaṇḍa'. They are said to preach as follows: "What (is the necessity) of gifts, or other vows, or the Vedas, or the sacrifices? The status of a Gaṇapati is sure to be attained as soon as the ashes are besmeared (on the body) . . . . . . (There is) no virtue like the ashes, no austerity like these . . . . . The blind, the humpbacked, the stupid, the illiterate or the (members of the different) castes such as the Śūdra, if (they are) characterised by matted hair, are undoubtedly worthy of respect. Viśvāmitra, though a Kṣatriya, became a Brāhman by austerity.

14 Aparārka's com. on Yāj., p. 16. 15 Jayākhya-saṃhitā VI, 4.

16 According to tradition there were 28 Śaiva Āgamas. 'Only fragments of 20 Āgamas have been preserved. Portions of two Upāgamas, Mṛgendra and Pauṣkara, are printed'. Cf. Eliot, Hinduism and Buddhism, II, pp. 204 ff.

17 Māgha-māhātmya, Uttara-kh., Ms No. 931 (dated 1311 Śaka) in the D. U. Mss Lib.

Vālmīki, a thief, became the foremost of Brāhmans. So, no discrimination should be made in this matter by the Śiva-worshippers. (One) becomes a Brāhman by means of austerity, and the determination of castes should be made in this way". From this it appears that these Śaivas cared little for the Vedas or the Brahmanical rules of castes and duties. From their view of castes and from the consmopolitan nature of their faith it seems that they did not recognise priesthood also.

The Tantric elements in the Pāñcarātra Saṃhitās and the Śaiva Āgamas, and the evidence of the Gangdhar stone inscription of Viśvavarman[18] prove that the Tantric cult attained popularity at a very early period. It is not, however, known when the Tantras began to be written. The discovery of a Ms of the Kubjikāmata-tantra written in Gupta characters proves that Tantric works began to be composed not later than the 7th century A.D.

The spread and popularity of the Tantric cult even among the Brāhmans and Kṣatriyas[19] were not at all favourable to the Brahmanical religion, because there are serious differences between the Tantra and the works of the Vedic tradition. 'In the first place the Śāstra (i.e., Tantra) contains provisions which are applicable for all without distinction of race, castes or sex. The Śāstra affords to all, with freedom from Vaidika exclusiveness, the practical method .... which qualifies the Sādhaka for the reception of the higher doctrine of the path of knowledge (Jñāna-mārga). The Śūdra and women are not, as in the case of Vaidikācāra, under any ban. As the Gautamīya Tantra (Chapter I) says, people of all castes, and whether men or women, may receive its Mantras .... In the Cakra there is no caste at all, even the lowest Cāṇḍāla being deemed, whilst therein, higher than Brāhmans. The Mahānirvāṇa Tantra (XIV, verses 187 and 184) says: 'That low Kaula who refuses to initiate a Cāṇḍāla or

[18] This inscription is dated about 424-425 A.D. Among the verses inscribed on it, there are two which run as follows:—

"*mātṛ(tṝ)ṇāñca (pramu) dita-ghanātyartha- nihrādinīnām|*
tantrodbhūta-prabala-pavanodvarttitāmbhonidhīnām||
. . . . . . gatam idaṃ ḍākinī-saṃprakīrṇam|
veśmātyugraṃ nṛpati-sacivo 'kārayat puṇya-hetoḥ||"

'Also, for the sake of religious merit, the counsellor of the king caused to be built this very terrible abode, ... (and) filled with female ghouls, of the divine Mothers, who utter loud and tremendous shouts in joy, (and) who stir up the (very) oceans with the mighty wind rising from the magic rites of their religion'.

Fleet, Gupta Inscriptions, pp. 76 and 78.

[19] Cf. Kūr I, 29, 25.

a Yavana into the Kaula-dharma, considering him to be inferior, or a woman, out of disrespect for her, goes the downward way. All two-footed beings in this world, from the Vipra to the inferior castes, are competent for Kulācāra'[20]'. According to the Tantras worthy women can serve as spiritual preceptors under certain conditions[21]. The freedom, which the Tantras allow to the members of all castes in worshipping the deities, seriously discourages priesthood. The rituals, which are all non-Vedic, do not require gifts to be made to Brāhmans. The circle-worship of the Left-hand Śāktas is really repulsive and demoralising. It requires, among other things, an equal number of men and women without distinction of caste or relationship, and the partaking of the five Tattvas, viz., wine, meat, fish, parched grain and sexual intercourse. The Tantriks believe in sorcery which may be meant for either white or black purposes.

The ideas, rites and practices of the Pāñcarātras, the Āgamic Śaivas and the Tantriks that have been described above, amply testify to their non-Brahmanical, or rather anti-Brahmanical, character. The spread of such ideas, rites and practices among the people could not but affect Brahmanism very seriously. So, the authors of the Purāṇas could not remain satisfied with introducing only those Smṛti-topics which came within the scope of the earlier Smṛti Saṃhitās; but they deemed it necessary to add chapters on Pūjā, Vrata, Homa, Saṃdhyā, Utsarga etc., which they rendered free from Tantric elements as far as practicable and infused with Vedic rituals. The occurrence of these topics in the comparatively late Purāṇas, or parts thereof, and the way in which the Purāṇas denounce the scriptures (not even excepting those of their respective sects) which imbibed Tantric influence, tend to support the above view. In Kūr I, 12, which was undoubtedly interpolated by the Smārta-Śāktas (i.e., those Śāktas who, like the Smārta-Vaiṣṇavas and Smārta-Śaivas, worshipped the Tantric deities, but observed the Smṛti rules with equal devotion), the literatures of the Kāpālas, Bhairavas, Yāmalas, Vāmas, Ārhatas, Kāpilas, Pāñcarātras and 'many others of this type' are called 'śruti-smṛti-viruddha' and are said to be intended to delude those who mislead others[22]. On the other hand, Devī is made to say in this very chapter: "Sacrifices etc., which are ordained by Śruti and Smṛti, are known as Dharma. Nothing else is the source of Dharma; it is the Veda from which Dharma originated"[23]. In Kūr I, 16, which was added

[20] Avalon, Principles of Tantra, Vol. I, Introduction, pp. lxix-lxx.

[21] Tantrasāra, edited and published by Pañca-śikha Bhaṭṭācārya, Calcutta, p. 8.

[22] Kūr I, 12, 257-259.

[23] Kūr I, 12, 251b-252.

by the Pāśupatas, the Śāstras of Kāpālas, Nākulas, Vāmas, Bhairavas, Pūrva-paścimas, Pāñcarātras, Pāśupatas (i.e., Āgamic Śaivas) and others are said to have been meant for the delusion of those outside the pale of the Vedas[24]. Similarly, in Kūr II, 37, 146-147, II, 21, 32 and II, 16, 15, all of which were added by the Pāśupatas, the scriptures of the Vāmas, Pāśupatas (i.e., Āgamic Śaivas), Lāṅgalas, Bhairavas, Pāñcarātras and others are said to be delusive, and the sectaries are called 'Pāṣaṇḍas' with whom none is advised to speak. In the Devībhāgavata, which belongs to the Smārta-Śāktas, Devī says to Himālaya: "What is ordained by Śruti and Smṛti is called Dharma. What the other scriptures say is the shadow of Dharma. The Veda arose from my omniscient and omnipotent self . . . . The king should banish from his kingdom those outlaws who forsake the Veda-dharma and take recourse to another . . . . The various other Śāstras found on earth, which are contradictory to Śruti and Smṛti, are Tāmasa pure and simple. Śiva composed the scriptures of the Vāmas, Kāpālikas, Kaulas and Bhairavas with the only intention of delusion. For the deliverance of those best Brāhmans who were burnt by the curses of Dakṣa, Bhṛgu and Dadhīca and were caused to deviate from the path of the Vedas, the Āgamas of the Śaivas, Vaiṣṇavas, Sauras, Śāktas and Gāṇapatyas were written as steps (sopāna) by Śaṃkara. In some places of these works there are some portions which do not go against the Vedas. By accepting these (portions) the Vaidikas do not incur sin"[25].

From the above discussion about the different religious movements and the foreign invasions it appears that the composite (vyāmiśra) character of the present Purāṇas is due to the attempt made by the Smārta Brāhman sectaries to preach and popularise their respective faiths against the heresies, and to establish the Brahmanical rules of castes and duties and the authority of the Vedas among the followers of at least their respective religions. It is to be noted that the composite Dharma, which the extant Purāṇas preach, has never been allowed by the orthodox Brahmanists to be identified with their own. However much the Smārta sectaries may have exalted the Purāṇic Dharma, it has been regarded by the orthodox Brahmanists as only inferior to the Vedic. As an example we may quote Vyāsa who says:

"dharma-śuddhim abhīpsadbhir na vedād anyad iṣyate|
dharmasya kāraṇaṃ śuddhaṃ miśram anyat prakīrtitam||

[24] Kūr I. 16, 115-117.

[25] Dbh VII, 39, verses 15-16a, 25a-b and 26-31. Also cf. XI, 1; 21-32.

ataḥ sa paramo dharmo yo vedād avagamyate|
avaraḥ sa tu vijñeyo yaḥ purāṇādiṣu sthitaḥ||" [26]

'Nothing other than the Veda is required by those who want purity of Dharma. (The Veda) is the pure source of Dharma; others are called composite. So, the Dharma, which is derived from the Veda, is the best. But that (Dharma), which is contained in the Purāṇas etc., is known to be inferior'. So, it is evident that the orthodox Brahmanists (i.e., those followers of Brahmanism who performed the Śrauta and Smārta rites only but did not worship the sectarian deities) continued to exist side by side with the followers of Purāṇic Hinduism though there was a continuous fall in their number, and that they must have had sympathy with the popularisation of the Purāṇic Dharma.

[26] Vyāsa quoted in Halāyudha's Brāhmaṇa-sarvasva, Ms No. K 554 (D. U. Mss Lib.), fol. 3b; in Aparārka's com. on Yāj., p. 9; and in Hemādri's Caturvarga-cintāmaṇi, Vol. II (Vrata-khaṇḍa), Part i, p. 22.

CHAPTER III

BRAHMANICAL ELEMENTS IN THE PURĀṆIC TEACHINGS

In the foregoing pages we have tried to find an explanation of the rise of the composite Dharma of the Purāṇas. We have also tried to explain why in the earlier Purāṇas the Smṛti-chapters deal with Varṇāśramadharma (consisting of Varṇa-dharma, Āśrama-dharma, Ācāra, Bhakṣyābhakṣya, Aśauca and Śrāddha), Naraka, Yuga-dharma, Karma-vipāka and Kali-svarūpa, whereas in the later Purāṇas, or in such portions thereof, the chapters on the glorification of the sectarian deities increase, and the Smṛti-chapters are added to by those on Pūjā, Vrata, Tīrtha etc. We shall now see how and to what extent the Purāṇic Brāhmans tried to establish the Varṇāśramadharma and the authority of the Vedas, and how much of the Vedic rituals they translated into those of the Purāṇas.

In the Purāṇas the Śruti and Smṛti are regarded as authorities on Karman (or Dharma). The Matsya-p. places Karma-yoga above Jñāna-yoga thus: "Karma-yoga is superior to a thousand Jñāna-yogas, because Jñāna-yoga arises from Karma-yoga, and through Jñāna-yoga one attains final emancipation. The divine knowledge of Brahma springs from Karma-yoga and Jñāna combined. Jñāna-yoga in its turn does not arise without Karma-yoga. Consequently, a person devoted to Karma-yoga attains to eternal truth"[1]. This Karman comprises the daily performance of the five great sacrifices, subjection to the sacraments, the culture of the eight Ātma-guṇas, doing good to Brāhmans and cows with money, and the worship of the sectarian deities (Mat 52, 12 ff.); and its sources are the Veda and the conduct of those versed in it (Mat 52, 7b).

The work enjoined by the 'Vedas' is of two kinds—Pravṛtti-mūlaka and Nivṛtti-mūlaka. Though the Purāṇas recognise that final emancipation is attainable only through renunciation and

[1] Mat 52, 5b-7a.

Yoga (i.e., through Nivṛtti-dharma), they do not wish, unlike the Buddhists, Jains and others, that anybody and everybody should accept Saṃnyāsa (complete renunciation) spontaneously without caring whether he is fit for it or not, because such Saṃnyāsa is very harmful to society. On the other hand, the Purāṇas hold that those people who lack extreme indifference should pass through the different stages of life, performing the duties enjoined by the Smṛtis, in order to reach that stage in which he will be fit for Saṃnyāsa. In the Mārkaṇḍeya-p. (chaps. 95 f.) there is an interesting story which states that Prajāpati Ruci was bent on attaining final release. Consequently, he left the house and the fire, took only one meal a day, slept on the bare earth, had no self-conceit, affection or attachment, and wandered about fearless like a Saṃnyāsin. Once his Pitṛs appeared before him and convinced him that the acquisition of a wife and the performance of the daily duties of a householder are necessary for freeing oneself from the debts one owes to the gods, fathers, men and others. They added: "Evil is driven away by means of disinterested gifts and by results and enjoyments which are good or ill according to former actions. Thus no bondage befalls him who acts with a tender heart, and such action being disinterested tends not to bondage. Thus a former action done, which consists of merit and demerit, is diminished day and night by enjoyments which consist of pleasure and pain . . . among mankind"[2]. They further continued: "Ignorance in very truth is this action thou mentionest—this maxim is not erroneous; nevertheless action is the cause undoubtedly of full acquisition of knowledge. On that view the restraint, which bad men observe because they do not perform what is enjoined, should tend immediately to final emancipation; on the contrary it produces a downward course"[3]. In the Devībhāgavata (I, 18 and 19) Śuka, who believed that the first three stages of life were obstacles to the attainment of Mokṣa, is instructed by Janaka to pass through all the stages in succession until he loses all attraction for the world, because 'the man who is totally free from worldly attachment is entitled to take up Saṃnyāsa, not otherwise'. Śuka, however, contends that there should be no objection if a man, even before he passes through all the stages, becomes indifferent to the world through knowledge and wants to become a Saṃnyāsin. To this Janaka says that a man, who wishes to rise high, should begin from the lowest rung of the ladder. He should pass through the stages in order and practise abstention while he is surrounded by things of enjoyment.

[2] Mārk 95. 14b-16. [3] Mārk 95, 19-20.

In this way he will get experienced in the real taste of wordly enjoyment and acquire greater strength of mind. Mind is the cause of bondage or release. Hence people should first try to control it by following the directions of the Veda. Mere physical abandonment of one's house and relatives cannot make one fit for final emancipation, because the physical needs continue to remain even after such abandonment, and in the forests also there are animals to attract the mind. Hence, Janaka adds, the mere acceptance of Saṃnyāsa is no guarantee for Mukti. Śuka next points out that the Vedic Dharma, by reason of its encouraging the slaughter of animals, cannot be expected to confer final release; but Janaka says that the killing of animals in sacrifices is equivalent to no killing at all, because there is no special intention on the part of the sacrificer. At last Śuka is convinced of the greatness of the Vedic Dharma. He, therefore, gives up the idea of taking up Saṃnyāsa and repairs to the hermitage of his father, Vyāsa, to live with him. There are other similar stories of great men in the Purāṇas denouncing spontaneous renunciation. These stories are clearly directed against the teachings of Buddhism and Jainism and also perhaps against those of popular Vaiṣṇavism, Śaivism and Brahmāism. We have said that these religions, especially the first two, attached great importance to renunciation, and, as a result, there was a great increase in the number of mendicants. The Purāṇas say that in the Kali age people 'would turn mendicants in hundreds and thousands' (cf. Kūr I, 29, 23; Vā 58, 50; and so on). Such increase of mendicants could not but affect the peace and discipline of society. So, we find that the Hindus adopted various means to check the people from giving themselves up recklessly to renunciation. Kauṭilya made laws thus: "When, without making provision for the maintenance of his wife and sons, any person embraces asceticism, he shall be punished with the first amercement"[4]. The authors of the Purāṇas also were not idle. They framed such stories of great men—because the conduct of the great has always the maximum of influence on the people—as would serve their purpose. They also took recourse to various other means. They glorified the service rendered to one's parents and relatives. Obedience to one's parents were said to be productive of all the fruits of Dharma (Kūr II, 12, 35). The people were advised not to do anything against their will (Kūr II, 12, 37). In the Padma-p. (Bhūmi-kh.) the parents and the spiritual preceptor are called Tīrthas, and stories are fabricated to show how one can

[4] Kauṭilya's Arthaśāstra, translated into English by Dr. Shama Shastry, p. 47; Ibid. (text), p. 48.

attain all kinds of pleasure in this life and the next by serving them.

It has been said above that the Buddhists and Śvetāmbara Jains converted women to asceticism. According to Kauṭilya such conversions were to be punished with the first amercement[5]. The numerous chapters on the duties of devoted wives and the glories of the same, as found in the Purāṇas, were perhaps meant for checking women from accepting asceticism. These chapters might also have been meant for checking the demoralisation of women caused by the influence of the casteless and immoral foreigners and by the Tantric cult. How greatly the circle-worship (cakra-pūjā) of the Tantras spread among the people is shown by the Kasmirian polymath Kṣemendra, who says:

> *"cakra-sthitau rajaka-vāyaka-carmakāra-*
> *kāpālika-pramukha-śilpibhir eka-pātre|*
> *pānena muktim avikalpa-ratotsavena*
> *vṛttena cotsavavatā guravo vadanti||"* [6]

The stories about the powers of chaste and devoted wives are full of supernatural occurrences. For instance, we may refer to the story of the Brāhmaṇ leper and his wife (Mārk 16, 14 ff.). The story runs as follows:

There was a Brāhman leper who had a very chaste and devoted wife. She served him wholeheartedly. Once the Brāhman was enamoured of a prostitute. Consequently, in order to fulfil his wishes, his wife was taking him at night to the house of the prostitute, when the leper's foot struck against the body of a sage who was lying pierced with a lance. The sage cursed him that he would die with sun-rise. At this the wife arrested the rise of the sun by virtue of her chastity, and, as a result, the whole creation was in danger. So, the gods sent Anasūyā who persuaded the leper's wife to allow the sun to rise and revived the dead leper by means of the merit gathered through service to her husband.

In the Purāṇas the second stage of life (i.e., the Gārhasthyāśrama) is very much lauded. The Matsya-p. says: "The holy places (tīrtha) are said to be in the houses of those who (abide by the rules) of the castes and stages (of life)" [7]. The Kūrma-p. says: "The householder is the source of the (other) three stages (of life). Others live on him. Therefore, the householder is the best (of all). As it is found in the Vedas that, of the four stages of life, the householder's (is the) only stage (that is best), so the stage of the

[5] Arthaśāstra (translated into English), p. 47. Ibid. (text), p. 48.
[6] Daśāvatāra-carita, p. 162.
[7] Mat 22, 80.

householder should be known as the only means of attaining Dharma"[8]. In this stage of life a wife is highly necessary. Without her a householder becomes unfit for performing his daily duties and thus incurs sins. Hence, of whatever temperament the wife may be, she deserves to be protected very carefully. In the Mārkaṇḍeya-p. (69-72) there is a story of Uttama, who banished his wife and was not shown proper respect for this act. He was instructed by a sage thus:

"A wife is a potent cause of righteousness, wealth and love among men; and, in particular, one who forsakes her has in sooth abandoned righteousness. A wifeless man, O king, is not fit for his own works, be he Brāhman or Kṣatriya, Vaiśya or even Śūdra. No brilliant deed didst thou do, Sir, when thou didst abandon thy wife; for as women must not forsake a husband, so men must not forsake a wife"[9].

In the Padma-p. (Bhūmi-kh., chaps. 41 ff.) there is a story of one Kṛkala, who had a very chaste and devoted wife named Sukalā. Kṛkala left his wife at home and went out to visit the holy places. When, after some time, he was returning home he thought that he had acquired so much merit that his forefathers might attain heaven by virtue of it. He was, however, disappointed to find his forefathers bound by a heavenly being who told him that really he had acquired no merit by such pilgrimage. This heavenly being further added that 'the highest virtues of a man who leaves alone his pure and most virtuous wife become fruitless, and not otherwise'; that the gods, Pitṛs, holy rivers, oceans, sacrifices, cows, sages and holy places are always present in the house of a man who has got such a wife; that 'there is no holy place (tīrtha) like a wife, no happiness like her, and no such merit for deliverance and good'; and that one who performs the funeral sacrifices without a wife is no better than a thief.

The means adopted by the authors of the Purāṇas to establish and popularise the Varṇāśramadharma are various and interesting. Often the sages, gods and goddesses are made to extol the Varṇāśramadharma as the means of attaining the sectarian gods. In the Viṣṇu-p. Aurva, being asked by king Sagara as to how Viṣṇu can be worshipped, says: "The supreme Being is worshipped by him who is loyal to the duties required by his own caste and stage of life. There is no other way of satisfying him. By performing sacrifices he makes oblations to him, by muttering prayers he invokes him, and by hurting others he hurts him, because Hari resides in all. Therefore, Janārdana is worshipped by that man who is given to

[8] Kūr I. 2, 51-52. [9] Mārk 71, 9-11.

the rules of good conduct and performs the duties of his own caste"[10]. In the Kūrma-p. it is said that Indradyumna worshipped Viṣṇu in one of his previous births with a view to experiencing the supreme Brahma. Śrī, the Māyā of Viṣṇu, appeared before Indradyumna and said: "I fail to overpower those who worship Puruṣottama, the prop of all beings, through Jñāna and Karma-yoga. So worship the Eternal One devoting yourself to Karman and Jñāna, and you will attain final beatitude"[11]. In Kūr I, 12, which is a Śākta document, Devī (i.e., Durgā), being asked as to how she can be attained by the people, says: "I am attainable by means of meditation, work, devotion and knowledge, but not by crores of acts other than these. Practise the Varṇāśramadharma with self-knowledge as directed by the Vedas and lawbooks for final beatitude. From Dharma originates Bhakti (devotion), and by Bhakti is attained the best knowledge. Dharma, according to the Vedas and the lawbooks, is sacrifice etc. Dharma originated from the Vedas and from nothing else. So, one who is desirous of knowing Dharma or attaining final release should take recourse to the Vedas which are identical with myself". She further adds that there is no Śāstra except the Vedas which can claim to be the source of Dharma. There are, of course, the literatures of the Vāmas, Ārhatas, Kāpilas, Pāñcarātras and many other sects, but these were declared by Devī herself with a view to deluding those people who mislead others on the strength of bad scriptures.[12]

The incarnations of Viṣṇu and Śiva are said to be intended for the revival of Dharma and the performance of sacrifices. For example, the Vāyu-p. says: "When sacrifices grew rare, lord Viṣṇu was born again and again for establishing Dharma and destroying Adharma"[13]. The Viṣṇu-p. says: "When the parctices taught by the Vedas and the institutes of law shall nearly have ceased, and the close of the Kali age shall be nigh, a portion of that divine being who exists in his own spiritual nature (ātma-svarūpin) and in the character of Brahma, and who is the beginning and the end, and who comprehends all things, shall descend upon earth: he shall be born in the family of Viṣṇuyaśas,—an eminent Brāhman of the village Sambhala,—as Kalki, endowed with the eight super-human faculties. By his irresistible might he will destroy all the Mlecchas and thieves, and all whose minds are devoted to iniquity. He will, then, re-establish righteousness upon earth; and the minds of those who live at the end of the Kali age shall be awakened, and shall

[10] Viṣ III, 8, 9-11. [11] Kūr I, 1, 60-61.

[12] Kūr I, 12, 249 f.

[13] Vā 98, 69. Also cf. Vā 97, 65-66; 98, 97; and so on.

be as pellucid as crystal"[14]. Regarding the mission of the incarnations of Śiva the Kūrma-p. says: "The blue-red Śaṃkara will be incarnated for establishing the Śrauta and Smārta (Dharma) and for doing good to his devotees". Śiva is described in Vā 30, 218 as '*varṇāśramāṇāṃ vidhivat pṛthak karma-pravartin*'.

The performance of the Varṇāśramadharma is said to be elevating and productive of happiness both in this world and the next. It is said in the Purāṇas that Śrāddha, which is performed by those who are loyal to the duties of the stages of life and have acquired knowledge, gratifies the manes[15], and that those who practise the seven acts, viz., celibacy, penance, sacrifice, begetting children, funeral sacrifices, acquirement of learning, and making gifts of food throughout their life, live happily in heaven in company with the gods and manes[16]. We have seen how men can attain Viṣṇu, Śiva or other gods by observing the rules of the Varṇāśramadharma. They can also be saved from hells and the power of Yama. In the Viṣṇu-p. Yama advises his servants not to touch the Viṣṇu-worshippers, one of whose characteristics is their devotion to the Varṇāśramadharma[17]. In the Varāha-p. Yama enumerates to Nārada those people who do not go to hell. These people include the keepers of the sacred fire, the givers of land, sesamum, cow, gold and earth, the masters of the Vedas, those who respect the twice-born, the sacrificers, and those who study the Vedas daily[18]. Even the very presence of those who are given to the Śrauta and Smārta Dharma is said to be highly pleasing. The Mārkaṇḍeya-p. (15, 52-55) says that the wind, that touched the body of the pious king Vipaścit, gladdened the people who were living in the hells, and mitigated their sufferings; because this king used to take food after offering it to the manes, gods, guests and servants, and performed various kinds of sacrifices.

In order to warn the people against violating the rules of the Varṇāśramadharma numerous stories have been fabricated to show the results of violation. For example, we may refer to the story of the sons of Raji who were deluded by Bṛhaspati, made to accept the Jina-dharma after giving up the Vedic Dharma, and were killed by Indra[19]; to the story of Vena who was killed by the sages for his neglect of the Varṇāśramadharma[20]; to the story of the demons who became very powerful by practising the Veda-dharma

14 Viṣ IV, 24, 26-27.

15 Mat 144, 61; Vā 56, 68-69; etc.

16 Mat 141, 61-62; Vā 56, 69-71.

17 *na calati nija-varṇadharmato yaḥ* ......| . . . *tam avaihi viṣṇu-bhaktam*|| Viṣ III, 7, 20.

18 Var 207, 19-23.

19 Mat 24, 43-49.

20 Viṣ I, 13; Vā 62, 103-126; Bhāg IV, 14; and so on.

but were deluded by Māyāmoha only to be defeated and killed by the gods[21]; and so forth. Besides these and similar other stories, there are numerous chapters on the description of the ages (yuga), on hells, and on the results of actions. In the chapters on Yuga-dharma the easy and happy life of the people of the three preceding ages is attractively pictured in order to bring it into striking contrast with the miseries and degradation of the people of the Kali age, which are ascribed mainly to the neglectful tendency of the people towards the Varṇāśramadharma. As an example, we may refer to the Matsya-p. in which the sufferings of the people of the Kali age are described as follows:

"At the end of Dvāpara and by the beginning of the Kali age, Kali becomes very strong. During the Kali age, people indulge in Hiṃsā, theft, falsehood, deceit, vanity etc., and delusion, hypocrisy and vanity overshadow the people. And Dharma becomes very weak in the Kali age, and people commit sin in mind, speech and actions. And works done with the whole heart and body sometimes become accomplished and sometimes not. Quarrels, plague, fatal diseases, famines, drought and calamities appear. Testimonies and proofs have no certainty. There is no criterion left when the Kali age settles down. Some die in the womb, some in childhood, some in youth, and some in old age. People become poorer in vigour and lustre. They are wicked, full of anger, sinful, false and avaricious. Bad ambitions, bad education, bad dealings, and bad earnings excite fear. The whole batch becomes greedy and untruthful. The Brāhmans become demoralised. They have base ambitions. Their knowledge and learning are mostly defective. Their character is exceedingly low, and by such ignoble conduct they prove very disastrous to the people. The people become saturated with jealousy, anger, vindictiveness, cowardice, greed and attachment. Lust increases during this age. The Brāhmans do not read the Vedas, nor do they perform sacrifices, and the Kṣatriyas deteriorate with the Vaiśyas and become well nigh extinct. The Śūdras sleep with the Brāhmans, sit with the Brāhmans, eat and perform sacrifices with them, and hold relations of Mantra with them. Many Śūdras will become kings, and many heretics will be seen. There will arise various sects; Saṃnyāsins wearing clothes coloured red, Kāpālins and various others holding themselves followers of some Deva or other will find fault with Dharma. Many profess to have supreme knowledge, because thereby they will easily earn their livelihood. Some hypocrites will mark their bodies with Vedic symbols also. In the Kali age anybody will study the Vedas; the

[21] Viṣ III, 17-18; and Pd (Sṛṣṭi-kh.) 13, 348 ff.

Śūdras will be experienced in the Vedas. So there will be many false religionists. The Śūdra kings will perform Aśvamedha sacrifices, and the people will serve their ends even by killing women, children and cows. They will cheat each other to serve their ends. The country will become desolate by repeated calamities, short lives, and various kinds of diseases. Every one will be miserable and addicted to Adharma. Owing to the dominance of vice and Tamoguṇa (quality of darkness), people will freely commit the sin of abortion, on account of which there will be a decline in the longevity and strength of the people. The people will live up to 100 years at most. Inspite of all the Vedas being in existence, it would be as if there were no Vedas, and the performance of sacrifices would be stopped. This is about the Kali age"[22].

The motive underlying such descriptions is undoubtedly the attraction of the mind of the people towards the Vedic Dharma. The descriptions of hells and of the punishments inflicted there on the sinners are no less awful. In the hells, it is said, the sinners are punished with the utmost cruelty for neglecting the Varṇāśramadharma and the general rules of morality. The Vāyu-p. says: "Those, who are fallen from an Āśrama (stage of life), fall into the fire and are eaten by black and variegated crows with iron beaks; and (one who is guilty) of breach (in the performance) of a sacrifice or vow, is cooked in the hell called Saṃdaṃśa"[23]; and "All those, who, out of anger or delight, perform acts contradictory to the (rules of) castes and Āśramas, go to hell"[24]. The chapters on Karma-vipāka also are equally effective in preventing the people from violating the rules of the Varṇāśramadharma.

The doctrine of Ahiṃsā, preached by the Jains and Buddhists, was often responsible for depriving Brahmanism of popular favour, because the latter encouraged the slaughter of animals in sacrifices and funeral ceremonies. So, the authors of the Purāṇas felt it necessary to glorify the practice of one's Svadharma, and introduced numerous stories for the purpose. In the Vāmana-p. there is the story of Sukeśin, king of the Rākṣasas, who gave up his Svadharma and accepted Para-dharma (i.e. mānava-dharma). As a result, his moving city was brought down to earth by the Sun-god. It was, however, replaced afterwards in its former position. In the Varāha-p. there is the story of the Brāhman Saṃyamana and the fowler Niṣṭhuraka which runs as follows:

[22] Mat 144, 29 f. *Cf.* also Vā 58, 31 f. There are many additional verses in the Vāyu.

[23] Vā 101, 171-172.

[24] Vā 101, 174.

Once Saṃyamana went to the river Bhāgīrathī for a bath and saw there a herd of deer which Niṣṭhuraka was going to hunt. Saṃyamana asked Niṣṭhuraka not to kill them. At this, the latter gave a short lecture on the unity of Ātman (which he identified with Nārāyaṇa), and demonstrated it by kindling a fire, the flame of which was divided thousandfold by means of an iron sieve placed on it, adding at the end :

"ātmā sa prakṛtisthaś ca bhūtānāṃ saṃśrayo bhavet|
vikṛtād udbhavas tasya eṣā vai jagataḥ sthitiḥ||
piṇḍa-grahaṇa-dharmeṇa yad asya vihitaṃ vratam|
tat tad ātmani saṃyojya kurvāṇo nāvasīdati||"

As Niṣṭhuraka said this, there came down from heaven chariots in all of which Niṣṭhuraka was found sitting simultaneously.

There is another similar story in the same Purāṇa. According to it, a fowler named Dharmavyādha convinced the sage Mataṅga that there is no food which is totally devoid of life (caitanya), and that by avoiding animal food one can never avoid Hiṃsā[25].

These stories are clear protests against the spread of Ahiṃsā which affected the sacrificial religion. They show to the people that one's Svadharma, of whatever type it may be, is as good as that of another in attaining the highest state of existence.

The control of women and Śūdras was a very difficult problem. We have already mentioned that the Jains and Buddhists allowed greater freedom and facilities to women and Śūdras. We have also seen how the authors of the Purāṇas tried to check women from accepting asceticism by glorifying the devoted and chaste wives. Other means also were adopted for the purpose. The Purāṇas framed stories to show that for women, service to their husbands and for the Śūdras, service to the twice-born were the means of attaining the highest regions. For an example we may refer to the Visnu-p. (VI, 2) which contains the following story :

Once the sages were unable to decide the question as to when Dharma, though practised little, is capable of producing the greatest result, and went to Vyāsa for a solution. They found the latter bathing in the Ganges and heard him shouting, "Excellent, excellent is the Kali age", "Blessed, blessed are the Śūdras" and "Fortunate are women" each time he dived. When, after bath, Vyāsa repaired to his hermitage, the sages asked him the cause of his exclamation. Vyāsa explained it saying : "In truth, in the Kali age, duty is discharged with very little trouble by mortals whose faults are all washed away by the water of their individual merits ; by Śūdras, through diligent attendance (only) upon the

[25] Var 8.

twice-born; and by women, through the slight effort of obedience to their husbands. Therefore, Brāhmans, did I thrice express my admiration of their happiness"[26].

In numerous cases the authors of the Purāṇas are found to have attempted to establish the Varṇāśramadharma among women and Śūdras through the Purāṇic vows and worships. For instance, king Nṛga, who was a Śūdra in his previous birth, is said to have become a king by virtue of the observance of the Buddhadvādaśī-vrata[27]; king Bhadrāśva and queen Kāntimatī, who served in the house of a Vaiśya in their previous births, attained royalty by managing a lamp to burn throughout the whole night in a Viṣṇu-temple on the twelfth day of the bright half of the month of Āśvina[28]; Kuvera performed the Dhanya-vrata in his previous birth as a Śūdra[29]; and so on. The purpose underlying these stories is clearly the winning over of women and Śūdras to the composite Dharma of the Purāṇas.

The authors of the Purāṇas realised that unless the authority of the Vedas was established among the people, the popularisation of the Varṇāśramadharma was almost impossible. Hence they adopted various means for the purpose. In the Purāṇas the Vedas, Itihāsa, Upa-Veda, Vedāṅga, Dharma-śāstra, Purāṇa etc. are said to constitute the body of Viṣṇu[30]. Śiva also is indentified with the Vedas and the sacrifice[31]. There are stories in the Purāṇas identifying the three Vedas with Brahmā, Viṣṇu and Śiva. For an example, we may refer to the story of Nārada and Sāvitrī, the mother of the Vedas, in Var 2, 63 ff. This story, in which the Ṛg-veda is identified with Nārāyaṇa, the Yajur-veda with Brahmā, and the Sāma-veda with Rudra, is as follows:

Nārada once went to Śveta-dvīpa. There he saw an extremely beautiful woman at the side of a lake, and enquired her identity. At this she only gazed at Nārada and took away all the knowledge he had acquired. When the perplexed Nārada sought her shelter, he saw in her three men, one in the heart of another. At the next moment these three men vanished, and there remained that woman only. Nārada insisting upon an explanation of the matter, she said that she was the mother of the Vedas in the forms of the three men, viz., Nārāyaṇa, Brahmā and Rudra. She also blessed Nārada with the mastery of all the Vedas and the Śāstras and with omniscience, and asked him to bathe in the Veda-lake (veda-saras) to be able to remember his previous births.

26 Viṣ VI, 2, 34-36a.
27 Var 47, 20 ff.
28 Var 49, 6 ff.
29 Var 56, 16.
30 Viṣ I, 22, 81-83.
31 Vā 30, 243b-244a and 251b.

The motive underlying this story is to raise the position of the Vedas in public eye by identifying them with the triad of gods, to attract the people to the study of the Vedas by attributing to them the power of conferring omniscience on the reader, and to canvass more regard for the Sāvitrī (also called the Gāyatrī). The muttering of the Gāyatrī together with the performance of Prāṇāyāma is said to be able to purify one of all Pātakas[32]. In the Purāṇas there are stories of sages versed in the Vedas and attractive descriptions of hermitages in which the Vedic hymns were chanted and sacrifices performed. The daily study of the Vedas is enjoined, and the regular student of the Vedas is said to be free from sins even after committing hundreds of sinful acts[33]. We have seen that the Purāṇas recognise the Vedas as the sources of Dharma. In other matters also the Vedas were regarded as authorities; viz., in the rites for the pacification of the unfavourable planets the Purāṇas and the Vedas are the authorities[34]; initiation to the worship of Brahmā is to be done according to the directions of the Vedas[35]; and so on. The Brāhmans who are versed in the Vedas are assigned high position in the Purāṇas. The knowledge of the Vedas is the greatest qualification of those Brāhmans who are to be invited in a funeral ceremony. A Veda-knowing priest is desirable in vows, worships, etc. The consecrator of an image should be well versed in the Veda-mantras and the Purāṇas, and should lead a pure life[36]. Gifts to and feeding of the Veda-pāraga and Āhitāgni Brāhmans are deemed highly meritorious. Acts of violence done to those learned in the Vedas are decried. Those who abandon the Vedas and the sacrifices are hated much. Such people, and those who censure the Vedas and the Vedic Dharma are among those who go to hell[37]. "Those men who have given instruction in wicked Śāstras, and those who have advised such instruction for the purpose of completely destroying the sight even of their enemies; those who have repeated the Śāstra improperly; those who have given utterance to an evil word; those who have blasphemed the Veda, the gods, the twice-born and their Guru; for so many years these very terrible birds with adamant beaks tear out the very tongues of these men as they are continually renewed" [38]. We have seen how the non-Vedic scriptures are censured as delusive in the Purāṇas.

32 Var 68, 25-26.

33 Var 68, 28a.

34 Mat 93, 3.

35 Pd (Sṛṣṭi-kh.) 15, 100.

36 Cf. Mat 265, 2-3.

37 Pd (Sṛṣṭi-kh.) 15, 143b-147a. Var 195, 4b.

38 Mārk 14, 43-45.

The Purāṇic Brāhmans tried to popularise the sacrifices also. In the Purāṇas Viṣṇu, in his Boar incarnation, is identified with the Vedic sacrifice, his different limbs representing the different requisites of the latter[39]. Śiva also is identified with the sacrifice[40]. There are names and stories of kings of different ages who performed numerous sacrifices, gave heavy priestly fees to Brāhmans, and repaired to heaven to enjoy the fruit.

The establishment of the Varṇāśramadharma and the authority of the Vedas seems also to have been attempted through the Vratas, Pūjās, Utsarga, etc. It is perhaps for this reason that we find the Purāṇic rituals imbued with the Vedic ones. The main component parts of a Vrata are generally the following :—selection of a proper Tithi, determination of taking the vow, lying on the ground, bath, appointment of a Brāhman as priest, worship, muttering (japa), offering oblations to the fire (homa), fasting, abstinence (especially from food), making gifts, feeding Brāhmans, keeping awake during the night, and listening to tales (ākhyāna-śravaṇa). All these have their parallels in the Vedic rituals[41]. In the Vratas the methods of Homa etc. often resemble the Vedic sacrifices. For instance, the Bhīmadvādaśī-vrata (also called the Kalyāṇinī-vrata—Mat 69) requires, among other things, the performance of Homa for which a pandal (maṇḍapa) furnished with a portal (toraṇa) and a sacrificial pond (kuṇḍa) is to be erected, the dimensions of all these being particularly given. Then, after the rituals of Ekāgni, Homa is to be performed with Caru sacred to Viṣṇu and then with ghee with the citation of Vedic Mantras of which the deity is Viṣṇu. This Homa requires twelve Brāhmans, four of whom are to be Ṛg-vedins, four Yajur-vedins, and four Sāma-vedins. The Ṛg-vedin Brāhmans are to conduct the Homa, the Yajur-vedins to recite the Mantra sacred to Rudra, and the Sāma-vedins to chant Vedic hymns on Viṣṇu. After the Homa is over, the Yajamāna (worshipper) is to make suitable gifts to all the Brāhmans. In the Saptamī-vrata (Mat 68) the preparation of Caru for Sūrya and Rudra, offer of ghee to Rudra in fire with the citation of seven solar Ṛcs and the Rudra-sūkta, performance of Homa in which Arka (Calatropis gigantia) and Palāśa (Butea frondosa) are used as fuel, performance of Homa 108 times with barley and black sesamum, and the offer of ghee 108 times with the citation of the Vyāhṛti, are necessary. In other matters also the Vratas often approach the Vedic sacrifices.

[39] Mat 248, 67 ff.; Bhāg III, 13, 35 ff.; etc.

[40] Vā 30, 243 and 251.

[41] See, Keith, Religion and Philosophy of the Veda, Harvard Oriental Series, Vol. 31, pp. 300 ff.

In the Ādityaśayana-vrata, Śāli rice, with ghee and a piece of gold, is to be placed on a plate made of Udumbara wood and given to a Brāhman (Mat 55, 18) ; the Kṛṣṇāṣṭamī-vrata (Mat 56) betrays the belief in the sanctifying effect of the products of the cow in that the person who has taken the vow is to take the urine and milk of a cow, ghee, sesamum, barley, water raised with Kuśa grass, the water with which the horns of a cow have been washed, leaves of Śirīṣa, Arka and Bilva, curd, and the five products of the cows (pañca-gavya) before worshipping Śiva ; during the same Vrata the branches of Vaṭa, Aśvattha, Udumbara, Plakṣa, Palāśa, Jambu and Viduṣa are to be used for cleansing the teeth ; in the Rohiṇīcandra-śayana-vrata (Mat 57) a man is to bathe with 'pañca-gavya' and mustard before taking up the vow obviously to attain purity of body ; in the Anaṅgadāna-vrata (Mat 70), which is meant for prostitutes, the Brāhman, who must be well-versed in the Vedas, is to cite the Vedic Mantras '*ka idaṃ kasmād āt* etc.' when accepting the cow offered by the prostitute ; and so on. The methods of the consecration of tanks, reservoirs etc. are almost regular sacrifices except that there are some popular elements, viz., the worship of the sectarian gods, the drawing of a circle and painting it with powder of five hues, and the like. The consecration of tanks requires the following operations :—

Consulting a Brāhman ; making an altar, a pandal and nine, seven or five pits ; construction of arches with the branches of the Aśvattha, Udumbara, Plakṣa and Vaṭa trees in all the four directions of the pandal ; appointment of eight sacrificial priests (hotṛ), eight warders (dvārapāla), eight mutterers of prayers (jāpaka), and one priest ; furnishing the pits with pitchers, materials of sacrifice, fans, white chowries, and big dishes made of copper ; offering of boiled rice and barley (i.e., caru) to the gods ; making a sacrificial post ; appointment of 25 Ṛtvijs who are to be honoured with gold car-rings, armlets, rings and clothes ; honouring an Ācārya ; making gifts ; bathing the worshipper and other members of his family with water containing different herbs ; performance of the sacrifice (which is purely Vedic) ; and so on.

The methods of dedicating and consecrating trees and grooves are in many respects similar to that of the consecration of tanks. The methods of making ceremonial gifts also require the erection of pandals and the performance of Homa. In baths during eclipses, the gifts of cows and the use of Vedic Mantras are enjoined (Mat 67). Graha-yajña and the consecration of images also require pandals, altars and Homa. Even the Śākta worships of the Purāṇas are replete with Vedic rituals. There is a Devī-yajña (sacrifice to Devī) described in Dbh III, 12. This 'yajña' is of three kinds—'sāttvika' 'rājasa' and 'tāmasa'. The priests to be employed in these sacrifices should be highly learned in the Vedas *(vedavittamāḥ)*, and in them special importance should be attached to the purity of things (dravya-śuddhi, i.e., articles acquired through fair means), purity of action (kriyā-śuddhi) and purity of Mantra (mantra-śuddhi), otherwise the results will be unfavourable. The methods of performing these three kinds of Devī-yajña show that they are modified Vedic sacrifices, the difference being that they are meant for Devī. In Dbh III, 25 king Sudarśana is said to have consecrated an image of Devī through the Vedic Brāhmans, and during the worship Vedic hymns were recited and Homa was performed. Dbh III, 26-27 deal with the Navarātra-vrata in which there is much of Vedic rites, and the Tantric rites, which are retained, are much refined. In this worship the priest should have perfect knowledge about Devī. He should possess a good character, and be continent and well versed in the Vedas and the Vedāṅgas. On the previous day the worshipper should take rice mixed with ghee only once, construct a pandal and an altar, and summon the Brāhmans. On the day of the worship he should bathe in the morning and appoint a priest who should congratulate him with Veda-mantras, place the image of Devī on the altar, and perform Homa. In this worship the sacrifice of animals (viz., buffaloes, goats or boars) is optional, and it should be followed by the worship of virgin girls (kumārī-pūjana), music, dancing, etc.

The above accounts of the methods of worship, consecration etc. show that the Vedic rituals were made to play no insignificant part in their performance. One thing, which is specially remarkable in them, is that the necessity of priests is almost the same as in the Vedic rites.

It should be mentioned here that the Vedic rituals that we find in the Purāṇic chapters dating earlier than the beginning of the 9th century A.D. were not retained to the same extent in the chapters of later dates but were often replaced by popular elements.

CHAPTER IV

THE PURĀṆIC RITES AND CUSTOMS AS INFLUENCED BY THE ECONOMIC AND SOCIAL NEEDS OF THE SACERDOTAL CLASS

Though the real origin of the composite Dharma that we find in the Purāṇas and call Purāṇic rites and customs is to be traced to the ideas, beliefs and practices of the Smārta Brāhman sectaries and not to the inventive power of any superior brain, the development and spread of this Dharma are apparently connected with the attempt of these Brāhmans to establish, among the people, the authority of the Vedas and the Brahmanical rules of castes, duties and conduct. But if we study the Purāṇas a little more closely we can also discover a distinct personal interest behind the attempt, and the Purāṇic Dharma appears to be due to a struggle of these Brāhmans no less for their own economic and social recovery than for saving the Brahmanical culture in general. How these Brāhmans were subjected to economic depression and social degradation and what measures they adopted for redress, we shall see in the following pages.

From very ancient times the Brāhmans were reduced generally to a priest class. In the period of the later Vedic Saṃhitās, the Brāhmaṇas, the Āraṇyakas and the Upaniṣads 'we can distinguish . . . . two classes of Brāhmans, the priests who, as Purohitas of the kings or belonging to his entourage, took part in the vast sacrifices, some of them lasting for at least a year, which they offered for their masters, and the priests of the village who lived a humble and more restricted existence, except when they might be called on to serve at the sacrifice instituted by some rich noble or merchant'[1]. The strict life of these priestly Brāhmans is reflected in the Brahmanical literature, the epics and the Purāṇas. Simplicity, culture and religion were the guiding principles of their life. They valued most the old means of livelihood, viz., 'yājana'

[1] CHI, Vol. I, pp. 127-128.

(officiating as priest in the sacrifices instituted by others), 'adhyāpana' (teaching) and 'pratigraha' (acceptance of gifts), the second of these being regarded as the best of all. They avoided service, trade, agriculture etc. until and unless they were in distress. In cases of economic crises which could not be redressed through the purer means, the Brāhmans could follow the profession of the Kṣatriyas. Even if that profession failed to give them the bare maintenance, they could take up the profession of the Vaiśyas, but in no case the profession of the Śūdras was acceptable. The Brāhmans could follow the profession of the Vaiśyas only under certain restrictions. They were not allowed to sell anything and everything they liked. The lawbooks enumerate numerous things by selling which the Brāhmans were degraded. In barter also there were restrictions. The Brāhmans were advised to follow agriculture through representatives, because it involved cruelty to animals and the death of innumerable insects[2]. The social position of those Brāhmans who took to the means of livelihood other than the purer three (i.e., 'yājana', 'adhyāpana' and 'pratigraha') was deemed low. Such Brāhmans were looked down upon and were considered unfit for invitation in a funeral ceremony[3]. As priests also they were often disqualified.

Even before the period of the Brāhmaṇas, the elaborate speculations of the priests began to cause a gradual increase in the number and intricacy of the Vedic rites and rituals on the one hand, and the Smṛti rules on the other. The growing mass of these engaged not only more time but also required more energy and expense. Yet the income of the Brāhmans does not seem to have increased in the same proportion, but appears rather to have decreased. The causes of this decrease are not far to seek. Buddhism, Jainism and other heresies preached against Brahmanism. Their doctrine of Ahiṃsā, their disbelief in the efficacy of funeral rites, sacrifices etc., their disregard for the Vedas and the Brāhmans, and their allowance of (apparently) equal status to all their followers affected the economic condition and the social position of the Brāhmans. The spread of the doctrine of Ahiṃsā was the foremost cause of the unpopularity of Vedic sacrifices which were the main sources of income to the priests. How greatly this doctrine influenced the minds of kings and commoners is shown by Aśoka's categorical prohibition of bloody sacrifices in his empire.

[2] Manu X, 75 ff.; Gaut. VII; Viṣ III, 8, 38 to the end; Kūr II, 25, 2-12; and so on.

[3] Manu III, 150 ff.; Gaut. XV, 18; Viṣ III, 15, 5-7; Kūr II, 21, 27 ff.; and so forth.

This prohibition must have made the economic condition of the priestly Brāhmans much worse. The popular forms of the sectarian religions (viz., Vaiṣṇavism, Śaivism, etc.) also were not very favourable to the priests. These were rather cosmopolitan in their attitude. Even the Śūdras and women could worship their deities themselves. The influence of Tantra on these religions made them far more dangerous to the priests. From the analysis of the contents of the Jayākhya-saṃhitā we have seen that it ignored priesthood and gifts to non-sectarian Brāhmans. The gifts, in the great majority of cases, went to the spiritual preceptors who were not always Brāhmans. The non-Brāhmans also, not excepting the Śūdras and women, were allowed to act as spiritual preceptors in certain cases. Therefore, these gifts also were not the monopoly of the Brāhmans.

The political supremacy of the Śūdras, of the casteless foreign races, and of the followers of the heresies was highly detrimental to the interests of the priestly Brāhmans. The 'Śūdra' monarchs, especially of the Nanda and the Maurya dynasty, were mostly the followers of one or other of the heresies and tried to preach their faiths among the people. Many Śūdras accepted the heresies and got out of the power of the Brāhmans. Such acceptance of the heretical religions by the Śūdras meant economic loss to the Brāhmans. According to orthodox opinion, the Brāhmans could make the Śūdras, whether slaves or not, do their menial work, because it was believed that the Śūdras were created by Svayaṃbhū only to serve the Brāhmans[4]. Further, they had, or at least claimed, absolute right over the earnings and belongings of their Śūdra slaves. Manu says: "A wife, a son, and a slave,—these three are declared to have no property; the wealth which they earn is (acquired) for him to whom they belong. A Brāhman may confidently seize the goods of (his) Śūdra (slave); for, as that (slave) can have no property, his master may take his possessions"[5]. Gautama also says that the savings of a Śūdra slave should be meant for his master[6]. Sometimes the twice-born masters forced their slaves to earn money for them. The Nāmasiddhika-jātaka (Faus. No. 97) states that the master and

[4] Cf. Manu VIII, 413.

[5] *bhāryā putraś ca dāsaś ca traya evādhanāḥ smṛtāḥ|*
yat te samadhigacchanti yasya tat tasya tad dhanam||
viśrabdhaṃ brāhmaṇaḥ śūdrād dravyopādānam ācaret|
na hi tasyāsti kiñcit svaṃ bhartṛ-hārya-dhano hi saḥ||
Manu VIII, 416-417.

[6] Gaut. X, 65—*tadartho 'sya nicayaḥ syāt.*

the mistress of a slave woman named Dhanapālī compelled her to work in others' houses to earn money. One day she failed to earn anything and was consequently beaten. After the death of a slave, his property passed into the hands of his kinsmen, and in the absence of the latter it could be taken by his master[7]. These and similar other privileges which the Brāhmans claimed, and also perhaps enjoyed, over their Śūdra slaves were prejudiced by the conversion of the latter to the heretical religions. The political power of the casteless foreigners, viz., Greeks, Scythians, Hūṇas, Ābhīras and others, does not seem to have been very favourable to the Brāhmans. Those foreign kings who retained their own religions or became Buddhists could not be expected to have acknowledged fully the supremacy of the Brāhmans from the very beginning and to have deemed it pious to make gifts to them. We are also not sure whether those foreigners who accepted Vaiṣṇavism or Śaivism came to value the directions of the Brāhmans from the very time of their entrance into India. The evidence of the inscriptions belonging to the Mauryas, Āndhras, Kṣaharātas, Kushans, Ābhīras and others shows that the donations made by them to the Buddhists were much greater than those made to the Brāhmans[8]. The donations made to the Buddhists even by the Gupta emperors were not small.

In the foregoing pages we have enumerated the principal causes which were connected with the economic depression of the priestly Brāhmans. Regarding the causes of their social degradation we have already said enough in the preceding chapters, which need not be repeated. We shall, therefore, turn our attention to the measures adopted by the Brāhmans for redress.

The priestly Brāhmans have always set much store by the rules of the Dharmaśāstras. Hence in the Purāṇas also they (i.e., the Smārta Brāhman sectaries) are found to try to better their economic condition through lawful means, viz., the acceptance of gifts, priesthood, teachership, etc. The first of these means being considered the best and most effective, the Brāhmans strain every nerve to urge the people to make gifts to themselves on any and every occasion. Such strenuous efforts are undoubtedly at the basis of the introduction of the numerous chapters on gifts in the Purāṇas. Let us first examine the chapters on the ceremonial gifts.

Though from the Vedas, the Brāhmaṇas, the Dharmasūtras and the earlier Dharmaśāstras we know that huge gifts used to be made occasionally to the Brāhmans in ancient times, that the priests tried

[7] Arthaśāstra of Kauṭilya, text, p. 183.

[8] See, Rapson, Cat. of Ind. Coins in the Brit. Mus., Introduction, pp. 45-63. Ep. Ind., VIII, 1905-6, pp. 59-96.

to extract from their clients the highest amount as priestly fees[9], and that the act of making gifts was looked upon as religious, there is no evidence to show that any vigorous propaganda was made by the Brāhmans to popularise the piety of making gifts earlier than the time of the Yājñvalkya-smṛti. Nor do the ancient people seem to have been familiar with the great variety of gifts that we find in the Purāṇas. In the works earlier than Yājñavalkya there is mention of the simple gifts of land, gold, silver, cows, horses, slave girls, houses, clothes, food, drink etc.[10], but in the Purāṇas the Brāhmans take advantage of the belief of the people in the merits of making gifts of cows etc. to multiply the number of gifts by many new inventions. For instance, the Purāṇas speak of the gifts of artificial cows made of paddy, raw sugar (guḍa), sesamum, water, ghee etc.; of hillocks made of gold, silver, gems, salt, sesamum, ghee, sugar, cotton etc.; of Tulā-puruṣa, Kalpa-pādapa, Kāma-dhenu, horse, universe (brahmāṇḍa), earth, horse and chariot, elephant and chariot, five ploughs, Kalpa-latā, cows, etc.—all made of gold; and so forth. Some of these gifts seem to have been invented even earlier than the beginning of the Christian era, for Khāravela, king of Kaliṅga, is said to have given away a Kalpa-pādapa[11].

The methods of making the artificial cows, hillocks etc. in the ceremonial gifts testify to their highly expensive nature. For example, in the Guḍadhenu-dāna (i.e., the gift of a cow made of raw sugar) the cow is to be made in the following way:

"The floor should be plastered with cowdung, the Kuśa grass should be spread on all sides, and then over it should be placed a black antelope-skin, four cubits in length, with its neck towards the east. This is meant for the cow. A small deer-skin should be meant for her calf. The cow, with her calf, should be made to face the east, and their legs should be turned towards the north. The image of the Guḍa-dhenu should be made of four maunds of raw sugar, and the calf of one maund of raw sugar,—this is considered to be the first best; the image of the cow made of two maunds, and of the calf of half a maund of raw sugar, is considered to be the next best; and the image of the cow made of one maund, and of the calf of ten seers of raw sugar, is considered to be the last best. The devotee is to choose between the three, according to his means. The mouths (of the images) of

[9] Cf. Aitareya-brāhmaṇa, AnSS ed., XXXIX, 6, 2; XXXIX, 8 and 9 wherein huge gifts made by early kings are referred to by the priests.

[10] Cf. the Dāna-stutis in the Vedas; Aitareya-brāhmaṇa XXXIX, 6 and 8-9; Manu IV, 227-235; Yāj. I, 198-216; and so on.

[11] JBORS, III, 1917, p. 432.

the cow and the calf should be made of clarified butter, and both should be covered with (pieces of) fine white cloth. Their ears should be made of oyster-shells, their legs of sugarcanes, and their eyes of good pearls. The tendons, nerves etc. (of these images) should be made of white threads, their dew-laps of white blankets, their cheeks and backs of copper, and their furs should be represented by white chowries. Their eyebrows should be made of corals, their udders of fresh butter, and their tails of (pieces of) silk cloth; a vessel of bell-metal should be placed to represent the milking vessel; the pupils of their eyes should be made of sapphire, and they should be adorned with horns of gold; their hoofs should be made of silver, and their nostrils, represented by scents, are to be furnished with various kinds of fruits"[12].

In the Dhānyācala-dāna (i.e., gift of a hillock made of paddy) the method of making the hillock is given by the Matsya-p. (83, 12-26a) as follows

"The hill of 1000 Droṇas of paddy is the first best, of 500 Droṇas the second best, and of 300 Droṇas the last best. The Sumeru hill in the centre should be made of rice, and three trees of gold should be on it. Pearls and diamonds should be placed on the east side of the hill, cat's-eyes and topazes on the south, emarlds and sapphires on the west, and lapislazuli and ruby on the north. Pieces of sandal wood should be placed on all sides. So also a creeper of corals should surround it, and the surface and the bottom of the rock should be bedecked with oyster-shells. The images of Brahmā, Viṣṇu, Śiva and the Sun should be made of gold by holy Brāhmans and placed on the summit of the hill. The four peaks should be made of silver, and silver should also be used to make the slopes. Sugarcanes, representing bamboos, should cover the caves, and streams of clarified butter should be on all sides. The clouds surrounding this hill on four sides should be made of cloths of four colours, viz., those on the east, of white cloth, those on the south, of yellow, those on the west, of pigeon-grey, and those on the north, of red-coloured cloths. Fruits of different kinds, fine garlands of flowers, and sandal should be placed on all sides. Eight silver Lokapālas . . . . . should be made . . . . . Then the Mandarācala should be erected with barley in the east and adorned with rows of fruits, and on the top should be planted a tree of gold . . . . . That hill should be adorned with a golden image of Cupid, arrayed in beautiful dresses, garlands of flowers, and sandal. There should be on one side of it a vessel containing milk and representing the sea of milk, and on the opposite side,

[12] Mat 82, 3-10a.

another vessel representing the sea called Aruṇoda. The forests of the hill should be represented by silver trees, according to the means of the devotee. On the south, the Gandhamādana hill should be made of wheat, with some gold in it; on its top should be placed a golden image of Yajñapati; and the lake Mānasa of clarified butter, and a garden of white cloth and silver should adorn it. On the west, a hill of sesamum should be made and adorned with scented flowers. Fig trees and swans of gold, a garden of silver-flowers, a pond of curds representing a lake of cold water, and clouds represented by white cloths, should also be made. On the north, the Supārśva hill of Māṣa (Phaseolus radiatus) should be made. A golden Vata tree and a cow of gold should be placed on the top of the hill. A pond of honey, representing an auspicious lake, and a garden of silver trees, should also be made at the bottom of it".

The gifts of the Tulā-puruṣa, Hema-kalpa-pādapa etc. require greater expenses. The encouragement to these expensive gifts means maximum extortion. Though the nature of these gifts shows that they are possible only for kings and emperors, there are provisions for adapting them to the circumstances of less wealthy people.

The occasions on which gifts are directed to be made are various and numerous. The Matsya-p. (274, 19b-23) says: "The great gifts (Mahādāna) should be made on the days of the Ayana, Viṣuva, Vyatipāta, Dina-kṣaya, on the first days of the Yugas and Manvantaras, on Saṃkrānti, Vaidhṛti, Caturdaśī, Aṣṭamī, Śuklā Pañcadaśī, on the Parvan days, on Dvādaśī, Aṣṭakā, the occasions of sacrifices, festivities, marriages, after dreaming bad dreams or seeing wonderful things, on getting wealth and (worthy) Brāhmans, on the occasion of funeral sacrifices, in desired times, in a sacred place, in temples, cowsheds, near a well or a garden or a beautiful tank, etc". Such varieties of occasions seem to be based on the principle that the more the people give, the better.

In the Purāṇas great attempt has been made to popularise gifts. It is preached that making gifts is the only piety in the Kali age[13], and that 'the creatures have no other piety on earth than that of making gifts'[14]. The merits of gifts made to Brāhmans are extolled with a view to attracting the notice of the people. Such gifts are said to give pomp and pleasure to the donor both in this life and the next. He is said to have health, wealth, a beautiful wife, and children on earth[15], and after death, to attain, without the least

[13] *'dānam ekaṃ kalau yuge'*—Kūr I, 28, 17; Manu I, 86; cf. Var 68, 8; etc.
[14] *'dāna-dharmāt paro dharmo bhūtānāṃ neha vidyate'*—Kūr II, 26, 56a.
[15] Mat 206, 30.

difficulty, the highly desired regions named Brahma-loka, Viṣṇu-loka etc., where the objects of enjoyment are very easily available. In these regions 'there are rivers flowing with clarified butter and milk and having curds and condensed milk as mud, and there are trees that grant the desires'[16]. Here the donor lives in full liberty for innumerable years 'being served incessantly by ladies having faces like the moon, complexion like burnished gold, broad buttocks, slender and rounded waists, and eyes tinged like a lotus'[17]. At the end of the period of enjoyment he is 'born again on earth as a king of kings, his foot-stool is tinged with (the rays of) the gems on the crests of the feudatory princes, and he becomes the performer of a thousand sacrifices . . . . . and conquers all other kings by dint of his great prowess'[18]. The above pictures of earthly and heavenly enjoyments, which are met with in almost all the Purāṇas, are undoubtedly meant for appealing to the popular psychology which always values physical enjoyment over final emancipation. The Purāṇas say that the people fail to get those things in the next world which they do not give to the Brāhmans on earth[19]. "What are given to Brāhmans become treasures in the next world, and there is no end of the fruits produced by the seed-like gifts sown in the land-like Brāhmans cultivated with the ploughs in the forms of the Vedas"—says the Viṣṇu-dharmottara (II, 32, 2b-3). By giving food and artificial cows of sesamum, clarified butter etc. to Brāhmans, the donor overcomes hunger and thirst which, consequently, cannot trouble him in heaven[20]. In the Purāṇas, gifts to Brāhmans are further said to please God[21] and to have great purificatory powers. They are said to be capable of destroying whatever sins the donor may have committed in any of his births. Even those donors who are guilty of adultery and murder of Brāhmans can get rid of their sins by making gifts[22]. The wonderful results of gifts on the donors, recipients and spectators, and of the topics on gifts on those who study or narrate or listen to them are described in almost all the Purāṇas in highly extravagant language. For example, the Varāha-p. (100, 12-13) says: "The man who makes gifts, the man who sees (them), the man who hears (about them), and the Vipra who accepts them—all become free from sins. The murderer of a Brāhman or the father, and the man who has killed a cow, drunk wine, or violated

16 Mat 205, 8. Also cf. Pd (Sṛṣṭi-kh.) 45, 176.
17 Mat 205, 9.
18 Mat 274, 77.
19 Pd (Sṛṣṭi-kh.) 31, 124a. Manu IV, 234.
20 Cf. Pd (Sṛṣṭi-kh.) 31, 135-136.
21 '*īśvara-prīṇanārtham*'—Kūr II, 26, 8.
22 Mat 206, 16; 90, 11; etc.

the bed of a superior person (guru-talpaga), get rid of all sins and attain the abode of Viṣṇu". The Matsya-p. also says: "One who witnesses the gifts with reverence, thinks of it at other times, repeats it to others, hears of it, or reads about it, becomes as beautiful as Indra and attains the region adorned by the god Puraṃdara"[23]; and "One who advises others (to make gifts) for their own good, invariably becomes the leader of the hosts of the Lord of the gods"[24]. Further, in the realm of Yama honour is said to be shown by Citragupta to those who repeatedly give food materials, foot-wears, umbrellas, water-pots etc., to Brāhmans[25]. According to Mārk 10, 51-55 those, who give water, food and drink, who worship the gods and the Brāhmans, and who do not forsake their own Dharma through anger, malice etc., are among those who die peacefully. In the different kinds of Dhenu-dāna and Acala-dāna, the cows and hillocks made are often identified with some prominent god or goddess, and are said to have the power of conferring the desired objects[26]. Such identification and ascription of power are obviously intended to attract the mind of the people to these gifts and also to make them have greater faith in their unfailing efficacy.

The Purāṇas narrate fictitious stories of kings and others who made gifts with great effect. For instance, in the Matsya-p. (274, 11-13) Vāsudeva, Bhārgava, Ambarīṣa, Kārtavīryārjuna, Prahlāda, Pṛthu, Bharata and others are said to have made gifts with the result that they were all guarded by the gods. There is also the story of the prostitute Līlāvatī and the Śūdra goldsmith. The former gave away a hillock of salt, and the latter made, without charging any fee, a golden tree and some images of gods required in the gift. As results of these pious acts, the prostitute attained the region of Śiva after death, and the Śūdra goldsmith became a paramount sovereign named Dharmamūrti in his next birth[27].

The authors of the Purāṇas try to impart a semblance of holiness and importance to the topics on gifts by calling the latter 'secret' (guhya, rahasya) and 'old' (purātana)[28]. Moreover, these topics are always ascribed to some prominent god or sage in order that they may have unquestionable authority.

Miserly habits and deceitful economy (vitta-śāṭhya) in gifts are repeatedly condemned in the Purāṇas[29], probably because these

[23] Mat 274, 78. [24] Ibid., 275, 29b.

[25] Cf. Var 206, verses 2, 11, 14-15 and 18; 205, 20 ff.; and so on.

[26] Cf. Mat 83; Var 99-112; and so forth.

[27] Mat 92, 17-31.

[28] Mat 274, 18; Var 112, 48; and so on.

[29] Mat 277, 17; Var 109, 5, and 110, 5; and so on.

are highly detrimental to the interests of the Brāhmans. Those who are misers and do not give anything to the Brāhmans, are condemned to hell and its severe tortures[30]. The Brahma-p. (chap. 215) gives a horrible picture of hellish tortures inflicted on sinners by the hell-guards. When these afflicted sinners hanker after food and drink, the guards remind them that as they did not give anything to the Brāhmans on earth, they can have nothing to eat or drink in the hells. They then begin punishing the poor souls afresh.

From what has been said above it is clear that in the Purāṇas the Brāhmans adopt every possible means to make the people bounteous to themselves. They are not, however, satisfied with this even. They become so greedy for gifts that they call upon the administrative power of the king to force the people to be charitable to themselves in normal times as well as in famines. In the Kūrma-p. the king is advised to confiscate all the belongings of a man and banish him from his kingdom, if the latter does not, after earning money, satisfy the gods and the Brāhmans[31]. This Purāṇa further says: "The man who does not give food etc. to the starving Brāhmans in times of famine is a hateful murderer of Brāhmans. Nothing should be accepted from him, nor should anything be given to him. The king should brand such a man and drive him out of his territory"[32]. The avaricious character of the gift-seeking Brāhmans seems also to be indicated by the stories of fatal quarrels over the possession of gifts. As an instance the story of Yājñavalkya and Śākalya in Vā 60, 35 ff. (= Bd II, 34, 36-68) may be cited. This story states that Janaka once celebrated a horse-sacrifice which was attended by thousands of Brāhman ascetics. Out of curiosity to know who was the most learned among them, Janaka thought out a plan. He offered a thousand cows, gold coins (suvarṇa) of a greater number, villages, gems and slaves to the sages and said that these were to be accepted by that person who was the most learned among them. This set on foot a quarrel among the sages. Each of them wanted to possess the wealth and challenged others in debate in order to establish his superior knowledge of the Vedas. When the other sages were thus quarrelling, Yājñavalkya ordered one of his students to take the wealth to his house, because, he boasted, he was the only man who had mastered all the Vedas and was able to defeat all the sages present. The interests of all other sages being thus jeopardised, they stood in a body against Yājñavalkya; but they were silenced by the latter with questions. One Śākalya among these defeated sages got furious at this insult. He

[30] Var. 198, 76-78; Br 214; and so forth.

[31] Kūr II, 26, 59. [32] Kūr II, 26, 60-61.

challenged Yājñavalkya again in debate. Yājñavalkya answered the questions asked by Śākalya, and then put a question to the latter with the curse that if he could not answer it, he would die. Śākalya failed to answer it and died. The Brāhmans are, again, sometimes found to take recourse to apparently deceitful means to extract money from others. For example, the Kūrma-p. (II, 26, 19-38) describes some gifts in which the people are made to understand that they are worshipping their respective deities and offering things to them, when they are really worshipping some Brāhmans and making gifts to the latter. The Purāṇa further adds: "A wise man should worship the Brāhmans to please the god whom he wishes to adore. The gods always dwell in the bodies of the Brāhmans .... ; so, they should be worshipped in the Brāhmans very carefully by those who desire the fulfilment of their wishes"[33]. Such identification of the Brāhmans with gods seems to be another means of exploitation.

In order that the gifts may be monopolised by the Brāhmans who are within the Brahmanical and the Hindu fold, the Purāṇas advise the people not to be liberal to those Brāhmans and non-Brāhmans who follow other religions. The Kūrma-p. says: "A person versed in the laws should not offer even water to an infidel, a rationalist, the Pāṣaṇḍas and one who is not learned in the Vedas"[34]. It adds: "A man should feed a pious (dhārmika—practising 'Dharma') and learned Brāhman even if the latter has already got a full meal, but never an illiterate and undutiful one who has been fasting for ten nights"[35]. Such preachings and prohibitions are directed mainly against the Jains and Buddhists who are the most formidable rivals to the Brāhmans in the field of gifts.

The characteristics of those Brāhmans who are the worthy recipients of gifts are laid down in the Purāṇic chapters on gifts. These characteristics are important in that they point not only to the economic condition of the priestly Brāhmans but also to the causes which compelled them to be hunters of gifts. The Purāṇas say that the recipients of gifts should be 'śrotriya' (versed in Śruti), 'kulīna' (of high lineage), 'vinīta' (well disciplined), 'vratastha' (observing a vow), 'tapasvin' (practising penance), 'sāgnika' or 'āhitāgni' (maintaining the sacred fire in the house, i.e., preforming sacrifices), 'veda-pāraga' (master of the Vedas), 'sadācāra' (of good conduct), 'annārthin' (wanting food), 'kuṭumbin' (burdened with families), 'daridra' (poor), and so forth[36]. The encouragement to

[33] Kūr II, 26, 36-38.
[34] Kūr II, 26, 68.
[35] Kūr II, 26, 64.
[36] Cf. Mat 72, 35, and 97, 15; Kūr II, 26, 11 and 14; Var 58, 15-16; 101, 7; 103, 9; 104, 9; and so forth.

making gifts to the 'śrotriya', 'āhitāgni' and 'sadācāra' Brāhmans is due to the fact that such Brāhmans need help for the proper conduct of their expensive sacrificial rites. There are inscriptional records of grant of land solicited by, and also made to, Brāhmans for the proper conduct of their Vedic rites. As examples, the Dāmodarpur Copper plates of the Gupta kings[37] may be referred to. Of these plates, two were inscribed in 443-444 and 447-448 A.D. The first plate states that a Brāhman Karppaṭika applied to the local government for a permanent grant to him, according to Nīvidharma, of one Kulyavāpa of untilled, 'aprada', 'khila' land for the convenient performance of his Agnihotra rites *(mamāgnihotropayogāya)*. According to the second plate, a person, whose name is illegible and who was in all probability a Brāhman, was granted five Droṇas of land for the conduct of his five daily sacrifices [*pa(ñca)-mahāyajña-pravartanāya*]. In the Purāṇas such grants are said to be highly meritorious. The Kūrma-p. (II, 26, 12) says: "The man who, out of devotion, gives the earth *(mahīṃ*, i.e., land*)* to a Brāhman maintaining the sacred fire, attains the highest region where sorrow is unknown". The frequent occurrence of the word 'daridra' and the expressions '*kuṭumbine deyaṃ*', '*kuṭumbine pradātavyā*' etc. in the chapters on gifts, and the recipients' citations of the Mantra in which they are to say that they are accepting the gifts especially for the maintenance of their dependants[38], show that the poor priests were burdened with families which they often supported with great difficulty, and were, consequently, compelled to accept gifts for their bare maintenance and not for luxury. In numerous cases the condition of the priests became so much straitened that they turned professional beggars and disturbed the people by continued begging[39]. The poverty of the priestly Brāhmans seems further to be indicated by their acceptance of gifts and food offered by prostitutes in the Anaṅgadāna-vrata (Mat 70, 42-45). According to Yājñavalkya (I, 215) such gifts are always to be rejected.

Though the priestly Brāhmans stand in great need of gifts, they hesitate to accept these from any and every person without discrimination. In their opinion, those members of the upper three castes who follow their respective duties are the best people from whom gifts are acceptable[40]. It is mainly in the case of Śūdras

[37] Ep. Ind., Vol. XV, pp. 113 ff.

[38] *ahaṃ gṛhṇāmi tvāṃ devi kuṭumbārthe viśeṣataḥ*|—Var 104, 12. Also cf. Var 99, 91-92 and Pd (Sṛṣṭi-kh.) 31, 143-144.

[39] Cf. *yas tu yācanako nityaṃ na sa svargasya bhājanaṃ*|
udvejayati bhūtāni yathā cauras tathaiva saḥ|| Kūr II, 26, 74.

[40] Cf. Kūr II, 26, 70.

that restrictions are to be followed more strictly. Inspite of all the theoretical restrictions, it is doubtful whether those members of the four castes who were neglectful of their duties were excluded in practice from being donors. From the evidence of the Purānas and the Buddhist literature we learn that priesthood ceased to be the only means of livelihood of the Brāhmans, and that many of them became state officials, traders, agriculturists and artisans. The Kṣatriyas, the Vaiśyas and the Śūdras also not seldom abandoned their respective hereditary professions for other occupations according to their own choice. From the facts that the Veda-knowing Brāhmans are allowed by the Purāṇas to accept gifts from even public women, and that the former are said to hanker after the favour of the Śūdras, it seems highly probable that in practice the priestly Brāhmans did not reject the gifts made to them by the 'fallen' members of the four castes.

Inspite of all their preachings for gifts, the Brāhmans seem never to have ignored the ideal life of simplicity and asceticism. They formulate that a Brāhman should live a simple life in which excess of wealth should have no place. He should not be greedy, nor should he be anxious for the acceptance of gifts, because greed of money causes degradation. He should accept from others only that amount which will give him a bare subsistence[41]. As to the expending of the money received, the Brāhmans are advised not to be reckless. They are to spend it for the maintenance of their dependants, for the worship of gods, for entertaining guests, for performing sacrifices and for making gifts, but never for enjoyment[42].

Besides the ceremonial gifts, of which much has been said above, there were other sources of income to the priestly Brāhmans. These are the vows (vrata) and worships, funeral ceremonies, penances, etc.

The way in which the gifts are connected with vows in the Purānas, proves definitely that one of the main objects of encouraging the latter is inducement to making gifts[43]. This fact is further evidenced by the description of many vows in which gifts are of primary importance[44]. The variety and the expensive nature of the articles of gifts also seem to point to the same fact. In order

[41] Cf. Kūr II, 26, 71-73.

[42] Cf. Kūr II, 25 18-21, and II, 26, 75.

[43] Cf. *ataḥ paraṃ pravakṣyāmi dāna-dharmān aśeṣataḥ|*
vratopavāsa-saṃyuktān yathā matsyoditān iha|| Mat 54, 1.
vrata-rūpāṇi dānāni nānā-rūpāṇi pārthiva|
tāni te'haṃ pravakṣyāmi lokānāṃ hita-kāmyayā||
Agni-p., quoted in Caṇḍeśvara's Kṛtya-ratnākara, fol. 189b.

[44] Cf. Mat 101 in which 62 different vows have been described.

to acquaint ourselves with the extent of taxation made through the vows, the direction of the Matsya-p. in connection with the Āditya-śayana-vrata is given below as an example. This Purāṇa says: "On the day of the fourteenth repast after the fast, the worshipper should feed the Brāhmans with raw sugar, milk and clarified butter. And after that, he should get a golden lotus, eight 'aṅgulas' in length, furnished with eight leaves and studded with gems, and bedecking it with nice cloth, should give it away to a Brāhman, along with bedsheet, pillow, utensils, shoes, chowries, a piece of mattress, looking-glass, garments, fruits, incense, bedstead, a cow with her horns covered with gold and hoofs with silver, along with her calf, and a vessel of bell-metal for milking the cow. The cow must necessarily be given away on that occasion"[45]. This multiplication of gifts in the Purāṇic vows stands in striking contrast with the simple priestly fees prescribed in the Ṣaṣṭhī-kalpa of the Mānava-gṛhya-sūtra[46]. In this Ṣaṣṭhī-kalpa, which is almost a regular Vrata, Ṣaṣṭhī is called Śrī, Lakṣmī, Kāma-patnī, Devī etc., and is thus deified. This Kalpa is meant for the attainment of progeny and wealth; and in it the priestly fee is only a cow and a bull *(gaur anaḍvāṃś ca dakṣiṇā)*.

Great attempt has been made in the Purāṇas to popularise the vows, which, the authors of the Purāṇas say, are to be observed by all without discrimination (*avicāreṇa .... anuṣṭheyaṃ ......* Mat 70, 32). Just as in the case of the ceremonial gifts, the observance of the vows also is said to be capable of conferring both Bhukti (objects of enjoyment) and Mukti (final release) and of destroying all sins; the secret and the highly effective topics on vows are always ascribed to some god or sage so that they may have unquestionable authority; stories of ancient kings and commoners are fabricated to show the great powers of the vows[47]; miserly economy (vitta-śāṭhya) is severely condemned; and so forth.

Of the gifts in penances and funeral sacrifices we scarcely need anything to add. From very ancient times, these have played an important part in the economic life of the priesthood[48]. In the Purāṇas also their necessity is not at all overlooked. A comparison between the Smṛti Saṃhitās and the Purāṇas shows how the gifts in penances and funeral ceremonies have been multiplied in the latter.

[45] Mat 55, 20-25.

[46] Mānava-gṛhyasūtra (Gaekwaḍ's Oriental Series, No. XXXV), pp. 176-179.

[47] Cf. Mat 55, 32; and 100. Var 41, 17 ff.; 42, 7 ff.; 43, 9 ff.; etc.

[48] Keith, Religion and Philosophy of the Veda (Harvard Oriental Series, Vol. 31), pp. 265-266. J. Jolly, Hindu Law and Custom (English translation by Batakrishna Ghosh), p. 255.

Besides the occasions mentioned above, there are numerous others on which the Brāhmans have to be satisfied with money or food or both; viz., visits to holy places are to be attended with gifts and feasts to Brāhmans; in almost all religious ceremonies the Brāhmans are to be sumptuously fed; gifts are to be made to them after noticing an evil omen, dreaming bad dreams, and listening to the Purāṇas; valuable gifts are invariably to be made to the priests and the spiritual preceptor in Vrata, Pratiṣṭhā, Mahādāna, etc.; and so forth.

The measures noticed above are not all that the Brāhmans adopt for their own interests. They also try to better their social position by various means, which we shall briefly notice here.

The Brāhmans knew well that the establishment of the Varṇāśramadharma and the authority of the Vedas is intimately connected with that of their own supremacy, and that if they would succeed in the former, the latter would follow as a direct consequence. This conciousness is most probably one of the causes why in the Purāṇas they strain every nerve to establish the Varṇāśramadharma and the authority of the Vedas first; and we have seen how seriously they try to achieve this end. They are, however, not satisfied with this much. They preach: "The Brāhmans who have mastered the Vedas are incomprehensible by all beings; Brāhmans deserve always to be worshipped; Brāhmans are all gods. None should cherish wrathful jealousy towards these twice-born"[49]. They also introduce many stories of Brāhmans who possessed miraculous power of favour and curse. As an example, we may refer to Var 37 containing the story of king Dīrghabāhu who neglected the Brāhmans and became a tiger as a result of their curse. Being pacified by Dīrghabāhu the Brāhmans said that he could get rid of his tigerhood when an arrow would pierce his body and the words '*namo nārāyaṇāya*' uttered by a Brāhman would enter his ears. In course of time all these happened, and Dīrghabāhu got back his former existence. Before going to heaven he said: "The person who, after worshipping the Brāhmans and uttering the word '*namas*' to Hari, gives up his life, becomes free from all sins and attains final release. 'It is true, it is true, and again, it is true', I declare by raising my arms, 'that the moving gods in the forms of Brāhmans are the same as Puruṣottama, the supreme Being'[50]". One of the intentions underlying the above story is to raise the position of the Brāhmans in the public eye by making the people believe in the fierceness of

[49] Var 208, 19b-20. There are innumerable such passages in the Purāṇas. It is needless to refer to them all.

[50] Var 37, 33-34.

their curse, by making them understand that the Brāhmans can do immense good when pleased, and by showing the power of the Mantras uttered by them. Not to speak of men, even gods and objects of Nature are said to be controlled by Brahmanical power. In the Viṣṇudharmottara Pauṣkara, who warns Paraśurāma against hurting, insulting, killing, or doing anything objectionable to, Brāhmans, refers to the powers of the latter, saying: "(It is the Brāhmans) who have made the Fire omnivorous, (the waters of) the great ocean undrinkable, the Moon a phthisical patient, and Śatakratu have the scrotum of a he-goat; the fire produced by whose anger does not cease (to burn) in the Daṇḍaka forest even to this day; whose favour, O son of Bhṛgu, is equally great; through whose grace, the Moon, though waned, attains fullness, the Sun is not overpowered by the Rākṣasas, Kārtavīrya attained great prosperity, and Dhanada became the owner of riches"[51]. All these allusions are based on elaborate stories narrated in one or other of the Purāṇas.

In the majority of the Purāṇas, the Brāhmans are called the visible gods of the earth and are indentified with Viṣṇu or some other prominent deity[52], so that any ill-treatment of them means the same to these deities. The Brāhmans are also often directed to be utilised as one of the mediums of worship[53]. This use is certainly due to their ascribed divinity.

The sanctity of Brāhmans is set forth in many of the Purāṇas in highly extravagant language so much so that the people are directed to drink the water with which the holy feet of the Brāhmans are washed, because 'all the holy places on (the surface of) the earth exist in a sea, and those in the seas exist in the feet of a Brāhman'[54]. The miraculous powers of this water are also described in the same strain.

It is to be noted that though in the later Vedic period claim had already begun to be made for the divinity of Brāhmans[55], it

[51] Viṣṇudh. II, 32, 25b ff.

[52] Var 125, 169; 37, 34; etc.; Bv I, 1, 141; Pd (Brahma-kh.) 14, 2; and so forth.

[53] For instance, in the Rohiṇīcandraśayana-vrata (Mat 57) a Brāhman is to be considered as the Moon and worshipped; in the Nāndīmukha-śrāddha 'the Mātṛs and Gaṇeśa are first to be worshipped on variegated altars, on images, or in Brāhmans' (Kūr II, 22, 100); and so on.

[54] Bv I, 11, 26; Pd (Brahma-kh.) 14, 12; and so forth.

[55] See Śatapatha-brāhmaṇa II, 2, 2, 6-7 wherein the Brāhmans, who have studied and teach the sacred lore, are called human gods and are said to have the power of placing the sacrificer, who gratifies them with gifts, in the heavenly world as well as in a state of bliss (sudhā).

See also *Ibid.*, IV, 3, 4, 4-5; Taittirīya-saṃhitā I, 7, 3, 1; Taittirīya-āraṇyaka II, 15; Viṣṇu-dharmasūtra 19, 20-24; and so on.

is in the Purāṇas that we notice a remarkably vigorous attempt made in this direction; and the later the Purāṇa the greater the claim to their divinity, so much so that they are raised at times even higher than the gods and their worship is preached in highly extravagant language.

CHAPTER V

ABSORPTION OF TANTRICISM BY THE PURĀṆIC RITES AND CUSTOMS

It has already been said in chapter II of this part of our work that the Tantras (including the Pāñcarātra Saṃhitās and the Śaiva Āgamas) preached ideas and practices which often went against the Brahmanical ones, that these non-Vedic works are often denounced in the Purāṇas as 'Mohana-śāstra', and that at the time the chapters on vows, worship etc. first began to be included in the Purāṇas, the Tantric elements were eliminated as far as possible. It is due most probably to this originally strained relationship between the Tantras and the Purāṇas that the Purāṇic chapters on vows, worship etc., which were added before 800 A.D., are almost totally free from Tantric influence. The few Tantric elements which are found in these chapters consist of Mantra-nyāsa[1], the occasional use of Tantric Mantras for Abhicāra only[2], the drawing of coloured lotuses (padma) or circles (maṇḍala, cakra) during worship in vows, consecration etc.,[3] and the worship of virgin girls in the Vīra-vrata[4]. The retention of these few Tantric traces show how greatly the mystic rites and practices of the Tantras influenced the minds of the Brāhmans, who seem to have such a firm belief in their unfailing efficacy that, inspite of all their antagonistic attitude towards the Tantras, they could not free themselves totally from the influence of these works.

Our analysis of the Purāṇas shows that from about the end of the eighth or the beginning of the ninth century A.D., some of these works began to recognise the Tantras as one of the authorities on religious matters. This recognition must have been effected by the great spread of Tantricism among the people including even the Buddhists. But at first the recognition seems to have been made under restrictions, for the Devībhāgavata says: "For the deliverance of those best Brāhmans who were burnt by the curses

[1] Cf. Mat 266, 29-30. [2] Cf. Mat 93, 150 ff.

[3] Mat 58, 21-22; 62, 16-19; 64, 12; 72, 30; 74, 6-7; and so on.

[4] Mat 101, 27-28.

of Dakṣa, Bhṛgu and Dadhīca, and were caused to deviate from the path of the Vedas, the Āgamas of the Śaivas, Vaiṣṇavas, Sauras, Śāktas and Gāṇapatyas were written as steps (sopāna) by Śaṃkara. In some places of these works there are some portions which do not go against the Vedas. By accepting these (portions) the Vaidikas do not incur sin"[5]. The Varāha-p. goes a step further. In it Nārāyaṇa is found to recommend, next to the Vedas, the sectarian scriptures of the Pāñcarātras thus: "By worshipping me through the Pauruṣa Sūkta and the study of the Saṃhitās, O twice-born, people always attain me in no time. I am attainable to those people (also) who, being unable to acquire (knowledge of) the Vedas, worship me after the direction of the Pāñcarātras"[6]. The Bhaviṣya-p. recognises the Tantras as an authority on the consecration of trees, parks, tanks, etc[7]. The Skanda-p. says that Śambhu can be realised through the Vedas, Purāṇas, Upaniṣads and the various Āgamas[8]. The Brahma-p. speaks of a king named Indradyumna who consulted the Tantras, Itihāsa, Purāṇas etc. to learn the method of worshipping Hari[9]. This gradual recognition of the authority of the Tantras is also reflected in those chapters on initiation, worship etc. which were added to the Purāṇas later than the beginning of the ninth century A.D. For instance, in the Purāṇic initiation (dīkṣā) as described in Var 127-129, some of the elements of Vedic Upanayana are introduced and the use of Tantric Mantras is carefully avoided, though the procedure is derived clearly from the Tantras, and the 'Āgama' is recognised as the authority[10]. On the other hand, Tantric elements are found to abound in the initiation described in the Garuḍa-p. (I, 9), Padma-p. (Sṛṣṭi-kh., 31, 8-75), Agni-p. (chaps. 27 and 81-89), etc. Similarly, in the consecration of images as described in Var 181-186 the sectarian Mantra is often used together with the Purāṇic and Vedic ones, whereas in Gd I, 48 this ceremony requires the performance of Nyāsas and the use of Tantric Mantras.

The liberal idea that the Brāhmans came to entertain about the Tantras was responsible for the inclusion of Tantric practices

[5] Dbh VII, 39, 28-31. The above mentioned direction of the Devībhāgavata is not a mere theory, but was often followed in practice. We learn from Aparārka (com., p. 17) that he was liberal enough to supplement the Vedic coustoms and rituals with those from the sectarian literatures of the Vāmas, Dakṣiṇas and others, if the latter did not go against his own; but the customs which were contradictory to those recommended by his own Śāstras were to be discarded.

[6] Var 66, 10-11b.

[7] Cf. Bhav II, i, 11, 1.

[8] Sk I, i, 5, 109-110.

[9] Br 44, 9-10.

[10] Var 127, 63a—*eṣāgame brāhmaṇasya dīkṣā bhūme hy udāhṛtā.*

in the Purāṇic religious rites. The extent of this inclusion even as early as about the tenth and eleventh centuries A.D. is found best in the Garuḍa and the Agni-purāṇa, which show that the frequent performance of Nyāsas and Mudrās and the use of mystic Tantric spells at every step constitute mainly the practical side of the rites. In these two Purāṇas as well as in a few others, the Yantra is recognised as a medium of worship[11], and rules are given for its painting.

The inclusion of Tantric practices is not limited to the Purāṇic rites only. The Vedic rites also are sometimes found influenced by these. Thus, the Vaidikī Saṃdhyā requires the performance of Nyāsa[12]. In some Purāṇas there is also the method of Gāyatrī-uddhāra—a mystic Tantric performance which is to precede the repetition of Gāyatrī[13].

The influence of the sectarian scriptures on the Purāṇic Brāhmaṇs seems to have liberalised, in certain cases, their idea about the lower castes. The Varāha-p. says: "Being remembered, or talked of, or seen, or touched, a devotee of the Bhagavat, even if he be a Cāṇḍāla, purifies (the people) easily"[14]. This Purāṇa also recommends that in religious ceremonies such as the consecration of images, the Bhāgavatas should be given preference even over the Brāhmans[15].

In the comparatively late portions of the Purāṇas the position of the spiritual preceptor is raised high, so much so that he is often indentified with the highest deity of a sect. Thus, in Var 99 a devotee, who is willing to have 'vrata-dīkṣā', is to identify his preceptor with Viṣṇu and honour him accordingly. The Bṛhan-nāradīya-p. says that there is no truth (tattva) higher than the preceptor. This high idea about the preceptor is perhaps one of the reasons why he is found to play an important part in the Purāṇic religious rites.

The gradual recognition of the authority of the Tantras by the Purāṇas, and the latter's absorption of Tantric elements enabled the former to exercise remarkable influence even on the Smṛti-Nibandhas. The writers on Smṛti, which is a continuation of a branch of the Vedic literature, can be divided into two sections, viz., (i) those who adhered to the Vedic customs and rituals, and regarded the orthodox Brahmanical works as authorities, and (ii) others who were liberal enough to admit the influence and authority of the

[11] Cf. Gḍ I, 17, 2—'. . . *karim* . . . *yantra-rūpiṇam*'; Padma-p. (Pātāla-kh.) 79, 1; and so on.

[12] Cf. Gḍ I, 221.

[13] Cf. Kūr II, 14, 57-61.

[14] Var 211, 88.

[15] Var 181, 20; 183, 25; 186, 23; and so on.

present Purāṇas professing sectarian Hinduism. This division, which is clearly perceptible in the Nibandhas, should be traced to the Smṛti Saṃhitās certainly posterior in time to those of Manu and Yājñavalkya. As we possess very few of the Smṛti works which were written between Yājñavalkya and the Nibandhas, we are not sure when this division began. The later Saṃhitās, found embodied in the Ūnaviṃśati Saṃhitā (Vaṅga. ed.) and betraying the influence of the Purāṇic Dharma by their references to and enumerations of holy places, their direction regarding the worship of Gaṇeśa, the fourteen Mātṛkās, Yama, Śiva and other deities, and the like, seem to point to a fairly early date. Whatever the period of this division may be, it is doubtless that the influence of the Purāṇas on Smṛti was due to the spread and popularity of Purāṇic Hinduism. The mention of the 'Purāṇa' as one of the fourteen sources of 'Dharma' [16] might also work at the basis of this influence.

The somewhat liberal idea held by the authors of the Purāṇas towards the popular practices was mainly responsible for liberalising the views of a very small number of Smṛti-writers who valued the Purāṇic Dharma. Consequently, a few of the comparatively late Smṛti Saṃhitās, which must be dated earlier than the Nibandhas, imbibed Tantric practices to supplement those of Saṃdhyā, Pūjā, etc.

The number of the Smṛti Saṃhitās, which valued the Purāṇas as a source of Dharma and imbibed Tantric practices, was so small that they could affect the Nibandhas very little. Hence in the Nibandhas the influence of the Purāṇas is slow to emerge. There are some commentators on Smṛti Saṃhitās and authors of digests who have intentionally avoided the quoting of passages from the Purāṇas. For instance, Viśvarūpācārya, in his commentary on the Yājñavalkya-smṛti, quotes not even a single line from any Purāṇa, though he profusely draws upon both Sūtra and Saṃhitā works of no less than 37 Smṛti-writers. It is not that before Viśvarūpa the Purāṇas did not contain any Smṛti-matter, but the fact seems to be that Viśvarūpa was quite unwilling to regard the Purāṇas as one of the sources of 'Dharma' perhaps on account of the latter's professing a Dharma which is composite (vyāmiśra) and, consequently, inferior (avara) to the Vedic. Vijñāneśvara, in his Mitākṣarā, follows his predecessor Visāvarūpa in avoiding the Purāṇic passages to a great extent but not totally. The few verses quoted by him from the Purāṇas show that he could not fully ignore the authority of the Purāṇas, though he tried to do so. On the other hand, Bhavadeva quotes, in his

[16] Cf. Yāj. I. 3.

Prāyaścitta-prakaraṇa, a few verses from the Matsya and the Bhaviṣya-purāṇa. There are also other Nibandha-writers who regard the Purāṇas as a source of Dharma, and have no hesitation in drawing upon them; but even in their works the influence of the Purāṇas is not very great in the beginning, but increases with the progress of time. Such a gradual increase in the Purāṇic influence is due most probably to the growing popularity of Purāṇic Hinduism and thereby of the Purāṇas themselves. But the credit of liberalising the views of the Nibandha-writers should perhaps be given to those few authors of Smṛti Saṃhitās who first acknowledged the authority of the Purāṇas and imbibed certain Tantric practices.

Thus, primarily the Purāṇas and secondarily the comparatively late Smṛti Saṃhitās were the causes of the Tantric influence on the Nibandhas. The authorities, viz., the Purāṇas and Smṛti Saṃhitās, quoted by the authors of the comparatively early Nibandhas to sanction the Tantric practices and the Śākta forms of worship, strengthen this supposition.

It has already been said that, inspite of all their abhorrence of the Tantras, the Purāṇas retained some Tantric elements. The great spread of the Tantric cult among the Hindus and the Buddhists made its influence felt more and more by the Purāṇas. Consequently, the Tantric elements made their way into the Purāṇas in a greater degree as the interpolations in these works were later. On the other hand, Tantric influence on the Nibandhas increased with the greater recognition of the authority of the Purāṇas by the Nibandha-writers, so much so that the Nibandhakāras like Vidyākara Vājapeyin, Raghunandana and others recognise fully the authority of the Tantras and draw profusely upon them on almost all matters concerning Dharma[17].

[17] See my articles in ABORS, Vol. XV, 1934, pp. 220 ff., and Vol. XVI, 1935, pp. 202 ff.; and IHQ, Vol. IX, 1933, pp. 678 ff.

APPENDIX I

From early times the Purāṇas have been regarded as one of the sources of Dharma (cf. Yāj. I, 3). This tradition is the main cause why the Nibandha-writers have drawn so frequently upon the Purāṇas in their respective works[1]. The numerous verses quoted by them from the different Purāṇas help us in forming an idea of the Smṛti materials these works contained during the ages they were used. The importance of these quotations is also keenly felt in determining the dates of the different units of the individual Purāṇas. Hence we have traced a good number of them in the extant Purāṇic works. A list of these traced verses, mainly on Dharma, is given below.

Besides the quotations noted in the following list, there are also others which, being absent from those editions of the extant Purāṇas which we have used in this work, are not mentioned here for want of space. The more important of these untraceable verses will, however, be given in a separate list.

As it was not possible for us to prepare, in all cases, the indexes of texts and authors quoted or referred to in the numerous commentaries and Nibandhas which we used in preparing the following list, we had to depend on those given in some of the printed editions of these works. So, if there are any defects in this list, which, we believe, are not many, they are due more to these indexes than to ourself.

It is to be noted that the following list does not include those verses which, though quoted in the commentaries and Nibandhas without any express mention of the respective sources, are traceable in the extant Purāṇas; because lines are often found common to the Smṛti Saṃhitās, epics, Purāṇas and other works of the Sanskrit literature. (See footnote 31 in Part I, chap. 2).

[1] Cf., for example, the discussion on the sources of Dharma in Smṛti-candrikā, I, pp. 3 ff.

I. VERSES QUOTED FROM THE 'MĀRKAṆḌEYA-P.' OR (IN A VERY FEW CASES) 'MĀRKAṆḌEYA'[2] IN

1. Aparārka's com. on Yāj.,	Mārkaṇḍeya-p.
p. 2	= 40, 29-34a.
p. 39	= 34, 109.
p. 146	= 29, 33.
p. 153	= 29, 35-36.
p. 173	= 34, 53b-54.
p. 279	= 34, 63.
p. 385	= 131, 25. The verse '*yajña-dāna*' is not found.
p. 434	= 30, 19 and 22-23.
p. 541	= 30, 17.
p. 554	= 32, 10.
p. 923	= 35, 36-38a.
pp. 968-970	= 11, 1-19.
p. 1022 (twice)	= 39, 12b and 13-15a.
pp. 1023-5	= 39, 16-38a.
pp. 1025-6	= 40, 15-25.
p. 1031	= 10, 26-28a.

2. Adbhutasāgara of Ballālasena,	Mārkaṇḍeya-p.
pp. 253-254	= 58, 55.
pp. 254-255	= 58, 6-9.
p. 256	= 58, 11-13a.
p. 257	= 58, 16-19a.
p. 259	= 58, 20b-28.
p. 261	= 58, 30-33a.
p. 262	= 58, 34-36a and 37.

[2] The verses of 'Mārkaṇḍeya' (the word '*mārkaṇḍeya*' being often used in the masculine gender), quoted in the commentaries and Nibandhas, are, except in a very few cases, not found in the present Mārkaṇḍeya-p. For instance, the verses of 'Mārkaṇḍeya', quoted in the Mitākṣarā on Yāj. I, 236 and 254 and III, 19, 287, 289, 316 and 324, are absent from the present Mārkaṇḍeya-p.

The facts that the great majority of the verses ascribed to 'Mārkaṇḍeya' is found in the Viṣṇudharmottara wherein the sage Mārkaṇḍeya is the speaker, that the same verses are sometimes quoted as from the 'Viṣṇudharmottara' in some places and from 'Mārkaṇḍeya' in others, and that in some cases verses of the Viṣṇudharmottara are quoted with the words *viṣṇudharmottare mārkaṇḍeyaḥ*', show that 'Mārkaṇḍeya', to whom these verses are ascribed in the Nibandhas, is, in the great majority of cases, identical with the sage Mārkaṇḍeya, the speaker in the Viṣṇudharmottara. In those cases in which the verses ascribed to 'Mārkaṇḍeya' are not found in the Viṣṇudharmottara, the changes in the text of the latter are to be held responsible. As to the few cases in which verses of 'Mārkaṇḍeya' are found in the Mārkaṇḍeya-p., it may be said that due to a confusion created by the similarity between the name of the sage and the title of the Purāṇa, verses of the Mārkaṇḍeya-p. were sometimes wrongly ascribed to 'Mārkaṇḍeya' or *vice versa*. For instance, the verses '*eka-bhaktena naktena*' and '*śukla-pakṣasya pūrvāhne*', which are quoted as from the 'Mārkaṇḍeya-p.' in Caturvarga-cintāmaṇi, II, i, p. 100 and III, i, p. 320 respectively but are not found in the present Purāṇa of the same title, are ascribed to 'Mārkaṇḍeya' (the word '*mārkaṇḍeya*' being used in the masculine gender) in Caturvarga-cintāmaṇi, III, ii, pp. 176 and 575 respectively. See also Aparārka's com., p. 206, Smṛti-candrikā, IV, p. 64, Smṛti-tattva, I, 109 and II, 88 and 95, and so on, wherein the former verse is ascribed to 'Mārkaṇḍeya'.

Mārkaṇḍeya-p.

	Mārkaṇḍeya-p.
p. 263	= 58, 38b-40a, 36b, 37a and 40b.
pp. 264-5	= 58, 40b-47.
pp. 266-7	= 58, 48b-53a.
pp. 267-8	= 58, 79b-80, 56, 75b-79a, 65-67, and 69-73a.
p. 506 (twice)	= 43, 4 and 20.
p. 507 (twice)	= 43, 19 and 15.
p. 508 (twice)	= 43, 27 and 16.
p. 509 (four times)	= 43, 17, 18a, 29 and 31. The line '*dṛṣṭvā tu tādṛśaṃ*' is not found.
p. 518	= 43, 35-37.
p. 523	= 43, 10.
p. 524	= 43, 24.
p. 525	= 43, 5.
p. 527	= 43, 32.
p. 528	= 43, 33.
p. 530	= 43, 28.
p. 531	= 43, 23a.
p. 535	= 43, 8.
p. 539	= 43, 26.
p. 541	= 43, 22 (Cf. also 43, 13a).
p. 542	= 43, 30.
p. 544	= 43, 7.
p. 545	= 43, 14.
p. 546	= 43, 6.
p. 548	= 43, 12.
p. 553 (twice)	= 43, 9b and 11.
p. 556	= 43, 9.
p. 557	= 43, 21.

3. **Dānasāgara of Ballālasena,**

fol. 20b	= 16, 36b-37a.
fol. 163b	= 10, 57a.
fol. 189b	= 10, 57a.

4. **Hāralatā of Aniruddhabhaṭṭa,**

p. 30	= 51, 105-107.

	Mārkaṇḍeya-p.
p. 160	= 10, 74.

5. Smṛti-candrikā of Devaṇabhaṭṭa,

II, 263	= 34, 67b-68a and 70b-71.
297	= 34, 52.
310	= 35, 36-37.
564	= 29, 33.
567	= 29, 29.
582	= 29, 22b-23a.
588	= 29, 24b-25a.
589 (twice)	= 29, 26b-27 and 28.
592	= 29, 46.
593	= 29, 31.
596	= 29, 39.
614	= 34, 59.
IV, 2	= 31, 3-15 (except verses 5 and 14).
3	= 31, 16.
8	= 30, 19-20 and 22-23.
21-22	= 33, 1-8a (except 6a).
27	= 31, 21-22.
97	= 33, 4b-5a.
213	= 32, 10.
V, 78	= 35, 39 and 40-41a.

6. Caturvarga-cintāmaṇi of Hemādri,

Vol. I,	
p. 61	= 46, 23-25.
p. 83	= 57, 34.
p. 118	= 49, 67-72.
pp. 121-122	= 49, 37-40.
p. 142	= 34, 109.
pp. 946-7	= 15, 60-61.
Vol. II, Part i,	
pp. 26-7	= 57, 1-3a, 7b-8a, 59-62a, 10a and 62b-63.
p. 34	= 34, 109.
p. 37	= 16, 36b-37a.
pp. 49-50	= 49, 66b-72.
p. 52	= 49, 37-40.
p. 326	= 16, 61 and 63. The line '*dharmārtha-kāma-saṃsiddhyai*' is not found.

Mārkaṇḍeya-p.

Vol. III, Part i,		
pp. 12-13	=	31, 8-10 and 12-17. The line *'piśācatvam anuprāptāḥ'* (on p. 13) is not found.
p. 81	=	31, 3-4.
p. 105	=	30, 5a.
p. 138	=	30, 6b-7a.
p. 151	=	31, 8 and 12.
p. 171	=	31, 20.
p. 193	=	33, 1 ff.
p. 197	—	(=Br 220, 45b-48a).
p. 250	=	31, 21-22.
p. 259	=	31, 21a and 22.
pp. 264-5	=	33, 1-5 and 6b-8a. The first two lines *'kanyā-gate savitari'* etc., which are not found in the Mārkaṇḍeya-p., are the same as Br 220, 14.
pp. 268-9	=	33, 8b to the end.
p. 276	=	31, 20-22.
p. 296	=	30, 12.
p. 411	=	32, 28.
p. 421	=	31, 34.
p. 427	=	29, 27.
p. 430	=	29, 26b.
p. 432	=	29, 28.
p. 437	=	29, 31.
p. 533	=	32, 14b-15a and 18b-c.
pp. 536-7	=	49, 64-72.
pp. 542-3	=	32, 9-10.
p. 549 (twice)	=	32, 11. The line *'varjyāś cābhiṣavā nityam'* is not found.
pp. 563-4	=	32, 12-13a and 14a.
p. 564	=	32, 25b-c.
pp. 572-3	=	32,17b-18.
pp. 801-2	=	35, 36-37.
p. 910	=	34, 52.
p. 931	=	34, 109,
p. 957	=	34, 67b-68a.
p. 961	=	34, 69-70.
p. 962	=	34, 63.
p. 1014	=	31, 31a.
p. 1063	=	31, 60a and 62.

Mārkaṇḍeya-p.

p. 1067	=	31, 60a and 62.
pp. 1082-1091	=	96, 7c to the end; 97, 1-26.
pp. 1097-8	=	32, 30-34.
pp. 1134-5	=	31, 30 and 32-34.
p. 1140	=	31, 37.
p. 1182	=	31, 36.
p. 1198	=	31, 39a.
p. 1203	=	31, 38.
p. 1210	=	31, 50b-51.
p. 1221	=	31, 40a.
pp. 1224-5	=	31, 40b-41a.
p. 1230	=	31, 40-41.
pp. 1241-2	=	31, 41b-42a.
p. 1252	=	31, 42b.
p. 1253	=	31, 43.
p. 1279	=	31, 44.
p. 1355	=	31, 46.
p. 1388	=	31, 48.
p. 1389	=	31, 50.
p. 1393	=	31, 52-53a.
p. 1424	=	31, 55a.
p. 1428	=	31, 54.
p. 1495	=	31, 59.
p. 1500	=	31, 56b-58a.
p. 1517	=	31, 62.
pp. 1539-1540	=	88, 14-18 and 20.
p. 1544	=	30, 7a.
p. 1546	=	30, 6a. The line *'vṛddhi-śrāddham'* is not found.
p. 1554	=	30, 5b.
pp. 1601-2	=	30, 8-11. The line *'iti brūyāt prayatnena'* is not found.
p. 1636	=	30, 12.
Vol. III, Part ii,		
p. 387	=	31, 21a and 22b.
p. 460	=	33, 1a
464	—	(=Br 220, 45b-48a).
p. 477	=	29, 14.
p. 503	=	31, 21-22.
pp. 503-4	=	31, 21a and 22.
pp. 510-511	=	33, 1-5 and 6a-8a. The verse *'kanyāgate savitari'*, which is not found in the Mārkaṇḍeya-p., is the same as Br 220, 14.

	Mārkaṇḍeya-p.
pp. 514-5	= 33, 8b to the end.
p. 522	= 31, 20-22.
p. 534	= 30, 12.
p. 608	= 31, 60a and 62.
p. 612 (thrice)	= 31, 60a and 62; 31, 61b and 60b-61a.
pp. 807-8	= 95, 7.
7. Kṛtyācāra of Śrīdatta Upādhyāya,	
fol 11a	= 34, 70-71.
fol. 22a	= 35, 36-37a.
fol. 28b	= 34, 52a.

	Mārkaṇḍeya-p.
fol. 65a	= 34, 94b.
fol. 67a	= 29, 35-36.
8. Madana-pārijāta of Madanapāla,	
p. 67	= 39, 12-14.
p. 119	= 34, 83-84.
pp. 122-123	= 35, 33-35 (expect 33b).
p. 125	= 34, 114 and 116. The other verses are not found.
pp. 473-474	= 31, verses 7-10, 12-13 and 15.

II. VERSES QUOTED FROM THE 'VĀYU-P'. OR 'VĀYAVĪYA' IN

1. Aparārka's com. on Yāj.,	Vāyu-p.
p. 258 (twice)	= 78, 51b-52a and 52b-54 (except 53a).
p. 387	= 77, 27.
p. 448	= 79, 67.
pp. 454-455	= 79, 68 and 78-80. (Three lines *'anāśrami tapas tepe'* etc. are not found).
p. 473	— Of the four lines quoted, only one tallies with Vā 78, 31b; the other three are not found.
p. 475	= 74, 4.
pp. 487-488	= 80, 39-40, 4, 37, 2, 5, 6, 7, 8, 16 and 19-21. 74, 1-2. Verses beginning with *'śrāddheṣū-pānahau dadyāt'*, *'tūla-pūrṇe tu yo dadyāt'*, and *'vyajanaṃ tāla-vṛntaṃ ca'* are found to tally with Bḍ III, 16, 8-9 and 10.

	Vāyu-p.
p. 490	= 75, 54b-55a.
p. 493	= 78, 48b-49a.
pp. 502-503	= 74, 20b-25a and 26-28. The lines *'svargāpavarga-sopānaṃ'* and *'bhrātaraḥ sarva-bhūtānāṃ'* are not found.
p. 506	= 75, 43.
p. 551	= 76, 31-33a and 34b-c.
p. 553	— Of the 21 lines quoted, only the first three and the last one tally with Vā 78, 8b-9a and 78, 10b respectively. These 21 lines are the same as Bḍ III, 14, 8b-9, 10b-12, and 14b-20.
p. 554	= 80, 42b-45a and 47-48.
p. 559	= 81, 18.
p. 560	= 82, 2a.
p. 924	= 79, 24b-25.
2. Adbhutasāgara of Ballālasena,	
p. 506.	= 19, 18.

Vāyu-p.

p. 507 (twice) = 19, 17 and 25.
p. 508 (thrice) = 19, 13, 27 and 14.
p. 509 (four times) = 19, 16, 33 and 15. The verse *'nagnaṃ śravaṇakaṃ'* is not found.

3. Dānasāgara of Ballālasena,

fol. 187a = 80, 59.

4. Kullūkabhaṭṭa's commentary,

on Manu III,
p. 267 — (*cf.* Bḍ III, 14, 11b).
on Manu IV,
49 = 78, 60.

5. Smṛti-candrikā of Devaṇabhaṭṭa,

II, 589 = 79, 18.
IV, 25 = 80, 45
203-204 — These verses tally with Bḍ III, 14, 14b-15, 16b and 17b-20.

208 (twice) = 78, 31b-32a and 40.
331 = 75, 54b-55a.
366 = 75, 43.
370-371 = 75, 22.
392-393 = 80, 2.
393 = 59, 49.

6. Caturvarga-cintāmaṇi of Hemādri,

Vol. I,

p. 90 = 79, 46b-47a.
p. 100 = 79, 38-39.
pp. 138-9 = 75, 20.

Vol II, Part i.

pp. 34-5 = 79, 46b-47a.

Vāyu-p.

p. 38 = 79, 38-39.

Vol. III, Part i,

p. 10 = 73, 55.
p. 17 — (=Bḍ III, 20, 12b-14a. The first verse is not found).
p. 25 = 81, 7-9a. The line *'pūjakānāṃ sadotkarṣaḥ'* is not found.
pp. 27-8 — (=Bḍ III, 20, 2b-5; 19, 50-53a; and 16, 55b-56a and 59. The remaining lines are not found).
pp. 37-8 = 31, 29a. Cf. also 30, 22-24.
p. 80 (twice) = 75, 22a. The line *'prāgdakṣiṇābhimukho'* is not found.
p. 162 = 78, 23.
pp. 186-7 = 81, 1-9a.
p. 213 = 81, 18.
p. 246 = 80, 45.
p. 279 = 81, 1-2a.
p. 368 = 79, 80.
p. 413 = 71, 69-71.
p. 419 = 79, 53-55a.
p. 428 = 79, 16b-17a.
p. 430 = 79, 18.
p. 432 = 79, 7 and 9.
p. 435 = 79, 8, 19 and 48b-49a.

pp. 439-440 = 79, 13 and 15b-16.
p. 467 = 79, 78.
p. 474 = 79, 79-81.
pp. 475-6 = 79, 67-68. Four lines *'ugreṇa tapasā'* etc. (on p. 475), which are not found in the present Vāyu-p., are the same as Bḍ III, 15, 40a, 39a and 41.
p. 504 = 83, 60b-66, 67b-68a and 69b.
p. 511 = 79, 5.
p. 590 = 78, 31b-32a.

		Vāyu-p.
pp. 522-3	=	78, 32b-36a and 38-39. Four lines from '*vaidikaiś cāpi*' on p. 522 and the verse '*pūjayiṣyanti*' on p. 523 are not found.
p. 544 (twice)	=	78, 8b-c. The verse '*akṛtāgrayaṇaṃ*' is not found.
p. 554	=	78, 9b-10.
p. 555	=	78, 11b-14, 9a, 11a and 15.
pp. 597-8	=	83, 3-9. The verse '*gayāyām akṣayaṃ śrāddhaṃ*' which is not found in the Vāyu-p., is the same as Bḍ III, 19, 13.
pp. 602-3	=	80, 42b-43.
p. 604 (twice)	=	80, 44; 80, 45a and 47-48.
p. 643	=	75, 51.
p. 672	=	80, 20-21. The verse '*rājatair bhājanaiḥ*' is not found.
p. 681	=	75, 7.
p. 682	=	75, 33.
p. 684	=	75, 34-35.
p. 686	=	75, 9a-b and 8.
p. 689	=	75, 10-11.
p. 694 (twice)	=	80, 37; 80, 39-40.
p. 698	=	80, 5.
p. 702	=	80, 7.
p. 703 (twice)	=	80, 16; 80, 8.
p. 705	—	(=Bḍ III, 16, 10).
p. 706	—	(=Bḍ III, 16, 8).
pp. 712-3	—	(=Bḍ III, 16, 9).
p. 719	=	80, 20-21; 74, 1a and 2c; 80, 19. The verse '*tila-pūrṇāni yo dadyāt*' is not found.
p. 722	=	74, 2a-b.
p. 734	=	75, 59b-60.
pp. 734-5	=	75, 31.

		Vāyu-p.
p. 737 (twice)	=	75, 12-13 and 14-15.
p. 746	=	80, 22, 26b-27a, 28b-29a, 30 and 31b-33a.
pp. 1006-7	=	79, 60.
p. 1011	=	75, 44.
p. 1016	=	79, 61.
p. 1019	=	79, 87.
pp. 1079-1080	=	74, 15a, 15c-17a, 15b and 17c-20a.
p. 1097	=	83, 10-12.
pp. 1127-8	=	83, 52-56.
p. 1179	=	74, 4.
p. 1208	=	74, 15a and 15c-17b.
p. 1330	=	75, 54b-55a.
p. 1397	=	76, 42a.
p. 1420	=	75, 43.
p. 1428	=	75, 22a.
p. 1431	=	75, 22.
pp. 1466-7	=	75, 52.
p. 1497	=	76, 43.
p. 1509	=	76, 31-33 and 34b-c.

Vol. III, Part ii.

pp. 453-4	=	81, 1-9a.
p. 455	=	81, 9a.
p. 492	=	81, 18.
p. 524	=	81, 1-2a.
pp. 561-2	—	(=Bḍ III, 17, 21b-22a; the remaining lines are not found).

7. Kṛtyācāra of Śrīdatta Upādhyāya,

fol. 2a	=	78, 60.
„ 10a	=	79, 38 and 39b.
„ 12b	=	79, 33a and 34a.
„ 41a	=	79, 46b-47a.
„ 64a	=	79, 88.

8. Kṛtya-ratnākara of Caṇḍeśvara,

fol. 173b	=	81, 2-4.
fol. 188a	=	81, 4a.

9. Mādhavācārya's com. on the Parāśara-smṛti, — Vāyu-p.

Vol. I, part ii,

p. 369 — These verses, which are not found in the Vāyu-p., are the same as Bd III, 14, 14b-20 (except 16a and 17a).
p. 412 = 75, 54b-55a.
p. 431 = 75, 22.
p. 438 = 76, 31.

10. Madana-pārijāta of Madanapāla,

p. 486 = 81, 2-4a.
p. 552 — These verses are found not in the Vāyu but in the Brahmāṇḍa-p. (III, 14, 9b, 10b-12 and 14b-17a).
p. 558 = 79, 53a. The other two lines *'gṛhasthānām'* etc. are not found.
p. 579 = 80, 2.
p. 581 = 75, 54b-55a.
p. 591 = 75, 57b-58a, 71-72 and 75b-76a.
p. 600 = 75, 43.

11. Prāyaścitta-viveka of Śūlapāṇi,

p. 306 = 78, 48b-49a.
p. 347 = 18, 12.
pp. 429-430 = 78, 69. 79, 20-22a.
p. 474 = 79, 24b-25.

12. Tīrtha-cintāmaṇi of Vācaspatimiśra,

p. 7 = 110, 2-3.

Vāyu-p.

pp. 274-275 = 82, 9 and 43. 77, 96b-97a, 98-99, 101-103, 105-106a, (two lines *'snātvā dina-trayam'* etc. on p. 275 of the Tīrtha-c. are not found), 108a and 109.
pp. 280-281 = 108, 13a, 14-19, (one line *'rāma-tīrthe naraḥ snātvā'* is not found), 21b-23a, (one line *'āgatya ca'* on p. 281 of the Tīrtha-c. is not found), 22 and 28-30.
p. 282 = 108, 20.
pp. 284-285 = 110, 9-15b, 19-20b, 20c, (one line *'tilājya-dadhi'* is found in the footnote on p. 443 of the Vāyu-p.), 56-59a and 61a.
pp. 285-286 = 105, 18-19a, 26 and 33.
p. 286 = 108, 71b; (one line *'pūtaḥ* etc.' is not found). 111, 17.
p. 288 = 110, 17 and 21-22.
p. 289 = 110, 23-24 and 30-32.
pp. 290-292 = 110, 34-42 and 44-55.
p. 296 = 110, 8-9, 62a and 65.
pp. 298-301 = 111, 1-3. 110, 21, 17-18a and 23-24. 111, 4-6b, 7, 8-10a, 12, 10b-11a, 13-14 and 15-22. Some verses, which are not found in the running text, are given in the footnote on p. 443 of the Vāyu-p.
p. 303 = 109, 43. The other three lines are not found.
p. 309 = 111, 23a-b and 24-26.

Vāyu-p.

pp. 310-312 = 111, 30a, 31-32, 35-36, 33-34 and 38-40. One line '*śrāddhāya piṇḍadānāya*' and one verse '*āmrāś ca siktāḥ*' on p. 311 of the Tīrtha-c. are not found.

pp. 314-318 = 111, 41, 44a, 45a, 44b, 45b-c, 46-49a, 50-52, 54a, 56b-63, 69-71a, 64-68, 73, (two verses are found in the footnote on p. 449 of the Vāyu-p.), 74-75b.

p. 320 = 105, 26.

p. 321 = 107, 46 and 48.

pp. 321-323 = 111, 77, 78a, 79. Three lines '*dṛṣṭvā natvā tha*', '*gayāyām dharma-pṛṣthe*' and '*gayā-śīrṣe 'kṣaya-vaṭe*' are given in the footnote on p. 449 of the Vāyu-p.
111, 76, 82-84 and 75.
109, 5b and 7b-12. One line '*upendra tvam*' on p. 323 of the Tīrtha-c. is not found.

Vāyu-p.

pp. 325-333 = 112, 21-22b, 23-26, (two lines are found in the footnote on p. 451 of the Vāyu-p.), 34b, 44b, 46-49a,
30-31,
(four lines '*udbhijjāḥ*' etc. are not found),
49b-53,
(the lines '*śrāddhi nāma*' etc. on p. 327 of the Tīrtha-c. are not found),
56-58a, 60, and 58b-59.
108, 12, 24,
(five lines '*rāme vanam gate*' etc. on p. 328 of the Tīrtha-c. are found in the footnote of the Vāyu-p., p. 436),
32a,
43b-44a,
(Vāyu-p. pp. 436-7, footnote, verses 1-2, 5-15, 17, 16, 18-26a, 28-32, 34b-38a; three lines '*tam dṛṣṭvā*' etc. on p. 332 of the Tīrtha-c. are not found).

III. VERSES QUOTED FROM THE 'BRAHMĀṆḌA-P.' OR 'BRAHMĀṆḌA' IN

1. Kālaviveka of Jīmūtavāhana, — Brahmāṇḍa-p.

p. 99 = II, 24, 56b-57.
p. 347 = II, 28, 41.
p. 351 = II, 28, 41.
p. 354 (twice) = II, 28, 47-48.
p. 366 = III, 19, 48b-49a.
p. 390 = II, 21, 144a and 147.

2. Aparārka's com. on Yāj., — Brahmāṇḍa-p.

p. 42 = III, 14, 94b-95a.
p. 123 = III, 14, 70.
p. 279 = III, 14, 101-103a.

		Brahmāṇḍa-p.
p. 416	=	III, 19, 14c-19.
pp. 440-441	=	III, 15, 63a and 64a. III, 15, 7b-10a. III, 19, 22b-26a. III, 9, 73. One verse *'pratyāsannam adhīyānam'* on p. 441 is not found in the Bḍ.
p. 459	=	III, 14, 26.
p. 462	=	III, 14, 97b-98a.
p. 472	=	III, 14, 32-33. One verse *'go-gajāśvādi-pṛṣṭhesu'* is not found.
p. 473	=	III, 14, 34, 35b-36a and 43b-44a.
p. 478	=	III, 11, 81-82a. The verse *'tatra siddhārthakān'* is not found.
p. 486	=	III, 11, 69b-71a.
pp. 489-490	=	III, 11, 91a, 93-95, 99-100, 108b-111, 113b-115a, 115b-116a. III, 12, 37. The verse *'nivāsaś caiva kīṭānām'* is not found.
p. 506	=	III, 11, 52 and 56.
p. 507 (twice)	=	III, 11, 68a, 55 and 65b-66a. The line *'bilva-patreṇa dātavyam'* is not found.
p. 510	=	III, 16. 2; III, 11, 2. The line *'daridro 'pi yathāśakti'* is not found.

3. Adbhutasāgara of Ballālasena,

p. 524	—	(=Vā 19, 22).
p. 527	—	(=Vā 19, 31).
p. 531	—	(=Vā 19, 21b).
p. 537 (twice)	—	(=Vā 19, 23b and 23).
p. 538	—	(=Vā 19, 24b).
p. 539	—	(=Vā 19, 24).
p. 542	—	(=Vā 19, 30).
p. 544	—	(=Vā 19, 5).
p. 545	—	(=Vā 19, 12)

4. Smṛti-candrikā of Devaṇa-bhaṭṭa,		Brahmāṇḍa-p.
II, 237	=	III, 14, 70.
243 (twice)	=	III, 14, 72, 65b and 93b.
262	=	III, 14, 102b-103a.
270-1	=	III, 14, 94b-95a.
287	=	III, 11, 75b-76a. The verse *'chinna-mūlā gṛhītavyāḥ'* is not found.
IV, 157	=	III, 15, 64a.
157-158	=	III, 9, 73.
159	=	III, 15, 63a.
205	=	III, 14, 58b-59a.
208 (twice)	=	III, 14, 34 and 35b-36a.
263	=	III, 11, 69b-70a.
264	=	III, 11, 70b-71a.
270	=	III, 14, 97b. The line *'uccāvacaḥ'* is not found.
281	=	III, 11, 17b-18, 20b and 19b.
353	=	III, 11, 80b-c. The verse *'na cāśru'*, which is not found in the Bḍ. is the same as Vā 83, 77.
365 (twice)	=	III, 11, 52 and 56. The line *'vajreṇa vā kuśair vā'pi'* is not found.
372	=	III, 11, 61b.
377	=	III, 11, 62b-63a.

5. Caturvarga-cintāmaṇi of Hemādri,

I,

pp. 160-163	=	III, 16, 2-5a, 8b-13a, 16b-17a, 18b-21a, 23b-26a, 27b-28a, 29-31a, 32b-34a, 35b-36a and 41-

		Brahmāṇḍa-p.
		42a. The line '*dātāram upatiṣṭhanti*' and seven lines from '*rathyān āvasathān*' on p. 162 are not found.
p. 232	=	II, 19, 157.
pp. 296-7	=	II, 16, 5. For the remaining verses cf. Bd II, 15, 31b ff.
III, i,		
pp. 36-7	=	III, 9, 2b, 5b-6, 8b, 8a and 11-12. Also cf. III, 9, 40 ff.
pp. 40-41	=	III, 9, 16-19, 21-26a and 35b. The verse '*yūyaṃ śarīra-kartāraḥ*' is not found.
p. 44 (twice)	=	III, 9, 55-56; III, 10, 57b-59.
pp. 54-55	=	III, 10, 3-4a, 52b-53, 75-77a, 84a, 85-86a, 88-89, 93-94 and 96-97a.
pp. 60-61	=	III, 9, 52b-53a, 54, 59b-65, 29-30, 33b and 34b. (Also cf. III, 10, 5-6a).
p. 70	=	III, 10, 99-100.
p. 133 (twice)	=	III, 11, 93-94a; III, 12, 3a and 4a. The lines '*vidhinā sā tu*' and '*tasya putrāḥ*' are not found.
pp. 134-5	=	III, 12, 4b-6a and 7-16a. The line '*sarvāpsarobhiḥ*' is not found.
pp. 271-2	=	III, 17, 21b-22a.
p. 361	—	(=Vā 79, 80).
p. 386	=	III, 19, 22b-23a and 24b-26a.
p. 403	=	III, 15, 28.
p. 442	=	III, 9, 73.
p. 519	=	III, 14, 34.

		Brahmāṇḍa-p.
p. 520 (twice)	=	III, 14, 35b-36a; III, 14, 39b-40a.
p. 549	—	Cf. III, 14, 13.
p. 566	=	III, 14, 19b and 20.
pp. 608-9	=	III, 14, 53-56.
p. 621	=	III, 14, 26. The verse '*yanna sarvāya*' is not found.
p. 638	=	III, 11, 74b-75. The last line '*agnikārye ca yāge ca*' is not found.
p. 639	=	III, 11, 75b-76a.
p. 682	=	III, 11, 69b-70a.
p. 684	=	III, 11, 70b-72a.
p. 687	=	III, 11, 42b-43a.
p. 735	=	III, 11, 55 and 54.
p. 736	=	III, 11, 65b-66a. The verse '*dadyāt krameṇa*' is not found.
p. 737	=	III, 11, 47b-49.
p. 962	=	III, 14, 102b-103a.
p. 981	=	III, 14, 94b-95a.
p. 1043	=	III, 11,2.
pp. 1081-2	=	III, 11, 22b-33a.
p. 1097	=	III, 19, 9b-10, 8b and 11.
p. 1211	=	III,11, 81. The verse '*tatra siddhārthakān*' is not found.
pp. 1335-6	=	III, 11, 99, 103-104 and 100-102. The line '*evaṃ lakṣaṇake*' is not found.
p. 1348	=	III, 12, 37.
p. 1355	=	III, 11, 91a and 93-95.
p. 1396	=	III, 12, 44b.
p. 1397	=	III, 11, 44a.
p. 1414	=	III, 11, 56.
p. 1415 (twice)	=	III, 11, 52a. The line '*vajreṇa vā*' is not found.
p. 1429	=	III, 11, 61b.
p. 1431	=	III, 11, 58.
p. 1462	=	III, 11, 62b-63a.
p. 1472	=	III, 11, 33b-34a.
p. 1509	=	III, 12, 31b-34a and 35.
p. 1574	—	(=Vā 76, 21b-22).

IV. VERSES QUOTED FROM THE 'VIṢṆU-P.' IN

	Viṣṇu-p.
1. Kālaviveka of Jīmūtavāhana,	
p. 14	= II, 8, 64-65.
p. 17	= II, 8, 28-30.
p. 20	= III, 14, 16.
p. 389-390	= II, 8, 72-73. Many of the quoted lines are missing in our edition of the Viṣṇu-p.
2. Aparārka's com. on Yāj.,	
p. 6	= III, 6, 28-29.
pp. 20-21	= III, 8, 11b. The other quotation is not found.
p. 50	= III, 11, 98.
p. 79	= III, 10, 13-15a.
p. 126	= III, 11, 21.
p. 151	= III, 11, 88-95. The last three lines of the quoted passage are not found.
p. 172	= III, 18, 97-102.
p. 173	= III, 12, 2.
p. 174	= III, 12, 38-39.
p. 227	= III, 12, 22.
pp. 420-421	= III, 14, 26 to the end.
p. 425	= III, 14, 12-13 and 15.
pp. 433-434	= III, 13,30-38 (except 34b and 35a).
p. 502	= III, 15, 28b-34.
p. 514	= III, 15, 10.
p. 515	= III, 13, 5-6.
	III, 10, 5a.
p. 530	= III, 13, 29.
p. 892	= III, 11, 98.
p. 986	= VI, 7, 31.
p. 1022	= VI, 7, 40.
p. 1025	= VI, 7, 43-44.
p. 1026 (twice)	= VI, 7, 45 and 89.
3. Hāralatā of Aniruddha-bhaṭṭa,	
p. 156	= III, 13, 10.

	Viṣṇu-p.
p. 159	= III, 13, 16 and 11-12a.
4. Dānasāgara of Ballālasena,	
fol. 21a	= III, 12, 20.
5. Kullūka-bhaṭṭa's commentary, on Manu,	
I, 2	= VI, 5, 74.
I, 69	= I, 3, 12-13 and 10.
I, 71	= I, 3, 14.
II, 32	= III, 10, 9.
II, 94	= IV, 10, 10.
III, 105	= III, 11, 105.
III, 280	= II, 8, 57.
IV, 151	= III, 11, 8b.
6. Smṛti-candrikā of Devaṇa-bhaṭṭa,	
I, 28	= VI, 2, 15.
52	= III, 10, 8a.
157	= III, 14, 12.
193	= III, 10, 23-24.
201	= III, 10, 18b-23a.
214	= III, 10, 16a.
II, 242	= III, 11, 15-16.
255	= III, 11, 19.
300	= III, 12, 20.
333-4	= III, 11, 24-25.
366 (twice)	= III, 11, 101. The other quotation is not traceable.
367	= III, 11, 98.
510-511	= III, 11, 26-28a.
525	= III, 11, 31-35.
528	= III, 11, 38b-39a.
582-583	= III, 11, 49-54.
588	= III, 11, 56.
594	= III, 11, 105.
596	= III, 11, 69.

	Viṣṇu-p.
608	= III, 11, 84-85.
611-612	= III, 11, 88-95.
613	= III, 11, 74b and 82b.
630	= III, 11, 109.
IV, 8-9	= III, 13, 30-38a.
22	= III, 14, 15.
28	= III, 14, 12 and 15b-c.
35-36	= III, 14, 7-9 and 16-18.
317 (twice)	= III, 15, 24. The other quotation is not found.
348	= III, 15, 32-34.
433	= III, 10, 4.
436	= III, 10, 5a

7. Śrī-bhāṣya of Rāmānuja,

p. 12, lines 14-15	= VI, 6, 12.
p. 14, lines 15-19	= VI, 7, 53; I, 2, 6; I, 4, 38.
&c.	&c.

Many quotations, which have been traced by the editor of the Bhāṣya.

8. Caturvarga-cintāmaṇi of Hemādri,

I,

p. 66	= III, 14, 7-9 and 16.
p. 90	= III, 12, 20.
p. 141	= III, 13,5-6.

II, i,

p. 18	= III, 6, 28-29.
pp. 20-21	= III, 6, 21b-24.
p. 27	= II, 3, 1 and 23-25.
p. 35	= III, 12, 20.

III, i,

	Viṣṇu-p.
p. 8	= III, 14, 22-25.
pp. 11-12	= III, 14, 1-2.
p. 37	= I, 5, 33-34a.
p. 105	= III, 13, 6b.
p. 171	= III, 14, 3.
pp. 174-6	= III, 14, 7-9 and 16-18.
p. 191 (twice)	= III, 10, 4; III, 13, 5-6.
p. 228	= III, 14, 15.
p. 252	= III, 14, 12 and 15b-c.
p. 259	= III, 14, 4.
p. 276	= III, 14, 3-6.
p. 431	= III, 11, 67.
p. 432	= III, 11, 61.
p. 438	= III, 11,105.
pp. 448-9	= III, 15, 2b-4.
p. 477	= III, 18, 103.
p. 738	= III, 14, 24. The line '*sa bhuktvā*' is not found.
p. 868	= III, 11, 24.
p. 874	= III, 11, 25.
p. 910	= III, 12, 24a.
p. 913 (twice)	= III, 12, 20. Cf. III, 17, 5 ff., and III, 18, 34 ff.
p. 924	= III, 11, 27-28a.
p. 929	= III, 11, 26.
pp. 943-4	= III, 11, 31-35.
pp. 991-2	= III, 11, 19.
p. 1015	= III, 15, 9-10.
p. 1033	= III, 14, 24.
pp. 1091-2	= III, 15, 29b-34. The line '*ślokān imāṃś ca*' and the verse '*mātāmahas tat-pitā ca*' are not found.
p. 1135	= III, 15, 8 and 10-11.
p. 1140	= III, 15, 13.
p. 1180	— Cf. III, 11, 104.
p. 1194	= III, 15, 12.
p. 1198	= III, 15, 15.
p. 1221	= III, 15, 17a.
p. 1222	= III, 15, 17b.
p. 1229	= III, 15, 17-18a.
p. 1241	= III, 15, 18b-19a.
p. 1252	= III, 15, 19a.
p. 1254	= III, 15, 19b-20a.
p. 1278	= III, 15, 20b.
p. 1388	= III, 15, 26b-27a.
p. 1389	= III, 15, 28b-29a.
p. 1495	= III, 15, 46b-47.

	Viṣṇu-p.
p. 1496-7	= III, 15, 41b-44.
pp. 1526-7	= III, 14, 26.
p. 1544	= III, 10, 5a.
p. 1555	= III, 13, 3.

III, ii,

pp. 138-9	= III, 8, 9.
p. 199 (twice)	= III, 18, 96 and 97b.
p. 457	= III, 10, 4.
p. 458	= III, 13, 5-6.
p. 500	= III, 14, 15.
p. 504	= III, 14, 3b-4.
p. 521	= III, 14, 3-6.
p. 643	= III, 14, 7-9 and 16.
p. 650	= III, 14, 12-13.
pp. 658-9	= VI, 2, 15.
p. 682	= III, 11, 115-116a.
p. 684	= III, 11, 116.
p. 696	= III, 11, 98.
p. 737	= III, 10, 8a.
p. 809	= III, 9, 25. The verse '*divā divye ca*' is not found.

9. Kṛtyācāra of Śrīdatta Upādhyāya,

fol. 1b (twice)	= III, 11, 5.
„ 4a	= III, 11, 14b.
„ 5a	= III, 11, 15-16.
„ 15b	= III, 11, 21.
„ 18b	= III, 12, 20b.
„ 28b	= III, 12, 24a.
„ 29b	= III, 11, 98.
„ 45b	= III, 11, 26.
„ 49b	= III, 11, 27a.
„ 54b	= III, 11, 31-35.
„ 55a	= III, 11, 39.
„ 57a	= III, 11, 40.
„ 64b	= III, 11, 102.
„ 65b	= III, 11, 48-55a.
„ 67a	= III, 11,64.
„ 71a	= III, 11, 77.
„ 71b (twice)	= III, 11, 78a and 86b.

	Viṣṇu-p.
„ 72b	= III, 11, 80a.

10. Prāyaścitta-viveka of Śūlapāṇi, Viṣṇu-p.

p. 7	= VI, 5, 26a.
p. 31	= II, 6, 35, 37 and 41.
p. 32	= II, 6, 34.
p. 285	= III, 11, 115-117.
pp. 367-368	= III, 11,115-116.
p. 368	= III, 15, 10.
p. 399	= III, 18, 39-42.
p. 474	= III, 17,6.

11. Madana-pārijāta of Madanapāla,

p. 43	= III, 11, 9.
p. 44	= III, 11, 12b and 14b.
p. 45	= III, 11, 15.
pp. 67-68	= VI, 7, 40. One verse is not found.
pp. 117-118	= III, 12, 22-23. The line '*jīveti* etc.' is not found.
p. 121	= III, 12, 14a.
p. 212	= III, 11, 22-23. The verse '*dhana-mūlāḥ kriyāḥ*' is not found.
p. 246	= III, 11, 25.
p. 276	= III, 12, 20.
p. 284	= III, 11, 27.
p. 325	= III, 11, 56.
p. 333	= III, 11, 84-85. The verse '*jaṭharaṃ* etc.' is not found.
p. 343	= III, 11, 102.
p. 344	= III, 11, 110. The prose portion is not found.
p. 349	= III, 11, 111a.
p. 420	= III, 11, 98.
p. 478	= III, 13, 33b-38a.
p. 515	= III, 14, 30-32.
p. 538	= III, 14, 12.

V. VERSES QUOTED FROM THE 'MATSYA-P.' OR 'MĀTSYA' IN

		Matsya-p.
1. Prāyaścitta-prakaraṇa of Bhavadeva,		
p. 5	=	227, 118b-120a.
2. Vijñāneśvara's Mitākṣarā,		
on Yāj. I, 297-8a	=	Chap. 94.
3. Kālaviveka of Jīmūtavāhana,		
p. 101	=	17, 9.
p. 292	=	61, 49a. The other line is not found.
p. 304	—	This verse, which is not found in the Matsya, is the same as Br 220, 14.
p. 321	=	274, 19b-22a.
p. 369	=	22, 83.
p. 370	=	22, 88.
p. 391	—	These lines, which are not found in the Matsya, are the same as Br 220, 53b-54.
p. 400	=	17, 4a. The other line is not found.
p. 418	=	17, 9.
p. 520	=	17, 5b-8.
4. Aparārka's com. on Yāj.,		
p. 16	=	265, 1b-5.
p. 139	—	(These verses are the same as Viṣ III, 11, 32-35).
p. 145	=	16, 5b-6a.
p. 301	=	Chap. 205 (except verse 1).
pp. 303-305	=	Chap. 82, verses 2-25 (except verses 12 and 24).
pp. 313-319	=	Chap. 274 (except verses 3a, 13b, and 28b).
pp. 320-323	=	Chap. 275 (except the last verse). Chap. 276 (except the last stanza; inserts a stanza after stanza 7).
pp. 324-326	=	Chap. 277 (except the last verse).
pp. 328-354	=	Chaps. 278 (except the last verse), 279, 280 (except the last two verses), 281-289, 83-87, 88 (except the first verse), 89-91, and 92 (except the last verse).
pp. 354-356	=	Chap. 206 (except the first and the last verse).
pp. 382-383	=	253, 19b-33.
pp. 392-396	=	Chap. 53 (except verses 1, 2, 5-10, 21, 25b-26a and 56b to the end).
pp. 403-404	=	Chap. 290 (except verses 1, 13-17 and 20 to the end).
pp. 409-413	=	Chap. 58 (except verses 1-3).
pp. 414-415	=	Chap. 59 (except verses 1 and 19).
p. 441	=	16, 11b-12a. The other stanza is not traceable.
p. 443	=	16, 8b-10a.
p. 456	=	16, 19-20.
pp. 466-467	=	22, 88.
p. 475 (twice)	=	15, 34a and 35b-36a. 16, 26-29 (except 26b).
p. 485	=	17, 26-27a.
p. 491	=	15, 32b-33a.
p. 507	=	18, 30.

		Matsya-p.
p. 511 (twice)	=	17, 52b-55 and 59.
p. 512	=	17, 60-61.
p. 514	=	16, 56-57a.
p. 515	=	17, 65b-66.
p. 523	=	18, 8-9a.
p. 550 (twice)	=	16, 52b-54a. The other quotation is not found.
p. 554	=	17, 36.
pp. 557-558	—	One line tallies with Mat 17, 4a; the substance of another quoted stanza is found in Mat 17, 2a.
p. 564	=	267, 12b-13.
p. 569	=	Chap. 94. The quoted passage has two verses more than Mat 94.
p. 572	=	93, 7b-9a and 11-12.
p. 575	=	93, 59-63a.
p. 800	=	227, 6.
p. 835	=	227, 8.
p. 856	=	227, 120b-121a and 126b-127a.
p. 889	=	18, 5-6.
p. 890	=	18, 7.
p. 954	=	184, 21b-23a.
p. 1043	=	227, 118b-120a.

5. An anonymous commentary on the Trikāṇḍa-maṇḍana of Trikāṇḍa-maṇḍana Bhāskara-miśra,

p. 238	=	93, 111.

6. Hāralatā of Aniruddha-bhaṭṭa,

p. 98	=	18, 30.
p. 162	=	18, 5-7.
p. 198	=	18, 12b-14a.

7. Dānasāgara of Ballālasena,

		Matsya-p.
fol. 6a	=	274, 1.
„ 15b-16a	=	22, 27b-28, 30b-36, 49-55a, 57-59, 68, 73b-75a and 71a.
„ 18a	=	206, 23b-24a.
„ 23a	=	115, 14.
„ 27a-31b	=	Chap. 274.
„ 39b-41a	=	„ 275
„ 42b-44a	=	„ 276.
„ 45b-46b	=	„ 277.
„ 48b-50a	=	„ 278.
„ 52a-53a	=	„ 279. (For '*guruṇokta-mantraiḥ*' in Mat 279, 10, the Dānasāgara reads '*guḍa-dhenu-mantraiḥ*' and supports this reading by saying that it was found in the majority of the Mss of the Matsya-purāṇa. Cf. fol. 52b).
„ 54a-55a	=	Chap. 280.
„ 56a-57a	=	„ 281.
„ 58b-59b	=	„ 282.
„ 61a-62a	=	„ 283.
„ 63b-64b	=	„ 284.
„ 66a-67b	=	„ 285.
„ 69a-70a	=	„ 286.
„ 71a-72a	=	„ 287.
„ 73a-74a	=	„ 288.
„ 77a-77b	=	„ 289.
„ 79a-81b	=	„ 83.
„ 87a-87b	=	„ 84.
„ 88a	=	„ 85.
„ 88b-89a	=	„ 86.
„ 89a-89b	=	„ 87.
„ 89b-90a	=	„ 88 (except the first line).
„ 90a-90b	=	„ 89.
„ 91a-91b	=	„ 90.
„ 92a-92b	=	„ 91.
„ 93a-93b	=	„ 92 (except verses 17-33).
„ 94a-95a	=	Chap. 82 (except verses 1, 20a, 23a, 24 and 26-31).
„ 115a-115b	=	Chap. 205 (except verse 1).

		Matsya-p.
fol. 117a-117b	=	207, 10-12.
„ 191b-193b	=	53, 3-4 and 11-56.
„ 203a-203b	=	290, 2-19.
„ 214a-215b	=	Chap. 206 (except the last verse).
8. Adbhuta-sāgara of Ballālasena,		
p. 5	=	229, 5.
p. 6 (twice)	=	229, 6-9a and 9b-10a. The line *'divyam tivra-phalam'* is not found.
p. 9 (twice)	=	228, 2-3a; 229, 12b-13a.
p. 20	—	Cf. 163, 37a.
p. 23	=	163, 38a.
p. 43	=	163, 35.
p. 50	=	163, 38b-39a.
pp. 87-88	=	67, 2-6.
p. 141	=	163, 39b.
p. 275	=	231, 5.
p. 290	=	163, 37b.
p. 296	—	Cf. Chap. 229.
p. 302	=	233, 7 and 8b.
p. 318 (twice)	=	233, 6; 163, 50.
p. 319 (thrice)	=	172, 19; 231, 4a (the second *pāda* differs); 172, 18b.
p. 320	=	238, 2; 163, 48b.
p. 336	=	163, 42b.
p. 337	=	163, 42a.
p. 353	=	243, 23a and 22.
p. 356	=	228, 11; 236, 5.
p. 358	=	172, 13-14a.
p. 375	=	233, 1a.
p. 376 (twice)	=	233, 1b and 2a.
p. 378 (twice)	=	233, 3a; 163, 43a.
p. 379	=	233, 3b-4a.
p. 380	=	Cf. 233, 4b.
p. 381	=	233, 9.

		Matsya-p.
p. 386	=	228, 21a.
p. 388	=	228, 21-22a.
p. 391	=	228, 22b-23.
p. 398	=	228, 24-25.
p. 401	=	228, 26-27.
pp. 408-409	=	240, 8b-9a.
p. 410	=	234, 1-3a. The line *'aśoṣyā vā'* is not found.
p. 412	=	234, 3b-5a.
p. 413 (twice)	=	228, 12b; 234, 5b-7.
p. 416	=	231, 1.
p. 417	=	231, 2b-3.
p. 418	=	231, 6b and 8a.
p. 419	=	231, 9b-11.
p. 425	=	230, 1-5a.
p. 426	=	163, 45b-46.
p. 427	—	230, 6a.
p. 428 (twice)	=	230, 8a and 7a.
p. 429 (twice)	=	230, 6b and 7b.
p. 430	=	230, 5b.
pp. 431-432	=	230, 9b-12. The line *'tallingena'* is not found.
p. 441	=	232, 5b-6a and 11a.
p. 442 (thrice)	=	232, 10a, 9b and 9a.
p. 443 (twice)	=	163, 44; 232, 6b.
p. 444	=	232, 7b-8.
p. 445	=	232, 11b-12a.
p. 446	=	163, 40.
p. 447	=	232, 12b-14.
p. 458	=	238, 1.
p. 459 (twice)	=	238, 15a-b and 16. The verse *'svayam udghāṭite'* is not found.
p. 460	=	237, 12 and 7-8. Four lines from *'dvāra-prākāra-geheṣu'* are not found.
p. 461	=	163, 51.
p. 468	=	228, 11b.
p. 469	=	236, 2a, 3a and 4b.
p. 470	=	236, 2b and 4b.

		Matsya-p.
p. 471 (twice)	=	236, 1 and 3b-4.
p. 472	=	228, 14a.
p. 478 (twice)	=	231, 7 and 8b-9a ; 153, 175a.
p. 483	=	134, 12b.
p. 484	=	238, 10a, 9a, 10b-11a, 6b, 8, 5b and 11b.
p. 486	=	238, 15a-b and 16.
p. 490	—	Cf. 241, 13.
p. 492	=	241, 12.
p. 493	=	241, 14.
pp. 501-502	=	242, 19b-20.
pp. 502-503	=	242, 2b-15a.
p. 514 (twice)	=	242, 17b-18 and 15b-16.
p. 560	=	235, 1-3.
p. 564	=	235, 4.
p. 583	=	237, 1-3a.
p. 584	=	237, 3b.
p. 585	=	237, 4.
p. 587 (twice)	=	237, 9a and 13-14.
p. 654	—	Cf. 237, 9b.
p. 663	=	237, 5b.
p. 689	=	237, 10.
p. 698	=	237, 11.
p. 701	=	172, 15.
pp. 701-702	=	233, 7-8.
p. 713	=	233, 2b.
p. 714	=	233, 9a.
pp. 733-736	=	Chap. 228 (except verses 1, 25b-26a and 29). Two of the quoted lines, viz., '*ārogya-dhana-kāmaś ca*' (Adbhs., p. 733) and '*kāryā mā-rudgaṇī*' (Adbhs., p. 734) are not found.
p. 736	=	228, 29.
pp. 743-4	=	229, 13b-20a, 22b-24a, 20b-22a, and 24b-25.
p. 751	=	229, 10b-11a.

		Matsya-p.
9. Kullūkabhaṭṭa's commentary,		
on Manu		
III, 265	=	17, 61.
V, 60	=	18, 30.
10. Haradatta's commentary,		
on Gaut.		
XIV, 12	=	18, 30.
11. Smṛti-candrikā of Devaṇabhaṭṭa,		
I,		
46-7	=	7, 37b-38a, 40b, 44b 45a and 46-47.
157	=	17, 6-8.
180	=	18, 30.
II,		
296	=	102, 13.
322	=	101, 37.
419	=	93, 111.
486	=	102, 2-8.
487	=	102, 9c-10a.
517	=	102, 14-21 and 23b.
III, ii,		
481	=	227, 146a. The other line differs.
IV,		
28	=	17, 4-5a.
29	=	17, 6-8.
82	=	22, 84.
83 (twice)	=	16, 21 ; 22, 85.
84 (twice)	=	22, 88 and 83.
121	=	22, 88.
156 (twice)	=	16, 8b-10a. The other quoted stanza is not found.
191	=	16, 19a.
194-195	=	16, 19b-20.
215	=	15, 39a. The first line is not found.

	Matsya-p.
255	= 17, 30.
265	= 15, 37b-38a.
270-271	= 16, 27b-28a.
271	= 16, 28b-29a.
272	= 19, 4a.
290-291	= 17, 14b-15a.
291	= 17, 23.
298	= 19, 4-11a (except 4b and 5a).
340	= 17, 28b.
358	= 17, 40b-41.
375	= 17, 47b.
388	= 17, 49b.
389 (twice)	= 16, 47a, 17, 53a-55 (except one line after verse 54).
406	= 17, 61b.
409	= 17, 62.
412	= 16, 56-57a.
438-430	= 17, 08.

12. Caturvarga-cintāmaṇi of Hemādri,

Vol. I,

	Matsya-p.
p. 68	= 17, 6-8. The verse *'snānaṃ dānaṃ japo'* is not found.
pp. 166-170	= 274, 3-30a (except 4a).
pp. 172-3	= 274, 30b-35a.
pp. 177-8	= 274, 35b-38.
pp. 178-9	= 274, 39-41a.
pp. 179-181	= 274, 41b-57.
pp. 182-3	= 274, 58-68a.
p. 184	= 274, 68b-70.
p. 185	= 274, 71-72a.
p. 186	= 274, 72b-73a.
p. 187	= 274, 73b-74 and 75-78.
pp. 218-222	= 275, 1-25 (except 22a).
p. 225	= 275, 26-29.
p. 232	= 276, 1-4a.
pp. 232-3	= 276, 4b-6a.
236	= 276, 6b-10.
p. 238	= 276, 11-12.
p. 239	= 276, 13-16.
p. 240	= 276, 17-19.
p. 245	= 277, 1-3a.
p. 246	= 277, 3b-6.
p. 247	= 277, 7b-9a.
pp. 247-8	= 277, 9b-16.
pp. 248-9	= 277, 17.
p. 249	= 277, 18-22.
p. 251	= 278, 1-4. The line *'go-sahasrāt'* is not found.
pp. 252-3	= 278, 5-11.
pp. 253-5	= 278, 12-22a.
pp. 256-7	= 278, 22b-24a and 26b-29.
pp. 265-8	= 279, 1-13.
pp. 274-7	= 280, 1-15.
pp. 279-281	= 281, 1-11 (except 7b and 11a).
p. 281	= 281, 12-13.
pp. 282-3	= 281, 14-16.
pp. 283-4	= 282, 1-4a and 5.
p. 284	= 282, 4b and 6-10a.
pp. 285-6	= 282, 10b-14.
p. 287	= 282, 15-16.
pp. 287-8	= 283, 1-4b.
pp. 288-291	= 283, 5-19.
p. 294	= 284, 1-3.
pp. 298-9	= 284, 4-18.
pp. 300-301	= 284, 19-21.
p. 326	= 285, 1-5a.
p. 327	= 285, 5b-7a.
p. 328	= 285, 7b.
p. 329	= 285, 8-10a.
p. 331	= 285, 10b-13a.
pp. 332-3	= 285, 13b-23.
pp. 334-7	= 286, 1-17.
pp. 337-9	= 287, 1-15.
pp. 340-2	= 288, 1-17.
pp. 343-5	= 289, 1-17 (except 5b).
pp. 397-400	= 82, 17-19, 1-6a, 7-16a, 16b, 21b-22, 23b, 25 and 16b.
p. 401	= 82, 20a.
pp. 478-9	= 205, 2-9.
p. 530	= 53, 3-12a.
pp. 533-9	= 53, 59b-61, 62c-71, 1-2, 11b-25a and 26b-56.
pp. 588-9	= 17, 21b (?) and 23. The line *'rajataṃ dakṣiṇāṃ'* is not found.
p. 650	= 253, 19b-22.

		Matsya-p.
pp. 651-2	=	253, 23-27, 28b and 30-31a. Three lines from *'madhye nava-padaḥ'* and the verse *'phaṇāvān mukhya-bhalvāṭau'* are not found.
p. 652	=	253, 31b-33.
pp. 653-6	=	268, 2b-36. Twelve lines from *'prāk māṃsyaudanam'* (on pp. 655-6) and the line *'vāstūpaśamanaṃ kṛtvā'* (on p. 656) are not found.
pp. 695-8	=	206, 1-21a, 22b-24, and 27a.
p. 699	=	206, 27b-31.
pp. 846-7	=	290, 2-12 and 18-19. The line *'ityayaṃ brahmaṇo māsaḥ'* (on p. 847) is not found.
p. 1014	=	58, 1-4a.
p. 1015	=	58, 5-12.
p. 1016	=	252, 17b.
pp. 1016-7	=	58, 13-21a.
p. 1018	=	58, 21b-29a.
pp. 1019-22	=	58, 29b-40a.
pp. 1023-5	=	58, 40b-56.
pp. 1047-9	=	59, 1-18.

Vol. II, Part i,

p. 20	=	53, 64.
pp. 21-22	=	53, 59b-61 and 62c-63.
pp. 48-9	=	60, 2, 6-7, 8b and 9b.
p. 68	=	58, 11-12, 16a and 17b.
pp. 68-9	=	58, 27 and 29b-30a.
pp. 88-9	=	260, 55-63 and 64b.
p. 149	=	94, 1.
pp. 149-150	=	94, 2.
p. 150	=	94, 3.
p. 222	=	93, 11 and 12b-c.
pp. 287-306	=	93, 65-72. The other lines are not found.

		Matsya-p.
p. 308 (twice)	=	58, 11-12, 16a and 17b; 58, 27 and 29b-30a.
p. 331	=	115, 14.
pp. 375-6	=	71, 9-12a and 13b-18a.
p. 376	=	71, 18b-19.
p. 422	=	62, 7a.
pp. 444-450	=	60, 1-7 and 8b-48.
pp. 508-510	=	72, 27-35b and 36-43a.
p. 871	=	94, 4.
pp. 1057-60	=	99, 1-4a, 5-14b, 15b-19; 100, 37. Eight lines from *'prati-māsaṃ tu kartavyā mūrtayaḥ'* (on p. 1058), the lines *'nivartanaṃ kṣetra-patiḥ'* (on p. 1058) and *'yatra sattvaṃ tatra'* (on p. 1059), and six lines from *'sapta-janmāny asau'* are not found.
pp. 1194-8	=	7, 2-12, 14b-31a and 57b-61a. The lines *'evaṃ prajāgaraṃ kṛtvā'* (on p. 1196) *'tataḥ sā'* (on p. 1197), *'kadācil-labdha-saṃcāraṃ'* (on p. 1197) and *'tat-prabhāvena jīvanti'* (on p. 1198) and the verse *'aho māhātmyam'* (on p. 1198) are not found.

Vol. II, Part ii,

pp. 58-61	=	95, 5-20a and 21 to the end. The line *'priyatāṃ deva-devo 'tra'* (on p. 59) is not found.

	Matsya-p.
pp. 538-541	= 97, 1 to the end. The lines *'utpadyate yadā'*, *'tadārabhya'* (on p. 538), *'prāktane 'hni'* (on p. 539) and *'trayīmayāyā'* (on p. 540) are not found.
pp. 699-703	= 54, 4b to the end.
pp. 842-3	= 101, 31-32.
pp. 906-9	= 96, 1-20 and 22b-24.
pp. 985-9	= 207, 1 to the end (except 40b).
pp. 1021-3	= 67, 1-12, 14-16, 18a and 20 to the end. The verses *'rakṣogaṇādhipaḥ'* (on p. 1022) and *'candra-grahe nṛpa ravi-grahaṇe'* (on p. 1023), and the lines *'kalaśaṃ dravya-saṃyuktaṃ'* (on p. 1022) and *'dravyais tair eva'* (on p. 1023) are not found.
pp. 1072-1088	= 228, 1-5a and 8b to the end.
	229, 1-20a, 22b-24a, 20b-22a, and 24b to the end.
	230, 1a, 2-3, 1b and 4 to the end (the line *'tallingārcanamātreṇa'* on p. 1079 is not found).
	231, 1-5, 9-10a and 11.
	232, 1-7 and 9b to the end.
	233, 1-4a; 237, 1 to the end (the verse *'sudeva iti'* on p. 1083 is not found).
	238, 1-4.
	233, 4b to the end.
	234, 1 to the end.
	235, 1 to the end.
	236, 1-2 and 4b to the end.
	238, 5 to the end (except 15c).

Vol. III, Part i,

	Matsya-p.
p. 14	= 19, 2.
p. 15	= 19, 1.
p. 16	= 19, 4-6a.
p. 19	= 16, 18.
pp. 23-32	= 19, 11b-12a, 10-11a and 12b-c; 20, 2-15a, 17-18, 19b-20a, 19a, 21-22 and 24b-27; 21, 2-10 and 27-28. Three lines from *'nāmadheyāni'* and six lines from *'unmukho nityavitrastaḥ'* on p. 30, the line *'ye ca yogāt'* on p. 31 and the line *'tataḥ prabhāte'* on p. 32 are not found.
pp. 33-4	= 21, 29, 32-33, 35-36a and 39b-40a. The line *'saṃnatiś cātiyogena'* is not found.
pp. 52-4	= 13, 3b-4a; 14, 1-2a; 15, 1-4, 12-14, 16-17, 20-22, 25a and 26-27.
p. 72	= 16, 21.
p. 80	= 18, 30.
pp. 85-6	= 16, 34b-35.
p. 106	= 17, 65b-66.
p. 253	= 17, 4-5a.
pp. 254-5	= 17, 6-8. The verse *'snānaṃ dānaṃ japo'* is not found.
p. 256	= 17, 9-10.
p. 260	= 17, 1-3 and 11a.
p. 324 (twice)	= 22, 85 and 88.

		Matsya-p.
pp. 386-7	=	16, 8b-10. Five lines from *'etāṃs tu bhojayet'* are not found.
p. 404	=	16, 11b-12a.
p. 448	=	16, 10b-11a.
pp. 504-5	=	16, 13b-17a.
pp. 548-9	=	15, 36b-37a and 38b.
p. 564	=	15, 37b-38a.
pp. 606-7	=	17, 36.
pp. 657-8	=	17, 23 and 21-24a. The line *'rajataṃ dakṣiṇām āhuḥ'* is not found.
p. 685	=	15, 37b-38a.
pp. 744-5	=	17, 50b-52a.
p. 765	=	17, 14b-17a.
p. 892	=	102, 9c-10a.
pp. 894-5	=	102, 2a, 3a, 2b-c and 3b-8.
p. 909	=	102, 13a-b.
p. 944	=	102, 14-15, 16b, 17b-22 and 23c.
p. 1015	=	16, 55c-57a.
p. 1044	=	17, 50.
p. 1063	=	16, 54b-55a. Also cf. 17, 56.
p. 1070	=	17, 37.
p. 1073	=	17, 38a.
pp. 1074-5	=	17, 39-40a. The line *'bhāratādhyayanaṃ'* is not found.
p. 1077	=	17, 38b.
pp. 1095-7	=	204, 2, 4, 3, 5-11a, 13a, 12b, 12a, 11b and 14-16. Lines 20-21 on p. 1095 and lines 16 and 18-20 on p. 1096 are not found.
p. 1158	=	16, 17b and 1[illegible]-20.
p. 1162	=	16, 23.
p. 1164	=	16, 22.
p. 1169	=	102, 1.
p. 1175	=	15, 34a and 35b-36a.
p. 1176	=	16, 26-27a.
p. 1186	=	16, 28b-29a.
p. 1220	=	16, 29b-30a.

		Matsya-p.
p. 1226	=	17, 16b. The verse *'yavo 'si'* is not found.
p. 1230	=	17, 23.
p. 1232	=	17, 14b-15.
p. 1236	=	17, 15b-16a.
p. 1238	=	17, 17a.
p. 1250	=	17, 17b.
p. 1259	=	17, 25b.
p. 1284	=	17, 18-19a.
p. 1291	=	17, 24.
p. 1301	=	17, 26-27.
p. 1312	=	17, 26.
p. 1339	=	18, 27.
p. 1343	=	15, 32b-33a.
p. 1347	=	16, 32-33.
p. 1370	=	17, 28b-29a.
p. 1396	=	16, 46.
p. 1399	=	17, 41b-43.
p. 1413	=	17, 45b.
p. 1420	=	17, 46.
p. 1446	=	16, 41.
p. 1450	=	18, 30.
p. 1472	=	17, 47b-49a.
p. 1473	=	17, 47b and 49.
p. 1475 (twice)	=	16, 24b-25 and 34b-36a. The line *'piṇḍa-bhūmau prayatnena'* is not found.
p. 1480	=	17, 49b-50a. Also cf. 16, 47a.
p. 1482	=	16, 47a; 17, 52b-53a; and 17, 53b-55.
p. 1484	=	16, 48b-49a.
p. 1489	=	16, 47b.
p. 1491	=	17, 59b. The other two lines *'apasavyena'* etc. are not found.
p. 1495	=	17, 60.
p. 1504	=	16, 52b-53a.
p. 1507	=	16, 53b-54a.
p. 1513	=	17, 56.
p. 1518	=	17, 62.
p. 1541	=	260, 53b-54a and 54c.
p. 1542	=	17, 66.
p. 1566	=	16, 5b-6a.
pp. 1617-1620	=	207, 1-37.

		Matsya-p.
p. 1621	=	207, 38-40.
p. 1717	=	204, 18.

Vol. III, Part ii,

pp. 41-2	=	274, 17-18 and 6b-10.
p. 448	=	22, 84.
pp. 505-6	=	17, 1-3.
p. 548	=	22, 85.
p. 577	=	16, 21.
p. 580	=	22, 85.
p. 607	=	16, 54b-55a.
p. 624	=	17, 9. The verse *'ityeṣā kathitā'* is not found.
p. 649	=	17, 4-5a.
p. 669	=	17, 6-8. The verse *'snānaṃ dānaṃ'* is not found.

13. Kṛtyācāra of Śrīdatta Upādhyāya,

fol. 66b	=	16, 5b.

14. Kṛtya-ratnākara of Caṇḍeśvara,

fol. (?)	=	61, 43 ff.
„ (?), lines 1-2	=	53, 28-29.
„ 139b	=	53, 23-24.
„ 161b-162a	=	56, 1 to the end.
„ 169a-170b	=	95, 1 to the end.
„ 176b	=	53, 31-32b.
„ 177a	—	Refers to Mat 82, 18 ff. in which Tila-dhenu-dāna is dealt with.
„ 178a	=	107, 7-8. The verse *'sitāsite'* is not found. 101, 36.
„ 181a	=	101, 53a-b.

		Matsya-p.
fol. 181a-182a	=	63, 1 to the end (except verse 29).
„ 187a	=	53, 33-35.
„ 193a	=	101, 79.
„ 193a-b	=	53, 36-37.
„ 197b	=	17, 6-8.
„ 220b f.	=	70, 32-44 and 45 ff.

15. Madana-pārijāta of Madanapāla,

p. 13	=	52, 5b-13a (except 12b); one line *'tṛptiṃ karoti'* is not found.
p. 264	=	101, 37.
p. 375	=	134, 21b-23a.
p. 540	=	17, 6-8.
p. 558	=	16, 11b-12a.
p. 568	=	16, 27b-28a.
p. 575	=	17, 23.
p. 631	=	17, 65b-66.

16. Mādhavācārya's com. on the Parāśara-smṛti,

Vol. I, Part ii,

p. 58	=	18, 30.
p. 182-3	=	134, 21b-23a.
p. 222	=	18, 30.
p. 310	=	17, 4-5a.
p. 311	=	17, 6-8.
pp. 361 and 365	=	16, 19a and 19b-20.
p. 371	=	17, 30.
p. 396	=	16, 27b-28a.
p. 398	=	16, 28b-29a. 19, 4a.
p. 405	=	17, 23 and 14b-15a
p. 418	=	17, 28b.
p. 433	=	17, 36.
p. 434	=	17, 49b. 16, 47. 17, 53-55.
p. 438	=	16, 54a.
p. 440-1	=	16, 55.
p. 443	=	16, 56-57a.

		Matsya-p.
17. Vratakāla-viveka of Śūlapāṇi,		
fol. 2b	=	93, 140b-141a.
18. Saṃbandha-viveka of Śūlapāṇi,		
fol. 1b	=	18, 30.
19. Prāyaścitta-viveka of Śūlapāṇi,		
p. 416	=	206, 23b-24a.
20. Tīrtha-cintāmaṇi of Vācaspatimiśra,		
p. 8	=	106, 3, 4b-5 and 7.
p. 17	=	108, 33.
pp. 23-24	=	110, 1-11a. The verse '*tathā dṛṣṭvā*' is not found.
p. 26	=	104, 16-17.
pp. 27-29	=	107, 8. The other verses are not found.
pp. 29-31	=	106, 27-28, 30b-33 and 46-48. 107, 20-21. 108, 15 and 25-26a. Three verses are not found.
pp. 42-43	=	105, 13b-14a and 16-22.
p. 45	=	105, 13b-15
p. 47	=	104, 5-6a.
pp. 48-49	=	106, 34-39.
p. 49	=	106, 40-42 and 44-45.
pp. 49-50	=	107, 4-6 (except 5c).
p. 50	=	107, 9-11 and 17-19.
p. 200	=	104, 14.
p. 205	=	106, 49a.
p. 216	=	106, 49. The remaining three lines are not found.
p. 236-9	=	82, 2-6 and 7-25 (except 23a and 24).

		Matsya-p.
p. 267	=	105, 15. The other verses are not found.
p. 340	=	133, 61-62.
p. 342	=	180, 54 and 57a; (one line is not found). 184, 56-57a; (one verse is not found).
p. 345	=	182, 27a-b.
p. 349	=	183, 71-72 and 75.
p. 351	=	183, 73.
21. Nityācāra-pradīpa of Narasiṃha Vājapeyin,		
p. 18	=	53, 59b-63.
p. 21	--	Reference to the chapters on Vāstu in the Matsya-p.
p. 104	=	18, 30.
p. 209	=	93, 83b-84a.
22. Dānakriyā-kaumudī of Govindānanda,		
p. 24 (twice)	=	18, 8b and 12b-14a.
p. 56	=	205, 4b-6.
p. 70 (thrice)	=	53, 17a-b, 20, 22a-b and 51.
p. 81	=	Chap. 206 (except verses 1,3-4a, 9a, 10-19, 20b-22, 23b-28a and 30-31).
p. 84	=	206, 23b-24a.
p. 86	=	18, 12b-14a.
p. 94 (twice)	=	207, 18-19a and 38.
p. 100	=	18, 16b.
p. 125	=	58, 55-56.
p. 130	=	58, 18a-b.
p. 157-8	=	58, 42b-43.
p. 161	=	17, 65b.
p. 164	=	58, 43b.

23. Śūddhikriyā-kaumudī of Govindānanda,

		Matsya-p.
p. 49	=	18, 30.
p. 74	=	18, 12b.
p. 139	=	18, 7a.
p. 163	=	18, 12b-14a.
p. 165	=	207, 38-41.
p. 169	=	207, 18-19a.
p. 177	=	17, 70.
p. 178	=	18, 26.
p. 182	=	18, 16a and 22b-23a.
p. 183	=	18, 22b-23a.
p. 184	=	18, 16.
p. 194	=	22, 82-84a.
p. 284	=	274, 6b-10.
p. 350	=	102, 31.

24. Śrāddhakriyā-kaumudī of Govindānanda,

p. 11	=	17, 30-36.
p. 27	=	17, 63-64.
p. 28	=	17, 70.
p. 32	=	17, 70.
p. 35-6	=	16, 8-12a. Six lines *ṣaḍaṅgavit'* etc. are not found.
p. 41	=	16, 14 and 15b-16. The line *'para-purvā-patiḥ'* and the verse *'karṇā-ṭāś ca'* are not found.
p. 59	=	17, 14b.
p. 81	=	16, 20 and 19.
p. 84	=	16, 19a and 29b-30a.
p. 98	=	16, 56-57a.
p. 103	=	184, 33a. 17, 11b-12a. 16, 27b-29a.
p. 122	=	17, 16b.
p. 126	=	17, 19b-23.

		Matsya-p.
p. 127	=	17, 14b-15a.
p. 128	=	17, 15b-16a and 17b.
p. 137	=	17, 26b-27a.
p. 142	=	15, 37b-38a.
p. 150	=	15, 32b-33a.
p. 186	=	17, 46.
p. 192	=	16, 39a.
p. 194	=	16, 38b-39.
p. 196	=	17, 47b and 49a.
p. 207	=	17, 52b-55a.
p. 208	=	17, 55a.
p. 212	=	17, 52a and 23.
p. 214	=	17, 59-60a.
p. 252	=	16, 57b-58a.
p. 259	—	cf. 17, 63a.
p. 300	=	18, 22b-23a.
p. 306	=	22, 82-85.
pp. 312-313	=	22, 2.
p. 319	=	18, 16a.
p. 326	=	16, 43.
p. 336	=	18, 8b-9a.
p. 337	=	18, 22b-23a.
pp. 345-346	=	18, 22b-23a.
p. 357	=	18, 16.
p. 362	=	18, 16a.
p. 389	=	17, 27 and 25.
p. 398	=	18, 26.
p. 425	=	18, 19b-22a.
pp. 433-434	=	18, 16.
p. 435	=	18, 28-29.
p. 436	=	18, 20a and 21b.
p. 471	=	16, 58b-c.
p. 474	=	18, 23a
p. 488	=	17, 65b-66.
p. 557	=	16, 5b.

25. Nityācāra-paddhati of Vidyākara Vājapeyin,

p. 127	=	182, 12b.
p. 530	=	258, 13a.

VI. VERSES QUOTED FROM THE 'BHĀGAVATA-P.' OR 'BHĀGAVATA' IN

1. Adbhutasāgara of Ballālasena, — Bhāgavata-p.

p. 354	=	I, 14, 16a.
p. 355	=	III, 17, 5.
p. 378	=	I, 14, 16b.
p. 410 (twice)	=	III, 17, 7; I, 14, 18a.
p. 426	=	I, 14, 20a.
p. 481	=	I, 14, 20b-c.
p. 625	=	I, 14, 13b.
p. 642	=	I, 14, 19b.
p. 643	=	III, 17, 13a.
p. 645	=	I, 14, 19b.
p. 653 (twice)	=	III, 17, 11b and 10.
p. 654	=	I, 14, 12b-13a.
p. 658 (twice)	=	III, 17, 9; I, 14, 12a.
p. 709	=	III, 17, 13.
p. 710	=	I, 14, 15 and 17b.
p. 712	=	III, 17, 4.

2. Caturvarga-cintāmaṇi of Hemādri,

Vol. II, Part i,

p. 7	=	I, 4, 25.

Vol. III, Part ii,

pp. 659-660	=	XI, 5, 20-32 and 35.
p. 664	=	XI, 5, 36-37.

3. Madhvācārya's com. on the Bhagavad-gītā, — Bhāgavata-p.

p. 64	=	I, 2, 30b.
p. 152	=	I, 2, 11b.
p. 410	=	III, 5, 46-47.
p. 439	=	VI, 4, 48a.
p. 444	=	XI, 5, 48; IV, 21, 47; VII, 10, 15b-17a.
p. 470	=	XI, 19, 36a.
p. 472	=	III, 20, 49b.
p. 497	=	I, 3, 27-28a.
p. 512	=	X, 16, 31a.
p. 546 (twice)	=	III, 26, 10; II, 2, 31a (second half).
p. 550	=	I, 17, 20a
p. 664 (twice)	=	VIII, 6, 10b; XI, 28, 17b.

4. Haribhakti-vilāsa of Gopālabhaṭṭa,

p. 21	=	I, 2, 28.
p. 412	=	I, 6, 34.
p. 557	=	I, 18, 13.
pp. 574-577	=	I, 1, 2; I, 3, 40-42a; I, 3, 45; and I, 7, 6-7.
p. 581	=	I, 2, 17.
p. 583	=	I, 2, 8.
pp. 590-591	=	I, 1, 19; and I, 18, 14.
p. 592	=	I, 18, 10.
pp. 607-608	=	I, 5, 22; and I, 6, 35.
p. 675	=	I, 1, 14.
p. 703 (twice)	=	I, 5, 17; and I, 2, 6.
p. 707	=	I, 2, 7.
p. 710	=	I, 7, 10.
p. 110	=	II, 1, 6.
pp. 577-578	=	II, 1, 9-10.
p. 584	=	II, 3, 17.
p. 586	=	II, 3, 12.
p. 587	=	II, 2, 37.
p. 594	=	II, 3, 20.
p. 673	=	II, 1, 11.
p. 690	=	II, 3, 24.
p. 706	=	II, 2, 33-34.
p. 708	=	II, 3, 10.
p. 731	=	II, 4, 18.

	Bhāgavata-p.
p. 120	= III, 9, 25. The verse 'deva prapannārti-hara' is not found.
p. 374	= III, 24, 31 ; and III, 9, 11b.
p. 500	= III, 25, 21.
p. 506	= III, 25, 23.
p. 554	= III, 25, 25.
p. 556	= III, 7, 19.
p. 558	= III, 7, 20.
p. 560	= III, 31, 33-35.
p. 561	= III, 9, 10.
p. 583	= III, 6, 36.
p. 584	= III, 5, 13.
p. 587	= III, 25, 34.
p. 588	= III, 5, 46.
p. 590	= III, 15, 48.
p. 591	= III, 5, 7.
p. 593	= III, 32, 19.
pp. 594-595	= III, 9, 7 ; III, 5, 14; and III, 13, 50.
p. 616	= III, 9, 41.
p. 668	= III, 33, 7.
p. 675	= III, 9, 15.
p. 706	= III, 25, 19.
p. 708	= III, 25, 32c-33.
p. 711	= III, 15, 25.
p. 715	= III, 29, 13.
p. 718	= III, 25, 32.
p. 734	= III, 2, 23.
p. 1064	= III, 9, 25.

	Bhāgavata-p.
p. 110	= IV, 20, 29.
p. 547	= IV, 31, 22.
p. 551	= IV, 9, 12.
p. 552	= IV, 30, 35-37.
p. 554	= IV, 29, 39-40.
p. 557	= IV, 24, 57.
p. 558	= IV, 9, 11.
p. 567	= IV, 22, 11.
p. 568	= IV, 22, verses 7, 10 13 and 14.
p. 584	= IV, 23, 12.
p 595	= IV, 20, 26.
p. 644	= IV, 21, 31 ; and IV, 31, 14.
p. 705	= IV, 11, 30.
p. 500	= V, 5, 2.
p. 555	= V, 12, 13.
p. 597	= V, 19, 23.
p. 708	= V, 6, 17.
p. 709	= V, 14, 44.
p. 713	= V, 19, 7.
&c.	&c.

Gopālabhaṭṭa has quoted numerous verses from the other Skandhas also; and these verses are almost all found in the extant Bhāgavata.

The 'Bhāgavata' verses quoted by Raghunandana and others also are in the majority of cases found in the present Bhāgavata, but it is needless to enlist them here.

VII. VERSES QUOTED FROM THE KŪRMA-P.' OR 'KAURMA' IN

1. Hāralatā of Aniruddhabhaṭṭa.	Kūrma-p.
p. 8	= II, 23, 1-2.
p. 9	= II, 23, 27.
p. 12	= II, 23, 3-4.
p. 15	= II, 23, 9.
p. 18	= II, 23, 5.
p. 31	= II, 23, 75-76.
p. 32-3	= II, 23, 25-26.

	Kūrma-p.
p. 38	= II, 23, 13 and 10b.
p. 39	= II, 23, 12.
p. 44	= II, 23, 14-17.
p. 50	= II, 23, 33b.
p. 53 (twice)	= II, 23, 28-29 and 30.
p. 56	= II, 23, 39-41.
p. 57-8	= II, 23, 42-45.
p. 63	= II, 23, 22-23a.

	Kūrma-p.
p. 66-7	= II, 23, 23b-24.
p. 72	= II, 23, 19-21.
p. 78	= II, 23, 31-33a.
p. 83 (twice)	= II, 23, 46-48a and 59.
p. 84 (twice)	= II, 23, 58 and 60.
p. 86	= II, 23, 53-54.
p. 87	= II, 23, 51.
p. 89	= II, 23, 48b-50.
p. 90	= II, 23, 52.
p. 93	= II, 23, 55-57.
p. 98	= II, 23, 62-63.
p. 114	= II, 23, 66-74.
p. 131	= II, 23, 77.

2. Dānasāgara of Ballālasena,

fol. 9b	= II, 26, 57.
„ 21a	= II, 18, 53.
„ 25a	= II, 18, 81-82.
„ 137a	= II, 26, 13.
„ 149b	= II, 26, 18.
„ 154a	= II, 26, 17.
„ 195a	= II, 44, 123 and 125-127.
„ 242b-243a	= II, 26, 30-31.
„ 246a	= II, 26, 25-26.
„ 252b-253a	= II, 26, 23 and 19-21.
„ 285a	= II, 26, 35.

3. Smṛti-candrikā of Devaṇa-bhaṭṭa,

Vol. I,

42	= II, 15, 11a.

Vol. II,

234	= II, 18, 3.
261	= II, 13, 4-5a and 6b-7a.
265	= II, 12, 64a; II, 13, 1b-3.
273	= II, 16, 77a.
274-275	= II, 13, 31-32.
278	= II, 18, 19.

	Kūrma-p.
291	= II, 18, 18.
350	= II, 18, 11.
356	= II, 18, 26-28a.
357	= II, 18, 9.
363-364	= II, 18, 23b-28a and 33-34.
365	= II, 18, 30.
366	= II, 18, 31.
368	= II, 18, 28b.
397	= II, 18, 82.
417	= II, 24, 7 and 10.
432-433	= I, 3, 14-18 and 27.
448	= II, 18, 55b-56.
454	= II, 25, 7-8. II, 25, 2, 10a and 11-12.
470	= II, 25, 2c-3a.
471	= II, 25, 4.
482	= II, 18, 58a.
485	= II, 18, 62.
488-489	= II, 18, 73.
495-496	= II, 18, 58-77a (except verses 59-60, 63a, 68 and 71-74).
505	= II, 18, 104.
510	= II, 18, 104.
511	— One of the quoted lines occurs after Kūr II, 18, 113, the other line missing, as is evidenced by the fact that Kūr II, 18, 114 consists of three lines.
516	= II, 18, 88a-b.
519	= II, 18, 87.
534-5	= II, 18, 94-99 (except 96 and 99a).
539	= II, 18, 121.
563	= II, 18, 111.
565	= II, 18, 112.
566 (twice)	= II, 18, 106 and 108.
568	= II, 18, 114.
569	= II, 18, 118a.
571	= II, 18, 107.
603	= II, 19, 3.
621	= II, 19, 15-16.
631	= II, 19, 30-32.

Vol. V,	Kūrma-p.
27	= II, 20, 6-7a.
177	= II, 23, 80b-82.
4. Caturvarga-cintāmaṇi of Hemādri,	
Vol. I,	
p. 6	= II, 26, 56.
p. 9	= II, 26, 59.
p. 17	= II, 26, 4-8.
p. 24	= II, 26, 63 and 11.
p. 38	= II, 26, 68.
p. 504	— Cf. II, 26, 14.
pp. 532-3	= I, 1, 16a and 17-21.
p. 540	= II, 44, 133a and 125-126.
p. 859	= II, 26, 33-35. The line *'tasmād asyām'* is not found.
p. 862	= II, 26, 29-31.
p. 868	= II, 26, 27-28.
Vol. II, Part i,	
p. 13	= I, 2, 54.
p. 21	= I, 1, 16a and 17-21a. Four lines from *'vedārthavittamaiḥ kāryam'* are not found.
p. 322	= I, 1, 52b and 53b. Five lines from *'brāhmaṇāḥ kṣatriyā vaiśyāḥ'* are not found.
p. 1158	= II, 26, 33-34.
Vol. II, Part ii,	
p. 156	= II, 26, 29.
p. 257	= II, 26, 27-28.
Vol. III, Part i,	
p. 9	= II, 22, 86.
p. 19	= II, 22, 3-4.

	Kūrma-p.
p. 24.	= II, 20, 5b-6.
p. 185	= II, 20, 4.
p. 250	= II, 20, 4-8.
p. 271	= II, 20, 9-15.
p. 272	= II, 20, 16-17.
p. 293	= II, 23, 80b-82.
p. 365	= II, 21, 32 and 34.
p. 391	= II, 21, 14.
p. 403	= II, 21, 9b.
p. 413	= II, 21, 15 and 18.
p. 417	= II, 21, 17. The verse *'tasmād agrāsane'* is not found.
p. 447	= II, 21, 20.
p. 466	= II, 21, 27.
p. 476	= II, 21, 32-34.
pp. 500-501	= II, 21, 35a, 36-42 and 44-46.
p. 543	= II, 20, 37.
p. 550	= II, 20, 48.
p. 564	= II, 20, 46-48.
pp. 596-7	= II, 20, 37 and 40-44.
p. 602	= II, 20, 39.
p. 603	= II, 22, 57.
pp. 604-5	= II, 22, 54-56.
p. 674	= II, 22, 63.
p. 675	= II, 22, 61-62.
p. 737 (twice)	= II, 22, 40b. The other quotation is not found.
p. 890	= II, 18, 62.
p. 902	= II, 18, 73.
p. 922	= II, 18, 88a-b.
p. 929	= II, 18, 114a and 88c.
p. 938	= II, 18, 87.
p. 959	= II, 13, 4-5a and 6b-7a.
pp. 963-4	= II, 13, 31.
p. 964	= II, 13, 32.
p. 967	= II, 12, 64.
pp. 967-8	= II, 13, 1b-3.
p. 1002	= II, 22, 7.
p. 1004	= II, 22, 5.
p. 1007 (twice)	= II, 22, 9 and 10.
pp. 1007-8	= II, 22, 11.
p. 1010	= II, 22, 6.
pp. 1011-2	= II, 22, 8.
p. 1015	= II, 22, 12.

	Kūrma-p.
p. 1093	= II, 22, 69.
p. 1099	= II, 20, 29b-32.
pp. 1135-6	= II, 22, 2-4.
p. 1138	= II, 22, 1.
p. 1146	= II, 22, 28.
p. 1148	= II, 22, 26.
p. 1149	= II, 22, 27.
p. 1161	= II, 22, 18.
p. 1163	= II, 22, 19.
p. 1165	= II, 22, 14.
p. 1167	= II, 22, 20-21.
p. 1171	= II, 22, 13.
p. 1180	= II, 22, 22.
p. 1182	= II, 22, 37.
p. 1191	= II, 22, 23-24.
p. 1201	= II, 22, 25.
p. 1224	= II, 22, 38.
p. 1234	= II, 22, 39.
p. 1241	= II, 22, 40b.
p. 1258	= II, 22, 41a.
p. 1260	= II, 22, 41b-42a.
p. 1300	= II, 22, 43b-44a.
p. 1344	= II, 22, 48.
p. 1345	— Cf. II, 22, 44-45.
p. 1392	= II, 22, 70a.
p. 1395	= II, 22, 70b-71a.
p. 1510	= II, 22, 79b.
p. 1515	= II, 22, 78.
p. 1517	= II, 22, 79a.
p. 1523	= II, 22, 28.
p. 1524	= II, 22, 29.
p. 1525	= II, 22, 30a.
p. 1528	= II, 22, 83b-84a and 85b.
p. 1535	= II, 22, 88.
p. 1537	= II, 22, 100a.
p. 1547	= II, 22, 96b-97a and 99a.
p. 1563	= II, 18, 111.
p. 1564	= II, 18, 112.
p. 1582	= I, 36, 1. Five lines from '*pūrvedyuḥ kṛta-saṃkalpaḥ*' are not found.
p. 1589	= II, 23, 79b-80a.
pp. 1600-1601	= II, 23, 83-84.

	Kūrma-p.
p. 1639	= II, 23, 85-87.

Vol. III, Part ii,

p. 6	= I, 5, 20-21, 19b and 18-19a. The line '*tasmāt kālātmakaṃ*' is not found.
p. 387	= II, 20, 6-7a.
p. 452	= II, 20, 4-8.
pp. 516-7	= II, 20, 9-15.
p. 518	= II, 20, 16-17.
pp. 530-1	= II, 23, 80b-82.
p. 730	= II, 15, 11a.
p. 783	= I, 3, 2 and 8.
p. 809-810	= I, 3, 6b-7 and 10-11a. The first ten lines (*kiṃcic-chreyaskaraṃ* etc.) and the last line (*tadaiva saṃnyaset*) are not found.
pp. 810-1	= I, 3, 3-6. Four lines from '*prathamād āśramād vā 'pi*' are not found.

5. Madana-pārijāta of Madanapāla,

p. 74	= II, 18, 25.
p. 206	= II, 18, 19.
p. 282	= II, 18, 104.
p. 284	= II, 18, 114a and 88c.
p. 286	= II, 18, 88a-b.
p. 309	= II, 18, 112.
p. 312	= II, 18, 107.

6. Mādhavācārya's com. on the Parāśara-smṛti[a]

Vol. I, Part i,

p. 58	= II, 15, 28b-29.

[a] These verses were traced by Mr. V. S. Islampurkar in his edition of the Parāśara-smṛti.

Kūrma-p.

p. 70 = II, 36, 48-49.
pp. 94-95 = II, 43, 5-9a.
p. 146 = II, 14, 37-40.
p. 151 = II, 14, 86-88.
p. 156 = II, 14, 77-78.
p. 158 = II, 14, 79.
p. 159 = II, 14, 84.
p. 161 = II, 24, 7 and 10.
p. 215 = II, 18, 121 and 119.
p. 216 = II, 18, 120.
p. 220 = II, 18, 3.
p. 239 = II, 13, 4-7a (except 5b and 6a).
p. 242 = II, 12, 64 and II, 13, 1b-3.
p. 258 = II, 18, 18.
pp. 269-270 = II, 18, 58-60.
p. 278 = II, 33, 69-70.
p. 301 = II, 18, 31.
p. 307 = II, 18, 82.
p. 311 = II, 18, 50-51.
p. 320 = II, 18, 90.
p. 336 = II, 18, 55-56.
p. 338 = II, 18, 57.
p. 340 = II, 25, 2 and 10-12.
p. 344 = II, 18, 104.
p. 355 = II, 18, 88.
p. 365 = II, 18, 90b-91.
pp. 371-372 = II, 18, 94-95, and 97-101.
p. 376 = II, 18, 121.
p. 379 = II, 18, 106-107.
p. 383 = II, 18, 108.
p. 385 = II, 18, 109.
p. 387 = II, 18, 111.
p. 389 = II, 18, 112.
p. 392 = II, 18, 114.
p. 409 = II, 18, 117.
p. 415 = II, 19, 4.
p. 417 = II, 19, 3.
p. 419 = II, 19, 5.
p. 425 = II, 19, 20-22, (except 20b).
p. 430 = II, 19, 19.
pp. 431-432 = II, 19, 9-13.
p. 444 = II, 19, 30-32.

Vol. I, Part ii,

p. 4 = II, 25, 4.
p. 9 = II, 25, 7.

Kūrma-p.

p. 15 = II, 25, 8.
p. 46 = II, 14, 20a and 21a.
p. 54 = II, 15, 1.
II, 15, 3-7a (except 3a and 5b).
p. 104 = II, 15, 11a.
p. 127 = II, 14, 62.
p. 132 = II, 14, 65.
p. 133 = II, 16, 23-25, 89b, 90b, 91 and 94b.
pp. 144-145 = II, 27, 30b-31, 32a, 32c, 33a, 16-17 and 25-27.
p. 146 = II, 27, 38-39.
p. 154 = II, 28, 2.
p. 155 = II, 28, 4.
p. 193 = II, 29, 7b, 8 and 10.
p. 205 = II, 23, 1a.
p. 209 = II, 23, 38.
p. 212 = II, 23, 5a.
p. 218 = II, 23, 9.
p. 219-220 = II, 23, 45.
p. 220 = II, 23, 42.
p. 254 = II, 23, 71.
p. 265 = II, 23, 23.
p. 277 = II, 23, 49-50a.
p. 281 = II, 23, 53.
p. 282 = II, 23, 54.
p. 314-5 = II, 20, 16-17.
p. 360 = II, 22, 2.

Vol. II, Part i,

p. 404 = II, 33, 21.

Vol. II, Part ii,

p. 7 = II, 33, 38.
p. 8 = II, 39, 49.
p. 14 = II, 18, 13b.
p. 17 = II, 18, 11.
pp. 161-162 = II, 33, 108, 97-100, 107 and 101-102.

7. Prāyaścitta-viveka of Śūlapāṇi,

p. 149 = II, 30, 8-9.
p. 155 = II, 30, 10-11.
p. 157 = II, 30, 8-9.
p. 434 = II, 33, 48.

	Kūrma-p.
8. Tīrtha-cintāmaṇi of Vācaspatimiśra,	
pp. 45-46	= I, 36, 5a and 6; (one line *'putradārāṃś ca'* is not found).
	I, 37, 9-10.
p. 264	= I, 36, 30.
9. Nityācāra-paddhati of Vidyākara Vājapeyin,	
p. 127	= II, 37, 146-147.
p. 590	= I, 22, 39b and 47b.
10. Nityācāra-pradīpa of Narasiṃha Vājapeyin,	
p. 19	= I, 1, 16.
p. 117	= II, 23, 14-15a.
p. 118	= II, 23, 12.
p. 120	= II, 23, 12a.
p. 121	= II, 23, 30.
p. 126	= II, 23, 25.
p. 189	= II, 18, 82.
p. 331-332	= II, 37, 146-147a.

VIII. VERSES QUOTED FROM THE 'VĀMANA-P.' OR 'VĀMANA' IN

	Vāmana-p.
1. Aparārka's com. on Yāj.,	
pp. 364-365	= 95, 23b-27 and 38-45. The verse *'ghṛtaṃ ca kṣīra-kumbhāś ca'* has been lost; and the line *'athavā catuṣpādaḥ'* is not found.
2. Dānasāgara of Ballālasena,	
fol. 5a	= 95, 7-9.
„ 152a	= 95, 44.
„ 181a	= 95, 44.
„ 204b	= 95, 44. The other verses *'gṛha-karma-karīṃ'* is not found.
„ 235a-b	= 95, 23b-24a.
„ 236a	= 95, 24b-c and 25-26a.
„ 236b	= 95, 26b-27a and 27b-c.
„ 237a	= 95, 38. The other verse *'ghṛtaṃ ca'* has undoubtedly been dropped.
„ 237b	= 95, 39 and 40.
fol. 238a	= 95, 41 and 43.
3. Smṛti-candrikā of Devaṇa-bhaṭṭa,	
II, 327	= 14, 49b-51a. Two lines *'tailābhyaṅgo'* and *'parvasv aṣṭamyāṃ'* are not found.
343	= 34, 6b-9b.
446	= 14, 35b-37.
V, 52	= 13, 31-32a.
4. Caturvarga-cintāmaṇi of Hemādri,	
Vol. I,	
pp. 885-6	= 95, 23b-27 and 38-45. The verse *'ghṛtaṃ kṣīra-kumbhāś ca'* is not found.
Vol. II, Part i,	
pp. 849-853	= 16, 30-55 and 58 to the end.

	Vāmana-p.
pp. 1103-5	= 17, 1 and 11-25b. The line *'śṛṇu rājan'* is not found.
Vol. II, Part ii,	
p. 351	= 92, 56-58.
Vol. III, Part i,	
p. 872	= 34, 6b-9a.
Vol. III, Part ii,	
p. 617	= 92, 56b-58a.
pp. 688-9	= 14, 48b-51a. The verse *'caturdaśyaṣṭamī darśa'* is not found.
5. Kṛtyācāra of Śrīdatta Upādhyāya,	
fol. 16a	= 14, 35-38a.
" 18a	= 14, 53b-54a.
" 59b	= 95, 14b.
" 71a	= 14, 52a.
6. Kṛtya-ratnākara of Caṇḍeśvara,	
fol. 176b-177a	= 95, 23b-24a.
" 177a	= 95, 45.
" 187a	= 95, 24b-c.
" 199b	= 14, 48b-51a.
" 210a	= 95, 46b.
7. Mādhavācārya's com. on the Parāśara-smṛti,	
Vol. I, part i,	
pp. 220-221	= 14, 23.
p. 282	= 14, 49b-50a.
p. 321	= 14, 35b-37.

	Vāmana-p.
Vol. I, Part ii,	
p. 153	= 14, 116-118.
pp. 231-232	= 14, 99b-100a.
Vol. II, Part ii,	
p. 224	= 13, 36.
8. Śrāddha-viveka of Śūlapāṇi.	
fol. 15b	= 95, 21b-22a.
9. Tīrtha-cintāmaṇi of Vācaspatimiśra,	
p. 273	= 79, 62b, 64-65, 67 and 69b-72.
p. 279	= 83, 4b-5.
10. Nityācāra-paddhati of Vidyākara Vājapeyin,	
p. 495	— Reference to Vām 85 (on *gajendra-mokṣaṇa*). But the Stotras appearing to be different, it seems that the chapter has been rewritten.
11. Varṣakriyā-kaumudī of Govindānanda,	
p. 87-8	= 14, 50b-51a and 49b-50a.
p. 166	= 95, 14b. The other line *'arka-dhustūra'* is not found.
p. 173	= 95, 21b-22a.
p. 260	= 95, 27b-c. The line *'jyaiṣṭhe māsi'* is not found.

		Vāmana-p.
p. 286	=	16, 6b-7a and 8.
p. 298	=	95, 39.
p. 517	=	95, 25-26a.

12. Śuddhikriyā-kaumudī of Govindānanda,

p. 70	=	14, 95.
p. 182	=	14, 95.
pp. 356-357	=	14, 66b-67 and 73.

13. Śrāddhakriyā-kaumudī of Govindānanda,

p. 261	=	95, 21b-22a.

14. Kālasāra of Gadādhara,

p. 3	=	94, 60.

15. Smṛti-tattva of Raghunandana,

Vol. I,

p. 22	=	94, 60.
p. 27 (twice)	=	14, 48b-49a. The other quotation is not found.
p. 58	=	94, 61.
p. 111	=	16, 6b-7a and 8.
p. 263	=	94, 61.
p. 326	=	14, 20a and 23
p. 411 (thrice)	=	95, 15a; the line '*tulasī*' is not found. 95, 14b. 95, 13-14a.
p. 413	=	95, 20b-21a.
p. 414	=	95, 21b-22a.
p. 588	=	94, 61.

Vol. II,

		Vāmana-p.
p. 12	=	94, 60.
p. 66 (twice)	=	95, 14b. 95, 13-14a.
p. 69	=	95, 15.
p. 71	=	95, 20b-21a.
p. 101	=	16, 6b-7a and 8.
p. 144	=	14, 38a.
p. 276	=	14, 38a.
p. 436	=	16, 6b-7a and 8.
p. 627	=	95, 45.

16. Nityācāra-pradīpa of Narasiṃha Vājapeyin,

p. 56	=	14, 48b.
p. 321	=	14, 35a.
p. 630	=	95, 10 and 12-14.
p. 644	=	95, 20b-21a.
p. 665	=	95, 21b-22a.
p. 701	=	95, 43a and 45.

17. Haribhakti-vilāsa of Gopālabhaṭṭa,

p. 105	=	94, 61.
p. 108	=	94, 70.
p. 111	=	94, 60.
p. 326	=	95, 10 and 12-14.
p. 354	=	95, 15-16.
p. 377	=	95, 20b-21a.
p. 393	=	95, 21b-22a.
p. 407	=	95, 5. The verse '*atrā 'pi kecit*' is not found.
p. 666	=	94, 62a and 63b.
p. 677	=	94, 72b-73.
p. 711	=	94, 54.
p. 729	=	94, 30. The verse '*ye śaṅkha-cakrābja-karaṃ*' is not found.
p. 1288	=	95, 46-47 and 49.

IX VERSES QUOTED FROM THE 'LIṄGA-P.' OR 'LAIṄGA' IN

Liṅga-p.

1. Ṭīkāsarvasva of Vandyaghaṭīya Sarvānanda,

Part I,

p. 90 = I, 4, 24b-25a and 26b-30.
p. 91 = I, 4, 36b-37a and 41-43a.
pp. 91-92 = I, 4, 32b-35. The line *'manavaś ca brahmasutāḥ'* is not found.

2. Adbhutasāgara of Ballālasena,

p. 507 (twice) = I, 91, 9 and 27.
p. 508 (thrice) = I, 91, 15, 29 and 16.
p. 509 (four times) = I, 91, 17b (cf.), 35, 31 and 34.
p. 524 = I, 91, 24.
p. 525 — Cf. I, 91, 5.
p. 527 = I, 91, 33.
p. 531 = I, 01, 23b.
p. 533 = I, 91, 13b.
p. 537 (twice) = I, 91, 25b and 25.
p. 538 = I, 91, 26b.
p. 539 = I, 91, 26.
p. 541 (twice) = I, 91, 13a. The line *'pibataś ca'* and the verse *'sadyaḥ snātānuliptasya'* are not found.
p. 542 = I, 91, 32.
p. 544 = I, 91, 7.
p. 545 = I, 91, 14.
p. 546 — Cf. I, 91, 6.

Liṅga-p.

p. 548 — Cf. I, 91, 12.
p. 554 — Cf. I, 91, 11.
p. 556 = I, 91, 21.
p. 712 = I, 100, 9-10.

3. Dānasāgara of Ballālasena,

fol. 15a-15b = I, 77, 33b-35 and 52b-54a.
„ 28a = II, 28, 34b.

4. Smṛti-candrikā of Devaṇa-bhaṭṭa,

II, 508 = I, 26, 16a.
561 = I, 77, 65-66a.

5. Caturvarga-cintāmaṇi of Hemādri,

Vol. I,

pp. 188-9 = II, 28, 14b-31.
pp. 191-3 = II, 28, 32-36a and 38-46. The lines *'badhnīyāc cakra-pāśaṃ'* and *'sahasreṇa tu kartavyau'* on p. 192 are not found.
pp. 194-6 = II, 28, 47-63. The metrical line *'tat sarvaṃ sarva-home'* on p. 195 is not found.
pp. 197-9 = II, 28, 64-78.
pp. 199-201 = II, 28, 79-84 and 87 to the end. The line *'dakṣiṇāṃ ca'* on p. 200 is not found.

Liṅga-p.

pp. 202-212 = I, 65, 51b-72a, 73-81, 84-116a, 118-123a, 124-135a, 136-151a, 152-155, 157-159 and 161-175.
The line '*tad aham sampravakṣyāmi*' on p. 202 is not found.

pp. 227-8 = II, 29, 1-7.

pp. 230-231 = II, 29, 8 to the end. The line '*subhagāyai vidmahe*' is not found.

pp. 249-251 = II, 33, 1 to the end.

pp. 257 and 258 = II, 38, 1 to the end.

p. 272 = II, 35, 1-3.

p. 273 = II, 35, 4 to the end.

p. 277 = II, 39, 1-2.

pp. 278-9 = II, 39, 3 to the end. Four lines from '*ghṛtena snāpayed devam*' on p. 278 are not found.

p. 301 = II, 32, 1b to the end.

pp. 369-371 = II, 30, 1 to the end. The line '*yat kṛtvā mānavaḥ*' on p. 371 is not found.

pp. 408-410 and 411 = II, 37, 1 to the end.

pp. 485-7 = II, 41, 1 to the end.

p. 633 = II, 42, 1 to the end.

p. 677 = II, 40, 1a.

pp. 687-8 = II, 40, 1b to the end.

pp. 730-1 = II, 36, 1 to the end. The line '*lūtādi braṇa-nāśāya*' is not found.

pp. 754-5 = II, 26, 6.

pp. 779-780 = II, 44, 1 to the end. The line '*japtvā rudrāṃs tu*' is not found.

pp. 794-6 = II, 43, 1 to the end.

pp. 822 and 824 = II, 34, 1 to the end.

Liṅga-p.

Vol. II, Part i,

pp. 67-8 = II, 28, 79-82.
p. 307 = II, 28, 79-82.

Vol. II, Part ii,

pp. 197-212 = II, 81, 1-5, 8b-17a, 18-21, 22b-39a, 40, 41b-42a and 43 to the end.
I, 82, 1-7a, 10b-31, 34b-35a, 32b-66a, 47-48a, 66b, 49a, 67-69, 68, 70-88a, 89b, 91-101, 103b-107a, 108b-109a, 110-114 and 117 to the end.

p. 397 = I, 84, 15 and 17-18a.
p. 398 = I, 83, 3b-4.

Vol. III, Part i,

pp. 1710-5 = II, 45, 2 to the end.

6. Mādhavācārya's com. on the Parāśara-smṛti,

Vol. I, Part i,

pp. 82-83 = I, 39, 69b-70; I, 40, 1.
p. 94 = I, 4, 49.
p. 343 = I, 26, 16a.

Vol. I, Part ii,

pp. 110-111 = I, 89, 109-110, 112a and 114-118a.

Vol. II, Part ii,

p. 14 = I, 26, 37b-38.

7. Nityācāra-paddhati of Vidyākara Vājapeyin,

pp. 146-147 = I, 94, 21-26a (except 24a).

Liṅga-p.

p. 571 = I, 85, 39b-40a.

8. Nityācāra-pradīpa of Narasiṃha Vājapeyin,

pp. 692-693 = I, 92, 169b-172a, 173b-175 and 176b-178.

9. Haribhaktirasā-mṛtasindhu of Rūpa Gosvāmin,

p. 58 = II, 3, 110.

Liṅga-p.

10. Haribhakti-vilāsa of Gopālabhaṭṭa,

p. 27 = II, 7, 12b-14a.
p. 409 = II, 2, 6b-8a.
p. 498 = II, 4, 5a.
p. 500 = II, 4, 6b-7a.
p. 505 = II, 4, 8-10a and 13b-14a.
p. 511 = II, 4, 11b-13a.
p. 570 = II, 4, 14b-16a.

X. VERSES QUOTED FROM THE 'VARĀHA-P' OR 'VĀRĀHA' IN

Varāha-p.

1. Kālaviveka of Jīmūtavāhana,

p. 424 = 28, 40-41.
The verse *'mahānavamyāṃ'* is not found.

p. 425 = 29, 14b-15.
The verse *'kārttikasya'* is not found.

p. 450-1 = 30, 6.
The other lines are not found.

2. Aparārka's com. on Yāj.,

p. 12 = 70, 41-42; 71, 52-54; and 70, 35b-36.
The verse *'kuhakāś cendrajālāni'* is not found.

p. 13 = 66, 11-12a.
pp. 301-302 = 112, 31-40.
The line *'irāvatī* etc.' is not found.

p. 426 = 13, 33-35.

Varāha-p.

p. 456 = 190, 103b-104a.
The line *'vastra-śaucādi'* is not found.

p. 498 = 190, 125.
pp. 525-526 = 188, 12-32 (except 14b-15, 18b-24 and 27-30a).
The lines *'śvaḥ kariṣye'* and *'pūjayiṣyāmi'* are not found.

3. Hāralatā of Aniruddha-bhaṭṭa,

pp. 128-130 = 187, 88-109a (except 89b, 91b-92a, 93b, 98a and 104).

4. Pitṛ-dayitā of Aniruddha-bhaṭṭa,

p. 75 = 187, 101-103.
p. 77 = 187, 106-107.

Varāha-p.

5. Dānasāgara of Ballālasena,

fol. 117a = 205, 24-25.
„ 124a = 207, 26.
„ 129a (twice) = 207, 50a and 50b.
„ 136b (twice) = 207, 26. 205, 30.
„ 157b-158a = 206, 18b-22.
„ 158a-158b = 206, 18b-22.
„ 159a = 206, 18b-22.
„ 161b = 207, 52b.
„ 166b = 207, 52b.
„ 168a = 207, 45b.
„ 173a = 207, 26.
„ 190a — Cf. 207, 51.
„ 221a = 206, 14b-15a.
„ 223b = 206, 14b-15a.
„ 232b = 206, 13-14b.

6. Smṛti-candrikā of Devaṇabhaṭṭa,

IV, 189 = 190, 103b-104a. The line *'vastra-śaucādi'* is not found.

7. Caturvarga-cintāmaṇi of Hemādri,

Vol. I,

pp. 404-5 = 99, 82-83 and 85-88. The line *'ikṣudaṇḍa-mayāḥ'* on p. 404 and the verse *'tila-dhenuṃ tato datvā'* on pp. 404-5 are not found.
pp. 431-2 — Cf. chap. 109.
pp. 479-480 = 112, 31-40. The line *'irāvatī dhenumatī* is not found.
p. 531 = 112, 69b-72.
pp. 972-3 = 211, 8 and 9b-12.

Varāha-p.

Vol. II, Part i,

pp. 11-12 = 32, 1-9a.
p. 321 (twice) = 37, 4-5. The verse *'kiṃcid vrataṃ'* is not found.
pp. 355-6 = 56, 1-14.
pp. 377-9 = 57, 1a, 3-9 and 11b-15. The line *'anena khalu mantreṇa'* on p. 378 is not found.
pp. 479-480 = 58, 1-3a, 8-13a and 15 to the end.
pp. 524-5 = 59, 1-3a, 9, 3b, 5-6a, 7b-8, 10a and 6b. For the five lines from *'sauvarṇaṃ rāja-taṃ vāpi'* cf. Var 59, 4. The last verse *'vighnāni tasya na bhavanti'* is not found.
pp. 556-7 = 60, 1 to the end. Two lines from *'gāṃ savatsāṃ'* and the verse *'śeṣāhi-bhoga'* are not found.
pp. 515-6 = 61, 1-10.
pp. 734-5 = 63, 2-7 and 11b-12.
pp. 747-8 = 62, 1-5a. The verse *'tasyaiva māgha-māsasya'* is not found.
pp. 957-8 = 64, 1 to the end.
pp. 985-991 = 139, 21-91a. There are numerous differences in readings and numbers of verses in the corresponding passages.
pp. 1022-6 = 39, 26-39, 40b-54b, 59-60, 67-74 and 76-77. The line *'caturbhis tila-pātraiś ca'* on p. 1024 is not found.

Varāha-p.

pp. 1026-7 = 40, 2b-9 and 10b-11.

pp. 1027-9 = 41, 1-15.

pp. 1029-30 = 42, 1-7 and 14 to the end.

pp. 1030-32 = 43, 1-16.

pp. 1032-4 = 44, 1-10 and 15 to the end.

pp. 1034-5 = 45, 1 to the end.

pp. 1036-7 = 46, 1-8. For the last eleven lines (*'kathayāmāsa dharmajño'* etc.) cf. 46, 9 ff.

pp. 1037-8 — Cf. chap. 47.

pp. 1038-9 = 48, 1-6b, 23a, 24b; (for the three lines from *'pūjyate matsya-rūpeṇa'* cf. Var 48, 17); 48, 20-22a.

pp. 1039-41 = 49, 1-4, 6-8a, 10b-11a, 16b, 18b, 19b and 22-29a. The line *'iyaṃ vyuṣṭiḥ purā jātā'* on p. 1041 is not found.

pp. 1041-4 = 50, 4a-b, 5-19, 22-25 and 26b to the end. The verses *'yuvanāśvaś ca rājarṣiḥ'* and *'e k a i a k y ā p i v ā p a t s u'* on pp. 1043 and 1044 respectively are not found.

pp. 1101-3 = 55, 1-3, 4-20a and 59. Three lines from *'keśaveti hariṃ pūjya'* on pp. 1101-2 and the line *'yathāvibhava-sāreṇa* on p. 1103 are not found.

pp. 1161-2 = 65, 6b-7.

p. 1172 = 31, 17b-18.

Vol. II, Part ii,

pp. 244-5 — Cf. 65, 11-13.

Varāha-p.

pp. 991-2 = 190, 38-39b and 40b-43. The lines *'muktvā tu'* and *'teṣāṃ trātā'* are not found.

Vol. III, Part i,

p. 17 = 34, 9.

p. 37 = 34, 1b-5.

p. 45 = 34, 5-6a.

p. 49 = 13, 31.

p. 57 = 13, 26b.

p. 58 (twice) = 34, 6-7 and 8b. 34, 9-10a.

pp. 58-9 = 13, 23-26. The line *'bhūrlokavāsināṃ'* and seven lines from *'saptadhā saptalokeṣu'* are not found.

p. 59 = 13, 27-28a.

p. 61 = 34, 12.

p. 439 = 14, 17-19.

p. 738 = 188, 34a, 36b and 49a.

p. 1011 = 190, 104a.

p. 1020-21 = 190, 125.

p. 1033 = 188, 34a, 36b and 49a.

pp. 1091-2 = 14, 27, 26 and 28-31. The line *'ślokān imāṃś ca'* and the verse *'mātāmahas tatpitā ca'* are not found.

pp. 1098-9 = 14, 49-58. Five lines from *'sayavaṃ pāyasaṃ vāpi'* are not found.

p. 1139 = 14, 7. Four lines from *'kathayec ca tadaiveṣāṃ'* are not found.

p. 1150 = 190, 103b. The line *'vastraśaucādi'* is not found.

p. 1167 = 190, 107-108a. Cf. also 188, 16.

p. 1180 = 14, 8a.

		Varāha-p.
p. 1194	=	14, 8b.
p. 1198	=	14, 11.
p. 1204	=	190, 120.
pp. 1204-5	=	188, 64-65.
p. 1229	=	14, 13a and 14a.
p. 1241	=	14, 14.
p. 1252	=	14, 15a. The line *'udaṅmukas tu devānāṃ'* is not found.
p. 1254	=	14, 15b-16a.
p. 1278	=	14, 16b.
p. 1288	=	190, 96b.
p. 1388	=	14, 23.
p. 1389	=	14, 25.
p. 1392	=	14, 32.
p. 1495	=	14, 42-43a.
pp. 1496-7	=	14, 37b-40.
p. 1505	=	190, 121; also 190, 27a-b. The line *'kṣāmayec ca'* is not found.
p. 1510	=	190, 118b-119a.
p. 1517	=	14, 44. The line *'tathānyān'* is not found.
pp. 1526-7	=	13, 53.
pp. 1535-6	=	13, 54-59.
pp. 1588-9	=	188, 27-29.
pp. 1607-8	=	188, 6, 12-14a, 16-18a, 25-26 and 30b-32. The lines *'śvaḥ kariṣye'* and *'pūjayiṣyāmi bhogena'* on p. 1607 are not found.
pp. 1608-9	=	188, 34a, 36b, 41a, 44 and 46-50a. The line *'tilopacāraṃ'* on p. 1608 is not found.
p. 1613	=	188, 67b-68.
pp. 1622-3	=	190, 38.
pp. 1630-1	=	190, 39a. The verse *'narā ye cātra'* and the line *'kareṇa puccham ādāya'* are not found.
p. 1633	=	190, 39b.

		Varāha-p.
Vol. III, Part ii,		
pp. 724-5	=	116, 4.
8. Kṛtyācāra of Śrīdatta Upādhyāya,		
fol. 15a	=	210, 64a and 65a.
„ 16a	=	211, 14a and 15a-b. The line *'tatkṣaṇād eva'* is not found.
9. Madana-pārijāta of Madanapāla,		
p. 561	=	190, 103b-104a. The line *'vastra-śaucādi'* is not found.
p. 611	=	188, 12. The lines *'śvaḥ kariṣye'* and *'pūjayiṣyāmi'* are not found.
10. Mādhavācārya's com. on the Parāśara-smṛti,		
Vol. I, Part ii,		
p. 360	=	190, 103b-104a. The line *'vastra-śaucādi'* is not found.
Vol. II, Part ii,		
p. 268 (twice)	=	202, 71. The verses *'tṛṇagulma'* etc. are not found.
11. Kṛtya-ratnākara of Caṇḍeśvara,		
fol. 167a-169a	=	39, 26-77.
„ 175a-175b	=	40, 2b to the end.

Varāha-p.

„ 185b-186a = 41, 1-15. Five lines '*agamyā-gamanam*' etc. are not found.

„ 190a-190b = 58, 1 to the end (except verses 3b-7 and 14).

„ 192a-192b = Chap. 42 (except verses 8-13).

„ 199b (twice) = 139, 47 (=155, 34). 116, 4 ff.

„ (?) = 211, 16-18.

12. Vratakāla-viveka of Śūlapāṇi,

fol. 4a = 62, 3.

13. Prāyaścitta-viveka of Śūlapāṇi,

p. 367 = 116, 4.

14. Tīrtha-cintā-maṇi of Vācas-patimiśra,

pp. 270-272 = 7, 13-26 and 27b-c. The line '*samāgatas tīrthavaram*' is not found.

15. Dānakriyā-kaumudī of Govindānanda,

p. 36 = 187, 90b-91a and 92b.

p. 99 = 188, 13, 10b, 12 and 14a. Two lines '*śvaḥ kariṣye*' and '*pūjayiṣyāmi*' are not found.

16. Śuddhikriyā-kaumudī of Govindānanda,

p 107 = 187, 90-91a and 92b.

Varāha-p.

p. 109 (twice) = 187, 94b-95. 187, 97b-c.

p. 110 = 187, 99-103 (except 99b).

p. 171 = 188, 13, 10b, 12 and 14a. The lines '*śvaḥ kariṣye*' and '*pūjayiṣyāmi*' are not found.

p. 177 — Cf. 188, 36b, 41a and 44.

17. Śrāddhakriyā-kaumudī of Govindānanda,

p. 75 = 188, 50b-c.

p. 76 = 190, 103b-104a. The line '*vastra-śau-cādi*' is not found.

p. 79 = 190, 104a.

p. 81 = 188, 13a.

p. 83 = 190, 103b.

p. 377 = 188, 50b.

p. 380-1 = 188, 13, 12 and 16. The lines '*śvaḥ kariṣye*' '*pūjayiṣyāmi*' and '*pāda-mrakṣaṇam*' are not found.

p. 395 = 188, 64-66. The line '*namo'stu te*' is not found.

18. Nityācāra-paddhati of Vidyākara Vājapeyin,

p. 63 = 190, 104a.

p. 481 — Cf. chaps. 130-136.

p. 506 = 132, 11b-12.

p. 507 = 66, 11a-b.

p. 509 = 66, 18.

p. 590 = 70, 40.

19. Haribhakti-vilāsa of Gopālabhaṭṭa,

pp. 82-90 = 99, 7-52. A few lines are not found.

	Varāha-p.
p. 130	= 131, 1.
p. 153	= 139, 17a and 19a. Many lines are not found.
p. 154	= 139, 2, 8b-9, 11 and 13-14. A few verses are not found.
p. 206	= 129, 17. The other two verses are not found.
pp. 394-395	= 119, 5-10. Many verses are not found.
p. 396	= 119, 13a.
p. 411	= 139, 96-97a and 99c. The other lines are not found.
p. 414	= 139, 99. The other lines are not found.
p. 687	= 152, 26.
pp. 1087-1088	= 128, 45b and 48. Cf. 128, 69-70.

XI. VERSES QUOTED FROM THE 'PADMA-P.' OR 'PĀDMA' IN

	Padma-p. (Ādi-kh.)
1. Tīrtha-cintāmaṇi of Vācaspatimiśra,	
pp. 18-23	= 43, 49. The other verses are not found.
p. 47	= 43, 22 ff.
2. Haribhakti-vilāsa of Gopālabhaṭṭa,	
p. 26	= 31, 114-116.
p. 108	= 31, 103.
p. 136 (twice)	= 31, 55b-56. 31, 54-55a and 57-58. The line '*yāmyaṃ hi yātanā*' is not found.
p. 215	= 31, 81-85.
p. 311	= 31, 96-98.
p. 428	= 31, 149-150.
p. 451	= 31, 140-141 and 143.
p. 478	= 31, 112.
p. 529	= 31, 101 and 103.
p. 545	= 31, 102 and 104-105.
p. 599	= 31, 99.
p. 768-9	= 31, 154, 158-159 and 165.
p. 835	= 31, 163.

Though the above verses quoted by Vācaspatimiśra and Gopālabhaṭṭa from the Padma-p. are traceable in Ādi-kh., chapters 31 and 43, it is highly probable that they drew upon Uttara-kh., chaps. 243-246, in which all the verses of Ādi-kh., chap. 31, and a few of those of Ādi-kh., chap. 43, are found.

—:o:—

	Padma-p. (Pātāla-kh.)
1. Haribhakti-vilāsa of Gopālabhaṭṭa,	
p. 22	= 93, 26.
p. 38	= 84, 48 and 52-53.
p. 118	= 92, 11.
p. 139	= 89, 12-16a and 20b-23.
p. 150	= 87, 29 and 32.
p. 165	= 94, 7-8a.
p. 166	= 89, 17b-19a.

	Padma-p. (Pātāla-kh.)
p. 357	= 94, 4a and 5b.
p. 359	= 94, 6-7a.
p. 367	= 94, 9b-11a.
p. 464	= 94, 4b-5a and 8b-9a.
p. 499	= 88, 8.
p. 529 (twice)	= 88, 21. The line *'bhavyāni bhūtāni'* is not found.
p. 549 ff.	= 94, 55 and 76. 96, 4-5. The other lines are not found.
p. 552	= 94, 56.
p. 553	= 96, 2a and 3.
p. 554	= 84, 37.
p. 642 (twice)	= 84, 40 and 72. 93, 28.
p. 655 (twice)	= 87, 22 and 8. 92, 13 and 16.
p. 672	= 84, 45.
p. 676	— Cf. 88, 4.
p. 679	= 92, 12.
p. 684	= 92, 15.
p. 700	= 85, 25.
p. 715	= 85, 32.
p. 769 (thrice)	= 92, 24-25a. 92, 26 and 34b-35. 92, 36b-41a.
p. 917, (thrice)	= 89, 45-47, 50-51a and 54-56a. 91, 23 and 26.
p. 918	= 85, 54-55 and 62-65. The line *'avaiśākhī bhavec chākhī'* is not found.
pp. 919-920	= 85, 67 and 70. 86, 13-16. 85, 66. 89, 48-49. 91, 21b-22 and 24-25.

	Padma-p. (Pātāla-kh.)
pp. 920-921	= 86, 17; (two lines *'ambarīṣa'* and *'tat prātar mādhave'* are not found). 89, 52, 44, 59b-60 and 61b-64.
p. 921	= 91, 11 and 17b-18a. 89, 4-12.
p. 922	= 91, 14-16.
p. 923	= 85, 42-44.
pp. 931-933	= 94, 28b-29a and 30. 94, 36b-39a, 72-73, 88b-90a and 18-20a.

—:o:—

1. Kālaviveka of Jīmūtavāhana,	Padma-p. (Sṛṣṭi-kh.)
p. 51	= 27, 70-71.
p. 390	= 27, 75.

2. Aparārka's com. on Yāj.,

p. 138	= 20, 164b-165a.
p. 306	= 31, 138a.
p. 570	= 8, 66-67a.

3. Hāralatā of Aniruddha-bhaṭṭa,

p. 199	= 10, 13b. There is also reference to Padma-p. (Sṛṣṭi-kh.) 10, 15-20a in which the Pārvatīyas and the gifts of beds have been mentioned.

4. Dānasāgara of Ballālasena,

fol. 18b	= 10, 16b-18a.
„ 154a	= 15, 140b-141a.
„ 239a	= 31, 149.

5. Adbhutasāgara of Ballālasena,		Padma-p. (Sṛṣṭi-kh.)
p. 20	=	42, 128b.
p. 23	=	42, 129b.
p. 50	=	42, 130.
p. 290	=	42, 129a.
p. 319 (twice)	=	37, 134 and 133b.
p. 320	=	42, 140a.
p. 332	=	37, 131a.
p. 336	=	42, 134a.
p. 358	=	37, 128-129a.
p. 409	=	37, 164b.
p. 412	=	42, 139b.
p. 426	=	42, 137-138a.
p. 443	=	42, 135b-136a.
p. 446	=	42, 140b-141a.
p. 461	=	42, 142b-143a.
p. 701	=	37, 130.
6. Smṛti-candrikā of Devaṇa-bhaṭṭa,		
I, 45-46	=	7, 41-46 and 48a.
7. Caturvarga-cintāmaṇi of Hemādri,		
Vol. I,		
p. 58	=	31, 183b-184a.
p. 71 (twice)	=	47, 238b-239a; the verse *'candrasya yadi vā'* is not found. 47, 241b-242a.
pp. 243-5	=	31, 166-187a. The line *'ahatāmbara-saṃcchannān'* on p. 244 is not found.
pp. 346-356	=	21, 81-93a, 94b-96a, 93b-94a, 96b-101a, and 102-127a.
pp. 360-1	=	21, 127b-135.
pp. 361-2	=	21, 136-145a.
pp. 364-6	=	21, 145b-152a.
p. 366	=	21, 152b-159a.
p. 376	=	21, 159b and 161b-165a.

		Padma-p. (Sṛṣṭi-kh.)
pp. 378-9	=	21, 165b-176a.
pp. 379-381	=	21, 176b-187a.
pp. 381-2	=	21, 187b-197a.
pp. 382-4	=	21, 197b-213. For the lines *'paśyed imān adhano 'pi bhaktyā'* on pp. 383-4 cf. Sṛṣṭi-kh. 21, 291 and 321a.
pp. 406-7	=	31, 137b-149.
p. 962	=	31, 187b-189a.
pp. 1030-1	=	24, 212-221.
Vol. II, Part i,		
p. 67	=	31, 174-179a. The line *'ahatāmbara-saṃcchannān'* is not found.
pp. 306-7	=	31, 174-179a. The line *'ahatāmbara-saṃcchannān'* is not found.
pp. 356-7	=	20, 137.
pp. 375-6	=	24, 9-16a and 17.
p. 389	=	20, 135a and 136.
pp. 422-6	=	22, 61-62, 64-68a, 68b-83, 85-97a, 84, 98-102 and 104. The line *'brāhmaṇaṃ brāhmaṇīṃ caiva'* on p. 425 is not found.
pp. 461-5	=	22, 105-127 and 128b-135. The line *'mukuṭaṃ vindhya-vāsinyai'* on p. 462 is not found.
pp. 471-4	=	22, 136-164. The verses *'yām upoṣya naro yāti'* and *'ānandadāṃ sakala-duḥkha-harāṃ'* and the line *'rudrāṇī-lokam āpno'.'* on p. 474 are found.
p. 483	=	20, 89b-91a.
pp. 483-4	=	20, 131.

		Padma-p. (Sṛṣṭi-kh.)
p. 484 (twice)	=	20, 122-123a; 20, 103-104a.
p. 532	=	20, 113.
pp. 553-6	=	22, 176 to the end. The lines *'ebhir mantra-padaiḥ'* and *'viprāya veda-viduṣe'* on p. 554 and the verse *'sārasvata-vrata-vareṇa'* on p. 555 are not found.
pp. 638-640	=	21, 215-216a, 218-232a and 235a. The lines *'udyāpayed yathā-śaktyā'* and *kartā śivapure'* on p. 639 and the lines from *'rājā bhavati rājendra'* are not found.
pp. 640-642	=	21, 281-289 and 291. Twelve lines from *'ādhi-vyādhi-vinirmuktaḥ'* on p. 641 is not found.
pp. 642-3	=	21, 263b-275a and 276-280. The line' *'śayanaṃ vastra-saṃvītaṃ'* is not found.
pp. 648-650	=	21, 307-311a, 312-315a, 311b, 315b-318a, 319a and 320-321. Three lines from *'tataḥ punar ihāgatya'* on pp. 649-650 are not found.
pp. 650-2	=	21, 292-306. The line *'aiśānyāṃ mitra-nāmānaṃ'* on p. 651 is not found.
pp. 743-4	=	21, 249b-262. The line *'kurvāṇaḥ saptamīm etāṃ'* on p. 744 is not found.

		Padma-p. (Sṛṣṭi-kh.)
pp. 746-7	=	21, 235b-248a.
p. 786	=	20, 112.
p. 787	=	20, 113a and 114b-115a.
p. 788	=	20, 232.
p. 881	=	20, 107.
p. 958	=	20, 72-74a.
p. 983	=	20, 138-139a. The line *'tila-droṇī-parigatāḥ'* is not found.
pp. 1044-9	=	23, 11b, 13, 17-19b, 20-47a, 48b, 49b-65 and 69b-72a. Three lines from *tathaiva viṣṇoḥ śirasi'* on p. 1047 are not found.
p. 1059	=	20, 40b-41.
pp. 1075-8	=	21, 22-40a, 44b and 40b-50. The lines *'yac cīrtvā'* and *'prabhāte vimale'* on p. 1075, *'pūjayej jagatāṃ nāthaṃ'* on p. 1076, *'divā-svapnaṃ parānnaṃ ca'* and *'kṣaudraṃ tailāmiṣaṃ'* on p. 1077, and *'mantreṇānena rājendra'* on p. 1078 and the verses from *'viśoka-dvādaśī caiṣā'* on p. 1078 are not found.
p. 1161	=	20, 109b-110.
p. 1202	=	20, 115b-116.

Vol. II, Part ii,

p. 25	=	20, 52b-54.
p. 147	=	20, 119.
pp. 175-9	=	24, 101-130.
p. 239	=	20, 111.
p. 242	=	20, 117.
p. 254	=	20, 74b-76.
p. 322	=	20, 133.

		Padma-p. (Sṛṣṭi-kh.)
pp. 350-1	=	17, 250-259. The verse *'pratipadi brāhmaṇyaś ca'* on p. 350 is not found.
p. 394	=	20, 130.
pp 542-8	=	23, 94-107, 109-138, 140b-141, 139b-140a, 142b-143, 139a and 144b-145. A few lines on pp. 544, 545, 547 and 548 are not found.
pp. 680-4	=	24, 64-91, 93b-94 and 96.
p. 794	=	20, 82b-83b. The line *'saubhāgya-padam'* is not found.
p. 818 (four times)	=	20, 40-50a (the line *'pārite ca'* is not found); 20, 55-56; 20, 114-115a (the line *'sita-vastra-yugenātha'* is not found); and 20, 83c-84 (the line *ghṛta-kumbhaṃ tathā'* is not found).
p. 857	=	20, 77-78. The line *'jyaiṣṭhāṣāḍhe tathā māghe'* is not found.
p. 860 (twice)	=	20, 57-58 (the line *'śiraḥ-saugandhya-jananaṃ'* is not found); 20, 108-109a.
p. 862 (twice)	=	20, 44-45; 20, 61-62.
p. 863	=	20, 65. Cf. 20, 66. The line *'sa sarva-pāpa-nirmuktaḥ'* is not found.

		Padma-p. (Sṛṣṭi-kh.)
pp. 863-4	=	20, 67-69a. The line *'divi deva-vimānasthaḥ'* is not found.
p. 864	=	20, 69b-71. The line *'brāhmaṇo bhāskarasyāpi'* is not found.
p. 865 (four times)	=	20, 79-80; 20, 81-82a; 20, 127; 20, 47b-48.
p. 866 (four times)	=	20, 106; 20, 87b-89a; cf. 20, 121; 20, 46-47a.
p. 883 (twice)	=	20, 118; 20, 134.
p. 884 (twice)	=	20, 100b-101a; 20, 129.
pp. 884-5	=	20, 104b-105.
pp. 885 (twice)	=	20, 94b-97a; 20, 97b-98.
pp. 893-4	=	22, 1-3a, 39-45a and 46b-48.
p. 895-6	=	22, 50-54. The line *'nānābhakṣa-phalair yuktaṃ'* is not found.
p. 901	=	22, 55a.
pp. 902-3	=	22, 55 and 58-59. The line *'yāvad āyuś ca'* is not found.
p. 904	=	22, 60.
p. 905	=	20, 128.
p. 906 (twice)	=	20, 101b-102. The verse *'pṛthivī-bhājane'* is not found.
pp. 910-911	=	20, 99-100a.
p. 911 (twice)	=	20, 123b-124; 20, 125-126.

Vol. III, Part i,		Padma-p. (Sṛṣṭi-kh.)
p. 14	=	10, 36.
p. 15	=	10, 35.
p. 16 (twice)	=	10, 38; 10, 39b-40a.
pp. 20-21	=	28, 89-95a, 97b-98, 100-101a, 103a, 102a, 103b, 105a, 109a-110 and 111b.
pp. 28-32	=	10, 45b-46a, 44-45a and 46b-47. 10, 49-61a, 62-64a, 65, 64b, 66b-68a, 69b-72, 89-97 and 112b-114. Lines 2-7 and 10-14 on p. 30 and line 13 on p. 31 are not found.
pp. 33-34	=	10, 115, 118-119, 121-122a and 124b-125a. The line *'saṃnatiś cātiyogena'* is not found.
pp. 52-4	=	9, 3b-4a, 11-12a, 32-35, 42, 44-45, 48-50 and 53-55a. Four lines from *'amūrtimantaḥ pitaro'* on p. 53 are not found. [These four lines are the same as Mat 15, 12-13].
p. 72	=	9, 88b-89a.
pp. 168-9	=	9, 12 and 15b-18.
pp. 185-6	=	9, 12, 15b-17a, 19-20, 21a, 23b, 29a, 24, 28b and 29b.
p. 275	=	27, 44.
p. 548	=	9, 64b-65a and 66b-67a.
p. 564	=	9, 65b-66a.
p. 567	=	9, 158.
p. 682	=	9, 63b-64a
p. 685	=	9, 65b-66a
p. 1015	=	9, 123b-124
p. 1070	=	9, 165b-166a.
p. 1073	=	9, 166b.
pp. 1074-5	=	9, 167b-169a.

		Padma-p. (Sṛṣṭi-kh.)
p. 1077	=	9, 167a.
p. 1094	=	47, 301b-302.
p. 1134	=	9, 139b-140a.
p. 1148	=	9, 140b-141a.
p. 1158	=	9, 85a and 86b-88a.
p. 1162	=	9, 90b-91a.
p. 1164 (twice)	=	9, 138b-139a; 9, 89b-90a.
p. 1175	=	9, 61-62a and 63b-64a.
p. 1176	=	9, 93b-94.
p. 1186	=	9, 96.
p. 1220	=	9, 97.
p. 1226	=	9, 143b-144.
p. 1232	=	9, 141b-142.
p. 1236	=	9, 142b-143a.
p. 1238	=	9, 145a.
p. 1250	=	9, 145b.
p. 1259	=	9, 153b.
p. 1284	=	9, 146-147a.
p. 1291	=	9, 152.
p. 1301	=	9, 154-155.
p. 1312	=	9, 154.
p. 1370	=	9, 156b-157a.
p. 1396	=	9, 113b-114a.
pp. 1399-1400	=	9, 170b-172.
p. 1475 (twice)	=	9, 92-93a (the line *'piṇḍa-bhūmau prayatnena'* is not found); 9, 102-3.
p. 1480	=	9, 178b-179a.
p. 1504	=	9, 120.
p. 1507	=	9, 121.
p. 1517	=	9, 123a.
p. 1544	=	9, 197b.
p. 1550	=	9, 197a.
p. 1555	=	9, 196.
p. 1560	=	9, 199.
p. 1574	=	28, 96b-97a.
p. 1588	=	10, 5.
p. 1595	=	10, 6-7.
p. 1601	=	10, 8-12a.
p. 1613	=	10, 12b-16a. The line *'bhojayet prayataḥ'* is not found.

		Padma-p. (Sṛṣṭi-kh.)
p. 1614 (twice)	=	10, 16b-18a; 10, 21.
Vol. III, Part ii,		
p. 312	=	9, 12 and 15b-18.
pp. 452-3	=	9, 12, 15b-17a, 19-20a, 21a, 23b, 29a, 24, 28b and 29b.
p. 614	=	17, 254-258.
pp. 616-7	=	17, 250-253.
p. 641	=	27, 70-74. The verse *'kṛttikā-rohiṇya-yāmya-yuktā'* is not found.
p. 677	=	27, 73-74.
8. Kṛtyācāra of Śrīdatta Upādhyāya,		
fol. 27b-28a	=	20, 145-157a. The line *'āruhya mama gātrāṇi'* is not found.
„ 51a-b	=	20, 159-170a.
„ 57a	=	20, 170b-177a.
„ 67b	=	15, 140b-141a.
9. Kṛtya-ratnākara of Caṇḍeśvara,		
fol. (?)	=	31, 77b-80.
10. Mādhavācārya's com. on the Parāśara-smṛti,		
Vol. II, Part ii,		
pp. 219-220	=	27, 50 and 53.
11. Nityācāra-paddhati of Vidyākara Vājapeyin,		
p. 72	=	20, 146a.
p. 210	=	20, 163-164a.
12. Smṛti-tattva of Raghunandana,		Padma-p. (Sṛṣṭi-kh.)
Vol. I,		
p. 359	=	20, 145-157a. The line *'āruhya mama gātrāṇi'* is not found.
pp. 372-3	=	20, 159-170a.
p. 394	=	20, 170b-176.
Vol. II,		
p. 338	=	10, 13b-14a.

—:o:—

		Padma-p. (Uttara-kh.)
1. Tīrtha-cintāmaṇi of Vācaspatimiśra,		
pp. 18-23	=	246, 51 ff.
p. 26	=	246, 43.
p. 27	=	246, 60b-61a.
2. Varṣakriyā-kaumudī of Govindānanda,		
p. 491	=	25, 16b-17a (=246, 6). The other quoted verse is not found.
p. 492	=	246, 19b-21a. The first one of the quoted verses is not found.
p. 494	=	246, 43. The first two of the quoted verses are not found.
3. Smṛti-tattva of Raghunandana,		
Vol. I,		
p. 148	=	242, 29. 246, 19b-21a. The other verses are not found.

	Padma-p. (Uttara-kh.)		Padma-p. (Uttara-kh.)
p. 397	= 122, 35b-36a (=245, 67).	p. 136 (twice)	= 244, 68b-70a. 244, 66b-68a and 70b-72a.
p. 456	= 122, 38b (=245, 69a). The second of the quoted lines is not found.	p. 215	= 245, 6-9 and 11.
		p. 311	= 245, 23-25.
p. 673	= 88, 15b-18.	p. 359	= 244, 8.
		p. 363	= 244, 11 and 13.
Vol. II,		p. 428	= 245, 83-84. 249, 110.
p. 363	= 245, 79.	p. 451	= 245, 69 and 76-77.
		p. 461	= 244, 7.
4. Sāṃkhya-pravacana-bhāṣya of Vijñāna Bhikṣu,		p. 463	= 244, 1-6 and 9-10.
		p. 529	= 245, 28a-b, 34 and 37. The verse *'na śūdrā'* is not found.
		p. 545	= 245, 28c, 29a and 30b-31.
pp. 5-6	= 263, 66-75a.	p. 599	= 245, 26.
p. 23	= 263, 70b-71a and 74b.	p. 671	= 72, 98-99.
		p. 768	= 245, 88 and 92-93.
5. Haribhakti-vilāsa of Gopālabhaṭṭa,		p. 823	= 38, 22. The verse *'stuvanti na praśaṃsanti'* is not found.
p. 26	= 245, 40-42.	p. 835	= 245, 97-98a.
p. 101	= 72, 100.	p. 862	= 38, 2, 3a and 5-21a. A few lines disagree.
p. 108	= 245, 29b-30a.		

XII. VERSES QUOTED FROM THE 'BṚHANNĀRADĪYA P.' OR 'BṚHANNĀRADĪYA' IN

	Bṛhannāradīya P.		Bṛhannāradīya P.
1. Vratakāla-viveka of Śūlapāṇi,		p. 113	= 26, 36-37.
		p. 307	= 26, 26.
fol. 7a.	— Cf. 16, 4.	p. 328	= 27, 28.
		p. 335	= 27, 29.
2. Śrāddhakriyā-kaumudī of Govindānanda,		3. Varṣakriyā-kaumudī of Govindānanda,	
p. 78	= 26, 2.		
p. 98	= 26, 3. The line *'tataḥ prātaḥ samutthāya'* resembles Bnār 26, 22a.	p. 206	= 27, 21 and 23.
		p. 567-8	= 14, 39, 54-55, 58 and 64.

4. Śuddhikriyā-kaumudī of Govindānanda, — Bṛhannāradīya P.

p. 83 = 7, 65.
p. 196 = 25, 28.

5. Smṛti-tattva of Raghunandana,

Vol. I,

p. 398 = 14, 55 and 60.
p. 453 = 14, 39-40, 54a and 55b.

Vol. II,

p. 112 = 22, 13-16.
p. 236 = 7, 65.
p. 312 = 24, 25.
p. 505 = 14, 55.

6. Haribhakti-vilāsa of Gopālabhaṭṭa,

p. 104 = 11, 99; and 28, 97.
p. 106 = 38, 106.
p. 107 = 1, 67.
p. 108 = 1, 81.
p. 117 = 38, 102; and 37, 122.
p. 157 = 18, 3, 46-47 and 49.
p. 253 = 11, 12.
p. 273 = 37, 66-67. The verse '*śālagrāma-śilās tāś ca*' is not found.
p. 312 = 1, 57 and 61-64.
p. 356 = 37, 68.
p. 364 = 13, 69.
p. 385 = 37, 35.
p. 409 = 13, 196-197.
p. 417 = 13, 204 and 199.
p. 430 = 35, 3.
p. 432 = 13, 190.
p. 433 = 3, 78.
p. 434 = 3, 77.
p. 456 = 35, 15-16; 35, 60 and 63.
p. 461 = 37, 65.

Bṛhannāradīya P.

p. 465-6 = 6, 50; (the verse '*saṃsāra-pāpa-vicchedī*' is not found). 13, 59-60, 62-63 and 66-68.
p. 466 = 37, 52.
p. 468 = 6, 22.
p. 469 = 13, 65.
p. 504 = 5, 60.
p. 506 = 5, 53-54 and 40a. One line is not found.
p. 507 = 5, 64 and 52; 5, 49.
pp. 525-528 = 4, 102 and 104-106; 5, 35; 11, 3-4 and 11; 11, 55-56; 18, 117; 32, 5-6 and 61; 1, 83; 35, 9 and 12; 37, 3-4 and 8; 38, 105b and 123a; (the lines '*vāsudeva-parāḥ*' and '*atyanta-durlabhā*' and the verse '*veda-vāda-ratāḥ*' are not found); 3, 57.
pp. 546-547 = 21, 72 and 74-76.
p. 549 = 34, 61.
p. 553 = 4, 13.
p. 555 = 4, 33.
p. 561 = 28, 116.
p. 562 = 35, 5.
p. 565 = 23, 43-44. The verse '*vaiṣṇavaṃ cāgataṃ*' is not found.
pp. 569-570 = 34, 60 and 62; 37, 5; and 37, 60-62 and 64.
p. 581 = 37, 2.
p. 599 = 1, 65.
pp. 639-641 = 11, 7-8; 13, 174a and 173b; 18, 115 and 118; 18, 127;

	Bṛhannāradīya P.		Bṛhannāradīya P.
	28, 100, 104-105 and 115; 32, 10; 34, 59; and 37, 46, 59 and 63.	p. 676	= 11, 100.
pp. 654-655	= 35, 2. The verse *'hari hari sakṛd uccaritam'*, which is not found in the Bnār, resembles Nār II, 7, 6.	p. 678	— (= Nār I, 34, 23).
p. 660	= 32, 59.	p. 682	= 38, 126.
p. 662	= 38, 100 and 107.	p. 686	= 2, 43.
p. 671	= 32, 60; and 37, 7.	p. 698	= 37, 50-51.
		p. 707	= 4, 4 and 30. 18, 116.
		p. 728	= 38, 103.
		p. 730	= 28, 106.
		p. 739	= 23, 36a, 45, 40a, 30b, 41 and 46.
		p. 751	= 21, 2-3.
		p. 752	= 21, 5.
		p. 775	= 21, 10.

XIII. VERSES QUOTED FROM THE 'NĀRADĪYA P.' OR 'NĀRADĪYA' IN

1. Smṛti-candrikā of Devaṇa-bhaṭṭa,	Nāradīya-p.
II, 323	= II, 31, 9b-10a. The other verses are not found.
IV, 28	= II, 2, 33b.
47	= II, 2, 12.
51	= II, 2, 15.
53	= II, 1, 10-15a, 16-18 and 21b-22a.
60	= II, 23, 30b-34a and 41b. The verse *'aṣṭavarṣādhiko* etc.' is not found.
65	= II, 1, 26.
68-9	= II, 37, 16-17a. The other verses are not found.
79 (twice)	= II, 2, 21-24. II, 2, 15a.
121	= II, 2, 15.
123	= II, 2, 12.

2. Caturvarga-cintāmaṇi of Hemādri,	Nāradīya-p.
Vol. I,	
p. 529	= II, 24, 18 and 20-21a.
Vol. II, Part i,	
pp. 993-4	= II, 24, 23b-24a. The first three lines are not found.
p. 995	= II, 3, 16a; I, 23, 8. The line *'tāni pāpāni'* is not found.
p. 1003	= II, 3, 8b-9.
Vol. II, Part ii,	
pp. 772-5	= II, 22, 25-33, 34b-36, 37b-39, 40b-45a, 46-47, and 49-66a. The line *'gacched yasya'* on p. 774 is not found.
pp. 789-790	= II, 31, 7 ff. A few lines are not found.

Vol. III, Part i, Nāradīya-p.

p. 255 = I, 25, 52b-55.
p. 281 = II, 2, 15.
p. 283 = II, 2, 8b-9a.
p. 286 = II, 2, 12.
p. 330 = II, 2, 8b-9a.

Vol. III, Part ii,

p. 89 = II, 2, 12.
p. 104 = II, 2, 15.
p. 146 = II, 1, 10-15a, 16-18, 15b, 18b and 21b-22a.
p. 149-150 = II, 1, 8, 9b and 22b-24.
p. 153 (twice) = I, 23, 8 (the line *'tāni pāpāni'* is not found) and II, 24, 23b-24a. II, 3, 8b-9.
p. 163 = II, 1, 16.
p. 172 = II, 3, 8b-9.
pp. 197-8 = II, 2, 18-20a.
pp. 201-2 = II, 2, 21-23.
p. 202 = II, 2, 23.
p. 217 = II, 2, 22.
p. 230 = II, 2, 25.
p. 233 = II, 2, 26-29a and 30a. The line *'nirgatā cet'* is not found.
pp. 249-250 = II, 2, 38-39a.
p. 254 — For the verse *'bahu-vākya-virodhena'* cf. II, 2, 29b-30a.
p. 265 = II, 2, 30b-31a.
p. 281 = II, 2, 21-24.
p. 282 = II, 2, 15a.
p. 526 = II, 2, 8b-9a and 15b-16a.
p. 542 = II, 2, 15.
p. 545 = II, 2, 12.
p. 555 = II, 2, 12.
p. 556 = II, 2, 8b.
p. 650 = II, 2, 33b-34a.
p. 711 = II, 31, 7, 9-10a and 12b. The verse *'punīmaḥ'* and the line *'naḍ-valeṣu'* are not found.

3. Mādhavācārya's com. on the Parāśāra-smṛti, Nāradīya-p.

Vol. II, Part i,

p. 36 = II, 31, 48.
p. 59 = I, 7, 52.

Vol. II, Part ii,

p. 228 = II, 23, 11; and II, 27, 41b-42. Two verses *'vācā cākrośikā'* and *'na sādhayanti kāryāṇi'* are not found.
p. 267-8 = II, 7, 12b-14 and 15b.

4. Madana-pārijāta of Madanapāla,

p. 507 = II, 2, 15.
p. 530 = II, 2, 33b.

5. Tīrtha-cintāmaṇi of Vācaspatimiśra,

p. 193 = II, 38, 34.
p. 194 = II, 38, 38.
p. 202 = II, 39, 25b-26a.

6. Śrāddhakriyā-kaumudī of Govindānanda

p. 79 = I, 28, 2b.
p. 83 = I, 28, 20b.
p. 169 = I, 28, 63-64a.
p. 172 = I, 28, 67 and 69a.

7. Smṛti-tattva of Raghunandana,

Vol. I,

p. 87-88 — Cf. II, 2, 14.
p. 101 = II, 22, 83b-84a.
p. 108 = II, 24, 7a.
p. 109 = II, 24, 7b-8a.
p. 120 — Cf. II, 2, 14.

	Nāradīya-p.
p. 369	= I, 27, 66.
p. 450	= II, 22, 57b-58a.
p. 498	= II, 38, 38 and 40. The verse *'gaṅgām eva'* is not found.
p. 543	= I, 30, 9b-10a.
p. 822	= II, 22, 23b-24 and 38b-39. II, 22, 57b-58a. II, 22, 76b, 81, and 83-84a. The lines *'amāṃsāśī'*, *'nitya-snāne'*, and *'ekāntare'* and the verse *'niṣpāvān rāja-māṣān'* are not found.
p. 880	= II, 22, 83b-84a.
Vol. II,	
p. 12	= II, 22, 82b and 83-84a.
p. 28	= II, 1, 15b.
p. 41	— cf.. II, 2, 14.
p. 87	= II, 24, 7a. II, 24, 7b-8a.
p. 100	= II, 24, 6.
p. 365	= I, 13, 98a.
p. 449	= II, 22, 57b-58a.

8. Haribhakti-vilāsa of Gopālabhaṭṭa,

p. 360	= II, 38, 26.
p. 386	= II, 22, 34-35.
p. 428	= II, 6, 3.
p. 519	= II, 10, 37b-38a.
p. 634	= II, 3, 3 and 4b-5a.
p. 676	= II, 6, 5-6.
p. 752	= II, 24, 23b-24a.
p. 761	— cf. II, 3, 8b-9.
p. 779	= II, 2, 38-39a.

	Nāradīya-p.
p. 785	= II, 2, 29b-30a.
p. 786	= II, 2, 25.
p. 802	— (The first line is the same as Bnār 27, 48a).
p. 840	= II, 2, 21.
p. 891	= II, 31, 9b-10a.
p. 1034	= II, 22, 36.

9. Kālasāra of Gadādhara,

p. 24	= II, 22, 47.
p. 25	= II, 22, 23b-24, 18a and 19a. The verses *'māṃsāśino'* are not found.
p. 26	= II, 22, 53b. The line *'kārttike varjayet'* is not found.
p. 33	= II, 22, 47.
p. 39	= II, 31, 16a. II, 31, 15. The line *'punīmaḥ sarvapāpāni'* and the verse *'na vahniṃ sevayet'* are not found.
p. 40	= II, 31, 24b-25. The line *'savituḥ'* is not found.
p. 45	— cf. II, 2, 14.
p. 127	= I, 23, 8. II, 1, 15b. Three lines *'tāni pāpāni'* etc. are not found.
p. 128	= II, 2, 38-39a.
p. 382	= II, 2, 15; II, 2, 12. The line *'paitraṃ mūlaṃ'* is not found.
p. 439	= II, 2, 12.

XIV. VERSES QUOTED FROM THE 'AGNI-P.' OR 'ĀGNEYA' IN

	Agni-p.
1. Dānasāgara of Ballālasena,	
fol. 96a-97b	= 210, 13b-17a, 19-21 22b, 23 and 25-29a. Many of the quoted verses are not found.
2. Smṛti-candrikā of Devaṇa-bhaṭṭa,	
IV, 59	= 187, 2a. The other line '*gṛhastho brahmacārī*' is not found.
3. Mādhavācārya's com. on the Parāśara-smṛti,	
Vol. I, Part i,	
p. 268	= 155, 3b-4a.
4. Śrāddha-viveka of Śūlapāṇi,	
fol. 92b	— cf. 163, 28.
5. Varṣakriyā-kaumudī of Govindānanda,	
p. 323	= 192, 6b-7. Three lines '*gandha-puṣpādibhiḥ*' etc. are not found.
6. Dānakriyā-kaumudī of Govindānanda,	
p. 3	= 209, 56.
p. 5	= 209, 35.
p. 11	= 211, 30.
p. 12	— cf. 209, 49b-50.
p. 13	= 209, 57a, 60a, 58a, 59a, 61a, 62b and 63a.
p. 14	= 209, 22 and 37b-38.
p. 16	= 209, 60a.
p. 19	= 209, 57a.
p. 20 (twice)	= 209, 57a. The other quoted line is not found.
p. 58-61	= 210, 10b-31a.
p. 76	= 209, 22.
p. 124	= 209, 56.
7. Śuddhikriyā-kaumudī of Govindānanda,	
p. 160	= 211, 30a.
p. 181	— cf. 163, 28.
p. 185	— cf. 163, 28.
8. Śrāddhakriyā-kaumudī of Govindānanda,	
p. 116	= 117, 54-56a.
p. 187	= 117, 22b-23.
p. 210	= 117, 27b.
p. 301	= 209, 13.
p. 303	= 209, 14-15.
p. 360	— cf. 163, 28.
9. Kālasāra of Gadādhara,	
pp. 285-286	= 209, 2.
p. 305	= 158, 43.
p. 322	= 158, 43.
pp. 357-358	= 157, 36b-38.
p. 406	= 211, 42-43a.
10. Smṛti-tattva of Raghunandana,	
Vol. II,	
p. 36	= 187, 2a.

	Agni-p.
	The other line '*gṛhastho brahmacārī*' is not found.
p. 142	= 209, 57a.
11. Haribhakti-vilāsa of Gopālabhaṭṭa,	
p. 354	— cf., 248, 3-4. The readings and arrangement of lines differ.
12. Nityācāra-pradīpa of Narasiṃha Vājapeyin,	Agni-p.
p. 127	= 158, 43.
13. Haribhakti-rasāmṛta-sindhu of Rūpa Gosvāmin,	
p. 122	= 339, 34b-35a.

XV. VERSES QUOTED FROM THE 'GARUḌA-P.' OR 'GĀRUḌA' IN

	Garuḍa-p.
1. Tīrtha-cintāmaṇi of Vācaspatimiśra,	
pp. 268-270	= I, 82, 1 to the end (except 6b).
p. 319	= I, 84, 20.
2. Śrāddhakriyā-kaumudī of Govindānanda,	
p. 53	= I, 222, 1b-2.
p. 54	= I, 222, 2b.
p. 83	= I, 222, 1b.
p. 119	= I, 222, 9 (partly)-10.
p. 123	= I, 222, 9-10.
p. 124	= I, 222, 9 (last portion).
p. 129	= I, 222, 11.
p. 138	= I, 222, 21 (last part).
p. 141	= I, 222, 16 (latter half).
p. 148	= I, 222, 23 (former half).
p. 155	= I, 222, 23 (latter half).
p. 157	= I, 222, 30 (first part).
p. 162	= I, 222, 25.
p. 173	= I, 222, 33.
p. 178	= I, 222, 35-37.
p. 180	= I, 222, 38.
p. 184	= I, 222, 40.
p. 191	= I, 222, 39 (last portion) to 41 (first portion).
p. 192	= I, 222, 40.
p. 193	= I, 222, 41 (latter half) to 42 (former half).
p. 199	= I, 222, 42 (last portion) to 43.
p. 204	= I, 222, 45-46 (former half).
p. 206	= I, 222, 47.
p. 210	= I, 222, 51 (former half).
p. 319	= I, 224, 1a and 2.
p. 346	= I, 224, 1a and 2.
p. 389	= I, 222, 19.
p. 560	= I, 222, 57-58a.
3. Śuddhikriyā-kaumudī of Govindānanda,	
p. 196	= I, 84, 5a.
4. Varṣakriyā-kaumudī of Govindānanda,	
pp. 42-43	= I, 125, 1 to the end.
p. 62	= I, 128, 5.

		Garuḍa-p.
pp. 68-9	=	I, 128, 18-19. The last verse is not found.
p. 175	=	I, 31, 23.
p. 295	=	I, 129, 23b-24a.
pp. 313-314	=	I, 131, 11-20. The line *'prapadye 'haṃ'* is not found.
p. 319	=	I, 131, 1-2 (except 2b).
p. 321	=	I, 140, 4-5 (except 4c).
p. 322	=	I, 140, 6 to the end.
pp. 456-457	=	I, 123, 1-2.
p. 494	=	I, 217, 127.
pp. 504-5	=	I, 127, verses 1-2, 3b, 9, 8b, 10b-17a and 18-20a.
p. 508	=	I, 124, 11b-18 and 21. The line *'bilvapatrayutaṃ'* and the verse *'visarjayet paredyuś ca'* are not found.

5. Smṛti-tattva of Raghunandana,

Vol. I,

p. 33	=	I, 129, 25-26.
p. 42	=	I, 131, 3a.
p. 44-5	=	I, 131, 11-15 and 17-20. The verse *'tam evopavaset kālaṃ'*, three lines beginning with *'prapadye 'haṃ sadā* etc.', and two lines *'sarvalokeśvara'* and *'trāhi maṃ sarvaduḥkhaghna'* are not found. Three lines *'sūryaḥ somo yamaḥ'* etc. also are not found.
p. 58-9	=	I, 133, 1-2.
p. 127 (twice)	=	I, 124, 13. I, 124, 16b-19a.
p. 206	=	I, 221, 2.
p. 346	=	I, 110, 24.

Agni-p.		Garuḍa-p.
p. 347	=	I, 217, 78-79. These verses greatly resemble Gḍ I, 98, 14 and 16 also.
p. 349	=	I, 217, 83.
p. 351	=	I, 110, 1.
p. 429	=	I, 68, 8-10.
p. 430	=	I, 217, 153.
p. 439	=	I, 172, 18-19a, 20a and 21b.
p. 440 (twice)	=	I, 173, 62, 56b, 63 and 5; (the lines *'grāhī śītaḥ'* and *'vātanut pittalo'* are not found). I, 173, 8a; (the other 8 lines are not found).
p. 752	=	I, 217, 127.

Vol. II,

p. 437	=	I, 129, 25-26.

6. Kālasāra of Gadādhara,

p. 89	=	I, 133, 1.
p. 146	=	I, 127, 1-3a.
p. 329	=	I, 52, 23. The line *'etad eva paraṃ'* is not found.

7. Haribhaktivilāsa of Gopālabhaṭṭa,

p. 28	=	I, 232, 8.
p. 103	=	I, 221, 2. The other verse *'yady apy upahataḥ pāpaiḥ'* is not found.
p. 110	=	I, 231, 2.
p. 113	=	I, 239, 58.
p. 279	—	cf. I, 66, 4b.
p. 505	=	I, 231, 8.
p. 512	=	I, 231, 14b-c.

		Garuḍa-p.
p. 580	=	I, 231, 13-14a. The line *'vaiṣṇavānām sahasrebhyaḥ'* is not found.
p. 653	=	I, 235, 8. The first three verses are not found.

		Garuḍa-p.
p. 689	=	I, 232, 18.
8. Haribhakti-rasāmṛta-sindhu of Rūpa Gosvāmin,		
p. 63	=	I, 232, 18.

XVI. VERSES QUOTED FROM THE 'BRAHMA-P.' OR 'BRĀHMA' IN

		Brahma-p.
1. Caturvarga-cintāmaṇi of Hemādri,		
Vol. I,	—	Numerous verses have been quoted in connection with donations, but not a single is found in the extant Brahma-p.
Vol. II, Part i,		
p. 226	=	60, 32b-33, 35b and 36-43.
pp. 788-9	=	29, 27b-29a.
&c.		&c.
Vol. III, Part i,		
p. 8	=	220, 99b-c.
p. 10	=	221, 1 ; 220, 210.
p. 11	=	220, 204.
pp. 12-13	=	220, 87b-99a. The line *'piśācatvam anuprāptāḥ'* is not found.
p. 45	=	220, 67.
p. 65	=	220, 77-78a.
p. 71	=	220, 77a. The other two lines are not found.
p. 138	=	220, 60a.

		Brahma-p.
p. 171	=	220, 10b-11a.
p. 189	=	220, 51b-52a.
p. 197	=	220, 45b-48a.
p. 213	=	220, 20b-21a.
p. 230	=	220, 53b-54a.
pp. 253-4	=	220, 55-56.
p. 259	=	220, 57-58.
p. 260	=	220, 10b-11, 13a and 14.
pp. 264-5	=	220, 14-19 and 20b-21.
p. 277	=	220, 44b-45a.
p. 279	=	220, 59.
p. 292	=	220, 62b and 64a.
p. 295	=	220, 64b-66.
p. 335	=	220, 53b-54a and 55-57.
p. 421	=	220, 109b-110a.
p. 458	=	220, 127a.
pp. 459-460	=	220, 136.
p. 500	=	220, 127b-135.
p. 542	=	220, 154-155a.
p. 549	=	220, 168.
p. 551	=	220, 156-158. The line *'cīnākam'* is not found.
p. 552	=	220, 161.
p. 557	=	220, 159b-160a. The line *'pavitre parame'* is not found.
p. 562	=	220, 170, 175b-176, 172b-175a, and 178-180a.
p. 601	=	220, 159.

		Brahma-p.
p. 602 (twice)	=	220, 181b-183a; 220, 184b-185a.
pp. 679-680	=	220, 165b-166. The verse *'śveta-candana'* is not found.
p. 680	=	220, 171b-172a.
p. 683	=	220, 161b-165a.
p. 687 (twice)	=	220, 167.
p. 736	=	220, 146. The other verse is not found.
p. 744	=	221, 161.
p. 1014	=	220, 106a.
pp. 1134-5	=	220, 105 and 107b-110a.
&c.		&c.

2. Mādhavācārya's com. on the Parāśara-smṛti,

Vol. II, Part ii,

p. 209	=	215, 136b-137a and 138b-139a.
p. 210-211	=	214, 29-31. Four lines are not found.
p. 224-6	=	217, 48-50, 75b-76a, 57, 59b, 80b-81a and 83a.
p. 266	=	217, 68-71a, 66-67, 77b-80a and 45-47.

3. Dolayātrā-viveka of Śūlapāṇi,

fol. 3b (line 4)	=	63, 18.

4. Rāsayātrā-viveka of Śūlapāṇi,

fol. 4a	=	67, 10-11.

5. Śrāddha-viveka of Śūlapāṇi,

		Brahma-p.
fol. 24b	=	220, 46b-47a.
" 25a	=	220, 45b-47a.
" 28b (twice)	=	220, 51b-52a. The other quoted passage is not found.

6. Tīrtha-cintāmaṇi of Vācaspatimiśra,

pp. 53-86	=	27, 2a.
		28, 1-2.
		Four verses from *'santi tīrthāni* etc.' on p. 53 of the Tīrtha-cintāmaṇi are not found.
		69, 14 to the end (except verses 26 and 39-40).
		70, 3-4a.
		42, 34b to the end (except 35b-36a).
		43, 1-13.
		45, 1-5a, 16b and 17b-c.
		45, 18-24, 53a, 54-79, 84b to the end, and 82a.
		48, 1-6, and 10 to the end.
		49, 1-40a, 41b-51, 54-56, and 57b to the end.
		50, 1-48, (one verse *'kuṇḍalābhyāṃ vicitrābhyāṃ'* is not found), 49-50a and 51 to the end.
		51, 1-33a and 37 to the end.
p. 87	=	57, 1-7.
pp. 88-92	=	57, 8-30a, 32b-42, 44-47 and 50-56.
pp. 92-103	=	57, 57 to the end.
		58, 1-7.

	Brahma-p.
	Four verses *'tasmāt taṃ muniśārdūla'* etc. on p. 94 of the Tīrtha-cintāmaṇi are not found.
	58, 12-27, 28b-29, 30b-58 and 62b to the end.
	59, 1.
	Two verses *'sarva-lakṣaṇa-saṃyuktaṃ'* etc. on p. 101 of the Tīrtha-cintāmaṇi are not found.
	59, 3-4, 6a, 27b, 28b-30a and 84b to the end.
	60, 1-11.
p. 104 =	57, 3-4.
p. 105 =	57, 8 and 13-14.
p. 106 =	57, 22-23.
pp. 107-108 =	57, 33-37 and 39-40.
p. 109 =	57, 58.
p. 111 =	60, 9-10.
pp. 112-128 =	60, 12 to the end.
	Two verses *'nārāyaṇa-paro dharmo'* etc. on p. 113 and one line *'aṅguṣṭhe haste'* on p. 114 of the Tīrtha-cintāmaṇi are not found.
	61, 1 to the end.
	62, 1-15 and 18 to the end (except 22a).
	Three lines *'nāstikāya na vaktavyaṃ'* etc. are not found.
	63, 1-7.
p. 130 =	60, 40-42a and 44-45.
p. 132 =	61, 14-16, 23a-b and 24.
p. 133 =	61, 25 and 27-30.
p. 134 =	61, 31-34.
p. 135 =	61, 35-38.
p. 138 =	63, 3 and 8-9.
pp. 139-143 =	63, 11 to the end.
	64, 1 to the end.
pp. 143-154 =	65, 1-13, 15b-41a, 43-59, 65, 71-72, and 74 to the end.
pp. 156-159 =	51, 29-32, 37, and 42-45.
	66, 1-2, 10-13a and 14 to the end.
p. 160 =	67, 3-5.
pp. 161-169 =	67, 2, 6-12, 13b-22a and 23-80.
	One verse *'durlabhaṃ pāvanaṃ'* on p. 167 of the Tīrtha-cintāmaṇi is not found.
	68, 28-31, 32b, 35, 69b-70, 72-75 and 76a.
p. 175 =	177, 19, 24 and 16-17.
	One verse *'kṣetrajñaṃ ca'* is not found.
pp. 176-180 =	41, 10b-11, 53b, 56-78a (six lines from *'bhuktvā tatra varān'* on p. 178 of the Tīrtha-cintāmaṇi are not found), 78b-88, 91b-92, 89-90 and 93.
pp. 180-182 =	28, 44-56a, 62b to the end, and 56b-62a.
pp. 183-184 =	42, 1-7 and 9-10.
p. 184 =	42, 11.

7. Śrāddhakriyā-kaumudī of Govindānanda,

p. 15 =	220, 28-30 (except 30a).
p. 16 =	220, 183b-184a.
	The line *'āma-māṃsaṃ'* is not found.
p. 17 =	220, 156-157a, 158b and 182b-183a.
p. 18 (twice) =	220, 170 and 197b-198a.

		Brahma-p.
p. 19	=	220, 180b-181a and 161. The line *'vetrāṅkuraṃ'* is not found.
p. 20	=	220, 159-160a.
p. 23	—	cf. 220, 162.
p. 28	=	220, 4.
p. 42	=	220, 127-129.
p. 43	=	221, 96a and 97a.
p. 64	=	219, 75b.
p. 74	=	220, 118b-119a.
p. 84-5	=	219, 46b-47a and 48.
p. 84	—	cf. 219, 54b and 62b.
p. 122	=	219, 48 and 51.
p. 141	=	220, 160b.
p. 142	=	220, 162-164.
p. 144	=	220, 167.
p. 145	=	220, 139-140. The line *'anaṅga-lagnaṃ yad vastraṃ'* is not found.
p. 148	=	219, 61b.
p. 172	=	219, 69-70a.
p. 187	=	219, 72b-73a.
p. 189	=	219, 75b.
p. 203	=	219, 78.
p. 206	=	219, 79.
p. 210	=	219, 81b-82a.
p. 212	=	219, 83.
p. 258	=	220, 51b-52a
p. 263	=	220, 51b-53a.
p. 285	=	220, 45b-48a.
p. 300	=	220, 53b-54a and 55-56.

8. Dānakriyā-kaumudī of Govindānanda,

p. 43	=	218, 26b-27a.
p. 49	=	216, 18.
p. 50	=	216, 12-13.
p. 52	=	216, 30.

9. Smṛti-tattva of Raghunandana,

Vol. I,

p. 216	=	220, 139.

		Brahma-p.
p. 404	=	29, 55-56. One verse is not found.
&c.		&c.

Vol. II,

p. 563	=	27, 2a and 11b; 28, 1-2a.
p. 564	=	42, 1-2, 4, 5 and 9-10; 46, 4; 70, 3-4a.
pp. 565-7	=	57, 2-42 (except 11b and 31).
p. 567	=	57, 57.
pp. 569-570	=	60, 47; 61, 1-3 and 57; 62, 1-2.
pp. 570-571	=	62, 3b-5a, 6b and 12b-13a; 62, 23; 63, 1-5, 13-14 and 8-9.
p. 571	=	60, 11.
pp. 571-2	=	63, 17-21.
p. 572	=	65, 3 and 57; 65, 83a; 66, 1-2; 70, 5-6a; 64, 18. The verse *'vārṣikāṃś caturo māsān'* is not found.
pp. 572-3	=	41, 10b-11, 53b, 56-57a, 59b-61a, 63b-64a, 67, 89b-90, 28, 64b-c, 43-44 and 48b. The verse *'pathi śmaśāne'* and the line *'tathā caivotkale deśe'* on p. 572 are not found. Four lines from *'dehaṃ tyajanti'* on p. 572 resemble Br 68, 75-77.
&c.		&c.

XVII. VERSES QUOTED FROM THE 'SKANDA-P.' OR 'SKĀNDA' IN

1. Kālaviveka of Jīmūtavāhana, — Skanda-p.

   p. 440 = VII, i, 208, 39.
   p. 448 = VII, i, 208, 38.

2. Aparārka's com. on Yāj.,

   p. 205 = VII, i, 208, 39.

3. Caturvarga-cintāmaṇi of Hemādri,

   Vols. I-III. — Hundreds of verses have been quoted by Hemādri from the 'Skanda-p.' or 'Skānda', and a good number of these quoted verses is found in the printed Skanda-p. For instance, Caturvarga-cintamaṇi,

   Vol III, Part i,

   p. 244 = Sk VI. 220, 43.
   p. 162 = Sk VII, i, 206, 29-30a.
   p. 316 = Sk VII, i, 206, 94.
   &c. &c.

4. Kālanirṇaya of Mādhavācārya,

   p. 98 = VII, i, 19, 2-3.
   p. 283 = VI, 226, 9-10a and 25-26a.
   The line '*śivarātris tu sā*' is not found.

4a. Mādhavācārya's com. on the Parāśara-smṛti, — Skanda-p.

   Vol. I, Part i,

   p. 185 = VII, i, 207, 70, 73 and 74b.
   p. 188 = VII, i, 207, 48.

5. Madana-pārijāta of Madanapāla,

   pp. 193-5 = IV, i, 4, 21-28, 36, 39 and 41-42.

6. Vratakāla-viveka of Śūlapāṇi,

   fol. 8a — Cf. IV, ii, 84, 51a.

7. Dīpakalikā of Śūlapāni,

   fol. 124a — the first two lines tally with V, iii, 209, 85, VI, 21, 71, VI, 37, 44 and so on, the remaining lines being not found.

8. Dolayātrā-viveka of Śūlapāṇi,

   fol. 1b ff. = II, ii, 42 (except lines 7a, 33b and 43b).
   fol. 3b-4a = II, ii, 42, 5.

9. Smṛti-tattva of Raghunandana,

   Vol. I,

   p. 29 (twice) = II, ii, 29, 33b-34 and 33a.
   p. 31 = II, ii, 29, 50.
   &c. &c.

(A). VERSES QUOTED FROM THE 'PURUṢOTTAMA-MĀHĀTMYA' IN

1. Dolayātrā-viveka of Śūlapāṇi, — Skanda-p.

fol. 3b (thrice) = II, ii, 29, 47. The other lines are not found.

(B). VERSES QUOTED FROM THE 'KĀŚĪ-KH.' IN

1. Tīrtha-cintāmaṇi of Vācaspatimiśra, — Skanda-p.

pp. 370-372 = IV, ii, 59, 104b-105, 115-117, 119-124, 126-133, 137-139 and 140-143.
The lines '*kṛte dharma-nadaṃ*' and '*dvā-pare bindu-tīr-thaṃ ca*' on p. 372 are not found.

2. Srāddhakriyā-kaumudī of Govindānanda,

p. 225 = IV, i, 38, 60.
p. 397 = IV, i, 35, 216b-217a.
p. 558 = IV, i, 35, 216b-217a

3. Varṣakriyā-kaumudī of Govindānanda,

pp. 280-1 = IV, i, 27, 152-154.
The last two lines '*e t ā n i daśa pāpāni*' etc. are not found.

Skanda-p.

p. 567 (twice) = IV, i, 40, 108 and 118. The two lines '*jāta-mātraṃ*' and '*bhakṣyābha-kṣye*' are not found.

p. 576 = IV, i, 4, 74-75, 77-81a and 82-83.

pp. 577-8 = IV, i, 4, 18, 22-23a and 33.
IV, i, 4. 34-35.
IV, i, 4, 36.
IV, i, 4, 60-61.
The first four lines '*pāṇipīḍitāḥ| tāsāṃ tuṣṭyā tu*' etc. are not found.

4. Smṛti-tattva of Raghunandana,

Vol. I,

pp. 370-1 = IV, i, 4, 80.
p. 422 = IV, i, 35, 199b-200 and 201b-203a.
p. 427 = IV, i, 35, 216b-217a.
p. 434 = IV, i, 35, 223-224a and 225a.

	Skanda-p.
p. 745	= IV, i, 35, 157.
Vol. II,	
p. 13	= IV, i, 4, 33.

5. Vidhāna-pārijāta of Anantabhaṭṭa,

	Skanda-p.
Vol. I,	
pp. 677-683	= IV, i, 37, verses 1, 3, 10-12, 14, 17-20, 22, 28, 30-32, 35, 37, 44-53, 55-57a, 58-59, 63-64, 66,
&c.	&c.

(C). VERSES QUOTED FROM THE 'REVĀ-KH.' IN

1. Mādhavācārya's com. on the Parāśara-smṛti,

	Skanda-p.
Vol. II, Part ii,	
pp. 231-2	.. The last four lines ('*gadgado*' *nṛtavādī*' etc.) are the same as Sk V, iii, 159, 12a, 16b, 17a and 18b. The rest are not found.
p. 253	— Cf. V, iii, 159, 12b.
p. 264 (twice)	— Of the 8 lines quoted, the last four tally with Sk V, iii, 159, 13a, 17b, 21a and 24a. The rest are not found.

(D). VERSES QUOTED FROM THE 'NĀGARA-KH.' IN

1. Caturvarga-cintamaṇi of Hemādri,

	Skanda-p.
Vol. II, Part i,	
pp. 485-497	= VI, 177, 14b to the end; 178, 1-74. A few lines are not found.
pp. 805-810	= VI, 162, 23-27 and 29-73.
Vol. II, Part ii,	
pp. 114-122	= VI, 266, 8 to the end.
Vol. III, Part i,	
p. 9	= VI, 215, 57b-60.
pp. 13-14	= VI, 218, 3b-5a, 6b-10a and 11b.
p. 16	= VI, 215, 40a and 41.
p. 22-23	= VI, 215, 38-39, 41, 43-50b and 55.
p. 24 (twice)	= VI, 215, 61 and 37.
pp. 45-46	= VI, 216, 9b-12a.
p. 48	= VI, 216, 14-16.
p. 66	= VI, 216, 67-68a.
p. 78	= VI, 216, 67-69a.
p. 152	= VI, 218, 3.
p. 169	= VI, 216, 7b-9a.
p. 172	= VI, 215, 32-37.
pp. 172-3	= VI, 215, 38-39.
p. 197	= VI, 216, 96b-97.
p. 199	= VI, 216, 99b-101.
pp. 200-201	= VI, 216, 124-130a.

		Skanda-p.
pp. 204-7	=	VI, 219, 14-15a; 220, 1, 7-8, 10a, 29, 32, 35a, 36b-37a, 39b-42, 48a, 47b, 51, 54b, 55b, 68-69 and 73-75; and 221, 2a, 3a. 5a and 6a. A few lines are not found.
p. 214	=	VI, 222, 1-3 (= 219, 19b-22).
pp. 219-221	=	VI, 222, 4-5, 7-14a. 16-28a and 30.
p. 229	=	VI, 217, 63b-65a.
p. 230	=	VI, 217, 65b-66a.
p. 252	=	VI, 217, 60-63a.
pp. 255-6	=	VI, 217, 52-59.
p. 390	=	VI, 217, 22 and 24-25.
p. 420	=	VI, 217, 7b-8a.
pp. 503-4	=	VI, 217, 11-15 and 17-20.
p. 523	=	VI, 217, 46.
pp. 538-540	=	VI, 221, 32, 33b-36a 37, 44, 38, 41-43 46, 49, 51-52 and 54-58. Three lines from *'tena te medhyatām'* on p. 539 are not found.
pp. 599-600	=	VI, 221. 23a, 24-26a and 27-30.
&c.		&c.

Vol. III, Part ii,

pp. 48-49	=	VI, 216, 96b-97. The verse *'nabho vātha'* is not found.
p. 304	=	VI, 266, 30-32. The verse *'māgha-phālgunayor madhye'* is not found.
p. 306 (twice)	=	VI, 266, 9-10a; and 266, 25-26a.

		Skanda-p.
pp. 309-310	=	VI, 266, 57-58a.
p. 312	=	VI, 216, 7b-8 (also cf. verse 83).
pp. 410-411	=	VI, 217, 65b-66a.
p. 411	=	VI, 217, 66b-67.
pp. 463-4	=	VI, 216, 96b-97.
pp. 465-6	=	VI, 216, 99b-102a.
p. 467	=	VI, 216, 124-130a.
pp. 473-5	=	VI, 219, 14-15a; 220, 1, 7-8, 10a, 29, 32, 35a, 36b-37a, 39b-42, 48a, 47b, 51, 54b, 55b, 68-69 and 73-75; and 221, 2a, 3a, 5a and 6a. A few lines are not found.
p. 493	=	VI, 222, 1-3 (= 219, 19b-22).
pp. 497-500	=	VI, 222, 4-5, 7-28a and 30.
p. 501	=	VI, 217, 63b-65a.
p. 649	=	VI, 217, 60-63a.

2. Kālanirṇaya of Mādhavācārya,

p. 290	=	VI, 266, 57. The line *'akṣayān labhate'* is not found.
p. 298	=	VI, 266, 30-32.
p. 310	=	VI, 216, 7b-8. The first and the third line tally with Sk VI, 216, 83 also.
p. 346	=	VI, 217, 66b-67.

3. Smṛti-tattva of Raghunandana,

Vol. I,

p. 125	=	VI, 266, 57. The line *'akṣayān labhate'* is not found.
p. 256	=	VI, 216, 96b-97. The verse *'nabho vātha'* is not found.

(E). VERSES QUOTED FROM THE 'PRABHĀSA-KH.' IN

1. Caturvarga-cintāmaṇi of Hemādri,

Vol. III, Part i,

		Skanda-p.
p. 280	=	VII, i, 205, 50b-51.
p. 291	=	VII, i, 205, 52.
p. 314	=	VII, i, 206, 51.
p. 316	=	VII, i, 205, 4-5a.
p. 319	=	VII, i, 205, 6.
p. 320	=	VII, i, 205, 8-9.
p. 330	=	VII, i, 205, 5a.
pp. 357-8	=	VII, i, 205, 77-81. The verse '*paradārābhigo mohāt*' is not found.
p. 370	=	VII, i, 206, 9-10a.
p. 389	=	VII, i, 205, 53 and 55a.
p. 448	=	VII, i, 205, 54b and 55b.
p. 455	=	VII, i, 205, 56b-57.
pp. 554-5	=	VII, i, 206, 83b-89a.
p. 641	=	VII, i, 206, 35b-37a. Three lines from '*prajā-puṣṭi-dyuti*' are not found.
p. 646	=	VII, i, 205, 11.
pp. 682-3	=	VII, i, 206, 47.
pp. 694-5	=	VII, i, 207, 4.
p. 702	=	VII, i, 207, 5. The lines '*cakra-baddhaṃ tu*' etc. are not found.
p. 717	=	VII, i, 207, 3.
p. 733	=	VII, i, 207, 6-7. The verse '*bandha-mokṣaṃ tu*' is not found.
p. 1019	=	VII, i, 206, 66.
p. 1021	=	VII, i, 206, 40.
p. 1070	=	VII, i, 336, 53b-54a.
p. 1073	=	VII, i, 336, 54b.
pp. 1074-5	=	VII, i, 336, 55b-56. The line '*bhāratā-dhyanaṃ*' is not found.
p. 1077	=	VII, i, 336, 55a.
pp. 1079-1080	=	VII, i, 206, 113-115 and 116b. Five lines from '*pitṝṇāṃ ca triṣu lokeṣu*' are not found.
pp. 1081-2	=	VII, i, 206, 117-124. Two lines from '*saptarṣīṇāṃ pitṝṇāṃ ca*' and four lines from '*devarṣīṇāṃ janetāraḥ*' are not found.
p. 1097	=	VII, i, 336, 259-260.
p. 1138	=	VII, i, 206, 3.
p. 1139	=	VII, i, 206, 4.
p. 1154	=	VII, i, 206, 2. The line '*savyena*' is not found.
p. 1160	=	VII, i, 208, 40.
p. 1168	=	VII, i, 206, 68.
p. 1176	=	VII, i, 206, 49.
p. 1179	=	VII, i, 205, 11.
p. 1193	=	VII, i, 206, 18b-c.
p. 1199	=	VII, i, 206, 46.
p. 1208 (twice)	=	VII, i, 206, 113-115a and 116a; and VII, i, 206, 118.
p. 1380	=	VII, i, 206, 39b-40a.
p. 1523	=	VII, i, 208, 42b-43.
p. 1525	=	VII, i, 208, 44-45a.
pp. 1525-6	=	VII, i, 208, 45b. The other two lines '*evam apy ācaret*' etc. are not found.
pp. 1571-3	=	VII, i, 336, 17, 34b-53a and 57-61a. The line '*jīvabhārgava*', eleven lines from '*āvāhayiṣye tān sarvān*', and the verse '*jātyantara-sahasrāṇi*' are not found.
p. 1574	=	VII, i, 336, 65b-67a.

		Skanda-p.
pp. 1574-5	=	VII, i, 336, 64-65a. Six lines from '*darbhās tilāḥ*' are not found.
Vol. III, Part ii,		
p. 9	=	VII, i, 19, 2-3.
p. 327	=	VII, i, 206, 94.
p. 540	=	VII, i, 205, 50b-51.
p. 561	=	VII, i, 205, 52.
p. 568	=	VII, i, 206, 51.
pp. 570-1	=	VII, i, 205, 4-5a.
pp. 574-5	=	VII, i, 205, 6.
p. 575	=	VII, i, 205, 8-9.

		Skanda-p.
p. 587	=	VII, i, 206, 93a and 92b.
2. Kālanirṇaya of Mādhavācārya,		
pp. 157-8	=	VII, i, 205, 50b-51.
3. Smṛti-tattva of Raghunandana,		
Vol. I,		
p. 1	=	VII, i, 19, 2-3.
p. 20	=	VII, i, 205, 52.
pp. 756-7	=	VII, i, 19, 2-3.

(F). VERSES QUOTED FROM THE 'CAMATKĀRA-KH.' IN

1. Caturvarga-cintāmaṇi of Hemādri,		Skanda-p.
Vol. III, Part i,		
p. 1162	=	VI (Nāgara-kh.), 20, 18.

Hemādri quotes 143 lines from the 'Camatkāra-kh.', and of these only two (as shown above) are found in the present Nāgara-kh. which contains chapters on a king named Camatkāra and a town named after him.

XVIII. VERSES QUOTED FROM THE 'BRAHMAVAIVARTA-P.' IN

1. Kālanirṇaya of Mādhavācārya,		Brahmavaivarta-p.
pp. 222-223	=	IV, 8, 54-55a.
p. 226	=	IV, 8, 67-68.
p. 227	=	IV, 8, 57b-58a.
2. Vratakāla-viveka of Śūlapāṇi,		
fol. 5b	=	IV, 8, 67-68.

3. Smṛti-tattva of Raghunandana,		Brahmavaivarta-p.
Vol. I,		
p. 38	=	IV, 8, 72. The verse '*catasro ghaṭikāḥ*' is not found.
p. 42	=	IV, 8, 6.
p. 44	=	IV, 8, 64-66.

	Brahmavaivarta-p.
p. 48 (twice)	= IV, 8, 62-63a. IV, 8, 62a.
p. 49	= IV, 8, 54-55a.
p. 51 (twice)	= IV, 8, 67-68. The verse '*kṛṣṇāṣṭamī*' is not found.
p. 53	= IV, 8, 72.
p. 54	= IV, 8, 57b-58a.
p. 104	= IV, 26, 39.
p. 109	= IV, 8, 84-85.
p. 326	= IV, 8, 72.
Vol. II,	
p. 37	= IV, 26, 39.
p. 52 (thrice)	= IV, 8, 72. The other verses are not found.
p. 87	= IV, 8, 84-85.
p. 99	= IV, 8, 84-85.

4. Haribhakti-vilāsa of Gopālabhaṭṭa,	Brahmavaivarta-p.
p. 794	= IV, 8, 72. The verse '*catasro ghaṭikāḥ*' is not found.
p. 979	= IV, 8, 54.
p. 985	= IV, 8, 67-68.
5. Kālasāra of Gadādhara,	
p. 55	= IV, 8, 57b-58a.
p. 87	= IV, 8, 72. The verse '*catasro ghaṭikāḥ*' is not found.
p. 97	= IV, 8, 54b.
p. 100	= IV, 8, 67-68.
p. 130	= IV, 26, 39.
p. 140-1	= IV, 8, 72. The other verses are not found.

XIX. VERSES QUOTED FROM THE 'BHAVIṢYA-P.' 'BHAVIṢYAT-P.' OR 'BHAVIṢYA' IN

1. Vijñāneśvara's Mitākṣarā,	Bhaviṣya-p.
on Yāj. III,	
6	= I, 32, 56b-57a.
2. Kālaviveka of Jīmūtavāhana,	
p. 408	= I, 21, 31 and 32b-34a.
pp. 411-412	= I, 31, 1-2, 4-10 and 16. The last line '*snāna dānādikaṃ karma*' is not found.
pp. 413-414	= I, 32, 1a and 3b-4a; I, 36, 67-69; I, 37, 1-2; I, 32, 1b-3a; I, 37, 3a. Four lines from '*supte janārdane deve*' are not found.

	Bhaviṣya-p.
p. 414	= I, 39, 1, 9b-10a and 12a. I, 46, 1a and 2a.
p. 415	= I, 81, 2-3, 14b and 15b-16a. I, 96, 3-4a.
pp. 415-416	= I, 97, 1; I, 98, 1; I, 99, 1-2; I, 100, 1; and I, 101, 1-2a and 20b-21a. The line '*snāna-dānādikaṃ sarvaṃ*' is not found.
p. 417	= I, 106, 4b-7a. Seven lines from '*śuklapakṣasya saptamyām upavāsaparo naraḥ*' are not found.

Bhaviṣya-p.

p. 492 = I, 81, 2. The verse '*amā vai soma-vāreṇa*' is not found.

pp. 507-508 = I, 99, 1-2. I, 106, 4b-6a.

3. Aparārka's com. on Yāj.,

p. 15 = I, 4, 87b-89.
p. 26 = I, 3, 6-7.
p. 39 = I, 3, 68b-69.
p. 41 = I, 3, 85b-86.
p. 52 = I, 4, 57. The verse '*savyāpasavya*' is not found.
p. 60 = I, 3 32b-33.
p. 239 = I, 184, 18b-19a.
p. 241 = I, 186, 20b-27a.
p. 283 = I, 184, 41 and 35b-37.
pp. 626-627 = I, 181, 23-24a and 26a. I, 181, 28-32.
p. 1186 = I, 65, 14, 16, 13a, 9b-10a and 15. The line '*triṣu varṇeṣu*' is not found.

4. Dānasāgara of Ballālasena,

fol. 14b = I, 181, 34.
" 23a = I, 64, 4 (= I, 103, 19b-20a).
" 276b = I, 93, 74b-75a.
" 287b-290a = I, 93, 58 and 59b; I, 93, 49-50; I, 93, 51; I, 93 69-71; I, 93, 45; I, 93, 42; I, 93, 43-44; I, 93, 68; (the verse '*bheryāṇi ca vādyāni*' is not found); I, 93, 60-61a; I, 93, 62; I, 93, 63; (three lines '*dhanadhānyaṃ*' etc. are not found); I, 93, 35; I, 93, 36; I, 118, 50b-52a; I, 103, 39b-41a; I, 93, 37; (three verses '*vimānam iti*' etc. are not found).

5. Smṛti-candrikā of Devaṇabhaṭṭa,

I, 53 = I, 3, 6-7a.
III, i, 54 = I, 181, 28-29.
IV, 163-164 — Of the five quoted verses, the verse '*vaiśvadevena*' is the same as Bhav I, 184, 5; the verse '*avratānāṃ*' is the same as Bhav I, 4, 117b-118a; and the verse '*brāhmaṇātikramo nāsti*' is the same as Bhav I, 4, 120b-121a or Bhav I, 184, 29b-30a.
230 = I, 186, 24.
231 = I, 186, 21b-22a.

6. Caturvarga-cintāmaṇi of Hemādri,

Vol. I,

p. 40 = I, 172, 22b-23a.
p. 62 = I, 31, 1-2, 6-7a and 16.
p. 63 = I, 81, 2; I, 96, 3-4a; I, 100, 1.
pp. 432-4 = IV, 155, 1-3, 7-10, 11b-12a, 11a and 13b to the end.
p. 466 = I, 170, 6-7. Also cf. IV, 158, 3a and 4b.
p. 467 = I, 169, 19-20.

	Bhavisya-p.
pp. 467-8	= I, 170, 1-2a and 3b-5.
p. 504	= I, 172, 23b-25a.
p. 663	= IV, 168, 45.
p. 664	= I, 169, 1-2.
p. 671	= IV, 168, 10b-12a.
p. 673	= IV, 168, 12b-13a.
pp. 680	= I, 172, 25b-26a. The verse *'dadyād guṇavate'* is not found.
pp. 1031-3	= IV, 128, 2-11 and 13-15. The line *'ato drumāḥ'* (on p. 1033) is not found.
&c.	&c.

Vol. II, Part i,

pp. 4-5	= I, 181, 10-14. Two lines from *'varṇa-dharmaḥ sa uktas tu'* are not found.
p. 10	= I, 181, 7a.
pp. 19-20	= I, 4, 87b-89.
p. 23	= I, 2, 1-3.
p. 27	= I, 181, 34.
pp. 31-2	= I, 181, 38b-40a.
pp. 50-51	= I, 97, 20; I, 98, 9-10a; I, 100, 8b-9a and 6b-7; I, 68, 3b-4. The verse *'saḍbhāga-kuṣṭhaṃ'* is not found.
pp. 229-231	= I, 214, 3 to the end.
pp. 345-8	= I, 18, 1 to the end.
pp. 381-2	= I, 19, 85b-90 and 91b-93a.
pp. 474-7	= I, 21, 1-12, 13b-14a, 15b-17a, 18-20, 24-31 and 34b-36. The verse *'yo 'syāṃ dadāti'* (on p. 477) is not found.
pp. 512-3	= I, 31, 1-5.
pp. 513-4	= I, 31, 6-10.

	Bhavisya-p.
pp. 514-9	= I, 31, 11-13, 14b-31a, 35b-36b and 37b-63. A few lines on pp. 517 and 519 are not found.
pp. 519-520	= I, 22, 1-2.
pp. 537-543	= IV, 37, 1-8 and 11 to the end. The line *'rasāj-jalaṃ'* (on p. 538) and the verse *'yad indreṇa purā cīrṇaṃ'* are not found.
pp. 557-560	= I, 32, 1-5a, 6b-16, 50-51a and 33b-41a. Eleven lines from *'evam uktvā'bhavat tuṣṇīṃ'* (on p. 559) are not found.
pp. 560-563	= I, 32, 42b-47a and 48-54a. Two lines from *'pūja-yitvā prayatnena'* (on p. 562) and seven verses from *'gāṃ ca dadyāt savatsāṃ vai'* (on p. 562) are not found.
pp. 563-4	= I, 37, 1 to the end; I, 38, 1-4 and 5b to the end. The line *'śacī dvi-bāhuḥ'* and the verse *'naktena bhakti-sahitaṃ'* are not found.
p. 567	= I, 37, 1 to the end. Two lines from *'pāya-sena ghṛtāḍhyena'* are not found.
pp. 604-5 (quoted as from Bhaviṣyotara-purāṇa')	= I, 39, 1-11 and 12b to the end. Three lines from *'tailaṃ ṣaṣṭhyāṃ'* are not found.
pp. 656-9	= I, 59, 1-25.
pp. 659-660	= I, 51, 1-15.

		Bhaviṣya-p.
pp. 660-663	=	I, 81, 1 ; I, 96, 3-4, 7-13a, 15b-16a and 17 to the end. Two lines *'sauvarṇaṃ kārayed bhaktyā'* and *'loke prasiddhaḥ'* (on p. 661) are not found.
pp. 663-4	=	I, 81, 2-4, 7-11a and 12-15a.
pp. 664-7	=	I, 97, 1-11a and 12 to the end.
pp. 667-9	=	I, 98, 1-14, 15b-16 and 18 to the end.
p. 669	=	I, 99, 1-4 and 6 to the end.
pp. 669-671 (quoted as from 'Bhaviṣyottara')	=	I, 100, 1-2 and 3b to the end. Three lines from *'putra-kāmo labhet putraṃ'* (on p. 671) are not found.
pp. 671-4	=	I, 101, 1, 7, 2-6, 8-9, 11b-12a and 13-22a.
pp. 674-6	=	I, 166, 1-15a. Six lines from *'kartavyo nikṣubhārkas tu'* (on p. 674), two lines from *'bhaktyā ca dakṣiṇāṃ'* and the line *'gandharva-rāja-patinā'* (on p. 675) and eight lines from *'mahāratna-prabhāveṇa'* (on p. 676) are not found.
pp. 676-9	=	I, 167, 1 to the end. The lines from *'kulīnaṃ rūpasaṃpannaṃ'* (on p. 677) and the lines *'kulīnaṃ rūpa-saṃpannaṃ'*, *'mahotsāhaṃ mahāviryam'*, *'itihāsavidaṃ'* and *'prabhayā sūrya-saṃkāśaḥ'* (on p. 678) are not found.

		Bhaviṣya-p.
pp. 679-685	—	Cf. I, 68 ; I, 69 ; I, 70, 1-11. (There are many verses common to the Bhaviṣya-p. and the Caturvarga-cintāmaṇi).
pp. 685-7	—	Cf. I, 70.
pp. 687-690	=	I, 208, 3-22a and 30b-34a.
pp. 690-696	—	Cf. I, 212 and 213 (verses 1-40a).
pp. 696-7	=	I, 213, 40b to the end.
pp. 724-6	=	I, 209, 1-14. Two lines *'mitraś cāśvayuje'* and *'tejasā hari-saṃkāśaḥ'* (on p. 725) are not found.
p. 726	=	I, 197, 25b-27.
pp. 726-8	=	I, 65, 1-7a, 19-20, 21b-23, 21a and 24 to the end. The line *'pavitrā hi pavitrāṇāṃ'* (on p. 726) is not found.
pp. 728-731	=	I, 105, 1-14a, 15b-16, 12b, 14b-15a, 17-20a, 25-26 and 29.
pp. 731-4	=	I, 64, 36b-60 and 61b to the end. The line *'śarkarā-khādya-miśrāṇi'* (on p. 732) is not found.
pp. 735-6	=	I, 108, 1-11.
pp. 736-8	=	I, 104, 2 to the end.
pp. 740-741	=	I, 106, 4b-10a and 11b-14.
p. 741	=	I, 110, 1-5, 7a and 8b.
pp. 741-3	=	I, 111, 1 to the end. The verse *'prāpyeha vipulaṃ devaṃ'* (on p. 742) and the *'homārcā kriyate tatra'* (on p. 743) are not found.
pp. 744-6	=	I, 112, 10b-17.

Bhaviṣya-p.

pp. 748-753 = I, 165, 1-12, 15-17a, 18-21 and 22b to the end.
Eighteen lines from '*dadhyodanaṃ ca bhuñjāno*' (on pp. 750-1) and three lines from '*kāntyā vidhu-samo rājan*' (on p. 752) are not found.

pp. 754-6 = I, 109, 1a and 2b-13a.

pp. 760-3 = I, 47, 50b to the end.
The first five lines '*kṣamā satyaṃ*' etc. are not found.

&c. &c.

Vol. II, Part ii,

pp. 424-440 = I, 55-57 and 58 (verses 1-23).
There are many cases of disagreement.

pp. 520-1 = I, 82, 1, 3, 5-6a and 7b-8a.
The verse '*yo yaḥ sūrya-dine*' is not found.

pp. 522-3 = I, 82, 8b-10a, 12a, 13 and 15b-24.

pp. 523-4 = I, 83, 1-3.
I, 68, 3b-4a.
I, 83, 4b-5 and 6a.

p. 524 (twice) = I, 86, 11b-12a (the remaining lines are not found).
I, 86, 15b-17.

pp. 525-6 = I, 89, 2b-3 and 5-7.

p. 526 = I, 90, 1-3a and 5.

pp. 526-7 (quoted as from 'Bhaviṣyottara') = I, 91, 1-4a and 6.

&c. &c.

(The above list of the quotations from the 'Bhavisya-p.' in the Caturvarga-cintāmaṇi is not exhaustive).

Bhaviṣya-p.

In Caturvarga-cintāmaṇi, Vol. II, verses have been quoted from the 'Bhaviṣya-p.' in connection with vows on Tithis beginning with Aṣṭamī, but these verses are not found in our printed Bhaviṣya.

In Caturvarga-cintamaṇi, Vol. III, verses have been quoted from the 'Bhaviṣya-p.' on Srāddha etc., and many of these verses are found in our printed Bhaviṣya. But it is needless to enlist them here.

7. Mādhavācārya's com. on the Parāśara-smṛti,

Vol. I, Part i,

p. 324 = I, 4, 56.

Vol. I, Part ii,

pp. 24-25 = I, 3, 6-7a.

p. 347 = I, 4, 120b-121a (= I, 184, 29b-30a).

p. 378 = I, 186, 21b-22a.

p. 382 = I, 186, 24.

8. Madana-pārijāta of Madanapāla,

p. 355 = I, 3, 6-7a.

p. 411 = I, 82, 56b-57a.

p. 476 = I, 183, 9-21a.
The line '*haviṣyeṇa*' is not found.

9. Kullūkabhaṭṭa's commentary,

on Manu II, 1 = I, 181, 7-8.

on Manu II, 13 = I, 181, 17a.

on Manu II, 25 = I, 181, 10-14.
The line '*varṇa-dharmaḥ sa uktas tu*' is not found.

on Manu III, 7 = I, 181, 24a.

APPENDIX II.

We give below *a list of the more important of the untraceable Purāṇic verses* contained in the commentaries and Nibandhas. A good number of such verses has already been noted in Appendix I. In spite of repeated searches we could not trace these verses in the respective Purāṇas, especially in the editions mainly used in this thesis. It is, however, not possible to assert that not a single traceable verse has escaped our notice.

The untraceable Purāṇic verses in the Caturvarga-cintāmaṇi are too numerous to be noted here.

[The abbreviations used exclusively in the following list are as follows:

Acom.	= Aparārka's com. on Yāj.	Mcom. on PS	= Mādhavācārya's com. on the Parāśara-smṛti.
AS	= Adbhutasāgara (of Ballālasena).	Mit.	= Mitākṣarā (on Yāj.).
BS-bh. of AM	= Brahmasūtra-bhāṣya of Ānandatīrtha Madhva.	MP	= Madana-pārijāta (of Madanapāla).
DK	= Dīpa-kalikā (of Śūlapāṇi)	Npr	= Nityācārapradīpa (of Narasiṃha Vājapeyin).
DS	= Dānasāgara (of Ballālasena).	PV	= Prāyaścitta-viveka (of Śūlapāṇi).
DV	= Durgotsava-viveka (of Śūlapāṇi).	SC	= Smṛti-candrikā (of Devaṇabhaṭṭa).
HL	= Hāralatā (of Aniruddhabhaṭṭa).	SS	= Smṛtyarthasāra (of Śrīdhara).
HV	= Haribhaktivilāsa (of Gopālabhaṭṭa).	ST	= Smṛti-tattva (of Raghunandana).
KC	= Kṛtyācāra (of Śrīdatta Upādhyāya).	ŚV	= Śrāddha-viveka (of Śūlapāṇi).
Kcom. on M.	= Kullūkabhaṭṭa's com. on the Manu-smṛti.	TC	= Tīrtha-cintāmaṇi (of Vācaspatimiśra).
KR	= Kṛtya-ratnākara (of Caṇḍeśvara).	TV	= Tithi-viveka (of Śūlapāṇi).
KV	= Kālaviveka (of Jīmūtavāhana.	VV	= Vratakāla-viveka (of Śūlapāṇi).
		YT	= Yātrā-tattva (of Raghunandana).]

Verses quoted from the

1. 'Mārkaṇḍeya-p.' in—(*i*) Acom., pp. 421 (=Viṣ III, 14, 31-32), 960, 1202. (*ii*) AS, p. 487. (*iii*) SC, II, p. 261 and IV, pp. 263-4, 391-2. (*iv*) KC, fol. 14b. (*v*) MP, pp. 61, 248, 264, 308, 326, 329.

2. 'Vāyu-p.' or 'Vāyavīya' in—(*i*) Acom., pp. 51, 202-3, 203, 467, 491, 532, 535, 1022. (*ii*) DS, fol. 25b, 150a-b. (*iii*) SC, I, 87; II, 410; IV, 76, 82, 335, 339, 339-340, 352, 403, 404, 416-7. (*iv*) KV, pp. 303 369, 372, 428. (*v*) KC, fol. 3b. (*vi*) Mcom. on PS, I, i, p. 134; I, ii, pp. 40 78-79, 415, 417, 423; II, ii, pp. 249, 261. (*vii*) PV, p. 462. (*viii*) MP, pp. 24, 585, 596, 625. (*ix*) TC, pp. 4, 283, 318, 325.

3. 'Brahmāṇḍa-p.' or 'Brahmāṇḍa' in—(*i*) KV, pp. 346, 401, 440, 458, 494, 534. (*ii*) Acom., pp. 126, 143-4, 269, 424, 448, 488, 499, 509, 512. (*iii*) AS, pp. 524, 527, 531, 537, 538, 539, 541, 542, 544, 545, 546, 556. (*iv*) SC, I, 28; II, 294, 302-3, 311, 317, 323; IV, 61, 261, 269-270, 338, 344, 358. (*v*) Mit. on Yāj. III, 30.

4. 'Viṣṇu-p.' or 'Vaiṣṇava' in—(*i*) KV, pp. 330, 464, 493. (*ii*) Acom., pp. 139, 244, 883. (*iii*) Mit. on Yāj. III, 6(?). (*iv*) DS, fol. 25b. (*v*) AS, pp. 383, 499-500, 564. (*vi*) SC, I, 127; II, 331, 423, 526, 570, 617; IV, 48, 53, 160, 213, 223, 243. (*vii*) Kcom. on M. IV, 62. (*viii*) KC, fol. 57b, 60b, 68b. (*ix*) PV, pp. 255, 396, 398, 431. (*x*) MP, pp. 204, 211.

5. 'Matsya-p.' or 'Mātsya' in—(*i*) KV, pp. 62, 177, 304, 391, 426, 447, 462, 523. (*ii*) Acom., pp. 201, 207, 209, 295, 370, 380-382, 427, 429, 442, 488, 549, 1225. (*iii*) HL, p. 169 (*iv*) AS, pp. 405, 409. (*v*) DS, fol. 26a. (*vi*) SC, II, 285, 565; IV, 53, 72, 76, 77-78, 198, 451-2; V, 86, 112. (*vii*) Kcom. on M. VIII, 92. (*viii*) MP, pp. 308, 525, 534, 537. (*ix*) PV, p. 405. (*x*) TC, pp. 25, 42, 192, 233, 268, 279, 352. (*xi*) Npr, p. 86.

6. 'Bhāgavata-p.' or 'Bhāgavata' in—(*i*) AS, pp. 427, 553. (*ii*) Madhva's com. on the Bhagavadgītā, pp. 101, 136, 168, 394, 440, 462, 525, 531, 613, 704. (In his Brahmasūtra-bhāṣya Madhva quotes, from a 'Bhāgavata-tantra' and 'Bhāgavata', verses which are not found in the present Bhāgavata-p. It is likely that in the above mentioned untraceable verses also there are some which were taken from the 'Bhāgavata-tantra').

7. 'Kūrma-p.' or 'Kaurmya' in—(*i*) KV, pp. 441, 444, 448, 508. (*ii*) Acom., pp. 201, 201-2, 204, 205, 207. (*iii*) DS, fol. 172b, 246b. (*iv*) For the verses quoted in Mcom. on PS see Islampurkar's edition. (*v*) MP, pp. 258, 272, 878. (*vi*) TC, p. 265. (*vii*) Npr, pp. 80, 85, 132. (*viii*) VV, fol. 3a, 6b. (*ix*) SC, IV, pp. 27, 61, 66, 71, 73, 75, 78, 79.

8. 'Vāmana-p.' or 'Vāmana' in—(*i*) KV, p. 360. (*ii*) SC, II, 363. (*iii*) MP, p. 62. (*iv*) ST, I, 356, 415, 840; II, 76, 139, 148, 563, 632. (*v*) YT, p. 19.

9. 'Liṅga-p.' or 'Laiṅga' in—(*i*) KV, pp. 352, 407, 414, 422, 466, 528, 535. (*ii*) Mit. on Yāj. I, 16, and III, 30. (*iii*) Acom., pp. 212, 428, 430. (*iv*) AS, p. 513. (*v*) SC, II, 623. (*vi*) SS, p. 66. (*vii*) Mcom. on PS, I, ii, 181-2. (*viii*) MP, pp. 535, 538. (*ix*) KR, fol. 149b. (*x*) DV, pp. 2, 5, 8, 22. (*xi*) TC, pp. 192, 341, 343, 344, 345, 347, 348, 351, 353, 356, 359. (*xii*) ST, I, 180, 198, 351, 396, 396-7, 650, 657, 678, 825; II, 63, 299, 412, 627.

10. 'Varāha-p.' or 'Vārāha' in—(*i*) KV, pp. 183, 441, 445, 447, 449, 450, 455, 456. (*ii*) Acom., pp. 126, 202, 497, 1052. (*iii*) SC, II, 548; IV, 63. (*iv*) Mcom. on PS, I, i, 296 and 476. (*v*) MP, p. 210. (*vi*) KR, fol. 167a, 186a. (*vii*) VV, fol. 2a. (*viii*) TC, pp. 191, 203.

11. 'Bṛhannāradīya-p.' or 'Bṛhannāradīya' in—(*i*) ST, I, 187. (*ii*) HV, pp. 664, 674, 712.

12. 'Nāradīya-p.' or 'Nāradīya' in—(*i*) KV, pp. 182, 442. (*ii*) SC, IV, 74, 75. (*iii*) Mcom. on PS, II, i, 34. (*iv*) MP, p. 265. (*v*) VV, fol. 5a, 5b. (*vi*) ST, I, 52, 107, 110, 112, 114, 147, 376, 786; II, 46, 79, 80, 101, 346, 428, 436, 507, 560, 648, 649.

13. 'Padma-p.' or 'Pādma' in—(*i*) KV, pp. 61, 288, 497, 498, 502. (*ii*) Acom., pp. 211, 212, 279. (*iii*) SC, II, 262, 321, 541, 545, 546, 547, 600, 629; IV, 389; V, 66, 194. (*iv*) Mcom. on PS, I, i, 239; I, ii, 165, 434; II, ii, 240, 269. (*v*) KC, fol. 33a. (*vi*) MP, p. 299. (*vii*) VV, fol. 2b, 4a, 7b. (*viii*) PV, p. 46. (*ix*) ŚV, fol. 87a. (*x*) DK, fol. 126b.

14. 'Agni-p.' or 'Āgneya' in—(*i*) BS-bh. of AM, pp. 53a, 68a. (*ii*) AS, pp. 19, 23, 50, 320, 378, 412, 426, 443, 453, 461, 488, 500, 501, 512, 513, 657, 708. (*iii*) DS, fol. 18a-b, 20a, 99a-b, 100a-b 113b-114b, 115a, 122b-123a, 123b, 127b-128a, 129b, 131a, 149a-b, 153b, 168b, 174a-177a, 180a, 181b, 187a, 189a, 204a, 209b, 216b-217a, 221a. (*iv*) SC, V, 122, 123, 123-4, 163 (in all these cases the title 'Vahni-p.' occurs). (*v*) Mcom. on PS, I, i, 351, 365, 366-9, 178 (Vahni-p.); II, ii, 221. (*vi*) KR, fol. 189b, 177b. (*vii*) DV, p. 12. (*viii*) TV, fol. 3b. (*ix*) TC, pp. 206, 263. (*x*) ST, I, 31, 93, 100, 130, 198, 371, 410, 411, 432, 483, 495, 498, 519, 810, 839; II, 37, 64, 65, 66, 147, 238, 286, 339, 349, 365, 529, 559, 571, 627. (*xi*) HV, pp 261, 296, 301, 320, 377, 487, 618, 751, 752, 775, 943, 977, 984, 1089, 1103, 1289, 1325. (From Vahni-p. on pp. 661, 977, 984). (*xii*) Npr, pp. 149-150, 183, 626. (*xiii*) Haribhaktirasāmṛtasindhu, p. 62.

15. 'Garuḍa-p.' or 'Gāruḍa' in—(*i*) BS-bh. of AM, pp. 2a, 4b-5a, 10a, 43b, 47a, 50b, 73a, 75a. (*ii*) SC, IV, 65, 67. (*iii*) Mcom. on PS, I, i, 198; II, ii, 226. (*iv*) VV, fol. 6a, 6b. (*v*) ST, I, 50, 54, 105-6, 106-7, 107, 109, 147, 148, 154, 358, 362, 413, 417, 750; II, 41-2, 48, 49, 53, 64, 70, 79-80, 87, 95, 143, 152, 424, 448, 527, 567-9. (*vi*) Npr, pp. 137, 190, 582, 596, 604. (*vii*) HV, pp. 143, 170-171, 182-3, 184, 192, 194, 273, 301, 318, 319, 322, 324, 333, 334, 356, 362, 363, 364, 365, 367, 368, 392, 393, 419, 444, 458, 460, 465, 468, 470, 487, 519, 561, 667, 673, 678, 757, 775, 779, 789, 790, 793, 798, 882, 934-5, 940.

16. 'Brahma-p.' or 'Brāhma' in (*i*) KV, (*ii*) Acom. etc. See under Brahmapurāṇa in Part I, Chap. III, sec. 8.

17. 'Bhaviṣya-p.' or 'Bhaviṣya' in—(*i*) KV, pp. 101, 173, 194-5, 300, 301-2, 302, 324-5, 325-6, 337, 372, 391-2, 401, 404-5, 406-7, 418, 420, 424, 438, 443, 447, 448, 451, 454, 485, 493, 512, 513, 527. (*ii*) Prāyaścitta-prakaraṇa, pp. 4, 6, 12, 13, 14, 17, 22, 25, 41. (*iii*) Acom., pp. 7, 51, 162, 211, 212, 215, 247, 421, 460, 471, 520, 522, 525, 538, 563, 564, 1037-8, 1055-6, 1056, 1056-7, 1059, 1060, 1061-2, 1065, 1066, 1067, 1067-9, 1071, 1075-7, 1081-2, 1193. (*iv*) DS, fol. 13b, 23b, 26b. (*v*) SC, I, 110, 175; II, 320, 600, 608; IV, 9-10, 17, 49-50, 68, 70, 122, 164, 236, 370, 405, 413, 437, 440; V, 104. (*vi*) Kcom. on M. III, 254; XI,

73, 74, 75-78, 83, 87, 91, 101, 102, 147. *(vii)* Mcom. on PS I, i, 419; I, ii, 40, 51, 291, 347, 378, 382, 444, 448, 452, 453, 460-461; II, i, 141. *(viii)* MP, pp. 33, 73, 262, 324, 325, 332, 355, 358, 411, 440, 543, 619, 630, 636, 791, 801, 802, 802-3, 816. *(ix)* VV, fol. 4b, 6a, 6b, 7a, 7b, 8a. *(x)* DK, fol. 3a, 4a, 28a, 33b, 45b, 115b, 116b

For the verses quoted from the 'Skanda-p.' or 'Skānda' and its different Khaṇḍas but not traceable in the printed Skanda, see under Skanda-p in Part I, Chap. III, sec. 9.

BIBLIOGRAPHY [1].

I. PRINTED TEXTS OF THE VEDIC, SANSKRIT, BUDDHIST AND JAIN LITERATURES

Adbhuta-sāgara of Ballālasena.—Edited by Muralīdhara Jhā and published by Prabhākarī & Co., Benares, 1905.

Agni-purāṇa.—Edited by Pañcānana Tarkaratna and published by the Vaṅgavāsī Press, Calcutta.

Ahirbudhnya-saṃhitā.—Edited by M. D. Rāmānujācārya. Adyar, Madras, 1916.

Aitareya-brāhmaṇa (with Sāyaṇācārya's commentary).—Edited and published by Hari Nārāyaṇa Āpte. Ānandāśrama Sanskrit Series. Poona, 1896.

Amarakoṣa of Amarasiṃha.—Edited by V. Jhalakikar under the superintendence of Sir R. G. Bhandarkar. Sixth edition. Bombay, 1907.

Āpastamba-dharmasūtra.—Edited and published by R. Halasyanātha Śāstrin, Kumbhakoṇam, 1895.

Arthaśāstra of Kauṭilya.—Edited by R. Shama Sastry. Mysore, 1924.

Atharva-veda.—Edited by R. Roth and W. D. Whitney. Berlin, 1924.

Āvaśyaka-sūtra.—Edited by Haribhadrasūri. Benares, 1905.

Baudhāyana-dharmasūtra.—Edited by L. Śrīnivāsācārya and published by the Government of Mysore, 1907.

Bhagavad-gītā with the commentaries of Śaṃkara, Madhva and others.—Edited by Viṭṭhala Śarman and published by the Gujarati Printing Press, Bombay, 1908.

Bhagavad-gītā with the commentaries of Śaṃkara, Abhinavagupta, Dhanapati and others.—Edited by Vasudev Laxman Sastri Pansikar and published by the Nirṇaya Sāgara Press, Bombay, 1912.

Bhāgavata-purāṇa.—Edited by Pañcānana Tarkaratna and published by the Vaṅgavāsī Press, Calcutta, 1315 B.S.

Bhaviṣya-purāṇa.—Published by Kṣemarāja Śrīkṛṣṇadāsa, Veṅkaṭeśvara Press, Bombay.

Brahmāṇḍa-purāṇa.—Published by Kṣemarāja Śrīkṛṣṇadāsa, Veṅkaṭeśvara Press, Bombay.

Brahma-purāṇa.—Edited by Pañcānana Tarkaratna and published by the Vaṅgavāsī Press, Calcutta, 1316 B.S.

1. Minor works, and those editions of the Purāṇas and the Mahābhārata which have been referred to only occasionally in the thesis, have not been mentioned in this Bibliography.

Brahmasūtra with the Bhāṣya of Bhāskarācārya.—Edited by Vindhyeśvarī Prasāda Dvivedin, Benares, 1915.

Brahmasūtra with Śāṃkara-bhāṣya and the commentary of Govindānanda.—Edited by Rāmanārāyaṇa Vidyāratna and published by the Asiatic Society of Bengal. Calcutta, 1863.

Brahmavaivarta-purāṇa.—Edited by Jīvānanda Vidyāsāgara. Calcutta, 1888.

Bṛhadāraṇyaka-upaniṣad with Śāṃkara-bhāṣya and Ānandagiri's commentary.—Published by Hari Nārāyaṇa Āpte. Ānandāśrama Sanskrit Series. Poona, 1914.

Bṛhaddharma-purāṇa.—Edited by Mm. Haraprasad Shastri. Bibliotheca Indica. Calcutta, 1897.

Bṛhannāradīya Purāṇa.—Edited by Pañcānana Tarkaratna and published by the Vaṅgavāsī Press. Second edition. Calcutta, 1316 B.S.

Bṛhat-saṃhitā of Varāhamihira.—Edited by Kern. Bibliotheca Indica. Calcutta, 1865.

Caturvarga-cintāmaṇi of Hemādri.—

Vol. I (Dāna-khaṇḍa)—Edited by Paṇḍita Bharatacandra Śiromaṇi. Bibliotheca Indica. Calcutta, 1873.

Vol. II (Vrata-khaṇḍa), Part i.—Edited by Paṇḍita Bharatacandra Śiromaṇi. Bibliotheca Indica. Calcutta, 1878.

Vol. II (Vrata-khaṇḍa), Part ii.—Edited by Paṇḍita Yajñeśvara Bhaṭṭācārya and Paṇḍita Kāmākhyānātha Tarkaratna. Bibliotheca Indica. Calcutta, 1879.

Vol. III (Pariśeṣa-khaṇḍa), Part i.—Edited by Paṇḍita Yajñeśvara Smṛtiratna and Paṇḍita Kāmākhyānātha Tarkaratna. Bibliotheca Indica. Calcutta, 1887.

Vol. III (Pariśeṣa-khaṇḍa), Part ii.—Edited by Paṇḍita Yajñeśvara Smṛtiratna and Kāmākhyānātha Tarkavāgīśa. Bibliotheca Indica. Calcutta, 1895.

Vol. IV (Prāyaścitta-khaṇḍa).—Edited by Paṇḍita Pramathanātha Tarkabhūṣaṇa. Bibliotheca Indica. Calcutta, 1911. It is very doubtful whether Vol. IV (Prāyaścitta-khaṇḍa) was really written by Hemādri.

Chāndogya-upaniṣad.—Published by Hari Nārāyaṇa Āpte. Ānandāśrama Sanskrit Series. Poona, 1913.

Dānakriyā-kaumudī of Govindānanda Kavikaṅkaṇācārya.—Edited by Kamala-kṛṣṇa Smṛtibhūṣaṇa. Bibliotheca Indica. Calcutta, 1903.

Daśāvatāra-carita of Kṣemendra.—Edited by Pandit Durgāprasāda and Kāśīnātha Pāṇḍuraṅga Parab. Kāvyamālā No. 26. Bombay, 1891.

Devībhāgavata.—Edited by Pañcānana Tarkaratna and published by the Vaṅgavāsī Press. Second edition. Calcutta, 1832 Ś.E.

Durgotsava-viveka of Śūlapāṇi.—Edited by Satīśa Candra Siddhāntabhūṣaṇa. Sanskrit Sāhitya Pariṣad. Calcutta.

Garuḍa-purāṇa.—Edited by Pañcānana Tarkaratna and published by the Vaṅgavāsī Press. Calcutta, 1314 B.S.

Gautama-dharmasūtra with the commentary of Haradatta.—Published by Hari Nārāyaṇa Āpte. Ānandāśrama Sanskrit Series. Poona, 1910.

Gopatha-brāhmaṇa.—Edited by Dr. Dieuke Gaastra. Leiden, 1919.

Hāralatā of Aniruddhabhaṭṭa.—Edited by Kamalakṛṣṇa Smṛtitīrtha. Bibliotheca Indica. Calcutta, 1909.

Haribhaktirasāmṛtasindhu of Rūpa Gosvāmin.—Edited by Gosvāmidāmodara Śāstrin. First edition. Acyuta-grantha-mālā (No. 6). Benares, Vikramābda 1988.

Haribhaktivilāsa of Gopālabhaṭṭa.—Edited by Śyāmācaraṇa Kaviratna and published by Gurudas Chatterjee & Sons. Calcutta, 1318 B.S.

Hārīta-saṃhitā.—Ūnaviṃśati Saṃhitā (pp. 127-139), second edition, edited by Pañcānana Tarkaratna and published by the Vaṅgavāsī Press, Calcutta, 1316 B.S.

Harivaṃśa with the commentary of Nīlakaṇṭha.—Edited by Pañcānana Tarkaratna and published by the Vaṅgavāsī Press. Calcutta, 1312 B.S.

Harṣa-carita of Bāṇabhaṭṭa.—Edited by A. A. Fürher. Bombay, 1909.

Jaiminīya-upaniṣad-brāhmaṇa.—Edited by Hanns Oertel. New Haven, 1894.

Jātakas.—Edited by V. Fausbôll. London, 1877-97.

Jayākhya-saṃhitā (with a Foreword by B. Bhattacharya).—Edited by Embar Krishnamacharya. Gaekwaḍ's Oriental Series, Vol. LIV. Baroda, 1931.

Kālanirṇaya (also called Kālamādhavīya or Kālamādhava) of Mādhavācārya.—Edited by Candrakānta Tarkālaṃkāra. Bibliotheca Indica. Calcutta, 1809 Śaka.

Kālasāra of Gadādhara.—Vol. I, edited by Sadāśiva Miśra. Bibliotheca Indica. Calcutta, 1904.

Kālaviveka of Jīmūtavāhana.—Edited by Pramathanātha Tarkabhūṣaṇa and published by the Asiatic Society of Bengal. Calcutta, 1905.

Kūrma-purāṇa.—Edited by Pañcānana Tarkaratna and published by the Vaṅgavāsī Press. Second edition. Calcutta, 1332 B.S.

Liṅga-purāṇa.—Edited by Jīvānanda Vidyāsāgara. Calcutta, 1885.

Madana-pārijāta of Madanapāla.—Edited by Madhusūdana Smṛtiratna. Bibliotheca Indica. Calcutta, 1893.

Madhva-vijaya of Nārāyaṇa Paṇḍitācārya.—Edited by T. R. Krishnacharya and published by the Nirṇaya Sāgara Press, Bombay, Śaka 1834.

Mahābhārata with the commentary of Nīlakaṇṭha.—Edited by Pañcānana Tarkaratna, and published in two parts by the Vaṅgavāsī Press, Calcutta. 1826-1830 Śakābda.

Mahābhāṣya of Patañjali.—Edited by F. Kielhorn. Second edition. Bombay.

Mānava-gṛhyasūtra.—Edited by Rāmakṛṣṇa Harṣajī Śāstrin. Gaekwaḍ's Oriental Series, No. XXXV. Baroda, 1926.

Manu-smṛti with Kullūkabhaṭṭa's commentary.—Edited by Pañcānana Tarkaratna and published by the Vaṅgavāsī Press. Fourth edition. Calcutta, 1320 B.S.

Manu-smṛti with Medhātithi's commentary.—Edited by Gaṅgānātha Jhā and published by the Asiatic Society of Bengal. Calcutta, 1932.

Mārkaṇḍeya-purāṇa.—Edited by Pañcānana Tarkaratna and published by the Vaṅgavāsī Press, Calcutta. Fourth edition. 1316 B.S.

Matsya-purāṇa.—Edited by Pañcānana Tarkaratna and published by the Vaṅgavāsī Press. Calcutta, 1316 B.S.

Mudrā-rākṣasa of Viśākhadatta.—Edited by A. Hillebrandt. Breslau, 1912.

Nāradīya Purāṇa.—Published by Kṣemarāja Śrīkṛṣṇadāsa, Veṅkaṭeśvara Press, Bombay.

Nityācārapaddhati of Vidyākara Vājapeyin.—Vol. I, edited by Vinoda-vihārī Bhaṭṭācārya. Bibliotheca Indica. Calcutta, 1903.

Nityācārapradīpa of Narasiṃha Vājapeyin.—Part I., published by the Asiatic Society of Bengal, Calcutta.

Padma-purāṇa.—Published by Hari Nārāyaṇa Āpte. Ānandāśrama Sanskrit Series. Poona, 1893.

It is printed in 4 volumes, Vol. I consisting of the Ādi and the Bhūmi Khaṇḍa, Vol. II of the Brahma and the Pātāla Khaṇḍa, Vol. III of the Sṛṣṭi Khaṇḍa, and Vol. IV of the Uttara Khaṇḍa.

Parāśara-smṛti (also called Parāśara Dharma-saṃhitā) with the Bhāṣya of Mādhavācārya.—Edited by Vāmana Śāstrī Islampurkar. Bombay Sanskrit Series, Bombay, 1893-1911.

Pitṛ-dayitā of Aniruddhabhaṭṭa.—Published by the Sanskrit Sāhitya Pariṣad, Calcutta.

Prāyaścitta-prakaraṇa of Bhavadeva.—Edited by Girīśa Candra Vedāntatīrtha and published by the Varendra Research Society, Rajshahi, Bengal, 1927.

Prāyaścitta-viveka of Śūlapāṇi.—Edited by Jīvānanda Vidyāsāgara. Calcutta, 1893.

Sāṃkhya-pravacana-bhāṣya (on the Sāṃkhya-darśana) of Vijñāna Bhikṣu.—Edited by Ratna Gopāla Bhaṭṭa and published by the Vidyā Vilāsa Press. Benares, 1909.

Sāṅkhyāyana-śrautasūtra.—Edited by A. Hillebrandt. Bibliotheca Indica. Calcutta, 1888.

Śatapatha-brāhmaṇa.—Edited by A. Weber. Leipzig, Otto Harrassowitz, 1924.

Śiva-purāṇa.—Edited by Pañcānana Tarkaratna and published by the Vaṅgavāsī Press. Calcutta, 1314 B.S.

Skanda-purāṇa.—Published by the Vaṅgavāsī Press, Calcutta, 1318 B.S.

It consists of seven Khaṇḍas or books (viz., Māheśvara, Viṣṇu, Brahma, Kāśī, Āvantya, Nāgara and Prabhāsa) printed in seven volumes respectively.

Smṛti-candrikā of Devaṇabhaṭṭa.—Edited by L. Śrīnivāsācārya and published in five volumes by the Government of Mysore. Mysore, 1914-21.

Smṛti-tattva of Raghunandana.—Edited by Jīvānanda Vidyāsāgara. Calcutta, 1895. This work has been printed in two volumes. Vol. I consists of (*i*) Tithi-tattva (pp.1-188), (*ii*) Śrāddha-tattva (pp. 189-325), (*iii*) Āhnika-tattva (pp. 326-465), (*iv*) Prāyaścitta-tattva (pp. 466-558), (*v*) Jyotistattva (pp. 559-735), (*vi*) Malamāsa-tattva (pp. 736-856), and (*vii*) Saṃskāra-tattva (pp. 857-948). Vol. II consists of (*i*) Ekādaśī-tattva (pp. 1-105), (*ii*) Udvāha-tattva (pp. 106-150), (*iii*) Vrata-tattva (pp. 151-161), (*iv*) Dāya-tattva (pp. 161-197), (*v*) Vyavahāra-tattva (pp. 197-233), (*vi*) Śuddhi-tattva (pp. 233-412), *(vii)* Vāstu-yāga-tattva (pp. 412-423), *(viii)* Kṛtya-tattva (pp. 423-483), *(ix)* Yajurvedi-śrāddha-tattva (pp. 483-502), *(x)* Deva-pratiṣṭhā-tattva (pp. 502-513), *(xi)* Jalāśayotsarga-tattva (pp. 513-528), *(xii)* Chandoga-vṛṣotsarga-tattva (pp. 528-562), *(xiii)* Śrī-puruṣottama-tattva (pp. 563-573), *(xiv)* Divya-tattva (pp. 574-613), *(xv)* Maṭha-pratiṣṭhādi-tattva (pp. 613-633), *(xvi)* Śūdra-kṛtya-vicāraṇa-tattva (pp. 633-636), *(xvii)* Yajurvedi-vṛṣotsarga-tattva (pp. 636-644), *(xviii)* Dīkṣā-tattva (pp. 645-659), and *(xix)* Śrī-durgārcana-paddhati (pp. 659-683).

Śrāddhakriyā-kaumudī of Govindānanda Kavi-kaṅkaṇācārya.—Edited by Kamala-kṛṣṇa Smṛtibhūṣaṇa. Bibliotheca Indica. Calcutta, 1904.

Śrī-bhāṣya of Rāmānuja.—Edited by Vāsudeva Śāstrī Abhyaṅkara. Bombay, 1914.

Śuddhikriyā-kaumudī of Govindānanda Kavi-kaṅkaṇācārya.—Edited by Kamala-kṛṣṇa Smṛtibhūṣaṇa. Bibliotheca Indica. Calcutta, 1905.

Taittirīya-āraṇyaka with the Bhāṣya of Sāyaṇācārya.—Edited and published by Hari Nārāyaṇa Āpte. Ānandāśrama Sanskrit Series. Poona, 1898.

Tantrasāra of Kṛṣṇānanda Āgamavāgīśa.—Edited and published by Pañcaśikha Bhaṭṭācārya. Fourth edition. Calcutta, 1318 B.S.

Tantravārttika of Kumārilabhaṭṭa.—Edited by Pandit Gaṅgādhara Śāstrin. Benares, 1903.

Ṭīkāsarvasva (a com. on Amarasiṃha's Nāmaliṅgānuśāsana) of Vandyaghaṭīya Sarvānanda.—Edited by T. Ganapati Shastri and printed at the Travancore Government Press, 1914-17.

Tīrtha-cintāmaṇi of Vācaspatimiśra.—Edited by Kamala-kṛṣṇa Smṛtitīrtha and published by the Asiatic Society of Bengal. Calcutta, 1912.

Trikāṇḍa-maṇḍana (of Trikāṇḍa-maṇḍana Bhāskaramiśra) with an anonymous commentary.—Edited by Candra-kānta Tarkālaṃkāra Bhaṭṭācārya and published by the Asiatic Society of Bengal. Calcutta, 1903.

Ūnaviṃśati Saṃhitā.—Edited by Pañcānana Tarkaratna, and published by the Vaṅgavāsī Press. Second edition. Calcutta, 1316 B.S.

Uśanas-saṃhitā.—Ūnaviṃśati Saṃhitā (pp. 226-271), second edition, edited by Pañcānana Tarkaratna and published by the Vaṅgavāsī Press, Calcutta, 1316 B.S.

Uttara-gītā with the Bhāṣya of Gauḍapāda.—Published by the Śrī Vāṇī Vilāsa Press, Śrīraṅgaṃ, 1926.

Vāmana-purāṇa.—Edited by Pañcānana Tarkaratna and published by the Vaṅgavāsī Press. Calcutta, 1314 B.S.

Varāha-purāṇa.—Edited by Pañcānana Tarkaratna and published by the Vaṅgavāsī Press. Calcutta, 1313 B.S.

Varṣakriyā-kaumudī of Govindānanda Kavi-kaṅkaṇācārya.—Edited by Kamalakṛṣṇa Smṛtibhūṣaṇa. Bibliotheca Indica. Calcutta, 1902.

Vāyu-purāṇa.—Edited and published by Hari Nārāyaṇa Āpte. Ānandāśrama Sanskrit Series. Poona, 1905.

Vidhāna-pārijāta of Anantabhaṭṭa.—Vol. I, edited by Paṇḍita Tārāprasanna Vidyāratna. Bibliotheca Indica. Calcutta, 1905.

Viṣṇu-dharmasūtra.—Ūnaviṃśati Saṃhitā (pp. 26-126), second edition, edited by Pañcānana Tarkaratna and published by the Vaṅgavāsī Press Calcutta, 1316 B.S.

Viṣṇudharmottara.—Published by Kṣemarāja Śrīkṛṣṇadāsa, Veṅkateśvara Press, Bombay.

Viṣṇu-purāṇa.—Edited by Pañcānana Tarkaratna and published by the Vaṅgavāsī Press. Second edition. Calcutta, 1331 B.S.

Yājñavalkya-smṛti with the Mitākṣarā of Vijñāneśvara.—Edited by Vāsudeva Lakṣmaṇa Śāstrī Paṇaśīkara and published by Pandurang Jawaji. Third edition. Bombay, 1926.

Yājñavalkya-smṛti with the commentary of Aparārka.—Edited and published in two parts by Hari Nārāyaṇa Āpte. Ānandāśarma Sanskrit Series. Poona, 1903 and 1904.

Yātrā-tattva of Raghunandana.—Edited by Dvārikā Nātha Nyāyaśāstrin. Sanskrit Sāhitya Pariṣad, Calcutta.

II. WORKS IN MANUSCRIPTS

Brāhmaṇa-sarvasva of Halāyudha.—Ms No. K554, Dacca University Mss Library.

Brahma-purāṇa.—Ms. No. 2337, dated 1616 Śaka, Dacca University Mss Library.

Bṛhannāradīya Purāṇa.—Ms No. 1667, dated 1578 Śaka, Dacca University Mss Library.

Dānasāgara of Ballālasena.—Mss Nos. 719-720. India Office Library, London. (Eggeling, India Office Catalogue, Nos. 1704-5).

Dīpa-kalikā (a com. on Yāj.) of Śūlapāṇi.—Ms No. 602. Dacca University Mss Library.

Dolayātrā-viveka of Śūlapāṇi.—Ms No. 177C, dated 1710 Śaka, Dacca University Mss Library.

Harivaṃśa.—Mss No. 508 (dated 1549 Śaka), No. 514 A (dated 1765 Śaka), No. 1041 and No. 1718 in the Dacca University Mss Library.

Kṛtyācāra of Śrīdatta Upādhyāya.—Ms. No. 4339, Dacca University Mss Library.

Kṛtya-ratnākara of Caṇḍeśvara.—Ms No. 1055C, Dacca University Mss Library. This is a very badly damaged palm-leaf Ms, many of its folios being lost and many others damaged at the sides.

Māgha-māhātmya of the Padma-purāṇa.—Ms No. 931, dated 1311 Śaka, Dacca University Mss Library.

Padma-purāṇa, Sṛṣṭi-khaṇḍa.—Ms No. 1621, Dacca University Mss Library.

Padma-purāṇa, Bhūmi-khaṇḍa.—Ms No. 1622, Dacca University Mss Library.

Padma-purāṇa, Pātāla-khaṇḍa.—Ms No. 1623, Dacca University Mss Library.

Padma-purāṇa, Uttara-khaṇḍa.—Ms No. 1624, Dacca University Mss Library.

Padma-purāṇa, Svarga-khaṇḍa.—Ms No. 1625, Dacca University Mss Library.

Rāsayātrā-viveka of Śūlapāṇi.—Ms No. 3350, Dacca University Mss Library.

Saṃbandha-viveka of Śūlapāṇi.—Ms No. 403C, Dacca University Mss Library.

Śrāddha-viveka of Śūlapāṇi.—Ms No. 151A, Dacca University Mss Library.

Uttara-gītā with the Bhāṣya of Gauḍapāda.—Mss Nos. 4504 and K558E, Dacca University Mss Library.

Vratakāla-viveka of Śūlapāṇi.—Ms No. 1578C, Dacca University Mss Library.

Yathārtha-mañjarī of Śrītīrtha Svāmin or Rāmānandatīrtha.—Ms No. 4093, dated 1734 Śaka, Dacca University Mss Library.

III. ANCIENT WORKS IN TRANSLATION

Arthaśāstra of Kauṭilya.—Translated into English by R. Shama Sastry. Third edition. Mysore, 1929.

Jātaka.—Translated into English by various scholars and edited by E. B. Cowell. Cambridge, 1895-1913.

Jātaka.—Translated into Bengali by Isan Chandra Ghosh and published by Anukul Chandra Ghosh, Calcutta, 1323-37 B.S.

Kalhan's Chronicle of the Kings of Kasmir (in 2 volumes).—This is a translation of Kalhan's Rājataraṅgiṇī by M. A. Stein. Westminster, 1900.

Mahāvagga.—Translated from Pāli by V. Fausbôll. Sacred Books of the East, Vol. X, part 2 (pp. 67-145). Oxford, 1881.

Mārkaṇḍeya-purāṇa.—Translated into English by F. E. Pargiter. Bibliotheca Indica. Calcutta, 1904.

Viṣṇu-purāṇa.—Translated into English by H. H. Wilson and edited by F. Hall. Vols. I-V. London, 1864-70.

IV. WORKS ON EPIGRAPHY

Corpus Inscriptionum Indicarum, Vol. I (Inscriptions of Aśoka). New edition by E. Hultzsch. Oxford, 1925.

Corpus Inscriptionum Indicarum, Vol. II, Part I (Kharoṣṭhi Inscriptions). Edited by Sten Konow. Calcutta, 1929.

Epigraphia Indica, Bombay.

Gupta Inscriptions (or Corpus Inscriptionum Indicarum, Vol. III). Edited by J. F. Fleet. Calcutta, 1888.

The Memoirs of the Archaeological Survey of India.

V. WORKS ON NUMISMATICS

Cunningham, A.—Coins of the Indo-Scythians (Śakas and Kushans). London, 1888.

Rapson, E. J.—A Catalogue of Indian Coins in the British Museum. London, 1908.

VI. VARIOUS MODERN WORKS

Aufrecht, Th.—Catalogus Codicum Manuscriptorum Sanscriticorum Bibliothecae Bodleianae, Oxonii, MDCCCLXIV.

Avalon, Arthur.—Principles of Tantra. Published in two volumes. London, 1914 and 1916.

Basu, Nagendra Nath.—Viśvakoṣa (a Bengali encyclopaedia in 22 volumes). Calcutta, 1293-1318 B.S.

Belvalkar, S. K.—Basu Mallik Lectures on Vedānta, 1925.

Bhandarkar, R. G.—Vaiṣṇavism, Śaivism and Minor Religious Systems. Strassburg, 1913.

Cambridge History of India.—Vol. I (Ancient India), edited by E. J. Rapson. Cambridge, 1922.

Chatterjee, J. C.—Kashmir Śaivism. Srinagar, Kashmir, 1914.

De, S. K.—Sanskrit Poetics (Studies in the History of). Published in two volumes. Luzac & Co., London. 1923 and 1925.

Eggeling.—A Descriptive Catalogue of the Sanskrit Mss in the Library of the India Office. Parts I-VII. London, 1887-1904.

Eliot, Charles.—Hinduism and Buddhism. Published in 3 volumes. London, 1921.

Encyclopaedia of Religion and Ethics. (In 12 volumes). Edited by James Hastings. Edinburgh, 1908-1921.

Farquhar, J. N.—An Outline of the Religious Literature of India. Oxford, 1920.

Fick, Richard.—Social Organisation in North-east India in Buddha's time. Translated from the German original by S. K. Maitra. Calcutta, 1920.

Hoernle. A. F. R.—Medicine of Ancient India (Studies in the). Clarendon Press, Oxford, 1907.

Hopkins, E. W.—The Great Epic of India. New Haven, Yale University Press, 1920.

Jolly, J.—Hindu Law and Custom. Translated from the German original by Batakrishna Ghosh. Published by the Greater India Society, Calcutta, 1928.

Kane, P. V.—History of Dharmaśāstra, Vol. I. Bhandarkar Oriental Research Institute. Poona, 1930.

Kane, P. V.—History of Sanskrit Poetics (or History of Alaṃkāra Literature), annexed, as an introduction, to the author's edition of the Sāhityadarpaṇa. Bombay, 1923.

Keith, A. B.—The Religion and Philosophy of the Veda and the Upaniṣads. Harvard Oriental Series, Vols. 31 and 32. 1925.

Law, Bimala Charan.—Women in Buddhist Literature. Colombo (Ceylon), 1927.

Macdonell, A. A.—A History of Sanskrit Literature. London, 1925.

McCrindle, J. W.—Ancient India as described by Megasthenes and Arrian. Bombay, 1877.

Mitra, R. L.—Notices of Sanskrit Mss. Published under Orders of the Government of Bengal. Calcutta, 1871-88.

Mitra, R. L.—A Catalogue of Sanskrit Mss in the Library of His Highness the Mahārājā of Bikaner, Calcutta, 1880.

Pargiter, F. E.—Ancient Indian Historical Tradition. Oxford, 1922.

Pargiter, F. E.—The Dynasties of the Kali age (The Purāṇa Text of). Oxford, 1913.

Rhys Davids, T. W.—Buddhist India. London, 1917.

Roy Choudhury, H. C.—The Early History of the Vaiṣṇava Sect (Materials for the Study of). Published by the University of Calcutta, 1920.

Sachau, E. C.—Alberūnī's India. (In two volumes). London, 1888.

Schrader, F. O.—Introduction to the Pāñcarātra and the Ahirbudhnya Saṃhitā. Adyar, Madras, 1916.

Shastri, Haraprasad.—A Descriptive Catalogue of Sanskrit Mss in the collections of the Asiatic Society of Bengal, Vol. V (Purāṇa Mss), Calcutta, 1928.

Shastri, Haraprasad.—Catalogue of Palm Leaf and Selected Paper Mss belonging to the Durbar Library, Nepal. Calcutta, 1905.

Shastri (Hrishikesh) and Gui (Siva Chandra).—A Descriptive Catalogue of Sanskrit Mss in the Library of Calcutta Sanskrit College, Vol. IV (Purāṇa Mss), Calcutta, 1902.

Smith, V. A.—The Early History of India (including Alexander's Campaigns). Fourth edition, revised by S. M. Edwards. Oxford, 1924.

Vaidya, C. V.—History of Mediaeval Hindu India, I, Poona, 1921.

Wilson, H. H.—Essays Analytical, Critical and Philological (collected and edited by Dr. Reinhold Rost), Vol. I, London, 1864.

Winternitz, M.—A History of Indian Literature. Vol. I, translated into English from the original German by Mrs. S. Ketkar and published by the University of Calcutta, 1927.

INDEX

L

R

S

W

Y

ERRATA

Page	Line	Incorrect	Correct
11	32	*śrādhānāṃ*	*śrāddhānāṃ*
19	10	Sapta-dvipa	Sapta-dvīpa
21	36	Sankrit	Sanskrit
27	34	the story	on the story
27	40	*Kaṭhitān*	*kathitān*
27	43	*prasaṃkhātaḥ*	*prasamkhyātaḥ*
28	36	‖	=
33	2	*vice verse*	*vice versa*
73	39	hiṃ	them
133	25	'Nāradīya P.	'Nāradīya P.'
136	21	chaps,	chaps.
140	20	ganges	Ganges
168	12	Śātras	Śāstras
206	13	morarch	monarch
216	12	discribed	described
217	34	at last	at least
227	8	Bramhanists	Brahmanists